History of the Jews

by Heinrich Graetz

ONE-VOLUME ABRIDGED EDITION

EDITED BY RANDOLPH PARRISH

Resource *Publications*

An imprint of *Wipf and Stock Publishers*
150 West Broadway • Eugene OR 97401

Resource Publications
An imprint of *Wipf and Stock Publishers*
150 West Broadway
Eugene, Oregon 97401

A History of the Jews
Edited by Graetz, Heinrich

ISBN: 1-57910-893-8
Publication date: February, 2002
Previously published by NPP/Public Domain, 1894.

INTRODUCTION

In the middle of the 19th century, in the middle of the most progressive and modern country of Europe, and in the middle of the great struggle to establish Reform Judaism as a viable alternative to traditional Orthodoxy, Heinrich Graetz undertook to compile his complete and massive History of the Jews. This, when finished, reach to eleven volumes, all in German. For the English edition, these were reduced to five, with another volume to contain the index. A later three-volume abridgment was circulated to great success. For this one-volume abridgment, it has been decided to omit all material relating to the Biblical and Roman periods, as this is already well-covered in the Bible or through such sources as Josephus. For the Talmudic era, and the times immediately following the destruction of the Temple and the start of the Diaspora, the reader has recourse to ***The History of the Jewish Nation After the Destruction of Jerusalem***, by Alfred Edersheim; a work which the editor highly recommends.

This work, then, begins with Maimonides, in the twelfth century; and traces the development of the great ideas and conflicts within Judaism itself--the Zohar; the Kabbala; Joseph Karo and the Shulhan Aruch; the rise of Chasidism; the Besht; Spinoza; and modern Reform. Graetz is permitted to speak for himself. He was a man of deep passions, great feelings, and a love for his people; and of great hopes for their future. He lets his heart show in his writings. He is articulate, learned, scholarly, and his work is suffused with his fervor. He loves, he hates, he chastens; he condemns, he praises. Isabella of Spain, who expelled the Jews from her realms in 1492, is not, as elsewhere, "Isabella the Catholic", but, for Graetz, "Isabella the Bigot". The Chasidic rabbis who claimed to be able to foresee the future and read minds, are for Graetz not mystics, but charlatans, and he takes it as his duty to expose them. Jews who came to the conclusion that Jesus from Nazareth was really the Messiah, he contends must have been dupes, or worse. As a result, he is never dull; and his recountings of historical events are often as entertaining as they are informative. But such is the sweep of his work, and the giant canvas upon which he writes, that we can look upon his prejudices with a gentle indulgence, while remaining grateful to him for undertaking his great work in the first place.

TABLE OF CONTENTS

EXPULSION OF THE]EWS FROM SPAIN

126

Friendship of Marranos and Jews--Torquemada demands of the Rabbis of Toledo the Denunciation of Marranos--Judah Ibn Verga-Jewish Courtiers under Ferdinand and Isabella--Isaac Abrabanel: his History and Writings--The Jews of Portugal under Alfonso V-The Ibn-Yachya Brothers-Abrabanel's Flight from Portugal to Spain--The Jews of Granada: Isaac Hamon--Edict of Banishment promulgated by Ferdinand and Isabella--Its Consequences-Departure from Spain--Number of the Exiles--Decline in the Prosperity of Spain after the Banishment of the Jews--Transformation of Synagogues and Schools into Churches and Monasteries--The Inquisition and the Marranos-Deza, the Successor of Torquemada.

EXPULSION OP THE JEWS FROM NAVARRE AND PORTUGAL

139

The Exiles from Navarre--Migration to Naples--King Ferdinand I of Naples and Abrabanel--Leon Abrabanel-Misfortunes of the Jews in Fez, Genoa, Rome, and the Islands of Greece--The Sultan Bajazet--Moses Kapsali--Spanish Jews in Portugal--The Jewish Astronomers, Abraham Zacuto and Jose Vecinho-The Jewish Travelers, Abraham de Beya and Joseph Zapateiro-Outbreak of the Plague among the Spanish Jews in Portugal-Sufferings of the Portuguese Exiles--Judah Chayyat and his Fellow-Sufferers-Cruelty of Joao II--Kindly Treatment by Manoel changed into Cruelty on his Marriage--Forcible Baptism of Jewish Children--Levi ben Chabib and Isaac Caro-Pope Alexander VI--Manoel's Efforts on Behalf of the Portuguese Marranos-Death of Simon Maimi and Abraham Saba.

RUCHLIN AND THE TALMUD

154

Antecedents of the Convert John Pfefferkorn--Pfefferkorn and the Dominicans of Cologne--Hoogstraten, Ortuinus Gratius and Amold of Tongern--Victor von Karben-Attacks on the Talmud and Confiscation of Copies in Frankfort--Reuchlin's Hebrew and Kabbalistic Studies--The Controversy conceming the Talmud--Activity on both Sides--Public Excitement--Complete

SETTLEMENT OF THE JEWS IN ENGLAND AND MANASSEH BEN ISRAEL

SPINOZA AND SABBATAI ZEVI

THE AGE OF LUZZATTO AND FRANK

HISTORY OF THE JEWS

VOL. III

CHAPTER XIV

MAIMUNI (MAIMONIDES)

Early years of Maimuni--His journey to Fez--Letter of Consolation of Maimun (father of Maimonides)--Maimuni and the Jewish Converts to Islam--The Maimun Family in Palestine and Egypt--Maimuni's Commentary on the Mishnah--Saladin and the Jews--Letter of Maimonides to Yemen--The Mishne-Torah of Maimuni--Controversies with Reference to this Work--Joseph Ibn-Aknin--Maimuni as a Physician--Maimuni attacked by Samuel ben Ali--Maimuni and the Jews of Provence--the More Nebuchim and its importance--Death of Maimonides

1171-1205 C.E.

Moses Ibn-Maimun (with the long Arabic name Abu-Amram Musa ben Maimun Obaid Allah) was born on the Eve of Passover (30th March, 1135, at one o'clock p.m.) in Cordova. The early training of Maimonides, as he is often called, was calculated to strengthen his character in a most emphatic manner. His father, Maimun ben Joseph, a pupil of Ibn-Migash, was, like his ancestors for eight generations back, as far as his progenitor Obadiah, a learned Talmudist and a member of the Rabbinical College of Cordova. Maimun also took an interest in the sciences, knew mathematics and astronomy, and wrote books on those subjects, as well as on Talmudical topics. It was he who imbued his son with an enthusiastic love for learning, and awakened his feeling for an ideal life. Maimuni had scarcely passed his thirteenth year when great misfortune broke over the community of Cordova. The city was captured by the Almohades (May or June, 1148), who forthwith promulgated fanatical edicts against Jews and Christians, giving them the alternatives of conversion to Islam, expulsion, or death. Maimun and his family went into exile with the great majority of the Cordovan congregation. They are said to have established themselves at Port Almeria, which a year before had been conquered by the Christians. In the year 1151, Almeria also fell into the power of the Almohades, whose fanatical king, of course, did not fail to impose on the Jewish and Christian inhabitants of the city a change of religion, as he had done in the other conquered cities of southern Spain. From that time the family of Maimun was obliged to lead a wandering life for many years, without being able to find a permanent residence anywhere.

From his father, Maimuni learned the Bible, the Talmud, the Jewish branches of learning, mathematics and astronomy; he attended lectures on science and medicine by Mahometan professors, and was introduced into the temple of philosophy. Through reading and contacts, he obtained a fund of solid information, and his clear intellect regulated his knowledge, however various and diverse it was. His was a thoroughly logical and systematic mind, which had the power of grouping and arranging the greatest and the smallest things, and he was a sworn enemy of disorder and chaotic confusion. In this respect he may justly be called the Jewish Aristotle. Perhaps no one before Maimuni had so thoroughly absorbed and assimilated Aristotle's philosophical system. He made it a part of his own intellectual possession.

Although he was attracted by many branches of learning, still there were four special subjects on which he centered most of his attention: the whole range of Biblical and Talmudical writings; philosophy; medicine; and mathematics, together with astronomy. In his twenty-third year, he prepared in Hebrew for a friend a thesis on the Jewish calendar, based on astronomical principles (1158). Although this little book has no special importance in itself, it is yet interesting, in that it reveals to us that his love of methodical regularity dominated him even in his earliest youth. In that same year he commenced a work, the undertaking of which in itself gives evidence of greatness and boldness of intellect. He began to explain the Mishnah independently and in a new light, at an age when most men have scarcely finished their college career--a gigantic task in which he had no model to guide him. He worked at it amid continual wanderings and while battling with hardships; but so thoroughly was the whole compass of the Talmud before hi, that he could manage to dispense with books. A year or two later (1159-1160) his father emigrated with him, his younger brother, David, and his sister, from Spain to Fez. What led Maimuni's family to remove to the land of the greatest intolerance is a matter that has not yet been cleared up. In Fez, as in the whole of northern Africa, wherever the bigoted Abdulmumen ruled, no Jews were allowed to profess their faith, but had to declare their belief in the first article of the Mahometan faith, that Mahomet, its founder, was a prophet; and even the family of Maimun had to assume the mask of Islam. As the religious persecution had now lasted for a decade, the African communities had begun to waver in their religious convictions. Only the strongest minds could continue to practice a religion which was forced upon them, and still inwardly remain faithful to their hereditary religion. The thoughtless multitude gradually became accustomed to the enforced religion, saw in the merciless oppression of Judaism its dissolution, and changing pretense into reality, came near to lending themselves to the notion that God had, through Mahomet, superseded His revelation on Mount Sinai by another in Mecca, and almost believed that He had chosen the Arabs instead of the Jews. This self-abandonment and overwhelming despair filled Maimun the elder with pain, and he sought to counteract their apathy as much as lay in his power, and to confirm the belief in Judaism in the hearts of the pseudo-Mahometan Jews. With this object he wrote in Arabic an exhortation to the community (1160), which is full of mournfulness, and instinct with a deep sense of religion. It warns the community to reflect that their sufferings did not arise from a feeling of revenge on the part of God, but from a desire to chasten the sinners. Moses in his Law had promised Israel a dazzling future which would assuredly not fail. It was accordingly the duty of the sons of his race to adhere firmly to their God and His Torah. The occupation with religion and the practice of what it enjoined were the ropes to which those who were sinking in the sea of trouble should cling. Every one should, as far as he was able, observe the religious precepts of Judaism, and turn himself in prayer to his God, and whoever was prevented from praying in the prescribed form should, at least, say a short prayer in Hebrew three times a day. Like the Jews who had been forced to baptism under the Spanish Visigothic kings, those who had been converted under compulsion

to Islam now exhorted one another to remain faithful to their ancient religion. Soon Maimun's son found an opportunity to enter the arena, to give expression to his original views on Judaism, to offer encouragement to his comrades in affliction, and to point out to them the course which they should pursue.

A Jewish writer of excessive piety had declared that all Jews who pretended to have adopted Mahometanism were to be treated as apostates and idolaters. He who publicly acknowledged Mahomet's mission as a prophet was to be regarded as a non-Jew, even though he privately fulfilled all the duties of Judaism, and he belonged to that class whose testimony had no validity in a Jewish court, particularly in affairs of marriage. He who visited a mosque, pretending to be a Mahometan, made himself guilty of blasphemy, even though he did not take part in prayer; and he only accentuated his offense, when, in the privacy of his own chamber, he recited the Jewish prayers. This zealot, in fine, asserted that every true Jew was bound to sacrifice his own life and that of his children rather than embrace the faith of Islam, even ostensibly. His theory rested on the assumption that Mahometanism is nothing more nor less than idolatry, for in Mecca, the holy city of the Mahometans, an idol was worshipped in the temple of the Kaaba. If Islam is so reprehensible--so continued the zealot, whose name has not come down to us--then the Talmudical precept, that every Jew should suffer martyrdom rather than be forced to idolatry, would apply to that creed, and he who in such circumstances shrank from death was to be considered an apostate.

This document appears to have produced considerable excitement among the secret Jews in Africa. The conscientious felt themselves crushed down by a burden of sin, the multitude became still more uncertain whether they should not secede to Islam altogether, since, however strictly they observed the ordinances of their religion, they were still considered idolaters and sinners, and could expect no pardon.

Moses Maimuni, who felt the whole weight of the accusation against himself and his brethren in suffering, and was apprehensive of evil consequences, thought that it behooved him to write a letter in refutation of the arguments of their assailant, and to justify the conduct of the pseudo-Mahometans. It was his first step into publicity, but this maiden effort bore the impress of his clear, comprehensive mind, which mastered a subject in all its aspects. He argued from new points of view, which had escaped the zealot, and the whole letter was so striking that it brought conviction to all minds. Maimuni, in this vindication, which he wrote in Arabic, that all men might be able to read it, took up a Talmudical standpoint, equally with the zealot, but he proved contrary results from the very passages adduced by his adversary.

He first of ail showed that partial transgression of the duties of Judaism did not constitute absolute departure from it. The idolatrous Israelites in the times of the prophets were always considered as members of the people of the Lord. Meir, a highly esteemed doctor of the Mishnah, had feigned heathenism during a time of persecution, and when put to the test, had even partaken of forbidden food. "We, however," continues Maimuni, "in no wise pay homage to heathenism by our actions, but only repeat an empty formula, which the Mahometans themselves know is not uttered by us in sincerity, but only from a wish to circumvent the bigoted ruler." Then he enters deeper into the matter. The Talmud ordains that all Jews should suffer martyrdom rather than let themselves be compelled to commit three capital sins--idolatry, unchastity, and murder. It was indeed highly meritorious to

suffer death rather than violate any commandment of the Law, so as to keep the name of God holy. But he who does not possess the resolution of a martyr, even in regard to committing the three capital sins, does not render himself liable to the punishment attached to idolatry, and moreover is in no wise regarded as a transgressor of the Law. For in the case of compulsion, the Torah has revoked all obligations. He, then, who lacks the courage to sacrifice himself for Judaism has transgressed only one precept, that of sanctifying the name of the Lord, but he still does not belong to those whose testimony has no validity in a law court. Even if any one should, by compulsion, actually worship an idol, he would by no means be exposed to punishment for idolatry, for how could the involuntary transgressor be compared with the willful violator of his religion ? "Then there is something else to consider," said Maimuni. " We must make a distinction between a transgression by mere word, and one by deed. The Mahometan authorities by no means demand of Jews a denial of Judaism, but a mere lip utterance of a profession of faith that Mahomet was a prophet, and this having been done, they do not offer much objection if the Jews conform to their own laws. Such compulsion, where nothing more than a word is demanded, is, in reality, without parallel. He who sacrifices himself as a martyr, rather than acknowledge Mahomet as the messenger of God, certainly performs a most meritorious action. But if a person puts the question whether he is bound to give up his life in a case of that kind, then we must answer conscientiously according to the precepts of Judaism, 'No.' But we ought to and must advise him to leave a country where such religious coercion prevails. This advice I give also to myself and my friends, to remove to some place where there exists religious freedom. Those, however, who have been compelled to stay, should consider themselves as exiles from whom God has turned His face, and should strive to discharge their religious duties ; but we should not despise those who, out of necessity, have been obliged to violate the Sabbath, but must gently admonish them not to forsake the Law. Those are in error who believe that they need not make any preparations for a departure on the ground that the Messiah will soon appear, and redeem them, and lead them back to Jerusalem. The coming of the Messiah has nothing to do with religious obligations; his advent has no absolving power." This reply of Maimuni, which was in reality an apology for his conduct and that of his friends (written about 1160-1164), displays the germs of his original conception of Judaism. Moses Maimuni appears to have zealously endeavored to induce the Jewish pseudo-Mahometans to retain their ancient religion, to combat their lukewarmness, and to urge them to abandon their equivocal life. On this account he exposed himself to extreme danger, and might have been put to death, if a Mahometan theologian and poet, named Abul-Arab Ibn-Moisha, had not interceded for him, and saved him. The feeling of insecurity, together with the pricks of conscience, when compelled publicly to deny Judaism, which they held as their most precious treasure, induced the family of Maimun to leave Fez, and travel to Palestine. In the depth of night they embarked (4th Iyar--18th April, 1165). After they had sailed for six days on the Mediterranean, there arose a terrible storm, gigantic waves tossed the vessel about like a shuttlecock, and rescue seemed impossible. But the storm abated, and, after a journey of one month, the ship sailed into the harbor of Accho (3rd Sivan--16th May). This day Maimun dedicated as a family festival, for having escaped religious intolerance and the dangers of the sea. The emigrants from Spain were

received in a friendly manner by the congregation of Accho. After a residence of nearly half a year in this town, the family traveled amid dangers to Jerusalem to pray at the ancient site of the Temple (4th Marcheshvan-- 14th October). They remained in Jerusalem for three days, then journeyed to Hebron, and from that place to Egypt, which at that time bade fair, through the Ajubides, to become the center of Islam. Some months after their arrival in Egypt the head of the family died (beginning of 1166). So highly esteemed were both father and son by all who knew them, that letters of consolation were sent to the latter by his friends in Africa and Christian Spain.

On the other hand, in Egypt, in old Cairo (Fostat), where the family of Maimun had settled, Maimuni's name had not as yet become famous. The two brothers lived quietly, and carried on the jewelry trade, the younger brother taking a far more active share, and traveling on business as far as India. Moses Maimuni, on the other hand, devoted himself to study. Severe misfortunes, which would have brought a mind less strong than his to despair, tore him from this quiet life. Physical sufferings threw him on a bed of sickness; heavy losses diminished his fortune, and informers appeared against him, and brought him to the brink of death. Lastly, his brother David perished in the Indian Ocean, and with him not only their fortunes, but also the money which had been entrusted to them by others for business purposes. These accumulated misfortunes aggravated his sufferings, and filled him with melancholy. The death of his brother afflicted him most. His unbounded trust in God, his enthusiastic love for learning, and his anxiety for his family, and for the widow and daughter of his brother, roused his courage once more, and moved him to enter on an active life. Maimuni appears from this time to have gained a livelihood by the practice of medicine. Nevertheless, as he was still unknown, his practice at first did not prove very lucrative. About this time he also gave public lectures on philosophical subjects. His whole mind, however, was bent on the completion of the gigantic work with which he had been occupied since his twenty-third year, during all his travels, in Mahometan disguises, on sea voyages, and in the midst of numerous adversities. He finished this his first great work in the year 1168, in Arabic, under the title of "Siraj" ("Illumination"). The object of this work was to facilitate the study of the Talmud, which had become difficult through its diffuse discussions, through the interpolated explanations of the Geonim, and through the commentaries of his predecessors, which were not always pertinent to the subject; to determine the right practice (Halacha) from the confusion of diverse arguments, and to define his position by short but comprehensive explanations of words and things.

Maimuni's commentary on the Mishnah arose out of the author's mental organization, which ever strove for clearness, method and symmetry. It was the first scientific treatment of the Talmud, and only so clear and systematic a thinker as Maimuni could have originated it, for the construction of the Talmud seems to be directly opposed to an orderly arrangement. The luminous introductions to the several parts of the commentary especially give evidence of its scientific character. In them he reveals complete command over the material, as well as a logical conception of the method to be pursued.

Maimuni treated, with special predilection, those points of the Mishna which have a scientific coloring, and into the treatment of which the principles of mathematics, astronomy, physics, anatomy, ethics and philosophy could be introduced. Here he was in his element. In such parts he could show that the doctors of the Mishnah, the upholders of tradition, knew science also, and based their works upon it. Especially did he aim at establishing that the Mishnah contains a sound ethical and a deep philosophical conception of God. To this end he turned his attention with particular interest and thoroughness to the Agadic elements in the Mishna, which till then had been little or only occasionally noticed. He further explained the nature of tradition, maintaining that not all that is contained in the Mishnah is tradition. For a traditional doctrine must be positive, and ought not to be open to doubt or uncertainty. Unconsciously Maimuni by this theory put himself in opposition to the Talmud, and undermined its firm position.

The tractate of the Mishnah, which combines, like a string of pearls, the sayings of the fathers (Aboth), appeared in the eyes of Maimuni a veritable treasure-trove. In explaining these he could display the whole wealth of his world of thought, and he thus saturated Talmudical Judaism with philosophical ideas. But he thereby became the victim of self-delusion. It was important for the future that Maimuni, in his unconscious self-deception, undertook for the first time to develop a Jewish system of belief. Since Judaism, according to his views, was nothing more than revealed philosophy, it ought to dominate the beliefs and opinions of men as well as their religious and moral conduct; aye, the one more than the other, as morality has no value in itself, and is only the fruit of right knowledge. He, accordingly, assumed as certain and positive that Judaism defines for us not only what we must do, but what we must believe; that it asserts certain ideas as irrefrutable truth. Maimonides drew up thirteen of such doctrines or articles of belief:--The belief in the existence of God; in His indivisible unity ; in His incorporeality and insusceptibility of change; in His eternity and existence before the world; in His absolute claim to our adoration (Monotheism); in the prophetic inspiration of chosen men; in Moses as the greatest prophet, with whom no other prophet can be compared; in the divinity of the Torah; in its inalterability; in God's providence; in His just reward and punishment; in the future appearance of the Messiah; and, finally, in the resurrection of the dead. Although these articles of faith rest on investigation, and therefore cannot claim unquestioning acceptance, yet, according to Maimuni, no one can be considered a true Israelite or Jew who does not acknowledge them all as true; he who denies a single one of them is a heretic (Min, Epicoros), he does not belong to the community of Judaism, and cuts himself off from the hope of future bliss.

Maimuni thus, on the one hand, raised the Jewish creed to the height of rational knowledge, and, on the other, set bounds to the free development of thought. Hitherto religious action only was valued as the characteristic of Jewish life. Maimuni now called a halt to free thought, marked the boundary line between belief and heresy, not in the firm province of religious practice, but in the shifting ground of religious belief, and brought the ethereal element of thought under rigid formulae.

Great as the work of Maimuni in his commentary on the Mishnah undoubtedly is, although he applied to it infinite learning, wealth of intellect, and systematic arrangement, yet he did not obtain a reputation corresponding to its merit. The reason of this was that among the Jews of Egypt and the East, to whom the work, being in Arabic, was most of all accessible, there was but the faintest appreciation of scientific treatment. The great work was at first scarcely noticed in the East. His pupils, to whom he gave lectures on the same plan, and who revered him as the incarnation of wisdom, spread

SALADIN AND THE JEWS.

his reputation abroad. One of his earliest disciples, Solomon Kohen, who traveled to southern Arabia (Yemen), was full of his praise, and impressed on the congregation there that, in time of need, they should apply to Maimuni for consolation and support.

In Egypt far-reaching changes had crept in, which produced a favorable turn In the fortunes of the Jews of that empire and the neighboring countries. The Fatimide Caliph died, or was deposed, and the great Saladin, the model of royal magnanimity and chivalry in that barbarous age, succeeded to the government (September, 1171)· At first the celebrated Ajublde only held the office of Vice-Field-Marshal of Nureddin; gradually he acquired absolute supremacy over Egypt and a part of Palestine, Syria, and even the districts about the Euphrates, and the Caliphate of Bagdad obeyed his rule. His empire became a safe asylum to the oppressed Jews. Saladin was just to the Jews, as indeed towards every one, even his bitterest enemies. Under him the Jews rose to great prosperity and distinction.

At first the fall of the Fatimide Caliphate, and the subjection of the surrounding countries belongIng to it, under the Abbasid or Sunnite Caliphs of Baghdad, set loose fanaticism which was felt by the Jewish congregations of Yemen. In that place two Shiites had seized upon the government, and they compelled the Jews to embrace Islam under threat of great suffering. Here also, as in Africa and southern Spain, the Jews outwardly pretended to adopt the Mahometan religion (about 1172). But as the grossest ignorance prevailed among them, there was danger that the unthinking multitude would proceed from pretense to reality, and fall away from Judaism altogether. This fear became real when a Jewish apostate preached to the congregation that Mahomet is mentioned in the Torah, and that Islam was a new, divinely announced revelation, which was intended to supersede Judaism. In addition, at just about this time, there appeared a Jewish enthusiast in Yemen, who proclaimed himself to be the forerunner of the Messiah, endeavored to instill in the Jews the belief that their affliction was the harbinger of the speedy approach of the Messianic empire, and bade them hold themselves in readiness for that event, and divide their property with the poor. This enthusiastic hope, to which many clung as drowning men to a straw, threatened to bring the direst misfortune on the heads of the Yemen Jews. The pious abandoned themselves to despair in the contemplation of these proceedings, altogether lost their heads, and knew not what plan they should adopt. At this point, Jacob Alfayumi, the most learned and most respected man among them, turned to Maimuni, of whom he had heard through his disciples, for counsel and consolation, described to him their sufferings and apprehensions, and begged him to send a reply.

Maimuni accordingly sent a letter of consolation, in Arabic, to the congregation of Yemen, directed personally to his correspondent, but having reference to all the members (Iggeret Yemen). In spite of its small compass, it contains valuable matter, and bears witness to the writer's lofty soul and spiritual refinement. He sought in it to elevate the sufferers to the height of spiritual consciousness, on which suffering for religion's sake loses its sting, and darkness appears as the inevitable antecedent of the break of day. He expressed himself on the relation of Judaism to Christianity and Islam with an acuteness and precision which reflect his profound conviction. It was certainly sad to reflect, remarks the sage of Cairo, that there should have occurred cruel persecutions of the Jews in two opposite directions ; in the West by the Almohades,

and in the East by the Mahometans of Yemen. Nevertheless they were not unexpected, for the prophets had announced them quite distinctly. "Because God has specially distinguished us, sons of Israel, through His grace, and has appointed us the upholders of the true religion and the true creed, the nations hate us, not only on our own account, but on account of the divinity which lives in our midst, in order to thwart in some measure the divine will." Since the revelation on Sinai there had never been a time when Judaism and its professors had not been exposed to sufferings and persecutions. The nations had manifested their hate in three different forms; either with the sword, like Amalek, Sennacherib, Nebuchadnezzar, Titus, and Hadrian, in order utterly to root out from the earth the nation that possessed the truth; or with the false tricks of sophistical persuasion, like the Persians, Greeks, and Romans, with a view to refute and falsify the doctrines of Judaism; or finally under the mask of revelation, as it were, in the garb of Judaism, in order to juggle it out of existence. The principle inimical to Judaism had at length discovered that it was unable to annihilate the upholder's of God's religion, or to tear it out of their hearts ; and now it hoped to destroy them by a crafty device. It pretended also to have received a revelation acknowledging that on Sinai to have been authorized for a time, but declared that it now had no further validity. This hostile principle, which sought the banishment of the divine from earth, attempted to substitute a stuffed figure for a godly child, and falsify Judaism. The new revelations of Nazareth and Mecca, compared with Judaism, were like well-executed statues of a man, compared with a real man full of life and energy. All this bitter enmity of the nations of the earth against Israel and its divine religion had been foreseen by the prophets, especially by Daniel, who at the same time foretold the victory of Judaism over superstition. "And now, brethren," so Maimuni addressed the congregation of Yemen in his letter, "consider. well these truths, and do not let yourselves be discouraged by the superabundance of your woe. Its purpose is to test you, and to show that the posterity of Jacob, the descendants of those who received the Law on Sinai, are in possession of the true Law." Furthermore, he pointed out that it was wrong to calculate the Messianic period, as the Yemen enthusiast thought he had succeeded in doing; for it can never be exactly determined, it having been purposely concealed as a deep secret by the prophets.

Lastly, Maimuni exhorted Jacob Alfayumi to circulate his letter among the congregations of Yemen, that it might strengthen them in their faith, but to take great precautions when reading it that no traitor might be given the opportunity of making it the pretext for an accusation. He himself, said Maimuni, wrote in anxiety as to the evil consequences which might ensue for him; but he considered that he who wished to work for the general good must not be deterred by apprehensions of danger. This interesting letter of consolation, which was written with much warmth, made so favorable an impression on the Jews of southern Arabia, that they, far from growing indifferent to their religion, were strengthened in it, and were moved to take an energetic share in all the events affecting the welfare of the whole body of Jews. In later times, when Maimuni attained greater importance, he found the means of putting a stop to the political oppression and bigoted persecution suffered by the Jews. For this the congregation of Yemen clove to him with enthusiastic love and veneration. They included his name in their daily prayer, a demonstration of honor which had been accorded only to the Exilarchs at their zenith.

FAME OF MAIMONIDES.

Maimuni's greatness only gradually obtained acknowledgment. As early as the year 1175, he was looked upon as an authority in the determination of rabbinical laws; and religious-legal questions were addressed to him from all parts, a circumstance from which we may infer the universal recognition of his authority. Maimuni appears to have been officially recognized in 1177 as rabbi of Cairo, on account of his profound knowledge of the Talmud, his character, and his fame. He, with nine colleagues, formed an ecclesiastical board. His office he regarded as a holy priesthood, and exercised it with characteristic conscientiousness and circumspection. Where he perceived any abuses, he placed himself boldly in the breach. Although Maimuni worked hard in eliminating from the rabbinical world all Karaite customs which had crept in, he, nevertheless, always showed great tolerance toward the followers of Anan. Being asked how Rabbanites should behave towards Karaites, he replied that as long as they kept within the bounds of decency, and did not scoff at the Talmud, they were to be treated respectfully, and to be approached with friendliness, humility, and in a pacific spirit. Rabbanites might visit them in their houses, bury their dead, comfort their mourners, and initiate their children into the covenant of Abraham. The Talmud enjoins that we must observe a friendly demeanor towards heathens and idolaters, how much more so towards those who spring from the seed of Jacob, and acknowledge only one God. By virtue of his office,

Maimuni tried hard to secure decorum in the synagogue, and also to remove many long-continued abuses. He noticed, for instance, that when the congregation had finished saying the silent prayer, thinking that they had performed their duty, they did not listen to its audible repetition by the reader, but chatted with one another, and generally behaved in an unbecoming manner. The Mahometans mocked at them, and with justice too, for they were accustomed to conduct their own divine service with concentrated devotion. Maimuni, who always felt deeply mortified when Judaism was exposed to ridicule, was anxious to put a stop to such offensive behavior in the synagogues, and with this motive abrogated the silent prayer altogether, without considering that it is expressly prescribed by the Talmud. Sincere prayer was to him of higher importance than mere mechanical fulfillment of precept. This practice, instituted by Maimuni, according to which the reader alone said the chief prayer, was followed, not only in the whole of Egypt, but even in several congregations of Palestine, in Damascus, and Haleb, and was continued among the native congregations for three centuries.

In the midst of his energetic activity in communal affairs, practicing as a physician, and devoting himself to the constant study of philosophy and science, Maimuni completed his second great work (8 Kislev --7 November, 1180), his epoch-making "Mishne Torah," or Religious Code. If, as he states, he labored at it continuously for ten successive years, the time stands in no relation to the magnitude of the performance. It is impossible to give the uninitiated an idea of this gigantic work, in which he collected the most remote things from the vast mine of the Talmud, extracting the fine metal from the dross, classifying all details under their appropriate heads, showing how the Talmud was based on the Bible, bringing its details under general rules, combining apparently unconnected parts into one organized whole, and cementing it into a work of art. He justly laid special emphasis, in the Mishne-Torah, on the necessity of skillful grouping, the difficulties of which can be estimated only by a specialist deeply versed in the subject. The Talmud resembles a Daedalian maze, in which one can

scarcely find his way even with Ariadne's thread, but Maimuni designed a well-contrived ground-plan, with wings, halls, apartments, chambers, and closets, through which a stranger might easily pass without a guide, and thereby obtain a survey of all that is contained in the Talmud. Only a mind accustomed to think clearly and systematically, and filled with the genius of order, could have planned and built a structure like this.

Apart from the technical excellences, and the incomparably well proportioned architecture, the work had, as far as the contents are concerned, a most important influence on the development of Jewish history. All the various lines which his predecessors had partially traced out on the ground of Judaism, Maimuni united in the greatest harmony. Nothing therein is given undue prominence, and nothing is neglected. The philosophical, the ethical and the ceremonial sides, and, so to speak, the emotional side of Judaism which the aspiration for a Messianic period of redemption expresses, are treated in this work as of equal worth and prominence. Maimuni united the divergent roads on which Judaism had been led, and made them meet together in one point. He worked out to final perfection all the efforts which, since Saadiah had tried to give a philosophical basis to Judaism, and to make clear its import, had been embodied in writing. His work was the necessary center of gravity of the tremendous intellectual structure of three centuries.

It may almost be said that Maimuni created a new Talmud. The old elements are certainly there; we know their source, their occurrence, and their original application, but under his treatment, grouping, and elaboration they assume a new shape. The rust is removed, the confusing non-essential matter is taken out, and everything appears newly cast, polished, fresh, and original. The Mishnah, the groundwork of the Talmud, begins with the question, "At what time is the Shema to be said in the evening?" and concludes with a discussion as to what things are unclean according to Levitical law. Maimuni, on the other hand, thus commences his Talmudical Code, "The foundation and pillar of all wisdom is to recognize that there is an original Being, who called all creatures into existence," and ends with the words, "The earth shall be full of the knowledge of the Lord as the waters cover the sea." Maimuni, so to speak, talmudized Philosophy, and philosophized the Talmud. He admitted philosophy into his religious Code, and conceded it a place of equal importance with the Halacha. From the time of Philo till Abraham Ibn-Daud, philosophy had always been treated as something secondary, which had nothing to do with practical Judaism, as it is daily and hourly practiced. Maimuni, on the other hand, introduced it into the holiest place in Judaism, and as it were gave Aristotle a place next to the doctors of the Law. A great portion of the first book of his work (Sepher Madda) is of a philosophical character. The object of his work was to simplify the knowledge of the whole of Judaism, both Biblical and Talmudical, which in his judgment were of equal value. He wanted to clear up the diffuseness and obscurity, which arise from Talmudical idiom, the discussions, the incomplete explanations of the Geonim, and render the study of the Talmud so difficult; to illumine chaos, and put confusion into order. The rabbi who had to determine questions of a religious or legal character, the pious man who desired to discharge his religious duty of knowing the Law, the student who desired to obtain knowledge of the Talmud, had no more need to struggle through the thorny underbrush of Halachic discus-

sions, but in addition to Holy Writ had simply to refer to the Code of the Mishne-Torah, in order to acquire complete information. He hinted rather broadly that his work was intended to render the Talmud less necessary, if not to supersede it. For this reason he wrote it in the neo-Hebrew language (Mishnah idiom), which was easily understood, so as to make it accessible to all people, and thus spread the knowledge of the Law, and the principles of Judaism generally. It is true that he came into collision with the views of his rabbinical contemporaries, who expected the Talmud to be treated with the same respect as the Holy Scriptures, wherein no word is superfluous, and which, therefore, must be studied in the original text.

In consistently carrying out his principle that all details should be brought under comprehensive heads, and that nothing should be admitted without conclusive grounds, Maimuni could not help deviating occasionally in his decisions from the Talmud method of determining the case, and striking out into a path peculiar to himself. In one particular point he stepped beyond the bounds of the Talmud. The Talmud treats as Biblical many decisions which were inferred from verses of Scripture by an application of the accepted rules of interpretation. Maimuni, however, advanced the principle that only those laws were Biblical which the Talmud distinctly claimed to be so without recording any difference of opinion on the subject.

In this bold view Maimuni was manifestly influenced by the objection of the Karaites against the Oral Law. Without being himself clearly aware of it, he conceded that a genuine tradition could not be amenable to differences of opinion, and must never, during its transmission from generation to generation, be exposed to doubt.

Although Maimuni's theory, consistently followed out, is calculated to undermine Talmudical Judaism, that Judaism, nevertheless, was in practice held by him in such estimation that he regarded nothing to be of higher importance. The Talmudical sages were, in his eyes, authorities who occupied a position only a step lower than the prophets. He regarded them as ideals, to emulate whom would lead to a virtuous, religious, and perfect life. The legal decisions proceeding from them, whether mandatory or prohibitory, could be abrogated only under circumstances specified in the Talmud itself. In practice, accordingly, it made no difference whether a law was Biblical or rabbinical; both were to be observed with equal conscientiousness.

Maimuni, through his religious Code, gave rabbinical Judaism a strong hold, and on the other hand he helped to ossify it. Much in the Talmud that was still unsettled and open to explanation he crystallized into unchangeable law. As he introduced into Judaism articles of belief, which were to limit thought by thought, so by his codified determinations of the laws, he robbed it of its mobility. Without considering the condition of the times in which the Talmudical decisions had arisen, he laid them down as binding for all times and circumstances. In this respect he was much stricter than the Tossafist school, who took the sting out of a too burdensome law by proving after elaborate examination that it was not applicable to changed circumstances and times, If Maimuni's Code had acquired absolute supremacy, as it at first seemed likely to do, and had dislodged the Talmud from the schools, from the hands of the religious authorities, and from the Jewish courts of law, Talmudical Judaism would have succumbed to petrifaction, notwithstanding the rich thought and the scientific treatment which Maimuni bestowed on it.

However, as soon as the Jews obtained possession of Maimuni's Code, which was accessible to them by reason of its simple language and arrangement,

EFFECTS OF THE "MISHNE-TORAH."

they began to see clearly its high importance. In Spain, it was said, every one copied it for himself; the Jewish mind was absorbed in it, young and old gathered together in order to master its contents. There were now many doctors of the Law who could pass an original opinion on any controversial point of law, and check the decision of the judge. And as in Spain, so it was in all countries, even in the East, where the study of the Talmud was more energetically pursued. The reverence for the great master increased every day, especially when it became known that his private life corresponded to the ideal which he had delineated of a Jewish sage. His people lavished on him the most enthusiastic of praises. " The only one of his time," "The banner of the rabbis," "The enlightener of the eyes of Israel," were modest titles. It required all Maimuni's moral force not to be overpowered by the incense burned before him. Maimuni's name rang from Spain to India, and from the sources of the Euphrates and the Tigris to southern Arabia, and eclipsed all contemporary celebrities. The most learned men subordinated themselves to his judgment, and solicited his instruction in the most humble manner; he was regarded as chief authority for the whole Jewish world, which revered him as its noblest representative.

He did not escape the attack of petty opponents, who were jealous of his towering greatness, Insignificant rabbis, who, being superficially familiar with the text of the Talmud, thought themselves in possession of all wisdom, and were unpleasantly awakened from their dream by Maimuni's work. In Cairo itself some Talmudists would not deign to bestow a glance on the Code, lest it might be said that they had learned something out of it. Others argued that the College of Baghdad was the only seat of Talmudical knowledge, and that he who had not studied in this school could not be recognized as thoroughly initiated, and, consequently, Maimuni's decisions did not deserve unconditional acceptance. Such little minds persuaded themselves that it lay in their power to compose a like or even a better work on all the laws of Judaism. The head of this petty opposition was Samuel ben Ali, of Baghdad, who, on his richly embellished Gaonate throne, surrounded by his slaves armed with scourges, would not acknowledge any one his equal, much less his superior. Maimonides opposed a contemptuous silence to detractors of this class. However, he also had honorable adversaries, who feeling that Maimuni's conception of Talmudical Judaism was not flesh of their flesh, scented heresy in the Code, and perceived danger therein to the practice of the religion. But wherein the strange and inconsistent elements lay only the more learned understood; the simple, on the other hand, lit upon secondary and quite unessential points, and excited themselves about them, as if the fundamental principles of the religion were in danger.

Thus, in Alexandria, after the publication of Maimuni's work, there broke out against it a popular insurrection, because it was taught therein that bathing before prayer, which the Eastern Jews had adopted from their Mahornetan neighbors, was not essential. Members of the congregation combined, and threatened to lay information against it before the Mahometan authorities, on the ground that those who had adopted Maimuni's Code as law wished to introduce innovations into the religion.

It was only after a residence in Egypt of more than twenty years that Maimuni obtained an appointment as physician at the court of Saladin; up to that time he had acquired only a slight practice. He was not Saladin's physician in ordinary, for the Sultan, on account of the constant wars with the adherents of Nureddin and with the Christians, could not visit his capital for a long time. But the favor of the noble vizier, the wise and mighty Alfadhel,

MAIMONIDES AS A PHYSICIAN.

who was also a great promoter of learning, and of whom a contemporary said, "he was entirely head and heart," was of as much value as the distinguished recognition of the sovereign. Alfadhel caused Maimuni to be placed on the list of physicians, settled upon him a yearly salary, and loaded him with favors. Inspired by his example, the great men of the country who lived in Cairo likewise bestowed upon him their patronage, so that Maimuni's time was so fully occupied that he was obliged to neglect his studies. Maimuni was indebted for his elevation more to his medical learning than to his skill as a physician; for he pursued this profession as a learned science, and prescribed no recipe for whose efficacy he could not cite the judgment of medical authorities. He treated the facts of scientific medicine in the same spirit as he had treated the Talmud. In this manner he elaborated the writings of Galen, the medical oracle in the Middle Ages; he abridged and arranged them, without permitting himself to deviate from the original in the slightest particular. The same character is borne also by his medical aphorisms, which are nothing further than extracts from and classifications of older theories. In spite of his almost absolute lack of originality in the province of medicine, Maimuni nevertheless enjoyed a wide reputation as a medical author. The celebrated Mahometan physician and theologian, Abdel-latif, of Baghdad, who enjoyed the favor of Saladin in a high degree, confessed that his wish to visit Cairo was prompted by the desire to make the acquaintance of three men, among whom was Musa ben Maimun. The poet and kadhi, Alsaid Ibn-Sina Almulk, sang of Matmuni's greatness as a physician in ecstatic verse:

" Galen's art heals only the body,
But Abu-Amran's (Maimuni's) the body and soul.
With his wisdom he could heal the sickness of ignorance.
If the moon would submit to his art,
He would deliver her of her spots at the time of full moon,
Cure her of her periodic defects,
And at the time of her conjunction save her from want"

Maimuni's reputation was so great that the English king, Richard Coeur-de-Lion, the soul of the third crusade, wanted to appoint him his physician in ordinary, but Maimuni refused the offer.

His patron, the chief judge and vizier Alfadhel, acquitted him at about this time of a grave charge, for which, under a less mild Mahometan, or even a Christian judge, he would have incurred the penalty of death. The same Abulalarab Ibn-Moisha who had befriended Maimuni in Fez, had come from Maghreb to Egypt, and when he saw Maimuni, whom he had known as a Mahometan, at the head of the Jewish community as spiritual chief, he appeared against him as an accuser, and averred that Maimuni had for a long time professed the religion of Islam, and consequently ought to be punished as a renegade. Alfadhel, before whose tribunal the accusation was preferred, decided rightly that the compulsory adoption of a creed could have no value, and, therefore, could involve no penalties (about 1187). In consequence of his favor with the vizier, Maimuni was appointed supreme head of all the Egyptian congregations, and this dignity descended in his family from father to son and grandson. It is certain that Maimuni drew no salary for this office, for nothing appeared to him more discreditable and sinful than to receive payment for the discharge of spiritual duties, or to degrade knowledge into a money-making business. He sought this prominent position not for himself, but for the sake of his co-religionists, in order to save them from injustice. It was through him that the heavy yoke of persecution was removed from the congregation of Yemen. When Saladin had once more wrested Jerusalem from the hands of the Christians, who had held it for nearly a century, he allowed the Jews to settle in the city of their fathers (October, 1187)· And from all sides there came devoted sons to visit their mourning and forsaken

mother. Possibly Maimuni was not unconnected with this act of noble-minded tolerance. Lastly, he endeavored to obtain for his brethren in faith precedence in the state over the Karaites, and gradually to oust the latter from their favorable position at court, so that many of them reverted to Rabbanism. This was accounted to Maimuni as a most meritorious deed in his time.

The higher Maimuni advanced in the esteem of his contemporaries, the more his extraordinary ability was acknowledged, and the louder his fame resounded, the more did the arrogant Samuel ben Ali, of Baghdad, feel himself belittled, and the more did he become filled with envy. Samuel accordingly took every opportunity to depreciate Maimuni's merit, and rob him of his fame. Samuel and his friends whispered to one another that Maimuni was by no means a strictly religious Jew, nor a true follower of the Talmud, and they spread many calumnies about him. Some mistakes which he had made in his youthful work, the Mishnah Commentary, were used by these malevolent people with a view to brand him as ignorant of the Talmud, and without claim to authority in this province.

In Damascus and Yemen there appeared religious teachers, who drew from Maimuni's writings logical conclusions which he himself did not care to deduce. As he strongly affirmed, and repeatedly insisted, that by the immortality of the soul a purely spiritual existence in another world was to be understood, whereas he passed over the resurrection of the dead as of only secondary importance, his disciples concluded that he was not thoroughly convinced of the resurrection, and forthwith began to teach that after death the body sinks into dissolution and decay, and that only the soul becomes elevated to a purely spiritual life. This liberal view clashed with explicit declarations in the Talmud, and consequently aroused general opposition. Samuel ben Ali was requested by someone in Yemen to give his opinion on this question of the belief in the resurrection. Samuel wrote a whole treatise upon it, with philosophical flourishes, in order to appear a worthy rival of Maimuni, and seized the opportunity of criticizing the latter's writings, hoping to heighten the effect of the criticism by according partial praise to Maimuni. On another occasion, Samuel ben Ali directed a letter to Maimuni, in which, amid much flattery and fawning, he reproached him with having committed an error in interpreting the Talmud, which could scarcely have been made by a beginner, kindly adding that Maimuni must not fret himself about it. At the same time, he did not forget to promise graciously to take him under his protection against the congregation in Yemen. Maimuni replied with a heated letter, in which he showed his malicious opponent that it was he who had erred in the deeper conception of the Talmud. He also touched upon the secret attacks made against his great work from this quarter, some asserting that the book contained mistakes, others that it was superfluous, others, again, that it was dangerous. "You seem," Maimuni observed to him, " to reckon me among those who are sensitive to every word of blame. You make a mistake. God has protected me against this weakness, and I protest to you, in His name, that if the most insignificant scholar, whether friend or foe, would point out to me an error, I would be grateful for the correction and instruction."

SAMUEL BEN ALI.

Although Samuel ben Ali was readily refuted by Maimuni, he still continued to spread the report that the latter was no Talmudist, and that his code did not deserve the respect which it enjoyed. From another side, from Haleb, Mar Sacharya, a man of limited range of vision, and with a superficial knowledge of the Talmud, thinking himself eclipsed by Maimuni's pupil, Joseph Ibn-Aknin, worked with equal hostility against master and disciple. But, as the sage of Fostat had warm and disinterested adherents everywhere, Samuel ben Ali and his ally of Haleb were constrained to act cautiously. They organized an intrigue against him, into which they drew one of the two Exilarchs. Towards this cabal, Maimuni assumed an attitude of contemptuous indifference and unconcern, which altogether disarmed his opponents.

In spite of his collisions with the party of Samuel ben Ali, and his prodigious activity as a physician, which scarcely gave him time for study, he completed his religious philosophical work, "Guide of the Perplexed" (*Moreh Nebuchim, Dalalat al Hairin*) in about 1190. This treatise became of extraordinary importance, not only for Judaism, but for the history of philosophy in the Middle Ages generally. Maimuni appears at the summit of his intellectual power in this work, and it contains the vindication of his profoundest convictions. The questions which the human mind starts ever anew, about the existence of a higher world, the destiny of our being, and the imperfection and evil of the earthly world, Maimuni sought to answer in a manner which was at that time considered convincing. The doubts which the thinking Jew may conceive of the truth of his hereditary religion, he endeavored to remove in a persuasive manner. He, whose thoughts were ever directed to the loftiest subjects, could with justice assume the character of guide to the perplexed and wavering. The external form of this epoch-making work would make it appear that the author had elaborated, for his favorite disciple, Joseph Ibn-Aknin, of Fez, separate treatises on important points which had disquieted and tortured the latter. But it was actually dictated by the desire to express clearly his philosophical conception of the world, and his views of the place which Judaism finds in it, and thoroughly to analyze their mutual relation.

Maimuni was, on the one hand, firmly convinced of the truth of the Aristotelian philosophy, as the Mahometan philosopher Ibn-Sina and others had formulated it. On the other hand, Judaism was to him a body of truths not less irrefutable. Both seemed to him to have the same conclusion and a common aim. Philosophy recognizes as the principal of all essences one indivisible God, the governor of the world. Judaism likewise teaches with emphatic attestation the unity of God, and abhors nothing more thoroughly than polytheism. Meta-physics knows no higher aim for man than that he should perfect himself intellectually, and work his way up to the highest knowledge. Judaism also, even Talmudical Judaism, places understanding and knowledge, the understanding of God, at the head of its precepts. If the truth which the human mind in the fullness of its power evolves from itself, and the revelation which the Deity vouchsafed to the Israelitish nation on Sinai, resemble each other in beginning and end, then their separate parts must correspond with each other, and be as one and the same truth, arrived at in different ways. Judaism cannot be in contradiction with philosophy, as both are emanations from the divine spirit. The truth which God has revealed must also agree with that which lies in the human reason, since the latter is a power originating from God, and similarly all truths which metaphysical thinking can bring to light must exist in the revelation--that is,

MAIMONIDES' "GUIDE FOR THE PERPLEXED."

in Judaism. Hence, Maimuni believed that originally, besides the written revelation in the Pentateuch, there were also communicated to the greatest of prophets oral doctrines of a philosophical character, which were transmitted by tradition to posterity, and which were lost only in consequence of the troubles and afflictions which the Israelites experienced in the course of ages. Traces of this old Israelitish wisdom are found, according to Maimuni, in the scattered utterances of the prophets, and in the reflections of the Agada. When, therefore, the thinking Jew borrows the truths of Greek philosophy, and adopts the theories of Plato and Aristotle, they are not altogether strange elements to him, but only a reminder of his own forgotten treasure.

The whole universe, which must be considered as a single organic whole, consisting of spheres suspended over one another working in harmony, is nothing more than the realized thoughts of God, or rather than the ideas of God ever tending to realization. He continually imparts to it new forms and shapes, and implants order and regularity in the world Everything is arranged therein in accordance with a final purpose. The Greek philosophy, it is true, assumes that the universe shares in the eternity of God; but it can neither irrefutably prove the eternity of the world, nor remove any of the difficulties which oppose the acceptation of the original existence of the universe. The doctrine of Judaism is much more reasonable, that the world had a positive beginning, and that time itself, which, indeed, is a form of the world and its motion, is not without beginning, but was called into being by the determining will of God.

The organically formed universe, created and made to cohere by God, consists of a series of entities of different degrees. Next to the Deity are the pure spirits, which are simple, and not composed of matter and form, and consequently partake most of the divine nature. Their necessary existence is proved philosophically, because many phenomena in the universe best admit of explanation through them. These pure spirits, these "forms free of matter," Judaism and Holy Writ call "angels." Among them must be assumed a spirit or angel who is the originator of thoughts or: ideas, the active world-spirit or creative reason (Sechel ha-Peel).

In the degree next to the pure spirits are entities which must certainly be considered as composed of matter and form, whose matter, however, is not heavy and coarse, but of an ethereal nature. These ethereal entities are the heavens and the brilliant world of stars, which possess an ever uniform motion, and are therefore not subject to the change of genesis and dissolution, but revolve in the firmament in constant brightness and with unbroken regularity. These form and influence the lower circle of entities. The stars are divided into four spheres--into the sphere of the fixed stars, of the moving stars (planets), of the sun and the moon. These spheres must be considered as endowed with life and intellectual power. Below the sphere of the moon there exists a grade of entities which are generated from coarser matter, but are susceptible of form, shape, and motion. This is the world of the four elements, which are in their turn fashioned into four spheres, one above the other. Within these spheres are formed, through manifold evolutions, influenced by the world of stars, lifeless minerals, plants, self-moving animals, and men capable of intelligence.

But how is the influence of God upon this multiform universe to be understood? The changes cannot proceed immediately through Him. The animated orbs of stars, which are the cause of all transformations on earth, are not set in motion by

God, but are impelled towards Him in longing and love, in order to partake of His perfection, His light, and His goodness. Through this ardent striving of the heavenly bodies to God comes their regular revolution, and in this manner they cause all changes in the world below the moon, in the circle of genesis and dissolution, through the reception and loss of peculiar forms and shapes. This theory of God, of the universe, and the various motions of the different beings, Maimuni found indicated in Holy Writ and in many utterances of the Agada, but only in obscure allusions, as these writings, being designed for every one, not solely for the philosopher, could not and durst not, at the risk of occasioning gross misunderstanding, unveil the complete image of truth.

More important than the analysis of this conception of the world is Maimuni's presentation of his ideas on matters more nearly concerning mankind. Since God, the creator of the world, is perfect and all-good, the world cannot have been made otherwise than good, and in accordance with a purpose. "God saw that all was good," "From on high there comes no evil." The evils which exist in the world are not to be looked upon as the work of God, but merely as the absence of the good and the perfect, since gross matter is incapable of partaking of the good and the divine. God did not create sin; but sin arises from the nature of the coarse matter, which is defective in its constitution, and which can only receive and retain defectively that which is good. But this evil must be overcome. God has implanted in the soul of man, who is superior to all entities composed of gross matter, the capacity and instinct for knowledge. If the soul follows this instinct, it is assisted by the active reason which has been specially created for the purpose of opening up to the soul the source of the divine spirit, in order that it may understand the structure of the world and God's influence upon it, and that it may be enabled to lead a worthy life. Man can thereby raise himself to the higher degree of the angels, and can conquer the frailties which arise out of his material body. Through this elevation to the higher abode of thought and to moral purity, and through mastery of his animal nature, man by his own will acquires a soul; he makes himself a super-earthly being, he wins for himself the immortality of the soul, and becomes united with the all-governing world-soul. The possibility of gaining this highest degree is vouchsafed to man with his freedom of will.

And man can acquire and in a manner win God's special providence in the same way as he can acquire and win immortality through the action of his soul. For God's care extends only to what remains and endures. Even in the lower world of the four elements, this is felt in the preservation of the species, which by reason of their form and purpose are of a spiritual nature. If man raises himself to the degree of a spirit, if he becomes master over matter, the providential eye of God will not pass him over. And as man can gain for himself, through moral and intellectual discipline, an immortal soul, so he incurs the highest penalty if his spiritual light is quenched through a sinful life, and is crushed by his material nature.

Man has the power of acquiring still more; he can, through an ideal life, come to possess the prophetic faculty, if he opens his mind by constant communion with God to the influences of the active reason. But it requires on the part of man cultivation and concentration of the imagination, and on the part of God the emanation of His spirit. Since a lively, continually active imagination is the chief qualification for prophecy, it can develop only in a state similar to a dream, when the disturbing activity of the senses is relaxed, and the mind may freely resign itself to the influences from above. The pro-

phesying of the prophets always occurred in a kind of dream. The Scriptural accounts of the actions and experiences of the prophets during their ecstatic condition, are not to be understood as being accounts of actual occurrences, but only of processes of the soul, as visions of the imagination. There are also different degrees of prophecy, according to the greater or less capacity requisite for them. Thus many miraculous tales in the Bible cease to appear supernatural and surprising, just as the hyperbolical style of the prophets is explicable on this theory. All this arises from the rule of the imagination and dream visions. Miracles are certainly not impossible. The same Creator who has established the laws of nature can also suspend them, but He does so only temporarily, that the old order may soon return, as when the waters of the Nile were changed into blood only for a short time, and the sea divided itself for the Israelites but for a few hours. The number of miracles in the Bible is, however, limited. Wonders are not, generally speaking, the means of verifying and confirming the declarations of the prophets; they must be proved by the prophecies themselves, and the fulfillment of what they predict. Miracles do not prove them true.

The most perfect of all prophets was that man of God with shining countenance, who brought to the world a religion which has exercised the profoundest sway over men's minds. The prophecy of Moses differed from that off other prophets in four essential points. He received the revelation without the mediation of another spiritual being, that is, without the influence of the active reason or of an angel, but communed with the Deity "face to face and mouth to mouth." Secondly, Moses communed with God, not in a dream, when all activity of the senses ceases, but the higher teaching was granted to him whilst he was in an ordinary frame of mind. Moreover, his being was not disturbed or dissolved by it, as in the case of other prophets when the spirit of God came upon them, but he could maintain himself under it. Finally, Moses was continually in the prophetic mood, whereas this power came upon other men of God only after longer or shorter intervals, and then only after careful preparation. Moses possessed this prophetic perfection only because, through the elevation of his mind, he had liberated himself from the tyranny of his senses, from desire, and even from his imagination, and had won for himself the degree of an angel, or of a pure spirit. [This picture of Moses, of course, is not the one presented in the scripture.--ed.] All coverings which blindfold the eye of the human mind, and disturb its view, he tore off, and penetrated to the fountain-head of truth. He attained to a degree such as no other mortal has reached, and therefore he was able also to recognize the Deity and His will with the undisturbed gaze of a pure spirit. The truth of the highest Being irradiated him without intermediation, and in transparent clearness, without word or speech. That which he perceived at such a height he brought to his people as a religion, as a revelation, and this truth, radiating immediately from the divinity, is the Torah.

This revealed religion, originating from God, is unique, just as the mediator, through whom the truth was conveyed to man, is the only one of his kind. Being a divine doctrine it is perfect, and consequently there can be none which can abrogate its authority, and supersede it, just as there was none previous to it.

The divinity of the Torah is proved by its contents as by its origin. It contains not only laws and precepts, but also dogmas upon questions most important for man, and this two-fold character is likewise a, mark to distinguish it at once from other codes and from other religions. Besides, the laws of the Torah aim at a higher purpose, so that there is nothing in it superfluous, nothing un-

necessary, nothing gratuitous. The design of the revelation brought down by Moses can be thus summarized: it was to promote the spiritual and physical welfare of those who received it, the one by inculcating correct ideas of God and His government of the world, the other by enjoining principles of virtue and morality. Maimuni made an attempt to show that the six hundred and thirteen laws of the Torah, or of Judaism, tend to establish a true theory as to the Deity and His relation to the world, to oppose false and pernicious opinions, to uproot false ideas, to remove wrong and violence, to accustom men to virtue, and finally to eliminate immorality and vice. Maimuni arranged all the obligations of Judaism under fourteen groups according to his scheme.

Maimuni's ideal labor, to raise Judaism to the height of a philosophical system, was of the most wide-spread effect. For the thinkers of his time, Maimuni's religious philosophy was, indeed,a "Guide of the Perplexed." For to these men, who were dominated by the same principles, whose thinking, on the one hand, was Aristotelian, and whose feeling, on the other hand, was Jewish, but who, nevertheless, were conscious of a deep gulf between their thinking and their feeling, nothing could have been more welcome than the discovery of a bridge which led from the one to the other. Many things which had appeared to them offensive, or at least trivial, in the Bible, received through Maimuni's ingenious manner of interpretation a higher importance, a deeper sense, and became clear to their understanding. To posterity his philosophical work was both stimulating and suggestive. Judaism, viewed in the light o Maimunl's philosophy, no longer appeared to Jewish students as something strange, belonging to the past, an extinct and mere mechanical system, but as something which belonged to themselves, a part of their consciousness, existing in the present, living in their thoughts and animating them. Jewish thinkers of all times after Maimuni have consequently had recourse to Maimuni's "Guide," have derived fruitful ideas from this source, and have even learnt from him to advance beyond his standpoint, and to combat him. And since in the end thinkers will always remain the guides and leaders; of men, and the designers of their future, it can be said with justice, that Judaism is indebted to Maimuni for its rejuvenescence. So exclusively did he hold sway over men of intellect, that for a long time his work completely supplanted the systems of his predecessors from Saadiah to Ibn-Daud.

Maimuni's philosophical work, being written in Arabic, also exercised considerable influence beyond the Jewish world. He had, it is true, composed it entirely for Jews, and it is said, moreover, that he strictly enjoined that it be copied entirely in Hebrew characters, so that it might not fall into the hands of the Mahometans, and provoke animosity against his own people. He even cautioned his favorite disciple to use the utmost care in handling the chapters sent to him, so that they might not be misused by Mahometans and wicked Jews; but nevertheless this work became known to the Arabs, even in Maimuni's lifetime. A Mahometan wrote a profound exposition of the premises established by Maimuni to prove the existence of God. The chief founders of the Christian scholastic philosophy not only used Malmuni's work, which was translated into Latin at an early period, but for the first time learnt from it how to reconcile the diverging tendencies of belief and philosophy.

It ought scarcely to be urged against Maimuni, as a reproach, that, led by the philosophy of his time, he introduced strange and even incompatible elements into his system; that he raised, instead of the God of Revelation, who is in complete sympathy

with the human race, with the Israelites, and with every individual, a metaphysical entity, who exists in cold seclusion and elevation, and who dare not concern Himself about His creatures, if His existence is not to evaporate as that of a mere phantasm. To this metaphysical God, he could attribute free-will only in a limited sense, whilst he practically denied Him altogether the possession of a complete personality. Judaism, however much Maimuni had its interests at heart, must be a loser by his system. As he could not accept the revelation of the Torah in the fullest sense as a communication of the Deity to His people, he had to consider the greatest prophet in the light of a demigod above mankind. The ideal of a perfectly pious man, according to Maimuni's conception, is attainable by very few, and only by disciplined thinkers, who have the power of raising themselves to that rank through the long succession of degrees of knowledge, which are not within the grasp of every one. A merely moral and religious course of life is not sufficient, since God can be adored only b a soul endowed with philosophical intuition, and consequently only the few can arrive at immortality and future bliss, and have divine care vouchsafed them. Thus, according to Malmuni's theory, there are but very few elect. Lastly, Maimuni had to put a forced interpretation on verses of Scripture, in order to make them harmonize with the results of philosophical thought.

Maimuni's intelligent contemporaries, and even his favorite pupil, Joseph Ibn-Aknin, felt that his theory was not quite consistent with Judaism. This feeling made itself especially noticeable in regard to the belief in the resurrection. Maimuni had certainly reckoned it among the articles of belief, but he had laid no stress upon it; there was no place for it in his philosophical system. From many sides, it was charged against him that, while he had made an exhaustive examination of the question of immortality, he had dismissed the doctrine of resurrection with a few words. Maimuni now felt that he owed it to himself to compose a vindication in the form of a treatise on the resurrection of the dead, which he wrote in Arabic in 1191. Therein he affirms that he firmly believes in the resurrection, and that it is a miracle whose possibility is assumed with the belief in a creation in time. He complains in the book of being misunderstood. This composition is written in an irritable mood, which contrasts greatly with the calmness of his former works. He was annoyed that he had to justify himself to " fools and women." Among the learned Mahometans, Maimuni's "Guide" made much stir, but was severely condemned by them, partly on account of his covert attacks upon Islam and the barren but orthodox philosophy which reigned at that time, and partly on account of his broad views. Abdel-latif, the representative of orthodoxy in the Islam world of the East, who had been patronized by Saladin, and had come to Egypt in order to make the acquaintance of Maimuni (probably early in 1192), speaks of him, it is true, with respect, but animadverts strongly upon his work. He expressed himself about him in the following manner: "Moses, the son of Maimun, visited me, and I found him to be a man of very high merit, but governed by an ambition to take the first place, and to make himself acceptable to men in power. Besides medical works, he has written a philosophical book for the Jews, which I have read; I consider it a bad book, which is calculated to undermine the principles of religion through the very means which are apparently designed to strengthen them."

Nowhere did Malmuni's ideas find more fruitful ground, and nowhere were they adopted with more readiness than in the Jewish congregations of

MAIMUNI AND THE FRENCH JEWS.

southern France, where prosperity, the free form of government, and the agitation of the Albigenses against austere clericalism, had awakened a taste for scientific investigation, and where Ibn-Ezra, the Tibbon and the Kimchi families, had scattered seeds of Jewish culture. The less the men of southern France were able of themselves to reconcile Judaism with the results of science, the more did they occupy themselves with the writings of the sage who in so convincing a manner showed that pure and earnest devotion to religion was compatible with a taste for free research, and whose works revealed circumspection, clearness, deliberation and depth. Not only laymen, but even profound Talmudists, like Jonathan Cohen, of Lunel, idolized him, eagerly absorbed his every word, and paid him profound homage. " Since the death of the last rabbis of the Talmud, there has not been such a man in Israel." Among the rules of health which Maimuni drew up for Alafdhal, who had become ruler of

Egypt, he threw in the observation that the strengthening of the soul through moral living and philosophical reflection was requisite for the preservation of a strong body; that immoderate enjoyment of wine and love destroyed vitality. He had the boldness to say to a wayward prince something that no courtier of the age had the courage to tell him. He was determined not to be unfaithful to his calling as a physician of the soul. Maimuni himself fell sick, and was much worn out by his medical practice, and much affected by political changes. As soon as he had recovered, and calm was restored, he answered certain questions which had some time before been directed to him from Lunel. In his missive he excuses himself on the ground that his senses were disturbed, his mental power weakened, and his capacities blunted, yet his arguments testify against him, for they display perfect clearness and freshness of mind.

The great veneration which the congregations of southern France felt for Maimuni's writings, and especially for his code, aroused against him a violent antagonist in the person of Abraham ben David, of Posquieres, whose inconsiderate manner of dealing with those who represented an opposite line of thought to himself had been experienced by Serachya Halevi Gerundi. This profound Talmudist subjected Maimuni's Mishne-Torah to scathing criticism, and treated him in a contemptuous manner. He maintained that the author had not thoroughly grasped many Talmudical passages, had misconstrued their sense, and had thus drawn many false conclusions. He reproached him for desiring to bring Talmudical authorities into oblivion by reducing the Talmud to a code, and lastly for smuggling philosophical notions into Judaism. But he by no means treated Maimuni as an innovator and a heretic; on the contrary, he did justice to his opinions and his noble aim. Abraham ben David's strictures (Hassagoth) upon Maimuni's work gave occasion to the Talmudists of a later time to indulge their casuistical tendencies, and gave a great impulse to the taste for disputation. The rich, learned, and impulsive rabbi of Posquieres also had his admirers. When he died (Friday, 26th Kislev-27th Nov., 1198), descendants of Aaron, who are not allowed to enter a cemetery, made his grave, since before such greatness as his the priesthood may sink its sacred character.

The polemic of Abraham ben David against Maimuni in no way prejudiced the latter's consideration among the congregations of Provence; he remained for them an infallible authority. The chief representative of Jewish-Provencal culture, Samuel Ibn-Tibbon, wrote to Maimuni that he was busying himself with the rendering of the "Guide " from Arabic into Hebrew, and that he longed to see the greatest man in the Jewish world face to

face. Ibn-Tibbon thereby anticipated a wish of Maimuni's, for the latter contemplated translating his work into Hebrew. Full of joy he replied to Ibn-Tibbon, and gave him some advice how to handle so difficult a theme (8th Tishri--10th September, 1199). He dissuaded him, however, from making the perilous voyage from France to Egypt on his account, as he would scarcely be able to devote to him an hour of his time. He took the occasion to inform him of his manifold occupations, which allowed him scarcely a moment's rest: "The Sultan (Alafdhal) lives in Cairo, and I in Fostat; the two towns lie at a distance of two Sabbath journeys (about a mile and a third) from each other. With the Sultan I have a hard time; I must visit him daily in the morning, and when he, or any of his children, or one of the women of his harem is suffering, I may not leave Cairo. Even when nothing particular happens, I cannot come home till after mid-day. When I enter my house, dying of hunger, I find the hall thronged with people-Jews, Mahometans, illustrious and otherwise, friends and foes, a motley crowd--who await my advice as a physician. There scarcely remains time for me to alight from my horse, wash myself, and take some refreshment. Thus it continues till night, and then, worn out with weakness, I must retire to bed. Only on Sabbath have I time to occupy myself with the congregation and with the Law. I am accustomed on this day to dispose of the affairs of the community for the following week, and to hold a discourse. Thus my days glide away." It may be that the congregation of Lunel was not aware that Samuel Ibn-Tibbon was engaged with the translation of the " Guide," or did not give him credit for ability in that direction; however it was, some of its members applied to Maimuni to translate this work for them into Hebrew. Maimuni pleaded want of time in excuse, and referred them to Ibn-Tibbon (about 1200). He seized the opportunity also to exhort the Provencal Jews to grapple with the scientific treatment of the Talmud. "You, members of the congregation of Lunel and of the neighboring towns, are the only ones who raise aloft the banner of Moses. You apply yourselves to the study of the Talmud, and also cherish wisdom. But in the East the Jews are dead to spiritual labors. In the whole of Syria only a few in Haleb occupy themselves with the study of the Torah, but even they have it not much at heart. In Iraq there are only two or three grapes (men of insight); in Yemen and the rest of Arabia they know little of the Talmud, and are acquainted only with the Agadic exposition. Only just lately have they purchased copies of my Code, and distributed them in a few circles. The Jews of India know little of the Bible, much less of the Talmud. Those who live among the Turks and Tartars have the Bible only, and live according to it alone. In Maghreb you know what is the position of the Jews (that they must affect the profession of Islam). Thus it remains with you alone to be a strong support to our religion. Therefore, be firm, and of good courage, and be united in your work." Maimuni felt that enlightened Judaism would have its chief advocacy in Provence. The congregation of Marseilles requested the poet Charisi to translate Mairnuni's Commentary to the Mishnah into Hebrew. The Provencals took this great man and his writings as a guide in all their actions.

When Maimuni dispatched his last missive to congregation of Linel, he felt the decadence of his powers: " I feel old, not in years, but on account of feebleness." He died from weakness at the age of seventy years (20th Tebet--l3th Dec., 1204), mourned by many congregations in all lands. In Fostat, both Jews and Mahometans publicly mourned for him for three days. In Jerusalem

DEATH OF MAIMONIDES.

the congregation held a special funeral service for him. A general fast was appointed, and the chapter containing the penalties for breaking God's commandments was read from the Torah, and from the Prophets the story of the capture of the Ark of the Covenant by the Philistines. His earthly remains were conveyed to Tiberias. Maimuni left only one son, Abulmeni Abraham, who inherited his father's character, his mildness, his sincere piety, his medical knowledge, his place as physician in ordinary, his dignity as chief (Nagid) of the Egyptian community, but not his intellect. His descendants, who can be traced till the fifteenth century, were distinguished for their piety and their knowledge of the Talmud. On the lips of all his reverers there hovered the brief but suggestive praise: "From Moses, the prophet, till Moses (Maimuni) there has not appeared his equal." An unknown person placed on his grave a short, almost idolatrous inscription :

> *"Here lies a man, and still no man; If thou wert a man, angels of heaven Must have overshadowed thy mother."*

These lines were afterwards effaced, and the following substituted:

> *"Here lies Moses Maimuni, the excommunicated heretic."*

These two inscriptions shadow forth the bitter differences which broke out after Maimuni's death, and divided Judaism into two camps.

HISTORY OF THE JEWS

VOL. IV

CHAPTER I.

CULTIVATION OF KABBALA

Progress of the Kabbala--Todros Halevi and his Sons--Isaac Allatif and his Kabbalistic Doctrines-Adventurous Career of Abraham Abulafia--He assumes the Character of Messiah--Opposition of Ben Adret--The Prophet of Avila--Joseph Jikatilla and his Kabbalistic Mazes--The Impostor Moses de Leon--Forgeries of the Kabbalists--Origin of the Zohar--Its Doctrines and Influence

1270--1328 C.E.

The secret science of the Kabbala, which hitherto had assumed a modest deportment and been of a harmless character, began to foment discord in Ben Adret's time, ensnare the intelligence and lead astray the weak. What it lacked in intrinsic truth and power of conviction, it endeavored to supply by presumptuousness. It had already spread from Gerona, its original seat, and from northern Spain by way of Segovia to southern Spain, as far as the Castilian capital, Toledo, the Jewish community of which had before strenuously opposed obscurantism. In the city of Toledo the Kabbala won the adherence, among others, of one man who, by his noble birth, his princely state, his high position, his wealth and learning, gave it great weight. This man, whose influence is even now not fully recognized, was Todros ben Joseph Halevi, of the noble Toledan family of Abulafia (born 1234· died after 1304)· He was a nephew of that Meir Abulafia who had been so obstinate an adversary of Maimuni and rationalistic thought. Todros Abulafia took as a model his uncle, who in his old age had laid his hands on his head, and blessed him. When he grew up, he applied himself to the Talmud and to secret lore ; but he must have been a man of affairs, too, for he obtained an honorable position at the court of Sancho IV, and was in special favor with the wise queen, Maria de Molina, as a physician and financier. By the Jews he was esteemed and venerated as their prince (Nasi). When the king and queen of Spain held a meeting in Bayonne with the king of France, Philip le Bel, to settle their mutual hostilities (1290), Todros Abulafia was in the train of the former, and received the most flattering homage from the Jews of southern France. Todros, like his uncle, was a determined opponent of philosophy and its devotees. He had no words bitter enough against the would-be wise people who hold everything which appears incompatible with logic as incredible and impossible. Even Maimuni, whom he highly respected, he censured for undervaluing the importance of the sacrifices so greatly as to explain them merely as a concession to the heathen propensities of the people, and for calling the offering of incense an expedient for purifying the air. He waged vehement warfare against the philosophy which denies the existence of evil spirits, which to him was identical with doubting the existence of angels. Having been initiated into the secret science by one of the earliest Kabbalists, perhaps by Jacob of Segovia, who formed a school of his own, Todros valued it as divine wisdom, to uncover whose veil to laymen was fraught with danger. The recognition of the secret doctrine by a person of so high a position could not but produce some effect. His sons, Levi and Joseph, likewise plunged headlong into its study. Two of the four Kabbalists of his

time, who developed the Kabbala, and extended its influence, ranged themselves under the banner of Todros Abulafia, and dedicated their compositions to him. These four Kabbalists of the first rank, who established new theories with more or less success, were Isaac Ibn-Latif, Abraham Abulafia, Joseph Jikatilla, and Moses de Leon, all Spaniards. They obscured the mental light, with which men of intellect, from Saadiah to Maimuni, had illumined Judaism, and substituted for a refined religious belief, fantastic and even blasphemous chimeras. The intellectual degradation of the Jews in the following centuries is to a large extent their work. They led astray both their own times and posterity through designed or unintentional imposition, and the injuries which they inflicted on Judaism are felt even at the present day.

The least harmful of these four was Isaac ben Abraham Ibn-Latif or Allatif (born about 1220, died about 1290). He no doubt owed his origin to the south of Spain, for he was acquainted with Arabic. Nothing is known of his history beyond the fact that he was on friendly terms with Todros Abulafia, to whom he dedicated one of his works. His writings, as has been said by one who came after him, seem to "stand with one foot on philosophy and with the other on the Kabbala." But Allatif only toyed with philosophical formulae, their meaning does not seem to have become known to him. He was not of a thoughtful nature, and did not enrich the Kabbala, although he attempted to give himself the appearance of following original methods, and avoided the usual Kabbalistic expressions. Allatif started with the thought that a philosophical view of Judaism was not the "right road to the sanctuary," and that it was, therefore, needful to seek a higher conception, but, instead of making the way clear, he concealed it by empty allusions and unmeaning phrases. Allatif laid more weight than his predecessors on the close connection between the spiritual and the material world--between God and His creation. For the Godhead is in all, and all is in it. In soul-inspiring prayers the human spirit is raised to the world spirit (Sechel ha-Poel),to which it is united "in a kiss," and, so influencing the Divinity, it draws down blessings on the sublunar world. But not every mortal is capable of such spiritual and efficacious prayer; therefore, the prophets, the most perfect men, were obliged to pray for the people, for they alone knew the power of prayer. The unfolding and revelation of the Deity in the world of spirits, spheres and bodies, were explained by Isaac Allatif in mathematical formulae. Isaac Allatif must, however, be considered a clear thinker, when compared with his enthusiastic contemporary, Abraham Abulafia, who endeavored to establish a new order of things by Kabbalistic sophisms.

Abraham ben Samuel Abulafia (born 1240, in Saragossa, died 1291) was an eccentric personage, full of whims, and fond of adventures. Endowed with a lively mind and with more than a moderate amount of knowledge, he renounced the ways of common sense to throw himself into the arms of enthusiasm. His whole life from his entry into manhood was a succession of adventures. His father, who had instructed him in the Bible and the Talmud, died when his son was a youth of eighteen, and two years later Abraham undertook a journey of adventure, as he relates, in order to discover the mythical river Sabbation or Sambation, and to become acquainted with the supposed Israelite tribes dwelling on its banks, no doubt with a Messianic purpose. His mind was in a constant tumult. He wrestled for clearness, but fell ever deeper into mazes and illusions. One thing, however, became evident to him, that the philosophy with which he had much occupied himself offered no certainty, and, therefore, no satisfaction to the religious mind thirsting after truth. Even the trite Kabbala as

commonly accepted, with its doctrine about the Sefiroth, did not satisfy his soul, since both only nursed the pride of knowledge. He, a Kabbalist, criticized the unsoundness of this mystic theory so severely and correctly that it is surprising that he should have conceived still more insane notions. Abraham Abulafia sought after something higher, for prophetic inspiration, which alone opens the fountain of truth, without traversing the laborious path of systematic application.

At length Abulafia believed that he had found what his soul was yearning for, and that through divine inspiration he had come upon a higher Kabbala, in relation to which the lower mystical doctrine and philosophy were only handmaids. This Kabbala alone, he maintained, offers the means of coming into spiritual communion with the Godhead, and of obtaining prophetic insight. This means was far from new, but the firm conviction of its effectiveness and his application of it are peculiar to Abulafia. To decompose the words of Holy Writ, especially the all-hallowed name of God, to use the letters as independent notions (Notaricon), or to transpose the component parts of a word in all possible permutations, so as to form words from them (Tsiruf), or finally to employ the letters as numbers (Gematria), these are the means of securing communion with the spirit-world. But this alone is not sufficient. He who desires to render himself worthy of a prophetic revelation, must adopt an ascetic mode of living, must remove himself from the turmoil of the world, shut himself up in a quiet chamber, deliver his soul from earthly cares, clothe himself in white garments, wrap himself up with Talith and Phylacteries, and devoutly prepare his soul, as if for an interview with the Deity. Besides, he must pronounce the letters of God's name at intervals, with modulations of the voice, or write them down in a certain order, at the same time making energetic movements, writhing and bending forward till the mind becomes dazed. In this condition, if it become lasting through practice, the divine grace is poured into the human soul, uniting with it in a kiss, and the prophetic revelation follows quite naturally. This means of working himself up into a state of ecstasy Abulafia certainly practiced, exciting his heated fancy to delirium. He considered his Kabbala to be prophetic inspiration, by means of which he alone could penetrate into the secrets of the Torah. For the plain sense of the words and the simple practice of the religious precepts were merely for the uninitiated, like milk for children. Experts, on the other hand, find the higher wisdom in the numerical value of the letters and in the manifold changes of the words.

In this way he laid down his Kabbala, in antithesis to the superficial or baser Kabbala, which occupies itself with the Sefiroth, and, as he said, erects a sort of Decem-unity instead of the Christian Trinity. He lectured on his Kabbala in Barcelona, Burgos, and Medina-Celi. So low was the general intelligence, that this half-insane enthusiast found old and young to listen to him. Two of his disciples, Joseph Jikatilla, and Samuel, alleged to be a prophet, both of Medina-Cell, proclaimed themselves to be prophets and workers of miracles. Abulafia appears, nevertheless, to have aroused opposition in Spain, or at least not to have found any real sympathy; he left his native country a second time, betaking himself once more to Italy, where he reckoned upon stronger support. In Urbino for the first time he produced prophetic writings, and alleged that God had spoken with him. At last he conceived the mad idea of converting the pope to Judaism (Sabbath-eve, 1281). The attempt

ABULAFIA IN ROME

cost him dear. He was arrested two days later in Rome, languished twenty-eight days in prison, and escaped the stake only through the circumstance that God, as he expressed it, had caused a double mouth (or tongue?) to grow in him. Possibly he told the pope that he, too, taught the doctrine of the Trinity. After this he was allowed to walk about Rome in freedom. Thence Abulafia proceeded to the island of Sicily, and in Messina he met with a favorable reception, gaining six adherents. Here he finally proclaimed that he was not only a prophet but the

Messiah, and set forth his claims in writing (November, 1284). God, he said, had revealed to him His secrets, and had announced to him the end of the exile and the beginning of the Messianic redemption. The gracious event was to take place in the year I290. Mysticism has always been the ground on which Messianic fancies have thriven.

Through strictly moral deportment, ascetic life and revelations veiled in obscure formulae, perhaps also through his winning personality and boldness, Abraham Abulafia found many in Sicily who believed in him, and began to make preparations for returning to the Holy Land. But the intelligent part of the Sicilian congregation hesitated to join him without investigation. They addressed themselves to Solomon ben Adret, to obtain information from him respecting Abraham Abulafia. The rabbi of Barcelona, who was acquainted with Abulafia's earlier career, sent an earnest letter to the community of Palermo, in which he severely condemned the self-constituted Messiah as illiterate and dangerous. Naturally, Abulafia did not allow this attack to remain unanswered, but proceeded to defend himself from the denunciation. In a letter he justified his prophetic Kabbala, and hurled back Ben Adret's invectives in language so undignified that many thought the letter not genuine.

But his abusive retort was of no avail, for other congregations and rabbis, who may have feared that a persecution might be the consequence of his fantastic doctrines, also expressed themselves against Abulafia. He was harassed so much in Sicily that he had to leave the island, and settle in the tiny isle of Comino, near Malta (about 1288). Here he continued to publish mystical writings, and to assert that he would bring deliverance to Israel. Persecution had embittered him. He leveled charges against his brethren in faith, who in their stubbornness would not listen to him : "Whilst the Christians believe in my words, the Jews eschew them, and absolutely refuse to know anything of the calculation of God's name, but prefer the calculation of their money." Of those who exclusively occupied themselves with the Talmud, Abulafia said that they were seized by an incurable disease, and that they were far inferior to those skilled in the higher Kabbala. Abraham Abulafia, besides twenty-six on other subjects, composed at least twenty-two so-called prophetic works, which, although the product of a diseased brain, were used by the later Kabbalists. What at last became of the prophetic and Messianic enthusiast and adventurer is not known.

His extravagant conduct did not fail to produce evil consequences, even in his own time, and was as infectious as an epidemic. About the same time there arose in Spain two enthusiasts, of whom one was probably Abraham Abulafia's disciple. One of them made his appearance in the small town Ayllon (in the district of Segovia), the other in the large congregation of Avila. Both proclaimed themselves to be prophets, and announced in mystic language the advent of the Messianic kingdom. Both found followers. The adherents of the prophet of Avila related, that in his youth he had been ignorant, and could neither read nor write; that an angel, who appeared to him in his sleeping, and sometimes also

THE PROPHETS OF AYLLON AND AVILA.

in his waking moments, suddenly endowed him through higher inspiration, with the power of writing a comprehensive work, full of mystical ideas, and a diffuse commentary (without which at that time no fairly respectable book could be conceived). When the people of Avila and remote congregations heard of this they wondered greatly. The story excited extraordinary interest, and the representatives of the congregation of Avila consulted Solomon ben Adret, the last commanding authority of that time, as to whether they should accept this new prophecy.

Himself a partial follower of the secret science, subscribing only to the Biblical and the Talmudical miracles, the rabbi of Barcelona replied that he would have considered the affair of the prophet of Avila as arrant fraud, if trustworthy people had not attested its truth. Still he could not possibly recognize him as a prophet, for he lacked the principal conditions which the Talmud lays down as essential to prophecy: outside of Palestine, prophecy is altogether impossible; the age is not suitable for prophetic revelation, and the prophetic spirit can not rest upon a perfectly ignorant person. It was incredible that a man should go to bed an idiot and get up a prophet. The story required the most painstaking and impartial investigation.

In spite of the warning of the most honored rabbi of the time, the prophet of Avila pursued his course, and fixed the last day of the fourth month (1295) as the beginning of the Messianic redemption. The easily influenced and ignorant multitude made preparations for its coming, fasted, and spent money lavishly in alms, that they might be found acceptable in the Messianic kingdom, and be permitted to partake of its bliss. On the appointed day, the deluded people, dressed as on the Day of Atonement, hastened to the synagogues, and waited there to hear the trumpet-blasts announcing the Messianic advent. But the expected Messiah did not show himself, nor was there any sign of him. Instead, they are said to have noticed on their garments small crosses, for which they were totally unprepared, and which partly sobered and partly terrified them. It is possible that some of the incredulous in the congregation had fastened the crosses secretly on their garments, either to practice a joke upon their credulous brethren, or to point out to what end Messianic charlatanry was destined to lead them, and thus cure them of their delusion. Some of the impostor's followers are said to have gone over to Christianity in consequence of this incident ; others, to have been plunged into melancholy, because they could not explain the presence of the crosses. What became of the prophets, or beguiled deceivers, of Ayllon and Avila is not related. Like Abraham Abulafia they were lost sight of, and have importance only as the excrescences of a diseased state. It is possible that another disciple of Abulafia, Joseph Jikatilla, who also was looked upon as a performer of miracles, and had his dwelling not far from Ayllon, played a part in the mad or deceitful pranks of the prophets of Ayllon and Avila. Joseph ben Abraham Jikatilla (born in Medina-Celi, died in Penjafiel, after 1305), heard, at the age of twenty years, an exposition of the bewildering secret doctrine of

Abulafia, and whilst the latter still was in Spain, he composed a Kabbalistic book of his own, in which he exhibits the same eccentricities as his master. He, too, occupied himself with the mysticism of letters and numbers, and with the transposition of letters. Joseph Jikatilla's writings are in reality only an echo of Abraham Abulafia's fancies; the same delusion is apparent in both. But far more influential and more pernicious than these three Kabbalists, Allatif, Abulafia, and Jikatilla, was Moses de Leon, whose ascendancy was felt both by his contemporaries and posterity. Although a contemporary and fellow-specialist unmasked his perform-

MOSES DE LEON

ances, Moses de Leon succeeded in introducing into Jewish literature and thought a book which gave the Kabbala a firm foundation and wide extension, in brief, raised it to the zenith of its power. The question about Moses ben Shem Tob de Leon (born in Leon about 1250, died in Arevalo, 1305) is only whether he was a selfish or a pious impostor. His intention was certainly to deceive and lead astray, and in this respect he appears much baser than Abulafia, who at all events was sincere and naive in his delusion. A sciolist, who had mastered neither the Talmud nor any other subject thoroughly, Moses possessed the skill to use deftly the little that he knew, to write easily and fluently, to discover a connection between the most remote things and verses of Scripture piled up in the chamber of his memory, and to couple them with playful wit. Even the Kabbala was not present to him as a system ; he knew merely its forms and technical terms, and employed them in a skillful manner.

Of careless prodigality, Moses de Leon expended everything that he had without reflecting what would remain for the morrow; he made use of the Kabbala which had come into fashion to procure for himself a rich source of revenue. He led a wandering life, lived a long time in Guadalajara, then in Viverro, in Valladolid, and finally in Avila. At first he published his intellectual productions under his own name (about 1285). His writings, however, were not sufficiently noticed, and brought him but little fame and money. Moses de Leon then hit upon a much more effective means for opening hearts and purses. He commenced the composition of books under feigned but honored names. If he put the doctrines of the Kabbala, worn threadbare, to be sure, into the mouth of an older, highly venerated authority, some imposing name from the dazzling past,--taking care, of course, to make the coloring and the method of presentation archaic--would not such a composition be eagerly swallowed! Would he not be richly rewarded if he hinted that he was in possession of so costly a treasure? Moses de Leon knew well the credulity of those who devoted themselves with more or less earnestness to the study of the Kabbala; how they eagerly sought for every word which they were led to think originated from ancient times. For, since the secret science had been promulgated, and had striven for recognition, doctrines which sounded Kabbalistic had been fathered upon old and illustrious names, and thus had found acceptance. But Moses de Leon did his work much more cleverly than most forgers. He found the most likely author for the secret doctrine, against whom there could be little or no objection, in the person of the Tanaite Simon bar Yochai, who is said to have spent thirteen years in a cave, solitary and buried in profound reflection, and whom ancient mysticism represented as receiving revelations. Simon bar Yochai was assuredly the right authority for the Kabbala. But he must not be permitted to write or speak Hebrew, for in this language the Kabbalists would recognize the echo of their own voices. He must express himself in Chaldee, in a half obscure language, peculiarly fit for secrets, and sounding as if from another world. And thus there came into the world a book, the book Zohar (brilliancy), which for many centuries was held by Jews as a heavenly revelation. But seldom has so notorious a forgery so thoroughly succeeded. Moses de Leon well knew how to produce the proper effect on credulous readers. He made Simon bar Yochai appear in splendor, surrounded by a halo, in the book Zohar, and impart his revelation to a circle of select pupils (sometimes twelve, sometimes six), "scholars who shine with heaven's light." "When they assembled to compose the Zohar, permission was granted to the prophet Elijah, to all the members of the celestial

SIMON BAR YOCHAI.

conclave, all the angels, spirits, and higher souls to act in sympathy with them, and the ten spiritual substances (Sefiroth) were charged with the duty of revealing to them deeply hidden secrets, reserved for the time of the Messiah." Or in another version : Simon bar Yochai summoned his followers to a great council, and heard the flapping of the wings of the celestial host, who also had assembled to listen to the disclosure of mysteries till then unknown even to the angels. The Zohar glorifies its author excessively. It calls him the holy light, who stands higher than the greatest prophet, Moses, "the faithful shepherd." "I swear by the holy heavens and the holy earth," the Zohar makes Simon bar Yochai exclaim, " that I behold now what no other mortal since Moses ascended Sinai for the second time has beheld, aye, even more than he. Moses knew not that his countenance shone; I, however, know that my countenance shines." On account of God's love for the writer of the Zohar, his generation merited the revelation of truths till then hidden. As long as he who illumines everything lives, the sources of the world are opened and all secrets are disclosed. "Woe to the generation forsaken by Simon bar Yochai." He is almost deified in the Zohar. His disciples once broke out into ecstatic praise that he had mounted the degrees to heavenly wisdom, which none of his predecessors had done; and of him it is written in Scripture, "All men are to appear before the lord," i. e., before Simon bar Yochai. This extravagant glorification and self-deification, sufficient to mark a forgery, are not without design. They were to meet the objection, how the Kabbala, so long unknown, and kept secret by the prudent Kabbalists--for they had hesitated to impart any of it in writing--how this mysterious wisdom could all at once come to light, and be revealed to every one's knowledge. The Zohar frequently uses the following excuse: As the time in which Simon bar Yochai lived was especially meritorious and rich in grace, and as the Messianic period was near, the veil which had concealed the book so long could now be drawn aside.

There are certainly very few compositions which have exercised so much influence as the Zohar, or which can be compared with it in regard to the remarkable nature of its contents and form. It is a book without beginning or end, of which it is unknown whether it once formed part of a whole, whether the extant portions originally belonged to it, or were added later, or whether at an earlier period more of it was in existence. It consists of three principal parts, with appendices and explanatory comments. The absence of form in this farrago made it possible for certain portions to be imitated. It is so easy and tempting to imitate its wild though sonorous style. Thus the forgery was counter-forged. It is not positively certain whether the Zohar is to be regarded as a running commentary to the Pentateuch, as a theosophic manual, or as a collection of Kabbalistic sermons. And its contents are just as curious, confused and chaotic as its form and external dress. The Zohar with its appendages in no wise develops a Kabbalistic system like Azriel's, neither does it unfold an idea like Abraham Abulaha, but plays with the Kabbalistic forms as with counters -- with the En-Sof, with the number of the Sefiroth, with points and strokes, with vowels, accents, with the names of God and the transposition of their letters, as well as with the Biblical verses and Agadic sayings -- casts them about in eternal repetition, and in this manner produces sheer absurdities. Occasionally it gives a faint suggestion of an idea, but in a trice it evaporates in feverish fancies, or dissolves in childish silliness.

The underlying principle of the Zohar (if we may speak of principles in reference to this book) is that the historical narratives and religious statutes of the

Bible were never intended to be understood in a plain, simple sense, but that they contain something higher, mysterious, supernatural. "Is it conceivable," the Zohar makes one of Simon bar Yochai's circle exclaim, "that God had no holier matters to communicate than these common things about Esau and Hagar, Laban and Jacob, Balaam's ass, Balak's jealousy of Israel, and Zimri's lewdness? Does a collection of such tales, taken in their ordinary sense, deserve the name of Torah ? And can it be said of such a revelation that it utters the pure truth ?" "If that is all the Torah contains," remarks Simon bar Yochai (or Moses de Leon), "we can produce in our time a book as good as this, aye, perhaps better. No, no! the higher, mystical sense of the Torah is its true sense. The Biblical narratives resemble a beautiful dress, which enraptures fools so that they do not look beneath it. This robe, however, covers a body, i. e., the precepts of the Law, and this again a soul, the higher soul. Woe to the guilty, who assert that the Torah contains only simple stories, and therefore look only upon the dress. Blessed are the righteous, who seek the real sense of the Law. The jar is not the wine, so stories do not make up the Torah." Thus the secret lore of Moses de Leon naturally has free play to pervert everything and anything, and give it the seal of sublimity, and in this manner to promulgate a false doctrine, not only absurd, sometimes even blasphemous and immoral. All laws of the Torah are to be considered as parts and constituents of a higher world; they resolve themselves into the mysteries of the masculine and feminine principle (positive and negative). Only when both parts meet, does the higher unity arise. Consequently, whenever any one transgresses one of the laws, he obscures the brilliant image of the higher world.

It is almost impossible to give an idea of the abuse which the Zohar, or Moses de Leon, practices in the interpretation of Holy Writ, and how he twists the sense of the words. In the verse, "Raise your eyes to heaven, and see who has created this," a profound mystery is supposed to reside, which the prophet Elijah learned in the celestial school, and revealed to Simon bar Yochai; namely, that God had been unknown and obscure before the creation of the world, in a manner existing, and still not existing. He was the "Who " (the unknown subject). The creation is part of His self-revelation. It was by the creation that He first proclaimed Himself as God.

The Zohar is particularly concerned with that side of man which is an eternal riddle to man--the soul, its origin and end. Like the older Kabbalists, the Zohar assumed the pre-existence of the souls in the brilliant world of the Sefiroth. They are there wrapped in a spiritual robe, and entranced in the contemplation of God's light. When the souls are about to enter this world they assume an earthly garment, the body; but as soon as they are to leave the earth, the angel of death divests them of this earthly garment. If a soul lives piously and morally here below, it receives its former heavenly robe, and can once more enjoy the blissful ecstasy of God's presence; if not, particularly if it departs from the world impenitent, it wanders about naked and ashamed till purified in hell. The nakedness of the soul, paradise and hell--depicted in fantastic, baroque, and terrible images--are themes for which the Zohar often and gladly makes digressions. What happens to the soul during sleep, and the shadows of life--sin, impurity in small and great things -- are likewise favorite subjects for discussion in the Zohar, to which it frequently reverts, presenting them in the greatest variety of guises and repetitions. One of the older Kabbalists arrived at the notion that to the higher world, the world of light, of holiness, and of angels, there was a sharp

antithesis--a world of darkness, of unholiness, of Satan, in short the principle of evil, which was likewise developed into ten degrees (Sefiroth) at the creation of the world. in spite of their opposite characters, the two worlds are of one origin, forming opposite poles, and are in the same relation other as the right side is to the left. Accordingly, evil is called in the language of the Kabbalists the left or other side. The Kabbalists gave another representation of the Satanic empire. On the border of the world of light, the world of darkness is situated, and encompasses it as the shell surrounds the kernel of the fruit. Hence the Zohar metaphorically designates evil, or sin, with its ten degrees, as shell (Kelifa). This side is the favorite topic of the Zohar; for here it can apply its peculiar exposition of the Scriptures. The ten Sefiroth of the left side, the Satanic kingdom, are enumerated and denominated by names which savor of barbarism. The names sound like those of the princes of the demons in the book of Enoch, and are perhaps borrowed thence: Samael or Samiel, Azael, Angiel, Sariel, Kartiel. The Zohar identifies all blasphemers and wicked people with the evil principle of the "shells" (Kelifoth)--the first serpent, Cain, Esau, Pharaoh, and Esau's empire, Rome, and the civil and spiritual power of Christendom in the Middle Ages, which rested on violence and injustice. Israel and righteous people, on the other hand, belong to the world of light, the right Sefiroth. "He who goes after the left side (sin), and defiles his actions, draws upon himself the impure spirits; they attach themselves to him, nor do they ever leave him." The laws of the Torah have no other object than to effect and cherish the union of the souls with the world of light. Every transgression of them brings the souls to the world of darkness, evil spirits, and impurity. The Zohar coarsely represents the connection of the souls with light or with darkness by the image of wedded union, as, in general, it asserts the masculine and feminine principle in the higher world, even in reference to the Deity. As long as Israel lives in exile, the divine unity is deficient and disrupted; God will become one only in those days when the Mistress (Matronita) will espouse the King.

Moses de Leon would have left a gap, if he had not spoken of the Messianic period--the keynote of the Kabbala--and determined its date. In fact, the sudden revelation of the doctrine so long held secret rests on the assumption that the time of the Messiah is near. But here the forger betrays himself. Instead of indicating a period or a year for the appearance of the Messiah approximating the age of Simon bar Yochai (in the second century), the Zohar, with its casuistical playing with letters and numbers, demonstrated that it would happen in the beginning of the fourteenth century, therefore in the lifetime of the author. "When the sixtieth or the sixty-sixth year will pass the threshold of the sixth thousand, the Messiah will show himself;" but some time will pass before all nations will be conquered, and Israel be gathered together. The Messiah will first be summoned to appear on earth from his secret abode in Paradise, "the bird's nest," where he has been dwelling in bliss since the beginning of the world. A bloody conflict will then break out in the world. Edom and Ishmael (Christian and Mahometan nations) will vehemently contend with one another, and eventually both will be annihilated by a mightier conquering people. Signs and miracles will presage the time, and the resurrection of the dead and a general diffusion of the Kabbalistic knowledge of God will constitute the end of the world. Moses de Leon intended to arouse in the minds of his contemporaries the hope that they would behold the time of the Messiah with their own eyes. He was perhaps as much a victim to Messianic

enthusiasm as Abraham Abulafia. Despite the Zohar's endeavor to exalt rabbinical Judaism and its law, and by a mystical explanation to give every custom, however trivial, a special signification and higher import, it carps at and criticizes the Talmud and its method, though in an obscure, equivocal manner, and with the most innocent air in the world. It represents the study of the Kabbala as of much higher importance than the study of the Talmud, and even of the Bible. The Kabbala has the power of soaring, and is able to follow the flight of the Deity in His inscrutable guidance of things; the Talmud, on the other hand, and its adherents, have clipped wings, and cannot elevate themselves to higher knowledge. The Zohar compares the Mishna (Talmud) with a lowly slave; the Kabbala, on the other hand, with a powerful mistress. The former has to do with inferior matters, with " clean and unclean," with "permitted and prohibited," with " what is and is not fit to be used." As long as this woman rules with her "now pure, at another time impure blood, "the union of the Father with the Matrona (God with Israel) cannot take place. In the Messianic period, on the other hand, when the higher knowledge will awake, and gain the ascendancy, the Kabbala will once more assert its dominion over the slave (Talmud), as in the time of the lawgiver Moses. The Zohar lastly compares the study of the Talmud with a rugged, unproductive rock which, when struck, gives out scanty drops of water, causing only disputes and discussions. The Kabbala, on the other hand, is like a spring flowing abundantly, to which only a word needs to be spoken to cause it to pour out its refreshing and vivifying contents.

When the Zohar or Midrash of Simon bar Yochai was published, it aroused the greatest wonder among the Kabbalists. They seized upon it with avidity. Moses de Leon received vast multitudes of orders to send copies. The question, whence all at once had come so comprehensive a work of an old teacher of the Mishna, not a trace of which had been known till then, was thus answered: Nachmani had exhumed it in Palestine, had sent it to his son in Catalonia, by a whirlwind it had been carried to Aragon or Alicante (Valencia), where it had fallen into the hands of Moses de Leon, who alone possessed the original document. The repute of the newly discovered Kabbalistic treasure soon spread through the whole of Spain. The school of Abulafia at once gave the Zohar the tribute of its acknowledgment, and considered it indisputably genuine. Moses de Leon's wildest hopes were more than realized. There were, of course, Kabbalists who doubted that the Zohar had originated with Simon bar Yochai and his school, but none the less did they pay homage to the book as to a pure source for Kabbalistic theories. When the Kabbalist Isaac of Accho,who had escaped the massacre that had ensued upon the capture of that city, arrived in Spain, and saw the Zohar, he was staggered, and became desirous of coming to the root of the question, whether this alleged ancient Palestinian work was really genuine, as he had been born and educated in the Holy Land, had associated with Nachmani's pupils, and yet had never heard a syllable about it. When he met Moses de Leon in Valladolid, the latter took a solemn oath that he had in his house at Avila an old copy of the book from the hand of Simon bar Yochai, and pledged himself to submit it to Isaac of Accho for examination. But Moses de Leon became ill on his journey home, and died in Arevalo (1305)· The veil around the origin of the Zohar was wrapped still closer. Two influential men of Avila, David Rafan and Joseph de Avila, had indeed discovered the simple truth from Moses de Leon's wife and daughter. Moses de Leon had never possessed the original copy,

but had evolved it out of his own inner consciousness, and had written it with his own hand. His wife frankly related that she had often asked her husband why he published the productions of his own intellect under a strange name, and that he had answered that the Zohar would not, under his own name, have brought him any money, but assigned to Simon bar Yochai it had been a lucrative source of income.

Thus wife and daughter, without being aware of the full gravity of their assuredly unassailable testimony, unmasked Moses de Leon as a forger. Nevertheless, the Zohar met with the unqualified applause of the Kabbalists, because it supplied a want which would have had to be provided for in one way or another. The Kabbalistic doctrine, which had already gained so much weight, had hitherto been without firm basis; it had no other authority than the very doubtful one of Isaac the Blind. Now the dignified figure of a teacher of the Mishna in communion with departed spirits and celestial hosts and angels confirmed the truths which were not only doubted by many at the time, but absolutely ridiculed. Should they, then, not cling to it and defend it ? What Moses de Leon put into the mouth of Simon bar Yochai, " Many will range themselves round the book Zohar, when it becomes known, and nourish their minds with it at the end of days," actually happened soon after his death. If the Zohar did not bring the Kabbalists anything essentially new, it exhibited to them what they did know in so peculiar a form and language, that they were wonderstruck. Everything in it is contrived for effect, for illusion, and for fascination. The long discussions which Simon bar Yochai holds with his circle or with the "faithful shepherd," have dramatic power, especially the scene in which, in premonition of his speedy dissolution, he imparts once more what he so often had proclaimed. Full of effect, and, upon minds easily accessible to faith, of transporting and overwhelming influence, are the oft-recurring exclamations in the Zohar: Woe, woe to those who believe, or do not believe, or fail to respect, this and that. Sometimes short prayers are interspersed, which, being elevated and imaginative, are peculiarly fitted to fill the soul with mysterious awe. Even the characteristic terms introduced instead of the usual Kabbalistic forms are calculated to arouse interest by their double sense. The author designated God and the higher spiritual substances (Sefiroth) collectively or in their single parts and effects, as father, mother, the prototype of man, bride, matron, the white head, the large and the small face, the mirror, the higher heaven, the higher earth, lily, apple-orchard, and so on. The pious were gained over to the side of the Zohar, as it attributes to every religious custom and every practice a higher import, a higher sanctity, and a mysterious effect.

So a new textbook of religion was by stealth introduced into Judaism. It placed the Kabbala, which a century before had been unknown, on the same level as the Bible and the Talmud, and to a certain extent on a still higher level.

The Zohar undoubtedly produced good, in so far as it opposed enthusiasm to the legal dry-as-dust manner of the study of the Talmud, stimulated the imagination and the feelings, and cultivated a disposition that restrained the reasoning faculty. But the ills which it has brought on Judaism outweigh the good by far. The Zohar confirmed and propagated a gloomy superstition, and strengthened in people's minds the belief in the kingdom of Satan, in evil spirits and ghosts.

Through its constant use of coarse expressions, often verging on the sensual, in contradistinction to the chaste, pure spirit pervading Jewish literature, the Zohar sowed the seeds of unclean desires, and later on produced a sect that laid aside all regard

for decency. Finally, the Zohar blunted the sense for the simple and the true, and created a visionary world, in which the souls of those who zealously occupied themselves with it were lulled into a sort of half-sleep, and lost the faculty of distinguishing between right and wrong. Its quibbling interpretations of Holy Writ, adopted by the Kabbalists and others infected with this mannerism, perverted the verses and words of the Holy Book, and made the Bible the wrestling-ground of the most curious, insane notions. The Zohar even contains utterances which seem favorable to the Christian dogma of the Trinity of the Godhead. The mystics dismembered the fair form of Holy Writ, indulged in mad sport, and stupefied all sense for truth, but they were scarcely more guilty in this respect than the so-called philosophers of the time. Maimuni's attempt to bring Judaism and its religious literature into consonance with reason, to give certain too realistic verses of the Bible a philosophical, or at least a tolerable sense, and place religious precepts on the basis of an intelligible, acceptable purpose, encouraged half-learned men to explain everything and anything in the same way. Hence the allegorizing of the Scriptures, the Agada, and the rites, was carried to an incredible extreme. These pseudo-philosophers divested the stories of the creation and of the patriarchs of their historical character, and interpreted them as philosophical commonplaces, in which they sported with Aristotelian and Maimunist terms, as the Zohar with Kabbalistic terms. Abraham and Sarah, for example, denote to the allegorists matter and form, Pharaoh denotes vicious desires, Egypt the body, the land of Goshen the heart, Moses the divine spirit, and the Urim and Thummim, which the High Priest wore on his breast in the Temple, were the astrolabe of the astronomers, with which they calculated time, longitude and latitude. If there had been at that time any Jewish thinkers of the first rank they would have made serious efforts to put a stop to this childish proceeding, whether Kabbalistic or pseudo-philosophical. But the age of Ben Adret happened to be poor in great intellects. Even the two chief representatives of the philosophy of that time, Shem-Tob Falaquera and Isaac Albalag, were not above mediocrity, and were themselves tainted with the current errors.

There were, however, certain men of bolder spirit, who from philosophical premises drew conclusions endangering the stability of Judaism. Like their predecessors, the Alexandrine allegorists, many Intelligent and consistent thinkers were induced at this time to disregard the ceremonies of Judaism by assigning erroneous purposes to religious precepts. As the ceremonies are intended simply to awaken certain religious, philosophical, or moral feelings, they argued, it is sufficient to call up these thoughts, to be penetrated by them, to occupy one's mind constantly with them, while the observance of religious customs is superfluous. Several members of this school denied Moses' prophetic character, accepting him only as an ordinary lawgiver, such as other nations had, and thus rejected the divinity of the Torah. The pseudo-philosophers cast a doubt upon the very fundamentals of Judaism, and thereby provoked a reaction injurious to free inquiry.

IV. CHAPTER II.

THE FIRST EXPULSION OF THE JEWS FROM FRANCE, AND ITS CONSEQUENCES.

Philip le Bel--The Jews of France plundered and banished--Estori Parchi; Aaron Cohen; Laments of Bedaresi--Eleazar of Chinon, the Martyr--Return of the Jews to France; their Precarious Position--Progress of the Controversy regarding the Study of Philosophy-Abba-Mari and Asheri--Death of Pen Adret--Rabbinical Revival in Spain--Isaac Israeli II--Samuel and the Queen Maria Molina--Don Juan Emanuel and Judah Ibn-Wakar--The Jews of Rome--Robert of Naples and the Jews-Peril of the Jews in Rome--Kalonymos hen Kalonymos, his Satires--Immanuel and Dante-The Poet Judah Siciliano-Leone Romano and King Robert--Shemarya Ikriti--Position of Karaism--Aaron the Elder and the Prayer-Book of the Karaites.

1306--1328 C.E.

PHILIP IV, le Bel, at that time the king of France, one of those monarchs who made arrogant and unprincipled despotism familiar to Europe, suddenly issued a secret order (21st January, 1306), imposing the strictest silence, to the higher and lower officials throughout his kingdom, to put all the Jews of France under arrest on one and the same day, without warning of any kind. Before the Jews had fully recovered from fasting on the Day of Lamentation in remembrance of the destruction of Jerusalem, and as they were about to begin their daily business, the constables and jailers appeared, laid hands upon them, and dragged young and old, women and children, to prison (10th Ab-22d July). There they were told that they had to quit the country within the space of a month, leaving behind both their goods and the debts owing to them. Whoever was found in France after that time was liable to the penalty of death. What could have induced this prudent rather than clerical prince so suddenly

EXPULSION OF THE JEWS FROM FRANCE.

to change his sentiments towards the Jews ? It was certainly not clerical intolerance, nor was it yielding to the will of the people. For the French, even in the Middle Ages, were not bigoted, and it was not their wish to remove the Jews to free themselves from usurers. Avarice was the first motive of this cruel order. For Philip's feud with the pope, and his war with the rebellious Flemish, had so exhausted his treasury, and had rendered necessary so unsparing an extortion of money that, as the ballads of the time scoffingly said, "The fowl in the pot was not secure from the king's grasp." The king wanted to replenish his coffers from the property of the Jews. Another circumstance is said to have moved him to this hard-hearted resolution. The German emperor Albrecht, who at that time was not on good terms with Philip, had demanded the surrender of the kingdom of Aries; and that he should acknowledge the authority of the successor of Vespasian, Titus, and Charlemagne over the French Jews, i.e., yield to him a portion of the hard-earned property of the Jews. Philip is said to have consulted his lawyers, to decide to whom the authority over the Jews appertained, and as they adjudged it to the German emperor, the idea occurred to him to fleece the Jews of their property, and to send his "servi camerae " naked and bare to Albrecht. Before the world the king covered his act of violence, inhuman as it was unstatesmanlike, with the excuse that incredible outrages of the Jews had rendered their expulsion imperative. That he had aimed at the possessions of the Jews was shown by his relentless plundering. The officials left the unhappy Jews nothing beyond the clothes they wore, and to everyone not more than seemed necessary for a day's living (12 gros Tournois). Wagonsful of the property of the Jews, gold, silver and precious stones were transported to the king; and less valuable objects were sold at a ridiculously low price. At the appointed time (September, 1306), they were banished, about 100,000 souls, from the country which their ancestors had inhabited, in part at the time of the Roman republic, long before Christianity had spread into France. Some who could not separate themselves from their property and the country which they loved went over to Christianity. The whole congregation of Toulouse is said to have been guilty of this cowardice, which scarcely seems credible. The celebrated seats, at which so much intellect had been displayed, the colleges of Rashi, Tam, and the Tossafists: Troyes, Paris, Sens, Chinon, Orleans; the places in which a higher culture had had its temple: Beziers, Lunel, Montpellier, whence the combatants for and against science were plunged into common misery--all these schools and synagogues were sold to the highest bidder or given away. A German or an English king might have destroyed the holy places of the Jews--King Philip le Bel made a present of a synagogue to his coachman. An approximate idea can be formed of the sums which the expulsion and robbery of the Jews brought in to the king, if it is kept in mind that the sale of the

Jewish goods in the house of the prefect of Orleans alone brought in 337,000 francs.

How many of the refugees, reduced to beggary, fell victims to the hardships of their journey cannot be known. The bitter plaints of those oppressed by the heavy affliction sound mournful and touching even at this distance of time. Estori Parchi, then a youth of many accomplishments and noble heart, a relative of Jacob ben Machir, whose parents had emigrated from Spain to southern France, thus describes his sorrow: "From the house of study have they torn me; naked was I forced as a young man to leave my ancestral home, and wander from land to land, from people to people, whose tongues

were strange to me." Parchi at length found a resting-place in Palestine. Another fugitive, the learned Aaron Cohen of Narbonne, poured forth this elegy: "Unhappy me, I saw the misery of the banishment of the sons of Jacob, like a herd of cattle driven asunder. From a position of honor I was thrown into a land of darkness." The sudden turn of fortune which changed rich men into beggars, and exposed the delicate and those used to the comforts of life to bitter privation, filled the bombastic poet Yedaya Bedaresi with gloomy reflections. In vivid colors he painted the trouble and pain of life, and man's helplessness and nothingness. His "Trial of the World" (Bechinath Olam), suggested by personal observation and bitter experience, consequently makes a depressing and mournful impression, and reflects faithfully the melancholy feelings of the ill-starred race.

The expulsion of the Jews from France by the stony-hearted Philip le Bel did not come off without martyred victims. Those who transgressed the time of grace, yet rejected solicitations to abjure their faith, were punished by death. A martyr of this time, Eleazar ben Joseph of Chinon, is specially famous. He was a learned, noble-minded man, a correspondent of Ben Adret, master of many distinguished disciples, among them the youthful Parchi, one of the last of the Tossafist school. He was condemned to the stake, although no crime could be laid at his door except that he was a Jew. With him died two brothers. The expatriated Jews dispersed in all parts of the world; many traveled to Palestine. But the majority remained as near as possible to the French borders, in Provence proper, at that time partly under German suzerainty, in the province of Roussillon, which belonged to the Aragonian king of Majorca, and in that island. Their Intention was to wait for a favorable change of fortune, which would permit them to return to the land of their birth. They had not speculated falsely. King Philip himself was induced by avarice to unbend from his severity.

The vehement struggle in Montpellier about permitting Jewish youth to engage in the study of the sciences, remarkable to relate, continued after the banishment from France (September, 1306), and the mutual hatred of the two parties was in no way abated by suffering. A portion of the Tibbonide party had settled in Perpignan, which belonged to the king of Majorca, who was no favorer of the Jews. At his command copies of the Talmud were once more delivered up to the auto-da-fe; but as he hoped to gain some advantage by the settlement of intelligent, industrious Jews, he suffered them. Abba-Mari and another portion of the congregation of Montpellier at first took up their abode in the town of Arles, but as he could not stay there, he, too, emigrated to Perpignan (January, I307)· But the opposing party, which had influence with the king or governor, endeavored to hinder his settlement in that place. Abba-Mari's partisans, by making representations to the king, succeeded in obtaining permission for him to live in Perpignan. Here the controversy raged anew. Solomon ben Adret and Asheri, particularly the latter, whose decision of character had acquired for him the chief authority, again interfered. Asheri declared that he had given his signature in a half-hearted manner to the decree prohibiting young men from occupying themselves with profane studies; for, according to his opinion, it was too great a concession to permit it at the age of twenty-five. Science ought to be prohibited altogether, for it inevitably lures on to unbelief. The defenders of science were to be condemned without mercy, since the afflictions of exile had made no impression on them, suffering had not broken their spirit of defiance, and had not chastened their hardness of heart.

ASHERI'S INFLUENCE.

This view, that qualities prejudicial to Judaism were inherent in science, gained supremacy after Ben Adret's death (1310), when Asheri was acknowledged in Spain and in the neighboring countries as the only authority in religious matters. Asheri, his sons and companions who had migrated with him from Germany, transplanted from the Rhine to vivacious Toledo that spirit of honest, but tormenting, narrow-minded and intolerant piety; that gloomy disposition which regards even harmless joy as a sin; that feeling of abjectness, which characterized the German Jews of the Middle Ages, and they inoculated the Spanish Jews with it. The free activity of the mind was checked. Asheri concentrated ail his mental power on the Talmud and its exposition. His chief work was a compilation of the Talmud for practical use (1307-1314). On all occasions he endeavored to enforce a difficult, painful, and severe discipline. If any one desired to express his thoughts on any department of knowledge whatsoever, he had to array his subject in the garments of contrite orthodoxy. When the erudite Isaac ben Joseph Israeli II, of Toledo, published an astronomical work (1310), he had to adjust it to Talmudical standards, and introduce it by a confession of faith, for only in this manner could he find grace in Asheri's eyes.

At about this time, during Asheri's rabbinate in Toledo, prominent Jews once more obtained influence at court. King Ferdinand IV (1295–1312) had a Jewish treasurer named Samuel, whose counsels he followed in political matters too. The dowager queen, Maria de Molina, who had held the reins of government during her son's minority, with feminine passionateness hated the favorite Samuel, who is said to have nourished the enmity between mother and son. One 'day, when Samuel was in Badajos, and was preparing to accompany the king to Seville, he was attacked by an assassin, and so severely wounded that he was left for dead. It is not known who instigated the deed. The king had such care and attention devoted to Samuel, that he recovered from his wounds.

Don Ferdinand's death brought in its train a time of unquiet, of civil war, and social anarchy for Spain. As the Infante Alfonso was still a child in the cradle, several persons, the clever Maria de Molina, the young queen-mother Constantia, and the uncles of the young king contended for the guardianship and the regency, and provoked faction feuds in the country (1312-1326), Donna Maria de Molina, who conducted the government, did not extend her hate against her son's Jewish counselor to the community to which he belonged. As in the lifetime of her husband she had had a Jewish favorite, Todros Abulafia, so during her regency she had a Jewish treasurer, Don Moses. When the council of Zamora (1313) renewed canonical laws hostile to the Jews, the cortes of Burgos demanded the exclusion of Jews from all honors and offices,and the pope issued a bull that Christians were to be absolved from their debts to Jews on account of usury, the wise regent submitted only in part. She ordered that Jews should not bear high-sounding Christian names, nor enter into close intercourse with Christians; but she most emphatically declared herself against the unjust abolition of debts, and published a law that no debtor could make himself free of his obligation to professors of the Jewish faith by appealing to a papal bull.

The regency of Don Juan Emanuel inaugurated an improvement in the condition of the Castilian Jews (1319--1325)· The regent was a friend of learning, himself an author and poet, and was consequently held in esteem by educated Jews. A Jew of Cordova, Yehuda ben Isaac Ibn-Wakar, found high favor in his eyes, and probably acted as his treasurer. At his solicitation Juan Emanuel once

more invested the rabbinate with penal jurisdiction, which the Jews had partly lost during the regency of Maria de Molina, and had practiced only privately.

Yehuda Ibn-Wakar, however, was an admirer of Asheri, and, like the latter, of excessive piety, desiring to have every religious transgression punished with the utmost severity. When a Cordovan uttered a blasphemy in Arabic, Ibn-Wakar asked Asheri what was to be done with him, and the latter replied that his tongue should be cut out. A beautiful Jewess having had intercourse with a Christian, Don Juan Manuel resigned her to the punishment of the Jewish court, and Yehuda Ibn-Wakar condemned her to have her face disfigured by the removal of her nose, and Asheri confirmed the sentence.

The southern Spanish and Castilian congregations still lived in peace, and in the undisturbed possession of their goods; on the other hand, the northern Spanish, and still more the southern French congregations were exposed to bloody attacks by fanatical hordes, which the church had unfettered, and then could not restrain. Jews once more lived in France. Louis X had recalled them nine years after their banishment (1315)· This king, himself seized by a desire to abrogate the ordinances of his father and indict his counselors, had been solicited by the people and the nobility, who could not do without the Jews, to re-admit them into France. He accordingly entered into negotiations with them in reference to their return. But the Jews did not accept his proposal without deliberation, for they well knew the inconstancy of the French kings, and the fanatical hatred of the clergy against them. They hesitated at first, and then submitted their conditions. These were, that they be allowed to reside in the same places as before; that they should not be indictable for former transgressions; that their synagogues, churchyards, and books be restored to them, or sites be granted for new places of worship. They were to have the right of collecting the money owing to them, of which two-thirds should belong to the king. Their former privileges, as far as they were still in force, were to be again extended to them, or new ones conceded. King Louis accepted all these conditions, and granted them also the right of emigration under certain restrictions. In order to conciliate the clergy, he, on his side, imposed the conditions that they wear a badge of a certain size and color, and hold neither public nor private disputations on religion. Two high officials (prud'hommes, auditeurs des Juifs) were appointed to superintend the re-settlement of the Jews. Their residence in France was fixed for twelve years ; if the king should resolve to expel them again after the expiration of that period, he put himself under the obligation to give them a year's warning that they might have time to make their preparations. The king published this decree, declaring that his father had been ill-advised to banish the Jews. As the voice of the people solicited their return, as the church desired a tolerant policy, and as the sainted Louis had set him the precedent of first banishing and then readmitting them, he had, after due consultation with the prelates, the barons, and his high council, permitted the return of the Jews. The French Jews streamed back in masses to their former dwelling places, regarding this event as a miraculous redemption. When Louis X died a year after, and his brother Philip V, the Long, ascended the throne, he extended their privileges, and protected them especially from the enmity of the clergy; so that they and their books could be seized only by royal officers. But they were not free from vexation by the degenerate clergy, who insisted that the Jews of Montpellier, who thought they could venture on certain liberties, should re-affix the Jew-badge on

their dress. At one time they accused the Jews of Lunel with having publicly outraged the image of Christ on the Purim festival; at another time they ordered that two wagonsful of copies of the Talmud be publicly burned in Toulouse. Such occurrences, however, were mere child's play compared with what they had to endure from the bigoted multitude.

Philip V had the idea, repugnant to the spirit of the time, of undertaking a crusade to wrest the Holy Land, after so many vain attempts, from the hands of the infidels. This enterprise appeared so foolish to the discerning that even Pope John XXII, the second of the popes that resided in Avignon instead of at Rome, dissuaded him from it. Nevertheless, the fancy, as soon as it was known, inflamed the minds of the rude populace. A young man of excited imagination gave out that a dove had settled at one time on his head, at another, on his shoulder, and when he had sought to seize it, it had transformed itself into a beautiful woman, who urged him to gather a troop of crusaders, assuring him of victory. His utterances found credulous hearers, and the lower people, children, and swine-herds attached themselves to him. A wicked priest and an unfrocked Benedictine monk used the opportunity to force their way to the front, and thus arose in northern France (1320) a numerous horde of forty thousand shepherds (Pastoureaux, Pastorelli, Roim), who moved in procession from town to town carrying banners, and announced their intention of journeying across the sea to deliver the so-called holy sepulcher. Their attention was immediately turned to the Jews, possibly because they wanted to raise money for the purchase of weapons by robbing the Jews of their possessions, or a Jew, as is related, had made sport of their childish heroism. The massacre of the Jews by the shepherds (Gesereth ha-Roim) is another bloody page in Jewish history, Nearly all the crusading enterprises had commenced with the murder of Jews; so this time. Thus perished almost all the Jews in the neighborhood of Bordeaux, Gascogne, Toulouse,

CALUMNIES OF THE "LEPERS."

Albi, and other towns of southern France. Altogether, more than 120 Jewish congregations in France and northern Spain were blotted out through the rising of the Shepherds, and the survivors were so impoverished by spoilation that they were dependent upon the succor of their brethren in other parts, which flowed to them in abundance even from Germany.

The following year, too, was very unfortunate for the Jews, the trouble beginning again in France. This persecution was occasioned by lepers, from whom it has its name (Gesereth Mezoraim). The unhappy people afflicted by leprosy in the Middle Ages were banished from society, declared dead as citizens, shut up in unhealthy quarters, and there tended after a fashion. Once, when certain lepers in the province of Guienne had been badly provided with food, they conceived and carried into effect the plan of poisoning the wells and rivers, through which many people perished (1321). When the matter was traced back to the lepers, and they were examined under torture, one of them invented, or somebody suggested to him, the lying accusation that the Jews had inspired them with the plan of poisoning the waters. The charge was generally believed; even King Philip V had no doubt about it. Sometimes it was asserted that the Jews wanted to take revenge for the sufferings experienced at the hands of the Shepherds the year before; again, that they had been persuaded by the Mahometan king of Granada to cause the Christians to be poisoned; or it was suggested that they had done it in league with the Mahometan ruler of Palestine, to frustrate the intended crusade of King Philip. In several places Jews were arrested on this accusation, unmercifully tortured, and some of them burnt (Tammuz--July, 1321). In Chinon a deep pit was dug, fire kindled in it, and eight Jewish men and women thrown in, who sang whilst dying. The mothers had previously cast in their children, to save them from forcible baptism. Altogether five thousand are said to have suffered death by fire in that year. Many were banished from France, and robbed by the heartless populace. Philip was convinced later on of the untruth of the accusation; but as the Jews had been accused, he seemed to think that the opportunity might be used to swell the treasury. Accordingly, the congregations were condemned by Parliament to a penalty of one hundred and fifty thousand pounds (Parisian); they were to apportion the contributions among themselves. Deputies (procureurs) from northern France (de la langue francaise) and from Languedoc, met and enacted that the southern French Jews, decimated and impoverished by the previous year's massacre, were to contribute forty-seven thousand pounds, and the remainder was to be borne by the northern French Jews. The wealthiest Jews were put under arrest as security for the payment of the fine, and their goods and debts distrained.

In the same year a great danger threatened the oldest of the European communities. Misfortune came upon it the more unexpectedly as till then it had tasted but little of the cup of misery which the Jews of England, France and Spain so often had to drink to the dregs. It was because Rome did not belong to the pope, but to the families of Orsini and Colonna, to the Ghibellines and Guelphs--the great and minor lords, who fought out their party feuds in that city--that the Jews were left untouched by papal tyranny. It was well for them that they were little considered.

At about this time the Roman Jews had made an advance in material welfare and intellectual culture. There were some who possessed houses like palaces, furnished with all the comforts of life. Since the time when, through the concurrence of favorable circumstances, they had tasted of the tree of knowledge,

learning and poetry were cherished by the Italian Jews. The seeds which Hillel of Verona, Serachya ben Shaltiel and others had scattered, commenced to bear fruit. When the flower of intellectual glory in southern France began to decay through the severity of Talmudical rigorists and the bloody persecutions, it unfolded itself in Italy, especially in Rome. At that time the first rays of a new cultural development, breaking through the gloom of priestcraft and the rude violence of the Middle Ages, appeared in Italy. A fresh current of air swept the heavens in Italy in the beginning of the fourteenth century, the epoch of Dante, thawing the icy coat of the church and of knightdom, the two Pillars of the Middle Ages. A sense of citizenship, the impulse towards liberty, enthusiastic love for science, were the striking symptoms of a new spirit, of a striving for rejuvenescence, which only the emperor, the embodiment of rude, ungainly knighthood, and the pope, the incarnation of the stern, unbending church, failed to perceive. Every greater or lesser Italian lord made it a point of honor to encourage art and science, and patronize poets, artists and learned men at his court. Nor were the Jews overlooked at this juncture. One of the most powerful Italian princes, Robert of Anjou, king of Naples, count of Provence (Arelat), vicar-general of the Papal States and for some time titular lieutenant of the Holy Roman empire, was a friend of science,a warm admirer also of Jewish literature, and consequently a protector of the Jews. Several Jewish litterateurs were his teachers, or at his instance undertook scientific and theological works.

Either in imitation of the current practice or from sincere interest in Jewish literature, rich Jews, who played the part of small princes, invited Jewish authors into their circle, lightened their material cares by liberal support, and stimulated their activity by encouragement. Thus it came to pass that three Jewish Italian men of letters had the courage to compete with the Spaniards and Provencals. These were Leo Romano, Judah Siciliano, and above all the poet Immanuel Romi, who once more ennobled neo-Hebrew poetry, and raised it to a higher level. The Roman congregation at that time displayed exceptional interest in Jewish writings. Of Maimuni, the embodiment of science for them as for the rest of the Jewish world, they possessed the copious Religious Codex, and the translation of his "Guide;" but of his luminous Mishna commentary, composed originally in Arabic, only those parts which Charisi and Samuel Ibn-Tibbon had done into Hebrew. The representatives of the Roman congregations, to whom probably the poet Immanuel also belonged, wished to have a complete edition of the work, and sent a messenger to Barcelona to Ben Adret expressly for the purpose of procuring the remaining parts. The affair was not so simple as the Roman Jews had imagined. The greater portion of the anxiously desired commentary of Maimuni on the Mishna, on account of peculiar difficulties, was not yet rendered into Hebrew. The greatest obstacle was the circumstance that the Spanish Jews, except those in Toledo and in the neighborhood of the kingdom of Granada, had forgotten Arabic. Ben Adret, who wished to oblige the Roman congregation, endeavored to get the required portions translated into Hebrew. He encouraged scholars, learned both in Arabic and the Talmud, to undertake this difficult task, and Joseph Ibn-Alfual and Jacob Abbassi of Huesca, Solomon ben Jacob and Nathaniel Ibn Almali, the last two physicians of Saragossa, and others divided the labor among themselves. Jewish literature is indebted for the possession of this most valuable work of Maimuni to the zeal of the Roman congregation, of Ben Adret, and these translators.

The Roman community was roused from its peaceful occupations and undisturbed quiet by a rough

SANGISA AND POPE JOHN XXII.

hand, and awakened to the consciousness that it existed under the scourge of priestcraft and the caprice of its rulers.

It is related that a sister of the pope (John XXII), named Sangisa, had repeatedly exhorted her brother to expel the Jews from the holy city of Christendom. Her solicitations had always been fruitless; she therefore instigated several priests to give testimony that the Jews had ridiculed by words and actions a crucifix which was carried through the streets in a procession. The pope thereupon issued the command to banish all the Jews from Roman territory. All that is certain is that the Jews of Rome were in great danger during that year, for they instituted an extraordinary fast, and directed fervent prayers to heaven (21 Sivan--18 June 1321), nor did they fail to employ worldly means. They sent an astute messenger to Avignon to the papal court and to King Robert of Naples, the patron of the Jews, who happened to be in that city on state affairs. The messenger succeeded, through the mediation of King Robert, in proving the innocence of the Roman Jews in regard to the alleged insulting of the cross and the other transgressions laid to their charge. The twenty thousand ducats,which the Roman community is said to have presented to the sister of the pope, silenced the last objections. The Jews of Rome entered their school of trouble later than the Jews of other countries. For that reason it lasted the longer.

Whilst King Robert was residing in southern France, he seems to have made the acquaintance of a learned, genial Jewish satirist, Kalonymos ben Kalonymos, and to have taken him into his service. This talented man (born 1287, died before 1337) possessed solid knowledge, was familiar with the Arabic language and literature (which was very remarkable in a Provencal), and in his youth (1307-1317) translated medical, astronomical, and philosophical writings from that language into Hebrew. Kalonymos ben Kalonymos was not merely a hewer of wood and drawer of water, an interpreter in the realm of science; he had intellect enough to make independent observations. Disregarding the province of metaphysical speculation, he was more interested in pure ethics, which he especially wished to inculcate in his co-religionists, "because neglect and ignorance of it leads men to all kinds of perversities and mutual harm." He did not treat the subject in a dry, uninteresting style, but sought to clothe it in attractive garments. With this end in view, Kalonymos adapted a part of the Arabic encyclopedia of science (which was in circulation under the name of "Treatises of the Righteous Brethren") for a dialogue between man and beasts, giving the theme a Jewish coloring.

In another work, "Touchstone" (composed at the end of 1322), Kalonymos ben Kalonymos held up a mirror for his Jewish contemporaries, in which they could recognize their perversities, follies, and sins. To avoid giving himself the appearance of an irreproachable censor of morals, he enumerated his own sins, more in satire than as a confession. Kalonymos whimsically satirized even Judaism. He wished he had been born a woman, for then he would not have had to bear the burden of six hundred and thirteen religious laws, besides so many Talmudical restrictions and rigorous ordinances, which could not possibly be fulfilled, even when a man tried with the most exacting conscientiousness. As a woman, he would not have to trouble himself with so much reading, to study the Bible, the Talmud, and the subjects belonging- to it, nor torment himself with logic, mathematics, physics, astronomy, and philosophy. By and by Kalonymos satire grew deeply serious. The degradation of his Jewish co-religionists, and the bloody persecutions occasioned by the Shepherds and the lepers, dispelled his mocking humor, and satire was changed into lamentation. In Rome, which King Robert assigned to him as a place of residence, Kalonymos, having been furnished with letters of recommendation, obtained entry into a joyous, vivacious, imaginative circle of men, by whom he was stimulated to write a peculiar parody. He composed a treatise for the Jewish carnival (Purim), in which he imitated the tenor and spirit of the Talmud, its method, controversies, and digressions, with considerable wit. It is a fine parody, exciting laughter at every step, and one can not tell whether it was intended as a harmless carnival joke or as a satire on the Talmud. Kalonymos occupied a position of importance in the Roman congregation. Handsome in form, of abundant accomplishments, solid character, all his excellencies enhanced by the good opinion of King Robert of Naples, he was everyone's favorite. The Italian Jews were proud of him. But Kalonymos was not a true poet, still less an artist.

Much more gifted, profound, and imaginative was his older friend and admirer, Immanuel ben Solomon Romi (born about 1265, died about 1330)· He was an anomaly in the Jewish society of the Middle Ages. He belonged to that species of authors whose writings are all the more attractive because not very decent. Of overflowing wit, extravagant humor, and caustic satire, he is always able to enchain his readers, and continually to provoke their merriment. Immanuel may be called the Heine of the Jewish Middle Ages. Immanuel had an inexhaustible, ready supply of brilliant ideas. And all this in the holy language of the Prophets and Psalmists. Granted that the neo-Hebrew poets and thinkers, the grammarians and Talmudists, had lent flexibility to the language, but none of Immanuel's predecessors had his power of striking from it showers of sparkling wit. But if, on the one side, he developed the Hebrew language almost into a vehicle for brilliant repartee, on the other side, he robbed it of its sacred character. Immanuel transformed the chaste, closely-veiled maiden muse of Hebrew poetry into a lightly-clad dancer, who attracts the attention of passers-by. He allows his muse to deal with the most frivolous and indelicate topics without the slightest concealment or shame. His collection of songs and novels tends to exert a very pernicious and poisonous effect upon hot-blooded youth. But Immanuel was not the hardened sinner, as he describes himself, who thought of nothing but to carry on amours, seduce the fair, and deride the ugly. He sinned only with the tongue and the pen, scarcely with the heart and the senses.

Though he often indulges in unmeasured self-laudation, this simple description of his moral conduct must still be credited: "I never bear my enemies malice, I remain steadfast and true to my friends, cherish gratitude towards my benefactors, have a sympathetic heart, am not ostentatious with my knowledge, and absorb myself in science and poetry, whilst my companions riot in sensual enjoyments." Immanuel belonged to those who are dominated by their wit, and cannot refrain from telling some pointed witticism, even if their dearest friends are its victims, and the holiest things are dragged in the mire by it. He allowed himself to be influenced by the vivacity of the Italians and the Europeanized Jews, and put no curb upon his tongue. What is remarkable in this satirist is that his life, his position, and occupation seem to have been in contradiction with his poetical craft. In the Roman community he filled an honorable position, was something like a president, at all events a man of distinction. He appears to have belonged to the medical profession, although he made sport of the quackery of physicians. In short, he led the domestic life of his time, a life permeated by morality

and religion, giving no opportunity for excess. But his honorable life did not prevent him from singing riotous songs, and from writing as though he were unconscious of the seriousness of religion, of responsibility and learning. Immanuel was acquainted, if not on intimate terms, with the greatest poet of the Middle Ages, the first to open the gates of a new epoch, and to prognosticate the unity of Italy in poetic phrase. Probably they came to know each other on one of Dante's frequent visits to Rome, either as ambassador or exile. Although their poetic styles are as opposite as the poles--Dante's ethereal, grave, and elevated; Immanuel's forcible, gay, and light--they, nevertheless, have some points of contact. Each had absorbed the culture of the past; Dante the catholic, scholastic, and romantic elements; Immanuel the biblical, Talmudical, Maimunist, philosophical, and neo-Hebraic products. Both elaborated this many-hued material, and molded it into a new kind of poetry. The Italians at that time were full of the impulse of life, and Immanuel's muse is inspired by the witchery of spring. He wrote ably in Italian, too, of which a beautiful poem, still extant, gives evidence. Immanuel was the first to adapt Italian numbers to the neo-Hebraic lyre. He introduced the rhyme in alternate lines (Terza rima in sonnet form), by which he produced a musical cadence. His poems are not equally successful. They are wanting not in imagination, but in tenderness and grace. His power lies in poetical prose (Meliza), where he can indulge in free and witty allusions. In this style he composed a host of short novels, riddles, letters, panegyrics, and epithalamia, which, by clever turns and comic situations, extort laughter from the most serious-minded readers.

In one of his novels he introduces a quarrelsome grammarian of the Hebrew language, a verbal critic who takes the field in grammatical campaigns, and is accompanied by a marvelously beautiful woman. Immanuel enters into a hair-splitting disputation that he may have the opportunity of coquetting with the lovely lady. He suffers defeat in grammar, but makes a conquest in love. Immanuel's description of hell and paradise, in which he imitated his friend Dante, is full of fine satire. Whilst the Christian romantic poet shows gravity and elevation in his poetical creation, represents sinners and criminals, political opponents and enemies of Italy, cardinals and popes, as being tortured in hell, metes out, as it were, the severe sentences of judgment day; his Jewish friend, Immanuel, invents scenes in heaven and hell for the purpose of giving play to his humorous fancy. Dante wrote a divine, Immanuel a human, comedy. He introduces his pilgrimage to heaven and hell by relating that he once felt greatly oppressed by the burden of his sins, and experienced compunction; at this juncture his young friend Daniel, by whose untimely death he had lately been deeply affected, appeared to him, and offered to guide him through the dismal portals of hell and the elysian fields of the blessed. In the chambers of hell Immanuel observes all the wicked and godless of the Bible. Aristotle, too, is there, " because he taught the eternity of the world," and Plato, "because he asserted the reality of species" (Realism). Most of all he scourges his contemporaries in this poem. He inflicts the torment of the damned upon the deriders of science; upon a Talmudist who secretly led a most immoral life; upon men who committed intellectual thefts, and upon those who sought to usurp all the honors of the synagogue, the one to have his seat by the Ark of the Covenant, the other to read the prayers on the Day of Atonement. Quack doctors are also precipitated into hell, because they take advantage of the stupidity and credulity of the multitude, and bring trusting patients to a premature grave. His

IMMANUEL AND DANTE.

young, beatified guide goes with him through the gates of Paradise. How the departed spirits rejoice at the poet's approach ! They call out, " Now is the time to laugh, for Immanuel has arrived." In the description of paradise and its inhabitants, Immanuel affects to treat his theme very seriously; but he titters softly within the very gates of heaven. Of course, he notices the holy men, the patriarchs, the pious kings and heroes of the Jewish past, the prophets and the great teachers, the poets, Jehuda Halevi and Charisi, the Jewish philosopher Maimuni. But next to King David, who fingers the harp and sings psalms, he observes the harlot Rahab who concealed the spies in Jericho, and Tamar who sat at the cross-roads waiting. Dante excludes the heathen world from paradise, because it did not acknowledge Christ, and had no share in the grace of salvation. Immanuel sees a troop of the blessed, whom he does not recognize, and asks their leader who they are. "These are," answers the latter, "righteous and moral heathens, who attained the height of wisdom, and recognized the only God as the creator of the world and the bestower of grace." The pious authors, David, Solomon, Isaiah, Ezekiel, on seeing Immanuel, darted forward to meet him; each one thanks him for having expounded his writings so well, and here older and contemporary exegetists come in for their share of Immanuel's sly satire.

Neo-Hebraic poetry, which began with Jose ben Jose, and reached its zenith in Ibn-Gebirol and Yehuda Halevi, attains its final stage of development in Immanuel. The gamut had now been run. After Immanuel, the Hebrew muse became silent for a long time, and it required a fresh and powerful stimulus to awaken it from slumber to new energy. Verses were, of course, written after his days, and rhymes polished, but they are as far removed from poetry as a street-song from a soul-stirring melody. The fate of Hebrew poetry is illustrated in Immanuel's career. For a long period he was popular, everyone sought his friendship, but in old age he fell into neglect and poverty. His own statement is that his generosity dissipated his means. He was as much derided as he had formerly been praised. He left Rome with his family, traveled about, and found repose at length at the house of a wealthy, influential friend of art (Benjamin?) in Fermo, who interested himself in him, and encouraged him to arrange the verses and poems written at different periods of his life into a symmetrical whole.

The praises which Immanuel bestows on his own productions, and his boast that he casts the old poets into the shade, certainly tend to produce a bad impression. Nevertheless, like every expert in his profession, he was far removed from that repulsive vanity which perceives its own depreciation in the recognition of another. To true merit Immanuel gave the tribute of his warmest praise, and modestly conceded precedence to it. Not only did he extol the highly honored Kalonymos, basking in the sunshine of the king's favor, with the most extravagant figures of speech, but he praised almost more heartily the poet Yehuda Siciliano, who lived in straitened circumstances. He gave him the palm for poetical verse, maintaining his own superiority in poetical prose. But for Immanuel, nothing would have been known of this poet. Poor Siciliano had to waste his power in occasional poems for his subsistence, and was thus unable to produce any lasting work. With glowing enthusiasm Immanuel eulogizes his cousin, the young and learned Leone Romano, Yehuda ben Moses ben Daniel (born about 1292), whom he calls the "Crown of Thought." In paradise he allots to him the highest place of honor. Leone Romano was the teacher of King Robert of Naples, and instructed him in the original language of the Bible. He knew the language of learned

LEONE ROMANO.

Christendom, and was probably the first Jew to pay attention to scholastic philosophy. He translated for Jewish readers the philosophical compositions of Albertus Magnus, Thomas Aquinas, and others. Leone Romano composed original works of exegesis, set forth in philosophical method. Greatly as his contemporaries admired his learning and intellect, which had achieved so much when he had scarcely arrived at man's estate, he exercised no influence whatever on posterity.

The Roman society which promoted science and poetry may be said to have included also the grandson of a Roman emigrant who took up his abode in Greece, Shemarya Ikriti (Cretan) of Negroponte (flourished 1290-1320). He stood in close relation with the Roman community and King Robert. Familiar with Talmudical literature, as he probably was rabbi in Negroponte, he devoted himself to philosophical speculations, and was, perhaps, well read in the Greek philosophical literature in its original language. In his youth, Ikriti, like many of his contemporaries, occupied himself with translations of philosophical works. Later on he conceived a plan of practical utility, in which he thought he could turn his knowledge to account. He sought to smooth over the difference between the Rabbanites and the Karaites, and lastingly to reconcile the sects at enmity with each other for centuries, "that all Israel may once more be united in one fraternal bond." Shemarya of Negroponte was the first, perhaps the only Rabbanite, who, if he did not extend the hand of reconciliation to Karaism, at least showed a friendly disposition towards it. He recognized that both parties were in error; Karaism was wrong in rejecting Talmudical traditions unconditionally; but the Rabbanites sinned against truth in placing the Talmud in the forefront,and overlooking the Bible. In Greece there may have been Karaites at that time who had come from Constantinople. To these Shemarya Ikriti addressed himself to incline their minds towards union with the mother community.

For the difficult task of bringing discordant faiths into harmony, much intelligence and energy were required, and Shemarya could furnish only good will. He was not deficient in knowledge, but his mental grasp was not sufficiently powerful. At the instance of King Robert, who interested himself in Jewish literature, he wrote a commentary on the Bible, and forwarded to him, with a dedication, the books first completed (1328). It read as follows: "To our noble king Robert, adorned like King Solomon with the crown of wisdom and the diadem of royalty, I send this exposition of the cosmogony and the Song of Songs." His Biblical commentaries were set forth with great diffuseness, covered a great range, and were not calculated to appeal to the Karaites, and draw them over to the side of rabbinical Judaism. His attempt at reconciliation miscarried, perhaps was not made in the proper spirit; for there was a disposition on the part of some Karaites to treat his overtures favorably, and his efforts would not have failed, if they had been conducted with skill. Nevertheless, Ikriti was held in such esteem in his time that the Roman congregation took an interest in his labors, entered into correspondence with him, while the Karaites assiduously read his works, and in later times considered him a member of their own party.

Karaism was still dragging itself along in its decaying, stiffening form. Internal schisms remained unaccommodated. Different Karaite congregations celebrated the festivals at different times: the Palestinians, according to the observation of the new moon, and the extra-Palestinian congregations, in common with the Rabbanites. Their extremely severe marriage laws were not finally settled even at this epoch. Karaism at that time had three

AARON BEN JOSEPH.

centers--Cairo in Egypt, Constantinople in the Byzantine Empire, and Sulchat (Eski-Crim) in the Crimean peninsula. Some importance was possessed by Aaron ben Joseph the Elder, physician in Constantinople (flourished about 1270--1300). He came originally from the Crimea, made extensive voyages, and acquired a knowledge of medicine and philosophy. Aaron I also made himself intimate with Rabbanite literature to a degree that few of his sect attained. He made use of Nachmani's commentary on the Pentateuch, and from this circumstance arose the mistake of later Karaites, that Aaron had sat at Nachmani's feet. His familiarity with Rabbanite literature had a beneficial effect on his style; he wrote much more clearly and intelligibly than most of the Karaite authors. He was even disposed to accept the tradition of the Talmud.

He completely fixed the Karaite prayer book (Siddur Tefila), hitherto in an unsettled condition, incorporating into it hymns written by Gebirol, Yehuda Halevi, Ibn-Ezra, and other Rabbanite liturgical poets. Aaron himself possessed very little poetical genius, and his metrical prayers, with which he enriched the prayer book of the Karaites, have no great poetical merit, but by the admission of hymns written by Rabbanites into his compilation, he showed that he knew how to appreciate the devout sublimity in the prayers of the Spanish Jews, and that he was not altogether devoid of taste. If Shemarya, of Negroponte, had undertaken to effect a reconciliation between the Rabbanites and the Karaites in a more intelligent and energetic manner, there can be no doubt that Aaron would willingly have offered his assistance, provided, of course, that he had known of Shemarya's attempt. There was not wanting among Karaites a strong inclination for union. Owing to the activity of Abraham Maimuni II, a great-grandson of the renowned Maimuni, who had succeeded to the post of Chief (Nagid) of the Rabbanite communities in Egypt after the death of his father David, an important Karaite congregation in Egypt on one day openly acknowledged the teachings of the Rabbanites. In Palestine, too, frequent conversions of Karaites to Talmudical Judaism took place. On this account the rabbis of the time were more favorably disposed towards them. On the one hand, the strict Talmudist Samson of Sens denounced the Karaites as heathens, whose wine was not to be partaken of by orthodox Jews; on the other hand, Estori Parchi,who had been banished from Provence, and who, emigrating to Palestine, had settled in Bethshan, recognized them as co-religionists, led astray by erroneous notions, but not to be rejected.

IV. CHAPTER III.

THE AGE OF THE ASHERIDES AND OF GERSONIDES.

Condition of Palestine--Pilgrims and Immigrants--Shem Tob Ibn Gaon-Favorable Position of the Jews in Castile under Alfonso XI--Joseph de Ecija and Samuel Ibn Waker-Increase of Anti-Jewish Feelings-Abner-Alfonso of Burgos, Convert to Christianity, and Persecutor of the Jews-Gonzalo Martinet--Fall of Martinet and Deliverance of the Jews--Decline of the Study of Science--The Study of the Talmud prosecuted with Renewed Vigor--Jacob and Judah Asheri-Isaac Pulgar, David Ibn-Albilla--The Provencal Philosophers Ibn-Kaspi, Leon de Bagnols, and Vidal Narboni--Decline of the Study of the Talmud in Germany--Emperor Louis of Bavaria and the Jews--Persecution by the " Leather-Arms."

1328--1350 C.E.

THE HOLY LAND was once more accessible to its children. The Egyptian sultans, into whose power it passed after the fall of Accho and the expulsion of the Christians, were more tolerant than the Christian Byzantine emperors and the Frankish crusading kings. They did not hinder the coming of Jewish pilgrims who desired to lighten their overburdened hearts by praying and weeping over the ruins of the past, so rich in recollections, or at the graves of their great men there interred; nor did they oppose the settlement of European exiles, who again cultivated the soil of the land of their fathers. The long, firm, yet mild, reign of the Mameluke sultan, Nassir Mahomet (1299--1341), was a happy time for the Jews who visited Palestine. Whilst under the rule of the Christian governors of the country no Jew was permitted to approach the former capital, at this time Jewish pilgrims from Egypt and Syria regularly came to Jerusalem, to celebrate the festivals, as in the time when the Temple shone in all its splendor. The Karaites established special forms of prayer for those who went on pilgrimages to Jerusalem: at their departure, the whole congregation assembled to give utterance in prayer to the bitter-sweet emotions connected with Zion. The immigrants who settled in Palestine engaged in agriculture. They came to feel so thoroughly at home there that the question was mooted whether the laws of tithes, of the year of release, and others ought not to be again carried into effect. In consequence of the freedom and tolerance which the Jews were enjoying, many enthusiastic spirits were again seized by the ardent desire to kiss the dust of the Holy Land. Emigration to Palestine, especially from the extreme west, became very common at this time.

A pupil of Meir of Rothenburg, named Abraham, a painstaking copyist of holy writings, considered his dwelling In the Holy Land a mark of divine grace. Two young Kabbalists, Chananel Ibn-Askara and Shem Tob Ibn-Gaon from Spain, also traveled thither, probably to be nearer the source of the mystic doctrines, which fancy assigned to this country, and took up their residence in Safet. But instead of obtaining fresh information upon the doctrines of the Kabbala, one of them--Ibn-Askara died in his youth--introduced new features of the science. Shem Tob ben Abraham Ibn-Gaon, from Segovia (born 1283, died after 1330), whose teacher in the Talmud had been Ben Adret, and in the Kabbala Isaac ben Todros, was a zealous adherent of the secret science, and described even Maimuni as a Kabbalist.

The congregation of Jerusalem was at this time very numerous. A large portion of the Rabbanite community led a contemplative life, studied the Talmud day and night, and became engrossed with the secret lore of the Kabbala. There were also handicraftsmen, merchants, and several acquainted with the science of medicine, with mathematics and astronomy. The artistic work of the famous calligraphers of Jerusalem was in great demand, far and near. Hebron, too, possessed a vigorous community, whose members engaged chiefly in the weaving and dyeing of cotton-stuffs, and in the manufacture of glass wares, exported in large quantities. In the south of Palestine, in company with Mahometans, Jewish shepherds again pastured their flocks after the manner of the patriarchs. Their rabbi was also a shepherd, and delivered discourses upon the Talmud in the pasture fields for such as desired to obtain instruction.

Although the Holy Land was the goal of ardent, longing hearts, yet it was no more a center for the dispersed of the Jewish race than it had been for a long time previous. It could not produce an original leader of any sort, and lived upon the crumbs of culture dropped by the Jews in Europe. The Kabbala, studied in Palestine since the time of Nachmani, was an exotic plant which could never flourish very well there, and degenerated into rankest superstition. The Holy Land did not even produce a Talmudical authority of widespread renown; also for earnest rabbinical studies it had become dependent upon Europe. The leadership of Judaism in the days after the death of Ben Adret and Asheri remained with Spain, not as formerly Aragon, but Castile, where the family of Asheri and their views prevailed. Here lived Talmudical authorities whose decisions were considered final. Here was still to be found, if not a flourishing state of science, at least appreciation of scientific research. In Castile, under the rule of the powerful and intelligent Alfonso XI, the Jews were in so prosperous a condition that, compared with other countries in Europe, this period may be called a Golden Age. Several clever Jews in succession, under the modest title of ministers of finance (Almojarif), exercised an influence upon the course of politics. Not only the court, but also the great nobles, surrounded themselves with Jewish counselors and officers. In place of the humble, servile bearing, and the degrading badge which the church decreed for the Jews, the Jewish Spaniards still bore their heads erect, and clothed themselves in gold and silk. Dazzled by the glitter of this favorable state of affairs, some recognized the fulfillment of the old prophecy, "the scepter shall not depart from Judah," which Christians had so often employed in their attacks on Judaism.

It is scarcely to be wondered at, if the Spanish Jews were unduly elated because of the promotion of a few from their midst to state offices. Such prominent public men were for the most part a protecting shield for the communities against the avaricious and turbulent lower orders of the nobility, against the stupid credulity and envy of the mob, and the serpent-like cunning of the clergy, lying concealed but ready to attack the Jews. Jewish ministers and counselors in the service and the retinue of the king, clothed in the costume of the court, and wearing at their sides the knightly sword, by these very circumstances, without special intercession, disarmed the enemies of their brethren in faith and race. The impoverished nobles, who possessed nothing more than their swords, were filled with envy of the rich and wise court Jews; but they were compelled to stifle their feelings. The masses, guided by appearances, did not venture, as was done in Germany, to ill-treat or slay any Jew they chanced across, as an outlaw and a pariah, because they knew that the Jews were held in high favor at court. They often overrated their influence, believing that the Jews at court could obtain a hearing with the king at any time. Even the haughty clergy were obliged to restrain themselves so long as Joseph of Ecija, Samuel Ibn-Wakar, and others, were in a position to counteract their influence.

JOSEPH OF ECIJA.

The sun that was shining upon them in Castile at this time was, strictly speaking, only a false sun, but its glimmer, compared with the gloom wherein the congregations of other countries were steeped, gives at least momentary pleasure. Alfonso XI, as soon as he came of age, and obtained the sovereignty (1325--1380), had two Jewish favorites, Don Joseph of Ecija and Samuel Ibn-Wakar. The former, whose full name was Joseph ben Ephraim Ibn-Benveniste Halevi, had a pleasing exterior, understood music, and knew how to ingratiate himself with those in power. At the recommendation of his uncle, the king had made him not only minister of finance (Almojarif), but also his confidential counselor (privado), whose opinion he highly valued. Joseph of Ecija possessed a state carriage, knights accompanied him as an escort on his journeys, and hidalgos dined at his table. On one occasion the king dispatched him on a very important and honorable mission which almost cost him his life. He was besieged by the citizens of Valladolid in the palace of the Infanta, and they demanded his surrender with tumultuous clamor. Some of Joseph's retinue succeeded in escaping from the city, and they hastened at full speed to the king, to whom they related what had taken place. Alfonso rightly considered this a revolt against his sovereignty. He marched rapidly against Valladolid, and summoned the knights of Old Castile to join him. For the sake of his Jewish favorite, he besieged the former capital of his kingdom, burnt many houses, and would have destroyed the place entirely, had not more moderate persons intervened, and explained to the king that the people were not so much embittered against Don Joseph as against Don Alvar Nunez, whose influence was most hateful to them. Don Alfonso thereupon condescended to remove Alvar from his public offices, whilst Don Joseph continued in favor with the king.

The other favorite of King Alfonso was his physician, Don Samuel Ibn-Wakar (Abenhuacar). This man had a scientific education, was an astronomer, and perhaps the astrologer of his master. Although he occupied no public office, and took no part in state affairs, yet, through the favor of the king, he possessed very great influence. There existed between Don Joseph of Ecija and Ibn Wakar the jealousy which is common among courtiers who bask in the rays of the same sun. On account of their rivalry, these two favorites sought to injure each other, and thus they and their co-religionists incurred the hatred of the people.

Some wealthy Jews, probably relying upon the favorable position of their friends at court, carried on money transactions in an unscrupulous manner. They extorted a high rate of interest and mercilessly persecuted their dilatory Christian debtors. The king himself encouraged the usury of the Jews and Moors, because he gained advantage therefrom. The complaints of the people against the Jewish and Mahometan usurers grew very numerous. The cortes of Madrid, Valladolid and other cities made this point the subject of petitions presented to the king, demanding the abolition of these abuses, and the king was compelled to yield to their entreaty.

The minds of the people, however, remained embittered against the Jews. The cortes of Madrid thereupon called for several restrictive laws against the Jews, such as, that they should not be allowed to acquire landed property, and that Jewish ministers of finance and farmers of taxes should not be appointed (1329). Alfonso replied, that, in the main, things should continue as they had been before. Don Samuel Ibn-Wakar rose even higher in the royal favor. Don Alfonso entrusted him with the farming of the revenues derived from the importation of goods from the kingdom of Granada.

SAMUEL IBN-WAKAR.

He, moreover, obtained the privilege empowering him to issue the coinage of the realm at a lower standard. Joseph of Ecija now became jealous and offered a higher sum for the right of farming the import-taxes from Granada. When he thought he had supplanted his rival, the latter dealt him a severe blow. Ibn-Wakar succeeded in persuading the king that it would be more advantageous to the people of Castile to carry the protective system to its uttermost limits, and prohibit all imports from the neighboring Moorish kingdom (1330-1331).

Whilst the two Jewish courtiers were striving to injure each other, the enemies of the Jews were busily at work to imperil their reputation and the existence of all the Castilian congregations. They inflamed the minds of the people by representing to them that, owing to the depreciation in the value of money, brought about by the farmer of the coinage, Ibn-Wakar, the price of the necessaries of life had risen, these articles being exported to the neighboring countries, where they were bartered for silver, which had a higher value in their own land. The enemies of the Jews also brought the influence of the church to bear to arouse the prejudices of the king against all the Jews. Their champion was a Jew, who no sooner had embraced Christianity, than he became a fanatical persecutor of his brethren. This was the infamous Abner, the forerunner of the baptized and unbaptized Jew-haters, who prepared, and at length accomplished, the humiliation and banishment of the Spanish Jews.

Abner of Burgos, or as he was afterwards called, Alfonso Burgensis de Valladolid (born about 1270, died about 1346), was well acquainted with biblical and Talmudical writings, occupied himself with science, and practiced medicine. His knowledge had destroyed his religious belief, and turned him not only against Judaism, but against all faiths. Troubled by cares for his subsistence, Abner did not obtain the desired support from his kinsmen in race. He was too little of a philosopher to accept his modest lot. His desires were extravagant, and he was unable to find the means to satisfy them. In order to be able to live in ease and splendor, Abner determined, when nearly sixty years of age, to adopt Christianity, although this religion was as little able to give him inward contentment as that which he forsook. [These were the charges that were leveled against him by his foes, as an apostate; charges which unfortunately have been brought against many Jews who sought to find in Jesus the true Messiah of Israel. Whether there is any truth in them, or whether the author here paints a too-dark portrait of Abner's motives, is for the reader to decide.--ed] As a Christian, he assumed the name of Alfonso. The infidel disciple of Aristotle and Averroes accepted an ecclesiastical office; he became sacristan at a large church in Valladolid, to which a rich benefice was attached, enabling him to gratify his worldly desires. He attempted to excuse his hypocritical behavior and his apostasy by means of sophistical arguments.

Alfonso carried his want of conscientiousness so far that not long after his conversion to Christianity he attacked his former brethren in faith and race with bitter hate, and showed the intention of persecuting them. Owing to his knowledge of Jewish literature, it was easy for him to discover its weak points, employ them as charges against Judaism, and draw the most hateful inferences. Alfonso was indefatigable in his accusations against the Jews and Judaism, and composed a long series of works, in which he introduced arguments partly aggressive, partly defensive of his new faith against the attacks upon it by the Jews. In his abuse of Judaism, the Hebrew language, in which he composed with much greater ease than in Spanish, was made to do service.

Alfonso had the brazen impudence to send one of his hateful writings to his former friend, Isaac Pulgar. The latter replied in a sharply satirical poem, and pressed him close in his polemical writings. The Jews of Spain had not yet become so disheartened as to suffer such insolent attacks in silence. Another less renowned writer also answered Alfonso, and thus a violent literary warfare broke out.

ALFONSO OF VALLADOLID.

Alfonso of Valladolid, however, did not content himself with polemical writings ; he boldly presented himself before King Alfonso XI, and laid his accusations against the Jews before him. He raked up anew the remark of the Church Father Jerome and others, that the Jews had introduced into their book of prayer a formula of imprecation against the God of the Christians and his adherents. The representatives of the Jewish community in Valladolid, probably summoned by the king to justify themselves, emphatically denied that the imprecation originally leveled against the Minim (Nazarenes) referred to Jesus and his present followers. Alfonso, however, would not admit the validity of this exculpation, and pledged himself to prove his charges against the Jews in a disputation. The king of Castile thereupon commanded the representatives of the Valladolid community to enter upon a religious discussion with the sacristan. It took place in the presence of public officials and Dominicans. Here Alfonso Burgensis repeated his accusations, and was victorious, inasmuch as, in consequence of this disputation, King Alfonso issued an edict (25th February, 1336) forbidding the Castilian communities, under penalty of a fine, to use the condemned prayer or formula of imprecation. Thus the enemies of the Jews succeeded in winning over the king, who was really well-disposed towards the Jews. More ominous events were to happen.

King Alfonso was not very constant; he transferred his favor from one person to another. He took into his confidence a man unworthy of the distinction, named Gonzalo Martinet (Nunez) de Oviedo, originally a poor knight, who had been promoted through the patronage of the Jewish favorite, Don Joseph of Ecija. Far from being grateful to his benefactor, he bore deep hatred against him who had thus raised him, and his hostile feeling extended to all Jews. When he had risen to the post of minister of the royal palace, and later to that of Grand Master of the Order of Alcantara (1337), he revealed his plan of annihilating the Jews. He lodged a formal charge against Don Joseph and Don Samuel Ibn-Wakar, to the effect that they had enriched themselves in the service of the king. He obtained the permission of the king to deal with them as he chose, so as to extort money from them. There upon Gonzalo ordered both of them, together with two brothers of Ibn-Wakar, and eight relatives with their families, to be thrown into prison, and confiscated their property. Don Joseph of Ecija died in prison, and Don Samuel died under the torture to which he was subjected. This did not satisfy the enemy of the Jews. He now sought to destroy two other Jews, who held high positions at court-Moses Abudiel and (Sulaiman?) Ibn·Yaish. He implicated them in a charge, pretending all the while to be friendly towards them. Through their downfall Gonzalo Martinet thought to carry into effect his wicked plan against the Castilian Jews without difficulty.

The Moorish king of Morocco, Abulhassan (Alboacin), whose help was implored by his oppressed co-religionists in Granada, had sent a very large army under the command of his son, Abumelik, over the straits to undertake a vigorous campaign against Castile. On the reception of this news, terror spread throughout Christian Spain. King Alfonso forthwith appointed Gonzalo Martinet, Master of the Order of Alcantara, as general in charge of this war, and invested him with plenary power. But funds were wanting; at the deliberation on ways and means of procuring them, Gonzalo propounded his plan for depriving the Jews of their wealth, and then expelling them from Castile. By this means, large supplies of money would flow into the royal treasury; for all the Christians who were dunned by the Jews would willingly pay large sums of

money to rid themselves of their enemies. Fortunately this proposal met with opposition in the royal council, and even from the most prominent clergyman in Castile, the archbishop of Toledo. The latter urged that the Jews were an inexhaustible treasure for the king, of which the state should not deprive itself, and that the rulers of Castile had guaranteed them protection and toleration. Don Moses Abudiel, who obtained information concerning the council held to decide on the weal or woe of the Jews, advised the congregations to institute public fasts, and to supplicate the God of their fathers to frustrate the wickedness of Gonzaio. The latter marched to the frontier against the Moorish army, and secured an easy victory. It happened, fortunately for the Spaniard, that the Moorish general, Abumelik, fell pierced by an arrow, and his army, filled with dismay at this event, was defeated and put to rout. The vainglory of the Grand Master of Alcantara now attained a high pitch. He thought to obtain such great importance in Spanish affairs that the king would be compelled to approve of all measures proposed by him. He was, indeed, filled with that pride which precedes a fall.

The feeble hand of a woman was the cause of his downfall. The beautiful and sprightly Leonora de Guzman, who had so enthralled the king with her charms that he was more faithful to her than to his wife, hated the favorite Gonzalo Martinet, and succeeded in making the king believe that he spoke ill of him. Alfonso desiring to learn the real truth of the matter sent a command to Gonzalo to present himself before him in Madrid; he, however, disobeyed the royal command. To be able to defy the anger of the king, he stirred up the knights o~ the Order of Alcantara and the citizens of the towns assigned to his government, to rebel against his sovereign, entered into traitorous negotiations with the king of Portugal and with the enemy of the Christians, the king of Granada. Alfonso was forced to lead his nobles against him, and besiege him in Valencia de Alcantara. In mad defiance, Gonzalo directed arrows and missiles to be aimed at the king, which mortally wounded a man in the vicinity of Alfonso. But some of the knights of the Order of Alcantara forsook their Grand Master, and surrendered the stronghold to the king. There remained nothing for Gonzalo except to yield. He was condemned to death as a traitor, and was burnt at the stake (1336), and thus ended the man who had sworn to annihilate the Jews. The Castilian congregations thereupon celebrated a new festival of deliverance, in the same month in which the evil plans of Haman against the Jews had recoiled on his own head. Alfonso again received the Jews into his favor, and raised Moses Abudiel to a high position at his court. From this time till the day of his death, Alfonso XI acted justly towards his Jewish subjects.

It may be thought that, under these on the whole favorable circumstances, the Jews occupied themselves with their intellectual culture, which had already developed its full blossom; but it was not so. Castile in particular, and all Spain, at this epoch, were very deficient in men who cultivated Jewish science. The Talmud constituted the only branch of study which intellectual men attended to, and even here there was no particular fertility. Decrease in strength manifested itself even in the study of the Talmud. The most famous rabbis of this period had so great a mistrust of their own powers that they no longer dared take an independent view of anything, and relied more and more upon the conclusions of older authorities. They made it very convenient for themselves by slavishly following Maimuni's Code in practical decisions, deviating from it only in such particulars as Asheri had objected to. The latter had pretty well succeeded, if not in altogether destroying the inclination of the Spanish Jews to engage in scientific inquiry, at least in bringing science into disrepute, and thus weakening its study. The distinguished supporters of philosophy henceforth no more came from Spain; the few that came into prominence were from southern France. These were Ibn-Kaspi, Gersonides and Narboni. Asheri and his sons, who inherited his hostility to science, in causing the view to become general throughout Spain, that a man should not engage in higher questions concerning Judaism and its connection with philosophy, did not consider that by this means the spirit of the Spanish Jews would become enfeebled and incapacitated for Talmudical investigations, too. The Jewish sons of Spain were not so well suited for the study of narrow Talmudism as the German Jews. Prevented from occupying themselves with science, they lost their buoyancy of spirit, and became unfit for the studies permitted. Even their pleasure in song and their poetical talents died away. Occasionally a poem was still produced, but it consisted merely of rude and unimaginative rhymes. In time they were no better than the German Jews, whom they had before so greatly despised. Even their prose style, on which the Spanish Jews had formerly bestowed so much care, degenerated for the most part into spiritless verbosity. The charming writer, Santob de Carrion, who as early as the time of Alfonso XI had clothed his thoughts in beautiful Spanish verse, was a solitary poet, whose song awoke no echo.

The eight sons of Asheri, his relatives, who had emigrated with him from Germany to Toledo, together with his numerous grandsons, dominated Spanish Judaism from this time onwards. They introduced a one-sided Talmudical method of instruction deeply tinged with a gloomy, ascetic view of religion. The most famous of the sons of Asheri were Jacob (Baal ha-Turim) and Yehuda, both intensely religious, and of unselfish, self-sacrificing dispositions; they were, however, limited to a very narrow range of ideas. Both were as learned in the Talmud as they were ignorant in other subjects, and possessed every duality calculated to bring the decay of religion into accord with the increasing sufferings of the Jews in this third home of their race.

Jacob ben Asheri (born about 1280, died 1340) was visited by bitter misfortunes. His life was one chain of sufferings and privations; but he bore all with patience, without murmur or complaint. Although his father, Asheri, had brought much wealth with him to Spain, and had always been in good circumstances, yet his son, Jacob, had to suffer the bitterest pangs of poverty. Nevertheless, he received no salary as a rabbi: in fact, he does not appear to have filled that post at any time. As with all the family of Asheri, both sons and grandsons, the Talmud constituted his exclusive interest in life ; but he displayed more erudition than originality. His sole merit consists in the fact that he brought the chaos of Talmudical learning into definite order, and satisfied the need of the time for a complete code of laws for religious practice.

Owing to his German origin and to his residence in Spain, Jacob Asheri became familiar with the productions of the different schools and authorities in their minutest details. He was thus well suited to control this chaotic mass and reduce it to order. On the basis of the labors of all his predecessors in this field, especially of Maimuni, Jacob compiled a second religious code (in four parts, Turim, shortened to Tur, about 1340)· This work treated solely of religious practice, that is, of the ritual, moral, marriage and civil laws. He omitted all such things as had fallen into disuse since the destruction of the Temple and because of altered circumstances. With the composition of this work, a new phase in the inner development of Judaism may be said to begin.

JACOB ASHERI'S CODE.

Jacob's code forms part of a graduated scale, by means of which it can be ascertained to how low a level official Judaism had sunk since the time of Maimuni. In Maimuni's compilation thought is paramount; every ritual practice, of whatever kind, whether good or bad, is brought into connection with the essence of religion. In Jacob's code, on the other hand, thought or reasoning is renounced. Religious scrupulousness, which had taken so firm a hold of the German Jewish congregations, inspires the laws, and imposes the utmost stringency and mortifications. Maimuni, in accepting religious precepts as obligatory, was guided entirely by the Talmud, and but seldom included the decisions of the Geonim as invested with authority. Asheri's son, on the contrary, admitted into his digest of religious laws everything that any pious or ultra-pious man had decided upon either out of scrupulosity or as a result of learned exposition. In his code, the precepts declared to be binding by rabbinical authorities far outnumbered those of Talmudic origin. One might almost say that in Jacob Asheri's hands, Talmudical Judaism was transformed into Rabbinism. He even included some of the follies of the Kabbala in his religious digest.

Jacob's code is essentially different from that of Maimuni, not only in contents, but also in form. The style and the language do not manifest the conciseness and lucidity of Maimuni's. Notwithstanding this, his code soon met with universal acceptance, because it corresponded to a want of the times, and presented, in a synoptical form, all the ordinances relating to the ritual, to marriage, and civil laws binding on the adherents of Judaism in exile under the rule of various nations. Rabbis and judges accepted it as the criterion for practical decisions, and even preferred it to Maimuni's work A few of the rabbis of that age refused to forego their independence, and continued to pronounce decisions arrived at by original inquiry, and therefore paid little heed to the new religious code. The great majority of them, on the other hand, not only in Spain, but also in Germany, were delighted to possess a handy book of laws systematically presenting everything worth knowing, making deep, penetrative research superfluous, and taxing the memory more than the understanding. Thus Jacob's Tur became the indispensable manual for the knowledge of Judaism, as understood by the rabbis, for a period of four centuries, till a new one was accepted which far surpassed the old.

His brother, Yehuda Asheri, was on a par with Jacob in erudition and virtue, but did not possess similar power of reducing chaos to order. He was born about 1284, and died in 1349· After the death of his father, the community of Toledo elected him as Asheri's successor in the rabbinate of the Spanish capital. He performed the functions of his office with extraordinary scrupulousness, without respect of persons, and was able to call the whole community to witness that he had never been guilty of the slightest trespass. When Yehuda Asheri, on account of some small quarrel with his congregation, resolved to take up his abode in Seville, the entire community unanimously begged of him to remain in their midst, and doubled his salary. In spite of this show of affection, he did not feel comfortable in Spain, and in his will he is said to have advised his five sons to emigrate to Germany, the original home of his family. The persecution of the German Jews, during the year of the epidemic pestilence, probably taught them that it was preferable to dwell in Spain. By reason of his position in the most important of the congregations and of his comprehensive rabbinical learning, Yehuda Asheri was regarded as the highest authority of his age, and was preferred even to his brother Jacob.

Seeing that even the study of the Talmud, so

DECLINE OF SCIENCE

zealously pursued in Spain, had fallen into this state of stagnation and lassitude, the other branches of science could not complain that they made no progress, or were not attentively cultivated. The study of the Bible, Hebrew grammar, and exegesis were entirely neglected; we can recall hardly a single writer who earnestly occupied himself with these subjects. Owing to the energetic zeal of Abba-Mari, the interdict of Ben Adret, and the pronounced aversion of Asheri, reasoning had fallen into disrepute and decay. The truly orthodox shunned contact with philosophy as the direct route to heresy and infidelity, and pseudo-pious people behaved in a yet more prudish fashion towards it. It required courage to engage in a study inviting contempt and accusations of heresy. The Kabbala, too, had done its work, in dimming the eyes of men by its illusions. There were but few representatives of a philosophical conception of Judaism in those days; these were Isaac Pulgar, of Avila, David Ibn-Albilla of Portugal, and Joseph Kaspi of Argentiere, in southern France.

Levi ben Gerson, or Leon de Bagnols, was more renowned and more talented than any of these. He was also called Leo the Hebrew, but more usually by his literary name Gersonides (born 1288, died about 1345)· He belonged to a family of scholars, and among his ancestors he reckoned that Levi of Villefranche who had indirectly caused the prohibition of scientific study. In spite of the interdict of Ben Adret forbidding the instruction of youths in science, Gersonides was initiated into it at a very early age, and before he had reached his thirtieth year he was at work at a comprehensive and profound work upon philosophy. Gersonides was gifted with a versatile and profound intellect, and averse to all superficiality and incompleteness. In astronomy he corrected his predecessors, and made such accurate observations that specialists based their calculations upon them. He invented an instrument by means of which observations of the heavens could be made more certain. This discovery filled him with such ecstasy that he composed a Hebrew poem, a kind of riddle, upon it, though he was an unpoetical man, and had his head filled with dry calculations and logical conclusions. He also wrote works upon the science of medicine, and discovered new remedies. At the same time he was held in very high repute by his contemporaries as a profound Talmudist, and inspired by his love for systematic arrangement, wrote a methodology of the Mishna.

Maestro Leon de Bagnols, as he was called as a physician, fortunately did not belong to the Jews of France proper; he successively lived in Orange, Perpignan, and in Avignon, at this time the home of popedom. Therefore, he had not been a sufferer in the expulsion of his co-religionists from this land ; but his heart bled at the sight of the sufferings which the exiles were made to undergo. He moreover escaped from the effects of the rising of the Shepherds, and the subsequent bitter calamities. At about the same time, his fertile powers of production began to put forth fruit, and he began the series of writings which continued for more than twenty years (1321-1343). None of his writings created such a sensation as his work on the philosophy of religion (Milchamoth Adonai). In this he set forth the boldest metaphysical thoughts with philosophical calmness and independence, as if paying no heed to the fact that by his departure from the hitherto received notions upon these questions, he was laying himself open to the charges of heresy and heterodoxy. "If my observations are correct," he remarked, "then all blame leveled against me, I regard as praise." Leon de Bagnols belonged to a class of thinkers seldom met with, who, with majestic brow, seek truth for its own intrinsic value,

GERSONIDES.

without reference to other ends and results which might cause conflict. Levi ben Gerson thus expressed his opinion upon this subject: Truth must be brought out and placed beneath the glare of open daylight, even if it should contradict the Torah in the strongest possible manner. The Torah is no tyrannical law, which desires to force one to accept untruth as truth, on the contrary, it seeks to lead man to a true understanding of things. If the truth arrived at by investigation is in harmony with the utterances of the Bible, then so much the better. In his independence of thought, the only parallel to Gersonides among Jewish inquirers is Spinoza. Unlike many of his predecessors, he would not look upon science as a body of occult doctrines designed for an inner circle of the initiated. He moreover refused to follow slavishly the authorities in philosophy regarded as infallible. He propounded independent views in opposition not only to Maimuni and Averroes, but also to Aristotle. Leon de Bagnols did not establish a perfect and thoroughly organized system of the philosophy of religion, but treated of the difficulties which interested the thinkers of the age more incisively than any of his predecessors.

In spite of his great ability, Gersonides exercised very little influence upon Judaism. By the pious, he was denounced as a heretic, because of his independent research, and his ambiguous attitude towards the doctrine of the creation. They took the title of his chief work, "The Battles of the Lord," to mean

"Battles against the Lord." So much the warmer was his reception by Christian inquirers after truth. Pope Clement VI, during the lifetime of the author, commanded his treatise upon astronomy and the newly-invented instrument to be translated into Latin (1342).

Of a similar nature was another representative of philosophical Judaism of this age, Moses ben Joshua Narboni, also called Maestro Vidal (born about 1300, died 1362). His father Joshua, who belonged to a family in Narbonne, but resided in Perpignan, was so warmly interested in Jewish, that is to say Maimunistic, philosophy, that in spite of the interdict hurled against all who studied the subject, he instructed his son therein when he was thirteen years old. Vidal Narboni became an enthusiastic student. He divided his admiration between Maimuni and Averroes, his writings consisting chiefly of commentaries upon their works. His travels from the foot of the Pyrenees to Toledo and back again to Soria (1345-1362) enriched and amended his knowledge. He was interested in anything worth knowing, and made observations with great accuracy. No calamities or troubles succeeded in damping his zeal in the inquiry after truth. In consequence of the Black Death, an infuriated mob fell upon the community at Cervera. Vidal Narboni was compelled to take to flight with the rest of the congregation; he lost his possessions, and, what was more painful to him, his precious books. These misfortunes did not disturb him; he took up the thread of his work where it had been interrupted. He accomplished no entirely independent or original work; he was a true Aristotelian of Averroist complexion. Narboni conceived Judaism as a guide to the highest degree of theoretical and moral truth: the Torah has a double meaning--the one simple, direct, for the thoughtless mob, and the other of a deeper, metaphysical nature for the class of thinkers--a common opinion in those times, Gersonides alone demurring. Narboni, too, gave expression to heretical views, that is, such as are contrary to the ordinarily accepted understanding of Judaism, but not with the freedom and openness of Levi ben Gerson. He rejected the belief in miracles, and attempted to explain them away altogether, but defended

AARON BEN ELIA.

man's freedom of will by philosophical arguments. Death overtook him in the very midst of his labors when, advanced in years, he was on the point of returning to his native land from Soria, on the other side of the Pyrenees, where he had spent several years.

Though the Karaite, Aaron ben Elia Nicomedi, may be reckoned among the philosophers of this time, he can scarcely be admitted into the company of Levi ben Gerson and the other Provencal thinkers. His small stock of philosophical knowledge was a matter of erudition, not the result of independent thought. Aaron II of Nicomedia (in Asia Minor, born about 1300, died 1369), who probably lived in Cairo, was indeed superior to his ignorant brother Karaites, but several centuries behind the Rabbanite philosophers. His thoughts sound like a voice from the grave, or as of one who has slumbered for many years, and speaks the language of antiquity, not understood by the men of his own day.

Aaron ben Elia was not even able to indicate the end aimed at by his work, "The Tree of Life." Without being himself fully conscious of his motives, he was guided in its composition by jealous rivalry of Maimuni and the Rabbanites. It vexed him sorely that Maimuni's religious philosophical work, "The Guide," was perused and admired not only by Jews, but also by Christians and Mahometans, whilst the Karaites had nothing like it. Aaron desired to save the honor of the Karaites by his "Tree of Life." He sought to detract from the merits of the work of Maimuni, and remarked that some of the statements to be found in the book had been made by Karaite philosophers of religion. Notwithstanding this, he followed Maimuni most minutely, and treated only of those questions which the latter had raised; but he sought to solve them not by the aid of philosophy, but by the authority of the Bible.

The history of this period, when dealing with events in Germany, has nothing but calamities to record: bloody assaults, massacres, and the consequent intellectual poverty: Asheri and his sons were either deluded or unjust when they preferred bigoted Germany to Spain, at that time still tolerable, and cast longing looks thitherwards from Toledo. From the time of Asheri's departure till the middle of the century, misfortune followed upon misfortune, till nearly all the congregations were exterminated. On account of this state of affairs, even the study of the Talmud, the only branch of learning pursued in Germany with ardor and thoroughness, fell into decay. How could the Germans gather intellectual strength, when they were not certain about one moment of their lives, or their means of sustenance? Their state in a most literal way realized the prophetical threat of punishment: "Thy life shall hang in doubt before thee; and thou shalt fear day and night, in the morning thou shalt say, Would God it were even ! and at even thou shalt say, Would God it were morning ! for the fear of thine heart wherewith thou shalt fear." Emperor Louis, the Bavarian, is reported to have been favorably inclined towards the Jews, which is said to have made them proud. But this is idle calumny both against the emperor and the Jews. No German ruler before him had treated his "servi camerae" so badly, pawned them and sold them, as Louis the Bavarian. He also imposed a new tax upon the Jews, the so-called golden gift-pence. As the emperors had gradually pawned all the revenues derived from their "servi camerae" to enable them to satisfy their immediate necessity for money, Louis the Bavarian was driven to cogitate upon some new means of obtaining supplies from them. He promulgated a decree (about 1342) which commanded that every Jew and Jewess in the German Empire above the age of twelve, and possessed of at least more than twenty florins, should pay annually to

the king or the emperor a poll-tax of a florin. He probably derived his right, if, indeed, the question of right was considered in reference to the treatment of Jews, from the fact that the German emperors were in possession of all the prerogatives once claimed by those of Rome. As the Jews, since the days of Vespasian and Titus, had been compelled to pay a. yearly tax to the Roman emperors, the German rulers declared themselves the direct heirs to this golden gift-pence.

Hitherto the massacres of Jews in Germany had taken place only at intervals, and in a few places; but now, under the reign of Louis, owing to riots and civil wars, they became much more frequent. During two consecutive years (1336--1337), a regularly organized band of peasants and rabble, who called themselves " the beaters of the Jews," made fierce attacks upon them with unbridled fury and heartless cruelty. Two dissolute noblemen were at the head of this troop; they gave themselves the name of Kings Leather-arm (Armleder) from a piece of leather which they wore wound round the arm. In this persecution, as in that of Rindfleisch, the fanaticism and blind superstition inculcated by the church played an important part. Five thousand peasants, armed with pitchforks, axes, flails, pikes, and whatever other weapons they could lay hands upon, gathered around the Leather-arms, and inflicted a bloody slaughter upon the Jewish inhabitants of Alsace and the Rhineland as far as Swabia. As frequently happened during such barbarous persecutions, numbers of Jews, on this occasion also, put an end to their own lives, after having slain their children to prevent their falling into the hands of the Church. Emperor Louis the Bavarian did indeed issue commands to protect the heretic Jews (April, 1337), but his help came too late, or was of little effect. At length the emperor succeeded in capturing one of the Leather-arms, whom he ordered to be executed.

At about the same time a bloody persecution, prompted by the frenzy of avarice, was set on foot in Bavaria. The councilors of the city of Deckendorf (or Deggendorf) desired to free themselves and all the citizens from their debts to the Jews, and enrich themselves besides. To carry out this plan, the fable of the desecration of the host by the Jews, with the accompaniment of the usual miracles, was spread abroad. When the populace had been incited to a state of fanatical frenzy, the council proceeded to execute the project which it had secretly matured outside the town, so as not to arouse any suspicion among the Jews. On the appointed day (30th September, 1337), at a signal from the church bell, the knight Hartmann von Deggenburg, who had been initiated in the conspiracy, rode with his band of horsemen through the open gates into Deckendorf, and was received with loud rejoicing. The knight and the citizens thereupon fell upon the defenseless Jews, put them to death by sword and fire, and possessed themselves of their property. In honor of the miracles performed by the host that had been pierced by the knives of the Jews, a church of the Holy Sepulcher was erected, and appointed as a shrine for pilgrims; and the puncheons which the Jews had used, together with the insulted host, were placed beneath a glass case, and guarded as relies. For many centuries they were displayed for the edification of the faithful--perhaps are still displayed. The lust for slaughter spread abroad into Bavaria, Bohemia, Moravia, and Austria. Thousands of Jews perished by different forms of torture and death. Only the citizens of Vienna and Ratisbon protected their Jewish inhabitants against the infuriated mob. The friendly efforts of Pope Benedictus XII were of little avail against the brutal spirit of the then Christian world.

IV. CHAPTER VI.

JEWISH APOSTATES AND THE DISPUTATION AT TORTOSA.

The Marranos--The Satirists--Pero Ferrus of Alcala, Diego de Valencia,and Villasandino--Astruc Raimuch and Solomon Bonfed--Paul de Santa Maria and his Zealous Campaign against the Jews--Joshua Ibn-Vives--Profiat Duran (Efodi)-Meir Alguades--The Philosophy of Crescas--Death of Henry III of Castile and Unfavorable Change in the Position of the Jews-Messianic Dreams of the Kabbalists--Jews seek an Asylum in Northern Africa--Simon Duran--Geronimo de Santa Fe, Vincent Ferrer and Benedict XIII--Anti-Jewish Edict of Juan II--Special Jewish Costume--Conversion of Jews owing to Ferrer's Violent Efforts--Disputation at Tortosa-The Jewish Spokesmen at the Conference-Incidents of the Meeting--Geronimo instigates the Publication of a Bull for the Burning of the Talmud--Pope Martin V befriends the Jews.

139I--1420 C.E.

THE baptized Jews who had abandoned their faith during the terrible persecution of 1391 became a source of considerable trouble to their Spanish brethren. They had embraced the cross only to save their lives, or the lives of those dear to them; for, surely, they had found no convincing demonstration of the truth of the Christian religion in the violence of its missionaries, or in the death agonies of their brethren in race who had perished rather than apostatize. Dazed and broken-hearted, these forced converts (Anusim) to Christianity felt more intense antipathy to their new religion than when they had been openly opposed to it. It was natural for them to resolve to take the first opportunity of casting away their disguise, and returning to Judaism with increased zeal. Many of these new Christians emigrated to the neighboring Moorish countries; to Granada or across the straits to Morocco, Tunis, or Fez. The majority, unable to leave Spanish territory, yet averse to wholly discarding their ancient faith, joined in Jewish ceremonies and celebrations whilst outwardly appearing Christians. The kings of Castile, Aragon and Majorca, who had disapproved of conversions by mob violence, allowed the Jews to do as they pleased. The authorities either did not or would not see their relapse into Judaism, and the Inquisition had not yet been established in Spain. These forced converts gradually formed themselves into a peculiar class, outwardly Christians, at heart Jews. By the populace, who nicknamed them Marranos, or "The Damned," they were regarded with more distrust and hatred than the openly observant Jews, not because of their secret fidelity to Judaism, but on account of their descent and inborn intelligence, energy, and skill. Baptized Jews, who had been glad to disencumber themselves of their Judaism, shared in these feelings of aversion. They were the worldlings who valued wealth, rank, and luxury above religion, or the over-educated whose philosophy had led them to skepticism, and whose selfishness induced them to welcome a change which brought them out of the narrow confines of a small community, and opened up a wider world to them. For their own advantage they simulated devotion to Christianity, but were on that account neither better nor more religious men. The unscrupulous among them found special pleasure in the persecution of their former religion and its followers. To gratify their malice, they brought charges against rabbis and other representative Jews, or any member of the community, thus endangering

DON PERO FERRUS.

the existence of the whole body of Jews in the country. It was bad enough that the latter had been robbed of so many able and learned men --physicians, authors, poets--and that the church had been enriched by their wealth and intelligence; but these very forces were used to inflict further mischief on the Jews that had remained steadfast. Knowing the faults of their former brethren, the converts could easily attack them. Don Pero Ferrus, a baptized Jew, made the community and rabbis of Alcala the target for his ridicule. In a poem he represents himself exhausted from want of sleep finding repose at last in the synagogue of this town, when suddenly he is disturbed, and scared away without mercy by "Jews with long beards and slovenly garments come thither for early morning prayer." A sharp rejoinder to this effort of Ferrus' "buffoon tongue" was put forth by a Jewish poet in the name of the Alcala community. Spanish poetry reaped considerable advantage from these passages at arms. Verse, up to that period starched, solemn, and stately as the punctilious ceremonial of the Madrid court, in the hands of Judaeo-Christian satirists acquired the flexibility, wit and merriment of neo-Hebraic poetry at its best. This tone and style were gradually adopted by Christian poets, who borrowed expressions from Jewish writers to give point to their epigrams. Not only the apostate, the monk, Diego de Valencia, used Hebrew words in lampoons on the Jews, but the same practice was adopted with surprising dexterity by the Christian satirist, Alfonso Alvarez de Villasandino, the "poet prince" of his day. A malicious critic might have been inclined to say that Spanish poetry was in process of being Judaized.

A few of the new-Christians showed as active a zeal in the propagation of Christianity as if they had been born Dominicans, or as if they felt isolated in their new faith among the old Christians, and yearned for the companionship of their former friends. A newly-baptized physician, Astruc Raimuch, of Fraga, who, as a Jew, had been a pillar of orthodoxy, exerted himself to make converts, taking to himself the name of Francisco God-flesh (Dios-Carne). He spread his snares particularly with a view to entrapping one of his young friends. A fluent writer of Hebrew, Astruc-Francisco drew up a letter in that language, dwelling on the decline of Judaism and enthusiastically propounding the dogmas of Christianity. His applications of Biblical texts to the doctrines of the Trinity, Original Sin, Redemption, and the Lord's Supper, appear almost droll in Hebrew. His friend's answer was meek and evasive, every word carefully weighed to avoid offending the delicate sensibilities of the church and its zealous servants. More spirited was the reply of the satirical poet, Solomon ben Reuben Bonfed, who in rhymed prose set himself to confute Astruc-Francisco's arguments with unsparing incisiveness. Apologizing in his introduction for interfering between two friends, he proceeded to point out that as a Jew the questions discussed concerned him nearly, whilst the mis-statements made rendered it impossible for him to remain silent. Solomon Bonfed examined somewhat minutely the dogmas of the Incarnation, Original Sin, and Transubstantiation, showing them to be irrational and untenable. He justly said : " You twist and distort the Bible text to establish the Trinity." Of all the Jews baptized in 1391, however, none inflicted so much injury on his former brethren as Rabbi Solomon Levi Burgos (born 1351-1352, died 1435), who as a Christian rose to very important ecclesiastical and political dignities under the name of Paul Burgensis, or de Santa Maria. Previous to his change of creed he had been a rabbi,

PAUL DE SANTA MARIA.

and he was well versed in Biblical, Talmudical, and Rabbinical literature. As a Jew he was extremely orthodox and punctilious, passing in his own circle for a pillar of the faith. His nature was, however, shrewd and calculating. Ambitious and vain to the last degree, he soon began to regard as too narrow his sphere of action within the walls of the college, which during a long period counted him amongst its students and teachers. He longed for a life of bustling activity. To obtain a state appointment, he sought access to court, and began to live like a grandee, with equipage and horses and numerous retinue. It was his ambition to become a Jewish Almojarif or even to obtain a higher appointment. His occupations bringing him into daily contact with Christians, and frequently involving him in religious controversies, he devoted some attention to church literature, in order to be able to make a display of learning. The massacres of 1391 dissipated his last hope of obtaining high preferment as a Jew, and he consequently resolved, in his fortieth year, to be baptized. To derive the best advantage from his conversion, the new Christian, Paul de Santa Maria, caused it to be understood that he had embraced Christianity willingly, as a result of the convincing arguments put forth in the theological writings of the schoolman Thomas Aquinas. The Jews received such protestations with distrust. Knowing him well, they did not scruple to ascribe his conversion to a craving for rank and power. After his change of creed, his family, wife and sons, renounced him.

For a commoner, the only road to high office lay through the church. Solomon-Paul knew this well, and at once proceeded to Paris and attended the University, where he pursued theology. His knowledge of Hebrew gave him a great advantage, and helped him to distinguish himself. It was not long before the quondam rabbi became a duly ordained Catholic priest. Then he betook himself to the papal court at Avignon, where the haughty, obstinate, and proselytizing cardinal, Pedro de Luna, reigned as anti-pope under the title of Benedict. Here, during the stormy church schism, favorable opportunities for intrigue and personal advancement presented themselves. Paul won the pope's favor by his shrewdness, zeal, and eloquence. He was appointed archdeacon of Trevinjo and canon of Seville, his first steps on the ladder of the Catholic hierarchy. He abandoned himself to the most ambitious dreams: he might become a bishop,a cardinal, and why not the pope? The times were propitious. He boasted that he was descended from the most ancient and the noblest branch of the Hebrew race, the tribe of Levi, the same that had given birth to Mary, the mother of Jesus. He was not an ordinary priest sprung from the people, but had ancestors bound to be acknowledged and distinguished by the church. On the recommendation of the pope, he was later on overwhelmed with honors and favors by the king of Castile, Don Henry III, and his ambition was satisfied.

The apostasy of so respected a rabbi as Solomon Burgensis not only created the greatest astonishment among Jews, but filled them with anxiety. Would this example not find imitators in a time of so much trouble and temptation? Would it not bias waverers, or at least encourage pretending Christians to persevere in the course begun? The prevailing disquietude was increased when it was found that after his own conversion Paul considered it his duty to convert his former co-religionists. To this end he left no stone unturned. With voice and pen he assailed Judaism, seeking his weapons in Jewish literature itself. Not long after his conversion he addressed a letter to his former acquaintance, Joseph (Jose) Orabuena, physician in ordinary to King Charles III of Navarre, and chief rabbi of the Navarrese communities, in which he stated that

he acknowledged and honored Jesus as the Messiah whose advent had been foretold by the prophets, and invited Orabuena to follow his example. To another chief rabbi, Don Meir Alguades, physician in ordinary to the Castilian king, Don Henry III, Paul de Santa Maria addressed a Hebrew satire in prose and verse, in which he ridiculed the innocent celebration of the Jewish feast of Purim. As if grudging the Jews the moderate pleasures in which they indulged during this festival, he exaggerated their love of drink, and boasted of his own sobriety. Paul evinces in this satire considerable skill in handling the new-Hebrew language,but, notwithstanding his opportunities, he exhibits little wit.

As soon as he had acquired a position at the papal court at Avignon, he devoted himself to calumniating the Jews with a view to bringing about new persecutions. His purpose became so obvious that the cardinal of Pampeluna himself, and other ecclesiastics, ordered him to desist. It is true the Jews had to pay dearly for his silence. He also intrigued against Chasdai Crescas. So far did this apostate carry his enmity to Judaism that he advised the king, Don Henry III, to abstain from employing both Jews and new-Christians in state offices. While the Franciscan monk, Nicholas de Lyra, a born Christian, held up the works of Jewish commentators like Rashi as models of simple exegesis, the former rabbi found every observation of a Rabbinical writer insipid, nonsensical, and scandalous. On the other hand, the most ridiculous commentary of a church writer was to him a lofty, unsurpassable work.

Thoughtful Jews were not slow to recognize their bitterest foe in this new-Christian, and they prepared for a severe struggle with him, notwithstanding that their choice of weapons was limited. Christians were not only free to say what they pleased in demonstration and defense of their doctrines, but could appeal to the summary authority of the sword and the dungeon. Jews were forced to all kinds of circumlocution and ambiguity to avoid provoking the violence of their adversaries.

The campaign against Paul de Santa Maria was opened by a young man, Joshua ben Joseph Ibn Vives of Lorca (Allorqui), a physician and an Arabic scholar, who had formerly sat at the feet of the renegade rabbi. In an humble epistle, as though a docile pupil were addressing an illustrious master, Joshua Allorqui administered many a delicate reproof to his apostate teacher, and at the same time, by his naive doubts, dealt destructive blows at the fundamental doctrines of Christianity. He observes in his introduction that the conversion of his beloved teacher had to him more than to others been a source of astonishment and reflection, as his example had been a main support of his own religious belief. He was at a loss to conceive the motives of the sudden change. He could not think that he had been led away by desire for worldly distinction, "for I well remember," he says, "how, surrounded by riches and attendants, thou didst yearn for thy former humble state with its life of retirement and study, and how it was thy wont to speak of thy high position as empty mockery of happiness." Nor could he suppose that Paul's Jewish convictions had been disturbed by philosophic doubt, as up to the moment of his baptism he had conscientiously observed all the ceremonial laws, and had known how to discriminate between the kernel of philosophic truth which harmonizes with religion and the pernicious shell

JOSHUA ALLORQUI ATTACKS CHRISTIANITY

which so often passes for the real teaching. Could it be that the sanguinary persecution of the Jews had led him to doubt the possibility of the enduring power of Judaism? But even this theory was untenable, for Paul could not be unaware of the fact that only a minority of Jews live under Christian rule, that the larger numbers sojourn in Asia, and enjoy a certain degree of independence; so that if it pleased God to allow the communities in Christian lands to be extirpated, the Jewish race would not by any means disappear from the face of the earth. There remained, continued Joshua Vives of Lorca, the assumption that Paul had carefully studied Christianity, and had come to the conclusion that its dogmas were well founded. He begged him, therefore, to impart to him the convictions at which he had arrived, and thus dissipate the doubts which he (Joshua) still entertained as to the truth of Christianity. Allorqui then detailed the nature of his doubts, covertly but forcibly attacking the Christian system. Every sentence in this epistle was calculated to cut the Jew-hating new-Christian to the quick. The evasive and embarrassed reply, which Paul indited later on, clearly indicated how he had winced under this attack.

At about the same time an accomplished Marrano, who had relapsed into Judaism, published a pungent attack on Christianity and the new-Christians. During the bloody persecution of 1391 in Catalonia, Profiat Duran, otherwise Isaac ben Moses, or, as he called himself in his works, Efodi (Ephodaeus), had been forced to simulate conversion to Christianity. He was joined by his friend David Bonet Buen-Giorno. Both resolved at a convenient opportunity to abandon their hated mask and emigrate to Palestine, where they could freely acknowledge Judaism. Their affairs being arranged, Profiat Duran traveled to a seaport town in the south of France, and there awaited his friend. The latter, in the meantime, was sought out by or came across the Jew-hating apostate, Solomon Paul de Santa Maria, and was prevailed upon to remain a Christian. What was Profiat Duran's astonishment when he received a letter announcing, with much exultant vaporing, the definite acknowledgment of Christianity by En Bonet, who exhorted him also to remain in the pale of his adopted faith. The letter contained an enthusiastic panegyric of Paul de Santa Maria, who had been taken into the favor of the king of Castile. Profiat Duran could not remain silent. In reply, he inflicted punishment on his friend, and more particularly on the proselytizing Paul, in an epistle characterized by the keenest irony, which has not

PROFIAT DURAN'S SATIRE.

yet lost its sting. It pretends to assent to everything advanced by Bonet, and to confirm him in his resolve to remain a Christian. "Be not ye like your fathers" (Altehi ka-Abothecha) is the refrain throughout, and so artfully is this admonition employed that Christians used it (under the title Alteca Boteca) as an apology for Christianity. Whilst thus pretending to criticise the errors of the older faith, Profiat Duran dwells on the Christian dogmas, naively describing them in their most reprehensible form. A portion of the satire is directed against the Jew-hater Paul de Santa Maria, upon whom Benet had bestowed unstinted praise. "Thou art of opinion that he may succeed in becoming pope, but thou dost not inform me whether he will go to Rome, or remain at Avignon "--a cutting reference to the papal schism distracting the church. "Thou extollest him for having made efforts to free Jewish women and children from the obligation of wearing the Jew badge. Take the glad tidings to the women and children. For myself, I have been told that he preached mischief against the Jews, and that the cardinal of Pampeluna was compelled to order him to be silent. Thou art of opinion that he, thy teacher, will soon receive the miter or a cardinal's hat. Rejoice, for then thou also must acquire honors, and wilt become a priest or a Levite." Towards the end Profiat

Duran changes irony into a tone of seriousness : he prays his former friend not to bear as a Christian the name of his respected father who, had he been alive, would sooner have had no son than one faithless to his religion. As it is, his soul in Paradise will bewail the faithlessness of his son. This satirical epistle was circulated as a pamphlet. Its author sent copies not only to his former friend, but also to the physician of the king of Castile, the chief rabbi, Don Meir Alguades. So telling was the effect produced, that the clergy, as soon as they discovered its satirical character, made it the subject of judicial inquiry, and committed it to the flames.

Favored and promoted by the anti-pope, Benedict XIII, of Avignon, Paul of Burgos rose higher and higher; he became bishop of Carthagena, chancellor of Castile and privy counselor to the king, Don Henry III. His malice did not succeed in prejudicing the king against the Jews, or inducing him to bar them from state employment. Don Henry had two Jewish physicians, in whom he reposed especial confidence. One, Don Meir Alguades, an astronomer and philosopher, he appointed, perhaps in imitation of Portugal, to the chief rabbinate of the various Castilian communities. He was always in the king's train, and it is probable that to some extent he influenced him favorably towards his co-religionists. The other was Don Moses Zarzel (Carcal), who celebrated in rich Spanish verse the long wished for birth of an heir to the Castilian throne, borrowing the beauties of the neo-Hebraic poetry to do honor to the newly-born prince, in whose hands, he prophesied, the various states of the Pyrenean Peninsula would be united. The calm, as between two storms, which the Spanish Jews enjoyed during the reign of Don Henry was favorable to the production of a few literary fruits, almost the last of any importance brought forth in Spain. None of these works was epoch-making; they were useful, however, in keeping alive the

spirit of better times, and in preventing the treasures of Jewish literature from being forgotten. Profiat Duran managed to make people forget his baptism and to settle down quietly in Spain or Perpignan, where he commentated Maimuni's philosophy, and some of Ibn-Ezra's works. He also composed a mathematical and calendarial essay (Chesheb-Efod) and an historical account of the persecutions to which his race had been subjected since the dispersion. His best work is a Hebrew grammar ("Maasi Efod," written about 1403), in which he summarizes the results of older writers, rectifies their errors, and even attempts to formulate the principles of Hebrew syntax.

A production of more than common merit was written by Chasdai Crescas, now on the brink of the grave, his spirits shattered by persecution. He was a profound, comprehensive thinker, whose mind never lost itself in details, but was forever striving to comprehend the totality of things. His scheme for a work treating, in the manner of Maimuni, of all phases and aspects of Judaism, investigating the ideas and laws out of which Jewish teaching had gradually developed, and reharmonizing the details with the whole where the connection had ceased to be apparent, bears witness to the extraordinary range of his learning and the perspicacity of his mind. The work was to be at once a guide to Talmudical study and a practical handbook. Death appears to have prevented the accomplishment of this gigantic enterprise, only the philosophic portion, or introduction, being completed. In this introduction Chasdai Crescas deals, on the one hand, with the principles of universal religion, the existence of God, His omniscience and providence, human free-will, the design of the universe, and, on the other, with the fundamental truths of Judaism, the doctrines of the creation, immortality, and the Messiah.

Crescas was less dominated by the Aristotelian bias of mediaeval philosophy than his predecessors. It had lost its halo for him; he perceived its weaknesses more clearly than others, and probed them more deeply. With bold hands he tore down the supports of the vast edifice of theory constructed by Maimuni on Aristotelian grounds to demonstrate the existence of God and His relation to the universe, and, conversant with the whole method of scholastic philosophy, he combated it with destructive force.

While the philosophy of his day appeared to him thus vague and illusory, he considered the foundations of Judaism unassailable, and set himself to show the futility of the criticisms of the former. The acknowledgment of Divine omniscience led him to the daring statement that man in his actions is not quite free, that everything is the necessary result of a preceding occurrence, and that every cause, back to the very first, is bound to determine the character of the final action. The human will does not follow blind choice, but is controlled by a chain of antecedent circumstances and causes. To what extent can the doctrine of reward and punishment be admitted, if the will is not free? Chasdai Crescas' answer to this is that reward and punishment wait on intentions, not on actions. He who, in purity of heart, wishes to accomplish good--which must, of course, necessarily follow--deserves to be rewarded, as the man who willingly promotes evil, deserves punishment. The highest good to which man can aspire, and the end of all creation, is spiritual perfection, or bliss everlasting, not to be obtained, as the philosophers imagine, by filling the mind with metaphysical theories, but only through the active love of God. This is the substance of all religion and particularly of Judaism. From this point of view it may with justice be said that "the world was created for the sake of the Torah," for the aim of the Law is

DON MEIR ALGUADES.

to lead to immortality by means of ideas and commandments and the guidance of thoughts and actions.

Chasdai Crescas, was the first to distinguish between universal religion and specific forms, such as Judaism and Christianity. His just objection to Maimuni's thirteen articles of faith was that they were either too many or too few, inasmuch as they blended indiscriminately fundamental truths common to all religions, and teachings peculiar to Judaism.

Together with Profiat Duran and Chasdai Crescas, Don Meir Alguades, the Castilian chief rabbi, appeared, in the brief interval between two bloody persecutions in Spain, as a writer of philosophic works. He was not an independent inquirer; he merely translated the ethics of Aristotle (l405, in collaboration with Benveniste Ibn-Labi) into Hebrew, making the work accessible to Jews, who, in practical life, lived up to its principles better than the Greeks, who produced them, or the Christians, who, in the pride of faith and church doctrine, considered themselves above the necessity of conforming to the requirements of morality.

Throughout the reign of Don Henry III of Castile the life of the Jews was tolerable. The young but vigorous monarch severely punished Fernan Martinet, the prime mover In the massacres of 1391, as a warning against further excesses. He permitted the Jews to acquire land, renewed the law of his ancestor, Alfonso XI, and relieved his Jewish tax-farmers and finance administrators from restrictions. As soon as he died (the end of 1406) the affairs of the Jews again took an unfavorable turn, foreshadowing unhappy times. The heir to the crown, Juan II, was a child, barely two years old. The regency devolved on the queen-mother, Catalina (Catherine) of Lancaster, a capricious, arrogant and bigoted young woman, who imagined that she ruled, while she was herself ruled by her various favorites. The co-regent, Don Ferdinand, later king of Aragon, who was intelligent and kind, allowed himself to be guided by the clergy. By his side in the council of state sat the apostate rabbi, Solomon alias Paul de Santa Maria, another and more mischievous Elisha-Acher, in whose eyes Judaism was an abomination, and every Jew a stumbling-block. The deceased king, Don Henry III, had appointed him executor of his will and tutor to his heir; he consequently had an influential voice in the council of the regency. What a prospect for the Jews of Castile! It was not long before they were made to feel the hostile spirit of the court. First it exhibited itself in attempts to humiliate the more notable Jews who had intercourse with the court circle and the grandees of the kingdom, and occupied positions of distinction. The intention was to dismiss them from these positions with the reminder that they belonged to a despised caste.

An edict was issued (October 25th, 1408), in the name of the infant king, reviving the anti-Jewish statutes of the code of Alfonso the Wise. "Whereas the exercise of authority by Jews may conduce to the prejudice of the Christian faith," their occupation of posts in which they might possess such authority was forbidden for all future time. Every Jew permitting himself to be invested with official functions, either by a nobleman or a municipality, was to be fined twice the amount of the revenue of such post, and, if his fortune did not suffice to make up the required amount, it would be confiscated, and the delinquent become liable to a punishment of fifty lashes. A Christian appointing a Jew to a post of influence would also be punished with a fine. To insure the working of the edict, it was enacted that the informer and the court of law concerned in a case should secure each one-third of the confiscated

ARREST OF DON MEIR ALGUADES.

estates. Officials were charged to make the edict known everywhere, and carefully to watch that its injunctions were carried out. It is impossible not to suspect the hand of Paul de Santa Maria in this decree. No one knew better than he the strong and the weak points in the character of the Spanish Jews, and he doubtless calculated that Jewich notables, in danger of losing their official employment and high social position, would go over to Christianity, while the faithful, excluded from intercourse with Christian society and from participation in the public life of the country, would suffer a decline similar to that of the German Jews.

At the same time he vented his hate on Meir Alguades, the physician of the dead king. The queen-regent had no cause to injure this Jewish notable; only Paul could desire his ruin, because he was the mainstay of his opponents and the leader of those who held him up to contempt. With the object of procuring his downfall, a vindictive accusation was trumped up against him. While the queen-mother, with the infant king, was staying at Segovia, some priests charged a Jew of the town with having bought a consecrated host from the sacristan, in order to blaspheme it. They further stated that the holy wafer had worked such terrible wonders while in the possession of the Jew, that in fear and trembling he had delivered it up to the prior of a monastery. Whether this story was fabricated, or whether there was a grain of truth in a bushel of fiction, it is impossible to say; it sufficed, however, to attract the serious attention of the bishop, Velasquez de Tordesillas, who caused a number of Jews to be arrested as accomplices in the crime, among them Don Meir Alguades. Criminal proceedings were formally commenced by order of the queen-regent, and Alguades and his fellow-prisoners were subjected to torture, and confessed their guilt. It is stated that in his agony Meir Alguades made a confession of another kind--that the king, Henry III, had come by his death at his hands. Although everybody knew that the king had been ailing from his youth, Don Meir--who must have been specially interrogated while under torture as to whether he had poisoned the king--was put to death in the most inhuman manner. He was torn limb from limb. The same fate befell the other prisoners. Still not satisfied, the bishop of Segovia accused some Jews of having bribed his cook to poison his food, and they also were put to death. At about this time one of the synagogues in Segovia was transformed into a church.

The troubled times, projecting shadows of a still more unhappy future, produced the melancholy phenomenon of another Messianic frenzy. Again it arose in the minds of mystics. The Zohar having adroitly been raised to the dignity of an approved authority, the Kabbala daily acquired more influence, although it was not studied in proportion to the zeal with which its authority was advocated. Three Kabbalists were particularly active in exciting the emotions and turning the heads of the people--Abraham of Granada, Shem Tob ben Joseph, and Moses Botarel. The first composed (between 1391 and 1409) a Kabbalistic work, a farrago of strange names of the Deity and the angels, of transposed letters, and jugglery with vowels and accents. Abraham of Granada had the hardihood to teach that those who could not apprehend God by Kabbalistic methods belonged to the weak in faith, were ignorant sinners, and like the depraved and the apostate were overlooked by God, and not found worthy of His special providence. He thought that the relinquishment of their religion by cultured Jews was explained by their fatal application to scientific study, and their contempt for the Kabbala. On the other hand, he professed to see in the persecutions of 1391, and in the conversion of so many prominent

MOSES BOTAREI

Jews to Christianity, the tokens of the Messianic age, the suffering that must precede it, and the approach of the redemption. Shem Tob ben Joseph Ibn-Shem Tob (died 1430) accused the Jewish philosophers, Maimuni, Gersonides, and others, of seducing the people to heresy and infidelity, and with being the real cause of apostasy in troubled times. In a work entitled "Emunoth" he made violent attacks on Jewish thinkers and philosophic studies generally, and taught that the salvation of Israel lies in the Kabbala, the oldest Jewish tradition, and the genuine, pure truth. The entire book is composed of grave charges against the more enlightened school of Jewish thinkers, and panegyrics of Kabbalistic nonsense.

These two men, Abraham of Granada and Shem Tob, though narrow-minded, were sincere, differing in this respect from Moses Botarel (or Botarelo), also a Spaniard, from Cisneros, in Castile, who pursued his course with fraudulent intent. He gave out that he was a thaumaturge and prophet; he announced himself even as the Messiah. He prophesied that in the spring month of 1393 the Messianic age would be ushered in by extraordinary marvels. Later on he wrote a work full of lies and delusions. In his pride and boastfulness, he addressed a circular letter to all the rabbis of Israel, declaring that he was in a position to solve all doubts, and throw light on all mysteries, that he was the chief of the great Synhedrin, and a great deal more in the same charlatanic strain.

As in the days of the oppression by the Visigothic kings, an asylum for persecuted Jews was formed on that portion of the African coast facing Spain. Many of the north African towns, such as Algiers, Miliana, Constantine, Buja, Oran, Tenes, and Tlemcen, were filled with Jews fleeing from the massacres of 1391, and with new-Christians anxious to get rid of the Christianity which they had been forced to embrace, but which they hated cordially. Almost daily there came fresh troops of refugees from all parts of Spain and Majorca. They transplanted to their new fatherland their intelligence, wealth, industry, and commercial enterprise. The Mahometan Berber princes, then more tolerant and humane than the Christians, received them without imposing a poll tax. At first the Mahometan population grumbled a little at so sudden and considerable an increase in the number of inhabitants, fearing that the price of provisions would be raised. When, however, the narrow-mindedness and selfishness of their complaints were pointed out to them by an intelligent kadi they were satisfied, and the Jews were allowed to settle in their midst in peace. The small Berber communities formed since the cessation of the Almohade persecution a century before, acquired greater importance through this immigration. The new-comers preponderated in numbers over the native Jews, so that the latter, to a certain extent, were forced to adopt the Spanish communal organization and the Sephardic ritual. The Spaniards, in fact, became the leading element in the old African communities.

The distinguished rabbi, Isaac ben Sheshet-Barfat, who had escaped from Spain and settled in Algiers, was recognizod by the king of Tlemcen as chief rabbi and judge of all the communities. This he owed to the influence of one of his admirers, Saul Astruc Cohen, a popular physician and an accomplished man, who not only practiced his art gratuitously, but spent his fortune in relieving both Mahometan and Jewish poor. In the name of the king the local rabbis were forbidden to assume clerical or judicial functions without the authority of the chief rabbi, Isaac ben Sheshet. This in no way detracted from the esteem in which Ben Sheshet was held, and applications for the decision of difficult questions continued to pour in upon him. In

ISAAC BEN SHESHET-BARFAT.

Algiers he continued to oppose wrong-doing with the conscientiousness and impartiality that had always characterized him. Among the members of his community was a mischievous personage (Isaac Bonastruc?), who had considerable influence with the Algerian authorities. Actuated by self-interest he was desirous of stopping the daily increasing immigration of Marranos, and to this end persuaded the kadi to impose a tax of one doubloon on every immigrant. Finding that troops of fugitives continued to arrive, he set himself to work upon the selfishness of the community, so that they might oppose any further influx of their brethren. Fifty-five new-Christians, who had recanted, from Valencia, Barcelona, and Majorca, were waiting to land in the harbor of Algiers, but were refused permission by Jews. This was tantamount to throwing them on the mercy of Christian executioners. Such selfishness and injustice the chief rabbi, Isaac hen Sheshet, could not tolerate, and he laid the ban on the heartless Jews, who tried to escape the punishment. So determined was his attitude that, with the assistance of Astruc Cohen and his brother, the Marranos were ultimately brought safe to land. In Africa Ben Sheshet-Barfat worked for nearly twenty years, promoting the welfare of his co-religionists and the interests of religion and morality. His declining years were embittered by the persistent attacks of a young rabbi, Simon ben Zemach Duran, an able Talmudist, who had emigrated from Majorca.

Ben Sheshet was succeeded on his death by Simon Duran (born 1361, died 1444)· The community of Algiers elected him on condition that he did not seek a ratification of his appointment from the king, probably because the authority derived by his predecessor from the royal confirmation had been too uncontrolled. Simon Duran, an accomplished mathematician and physician, was the first Spanish-Jewish rabbi to take pay. He publicly excused himself for doing so, on the ground of his necessitous circumstances. During the persecutions in

Malorca a portion of his large fortune had been lost, and the remainder had been sacrificed in bribing the informers who threatened to deliver him as a Judaizing Christian to the Dominican Moloch. He had arrived in Algiers almost a beggar, and the healing art, by which he had hoped to earn a subsistence, had brought him nothing, physicians enjoying but little consideration among the Berbers. Subsequently Simon Duran justified the payment of rabbis from the Talmud. Were the abbots, bishops, and princes of the church equally conscientious?

As if the Jews of Spain had not had enough enemies in the poor, indolent burghers and nobles, who regarded their opulence with so much jealousy, in the clergy, who cloaked their immorality with zeal for the propaganda of the faith, or in the upstart converts, who sought to disguise their Jewish origin by a show of hatred of their former brethren, there arose at about the beginning of the fifteenth century three new Jew-haters of the bitterest, most implacable type. One was a baptized Jew, another a Dominican friar, and the third an abandoned anti-pope. On these three men, Joshua Lorqui, Fra Vincent Ferrer, and Pedro de Luna, or Benedict XIII, the responsibility must rest for the events which directly conduced to the most terrible tragedy in the history of the Jews of Spain. Joshua Lorqui of Lorca assumed on his baptism the name Geronimo de Santa Fe, became physician in ordinary to the Avignon pope, Benedict, and, like his teacher, Solomon-Paul de Santa Maria, considered it his mission in life to draw his former brethren over to Christianity by every possible means. Vincent Ferrer, afterwards canonized, was one of those gloomy natures to whom the world appears a vale of tears, and who would wish to make it one. In saint-like virtue, indeed, he stood alone among the clergy and monks of his day.

VINCENT FERRER.

The pleasures of life had no charm for him ; for gold and worldly distinction he thirsted not ; he was penetrated with true humility, and entered on his work with earnestness. Unfortunately, the degeneracy and foulness of society had impressed him with the fantastic idea that the end of the world was at hand, and that mankind could be saved only by adopting the Christian faith and a monastic mode of life. Vincent Ferrer consequently revived flagellation. He marched through the land with a troop of fanatics who scourged their naked bodies with knotted cords, and incited the masses to adopt the same form of penance, believing that it would-bring about the salvation of the world. Gifted with a sympathetic voice, an agreeable manner, and considerable eloquence, this Dominican friar soon obtained ascendancy over the public mind. When amid sobs he recalled the sufferings of Jesus, and depicted the approaching end of the world, the emotions of his auditors became violently agitated, and he could lead them to good or to evil. He had given up a high position at the papal court to lead the life of a flagellant and barefooted friar. This helped to increase the number of his admirers and disciples, for renunciation of position and wealth on the part of an ecclesiastic was without parallel. Ferrer, however, abused his power by the promotion of sanguinary deeds. He directed his fanatical denunciations not only against Jews and heretics, but even against friends who had helped to raise him from the dust. The terrible demoralization of the church is illustrated in this monk. The wrangling of three contemporary popes, each declaring himself to be the vice-regent of God, one of whom, John XXIII (1410-1415), had exhausted the catalogue of vices and deadly sins, a pirate, a trafficker in indulgences, an assassin, and a debauchee--all this did not so strikingly indicate the prevailing degeneracy as the fanatical excesses of one really pure, moral nature like Vincent Ferrer. The dove had become transformed into a venomous snake, the lamb into a rapacious beast. So much viciousness cannot be spontaneous in human character, in the adherents of Christianity; it must have been derived from the Christian teaching itself.

Unlike Wycliffe and other reformers, Ferrer did not raise his voice against the shortcomings of the church, but devoted himself to Jews and heretics, whom he hated as adversaries of Christianity and opponents of the infallibility of the pope. With pen and voice he opened a crusade against Jews, which he sustained for several years. His most vehement invective was aimed at the Spanish new-Christians, who during the massacres of 1391 had gone over to the church, but still largely conformed to Judaism. Partly from fear of incurring the severe punishment attaching to apostasy, partly won over by the fiery eloquence of the preacher, the Marranos made a contrite confession of faith, which Ferrer regarded as a great victory for the church, a triumph for the truths of Christianity, leading him to hope that the conversion of the entire body of Jews might be vouchsafed to him. By his influence with the people, who honored him as a saint, he was very useful to the kings of Spain in putting down popular risings during the civil wars without bloodshed. Encouraged-by the consideration of the Castilian royal family, Ferrer craved permission not only to preach in the synagogues and mosques, but to force Jews and Mahometans to listen to his addresses. A crucifix in one arm, the Torah in the other, escorted by flagellants and spearmen, he called upon the Jews, "with a terrible voice," to enrol themselves under the cross.

Seraphic as he was, Vincent Ferrer was not averse to the employment of force. He represented to the Spanish rulers that the Jews should be strictly isolated, as their intercourse with the Christian population was calculated to injure the true faith. His suggestions met with too ready a response. Through him and the other two conversionists, unspeakable sorrows were brought upon the Spanish Jews; indeed, the years from 1412 to 1415 may be reckoned among the saddest in the sorrowful history of the Jewish people. Shortly after Ferrer's appearance at the most Christian court, the regent Donna Catalina, the Infante Don Ferdinand, and the apostate Paul Burgensis de Santa Maria, in the name of the child-king, Juan II, issued an edict of twenty-four articles (January 12th, 1412), the aim of which was to impoverish and humiliate the Jews, and reduce them to the lowest grade in the social scale. It ordered that they should live in special Jew-quarters (Juderias), provided with not more than one gate each, under pain of confiscation of fortune and personal chastisement. No handicraft was to be exercised by them; they were not to practice the healing art, nor transact business with Christians. It goes without saying that they were forbidden to hire Christian servants and fill public offices. Their judicial autonomy was abolished, not only in criminal cases, in which they had long ceased to exercise it, but also in civil disputes. The edict prescribed a special costume for the Jews. Both men and women were to wear long garments, in the case of males, of coarse stuffs. Whoever dressed in the national costume, or in fine materials, became liable to a heavy fine; on a repetition of the offense, to corporal punishment and confiscation of property. The wearing of the red Jew badge was, of course, insisted upon. Males were prohibited from shaving the beard or cutting the hair under pain of one hundred lashes. No Jew was to be addressed, either in conversation or in writing, by the title "Don," to the infringement of which a heavy fine was also attached. They were interdicted from carrying weapons, and might no longer move from town to town, but were to be fixed to one place of abode. The Jew detected in an evasion of the latter restriction was to lose his entire property, and be made a bondman of the king: Grandees and burghers were sternly enjoined to afford not the slightest protection to Jews.

It is not unwarrantable to assume the influence of the apostate Paul de Santa Maria in the details of these Jew-hating laws. They singled out the most sensitive features of the Jewish character, pride and sense of honor. Wealthy Jews, in the habit of appearing in magnificent attire and with smoothly shaven chins, were now to don a disfiguring costume, and go about with stubbly, ragged beards. The cultivated, who as physicians and advisers of the grandees had enjoyed unrestricted intercourse with the highest ranks, were to confine themselves to their Jew quarter, or be baptized, baptism being the hoped-for result of all these cruel restrictions, enforced with merciless vigor. A contemporary writer (Solomon Alami) describes the misery caused by the edict: "Inmates of palaces were driven into wretched nooks, and dark, low huts. Instead of rustling apparel we were obliged to wear miserable clothes, which drew contempt upon us. Prohibited from shaving- the beard,we had to appear like mourners. The rich tax-farmers sank into want, for they knew no trade by which they could gain a livelihood, and the handicraftsmen found no custom. Starvation stared everyone in the face. Children died on their mothers' knees from hunger and exposure."

Amid this tribulation the Dominican Ferrer invaded the synagogues, crucifix in hand, preached Christianity in a voice of thunder, offering his hearers enjoyment of life and opportunities of preferment, or threatening damnation here and hereafter. The Christian populace, inflamed by the passionate, eloquence of the preacher, emphasized his teaching

by violent assaults on the Jews. The trial was greater than the unhappy Castilian Jews could bear. Flight was out of the question, for the law forbade it under a terrible penalty. It is not surprising, then, that the weak and lukewarm among them, the comfort-loving and wordly-minded, succumbed to the temptation, and saved themselves by baptism. Many Jews in the communities of Valladolid, Zamora, Salamanca, Toro, Segovia, Avila, Benavente, Leon, Valencia, Burgos,

Astorga, and other small towns, in fact, wherever Vincent Ferrer preached, went over to Christianity. Several synagogues were turned into churches by Ferrer. In the course of his four months' sojourn (December, 1412--March, 1413) in the kingdom of Castile, this proselyte-monger inflicted wounds upon the Jews from which they bled to death.

When, however, he repaired to the kingdom of Aragon-summoned thither to advise on the rival claims of several pretenders to the throne--and when through his exertion the Castilian Infante, Don Ferdinand, was awarded the Aragonese crown (June, 1414), a trifling improvement took place in the condition of the Castilian Jews. The regent, Donna Catalina, issued a new edict in the name of her son (17th July). In this document the Jews were still interdicted the exercise of handicrafts, but were allowed, under a multitude of conditions, to visit markets with their merchandise. The prohibition to hire Christian or Mahometan domestics was confirmed; but, on the other hand, the employment of day-laborers and gardeners for the fields and vineyards of Jews, and shepherds for their flocks, was permitted. The new law triflingly allowed Jews to trim their hair and to clip with shears, but not entirely remove, their beards; a fringe of hair was ordered to be left on the chin, and shaving with the razor was forbidden, as though the queen-regent and her sage counselors were anxious that Jewish orthodoxy should not be wronged. The new decree conceded the wearing of dress materials of a value of sixty maravedis (under the former edict the value had been fixed at half this sum), but imposed a funnel-shaped head-covering, to which it was forbidden to attach tassels. The vehemence with which the edict declaimed against the ostentation of Jewish women disclosed its female authorship. Under this decree, freedom of domicile was once more accorded to Jews. It is noteworthy that the new edict applied only to Jews, whereas its predecessor restricted Mahometans as well.

With the transfer of the fanatical Ferrer to Aragon, the communities of that kingdom began to experience trials and misfortunes. The newly-elected king, Don Ferdinand, owed his crown to Ferrer, for as arbitrator between the rival pretenders he had warmly espoused his cause, proclaimed him king, and united the populace in his favor. Ferdinand consequently paid exceptional veneration to his saintliness, appointed him his father-confessor and spiritual adviser, and granted him his every wish. Foremost among Ferrer's aspirations was the conversion of the Jews, and to advance it the king commanded the Jews of Aragon to give every attention to his discourses. The zealous proselytizer made a tour of the kingdom, vehemently denouncing the Jews in every town he visited. His intimidations succeeded in converting a large number, particularly in Saragossa, Daroca,Tortosa, Valencia, and Majorca. Altogether Ferrer's mission to the Jews of Castile and Aragon is said to have resulted in not less than 20,500 forced baptisms. [In fact Ferrer strongly denounced forced baptism and violence against Jews. He constanty recalled to Christians their own Jewish roots: "Jesus Christ was a Jew, and the Blessed Virgin was a Jewess. . . It is a great sin to vilify them (the Jews). This circumcised God is our God. . . " In 1411-1412 he is said to have arranged 35,000 baptisms; in Toledo in one month he made 4000 converts--ed.] This, however, did not end the woes of Spanish Jews. Pope

Benedict XIII had still worse troubles in store for them, employing as his instrument his newly-baptized Jewish physician, Joshua Lorqui, otherwise Geronimo de Santa Fe. This pope, deposed by the council of Pisa as schismatic, heretic

POPE BENEDICT XIII.

and forsworn, deprived of his spiritual functions and put under the ban, projected the conversion of the entire body of Jews in Spain to the church, at that time the object of universal opprobrium. On the Pyrenean peninsula he was still regarded as the legitimate pope, and from this base of operations he used every effort to procure a general acknowledgment of his authority. He was not slow to perceive that the general conversion of the Jews would powerfully assist his design. If it were vouchsafed to him to overcome at last the obstinacy, blindness and infidelity of Israel, and to bring it under the sovereignty of the cross--would it not be the greatest triumph for the church and for himself? Would it not put all his enemies to shame? Would not the faithful range themselves under the pope who had so glorified the church? What better proof could he give that he was the only true pontiff?

To promote this scheme, Benedict, by the authority of the king, Don Ferdinand, summoned (towards the end of 1412) the most learned rabbis and students of Scripture in the kingdom of Aragon to a religious disputation at Tortosa. The apostate Joshua Lorqui, who was well read in Jewish literature, was to prove to the Jews, out of the Talmud itself, that the Messiah had come in the person of Jesus. The design was to operate on the most prominent Jews, the papal court being convinced that, their conversion effected, the rank and file would follow of their own accord. Geronimo carefully selected the names of those to be invited, and the pope or the king attached a punishment to their non-attendance. What were the Jews to do? To come or to remain away, to accept or to refuse, was equally dangerous. About twenty-two of the most illustrious Aragonese Jews answered the summons. At their head was Don Vidal ben Benveniste Ibn-Labi (Ferrer), of Saragossa, a scion of the old Jewish nobility, a man of consideration and culture, a physician and neo-Hebrew poet. Among his companions were Joseph Albo, of Monreal, a disciple of Chasdai Crescas, distinguished for his philosophic learning and genuine piety; Serachya Halevi Saladin, of Saragossa, translator of an Arabic philosophic work; Matathias Yizhari (En Duran?),of the same town, also a polished writer; Astruc Levi, of Daroca, a man of position; Bonastruc Desmaestre, whose presence was most desired by the pope, because he was learned and distinguished; the venerable Don Joseph, of the respected Ibn-Yachya family, and others of lesser note.

Although the Jewish notables summoned to the disputation were men of liberal education, and Don Vidal even spoke Latin fluently, none of them possessed that stout-heartedness and force of character which impress even the most vindictive enemy, and which Nachmani so conspicuously displayed when alone he encountered two of the bitterest adversaries of Judaism--the Dominican General De Penyaforte and the apostate Pablo Christiani. A succession of humiliations and persecutions had broken the manhood of even the proudest in Jewry, and had transformed all into weaklings. They were no match for perilous times. When Benedict's summons reached them, they trembled. They agreed to act with circumspection and calmness, not to interrupt their opponent, and, above all, to be united and harmonious, but they disregarded these resolutions, exposed their weakness, and eventually broke up into factions, each of which took its own course.

Duly commissioned by his schismatic master, the renegade Geronimo drew up a program. In the first place, proofs were to be adduced from the Talmud and cognate writings that the Messiah had already come in the person of Jesus of Nazareth. The papal court flattered itself that this would bring about widespread conversion of the Jews, but, in case of failure, there was to follow a war of exter·

mination against the Talmud on account of the abominations it contained, and the support it afforded the Jews in their blindness. Geronimo de Sante Fe accordingly composed a treatise on the Messianic character and Divinity of Jesus as illustrated in Jewish sacred writings. He enumerated twenty-four conditions of the coming of the Messiah, and exerted himself to show that they had all been fulfilled in Jesus. His fundamental contention was that the Christians constituted the true Israel, that they had succeeded the Jewish people in Divine favor, and that the Biblical terms, mountain, tent, temple, house of God, Zion and Jerusalem were allegorical references to the church. An instance of his ridiculous arguments may be mentioned. Like John of Valladolid, he saw in the irregular formation of a letter in a word in Isaiah a deep mystery, indicating the virginity of Mary, and the realization of the Messianic period by the advent of Jesus. This treatise, which blended the Patristic and the Rabbinic spirit, having been examined by the pope and his cardinals, was ordered to serve as the theme of the disputation.

No more remarkable controversy was ever held. It occupied sixty-eight sittings, and extended, with few interruptions, over a year and nine months (from February, 1413,until the 12th November, 1414)· In the foreground stands a pope, abandoned by almost the whole of Christendom, and hunted from his seat, anxious for a favorable issue, not for the glorification of the faith, but for his own temporal advancement; by his side, a baptized Jew, combating Rabbinical Judaism with Rabbinical weapons; and in the background, a frenzied Dominican preacher with his escort of flagellants, promoting a persecution of the Jews to give force to the conversionist zeal of Tortosa. The helpless, bewildered Jews could only turn their eyes to heaven, for on earth they found themselves surrounded by bitter enemies. When, at their first audience with Pope Benedict (6th February, 1413), they were asked to give their names for registration, they were seized with terror; they imagined their lives in jeopardy. The pope quieted them with the explanation that it was only a customary formality. On the whole he treated them at first with kindness and affability, the usual attitude of princes of the church when they have an end to attain. He assured them that no harm would befall them; that he had summoned them merely to ascertain whether there was any truth in Geronimo's statement that: the Talmud attested the Messianic character of Jesus, and he promised them the fullest freedom of speech. At the end of the first audience he dismissed them graciously, assigned quarters to each of the notables, and gave instructions that their comfort should be cared for. A few prophesied from this friendly reception a successful issue for themselves and their cause, but they knew little of Rome and the vice-regents of God.

A few days later the disputation began. When the Jewish notables entered the audience hall, they were awe-struck by the splendor of the scene: Pope Benedict, on an elevated throne, clad in his state robes; around him the cardinals and princes of the church, resplendent in jeweled vestments; beyond them nearly a thousand auditors of the highest ranks. The little knot of defenders of Judaism trembled before this imposing and confident

array of the forces of Christianity. The pope himself presided, and opened the sitting with an address to the Jews. He informed them that the truth of neither Judaism nor Christianity was to be called into question, for the Christian faith was above discussion and indisputable, and Judaism had once been true, but had been abrogated by the later dispensation. The disputation would be confined to the single question, whether the Talmud recognized Jesus as the Messiah. The Jews were consequently limited to mere defense. At a sign from the pope, the convert Geronimo stood forth, and, after a salutation of the papal toe, delivered himself of a long-winded harangue, abounding in Christian, Jewish, and even scholastic subtleties, and full of praise of the magnanimity and graciousness of the pope in endeavoring to bring the Jews into the way of salvation. His text, applied to the Jews, was a verse from Isaiah: "If ye be willing and obedient, ye shall eat the good of the land; but if ye refuse and rebel, ye shall be devoured with the sword"--which disclosed the final argument of the church. In reply, Vidal Benveniste,who had been elected spokesman by the notables, delivered a speech in Latin, which evoked a compliment from the pope. Don Vidal exposed Geronimo's malignity in threatening the sword and other punishments before the arguments on either side were heard. The pope acknowledged the justice of the reproof, and said in extenuation that Geronimo had still the boorishness derived from his Jewish origin. The notables plucked up courage to petition the pope to release them from further controversy, giving as their reason that their opponent employed scholastic methods of reasoning, in which it was impossible for them to follow him, as their faith was founded not on syllogisms but on tradition. The pope naturally declined to accede to this request, but invited them to continue the discussion on the following day, and had them escorted to their quarters by officers of high rank.

For a time the controversy retained its friendly character. Geronimo quoted obscure Agadic passages from the Talmud and other Hebrew writings to establish his astounding contention that the Talmud attests that Jesus was the

Messiah. Generally the pope presided at the disputations, but occasionally grave matters affecting his own position necessitated his absence. The maintenance of his dignity was threatened by the convening of the council of Constance by the Christian princes, which constituted itself the supreme court in the conflict between the three popes. Consequently, Benedict had to hold frequent consultations with his friends. On these occasions, his place was taken by the general of the Dominicans or the chamberlain of the papal palace. The proofs adduced by Geronimo in support of his statements were so absurd that it should have been easy for the Jewish delegates to refute them. But their words were willfully misinterpreted, so that in several instances it was recorded in the protocol that they had conceded the point under discussion. A few of them consequently committed their refutations to writing; but they still met with arbitrary treatment. Some points raised by them were condemned as not pertinent to the discussion. The Jewish delegates, who had entered on the controversy with unwilling hearts, were exhausted by

the talking and taunting, and were anxious to avoid retort. Suddenly the pope threw aside his mask of friendliness, and showed his true disposition by threatening them with death. Sixty-two days the war of tongues had lasted, and the representatives of Judaism showed no sign of their much-hoped-for conversion. Their power of resistance appeared to grow with the battle. So, in the sixty-third sitting, the pope changed his tactics. At his command Geronimo now came forward as the censor of the Talmud, accusing it of containing all kinds of abominations, blasphemy, immorality and heresy, and demanding its condemnation. A few new-Christians, among them Andreas Beitran (Bertrand) of Valencia, the pope's almoner, valiantly seconded this demand.

Geronimo had prepared, at the instance of the pope, a treatise with this purpose in view. Every inimical reference in the Talmud to heathens or Jewish Christians, Geronimo interpreted as applying to Christians, a fabrication with disastrous consequences, inasmuch as the enemies of the Jews repeated these deadly charges without further inquiry. When the attacks on Talmud unexpectedly became the subject of discussion, the Jewish representatives defended the arraigned points, but were so hard pressed that they split up into two parties. Don Astruc Levi handed in a written declaration, setting forth that he ascribed no authority to the Agadic sentences quoted incriminating the Talmud; that he held them as naught, and renounced them. The majority of the notables supported him. To save the life of the whole they sacrificed a limb. Joseph Albo and Ferrer (Don Vidal) alone maintained their ground, declaring that the Talmudic Agada was a competent authority, and that the equivocal passages had a different meaning from that ascribed to them, and were not to be interpreted literally. So the machinations of the pope and his creatures had at least succeeded in bringing about a division in the ranks of the defenders of Judaism.

The principal object of the disputation--the conversion of the Jews en masse through the example of their most prominent leaders--was not attained. All the means employed failed--the benignant reception, the threats of violence, the attack on Jewish convictions. An expedient, calculated entirely for effect, had also been tried, which, it was thought, would so mortify the notables that, dazed and overwhelmed, they would throw down their arms and surrender at discretion. The fanatical proselytizer Vincent Ferrer had returned from Majorca to Catalonia and Aragon, and, surrounded by his terror-inspiring band of flagellants, had renewed his mission to the Jews, amid dismal chants and fiery exhortations to embrace the cross. Again he succeeded in winning over many thousands to Christianity. In the great Jewish communities of Saragossa, Calatajud, Daroca, Fraga and Barbastro, the conversions were limited to individuals; but smaller congregations, such as those of Alcaniz, Caspe, Maella, Lerida, Alcolea and Tamarite, hemmed in by hostile Christians,

went over in a body to Christianity. All these proselytes were gradually brought, in small and large troops, to Tortosa, and conducted, at the order of the pope, into the audience hall, where, before the entire assembly, they made public profession of the Christian faith. Living trophies, they were intended to shadow forth the impending victory of the church, dishearten the defenders of Judaism, and press upon them the conviction that, as in their absence the Jewish communities were melting away, all resistance on their part was in vain. It is no small merit that Don Vidal, Joseph Albo, Astruc Levi, and their companions refused to yield to the pressure. The pope saw his hopes shattered. Not a single notable wavered, and conversions of large masses did not take place. The great communities of Aragon and Catalonia remained true to their faith, with the exception of a few weaklings, amongst them some relations of Vidal Benveniste. [By the end of the "disputation", some 3000 had converted, and this included twelve of the fourteen learned rabbis arranged against Geronimo de Santa Fe.--ed.] The council of Constance would soon meet, and Benedict would be unable to appear before it as the triumphant conqueror of Judaism--would have no special claim to preference over the other two competing popes.

In his disappointment he vented his spleen on the Talmud and the already restricted liberties of the Jews. At the last sitting of the disputation he dismissed the Jewish notables with black looks, from which they easily divined his evil intentions. Various obstacles prevented him from putting them into force for six months, when (May 11th, 1415) they were embodied in a bull of eleven clauses. The Jews were forbidden to study or teach the Talmud and Talmudic literature; all copies of the Talmud were to be sought out and confiscated. Anti-Christian works, written by Jews, especially one entitled "Mar Mar Jesu," were not to be read under pain of punishment for blasphemy. Every community, whether large or small, was prohibited from possessing more than one simple, poorly appointed synagogue. The Jews were to be strictly separated from Christians, were not to eat, bathe, or do business with them. They were to occupy no official posts, exercise no handicrafts, not even practice medicine. The wearing of the red or yellow Jew badge was also enjoined by this bull. Finally, all Jews were to be forced to hear Christian sermons three times a year--during Advent, at Easter, and in the summer. In the first sermon the Prophets and the Talmud were to be used to prove that the true Messiah had come; in the second, their attention was to be directed to the abominations and heresies contained, according to Geronimo's treatise, in the Talmud, alone responsible for their infidelity; and in the third it was to be impressed upon them that the destruction of the temple and the dispersion of the Hebrew people had been predicted by the founder of Christianity. At the close of each sermon the bull was to be read aloud. The strict execution of this malignant edict was confided by the pope to Gonzalo de Santa Maria, son of the apostate Paul, who had been taken over to Christianity by his father.

Fortunately, the vindictive schemes of Pope Benedict never came into active operation. While he was still engaged in tormenting the Jews, the council of Constance decreed his deposition. As he had obstinately opposed the advice of the king, Don Ferdinand, and the German emperor, Sigismund, to lay aside the tiara of his own initiative, he was abandoned by his Spanish protectors. The weapons he had employed recoiled upon himself. His last adherents were drawn from him by Vincent Ferrer's fanatical preaching. The flagellant priest not only exhorted the king of Aragon to renounce "this unfrocked and spurious pope," but he held forth everywhere--in the churches and the open streets --that "a man like this pope deserves to be pursued

to death by every right-thinking Christian." Deserted by his protectors, his friends, and even his protectors, there now remained to Pedro de Luna, of all his possessions, only a small fortress, and even here King Ferdinand, urged on by Santa Maria, the pope's creature, threatened him with a siege. In the end this ambitious and obstinate man covered himself with ridicule by attempting to continue to play the part of pope in his tiny palace. He appointed a college of four cardinals, and pledged them before his death not to recognize the pope elected at Constance, but to choose a successor from among their own body. When he died, his college elected two popes instead of one. What became of the malicious apostate, Joshua Lorqui-Geronimo de Santa Fe, after the fall of his master, is not known. In Jewish circles he was remembered by the well-earned sobriquet of" The Calumniator " (Megadef). King Ferdinand of Aragon, who had always allowed himself to be influenced by enemies of the Jews, died in 1416. His death was followed, after a short interval, by that of the Jew-hating regent, Catalina of Castile, the instrument of Vincent's Jew-hunt (1418), and finally by that of Vincent himself (1419), who had the mortification to see the flagellant movement, to which he owed his saintly reputation, condemned by the council of Constance, he himself being compelled to disband his "white troop."

Although the chief persecutors of the Jews had disappeared, the unhappy conditions created by them remained. The exclusive laws of Castile and the bull of Pope Benedict were still in force. Ferrer's proselytizing campaigns had severely crippled the Spanish, and even foreign communities. In Portugal alone they met with no success. The Portuguese ruler, Don Joao I, had other interests to pursue than the conversion of Jews. He was then occupied in that first conquest on the coast of Africa, opposite to Portugal, which laid the foundation of the subsequent maritime supremacy of the Portuguese. When Vincent Ferrer petitioned King Joao for permission to come to Portugal in order to make the pulpits and streets resound with his dismal harangues on the sinfulness of the world and the blindness and obstinacy of the Jews, the Portuguese king informed him that he "might come, but with a crown of red-hot iron on his head." Portugal was the only refuge on the Pyrenean peninsula from the proselytizing rage of the flagellant preacher, and many Spanish Jews who had the means of escaping fled thither. Don Judah Ibn Yachya-Negro, held in high esteem by King Joao I, and, perhaps, appointed by him chief rabbi of Portugal, represented to him the horrors of enforced baptism, and the necessary insincerity of the professions of unwilling converts. The king consequently issued his commands that the immigrant new-Christians should not be interfered with or delivered up to Spain.

In other parts of Europe, where the fanatical Dominican had been, or whither reports of his deeds or misdeeds had penetrated, the Jews were forced to drain the cup of bitterness to the dregs. In Savoy, which Vincent Ferrer had visited, they were obliged to hide themselves with their holy books in mountain caves. In Germany, persecutions of Jews had always found a congenial soil, and they were promoted by the anarchy which prevailed during the reign of Sigismund and the sessions of the council of Constance. Even the Italian communities, though for the most part undisturbed, lived in continual anxiety, lest the movement strike a responsive chord in their politically distracted land. They convened a great synod, first at Bologna, then at Forli (1416-1418), to consider what measures might be adopted to avert the threatened danger.

POPE MARTIN V.

Happily, at this moment, after a long schism, bitter strife and a plurality of anti-popes, the council of Constance elected a pope, who, though full of dissimulation, was not the most degraded in the college of cardinals. Martin V, who was said by his contemporaries to have appeared simple and good before his election, but to have shown himself afterwards very clever and not very kind, received the Jews with scant courtesy when, during his progress through Constance, they approached him carrying lighted tapers in festive procession, and offered him the Torah with a prayer for the confirmation of their sufferance. From his white palfrey with silk and gold trappings he answered them: "You have the law, but understand it not. The old has passed away, and the new been found." Yet he treated them with leniency. At the request of Emperor Sigismund, he confirmed the privileges granted to the Jews of Germany and Savoy by the preceding emperor, Rupert, denouncing attacks on their persons and property, and the practice of converting them by force. The emperor, who may be accused of thoughtlessness but not of a spirit of persecution, thereupon issued his commands to all the German princes and magistrates, cities and subjects, to allow his "servi camerae" the full enjoyment of the privileges and immunities which had been given them by the pope (February 26th, 1418). A deputation of Jews, commissioned by the Italian synod, also waited upon the now generally acknowledged pope, and craved his protection. Even the Spanish Jews appear to have dispatched an embassy to him, consisting of two of their most distinguished men, Don Samuel Abrabanel and Don Samuel Halevi. When the Jews complained of the insecurity of their lives, the attacks on their religious convictions, and the frequent desecration of their sanctuaries, the pope issued a bull (January 3lst, 1419), with the following preamble:

> *" Whereas the Jews are made in the image of God, and a remnant of them will one day be saved, and whereas they have besought our protection, following in the footsteps of our predecessors we command that they be not molested in their synagogues ; that their laws, rights, and customs be not assailed; that they be not baptized by force, constrained to observe Christian festivals, nor to wear new badges, and that they be nor hindered in their business relations with Christians."*

What could have induced Pope Martin to show such friendly countenance to the Jews? Probably he had some idea of checkmating by this means the Jew-hating Benedict, who still played at being pope In his obscure corner. The principal consideration probably was the rich gifts with which the Jewish representatives approached him. Although at the council of Constance no cardinal was poorer than Martin, and his election was in great measure owing to this fact, on the throne of St. Peter he showed no aversion to money. On the contrary, everything might be obtained from him if money were paid down; without it, nothing.

IV. CHAPTER. VII

PROGRESS OF JEWISH LITERATURE

Anti-Christian Polemical Literature--Joseph Albo as a Religious Philosopher--Jewish Philosophical Systems

1420-1442 C.E.

From the Apennine Peninsula let us turn back to the Pyrenean, where the pulsation of historic life among the Jews, though gradually becoming weaker, still was stronger than in the other countries in which they were dispersed. The two branches of intellectual activity which formerly, in their palmy days, had exercised every mind--the severe study of the Talmud and the airy pursuit of the poetic muse--had lost their predominance in the Spanish Jewries. The systematic study of the Scriptures also was no longer properly cultivated. The literary activity of this period was almost exclusively directed towards combating the intrusiveness of the church, repelling its attacks on Judaism, and withstanding its proselytizing zeal. Faithful and strong-minded Jewish thinkers held it a duty to proclaim their convictions aloud, and to admonish waverers and strengthen them. The more the preaching monks, especially apostates of the stamp of Paul de Santa Maria, Geronimo de Santa Fe, and Pedro de la Caballeria, exerted themselves to prove that the Christian Trinity was the true God of Israel, taught and typified in the Bible and the Talmud, and the more the church stretched forth its tentacles towards the Jews, straining every nerve to fold them in its fatal embrace, the more necessary was it for the synagogue to watch over its sacred trust, and guard its holy of holies from idolatrous desecration. It was especially necessary that the weaker-minded should be spared confusion in religious and doctrinal matters. Hence Jewish preachers devoted themselves more than ever to expounding the doctrine of the unity of God in their pulpits. They pointed out the essential and irreconcilable difference between the Jewish and the Christian conception of the Deity, and characterized their identification as false and impious. Some preachers, in their zeal, went to extremes. Instead of relying exclusively on the convincing demonstrations in the Bible text, or on the attractive illustrations of the Agada, they resorted to the armory of scholasticism, employing the formula of philosophy and, in the presence of the Torah, and by the side of the Hebrew prophets and the Talmudical sages, quoted Plate, Aristotle, and Averroes.

This controversial literature, cultivated on a large scale, was designed to defend Judaism against calumny and abuse, rather than to convert a single Christian soul. Doubtless it also desired to stir up the new-Christians, and to re-animate their Jewish spirit beneath the disguise they had assumed to save their lives. Hence the majority of the polemical writings of the day were merely vindications of Judaism from the old charges fulminated by Nicholas de Lyra a century before, or more recently by Geronimo de Santa Fe and others, and widely circulated by the Christian clergy. Solomon-Paul of Burgos, who had been appointed bishop of his native town, wrote, in his eighty-second year (1434, a year before his death), a venomous tract against Judaism--"Searching the Scriptures" (Scrutinium Scriptuarum)--in the form of a dialogue between a teacher and his pupil, the unbelieving Saul and the converted Paul. Solomon-Paul does not seem to have retained much of the wit which, according to Jewish and Christian panegyrists, had at one time distinguished him--it had probably become blunted amid the luxurious ease of the episcopal palace-for his tract, devoutly Christian and Catholic in tone, is pointless and dull. Another ex-rabbi who devoted himself to attacking Judaism was Juan de Espana, also called Juan the Old (at Toledo), a convert who in old age had embraced Christianity under the influence of Vincent Ferrer's proselytizing efforts. He wrote a treatise on his own conversion and a Christian commentary on the seventy-second Psalm, in both of which he asserted the genuineness of his change of creed, and urged the Jews to abjure their errors.

Joseph Albo (born about 1380, died about 1444), of Monreal, one of the principal representatives of Judaism at the Tortosa disputation, who, probably through the intolerance of Pope Benedict, had emigrated to Soria, was a physician and a pupil of Chasdai Crescas, hence well acquainted with the physical sciences and the philosophic thought of his time. Although a strict adherent of Talmudical Judaism, he was, like his teacher, not averse to philosophic ideas. Indeed, he tried to reconcile them, without, of course, permitting Judaism to yield a jot to philosophy. Albo had not, however, the profundity of his teacher; as a thinker he was superficial, commonplace, and incapable of writing with logical sequence. On the advice of his friends, he undertook to investigate in how far freedom of inquiry in religious matters was possible within the limits of Judaism. At the same time he wished to fix the number of articles of faith and to decide the question whether the number thirteen adopted by Maimuni was correct, or whether it could be increased or lessened without justly bringing a charge of heresy on him who made the change. Thus originated his religio-philosophical system, the last on Spanish soil. Albo's style differs widely from that of his predecessors. He was a preacher--one of the cleverest and most graceful--and this circumstance exercised marked influence on his method of exposition. It is easy, comprehensible, popular and captivating. Albo has the knack of explaining every philosophic idea by a striking illustration, and of developing it by skillful employment of Bible verses and Agadic aphorisms. What his style thus gained, on the one hand, in intelligibility and popularity, it lost, on the other, through a certain redundancy and shallowness.

It is a remarkable fact that Albo, who thought that he was developing his religio-philosophical system exclusively in the native spirit of Judaism, placed at its head a principle of indubitably Christian origin; so powerfully do surroundings affect even those who exert themselves to throw off such influence. The religious philosopher of Soria propounded as his fundamental idea that salvation was the whole aim of man in this life, and that Judaism strongly emphasized this aspect of religion. His teacher, Chasdai Crescas, and others, had considered man's aim the bliss of the future life, to be found in proximity to the Deity and in the union of the soul with the all-pervading spirit of God. According to Albo highest happiness consists not so much in the exaltation of the soul as in its salvation. That is the nucleus of Albo's religio-philosophical system.

"IKKARIM"

Man attains only after death the perfection for which he is destined by God; for this higher life his mundane existence is but a preparation. How can he best utilize his term of preparation? There are three kinds of institutions for the reclamation of man from barbarism and his advancement to civilization. The first is Natural Law, a sort of social compact to abstain from theft, rapine and homicide; the second is State Legislation, which cares for order and morals; and the third is Philosophical Law, which aims at promoting the enduring happiness of man, or, at least, at removing obstacles in the way of its realization. All these institutions, even when highly developed, are powerless to assist the real welfare of man, the redemption of his soul, his beatitude; for they concern themselves only with actions, with proper conduct, but do nothing to inculcate the views or supply the principles which are to be the mainsprings of action. If the highest aim of man be eternal life or beatitude after death, then there must be a Divine Legislation, without which man in this world must always be groping in darkness and missing his highest destiny. This Divine Legislation must supply all the perfections lacking in its mundane counterpart. It must have for its postulate a perfect God, who both wishes and is able to promote the redemption of man; it must further bear witness to the certainty that this God has revealed an unalterable Law calculated to secure the happiness of man; and finally it must appoint a suitable requital for actions and intentions. Hence this Divine Legislation has three fundamental principles: the Existence of God, the Revelation of His Will, and Just Retribution after Death. These are the three pillars on which it rests, and it requires none other.

Judaism, then, according to Albo, is a discipline for eternal salvation. It is "the Divine Legislation"' (Dath Elohith), and, as such, comprises many religious laws--613 according to the customary calculation--to enable each individual to promote his own salvation. For even a single religious precept fulfilled with intelligence and devotion, and without mental reservation or ulterior motive, entitles man to salvation. Consequently, the Torah, with its numerous prescriptions, is not intended as a burden for its disciples, nor are the Jews threatened, as Christian teachers maintain, with a curse in the event of their not observing the entire number of commandments. On the contrary, the object is to render easy the path to higher perfection. Therefore, the Agada says that every Israelite has a share in Eternal Life (Olam ha-ba), for each one can obtain this end by the fulfillment of a single religious duty.

Arrived at this point, the religious philosopher of Soria propounds the question whether Judaism can ever be altered as previous dispensations were by the Sinaitic Revelation. This question required specially careful consideration, as Christians always maintained that Christianity was a new revelation, as Judaism had been in its time; that the "New Covenant" took the place of the "Old," and that by the Gospel, the Torah had been fulfilled. Albo had acknowledged the existence of rudimentary revelations previous to that of Sinai, and to avoid being entrapped by the consequences of his own system he put forward a peculiar distinction. That which God had once revealed by His own mouth direct to man was, by virtue of that fact, unalterable and binding for all time; but that which had been communicated only by a prophetic intermediary might suffer change or even annulment. The Ten Commandments which the Israelites had received direct from God, amid the flames of Sinai, were unalterable; in them the three cardinal principles of a divine legislation are laid down. On the other hand, the remaining prescriptions of Judaism, imposed on the people solely through the mediation of Moses, were open to change or even revocation.

WEAKNESS OF ALBO'S SYSTEM.

But this instability of a portion, perhaps a large portion, of the Jewish religious law was only a theory, propounded simply as a possibility. In practice the obligations of the Torah were to be regarded as binding and unalterable, until it should please God to reveal other laws through the medium of a prophet as great as Moses, and in as open and convincing a manner as on Sinai. Hitherto no prophet had made good his claim so far as to render necessary the rescinding of any portion of Judaism.

Albo's religious system is far from satisfactory. Based upon the Christian doctrine of salvation, it was compelled to regard faith, in a Christian sense, as the chief condition of the soul's redemption, and the ordinances of Judaism as sacraments, similar to baptism or communion, upon which salvation was dependent. Nor is the development of his theory strictly logical. Too often the arts of the preacher take the place of severe reasoning, and for the illustration of his ideas he indulges in prolix sermons in exposition of Biblical and Agadic texts.

A bolder thinker than Albo, but, like him, a preacher, was his junior contemporary, Joseph Ibn Shem Tob. At one time, when in disgrace with the king of Castile, and leading a wandering life, he held forth every Sabbath to large audiences. He had been well schooled in philosophy. His Kabbalistical, gloomy and fanatical father, who denounced philosophy as a primary source of evil, damned Aristotle to hell, and even accused Maimuni of heterodoxy, must have been scandalized when his son Joseph plunged deep, and with all his heart, into the study of Aristotle and Maimuni. But Joseph did not hesitate to stigmatize the error of his father and of those who thought the employment of philosophic methods opposed to the interests of religion. He, on the contrary, held that they were essential for the attainment of the higher destiny to which all men, especially Israelites, are called. The cultured, philosophical Jew who intelligently discharges all the religious duties of Judaism obviously realizes his high aim much sooner than the Israelite who practices his ceremonial blindly, without wisdom or understanding. Science is also of great value in enabling human intelligence to discriminate error. It is the nature of man's imperfect intellect to foster truth and error side by side; but knowledge teaches how to distinguish between the true and the false. On the other hand, gaps in philosophical teaching are bridged over by the Sinaitic Law. In so far as the latter conceives the happiness of man in the survival of the spirit after the destruction of the body, it is immeasurably the superior of philosophy. Judaism also names the means of attaining eternal happiness --the conscientious fulfillment of religious obligations.

On this point, Joseph Shem Tob's view approximates that of Joseph Albo. In his eyes, also, the commandments of Judaism have a sacramental character, but he does not emphasize salvation so much as Albo. Joseph Ibn-Shem Tob went so far, however, as to deny that the objects of the religious laws were knowable, and, to a certain extent, ascribed to them a mystical influence.

None of these writings of the first half of the fifteenth century, philosophical or polemical, was the fruit of leisure and an unfettered spirit. All were stimulated into existence by the urgent necessities of the times, and were put forth to protect the religious and moral treasure-house from pressing danger. In order not to succumb, Judaism was forced simultaneously to strengthen itself from within and ward off attacks from without.

IV. CHAPTER VIII

ASYLUM IN TURKEY

Capture of Constantinople By Mahomet II--The Jews find an Asylum in Turkey--The Karaites--Moses Kaspali

1441-1474 C.E.

It seems almost providential that, at a moment when the persecutions in Europe were increasing in number and virulence, the new Turkish empire should have arisen to offer an hospitable asylum to the hunted Jews. When, three days after the chastisement which he inflicted on Constantinople, the sultan, Mahomet II, proclaimed that all the fugitive inhabitants might return to their homes and estates without fear of molestation, he gave a benevolent thought to the Jews. He permitted them to settle freely in Constantinople and other towns, allotted them special dwelling-places, and allowed them to erect synagogues and schools. Soon after his capture of Constantinople, he ordered the election of a Greek patriarch, whom he invested with a certain political authority over all the Greeks in his new dominions, and also nominated a chief rabbi to preside over the Hebrew communities. This was a pious, learned, upright Israelite, named Moses Kapsali. Mahomet even summoned this rabbi to the divan, and singled him out for special distinction, giving him a seat next to the mufti, the Chief Ulema of the Mahometans, and precedence over the patriarch. Moses Kapsali (born about 1420, died about 1495), also received from the sultan a kind of political suzerainty over the Jewish communities in Turkey. The taxes imposed upon the Jews he had to apportion

among communities and individuals; he had to superintend their collection and to pay them into the sultan's exchequer. He was furthermore empowered to inflict punishment on his co-religionists, and no rabbi could hold office without his sanction. In short, he was the chief and the official representative of a completely organized Jewish communal system

This favorable situation of the Jews had a stimulating effect on the degenerate Karaites, who migrated in considerable numbers from Asia, the Crimea and southern Poland, to take up their abode with their more happily placed brethren in Constantinople and Adrianople. The Karaites, whose fundamental principle is the study and reasonable interpretation of the Bible, were in so lamentable a state of ignorance, that their entire religious structure had become a system of authorized dogmas and traditions more rigid even than that of the Rabbanites. The extent of their intellectual decline may be measured by the fact that in the course of a century they failed to produce a single moderately original theological writer. Those with a bent for study were compelled to sit at the feet of Rabbanite teachers and receive from them instruction in the Scriptures and the Talmud. The proud masters of Bible exegesis had become the humble disciples of the once despised Rabbanites. The petrifaction of Karaism is illustrated by an event in European Turkey. A Karaite college, consisting of Menachem Bashyasi, his son Moses Bashyasi, Menachem Maroli, Michael the Old, his son Joseph, and a few others, had permitted the lights necessary for the Sabbath eve to be prepared on Friday, so that the holy day need not be spent in darkness. The college gave adequate reasons for the innovation. According to a Karaite principle, not only an ecclesiastical authority, but any individual is justified in abolishing an ancient custom, or annulling former decisions, if he can cite sufficient exegetical authority. Nevertheless, stormy opposition arose (about 1460) against this decision, aimed at a custom derived, perhaps, from Anan, the founder of Karaism, and hence possessing the sacredness conferred by the rust of seven centuries. Schism and friction were the result. The section of the community which ventured to prepare the lights required for the Sabbath eve was abused, and charged with heresy. Moreover, the schism relating to the commencement of the festivals was still unhealed. The Palestinian Karaite communities and their neighbors continued to distinguish between an ordinary and a leap year by the state of the barley harvest, and to regulate their festivals by the appearance of the new moon. On the other hand, the communities in Turkey, the Crimea, and southern Poland, used the calendar of the Rabbanites. These hereditary differences were eating more and more into the solidarity of the sect, for there was no means of composing them, and agreeing upon uniform principles.

The conspicuous decrepitude of Karaism and the ignorance of its followers afforded the Rabbanites in the Turkish empire an opportunity for reconciling them to Talmudic Judaism, or, at least, overcoming their bitter hostility towards it. Rabbanite teachers, Enoch Saporta, an immigrant from Catalonia, Eliezer Kapsali, from Greece, and Elias Halevi, from Germany, stipulated that their Karaite pupils, whom they instructed in the Talmud, should thenceforward abstain, in writing and in speech, from reviling Talmudic authorities, and from desecrating the festivals of the Rabbanite calendar. In the difficult position in which studiously inclined Karaites found themselves, they could not do otherwise than give this promise. The Turkish chief rabbi, Moses Kapsali, was of opinion that, as the Karaites rejected the Talmud, they might not be taught in it.

TURKEY.

But he was a disciple of the strict German school, which, in its gloomy ultra-piety, would allow no concessions even though the gradual conversion of a dissenting sect could be effected.

When contrasted with the miserable condition of the Jews in Germany, the lot of those who had taken up their abode in the newly-risen Turkish empire must have seemed unalloyed happiness. Jewish immigrants who had escaped the ceaseless persecutions to which they had been subjected in Germany expressed themselves in terms of rapture over the happy condition of the Turkish Jews. Unlike their co-religionists under Christian rule, they were not compelled to yield up the third part of their fortunes in royal taxes; nor were they in any way hindered in the conduct of business. They were permitted to dispose of their property as they pleased, and had absolute freedom of movement throughout the length and breadth of the empire. They were subject to no sumptuary laws, and were thus able to clothe themselves in silk and gold, if they chose.

The fruitful lands taken from the slothful Greek Christians were occupied by them, and offered rich reward to their industry. Turkey was, in short, correctly described by an enthusiastic Jew as a land "in which nothing, absolutely nothing, is wanting." Two young immigrants, Kalmann and David, thought that if German Jews realized' but a tenth part of the happiness to be found in Turkey, they would brave any hardships to get there. These two young men persuaded Isaac Zarfati, who had journeyed in Turkey in earlier times, and whose name was by no means unknown in Germany, to write a circular letter to the Jews of the Rhineland, Styria, Moravia and Hungary, to acquaint them with the happy lot of Jews under the crescent as compared with their hard fate under the shadow of the cross and to call upon them to escape from the German house of bondage and emigrate to Turkey.

Isaac Zarfati's appeal induced many Jews to emigrate forthwith to Turkey and Palestine. Their grave demeanor, extreme piety, and peculiar apparel at once distinguished them from the Jews of Greece and the Orient, and ere long the newcomers exercised considerable influence upon the other inhabitants of the countries in which they settled.

There were peculiar circumstances connected with the prohibition of the emigration of Jews to Palestine. The Jewish inhabitants of Jerusalem had obtained permission from a pasha to build a synagogue on one of the slopes of

Mount Zion. The site of this synagogue adjoined a piece of land owned by Franciscan monks, or rather containing the ruins of one of their chapels, known as David's chapel. When this permission was given to the Jews, the monks raised as much clamor as though all Palestine, including the Holy City, had been their peculiar inheritance since the beginning of time. They forthwith carried their complaints to the pope, and represented that, if the Jews were permitted to take such liberties as this, it would not be long before they took possession of the Church of the Holy Sepulcher itself. The pope at once issued a bull directing that no Christian shipowner should convey Jewish emigrants to the Holy Land. As the Levantine trade was at that time almost entirely in the hands of the Venetians, the Doge was prevailed upon to issue stringent orders to all the shipmasters of the mainland and the islands not to give passage to Palestine to any Jews.

It is, indeed, strange that, while the Christian powers were under the impression that they had hemmed in the children of Israel on all sides like hunted animals, the Turks of Eastern Europe opened a way of escape to them. Ere another half century had passed, their Spanish brethren, savagely hunted from the Peninsula, were destined to seek the same asylum.

IV. CHAPTER IX

THE JEWS IN ITALY AND GERMANY BEFORE THE EXPULSION FROM SPAIN

Joseph Kolon, his Character and his Feud with Messer Leon--Simon of Trent--The Jews of Ratisbon

1474-1492 C.E.

The most distinguished rabbis of Italy were at that time Judah Menz and Joseph Kolon, and precisely these two were most inimical to any liberal manifestation within Judaism, and most strenuously opposed the advocates of freedom. Joseph ben Solomon Kolon (flourished 1460--1490) was of French extraction, his ancestors having been expelled from France; but he passed his youth in Germany, and belonged to the German school. He subsequently lived with his relatives in Chambery until the Jews were hunted out of Savoy. With many companions in misfortune he went to Lombardy, where he gained his living by teaching; finally he became rabbi of Mantua. Endowed with extraordinary penetration, and fully the equal of the German rabbis in the depth of his Talmudic learning, Joseph Kolon was celebrated in his day as a Rabbinical authority of the first magnitude, and his academy rivaled the German school itself. He was consulted by both German and Italian communities. On scientific subjects and all matters outside the Talmud he was as ignorant as his German fellow-dignitaries. A resolute, decided nature, Joseph Kolon was a man of rigid views on all religious matters. His ruggedness involved him in unpleasant relations with Moses Kapsali in Constantinople, and in a heated controversy with the cultured Messer Leon in his own community. However well they might agree for a time, Joseph Kolon, the strict Talmudist, and Messer Leon, the cultured man of letters, could not long tolerate each other. When the conflict between them broke out, the whole community of Mantua took sides in their feud, and split into two parties as supporters of the one or the other. The strife at length became so keen that in 1476-1477 Duke Joseph of Mantua banished them both from the city; after which Kolon became rabbi of Pavia.

Still more strained were the relations between the rabbi Judah Menz and the philosopher Elias del Medigo. The former (born 1408, died 1509), a man of the old school, of comprehensive knowledge of Talmudic subjects, and of remarkable sagacity, was most resolutely opposed to scientific progress and freedom in religious matters, and after his expulsion from Mayence transplanted the narrow spirit of the German rabbis to Padua and Italy in general.

The relatively secure and honorable position of the Jews in Italy did not fail to rouse the displeasure of fanatical monks, who sought to cover with the cloak of religious zeal either their dissolute conduct or their ambitious share in worldly affairs. The colder the Christian world grew towards the end of the fifteenth century with regard to clerical institutions, the more bitterly did the monastic orders rage against the Jews. Preaching friars made the chancels ring with tirades against them, and openly advocated their utter extermination. Their most desperate enemy at this time was the Franciscan Bernardinus of Feltre, a worthy disciple of the bloodthirsty Capistrano. The standing text of his sermons was: Let Christian parents keep a watchful eye on their children lest the Jews steal, ill-treat, or crucify them.

He held up Capistrano, the Jew-slayer, as the type and model of a true Christian. In his eyes friendly and neighborly intercourse with Jews was an abomination, a most grievous sin against canonical law. Christian charity, he admitted, directs that Jews, being human, be treated with justice and humanity; but at the same time the canonical law forbids Christians to have any dealings with them, to sit at their tables, or to allow themselves to be treated by Jewish physicians. As the aristocracy everywhere, in obedience to their own interests, took the part of the Jews, Bernardinus inflamed the lower classes against the Jews and their patrons. Because certain Jewish capitalists had been successful, he depicted all Jews as vampires and extortioners, and roused the ill will of the populace against them. "I, who live on alms and eat the bread of the poor, shall I be a dumb dog and not howl when I see the Jews wringing their wealth from Christian poverty? Yea! shall I not cry aloud for Christ's sake?" Such is a fair specimen of his preaching. The authorities sorely hindered Bernardinus in his business of Jew-baiting, and his bloodthirsty sermons mostly failed of effect. When he was conducting his crusade in Bertgamo and Ticini, Dyke Galeazzo,

of Milan, forbade him to proceed. In Florence, in fact everywhere in Tuscany, the enlightened prince and the senate took the part of the Jews with vigor. The venomous monk spread the report that they had allowed themselves to be bribed with large sums by Yechiel of Pisa and other wealthy Jews. As Bernardinus was inciting the youth of the city against the Jews, and a popular rising was imminent, the authorities ordered him to quit Florence and the country forthwith, and he was compelled to submit (1487). Little by little, however, by dint of untiring repetition of the same charges, he managed so far to inflame public opinion against the Jews that even the Venetian senate was not always able to protect them. Finally, he succeeded in bringing about a bloody persecution of the Jews, not, indeed, in Italy, but in the Tyrol, whence it spread to Germany.

While Bernardinus was preaching in the city of Trent, he remarked with no little chagrin the friendly relation between Jews and Christians. Tobias, a skillful Jewish physician, and an intelligent Jewess, named Brunetta, were on most friendly terms with the upper classes, enjoying their complete confidence. This roused his ire not a little, and he made the chancels of Trent ring with savage tirades against the Jews. Some Christians called him to account for his hatred of Jews, remarking that though they were without the true faith, those of Trent were worthy folk. The monk replied: "Ye know not what misfortune these good people will bring upon you. Before Easter Sunday is past they will give you a proof of their extraordinary goodness." It was easy for him to prophesy, for he and a few other priests had arranged a cunning plan, which not only brought about the ruin of the community of Trent, but also caused the greatest injury to the Jews of various countries. Chance aided him by creating a favorable opportunity.

In Holy Week of 1475 a three-year old child, named Simon, the son of poor Christian parents, was drowned in the Adige, and the corpse was caught in a grating close to the house of a Jew. In order to anticipate misrepresentation of the event, he hurried to Bishop Hinderbach to give him notice of the occurrence. The bishop took two men of high position with him, went to the place, and had the body carried into the church. As soon as the news spread, Bernardinus and other hostile priests raised a fierce outcry against the Jews, saying that they had tortured and slain the child, and then flung it into the water. The body of the supposedly ill-treated child was exhibited, in order to inflame the fury of the populace against them. The bishop had all the Jews of Trent, high and low, cast into prison, commenced proceedings against them, and called a physician, Matthias Tiberinus, to testify to the violent death of the child. A baptized Jew, one Wolfkan, from Ratisbon, an engrosser, came forward with the most fearful accusations against his former co-religionists. His charges the more readily found credence as the imprisoned Jews confessed under torture that they had slain Simon, and drunk his blood on the night of the Passover. Brunetta was said to have supplied the weapons for the purpose. A letter also was said to have been found in the possession of a rabbi, Moses, which had been sent from Saxony, asking for Christian blood for the next Passover. Only one of the tortured victims, a man named Moses, endured every torment without confirming the lying accusations of his enemies. The result was that all the Jews of Trent were burnt, and it was resolved that no Jew should thenceforth settle in the city. Four persons only became converts to Christianity, and were pardoned.

The bishop of Trent, Bernardinus, and the monks of all orders made every effort to utilize this occurrence for the general ruin of the Jews. The corpse

SIMON OF TRENT

of the child was embalmed, and commended to the populace as a holy relic. Thousands made pilgrimages to its remains, and ere long it was believed by the faith-drunken pilgrims that they had seen a halo about the remains of the child Simon. So much was said about it that even its inventors came to believe in the martyrdom. From every chancel the Dominicans proclaimed the new miracle, and thundered against the infamy of the Jews. Two lawyers from Padua who visited Trent in order to convince themselves of the truth of the occurrence were almost torn to pieces by the fanatical mob. It was imperative that the marvel be believed in, and so the Jews of all Christian countries were jeopardized anew. Even in Italy they dared not go outside the towns lest they be slain as child-murderers.

The Doge, Pietro Mocenigo, and the Venetian senate, on the complaint of the Jews about the insecurity of their lives and property, issued orders to the podesta of Padua energetically to defend them against fanatical outbreaks, and to forbid the preaching friars to inflame the mob against them. The Doge accompanied the orders with the remark that the rumor that Jews had slain a Christian child in Trent was a fabrication, a device invented.by their enemies to serve some purpose. When Pope Sixtus IV was urged to canonize little Simon he steadfastly refused, and sent a letter to all the towns of Italy, on October 10th, 1475, forbidding Simon of Trent to be honored as a saint until he could investigate the matter, and thus he allayed the popular excitement against the Jews. The clergy, nevertheless, permitted the bones of Simon to be held sacred, and instituted pilgrimages to the church built for his remains.

Through this circumstance Jew hatred in Germany gained fresh vigor. The citizens of Frankfort-on-the-Main exhibited, on the bridge leading to Sachsenhausen, a picture representing in hideous detail a tortured child, and the Jews leagued with the devil in their bloody work. The news of the child-murder in Trent spread like wildfire through the Christian countries, and became the source of new sufferings to Jews. Nowhere were these sufferings so severe as in the free city of Ratisbon, containing one of the oldest Jewish communities in South Germany. It was held to be not only very pious but of distinguished morality, and it was considered a high honor to intermarry with the Jews of Ratisbon. Within the memory of man no native Jew had been brought before a tribunal for any moral lapse. The community was regarded as the most learned in the land, and the parent of all German communities. It possessed chartered liberties, which the emperors, in consideration of a crown-tax, were accustomed to renew on their accession. The Jews of Ratisbon were half recognized as burghers, and mounted guard with the Christians as militia. One might almost say that the Bavarian princes and corporations vied with each other in favoring them --of course, merely to share their purses. In the latter half of this century they had become a veritable bone of contention between the Duke of Bavaria-Landsberg and Frederick III, who, hard pressed on all sides, not only in the empire, but even in his own possessions, hoped to fill his empty coffers with the wealth of the Jews.

In addition to these the Kamerau family made claims upon the Jews of Ratisbon, as well as the town council, and, of course, the bishop. These contradictory and mutually hostile demands made the position of the Jews anything but a bed of roses. First from one side and then from another came orders to the council to imprison the Jews, their chiefs, or their rabbi, at that time the sorely-tried Israel Bruna, until, worn out by confinement, they decided to pay what was claimed. The council did indeed seek to shield them, but only so long

as no danger threatened the citizens, or the Jews did not compete with the Christian guildmembers.

To escape these cruel and arbitrary extortions, prudence directed that they place themselves under the protection of one of the Hussite nobles or captains. They would thus enjoy more security than was possible under the so-called protection of the emperor, since the fiery Hussites were not a little feared by the more sluggish Germans. Although they had to some extent abandoned their heretical fanaticism, and had taken service under the Catholic sovereigns, their desperate valor was still a source of terror to the orthodox clergy. The event proved that the Jews had acted wisely in appealing to their protection.

A bishop named Henry was elected in Ratisbon, a man of gloomy nature, to whom the sentiment of mercy was unknown, and he naturally insisted on the enforcement of the canonical restrictions against the Jews. As examples to others, for instance, he mercilessly punished a Christian girl who had entered the service of a Jew, and a Christian barber who had let blood for a Jewish customer. His animosity was contagious. On one occasion, when the Jewish midwife was sick, and a Christian was about to attend some Jewish women, the council actually dared not give her the required permission without the episcopal sanction.

Bishop Henry and Duke Louis, one in their hatred of Jews, now pursued what seemed to be a preconcerted plan for the ruin or conversion of the Jews of Ratisbon. On the one hand, they obtained the acquiescence of the pope, and on the other, the assistance of influential persons on the city council. Their campaign began with attempts at conversions and false accusations, for which they availed themselves of the assistance of a couple of worthless converted Jews. One of these, Peter Schwarz by name, wrote slanderous and abusive pamphlets against his former cc-religionists. The other, one Hans Vayol, heaped the vilest calumnies upon the aged rabbi, Israel Bruna, amongst other things charging him with purchasing from him a seven year-old Christian child and slaughtering it, and the rabbi of Ratisbon, already bowed down by sorrow and suffering, was charged with the death of the child.

Israel Bruna (of Brunn, born 1400, died I480) was one of those sons of sorrow who seem to fall from one misfortune into another. He appears to have been exiled from Brunn, where he was recognized as a Rabbinical authority, and after many wanderings, to have traveled by way of Prague to Ratisbon. He settled there, and wished to perform the functions of rabbi for those who might place confidence in him. But a Talmudic scholar who resided in the city, one Amshel, a layman, not an elected rabbi, raised objections to his competitor, and forbade Israel Bruna to hold discourses before disciples, to deal with matters of divorce, to exercise any Rabbinical functions, or to divide the honors of the office with himself. As each had his followers, a schism arose in the community of Ratisbon. His two teachers, Jacob Well and Isserlein, upholders of the freedom of the Rabbinical office and pronounced opponents of spiritual officialism, took the part of the persecuted Israel Bruna, with whom David Sprint, a rabbi of Nuremberg, also took sides. These men proved in the dearest manner that any Jew is competent to assume Rabbinical functions, provided he possesses the requisite knowledge, is authorized by a recognized teacher, and leads a pious and moral life. They further adduced in favor of Israel Bruna the fact that he contributed his quota to the communal treasury, and was therefore a worthy member of the community. The breach nevertheless remained open, and Israel Bruna was often exposed to insults from the opposite

party. Once when he was about to hold a discourse, several of the ringleaders left the lecture room, and were followed by many others. Disciples of his opponent secretly painted crosses on his seat in the synagogue, wrote the hateful word "heretic" (Epicuros) beside them, and offered other insults to him. As time went on, after the death of the great rabbis, Jacob Well and Israel Isserlein, Bruna was recognized as a Rabbinical authority, and from far and near questions were sent to him. His misfortunes, however, did not cease. When Emperor Frederick demanded the crown-tax from the community of Ratisbon, Duke Louis opposed the payment, and the council was unable to decide which side to assist. The emperor thereupon threw Israel Bruna into prison to force him to threaten his people with the ban if they did not pay over the third part of their possessions. He was released only on bail of his entire property; and, in addition, the fearful charges of child-murder and other capital crimes were raised against the decrepit old man by the converted Jew, Hans Vayol. Bishop Henry and the clergy were only too ready to gratify their hatred of Jews by means of this accusation, and the besotted populace gave all the more credence to the falsehood, as rumors of the death of Christian children at the hands of Jews daily increased. No one in Ratisbon doubted that gray old Israel Bruna had foully murdered a Christian child, and he was on the point of being put to death on the demand of the clergy. To withdraw him from the fury of the mob, the council, which feared to be made answerable, imprisoned him.

In the meantime the anxious community appealed, not only to the emperor, but also to the Bohemian king, Ladislaus, more feared than the emperor; and ere long stringent directions came from both to release the rabbi instantly without ransom. The council, however, excused itself on the plea of fear of the bishop and the mob. Thereupon followed a mandate from the emperor to defer the execution of Israel Bruna until he came to the diet at Augsburg. The council was still less satisfied with this order, for it feared to lose its jurisdiction over the Jews. It accordingly prepared to take decisive action in the matter. The accuser, Hans Vayol, was led on the stone bridge, where the executioner stood in readiness. He was informed that he must die, and admonished not to go into eternity with a lie on his lips. The hardened sinner maintained his accusations against the Jews in general, but confessed that the rabbi, Israel Bruna, was innocent of the charge of child-murder, and on receipt of another rescript from the emperor, Vayol was banished, and the rabbi released from prison. He was, however, compelled to take an oath that he would not revenge himself for his long sufferings. This poor, feeble graybeard--how could he have avenged himself?

At this juncture the news of the martyrdom of Simon of Trent reached Ratisbon, and added fuel to the fire. Bishop Henry was delighted to have an opportunity of persecuting the Jews with impunity in the interest of the faith. He had heard something of this child-murder on his journey to Rome. On his return, he urged the council to institute a rigid inquiry respecting the Jews accused by Wolfkan. The result of the extorted confessions was the imprisonment of the whole community. Sentinels stood on guard day and night at the four gates of the Jewry of Ratisbon, and permitted no one to enter or go out. The possessions of the whole community were confiscated by the commissioners and judges who took an inventory of everything. A horrible fate threatened the unhappy children of Israel.

This trial, which caused considerable attention in its day, proved quite as prejudicial to the citizens as to the Jews themselves. Immediately after the inquiry

began, several Jews of Ratisbon had betaken themselves to Bohemia and to the emperor, and tried by every means to save their unhappy brethren. They knew that to explain their righteous cause gold, and plenty of it, would be above all things necessary. For this reason several Bavarian rabbis assembled in a synod at Nuremberg, and decided that the Bavarian communities and every individual not absolutely impoverished should contribute a quota to make up the amount necessary to free the accused Jews of Ratisbon. When the safety of their brethren was in question, the Jews, however fond they might be of money, were by no means parsimonious. The intercession of the Bohemian nobles under whose protection several of the Ratisbon community had placed themselves led to no result. Far more efficacious were the golden arguments which the ambassadors of the community laid before Emperor Frederick and his advisers. It is only just to say that this usually feeble sovereign displayed considerable ability and firmness in this inquiry. He was so strongly convinced of the falsehood of the blood accusation against the Jews that he would not allow himself to be deceived by any trickery. He dispatched rescript after rescript to the council of Ratisbon, ordering the immediate release of the imprisoned Jews, the cessation of the durance of the community, and the restoration of their property. The council, through fear of the bishop and the duke, delayed the execution of the order, and the emperor became furious at the obstinacy of the citizens when news was brought to him that, in spite of the imperial command, they had already executed some of the Jews. He thereupon declared the city to have fallen under the ban of the empire on account of its obstinate disobedience, and summoned it to answer for its contumacy. At the same time he sent the imperial chancellor to deprive the city of penal jurisdiction and to threaten it with other severe penalties.

Frederick, as a rule weak, showed surprising firmness on this occasion. New and shameless charges were nevertheless brought by the clergy against the Jews. In Passau they were accused of having bought consecrated wafers from a Christian, and profaned them; whereupon certain marvels were said to have occurred. For this the bishop of Passau had a great number of Jews put to death, some "mercifully" by the sword, others at the stake, and others by means of red-hot pincers. In memory of this inhumanity and "to the glory of God," a new church was built near the scene of the atrocities. A Jew and a Jewess of Ratisbon were accused of complicity in this crime, and thrown into prison with the others. All the details were brought to the notice of the emperor in order to rouse his anger. He, however, maintained his conviction that the Jews of Ratisbon were innocent, and issued a new order to the effect that those in prison on the charge of profaning the host were neither to be tortured nor put to death, but to be treated like other prisoners. In vain the council sent deputy after deputy to the imperial court. Frederick roundly declared, "In justice and honor I neither can nor will permit these Jews to be slain, and the men of Ratisbon who have so long hardened themselves in their disobedience shall certainly not sit in judgment upon them."

Thus, after long resistance, the council was compelled to kiss the rod, and give a written promise to release the imprisoned Jews, and not to drive any out of the city on account of this trial. Further, the city was sentenced to pay a fine of 8,000 gulden into the imperial exchequer and to find bail in 10,000 gulden--which latter burden, strangely enough, the Jews had to bear. An appeal to the pope was out of the question, since experience had taught that "the papal court was even more greedy of gold than the imperial."

THE RATISBON COMMUNITY SET FREE

When the community of Ratisbon was informed of this conclusion of the affair, and of the conditions under which it could gain its freedom--by paying not only the sum imposed upon itself, but also the fine of the city and the costs of the proceedings--it refused. The delegates said that the total exceeded the possessions of the Jews, as they had been deprived, for three long years, of freedom and all opportunity of earning money. They preferred their present miserable state to becoming beggars. So they remained two years longer in durance, partly on account of lack of money, and partly by reason of the excessive bail demanded. They were finally set at liberty on taking an oath that they would not take revenge, nor convey their persons or their goods out of the city of Ratisbon.

All the Jews living in Swabia were expelled, doubtless in consequence of false accusations in connection with the child-murder of Trent. As late as in the eighteenth century, the shameless falsehood was repeated, and in many parts entailed upon the Jews the sacrifice of life and property.

IV. CHAPTER X

THE INQUISITION 1N SPAIN.

Jewish Blood in the Veins of the Spanish Nobility--The Marranos cling to Judaism and manifest Unconquerable Antipathy to Christianity-Ferdinand and Isabella--The Dominicans, Alfonso de Ojeda, Diego de Merle, and Pedro de Solis--The Catechism of the Marranos-A Polemical Work against the Catholic Church and Despotism gives a Powerful Impulse to the Inquisition-The Tribunal is established in 1480--Miguel Morillo and Juan de San Martin are the first Inquisitors--The Inquisition in Seville--The " Edict of Grace"--The Procession and the Auto-da-fe--The Numbers of the Accused and Condemned--Pope Sixtus IV and his Vacillating Policy with Regard to the Inquisition-The Inquisition under the first Inquisitor General, Thomas de Torquemada; its Constitutions--The Marranos of Aragon--They are charged with the Death of the Inquisitor

Arbues--Persecutions and Victims--Proceedings against two Bishops Favorable to the Jews,.De Avila and De Aranda.

1474-1483 C.E.

A JEWISH poet called Spain the " hell of the Jews;" and, in very deed, those foul fiends in monks' cowls, the inventors of the Holy Inquisition, made that lovely land an inferno. Every misery, every mortal pang, conceived only by the most extravagant imagination of poet; every horror that can thrill the heart of man to its lowest depths, these monsters in the garb of humility brought upon the Jews of the Hesperian Peninsula.

These Calibans also said, "'Burn but their books; for therein lies their power." The Dominicans wished to destroy not only the bodies, but the very soul and spirit of the Jews. Yet they were not able to quench the life of Judaism. They only succeeded in transforming the Spanish paradise into one vast dungeon, in which the king himself was not free. The inquisition, created by the begging friars, wounded the Jew deeply, yet not mortally.

His wounds are now almost healed; but Spain suffers still, perhaps beyond hope of cure, from the wounds dealt by the Inquisition. Ferdinand the Catholic and Isabella the Bigot, who, through the union of Aragon and Castile, laid the foundation for the greatness of Spain, prepared the way, at the same time, by the establishment of the Inquisition, for her decay and final ruin.

The new-Christians, who dwelt by hundreds and thousands throughout the kingdoms of Aragon and Castile, were so many thorns in monkish flesh. Many of them held high offices of state, and by means of their wealth wielded great and far-reaching influence. They were also related to many of the old nobility; indeed, there were few families of consequence who had not Jewish blood in their veins. They formed a third part of the townspeople, and were intelligent, industrious, and peaceful citizens. These Marranos, for the most part, had preserved their love for Judaism and their race in the depths of their hearts. As far as they could, they observed Jewish rites and customs, either from piety or from habit. Even those who, upon philosophical grounds, were indifferent to Judaism, were not less irreconcilably hostile to Christianity, which they were compelled to confess with their lips. Although they did not have their children circumcised, they washed the heads of the infants immediately after baptism. They were, therefore, rightly looked upon by the orthodox clergy either as Judaizing Christians, or as apostate heretics. They took no count of the origin of their conversion, which had been accomplished with fire and sword. They had received the sacrament of baptism, and this condemned them and their descendants to remain in the Christian faith, however hateful it might be to them. Rational legislation would have given them liberty to return to Judaism, and, in any case, to emigrate, in order to avoid scandal. But the spiritual powers were full of perversity. That which demands the freest exercise of the powers of the soul was to be brought about by brute force, to the greater glory of God!

During the lifetime of Don Henry IV the clerical members of the cortes of Medina del Campo had persistently advanced the proposal that a court of Inquisition be instituted to bring recusant or suspected Christians to trial, and inflict severe punishment with confiscation of goods. Unfortunately for the clericals, the king was by no means zealous for the faith or fond of persecution; and so this decision of the cortes, like many others, remained a dead letter. The Dominicans, however, promised themselves greater results under the new sovereigns-Queen Isabella, whose confessors had reduced her to spiritual slavery, and Don Ferdinand, who, by no means so superstitiously inclined, was quite ready to use religion as the cloak of his avarice. It is said that the confessor, Thomas de Torquemada, the incarnation of the hell-begotten Holy Inquisition, had extorted from the Infanta Isabella a vow that, when she came to the throne, she would devote herself to the extirpation of heresy, to the glory of God and the exaltation of the Catholic faith. She was now queen; "her throne was established: and her soul was sufficiently beclouded to believe that God had raised her solely to cleanse Spanish Christianity from the taint of Judaism."

The prior of a Dominican monastery, Alfonso de Ojeda, who had the ear of the royal consorts, made fearful representations to them as to the offenses of the new-Christians against the faith. Aided by two others of like mind, he strained every nerve to set the Inquisition in motion against the Marranos; and the papal nuncio in Spain, Nicolo France, supported the proposition of the monk for a tribunal to call them to account for their transgressions.

Without further consideration Don Ferdinand, seeing that his coffers would be filled with the

SIXTUS IV'S BULL

plunder of the accused, gave his assent to the scheme. The more scrupulous queen hesitated, and the royal pair decided to appeal to the pope for advice. The two Spanish ambassadors at the court of Rome, the brothers Francisco and Diego de Santillana, earnestly pressed the pope and the college of cardinals to grant the request of their sovereigns. Sixtus IV, from whom anything, good or bad, could be obtained for gold, immediately grasped the money-making aspect of the Holy Inquisition. In November, 1478, he issued a bull empowering the sovereigns to appoint inquisitors from among the clergy, with full authority to sit in judgment on all heretics, apostates, and their patrons, according to the laws and customs of the ancient Inquisition, sentence them, and -- most important point of all--confiscate their goods.

Isabella, who had been somewhat favorably influenced in behalf of the new-Christians, was not inclined to adopt rigorous measures to begin with. At her direction, the archbishop of Seville, Cardinal Mendoza, prepared a catechism in 1478 for the use of new-Christians, and issued it to the clergy of his diocese, in order that they might instruct the Marranos in the articles, the sacraments, and the usages of the Christian religion. The authors of this measure displayed strange simplicity in believing that the baptized Jews would allow an antipathy, which every day found new incitement, to be appeased by the dry statements of a catechism. The Marranos naturally remained in what the church considered their blindness; that is to say, in the purity of their monotheism and their adherence to tneir ancestral religion.

It happened that a Jew or a new-Christian grievously offended the sovereigns by the publication of a small work in which he exposed at once the idolatrous cult of the church and the despotic character of the government. Hereupon the queen became more and more inclined to assent to the proposals for the establishment of the bloody tribunal. The work made so strong an impression that the queen's father-confessor, in 1480, published a refutation by royal command. The attitude of the court became more and more hostile to new-Christians, and when the commission appointed by the sovereigns to inquire into the improvement or obstinacy of the Marranos reported that they were irreclaimable, it was authorized to frame the statute for the new tribunal. The commission was composed of the fanatical Dominican, Alfonso de Ojeda, and the two monks--one in mind and order--Pedro de Solis and Diego de Merle.

Had demons of nethermost hell conspired to torment innocent men to the last verge of endurance and to make their lives one ceaseless martyrdom, they could not have devised more perfect means than those which the three monks employed against their victims.

The statute was ratified by the sovereigns, and the tribunal of the Holy Inquisition was appointed on September 17th, 1480. It was composed of men well fitted to carry out the bloody decree: the Dominican Miguel Morillo, inquisitor in the province of Roussillon, and renowned as a converter of heretics by means of torture; Juan de San Martin; an assessor, the abbot Juan Ruez, and a procurator fiscal, Juan Lopez del Barco. These men were formally confirmed by Sixtus IV as judges in matters of faith, and of heretics and apostates. The tribunal was first organized for the city of Seville and its neighborhood, as this district stood immediately under royal jurisdiction, and, therefore, possessed no cortes, and because it contained a great many Marranos. Three weeks later the sovereigns issued a decree calling upon all officials to render the inquisitors every assistance in their power.

It is noteworthy that as soon as the creation of

THE INQUISITION AT SEVILLE.

the tribunal became known, the populace everywhere looked upon it with displeasure, as though suspicious that it might be caught in the net spread for the Marranos. While the cortes of Medina del Campo proposed the establishment of a court for new-Christians, the great popular assembly at Toledo in the same year--the first after the accession of Ferdinand and Isabella--maintained absolute silence on the question, as though it desired to have no share in the unholy work. The mayor and other officials of Seville proved so disinclined to assist the inquisitors that it was necessary to issue a second royal decree on December 27th, 1480, directing them to do so. The nobles, allied with the converted Jews either through blood or friendship, stood stoutly by them, and sought by every means to protect them against the new tribunal.

As soon as the new-Christians of Seville and the neighborhood received news of the establishment of the Inquisition, they held a meeting to consider means of turning aside the blow aimed at them. Several wealthy and respected men of Seville, Carmona and Utrera, among them Abulafia, the financial agent of the royal couple, prepared to do battle with their persecutors. They distributed money and weapons among the people, to enable them to defend themselves. An old man urged the conspirators to armed resistance; but the conspiracy was betrayed by the daughter of one of its members, and all fell into the hands of the tribunal. Others, who had collected their possessions, and fled to the province of Medina-Sidonia and Cadiz, under whose governors they hoped to receive protection against the threatened persecution, were deceived, for the Inquisition went to work with remorseless severity. As soon as it had taken up its quarters in the convent of St. Paul at Seville, on January 2d, 1481, it issued an edict to the governor of Cadiz and other officials to deliver up the Marranos and distrain their goods. Those who disobeyed were threatened not only with excommunication, but also with the punishment assigned, as sharers of their guilt, to all who showed sympathy to heretics--confiscation of goods and deprivation of office.

The Inquisition inspired so much terror that the nobility lost no time in imprisoning those to whom they had lately promised protection, and in sending them in custody to Seville. The number of these prisoners was so great that the tribunal was soon obliged to seek another building for its functions. It selected a castle in Triana, a suburb of Seville. On the gate of this house of blood were inscribed, in mockery of the Jews, certain verses selected from their Scriptures:--"Arise, God, judge Thy cause;" " Catch ye foxes for us," which plainly showed the utter heartlessness of their judges. Fugitives when caught were treated as convicted heretics. So early as the fourth day after the installation of the tribunal, it held its first sitting. Six Marranos who had either avowed their old religion before their judges, or made horrible confessions on the rack, were condemned and burnt alive. The tale of victims grew to such proportions that the city authorities set apart a special place as a permanent execution ground, which subsequently became infamous as the Quemadero, or place of burning. Four huge caricatures of prophets distinguished this spot, existing to the present day to the shame of Spain anti Christianity. For three hundred years the smoke of the burnt-offering of innocence ascended to heaven from this infernal spot.

With that mildness of mien which skillfully covers the wisdom and the venom of the serpent, Miguel Morillo and his coadjutors gave to the new-Christians guilty of relapse into Judaism a certain time in which to declare their remorse. Upon doing this they would receive absolution, and be permitted to retain their property. This was the Edict of Grace; but it was not wanting in threats for those who should permit the time of respite to elapse, and be denounced by others as backsliders. The full vigor of the canonical laws against heresy and apostasy would then be exercised against them. The credulous in crowds obeyed the summons. Contritely they appeared before the tribunal, lamented the awful guilt of their lapse into Judaism, and awaited absolution and permission to live in peace. But now the inquisitors imposed the condition that they declare by name, position, residence and other particulars all persons of their acquaintance whom they knew to be apostates. This declaration they were to substantiate on oath. In the name of God they were asked to become accusers and betrayers--the friend of his friend, the brother of his brother, and the son of his father. Terror, and the assurance that the betrayed should never know the names of their betrayers, loosed the tongues of the weakhearted, and the tribunal soon had a long list of heretics upon whom to carry out its bloody work.

Not only the hunted Marranos, every Spaniard was called upon by an edict of the inquisitors to become an informer. Under threat of excommunication every one was bound to give, within three days, a list of acquaintances guilty of Jewish heresy. It was a summons to the most hateful vices of mankind to become allies of the court: to malice, hatred and revenge, to sate themselves by treachery; to greed, to enrich itself; and to superstition, to gain salvation by betrayal.

And what were the signs of this heresy and apostasy? The Inquisition had published a very complete, practical guide on the subject, so that each informer might find good grounds for his denunciation. The following signs of heresy were set forth: if baptized Jews cherished hopes of a Messiah; if they held Moses to be as efficacious for salvation as Jesus; if they kept the Sabbath or a Jewish feast; if they had their children circumcised; if they observed the Jewish dietary laws; if they wore clean linen or better garments on the Sabbath, laid tablecloths, or lit no fire on this day, or if they went barefoot on the Day of Atonement, or asked pardon of each other. If a father laid his hands in blessing on his children without making the sign of the cross; if one said his prayers with face turned to the wall, or with motions of the head; or if he uttered a benediction (Baraha, Beracha) over the wine-cup, and passed it to those seated at the table with him, he was to be deemed recalcitrant. As a matter of course, neglect of the usages of the church was the strongest ground for suspicion and accusation. Again, if a new-Christian repeated a psalm without adding the Gloria; or if he ate meat on fast days; or if a Jewish woman did not go to church forty days after her lying-in ; or if parents gave their children Jewish names, the charge of heresy was held proved.

Even the most innocent actions, if they happened to coincide with Jewish usages, were regarded as signs of aggravated heresy. If anyone, for instance, on the Jewish Feast of Tabernacles accepted gifts from the table of Jews, or sent them; or if a new-born child was bathed in water in which gold coins and grains of corn had been placed; or if a dying man in his last moments turned his face to the wall--all such actions were held to be signs of heresy.

By such means unscrupulous people were given ample opportunity for denunciation, and the tribunal was enabled to accuse of heresy the most orthodox proselytes when it desired to destroy their influence or confiscate their property. Naturally the dungeons of the Inquisition were soon filled with Jewish heretics. Fully 15,000 were thrown into prison at the outset. The Christian priests of Moloch inaugurated

THE FIRST AUTO-DA-FE.

the first auto-da-fe, on January 6th, 1481, with a solemn procession, repeated innumerable times during the following three hundred years. The clergy in their gorgeous vestments and with crucifixes; the grandees in black robes with their banners and pennons; the unhappy victims in the hideous San Benito, short and clinging, painted with a red cross, and flames and figures of devils; the accompanying choir of a vast concourse--so the executioners with proud bearing and the victims in most miserable guise marched to the place of torment. Arrived there the inquisitors recited their sentence on the victims. To the horror of the scene was added the ghastly mockery that the tribunal did not execute the sentence of death, but left it to the secular judge ; for the church, though steeped to the lips in blood, was supposed not to desire the death of the sinner. The Jewish heretics were given to the flames forthwith, or, if penitent, they were first strangled. In the first auto-da-fe, at which the bishop, Alfonso de Ojeda, preached the inauguration sermon, only six Judaizing Christians were burnt. A few days later the conspirators of Carmona, Seville, and other towns, and three of the most wealthy and respected of the Marranos, among whom was Diego de Suson, the possessor of ten millions, and Abulafia, formerly a Talmudic scholar and a rabbi, were burnt to death. On the 26th of March seventeen victims suffered death by fire on the Quemadero. In the following month a yet greater number were burnt; and up to November of the same year 298 burnt-offerings gasped out their lives in flame and smoke in the single district of Seville. In the archbishopric of Cadiz no less than 2,000 Jewish heretics were burnt alive in the course of that year, most of them being wealthy or well-to-do, their possessions, of course, going to the royal exchequer. Not even death afforded a safeguard against the fury of the Holy Office. These ghouls of religion tore from their graves the corpses of proselytes who had died in heresy, burnt them, confiscated their possessions in the hands of their heirs, and condemned the latter to obscurity and poverty that they might never aspire to any honorable office. Here was a splendid field for the avarice of the king. When it was impossible to convict a wealthy heir, it was only necessary to establish proofs of a relapse to Judaism against his dead father, and then the property fell partly to the king, partly to the Holy Inquisition !

Many Marranos saved themselves by flight from the clutches of the merciless persecutors, and took refuge in the neighboring Moslem kingdom of Granada, in Portugal, Africa, Provence, or Italy. Those who reached Rome approached the papal court with bitter complaints about the savage and arbitrary proceedings of the Inquisition against themselves and their companions in misery. As the complainants did not come with empty hands, their cause usually obtained a ready hearing. On the 29th of January, 1482, the pope addressed a severe letter to Ferdinand and Isabella, censuring the conduct of the Inquisition in no measured terms. He stated that he had been assured that the proceedings of the tribunal were contrary to all forms of justice, that many were unjustly imprisoned, and subjected to fearful tortures. Innocent people had been denounced as heretics, and their property taken from their heirs. In this letter the pope admitted that he had issued the bull for the institution of the Inquisition without due consideration !

Sixtus further stated that, in strict justice, he ought to depose the inquisitors, De Morillo and San Martin; but out of consideration for their majesties he would allow them to remain in possession of their offices, only so long, however, as no further complaints were made against them. Should protests again be raised he would restore the inquisitorial office to the bishops, to whom it properly belonged. The pope refused the request of Don Ferdinand to institute in the other provinces of the united kingdom extraordinary tribunals for the trial of heretics.

But Don Ferdinand also knew how to apply the golden key to the papal cabinet, and obtained a bull sanctioning the establishment of the Inquisition in the provinces of Aragon. In this bull, dated February 11th, 1482, Sixtus appointed six monks and clerics as chief inquisitors, among them Thomas de Torquemada, general of the Dominicans of Avilo, a monk already infamous for his bloodthirsty fanaticism. In another letter, of the l7th of April, he invested these men with discretionary powers, in virtue of which they were able to dispense with certain forms of common law, the hearing of witnesses and the admission of pleaders for the defense. Thus were fresh victims brought to the stake.

In the kingdom of Aragon, however, where the nobility and the middle class had a weighty voice in public matters, the condemnation of Jewish heretics without formal trial raised such formidable opposition that Cardinal Borgia, afterwards the infamous Alexander VI, and the king himself, petitioned the pope for a modification of the conditions governing the practice of the tribunal. In a letter of the 10th of October, Sixtus excused himself from making any radical changes in consequence of the absence of the cardinals, who had fled from Rome in mortal fear of the plague. But he abrogated the conditions which too flagrantly violated the principles of common law; that is to say, he ordered that accuser and witnesses should be confronted with the accused, and that the process should be conducted in public.

The Inquisition also met with great opposition in Sicily, an appendage of the kingdom of Aragon. The people and even the authorities took the part of the new-Christians, and shielded them from the persecution of their bloodthirsty judges. Christians themselves openly charged that the victims were not executed out of zeal for the faith, but from insatiable greed which sought ceaseless confiscations. The bigoted Isabella was sorely troubled at having her pious desire to devote the proselytes to death thus evilly represented, and even the pope behaved as though it wounded him to the heart. (February, 1483)

Sixtus IV had the greatest interest in maintaining friendly relations with the Spanish court, and, therefore, made every concession with regard to the Inquisition. As it often happened that Christian proselytes condemned by the tribunal, who had succeeded in escaping to Rome, purchased absolution from the papal throne, with the infliction of only a light, private penance, the sovereigns saw that their efforts to purge the Christian faith by the extermination of Jewish proselytes, especially by the confiscation of their goods, were most unpleasantly thwarted. The court, therefore, insisted that the pope appoint a judge of appeals in Spain itself, so that the rulings of the Inquisition might not be reversed in foreign countries, where all kinds of unfavorable influences might be brought to bear. The pope agreed to this proposition, and appointed Inigo Manrique chief judge of appeals in cases in which the condemned moved for a revision of their trial. This measure was, however, of very doubtful benefit to the unfortunate culprits, for upon what ground could they base their appeal when the trial had been conducted in secret, and neither accuser nor witnesses were known to them? It is altogether likely, too, that the tribunal did not leave them very much time to institute proceedings for the revision of the verdict. Between the passing of the sentence and the last act of the auto-da-fe only a very short interval elapsed.

DISQUALIFICATION OF NEW-CHRISTIAN BISHOPS.

Another measure of the Spanish court, calculated to deprive the accused of the last hope of acquittal, was approved by the pope. Baptized Jews, or new-Christians descended from them, frequently held bishoprics, and were naturally favorably inclined to their unfortunate and persecuted brethren in race. At the request of the Spanish court, the pope issued a bull decreeing that no bishop, vicar, or member of the upper clergy descended from a Jewish family, whether paternally or maternally, should sit as a judge in any court for the trial of heretics. From this prohibition there was only a step to the condemnation of clergy of Jewish blood to the stake

Had his Holiness, Sixtus IV, not been infamous as a monster of depravity, sensuality and unscrupulousness, who appointed boys to bishoprics and the cardinal dignity, and who bestowed no clerical office without payment--as his contemporary, Infessura, the chancellor of Rome, has recorded--his conduct with regard to the Holy Inquisition would have been sufficient to brand him with immortal infamy. Within a short period he published the most contradictory decisions, and did not take the trouble to veil his inconsistency with the most flimsy pretense. Scarcely had he proclaimed the utmost rigors against Judaizing heretics, and appointed a tribunal of appeals, than he partly abrogated these bulls, and issued another prescribing milder proceedings to the Inquisition, only to alter this policy in its turn.

The hated Marranos, among them the high-spirited Juan de Seville, had exerted themselves to procure from the papal court a decree to the effect that those who had undergone private penance in Rome should not be submitted to the oppression and persecution of the avaricious king and his bloodthirsty inquisitors, but should be regarded and treated as orthodox Christians. At first the pope consented, and issued a bull on August 2d, 1483, "to be held in eternal remembrance and as guide for the future," in which he especially directed that rigor be tempered with mercy in dealing with the new-Christians, seeing that the severity of the Inquisition had overstepped the bounds of justice. The bull enacted that all new-Christian who had confessed their remorse to the confessor-general in Rome, and had been assigned a penance, should not be pursued by the Inquisition, and should have their trials suppressed. It exhorted the king and queen, to remember that in mercy and kindness alone may man resemble God, and that, therefore, they might in this follow in the steps of Jesus, whose peculiar attribute it was to show mercy and to pardon. The pope permitted this bull to be copied indefinitely, each copy to have the authority of the original, in order that the papal attitude with regard to new-Christians might be made universally known. Sixtus concluded with the statement that he issued this bull entirely of his own motion, not in obedience to external influence, although it was well known in high circles that it had been bought with new-Christian gold. The sovereigns, however, would have nothing to do with mercy or forbearance; they desired the death of the culprits and the possession of their property. Nor was the pope really inclined to mild measures. A few days later, on August 13th, he recalled this

bull, excusing himself to the king for its tenor, and said that it had been issued in too great haste. Such was the consistency and infallibility of his Holiness, Pope Sixtus IV !

In vain Don Juan de Seville, who had procured the promulgation of the favorable bull, endeavored to circulate it. He failed to find any clerical official in Spain to copy and confirm it. He, therefore, applied to the Portuguese archbishop of Evora, who caused it to be copied by his notary and recognized as authentic. The Inquisition, however, was extremely suspicious of those who had sought and obtained indulgences at Rome, and Don Juan de Seville and his companions fell at length into its hands, and were severely punished.

Terrible though the tribunal had hitherto been; though many thousands of compulsory proselytes and their descendants, during its three short years of existence, had been cast Into the flames, left to rot in its dungeons, driven from their country, or reduced to beggary, it was child's play compared with what it became when placed under the control of a priest whose heart was closed to every sentiment of mercy, whose lips breathed only death and destruction, and who united the savagery of the hyena with the venom of the snake. Until now the Inquisition had been confined to southern Spain, to the districts of Seville and Cadiz, and the Christian province of Andalusia. In the remaining provinces of

Spain it had hitherto been unable to get a footing, in consequence of the resistance offered to its introduction by the cortes. Through the opposition of the people, the wicked will of the inquisitors Morillo and Juan de San Martin had remained inoperative; their uplifted arm was paralyzed by innumerable difficulties. If here and there a few courts were held in the remaining districts of Spain, they were isolated and without organization, and were thus unable to furnish each other with victims. King Ferdinand thus had not yet collected treasure enough, nor had the pious Isabella beheld a sufficient number of new-Christians writhing in the flames. For their joint satisfaction they now persuaded the pope to appoint an inquisitor-general who should constitute, direct, and supervise the several courts, that none of the suspected Marranos might avoid their fate, and that the opposition of the populace might be broken down by every species of terrorism. In cold blood, and with little interest even for the faith itself, the pope assented; and in May, 1483, appointed the Dominican, Thomas de Torquemada, hitherto prior of a monastery in Segovia, inquisitor-general of Spain. There are certain men who are the embodiment of good or evil sentiments, opinions and principles, and fully illustrate their extremist consequences. Torquemada was the incarnation of the Holy Inquisition with all its devilish malice, its heartless severity, its bloodthirsty ferocity.

TRIBUNALS IN THE GREAT TOWNS.

The inscription which the poet Dante placed upon the portal of Hell--

"All hope abandon, ye who enter here ! "

would have been even more suitable to the dungeons of the Holy Inquisition, which the cruel energy of Torquemada now established in nearly all the great towns of Spain. He at once instituted three new tribunals in Cordova,Jaen and Villareal (Ciudad Real), and, later on, one in Toledo, the capital of southern Spain. The offices of the Inquisition were entirely tilled by him with hypocritical and fanatical Dominicans, whom he made the tools of his will, so that they worked like an organism with a single head, ready at his word to perpetrate the most hideous barbarities with a composure that cannibals might have envied. In those days Spain was filled with the putrefaction of the dungeon, the stench of corpses, and the crackling of the flames in which were burning innocent Jews, forced into a faith the falsity of which was demonstrated by every action of the servants of the church. A wail of misery piercing bone and marrow went through that lovely land; but their Catholic majesties paralyzed the arm of every man prompted by mercy to put a stop to the butchery. At the court itself there sat a commission on the affairs of Jewish Christians, of which the inquisitor-general held the presidency.

Don Ferdinand wished to perpetuate the jurisdiction of the Inquisition in his hereditary lands, in order to till his purse with the spoils of the new-Christians settled there. During the assembly of the cortes at Tarazona, in April, 1484, he laid his plans before his privy council, and canceled the ancient privileges of the country, which had existed from the earliest times, and which provided that no native of Aragon, whatever his crime, should suffer confiscation of his property. The inquisitor-general accordingly appointed for the archbishopric of Saragossa two inquisitors who rivaled himself in bloodthirsty fanaticism, the canon, Pedro Arbues de Epila, and the Dominican, Gaspard Juglar. A royal ordinance was now issued to all officials and nobles, directing them to give every assistance to the inquisitors. The grand justiciary of Aragon, though of Jewish origin, and other dignitaries, were obliged to take an oath that they would spare no efforts to exterminate the culprits condemned by the tribunal.

Torquemada, the very soul of the Inquisition, now decided to publish a code for the guidance of the judges, so that the net might be drawn as closely as possible round his victims. The whole body of inquisitors was assembled to consider this design, and, under the title of "Constitutions," issued, on October 29th, 1484, a code of laws, calculated to inspire the utmost horror had no more been done than commit them to paper It has been asserted that the monkish inquisitors merely copied the anti-Jewish enactments of the councils under the Visigothic kings. It is true that the decrees of Receswinth threatened with death, by fire or stoning, all new-Christians convicted of adherence to Jewish customs. The comparison is, nevertheless, incorrect. For not the enactments against heresy, but their enforcement, distinguishes the "Constitutions" of the Inquisition as the most hideous ever fashioned by human wickedness. It was as though the most malicious demons had taken counsel to discover how they might bring innocent human beings to destruction.

One decree ordained a respite of thirty days for those who of their own free will would tender confession

of their relapse to Judaism. These were to be spared all punishment and confiscation of goods with the exception of a moderate fine. They were, however, compelled to put their confession into writing, to give exact answers to all questions put to them, and especially to betray their fellow-offenders, and even those whom they only suspected of Judaizing tendencies. Those who confessed after the expiration of the time of respite were to lose all their property, even that which they had possessed at the time of their falling away from Christianity, and though it had passed into other hands. Only new-Christians under twenty years old were exempted from loss of property in the event of later confessions; but they were compelled to bear a mark of infamy composed of flaming crosses, the San Benito, upon their clothing, and to take part in the processions and attend high mass in this guise. Those whose remorse awakened after the appointed day were indeed to receive indulgence, but they were to remain branded for life. Neither they nor their descendants were ever to hold any public office, nor to wear any garment embroidered with gold, silver or pearls, or made of silk or fine wool, and they were condemned to bear the "fiery cross " for ever. Should the inquisitors discover that the confession of a penitent was insincere, it was their duty to deny him absolution, to treat him as a recalcitrant, and to consign him to the flames. If a penitent made only a partial confession of his sins, he, too, was condemned to death. The evidence against a Judaizing Christian might, when not otherwise convenient, be taken through other persons. It was not necessary to place this testimony before the accused in full detail, but merely as an abstract. If, in spite of the evidence laid before him, he maintained that he had never relapsed into Judaism, he was condemned to the flames as impenitent. Inconclusive proofs of relapse brought against a Marrano stretched him upon the rack; in case he confessed under torture, he was submitted to a second trial. If he then adhered to what he had confessed under torture he was condemned; if he denied it, he underwent the torture again. In those cases in which an accused person failed to answer to the summons issued against him, he was condemned as a contumacious heretic, i. e., his property was confiscated.

In the face of such proceedings--the parody of a trial-and the pre-determination on the part of the judge to consider the accused guilty, how was it possible for any Marrano to prove his innocence! The dungeon and the rack frequently made the accused so indifferent to their fate and so weary of life that they made confessions as to themselves, their friends and even their nearest relatives which appeared to vindicate the necessity for the Inquisition. The trial of every new-Christian involved others in apparent guilt, and brought new examinations and new accusations in its train, thus furnishing an ever-increasing number of victims to the Holy Office.

The towns of the kingdoms of Aragon and Valencia had from the first manifested the greatest displeasure at the introduction of the Inquisition. Up to this period they had been less despotically governed than Castile, and were exceedingly jealous of their freedom. Above everything the Aragonese valued, as the apple of their eye, the privilege which forbade the confiscation of goods even on account of the gravest offenses. Now the officers of the Inquisition were to be invested with unlimited power over life and property. The new-Christians, who held high offices and influential positions in Aragon, were naturally eager to foment and increase the discontent. In Teruel and Valencia, in 1485, disastrous popular risings broke out against the Inquisition, and were quelled only after great bloodshed.

CONSPIRACY AGAINST ARBUES.

The Marranos and those of Jewish descent did not, however, surrender their project of paralyzing the Inquisition in Aragon. Some of the highest dignitaries of state were numbered among them ; as, for example, Luis Gonzalez, royal secretary of state for Aragon; Alfonso de Caballeria, the vice-chancellor; his brother, the king's major-domo; Philip Clemente, chief notary; and such high hidalgos as the Counts of Aranda, together with many knights, among whom were the valiant Juan de Abadia, whose sister was burnt for heresy, and Juan Perez Sanchez whose brothers were at court.

As soon as the first victims fell under the Inquisition in Saragossa, influential new-Christians brought pressure to bear upon the cortes to induce them to protest, both to the king and to the pope, against the introduction of the tribunal into Aragon. Commissioners were sent to the royal and papal courts to effect in person the repeal of the ordinances. They expected but little trouble in Rome, for there everything was to be had for money. With the king it seemed to be a matter of much greater difficulty. Ferdinand remained obstinately fixed in the resolution to exterminate the Jewish Christians by means of the Inquisition, and to acquire their property. When the commissioners sent news to their friends in Aragon of the failure of their efforts, Perez Sanchez conceived a plot to remove Pedro Arbues, chief inquisitor for Aragon, in order to cripple the activity of the Inquisition by terrorism, and to force the king to give way. He imparted his project to his friends, and many bound themselves to stand by him. In order to win over the entire body of new-Christians, and to induce them to stand firmly together, the leaders of the conspiracy laid them under contribution for the expenses of carrying out the project. A hidalgo, Blasco de Alagon, collected the money, and Juan de Abadia undertook to hire the assassins, and to see that the death of Arbues was achieved. This conspiracy was joined by many distinguished persons of Jewish descent in Saragossa, Tarazona, Calatayud, Huesca and Barbastro.

Juan de Abadia procured two trustworthy men, Juan de Esperaindo and Vidal de Uranso, with four assistants, to accomplish the death of the inquisitor Arbues. The intended victim appears to have suspected the plot, for he protected his body with a shirt of mail and his head with a species of steel cap. Before daybreak on the 15th of September, 1485, as he was entering the church with a lantern to hear early mass, the conspirators followed him. As soon as he had fallen on his knees, Esperaindo struck him on the arm with his sword, while Vidal wounded him in the neck. He was borne out of the church bathed in blood, and died two days later. The conspirators took instant flight. As soon as the news of the attack on the chief inquisitor spread in Saragossa it produced a violent reaction. The orthodox Christians assembled in crowds crying in tones of fury: "To the flames with the Jew-Christians! They have murdered the chief inquisitor!" The Marranos would have been massacred in a body there and then, had not the royal bastard, the youthful Archbishop Alfonso of Aragon, mounted his horse, and restrained the crowd by an armed force, promising them the fullest satisfaction by the severe punishment of the guilty persons and their accomplices.

King Ferdinand made good use of the unfortunate conspiracy in the establishment of the Inquisition in Aragon. The sovereigns carried public mourning for the murdered Arbues to the verge of idolatry. A statue was consecrated to his memory, in honor of his services to religion and the extermination of Jewish heretics. The Dominicans were by no means displeased at the death of the chief inquisitor. They were, in fact, in need of a martyr

PUNISHMENT OF THE CONSPIRATORS.

to enable them to surround their tribunal of blood with a halo of glory. They used every effort to raise Pedro Arbues to the rank of saint or Christian demi-god. It was not long before they fabricated a divine communication from the sainted heretic-slayer, in which he exhorted all the world to support and carry forward the Holy Inquisition, and soothed the scruples of the members of the tribunal, on account of the enormous number of men they had consigned to the flames, by assuring them that the most honorable places in heaven awaited them as the reward of their pious efforts.

The unsuccessful conspiracy of the Marranos in Saragossa afforded a vast number of fresh victims. A few of the conspirators made full confession, and so the inquisitors soon had a complete list of the culprits. These were pursued with redoubled vigor as Judaizing heretics and enemies of the Holy Office. Those who had borne a leading part in the conspiracy, as soon as they fell into the hands of their judges, were dragged through the streets of Saragossa, their hands were hewn off; and they were then hanged. Juan de Abadia escaped this dishonorable fate by killing himself in prison. More than two hundred Jewish Christians were burnt as accomplices, a yet greater number were condemned to perpetual imprisonment, among them a high dignitary of the Metropolitan Church of Saragossa, and not a few women of gentle birth. Francisco de Sante-Fe also died at the stake. Even those who had given shelter to the conspirators for a brief period during their flight were compelled to attend an auto-da-fe: as penitents, and lost their civil rights. How far the inhumanity of the persecutors went is especially shown by one of the punishments inflicted. A conspirator, Gaspard de Santa Cruz, had been successful in making his escape to Toulouse, and there died in peace. The Inquisition, not content with burning him in effigy, laid hands upon his son as an accomplice in his father's flight, and condemned him to travel to Toulouse to communicate his sentence to the Dominicans of that city, and to desire them to exhume the body of his father and burn it. The weak son performed his disgraceful mission, and brought back to Saragossa the certificate of the Dominicans to the effect that the corpse of the father had been dishonored on the prayer of the son.

Certain towns of northern Spain, such as Lerida and Barcelona, still obstinately resisted the introduction of the Inquisition. Their resistance proved vain. The iron will of Fernando and the bloodthirsty fanaticism of Torquemada overcame every obstacle, and the papal court was obliged to give its assent to every proposal. From that time forth the number of victims continued to increase. On the 12th of February, 1486, an auto-da-fe was celebrated in Toledo with 750 human burnt-offerings, while on the 2d of April in the same year, 900 victims were offered up, and on the 7th of May, 750· On the 16th of August twenty-five Jewish heretics were burnt alive in Toledo; on the following day two priests suffered; and on the 10th of December 950 persons were condemned to shameful public penance. In the following year, when the Inquisition was established in Barcelona and on the island of Majorca, two hundred Marranos suffered death by fire in these places alone. A Jew of that time, Isaac Arama, writes on this subject as follows: "In these days the smoke of the martyr's pyre rises unceasingly to heaven in all the Spanish kingdoms and the isles. One-third of the Marranos have perished in the flames, another third wander homeless over the earth seeking where they may hide themselves, and the remainder live in perpetual terror of a trial." So the tale of victims grew from year to year under the eleven tribunals which transformed the fair land of Spain into a blazing Tophet,

whose flames soon reached and devoured the Christians themselves.

The pitiless persecution of the new-Christians had its origin perhaps even more in the racial hatred of the pure-blooded Spaniards towards the children of Judah than in religious fanaticism. Persons of Jewish descent, whom it was impossible justly to accuse of heresy, were included in the accusations simply because they held high offices. They were not permitted to enjoy any dignity or to exercise any influence in the country. The inquisitor-general, Torquemada, even laid hands upon two bishops of Jewish blood, De Avila and De Aranda, so that, if it were impossible to consign them to the ffames, he might at least expel them from their sees.

IV. CHAPTER XI.

EXPULSION OF THE JEWS FROM SPAIN.

Friendship of Marranos and Jews--Torquemada demands of the Rabbis of Toledo the Denunciation of Marranos--Judah Ibn Verga-Jewish Courtiers under Ferdinand and Isabella--Isaac Abrabanel: his History and Writings--The Jews of Portugal under Alfonso V-The Ibn-Yachya Brothers-Abrabanel's Flight from Portugal to Spain--The Jews of Granada: Isaac Hamon--Edict of Banishment promulgated by Ferdinand and Isabella--Its Consequences-Departure from Spain--Number of the Exiles--Decline in the Prosperity of Spain after the Banishment of the Jews--Transformation of Synagogues and Schools into Churches and Monasteries--The Inquisition and the Marranos-Deza, the Successor of Torquemada.

1483-1492 C.E.

THE monster of the Inquisition, having poured out its wrath on the new-Christians, now stretched its arms over the Jews, and delivered them to a miserable fate. The connection between the Jews and the Marranos was too close for the former not to be made to participate in the misfortunes of the latter. They were in intimate relations with each other, were bound to each other by close, brotherly ties. The Jews experienced heartfelt pity for their unfortunate brethren, so unwillingly wearing the mask of Christianity, and strove to keep them in touch with the Jewish community. They instructed Christian-born Marranos in the rites of Judaism, held secret meetings with them for prayer, furnished them with religious books and wntlngs, kept them informed of the occurrence of fasts and festivals, supplied them at Easter with unleavened bread, and throughout the year with meat prepared according to their own ritual, and circumcised their new-born sons. In Seville, in fact in the whole of Andalusia, there were countless new-Christians, baptlzed at the

time of the furious attack upon the Jews by Ferdinand Martinez, and later during the persecution of 1391, so that it offered a good field for the activity of Jews who were endeavoring to bring back turncoat brethren into the ranks of Judaism.

The fiendish Torquemada strove by every possible means to destroy these ties. As soon as he had become grand inquisitor, he issued a command that Marranos should present themselves for confession, ordered the rabbis of Toledo to be convened, and exacted from them an oath that they would inform against new-Christians who observed Jewish rites and ceremonies, and would excommunicate Jews who refused to become witnesses against their own people. They were threatened with heavy punishment if they refused to take this oath (1485)· What a tragical struggle for the rabbis of Toledo ! They themselves were to lend a hand to wrench their faithful brethren from Judaism, and deliver them over to Christianity, or, rather, to the stake ! Surely, they could not be brought to this, and preferred to suffer punishment! Judah Ibn-Verga, ordered by the inquisitors to deliver over pseudo-Christians who secretly clung to Judaism, chose to leave his native Seville, and fled to Lisbon, where he eventually died a martyr's death. Since the inquisitors could not attain their ends through Jews, who, despite all measures, continued their secret intercourse with new-Christians, they urged the king and queen to issue a mandate for the partial expulsion of the Jews from Andalusia, especially from Seville.

The Castilian and Aragonese Jews might have known, from these sad events, that their sojourn could not be of long duration; but they loved Spain too dearly to part from her except under compulsion. Besides, the king and queen often protected them from unfair treatment. When they removed to special Jewish quarters, Ferdinand and Isabella were at great pains to shield them from annoyance and chicanery. Moreover, under the rule of these Catholic sovereigns there were Jewish tithe and tax collectors, and, finally, the Jews relied upon the fact that they were indispensable to the Christians. The sick preferred to seek advice with Jewish physicians, the lower classes consulted Jews on legal questions, and even asked them to read the letters or documents which they received from the clergy. In addition to all this, it happened that, at the time when Torquemada was casting his snares over the Moors and Jews, the celebrated Abrabanel received an important post at the court of Castile, and enjoyed unlimited confidence. Under his protection the Spanish Jews hoped to be able to defy the fury

ISAAC ABRABANEL.

of the venomous Dominicans. Abrabanel's favored position at court, the geniality of his character, his affection for the Hebrew race, his love of learning, and his tried wisdom, brought back the time of Samuel Nagrela, and lulled the Jews with false hopes.

Don Isaac Pen Judah Abrabanel (born in Lisbon 1437, died in Venice 1509) worthily closes the list of Jewish statesmen in Spain who, beginning with Chasdai Ibn-Shaprut, used their names and positions to protect the interests of their race. In his noble-mindedness, his contemporaries saw proofs of Abrabanel's descent from the royal house of David, a distinction on which the Abrabanels prided themselves, and which was generally conceded to them. His grandfather, Samuel Abrabanel, who, during the persecution of 1391, but probably only for a short time, lived as a Christian, was a large-hearted, generous man, who supported Jewish learning and its votaries. His father, Judah, treasurer to a Portuguese prince, was wealthy and benevolent. Isaac Abrabanel was precocious, of clear understanding, but sober-minded, without imagination and without depth. The realities of life, present conditions and events, he grasped with unerring tact; but what was distant, less obvious to ordinary perceptions, lay veiled in a mist which he was unable to penetrate or dispel. The origin of Judaism, its splendid antiquity, and its conception of God were favorite themes with Abrabanel from his youth upward, and when still quite a young man he published a treatise setting forth the providence of God and its special relation to Israel. Philosophical conceptions were, however, acquired, not innate with him; he had no ability to solve metaphysical questions. On the other hand, he was a solid man of business, who thoroughly understood finance and affairs of state. The reigning king of Portugal, Don Alfonso V, an intelligent, genial, amiable ruler, was able to appreciate Abrabanel's talents; he summoned him to his court, confided to him the conduct of his financial affairs, and consulted him on all important state questions. His noble disposition, his sincerely devout spirit, his modesty, far removed from arrogance, and his unselfish prudence, secured for him at court, and far outside its circle, the esteem and affection of Christian grandees. Abrabanel stood in friendly intimacy with the powerful, but mild and beneficent Duke Ferdinand of Braganza, lord of fifty towns, boroughs, castles, and fortresses, and able to bring 10,000 foot-soldiers and 3,000 cavalry into the field, as also with his brothers, the Marquis of Montemar, Constable of Portugal, and the Count of Faro, who lived together in fraternal affection. With the learned John Sezira, who was held in high consideration at court, and was a warm patron of the Jews, he enjoyed close friendship. Abrabanel thus describes his happy life at the court of King Alfonso:

> *"Tranquilly I lived in my inherited house in fair Lisbon. God had given me blessings, riches and honor. I had built myself stately*

buildings and chambers. My house was the meeting-place of the learned and the wise. I was a favorite in the palace of Alfonso, a mighty and upright king, under whom the Jews enjoyed freedom and prosperity. I was close to him, was his support, and while he lived I frequented his palace."

Alfonso's reign was the end of the golden time for the Jews of the Pyrenean Peninsula. Although in his time the Portuguese code of laws (Ordenacoens de Alfonso V), containing Byzantine elements and canonical restrictions for the Jews, was completed, it must be remembered that, on the one hand, the king, who was a minor, had had no share in framing them, and, on the other, the hateful laws were not carried out. In his time the Jews in Portugal bore no badge, but rode on richly caparisoned horses and mules, wore the costume of the country, long coats, fine hoods and silken vests, and carried gilded swords so that they could not be distinguished

from Christians. The greater number of the taxfarmers (Rendeiros) in Portugal were Jews. Princes of the church even appointed Jewish receivers of church taxes, at which the cortes of Lisbon raised complaint. The independence of the Jewish population under the chief rabbi and the seven provincial rabbis was protected in Alfonso's reign, and included in the code. This code conceded to Jews the right to print their public documents in Hebrew, instead of in Portuguese as hitherto commanded.

Abrabanel was not the only Jewish favorite at Alfonso's court. Two brothers Ibn-Yachya Negro also frequented the court of Lisbon. They were sons of a certain Don David, who had recommended them not to invest their rich inheritance in real estate, for he saw that banishment was in store for the Portuguese Jews.

As long as Isaac Abrabanel enjoyed the king's favor, he was as a "shield and a wall for his race, and delivered the sufferers from their oppressors, healed differences, and kept fierce lions at bay," as described by his poetical son, Judah Leon. He who had a warm heart for all afflicted, and was father to the orphan and consoler to the sorrowing, felt yet deeper compassion for the unfortunate of his own people. When Alfonso conquered the port of Arzilla, in Africa, the victors brought with them, among many thousand captive Moors, 250 Jews, who were sold as slaves throughout the kingdom. That Jews and Jewesses should be doomed to the miseries of slavery was unendurable to Abrabanel's heart. At his summons a committee of twelve representatives of the Lisbon community was formed, and collected funds; then, with a colleague, he traveled over the whole country and redeemed the Jewish slaves, often at a high price, The ransomed Jews and Jewesses, adults and children, were clothed, lodged, and maintained until they had learned the language of the country, and were able to support themselves.

When King Alfonso sent an embassy to Pope Sixtus IV to congratulate him upon his accession to the throne, and to send him tidings of his victory over the Moors in Africa, Doctor John Sezira was one of the ambassadors. One in heart and soul with Abrabanel, and friendly to the Jews, he promised to speak to the pope in their favor and behalf. Abrabanel begged his Italian friend, Yechiel of Pisa, to receive John Sezira with a friendly welcome, to place himself entirely at his disposal, and convey to him, and to the chief ambassador, Lopes de Almeida, how gratified the Italian Jews were to hear of King Alfonso's favor to the Jews in his country, so that the king and his courtiers might feel flattered. Thus Abrabanel did everything in his power for the good of his brethren in faith and race.

In the midst of prosperity, enjoyed with his gracious and cultured wife and three fine sons, Judah Leon, Isaac and Samuel, he was disturbed by the turn of affairs in Portugal. His patron, Alfonso V, died, and was succeeded by Don Joao II (1481-1495), a man in every way unlike his father--stronger of will, less kindly, and full of dissimulation. He had been crowned in his father's lifetime, and was not rejoiced when Alfonso, believed to be dead, suddenly re-appeared in Portugal. Joao II followed the tactics of his unscrupulous contemporary, Louis XI of France, in the endeavor to rid himself of the Portuguese grandees in order to create an absolute monarchy. His first victim was to be Duke Ferdinand of Braganza, of royal blood, almost as powerful and as highly considered as himself, and better beloved. Don Joao II was anxious to clear from his path this duke and his brothers, against whom he had a personal grudge. While flattering the Duke of Braganza, he had a letter set up against him, accusing him of a secret, traitorous understanding with the Spanish sovereigns, the truth of which has not to this day been satisfactorily ascertained. He arrested

him with a Judas kiss, caused him to be tried as a traitor to his country, sent him to the block, and took possession of his estates and wealth (June, 1483)· His brothers were forced to fly to avoid a like fate. Inasmuch as Isaac Abrabanel had lived in friendly relations with the Duke of Braganza and his brothers, King Joao chose to suspect him of having been implicated in the recent conspiracies. Enemies of the Jewish statesman did their best to strengthen these suspicions. The king sent a command for him to appear before him. Not suspecting any evil, Abrabanel was about to obey, when an unknown friend appeared, told him his life was in danger, and counseled him to hasty flight. Warned by the fate of the Duke of Braganza, Abrabanel followed the advice, and fled to Spain. The king sent mounted soldiery after him, but they could not overtake him, and he reached the Spanish border in safety. In a humble but manly letter he declared his innocence of the crime, and also the innocence of the Duke of Braganza. The suspicious tyrant gave no credence to the letter of defense, but caused Abrabanel's property to be confiscated, as also that of his son, Judah Leon, who was already following the profession of a physician. His wife and children, however, he permitted to remove to Castile.

In the city of Toledo, where he found refuge, Isaac Abrabanel was honorably received by the Jews, especially by the cultured. A circle of learned men and disciples gathered round the famous, innocently persecuted Jewish statesman. With the rabbi, Isaac Aboab, and with the chief tithe-collector, Abraham Senior, he formed a close friendship. The latter, it seems, at once took him into partnership in the collection of taxes. Abrabanel's conscience pricked him for having neglected the study of the-law in following state affairs and mammon, and he attributed his misfortunes to the just punishment 9flısaven. He at once began to write, at the earnest entreaty of his new friends, an exposition of the books of the earlier prophets, hitherto, on account of their apparent simplicity, neglected by commentators. As he had given thought to them before, he soon completed the work. Certainly, no one was better qualified than Abrabanel to expound historical biblical literature. In addition to knowledge of languages, he had experience of the world, and the insight into political problems and complications necessary for unraveling the Israelitish records.

He had the advantage over other expositors in using the Christian exegetical writings of Jerome, Nicholas de Lyra, and the baptized Paul of Burgos, and taking from them what was most valuable. Abrabanel, therefore, in these commentaries, shed light upon many obscure passages. They are conceived in a scholarly style, arranged systematically, and before each book appear a comprehensible preface and a table of contents, an arrangement copied from Christian commentators, and adroitly turned to account by him. Had Abrabanel not been so diffuse in style, and not had the habit of introducing each Scriptural chapter with superfluous questions, his dissertations would have been, or, at all events, would have deserved to be, more popular. Nor should he have gone beyond his province into philosophical inquiry. Abrabanel accepted the orthodox point of view of Nachmani and Chasdai, merely supplementing them with commonplaces of his own. He was not tolerant enough to listen to a liberal view of Judaism and its doctrines, and accused the works of Albalag and Narboni of heresy, classing these inquirers with the unprincipled apostate, Abner-Alfonso, of Valladolid. He was no better pleased with Levi ben Gerson, because he had resorted to philosophical interpretations in many cases, and did not accept miracles unconditionally. Like the strictly orthodox Jews of his day, such as Joseph

Jaabez, he was persuaded that the humiliations and persecutions suffered by the Jews of Spain were due to their heresy. Yet, did German Jews, wholly untouched by heretical philosophy, suffer less than their brethren in Spain? Only a brief time was granted to Abrabanel to pursue his favorite study; the author was once more compelled to become a statesman. When about to delineate Judean and Israelite monarchs, he was summoned to the court of Ferdinand and Isabella to be entrusted with the care of their finances. The revenues seem to have prospered under his management, and during his eight years of office (March, 1484-March, 1492) nothing went wrong with them. He was very useful to the royal pair by reason of his wisdom and prudent counsel. Abrabanel himself relates that he grew rich in the king's service, and bought himself land and estates, and that from the court and the highest grandees he received great consideration and honor. He must have been indispensable, seeing that the Catholic sovereigns, under the very eyes of the malignant Torquemada, and in spite of canonical decrees and all the resolutions repeatedly laid down by the cortes forbidding Jews to hold office in the government, were compelled to entrust this Jewish minister of finance with the mainspring of political life ! How many services Abrabanel did for his own people during his time of office, grateful memory could not preserve by reason of the storm of misfortunes which broke upon the Jews later; but in Castile, as he had been in Portugal, he was as a wall of protection to them. Lying and fearful accusations from their bitter foes, the Dominicans, were not wanting. At one time it was said that the Jews had shown disrespect to some cross;at another, that in the town of La Guardia they had stolen and crucified a Christian child. From this tissue of lies, Torquemada fabricated a case against the Jews, and condemned the supposed criminals to the stake. In Valencia they were declared to have made a similar attempt, but to have been interrupted in the deed (1488--1490). That the Castilian Jews did not suffer extinction for the succor they afforded the unfortunate Marranos, was certainly owing to Abrabanel.

Meantime began the war with Granada, so disastrous for the Moors and Jews, which lasted with intervals for ten years (1481--1491)· To this the Jews had to contribute. A heavy impost was laid upon the community (Alfarda--Strangers' Tax), on which the royal treasurer, Villaris, insisted with the utmost strictness. The Jews were, so to say, made to bring the fagots to their own funeral pyre, and the people, adding insult to injury, mocked them. In the province of Granada, which by pride had brought about its own fall, there were many Jews, their numbers having been increased by the Marranos who had fled thither to avoid death at the stake. Their position was not enviable, for Spanish hatred of Jews was strongly implanted there; but their creed was not attacked, and their lives were not in constant peril. Isaac Hamon was physician in ordinary to one of the last kings of Granada, and enjoyed high favor at court. One day a quarrel arose in the streets of Granada, and the bystanders implored the disputants to leave off in the name of their prophet, but in vain. But when they were bidden to give over in the name of the royal physician, they yielded. This occurrence, which testified that Isaac Hamon was held in more respect by the populace than the prophet Mahomet, roused certain bigoted Mahometans to fall upon the Jews of Granada and butcher them. Only those escaped who found refuge in the royal castle. The Jewish physicians of Granada came to the resolution henceforth not to clothe themselves in silken garments, nor ride on horseback, in order to avoid exciting the envy of the Mahometans.

FALL OF GRANADA.

After long and bloody strife the beautiful city of Granada fell into the hands of the proud Spaniards. Frivolous Muley Abu-Abdallah (Boabdil), the last king, signed a secret treaty with Ferdinand and Isabella (25th November, 1491) to give up the town and its territory by a certain time. The conditions, seeing that independence was lost, were tolerably favorable. The Moors were to keep their religious freedom, their civil laws, their right to leave the country, and above all their manners and customs, and were only required to pay the taxes which hitherto they had paid the Moorish king. The renegades-that is to say, Christians who had adopted Islam, or, more properly speaking, the Moorish pseudo-Christians, who had fled to Granada, and returned to Islam, were to remain unmolested. The Inquisition was not to claim jurisdiction over them. The Jews of the capital of Granada, of the Albaicin quarter, the suburbs and the Alpujarras, were included in the provisions of the treaty. They were to enjoy the same indulgences and the same rights, except that relapsed Marranos were to leave the city, only the first month after its surrender being the term allowed for emigration; those who stayed longer were to be handed over to the Inquisition. One noteworthy point stipulated by the last Moorish king of Granada, was that no Jew should be set over the vanquished Moors as officer of justice, tax-gatherer, or commissioner. On January 2d, 1492, Ferdinand and Isabella, with their court, amid ringing of bells, and great pomp and circumstance, made their entry into Granada. The Mahometan kingdom of the Peninsula had vanished like a dream in an Arabian Nights' legend. The last prince, Muley Abu-Abdallah, cast one long sad farewell look, "with a last sigh," over the glory forever lost, and retired to the lands assigned to him in the Alpujarras, but, unable to overcome his dejection, he turned his steps toward Africa. After nearly eight hundred years the whole Pyrenean Peninsula again became Christian, as it had been in the time of the Visigoths. But heaven could not rejoice over this conquest, which delivered fresh human sacrifices to the lords of hell. The Jews were the first to experience the tragical effect of this conquest of Granada.

The war against the Mahometans of Granada, originally undertaken to punish attempts at encroachment and breach of faith, assumed the character of a crusade against unbelief, of a holy war for the exaltation of the cross and the spread of the Christian faith. Not only the bigoted queen and the unctuous king, but also many Spaniards were dragged by this conquest into raging fanaticism. Are the unbelieving Mahometans to be vanquished, and the still more unbelieving Jews to go free in the land? This question was too pertinent not to meet with an answer unfavorable to the Jews. The insistence of Torquemada and friends of his own way of thinking, that the Jews, who had long been a thorn in their flesh, should be expelled, at first met with indifference, soon began to receive more attention from the victors. Then came the consideration that owing to increased opulence, consequent on the booty acquired from the wealthy towns of conquered Granada, the Jews were no longer indispensable. Before the banner of the cross waved over Granada, Ferdinand and Isabella had contemplated the expulsion of the Jews. With this end in view, they had sent an embassy to Pope Innocent VII, stating that they were willing to banish the Jews from the country, if he, Christ's representative, set them the example; but even this abandoned pope, who had seven illegitimate sons and as many daughters, and who, soon after his accession to the papal chair, had broken a solemn oath, was opposed to the expulsion of the Jews. Meshullam, of Rome, having

heard of the pope's refusal, with great joy announced to the Italian and Neapolitan communities that Innocent would not consent to the expulsion. The Spanish sovereigns decided on the banishment of the Jews without the pope's consent.

From the enchanted palace of the Alhambra there was suddenly issued by the "Catholic Sovereigns " a proclamation that, within four months, the Spanish Jews were to leave every portion of Castile, Aragon, Sicily and Sardinia under pain of death (March 31, 1492). They were at liberty to take their goods and chattels with them, but neither gold, silver, money, nor forbidden articles of export--only such things as it was permitted to export. This heartless cruelty Ferdinand and Isabella sought to vindicate before their own subjects and before foreign countries. The proclamation did not accuse the Jews of extravagant usury, of unduly enriching themselves, of sucking the marrow from the bones of the people, of insulting the host, or of crucifying Christian children--not one syllable was said of these things. But it set forth that the falling away of the new-Christians into "Jewish unbelief" was caused by their intercourse with Jews. The proclamation continued that long since it would have been proper to banish the Jews on account of their wily ways; but at first the sovereigns had tried clemency and mild means, banishing only the Jews of Andalusia, and punishing only the most guilty, in the hope that these steps would suffice. As, however, these had not prevented the Jews from continuing to pervert the new-Christians from the Catholic faith, nothing remained but for their majesties to exile those who had lured back to heresy the people who had indeed fallen away, but had repented and returned to holy Mother Church. Therefore had their majesties, in council with the princes of the church, grandees, and learned men, resolved to banish the Jews from their kingdom. No Christian, on pain of confiscation of his possessions, should, after the expiration of a certain term, give succor or shelter to Jews. The edict of Ferdinand and Isabella is good testimony for the Jews of Spain in those days, since no accusations could be brought against them but that they had remained faithful to their religion, and had sought to maintain their Marrano brethren in it. A legend relates that their majesties were embittered against the Jews, because the Infante had found the picture of a crucified Holy Child in an orange which a Jewish courtier had given him.

The long-dreaded blow had fallen. The Spanish Jews were to leave the country, round which the fibers of their hearts had grown, where lay the graves of their forefathers of at least fifteen hundred years, and towards whose greatness, wealth, and culture they had so largely contributed. The blow fell upon them like a thunderbolt. Abrabanel thought that he might be able to avert it by his influence. He presented himself before the king and queen, and offered enormous sums in the name of the Jews if the edict were removed. His Christian friends, eminent grandees, supported his efforts. Ferdinand, who took more interest in enriching his coffers than in the Catholic faith, was inclined to yield. Then the fanatical grand inquisitor, Torquemada, lifted up his voice. It is related that he took upon himself to rush into the presence of the king and queen, carrying the crucifix aloft, and uttering these winged words: "Judas Iscariot sold Christ for thirty pieces of silver; your highnesses are about to sell Him for 300,000 ducats. Here He is, take Him, and sell Him ! " Then he left the hall. These words, or the influence of other ecclesiastics, had a strong effect upon Isabella. She resolved to abide by the edict, and, of bolder spirit than the king, contrived to keep alive his enmity against the Jews. Juan de Lucena, a member

THE POSSESSIONS OF THE EXILES.

of the royal council of Aragon, as well as minister, was equally active in maintaining the edict. At the end of April heralds and trumpeters went through the whole country, proclaiming that the Jews were permitted to remain only till the end of July to set their affairs in order; whoever of them was found after that time on Spanish ground would suffer death.

Great as was the consternation of the Spanish was at having to tear themselves from the beloved land of their birth and the ashes of their forefathers, and go forth to an uncertain future in strange lands, among people whose speech they did not understand, who, perhaps, might be more unfriendly towards them than the Spanish Christians, they had to bestir themselves and make preparation for their exodus. At every step they realized that a yet more cruel fate awaited them. Had they been able, like the English Jews at the end of the thirteenth century, and the French a century later, to take their riches with them, they might have been able to provide some sort of miserable existence for themselves; but the Jewish capitalists were not permitted to take their money with them, they were compelled to accept bills of exchange for it. But Spain, on account of its dominant knightly and ecclesiastical element, had no places of exchange like those in Italy, where commercial notes were of value. Business on a large scale was in the hands, for the most part, of Jews and new-Christians, and the latter, from fear, had to keep away from their brethren in race. The Jews who owned land were forced to part with it at absurd prices, because no buyers applied, and they were obliged to beg the Christians for even the meanest thing in exchange. A contemporary, Andreas Bernaldez, pastor of Los Palacios, relates that the most magnificent houses and the most beautiful estates of the Jews were sold for a trifle. A house was bartered for an ass, and a vineyard for a piece of cloth or linen. Thus the riches of the Spanish Jews melted away, and could not help them in their day of need. In Aragon, Catalonia and Valencia, it was even worse with them. Torquemada, who on this occasion exceeded his former inhumanity, forbade the Christians to have any intercourse with them. In these provinces Ferdinand sequestrated their possessions, so that not only their debts, but also the claims which monasteries pretended to have upon them were paid. Torquemada imposed on the Dominicans the task of preaching Christianity everywhere, and of calling upon the Jews to receive baptism, and thus remain in the land. On the other side, the rabbis bade the people remain steadfast, accept their trials as tests of their firmness, and trust in God, who had been with them in so many days of trouble. The fiery eloquence of the rabbis was not necessary. Each one encouraged his neighbor to remain true and steadfast to the Jewish faith. "Let us be strong" so they said to each other, "for our religion, and for the Law of our fathers before our enemies and blasphemers. If they will let us live, we shall live; if they kill us, then shall we die. We will not desecrate the covenant of our God; our heart shall not fail us. We will go forth in the name of the Lord." If they had submitted to baptism, would they not have fallen into the power of the bloodstained Inquisition? One year before the proclamation of banishment was made, thirty-two new-Christians in Seville were bound living to the stake, sixteen were burned in effigy, and 625 sentenced to do penance. The Jews, moreover, were not ignorant of the false and deceitful

ways in which Torquemada entrapped his victims. Many pseudo-Christians had fled from Seville, Cordova and Jaen, to Granada, where they had returned to the Jewish faith. After the conquest of the town, Torquemada proclaimed that if they came back to Mother Church,"whose arms are always open to embrace those who return to her with repentance and contrition," they would be treated with mildness, and in private, without onlookers, would receive absolution. A few allowed themselves to be charmed by this sweet voice, betook themselves to Toledo, and were pardoned--to a death of fire. Thus it came about that, in spite of the preaching of the Dominicans, and notwithstanding their indescribably terrible position, few Jews passed over to Christianity in the year of the expulsion from Spain. [The position of those who converted was actually more dangerous than that of those who remained Jews; the latter could not be accused of heresy. It has been suggested that the aim of the Inquisitors was in fact racial: to destroy the Jews as a people, not a religion; and thus they endeavored to make any route of escape--even conversion--impossible.--ed] Among persons of note, only the rich tax-collector and chief rabbi, Abraham Senior, his son, and his son-in-law, Meir, a rabbi, went over, with the two sons of the latter. It is said that they received baptism in desperation, because the queen, who did not want to lose her clever minister of finance, threatened heavier persecution of the departing Jews, if these did not submit. Great was the rejoicing at court over the baptism of Senior and his family. Their majesties themselves and the cardinal stood as sponsors. The newly-baptized all took the family name of Coronel, and their descendants filled some of the highest offices in the state.

Their common misfortune and suffering developed among the Spanish Jews in those last days before their exile deep brotherly affection and exalted sentiments, which, could they have lasted, would surely have borne good fruit. The rich, although their wealth had dwindled, divided it fraternally with the poor, allowing them to want for nothing, so that they should not fall into the hands of the church, and also paid the charges of their exodus. The aged rabbi, Isaac Aboab, the friend of Abrabanel, went with thirty Jews of rank to Portugal, to negotiate with King Joao II, for the settlement of the Jews in that country, or for their safe passage through it. They succeeded in making tolerably favorable conditions. The pain of leaving their passionately loved country could not be overcome. The nearer the day of departure came, the more were the hearts of the unhappy people wrung. The graves of their forefathers were dearer to them than all besides, and from these they found parting hardest. The Jews of the town of Vitoria gave to the community the Jewish cemetery and its appertaining grounds in perpetuity, on condition that it should never be encroached upon, nor planted over, and a deed to this effect was drawn up. The Jews of Segovia assembled three days before their exodus around the graves of their forefathers, mingling their tears with the dust, and melting the hearts of the Catholics with their grief. They tore up many of the tombstones to bear them away as memorial relics, or gave them to the Moors.

At last the day arrived on which the Spanish Jews had to take staff in hand. They had been accorded two days respite, that is, were allowed two days later than July 31st for setting forth. This date fell exactly upon the anniversary of the ninth of Ab, which was fraught with memories of the splendor of the old days, and had so often found the children of Israel wrapped in grief and misery. About 300,000 left the land which they so deeply loved, but which now became a hateful memory to them. They wandered partly northwards, to the neighboring kingdom of Navarre, partly southwards, with the idea of settling in Africa, Italy or Turkey. The majority, however, made for Portugal. In order to stifle sad thoughts and avoid the melancholy impression which might have moved some to waver and embrace the cross in order to remain in the

land, some rabbis caused pipers and drummers to go before, making lively music, so that for a while the wanderers should forget their gnawing grief. Spain lost in them the twentieth part of her most industrious, painstaking, intelligent inhabitants, its middle class, which created trade, and maintained it in brisk circulation, like the blood of a living organism. For there were among the Spanish Jews not merely capitalists, merchants, farmers, physicians and men of learning, but also artisans, armor and metal workers of all kinds, at ail events no idlers who slept away their time. With the discovery of America, the Jews might have lifted Spain to the rank of the wealthiest, the most prosperous and enduring of states, which by reason of its unity of government might certainly have competed with Italy. But Torquemada would not have it so; he preferred to train Spaniards for a blood-stained idolatry, under which, in the sunlight of the Lutheran Reformation, pious men were condemned to chains, dungeons, or the galleys, if they dared read the Bible. The departure of the Jews from Spain soon made itself felt in a very marked manner by the Christians. Talent, activity, and prosperous civilization passed with them from the country. The smaller towns, which had derived some vitality from the presence of the Jews, were quickly depopulated, sank into insignificance, lost their spirit of freedom and independence, and became tools for the increasing despotism of the Spanish kings and the imbecile superstition of the priests. The Spanish nobility soon complained that their towns and villages had fallen into insignificance, had become deserted, and they declared that, could they have foreseen the consequences, they would have opposed the royal commands. Dearth of physicians was sternly felt, too. The town of Vitoria and its neighborhood was compelled, through the withdrawl of the Jews, to secure a physician from a distance, and give him a high salary. In many places the people fell victims to quacks, boastful bunglers, or to the superstition of deceiving or self-deceived dealers in magic. In one word, Spain fell into a condition of barbarism through the banishment of the Jews, and all the wealth which the settlement of American colonies brought to the mother country only helped to render its inhabitants more idle, stupid, and servile. The name of the Jews died out of the country in which they had played so important a part, and the literature of which was so filled with Jewish elements that men of intelligence were constantly reminded of them. Schools, hospitals, and everything which the Jews could not or dared not take away with them, the king confiscated. He changed synagogues into churches, monasteries or schools, where the people were systematically kept ignorant, and trained for meanest servility. The beautiful synagogue of Toledo, which Don Pedro's Jewish statesman, Samuel Abulafia, had erected about a century and a half before, was transformed into a church (de nuestra Senora de San Benito), and, with its Moorish architecture, its exquisite columns, and splendid proportions, is to this day a magnificent ornament to the city. In the other cities and towns of Spain, which live in the chronicles of Jewish history, in Seville, Granada, Cordova, in densely-populated Lucena, Saragossa and Barcelona, every trace was lost of the sons of Jacob, or of the Jewish nobility, as the proud Jews of Spain styled themselves. Jews, it is true, remained behind, Jews under the mask of Christianity, Jewish Christians, or new-Christians, who had afforded their departing brethren active help. Many of them had taken charge of their gold and silver, and kept it till they were able to send it on by the hands of trusted persons, or had given them bills of exchange on foreign places. These negotiations were often of no avail, for when the fanatical king and queen heard of them, they

PERSECUTION OF THE MARRANOS.

sent for the treasure left behind, or sought to prevent the payment of the checks.

Great as were the obstacles, the Marranos did not cool in their zeal for their exiled brethren. They pursued those guilty of inhuman brutality to the wanderers with bitter hatred, and delivered them over to the Inquisition-turning the tool against its makers. At the instigation of tile Marranos, the brother of Don Juan de Lucena, the powerful minister of Ferdinand, was thrown into the prison of the Inquisition, kept there under a strong guard, and none of his relatives allowed to see him, the minister, whose position exempted him from the power of the Inquisition, having counseled the banishment of the Jews, and practically assisted in it, and his brother having relentlessly confiscated the property they had left behind. Torquemada complained that Don Juan was persecuted by the new-Christians on account of his faith. The Marranos, now more than ever on their guard, lest they give the slightest offense, had to cross themselves assiduously, count their beads, and mumble paternosters, while inwardly they were attached more than ever to Judaism. Frequently their feelings outran their will, they broke the bonds of silence, and this was productive of heavy consequences. Thus a Marrano in Seville, on seeing an effigy of Christ set up in church for adoration, cried out, "Woe to him who sees, and must believe such a thing!" Such expressions in unguarded moments naturally afforded the best opportunity for inquiry, imprisonment, the rack and autos-da-fe, not merely for the individual caught in the act, but for his relatives, friends, and everybody connected with him who had any property. It is not astonishing that under the first inquisitor-general, Thomas de Torquemada, in the course of fourteen years (1485--1498) at least two thousand Jews were burned as impenitent sinners. He was so hated that he lived in constant fear of death. Upon his table he kept the horn of a unicorn, to which the superstition of the time ascribed the power of nullifying the effect of poison. When Torquemada went out, he was attended by a bodyguard (Familares) of fifty, and two hundred foot-soldiers,to protect him from assault. His successor,the second inquisitor-general, Deza, erected still more scaffolds; but it soon came to pass that the men of blood butchered each other. Deza before his death was accused of being secretly a Jew. When the persecutions against the remaining Moors and Moriscos, and against the followers of the German reformer Luther, were added to those of the Marranos, Spain, under the wrath of the Holy Inquisition, became literally a scene of human slaughter. With justice nearly all the European princes, and even the parliament of Paris, bitterly blamed the perverseness of Ferdinand and Isabella in having driven out so useful a class of citizens. The sultan Bajasid (Bajazet) exclaimed: "You call Ferdinand a wise king, he who has made his country poor and enriched ours ! "

IV. CHAPTER XII.

EXPULSION OP THE JEWS FROM NAVARRE AND PORTUGAL.

The Exiles from Navarre--Migration to Naples--King Ferdinand I of Naples and Abrabanel--Leon Abrabanel-Misfortunes of the Jews in Fez, Genoa, Rome, and the Islands of Greece--The Sultan Bajazet--Moses Kapsali--Spanish Jews in Portugal--The Jewish Astronomers, Abraham Zacuto and Jose Vecinho-The Jewish Travelers, Abraham de Beya and Joseph Zapateiro-Outbreak of the

Plague among the Spanish Jews in Portugal-Sufferings of the Portuguese Exiles--Judah Chayyat and his Fellow-Sufferers-Cruelty of Joao II--Kindly Treatment by Manoel changed into Cruelty on his Marriage--Forcible Baptism of Jewish Children--Levi ben Chabib and Isaac Caro-Pope Alexander VI--Manoel's Efforts on Behalf of the Portuguese Marranos-Death of Simon Maimi and Abraham Saba.

1492--1498 C.E.

THE Jews of northern Spain, in Catalonia and Aragon, who turned their steps to neighboring Navarre, with the idea of seeking shelter there, were comparatively fortunate. Here at least was a prospect of a livelihood, and a possibility of looking round for other places of refuge. The Inquisition had met with courageous resistance from the rulers and the people of Navarre. When some Marranos, concerned in the murder of Arbues, the inquisitor, fled to this kingdom, and the bloodthirsty heresy-mongers demanded that they be given up to the executioners, the town of Tudela declared that it would not suffer such unrighteous violence to people who had sought its protection, and closed the gates against their emissaries. In vain did king Ferdinand, who had an eye upon Navarre, threaten it with his anger. The citizens of Tudela remained firm. A Navarrese prince, Jacob of Navarre, suffered for the shelter he gave to a hunted Marrano. The inquisitors suddenly arrested, imprisoned, and sentenced him, as an enemy of the Holy Office, to shameful exposure in a church, where his list of offenses was publicly read out, and absolution promised him only if he submitted to flagellation from priestly hands. Several other towns of Navarre gave protection to the fugitives, and about 12,000 Castilian wanderers took up their quarters in Navarre. Count of Lerin probably received the greater number of these. But the Jews enjoyed only a few years of peace in Navarre; for upon the vehement urging of King Ferdinand, who followed the fugitives with bitterest enmity and persecution, the king of Navarre gave them the choice between wandering forth again and baptism. The greater number adopted Christianity, because there was only a short time for preparation, and no time for thinking. In the community of Tudela, so famous for steadfast piety, 180 families submitted to baptism.

Also those Castilian Jews were fortunate who, instead of indulging themselves in the vain hope that the edict would be recalled, did not stay until the last day, but made their way, before the end of the respite, to Italy, Africa, or Turkey. They did not lack the means of getting away. The Spanish Jews had such widespread repute, and their expulsion had made so much stir in Europe, that crowds of ships were ready in Spanish seaports to take up the wanderers and convey them to all parts, not only the ships of the country, but also Italian vessels from Genoa and Venice. The ship-owners saw a prospect of lucrative business. Many Jews from Aragon, Catalonia and Valencia desired to settle in Naples, and sent ambassadors to the king, Ferdinand I, to ask him to receive them. This prince was not merely free from prejudice against the Jews, but was kindly inclined towards them, out of compassion for their misfortunes, and he may have promised himself industrial and intellectual advantage from this immigration of the Spanish Jews.

KIND TREATMENT IN NAPLES

Whether it was calculation or generosity, it is enough that he bade them welcome, and made his realm free to them. Many thousands of them landed in the Bay of Naples (24th August, 1492), and were kindly received. The native Jewish community treated them with true brotherly generosity, defrayed the passage of the poor not able to pay, and provided for their immediate necessities.

Isaac Abrabanel, also, and his whole household, went to Naples. Here he lived at first as a private individual, and continued the work of writing a commentary upon the book of Kings, which had been interrupted by his state duties. When the king of Naples was informed of his presence in the city, he invited him to an interview, and entrusted him with a post, in all likelihood in the financial department. Probably he hoped to make use of Abrabanel's experience in the war with which he was threatened by the king of France. Whether from his own noble impulses, or from esteem for Abrabanel, the king of Naples showed the Jews a gentle humanity which startlingly contrasted with the cruelty of the Spanish king. The unhappy people had to struggle with many woes; when they thought themselves free of one, another yet more merciless fell upon them. A devastating pestilence, arising out of the sad condition to which they had been reduced, or from the overcrowding of the ships, followed in the track of the wanderers. They brought death with them. Scarcely six months had they been settled on Neapolitan soil when the pestilence carried numbers of them off; and King Ferdinand, who dreaded a rising of the populace against the Jews, hinted to them that they must bury their corpses by night, and in silence. When the pest could no longer be concealed, and every day increased in virulence, people and courtiers alike entreated him to drive them forth. But Ferdinand would not assent to this inhuman proceeding; he is said to have threatened to abdicate if the Jews were ill-treated. He had hospitals erected for them outside the town, sent physicians to their aid, and gave them means of support. For a whole year he strove. with unexampled nobility, to succor the unfortunate people, whom banishment and disease had transformed into living corpses. Those, also, who were fortunate enough to reach Pisa found a brotherly reception. The sons of Yechiel of Pisa fairly took up their abode on the quay, so as to be ready to receive the wanderers, provide for their wants, shelter them, or help them on their way to some other place. After Ferdinand's death, his son, Alfonso II, who little resembled him, retained the Jewish statesman, Abrabanel, in his service, and, after his resignation in favor of his son, took him with him to Sicily. Abrabanel to the last remained faithful to this prince in his misfortunes (January, 1494, to June, 1495).

After the conquest of Naples by the weak-headed knight-errant king of France, Charles VIII, the members of the Abrabanel family were torn apart and scattered. None of them, however, met with such signal misfortune as the eldest son, Judah Leon Medigo (born 1470, died 1530)· He had been so well beloved at the Spanish court that they were loath to part with him, and would gladly have kept him there--of course, as a Christian. To attain this end, a command was issued that he be not permitted to leave Toledo, or that his one-year-old son be taken from him, baptized immediately, and that in this manner the father be chained to Spain. Judah Abrabanel, however, got wind of this plot against his liberty, sent his son, with his nurse, "like stolen goods," secretly to the Portuguese coast; but as he himself did not care to seek shelter in the country where his father had been threatened with death, he turned his face towards Naples. His suspicions of the king of Portugal

were only too speedily justified. No sooner did Joao hear that a relative of Abrabanel was within his borders than he ordered the child to be kept as hostage, and not to be permitted to go forth with the other Jews. Little Isaac never saw his parents and grandparents again. He was baptized, and brought up as a Christian. The agony of the father at the living death of his lost child was boundless. It gave him no rest or peace to his latest hour, and it found vent in a lamentation sad in the extreme. Yet what was the grief for one child, compared with the woes which overtook the thousands of Jews hunted out of Spain?

Many of them found their way to the nearest African seaport towns, Oran, Algiers and Bugia. The inhabitants, who feared that their towns would. be overcrowded from such a vast influx, shot at the Jews as they landed, and killed many of them. An eminent Jew at the court of Barbary,however, addressed the sultan in behalf of his unhappy brethren, and obtained leave for them to land. They were not allowed to enter the towns, probably because the pestilence had broken out among them, too. They could only build themselves wooden huts outside the walls. The children collected wood, and their elders nailed the boards together for temporary dwellings. But they did not long enjoy even this miserable shelter, as one day a fire broke out in one of the huts, and soon laid the whole camp in ashes.

Those who settled in Fez suffered a still more terrible lot. Here also the inhabitants would not admit them, fearing that such an influx of human beings would raise the price of the necessaries of life. They had to encamp in the fields, and live on roots and herbs like cattle. On the Sabbath they stripped the plants with their teeth, in order not to desecrate the holy day by gathering them. Starvation, pestilence, and the unfriendliness of the Mahometan people vied with each other in inflicting misery upon the Jews. In their awful despair, fathers were driven to sell their children as slaves to obtain bread. Mothers killed their little ones that they might not see them perish from the pangs of hunger. Avaricious captains took advantage of the distress of the parents to entice starving children on board their vessels with offers of bread, and, deaf to the cries and entreaties of the parents, carried them off to distant lands, where they sold them for a good price. Later, the ruler of Fez, probably at the representation of the original Jewish inhabitants, proclaimed that Jewish children who had been sold for bread, and other necessaries of life, should be set at liberty.

The descriptions by their contemporaries of the sufferings of the Jews make one's hair stand on end. They were dogged whithersoever they went. Those whom plague and starvation had spared, fell into the hands of brutalized men. The report got about that the Spanish Jews had swallowed the gold and silver which they had been forbidden to carry away, intending to use it later on. Cannibals, therefore, ripped open their bodies to seek for coin in their entrails. The Genoese chip-folk behaved most inhumanly to the wanderers who had trusted their lives to them. From avarice, or sheer delight in the death agonies of the Jews, they flung many of them into the sea. One captain offered insult to the beautiful daughter of a Jewish wanderer. Her name was Paloma (Dove), and to escape shame, the mother threw her and her other daughters and then herself into the waves. The wretched father composed a heartbreaking lamentation for his lost dear ones.

Those who reached the port of Genoa had to contend with new miseries. In this thriving town there was a law that Jews might not remain there for longer than three days. As the ships which

were to convey the Jews thence required repairing, the authorities conceded the permission for them to remain, not in the town, but upon the Mole, until the vessels were ready for sea. Like ghosts, pale, shrunken, hollow-eyed, gaunt, they went on shore, and if they had not moved, impelled by instinct to get out of their floating prison, they might have been taken for so many corpses. Only a short time had been granted them on the Mole, but a great part of the winter passed before the repairs were completed. The longer they remained, the more their numbers diminished, through the passing over to Christianity of the younger members, and many fell victims to plagues of all kinds. Other Italian towns would not allow them to land even for a short time, partly because it was a year of famine, partly because the Jews brought the plague with them.

The survivors from Genoa who reached Rome underwent still more bitter experiences; their own people leagued against them, refusing to allow them to enter, from fear that the influx of new settlers would damage their trade. They got together 1,000 ducats, to present to the notorious monster, Pope Alexander VI, as a bribe to refuse to allow the Jews to enter. This prince, himself unfeeling enough, was so enraged at the heartlessness of these men against their own people, that he ordered every Roman Jew out of the city. It cost the Roman congregation 2,000 ducats to obtain the revocation of this edict, and they had to take in the refugees besides.

The Creek islands of Corfu, Candia, and others became filled with Spanish Jews; some had dragged themselves thither, others had been sold as slaves there. The majority of the Jewish communities had great compassion for them, and strove to care for them, or at all events to ransom them. They made great efforts to collect funds, and sold the ornaments of the synagogues, so that their brethren might not starve, or be subjected to slavery. Persians, who happened to be on the island, bought Spanish refugees, in order to obtain from Jews of their own country a high ransom for them. Elkanah Kapsali, a representative of the Candian community, was indefatigable in his endeavors to collect money for the Spanish Jews. The most fortunate were those who reached the shores of Turkey; for the Turkish Sultan, Bajazet II, showed himself to be not only a most humane monarch, but also the wisest and most far-seeing. He understood better than the Christian princes what hidden riches the impoverished Spanish Jews brought with them, not in their bowels, but in their brains, and he wanted to turn these to use for the good of his country. Bajazet caused a command to go forth through the European provinces of his dominions that the harassed and hunted Jews should not be rejected, but should be received in the kindest and most friendly manner. He threatened with death anyone who should ill-treat or oppress them. The chief rabbi, Moses Kapsali, was untiringly active in protecting the unfortunate Jewish Spaniards who had come as beggars or slaves to Turkey. He traveled about, and levied a tax from the rich native Jews "for the liberation of the Spanish captives." He did not need to use much pressure; for the Turkish Jews willingly contributed to the assistance of the victims of Christian fanaticism. Thus thousands of Spanish Jews settled in Turkey, and before a generation had passed they had taken the lead among the Turkish Jews, and made Turkey a kind of Eastern Spain.

ISAAC ABOAB'S MISSION.

At first the Spanish Jews who went to Portugal seemed to have some chance of a happy lot. The venerable rabbi, Isaac Aboab, who had gone with a deputation of thirty to seek permission from King Joao either to settle in or pass through Portugal succeeded in obtaining tolerably fair terms. Many of the wanderers chose to remain in the neighboring kingdom for a while, because they flattered themselves with the hope that their indispensableness would make itself evident after their departure, that the eyes of the now blinded king and queen of Spain would be opened, and they would then receive the banished people with open arms. At the worst, so thought the refugees, they would have time in Portugal to look round, decide which way to go, and readily find ships to convey them in safety to Africa or to Italy. When the Spanish deputies placed the proposition before King Joao II to receive the Jews permanently or temporarily in Portugal, the king consulted his grandees at Cintra. In presenting the matter, he permitted it to be seen that he himself was desirous of admitting the exiles for a pecuniary consideration. Some of the advisers, either from pity for the unhappy Jews, or from respect for the king, were in favor of granting permission; others, and these the majority, either out of hatred for the Jews, or a feeling of honor, were against it. The king, however, overruled all objections, because he hoped to carry on the contemplated war with Africa by means of the money acquired from the immigrants. It was at first said that the Spanish refugees were to be permitted to settle permanently in Portugal. This favor, however, the Portuguese Jews themselves looked upon with suspicion, because the little state would thus hold a disproportionate number of Jews, and the wanderers, most of them penniless, would fall a heavy burden upon them, so that the king, not of an amiable disposition, would end by becoming hostile to all the Jews in Portugal. The chief men, therefore, of the Jewish-Portuguese community met in debate, and many gave utterance to the cruel view that they themselves would have to take steps to prevent the reception of the Spanish exiles. A noble old man, Joseph of the family of Ibn-Yachya, spoke warmly for his unfortunate brethren; but his voice was silenced. There was no more talk of their settling in Portugal, but only of the permission to make a short stay, in order to arrange for their journey. The conditions laid down for the Spanish Jews were: Each one, rich or poor, with the exception of babes, was to pay a stipulated sum (eight gold-cruzados, nearly one pound) in four installments; artisans, however, such as metal-workers and smiths, who desired to settle in the country, only half of this amount. The rest were permitted to stay only eight months, but the king undertook to furnish ships at a reasonable rate for transporting them to other lands. Those found in Portugal after the expiration of this period, or not able to show a receipt for the stipulated payment, were condemned to servitude. On the promulgation of these conditions, a large number of Spanish Jews (estimated at 20,000 families, or 200,000 souls) passed over the Portuguese borders. The king assigned to the wanderers certain towns, where they had to pay a tax to the inhabitants. Oporto was assigned to the families of the thirty deputies, and a synagogue was built for them. Isaac Aboab, the renowned teacher of many disciples, who later took positions as rabbis in Africa, Egypt and Palestine, died peacefully in Oporto; his pupil, famous as a geographer and astronomer, Abraham Zacuto, pronounced his funeral oration (end of 1492). Only a few of his fellow-sufferers were destined to die a peaceful death.

The feverish eagerness for discovering unknown lands and entering into trading relations with them,

JEWISH ASTRONOMERS.

which had seized on Portugal, gave practical value to two sciences which hitherto had been regarded as the hobby or amusement of idlers and dilettanti--namely, astronomy and mathematics, the favorite pursuits of cultured Jews of the Pyrenean Peninsula. If India, the land of gold and spices, upon which the minds of the Portuguese were set with burning desire, was to be discovered, then coasting journeys, so slow and so dangerous, would have to be given up, and voyages made thither upon the high seas. But the ships ran the risk of losing their way on the trackless wastes of the ocean. Venturesome mariners, therefore, sought astronomical tables to direct their way by the courses of the sun and the stars. In this science Spanish Jews had the mastery. A Chazan of Toledo, Isaac (Zag) Ibn-Said, had published astronomical tables in the thirteenth century, known under the name of Alfonsine Tables, which were used with only slight alterations by the scientific men of Germany,France, England and Italy. As Joao II of Portugal now wished to send ships to the Atlantic for the discovery of India by way of the African sea-coast, he summoned a sort of astronomical congress for the working out of practical astronomical tables. At this congress, together with the famous German astronomer, Martin Behaim, and the Christian physician of King Rodrigo, there sat a Jew, the royal physician, Joseph (Jose) Vecinho, or de Viseu. He used as a basis the perpetual astronomical calendar, or Tables of the Seven Planets, which Abraham Zacuto, known later as a chronicler, had drawn up for a bishop of Salamanca, to whom he had dedicated it. Joseph Vecinho, together with Christian scientists, also improved upon the instrument for the measurement of the altitude of the stars, the nautical astrolabe, indispensable to mariners. By its aid Vasco da Gama first found it possible to follow the seaway to the Cape of Good Hope and India, and thus, perhaps, Columbus was enabled to discover a new continent. The geographical knowledge and skill of two Jews, Rabbi Abraham de Beya and Joseph Zapateiro de Lamego, were also turned to account by King Joao II, who sent them to Asia to obtain tidings of his emissaries to the mythical land of Prester John.

Although King Joao thus employed learned and skillful Jews for his own ends, he had no liking for the Jewish race: he was indifferent, or rather inimical, to them directly they came in the way of his bigotry. In the year in which he dispatched Joseph Zapateiro and Abraham de Beya to Asia, at the instigation of Pope Innocent VIII he appointed a commission of the Inquisition for the Marranos who had fled from Spain to Portugal, and, like Ferdinand and Isabella in Spain, delivered over those who had Jewish leanings, either to death by fire or to endless imprisonment. Some Marranos having taken ship to Africa, and there openly adopted Judaism, he prohibited, under penalty of death and confiscation, baptized Jews or new-Christians from leaving the country by sea. On the breath of this heartless monarch hung the life or death of hundreds of thousands of Jewish exiles.

Against those unfortunates in Portugal, not only evil-minded men, but nature itself, fought. Soon after their arrival in Portugal, a cruel pestilence began to rage among them, destroying thousands. The Portuguese, who also suffered from the plague, believed that the Jews had brought it into the country; and, indeed, all that they had suffered, the oppressive heat at the time of their going forth, want, misery, and all kinds of devastating diseases, may have developed it. A considerable number of the Spanish refugees died of the plague in Portugal. The population on this account murmured against the king, complaining that the pestilence had followed in the track of the accursed Jews, and established itself in the country. Don Joao, therefore,

had to insist more strenuously than he otherwise would have done upon the condition that all who had settled in Portugal should leave at the expiration of the eight months. At first he put ships at their disposal, at moderate rates of transportation, according to his agreement, and bade the captains treat their passengers with humanity, and convey them whither they wished to go. But these men, inspired by Jew hatred and avarice, once upon the seas, troubled themselves but little about the king's orders, since they had no need to fear complaints about their inhumanity They demanded more money than had originally been bargained for, and extorted it from the helpless creatures. Or, they carried them about upon the waste of waters till their stock of provisions was exhausted, and then demanded large sums for a fresh supply of food, so that at last the unfortunates were driven to give their clothes for bread, and were landed anywhere in a nearly naked state. Women and young girls were insulted and violated in the presence of their parents and relatives, and disgrace was brought upon the name of Christian. Frequently these inhuman mariners landed them in some desolate spot of the African coasts, and left them to perish from hunger and despair, or to fall a prey to the Moors, who took them prisoners.

The sufferings of the exiled Jews who left Portugal in ships are related by an eye-witness, the Kabbalist, Judah ben Jacob Chayyat, of a noble and wealthy family. The vessel on which he, his wife, and two hundred and fifty other Jews, of both sexes and all ages, had embarked, left the harbor of Lisbon in winter (beginning of 1493) and lingered four months upon the waves, because no seaport would take them in for fear of the plague. Provisions on board naturally ran short. The ship was captured by Biscayan pirates, plundered and taken to the Spanish port of Malaga. The Jews were not permitted to land, nor to set sail again, nor were provisions given them. The priests and magistrates of the town desired to incline them to the teaching of Christ by the pangs of hunger. They succeeded in converting one hundred persons with gaunt bodies and hollow eyes. The rest remained steadfast to their own faith, and fifty of them, old men, youths, maidens, children, among them Chayyat's wife, died of starvation. Then, at last, compassion awoke in the hearts of the Malagese, and they gave them bread and water. When, after two months, the remainder of them received permission to sail to the coasts of Africa, they encountered bitter sufferings in another form. On account of the plague they were not permitted to land at any town, and had to depend upon the herbs of the field. Chayyat himself was seized, and flung by a malicious Mahometan into a horrible dungeon full of snakes and salamanders, in order to force him to adopt Islamism; in case of refusal, he was threatened with death by stoning. These continuous, grinding cruelties did not make him waver one instant in his religious convictions. At last he was liberated by the Jews of a little town, and carried to Fez. There so severe a famine raged that Chayyat was compelled to turn a mill with his hands for a piece of bread, not fit for a dog. At night he and his companions in misery who had strayed to Fez slept upon the ash-heaps of the town.

Carefully as the Portuguese mariners strove to conceal their barbarities to the Jews, their deeds soon came to light, and frightened off those who remained behind from emigrating by sea. The poor creatures, moreover, were unable to raise the necessary money for their passage and provisions. They, therefore, put off going from day to day, comforting themselves with the hope that the king would be merciful, and allow them to remain in Portugal, Don Joao, however. was not a monarch whose heart

JEWISH CHILDREN SENT TO SAN THOMAS.

was warmed by kindness and compassion. He maintained that more Jews had come into Portugal than had been stipulated for, and insisted, therefore, that the agreement be strictly carried out. Those who remained after the expiration of eight months were made slaves, and sold or given to those of the Portuguese nobility who cared to take their pick from them (1493).

King Joao went still further in his cruel dealing with the unhappy Spanish Jews. The children from three to ten years of age whose parents had become slaves, he ordered to be transported by sea to the newly-discovered San Thomas or Lost Islands (Islas perdidas), there to be reared in the tenets of Christianity. The weeping of the mothers, the sobbing of the children, the rage of the fathers, who tore their hair in agony, did not move the heartless despot to recall his command. Mothers entreated to be allowed to go with their children, threw themselves at the king's feet as he came out of church, and implored him to leave them at least the youngest. Don Joao had them dragged from his path " like bitches who had their whelps torn from them." Is it to be wondered at that mothers, with their children in their arms, sprang into the sea to rest united in its depths? The Islands of San Thomas, whither the little ones were taken, were full of lizards and venomous snakes, and inhabited by criminals transported thither from Portugal. Most of the children perished on the journey, or became the prey of wild beasts. Among the survivors it happened that brothers and sisters, in ignorance of their relationship, married each other. Perhaps the king's barbarity to the Jews must be accounted for by the bitter gloom which mastered him at the death of his only legitimate son.

After the death of Joao II, who sank in wretchedness into his grave (end of October, 1495), he was succeeded by his cousin Manoel, a great contrast in disposition to himself--an intelligent, amiable, gentle-minded man, and a lover of learning. There seemed some prospect of a better star's rising upon the remnant of the banished Jews in Portugal. King Manoel, finding that the Jews had remained in his kingdom beyond the allotted time only from fear of many forms of death upon the ocean,gave all the slaves their freedom. The money which, beside themselves with joy, they offered him for this, he refused. It is true that his ulterior motive, as Bishop Osorius tells us, was to win them over to Christianity by clemency. The Jewish mathematician and astronomer, Abraham Zacuto, who had remained in Lisbon, having come thither from northern Spain, where he had taught his favorite science even to Christians, was made chief astrologer Zacuto served the king not merely in the latter capacity. Although a man of limited understanding, unable to rise above the superstition of his day, he had sound knowledge of astronomy, and published a work upon that science, besides preparing his astronomical tables. He also invented a correct metal in strument for measuring the altitude of the stars, to replace the clumsy and inaccurate wooden one used hitherto by mariners.

Under King Manoel, in whose reign Portugal's domains were enlarged by acquisitions in India and America, the Jews were able to breathe awhile. It appears that soon after ascending the throne he issued a command that the accusations against them for murdering children should not be recognized by courts of justice, since they were malicious, lying inventions. Nor would he allow the fanatical preaching friars to utter denunciations against them.

Very short, however, was the gleam of happiness for the Jews under Manoel: the somber bigotry of the Spanish Court changed it into terrible gloom. No sooner had the young king of Portugal mounted the throne than their majesties of Spain began to entertain the idea of marriage relations with him in

MANOEL AND ISABELLA.

order to turn an inimical neighbor into a friend and ally. They proposed marriage with their younger daughter, Joanna, who afterwards became notorious on account of her jealous disposition and her madness. Manoel lent a willing ear to the proposal of an alliance with the Spanish court, but preferred the elder sister, Isabella II, who had been married to the Infante of Portugal, and had soon after become a widow. Isabella had strong repugnance to a second marriage; but her confessor knew how to overrule her objections, and made her believe that if she consented she would have opportunity to glorify the Christian faith. The Spanish court had marked with chagrin and vexation that the Portuguese king had received the Jewish and Mahometan refugees, and King Manoel's friendly treatment of them was a thorn in their flesh. Ferdinand and Isabella thought that by falling in with the Portuguese king's wishes, they would attain their end. They, therefore, promised him the hand of their eldest daughter upon condition that he join with Spain against Charles VII, and send the Jews out of Portugal, both the native and the refugee Jews. The conditions were very disagreeable to King Manoel, who was on good terms with France, and reaped great advantage from the wealth, energy, intelligence, and knowledge of the Jews.

He consulted with his lords and council upon this question, fraught with such importance for the Jews. Opinions upon it were divided. Manoel hesitated for some time, because his noble nature shrank from such cruelty and faithlessness. The Infanta Isabella spoke the deciding word. She entertained fanatical, almost personal hatred against the Jews. She believed or was persuaded by the priests that the misfortunes and unhappiness which had befallen King Joao in his last days were occasioned by his having allowed Jews to enter his kingdom; and, nourished as she had been at the breast of superstition, she was afraid of ill-luck in her union with Manoel if Jews were permitted to remain in Portugal. What dreary lovelessness in the heart of a young woman! Irreconcilable strife of feelings and thoughts was thus raised in the soul of King Manoel. Honor, the interest of the state, humanity, forbad his proscribing and expelling the Jews; but the hand of the Spanish Infanta, and the Spanish crown were to be secured only by the misery of the Jews. Love turned the balance in favor of hate. When the king was expecting his bride to cross the borders of his kingdom, he received a letter from her saying that she would not set foot in Portugal until the land was cleansed of the "curse-laden" Jews.

The marriage contract between Don Manoel and the Spanish Infanta, Isabella, then, was sealed with the misery of the Jews. It was signed on the 30th of November, 1496, and so early as the 24th of the following month, the king caused an order to go forth that all the Jews and Moors of his kingdom must receive baptism, or leave the country within a given time, on pain of death. In order to relieve his conscience, he showed clemency in carrying his edict into effect. He lengthened the term of their stay until the October of the following year, so that they had time for preparation. He further appointed three ports, Lisbon, Oporto, and Setubal, for their free egress. That he sought to allure the Jews to Christianity, by the prospect of honor and advancement, was so entirely due to the distorted views of the times, that he cannot be held responsible for it; as it was, only a few submitted to baptism.

Precisely Manoel's clement behavior tended to the greater misery of the Jews. Having ample time to prepare for their departure, and not being forbidden to take gold and silver with them, they thought that there was no need to hurry. Perhaps the king would change his mind. They had friends at court

CHILDREN BAPTIZED BY FORCE.

who were agitating in their favor. Besides, the winter months were not a good time to be upon the ocean. The majority, therefore, waited until spring. In the meantime King Manoel certainly did change his mind, but only to increase their fearful misery. He was much vexed at finding that so few Jews had embraced Christianity. Very unwillingly he saw them depart with their wealth and their possessions, and sought ways and means to retain them, as Christians, of course, in his own kingdom. The first step had cost him a struggle, the second was easy.

He raised the question in council whether the Jews could be brought to baptism by force. To the honor of the Portuguese clergy it must be said that they expressed themselves as opposed to this. The bishop of Algarve, Ferdinand Coutinho, cited ecclesiastical authorities and papal bulls to the effect that Jews might not be compelled to adopt Christianity, because a free, not a forced, confession was required. Manoel, however, was so bent upon keeping the industrious Jews with him, that he openly declared that he did not trouble himself about laws and authorities, but would act upon his own judgment. From Evora he issued (beginning of April, 1497) a secret command that all Jewish children, boys and girls, up to the age of fourteen, should be taken from their parents by force on Easter Sunday, and carried to the church fonts to be baptized. He was advised by a reprobate convert, Levi ben Shem Tob, to take this step. In spite of the secrecy of the preparations, several Jews found it out, and were about to flee with their children from the "stain of baptism." When Manoel heard it, he ordered the forced baptism of children to be carried out at once. Heartrending scenes ensued in the towns where Jews lived when the sheriffs strove to carry away the children. Parents strained their dear ones to their breasts, the children clung convulsively to them, and they could be separated only by lashes and blows. In their despair over the possibility of being thus for ever sundered, many of them strangled the children in their embraces, or threw them into wells and rivers, and then laid hands upon themselves, "I have seen," relates Bishop Coutinho, "many dragged to the font by the hair, and the fathers clad in mourning, with veiled heads and cries of agony, accompanying their children to the altar, to protest against the inhuman baptism. I have seen still more horrible, indescribable violence done them." In the memory of his contemporaries lingered the frightful manner in which a noble and cultured Jew, Isaac Ibn-Zachin, destroyed himself and his children, to avoid their becoming a prey to Christianity. Christians were moved to pity by the cries and tears of Jewish fathers, mothers and children, and despite the king's commands not to assist the Jews, they concealed many of the unfortunates in their houses, so that at least for the moment they might be safe; but the stony hearts of King Manoel and his young wife, the Spanish Isabella II, remained unmoved by these sights of woe. The baptized children, who received Christian names, were placed in various towns, and reared as Christians. Either in obedience to a secret order, or from excessive zeal, the creatures of the king not only seized children, but also youths and maidens up to the age of twenty, for baptism.

Many Jews of Portugal probably embraced Christianity in order to remain with their children; but this did not satisfy the king, who, not from religious zeal, but from political motives, had hardened his heart. All the Jews of Portugal, it mattered not whether with or without conviction, were to become Christians and remain in the country. To attain this end, he violated a solemn promise more flagrantly than his predecessor. When the time of their departure came closer, he ordered the Jews to embark from one seaport only, that of Lisbon,

PORTUGUESE JEWS PERSECUTED.

although, at first, he had allowed them three places. Therefore, all who wished to go, had to meet in Lisbon--20,000 souls, it is said, with burning grief in their hearts, but prepared to suffer anything to remain true to their convictions. The inhuman monarch allowed them lodgings in the city, but he placed so many hindrances in the way of their embarkation, that time passed by, and the day arrived when they were to forfeit life, or at least liberty, if found upon Portuguese soil. He had all who remained behind locked in an enclosed space (os Estaas) like oxen in stalls, and informed them that they were now his slaves, and that he could do with them as he thought fit. He urged them voluntarily to confess the Christian faith, in which case they should have honor and riches; otherwise they would be forced to baptism without mercy. When, notwithstanding this, many remained firm, he forbade bread or water to be given them for three days, in order to render them more pliable. This means did not succeed any better with the greater number of them: they chose to faint with starvation rather than belong to a religion which owned such followers as their persecutors. Upon this, Manoel proceeded to extreme measures. By cords, by their hair and beard,they were dragged from their pen to the churches. To escape this some sprang from the windows, and their limbs were crushed. Others broke loose and jumped into wells. Some killed themselves in the churches. One father spread his tallith over his sons, and killed them and himself. Manoel's terrible treatment comes into more glaring prominence when compared with his behavior to the Moors. They, too, had to leave Portugal, but no hindrances were placed in their way, because he feared that the Mahometan princes in Africa and Turkey might retaliate upon the Christians living in their domains. The Jews had no earthly protector, were weak and helpless, therefore. Manoel, whom historians call the Great, permitted himself to perpetrate such atrocities. In this fashion many native Portuguese and refugee Spanish Jews were led to embrace Christianity, which they--as their Christian contemporaries relate with shame-had openly scorned. Some, at a later period, became distinguished Rabbinical authorities, like Levi ben Chabib, afterwards rabbi in Jerusalem. Those who escaped with their lives and their faith attributed it to the gracious and wondrous interposition of God. Isaac ben Joseph Caro, who had come from Toledo to Portugal, there lost his adult and his minor sons ("who were beautiful as princes"), yet thanked his Creator for the mercy that in spite of peril on the sea he reached Turkey. Abraham Zacuto, with his son Samuel, also was in danger of death, although (or because) he was King Manoel's favorite, astrologer and chronicler. Both, however, were fortunate enough to pass through the bitter ordeal, and escape from Portugal, but they were twice imprisoned. They finally settled in Tunis.

The stir which the enforced conversion of the Jews caused in Portugal did not immediately subside. Those who had submitted to baptism through fear of death, or out of love for their children, did not give up the hope that by appealing to the papal court they might be able to return to their own faith, seeing that, as all Europe knew, Pope Alexander VI and his college of cardinals, as base as himself, would do anything for money. Rome was a market of shame--a hill of Astarte--a mart of unwholesomeness--but there the innocent, also, could buy their rights. The Portuguese new-Christians now sent a deputation of seven of

MANOEL'S CONCESSIONS.

their companions in misery to Pope Alexander, and they did not forget to take a purse of gold with them. The pope and-the so-called holy college showed themselves favorably inclined towards them, especially Cardinal de Sancta Anastasia took them under his patronage. The Spanish ambassador, Garcilaso, however, was instructed by their Spanish majesties to oppose them. Despite his influence the affairs of the Portuguese Jews must have taken a favorable turn, for King Manoel decided to make concessions. He issued a mild decree (May 3oth, 1497), in which he granted amnesty to all forcibly baptized Jews, and a respite of twenty years, during which they were not to be brought before the tribunal of the Inquisition for their adherence to Judaism. It was said that it was necessary for them first to lay aside their Jewish habits, and accustom themselves to the ways of the Catholic faith, for which they needed time. Further, the decree ordered that, on the expiration of this term, a regular examination should be made of those accused of Judaizing practices, and if the case was decided against them, their goods should not be confiscated, as in Spain, but given over to their heirs. Finally, the decree ordained that those baptized physicians and surgeons who did not understand Latin might make use of Hebrew books of reference. Practically this allowed the enforced Christians to live in secret, without fear of punishment, as Jews, and to retain all their books. For, who, in Portugal, in those days, could distinguish a book of medicine from any other work in the Hebrew language? The students of the Talmud could thus follow their favorite researches and studies under the mask of Catholicism. This amnesty benefited the Portuguese Marranos, but not those who had immigrated into Portugal, by a clause which Manoel had inserted out of deference to the Spanish court, or, more particularly, to the Spanish Infanta Isabella. For she insisted that the Marranos who had fled out of Spain into Portugal should be delivered over to the Moloch of the Inquisition. In the marriage contract between the king of Portugal and the fanatical Isabella (August, 1497), it was expressly set down that all persons of the Hebrew race coming under condemnation of the Inquisition, who sought refuge in Portugal, must leave within a month's time.

Thus many thousand Portuguese Jews became pseudo-Christians, but with the firm resolve to seize the first opportunity to get away, so that in a free country they might openly practice a religion only the dearer to them for ail they had suffered for it. There were some Jews, however, who had refused baptism with all their might. Among them was Simon Maimi, apparently the last chief rabbi (Arrabi mor) in Portugal, a scrupulously pious man; also his wife, his sons-in-law, and some others. They were closely imprisoned, because they would not forswear Judaism, nor observe the rites of the church. To bring them to conversion, Simon Maimi and his fellow sufferers, official rabbis, were most inhumanly tortured. They were immured up to the neck in their prison, and left for three days in this fearful position. When they nevertheless remained firm, the walls were torn down; three had died, among them Simon Maimi, whose conversion was most important, because his example would have influenced the others. Two Marranos imperiled their lives to secure the corpse of the pious martyr, that they might inter it in the Jewish burial-ground, although it was strictly forbidden to bury the Jewish victims of Christian sacrifice otherwise than by the executioner's hands. A few Marranos secretly attended their deeply-lamented saint to his last rest, and celebrated a mourning service over his grave. Manoel permitted the few remaining Jews to depart

THE LAST PORTUGUESE JEWS SET FREE.

not long after, probably on the death of Isabella, the instigator of all his barbarities to the Jews. She died at the birth of the heir to the thrones of Portugal and Spain, August 24th, 1498, and the Infante died two years later. One of the remnant dismissed was Abraham Saba, a preacher and Kabbalist author, whose two children were baptized by force and taken from him. The companions of Simon Maimi and his sons-in-law remained in prison a long time, were afterwards sent to Arzilla, in Africa, there condemned to work at the trenches on the Sabbath, and died at last a martyr's death,

Eighty years later, Manoel's great-grandson, the adventurous king, Sebastian, led the flower of the Portuguese people to fresh conquests in Africa. In a single battle the power of Portugal was broken, her nobility slain, or cast into prison. The captives were earned to Fez, and there, in the slave-market, offered for sale to the descendants of the barbarously treated Portuguese Jews. The unhappy Portuguese nobles and knights were, however, glad to be bought by Jews, as they well knew the mild and humane nature of the followers of the " God of vengeance."

IV. CHAPTER XIV.

RUCHLIN AND THE TALMUD.

Antecedents of the Convert John Pfefferkorn--Pfefferkorn and the Dominicans of Cologne--Hoogstraten, Ortuinus Gratius and Amold of Tongern--Victor von Karben-Attacks on the Talmud and Confiscation of Copies in Frankfort--Reuchlin's Hebrew and Kabbalistic Studies--The Controversy conceming the Talmud--Activity on both Sides--Public Excitement--Complete Victory of Reuchlin's Efforts in Defense of Jewish Literature--Ulrich von Hutten--Luther-Revival of Hebrew Studies.

1500--1520 C.E.

WHO could have anticipated that from the German nation, everywhere considered heavy and stupid, from the land of lawless knights, of daily feuds about trifles, of confused political conditions, where everyone was both despot and slave, mercilessly oppressing his inferiors, and pitifully cringing to his superiors--who could have anticipated that from this people and this country would proceed a movement destined to shake European affairs to their center, create new political conditions, give the Middle Ages their death-blow, and set its seal on the dawn of a new historical era ? A reformation of church and politics, such as enlightened minds then dreamt of, was least expected from Germany. Yet there slumbered latent powers in that country, which only needed awaking to develop into regenerating forces. The Germans still adhered to ancient simplicity of life and severity of morals, pedantic, it is true, and ludicrous in manifestation; whilst the leading Romance countries, Italy, France and Spain, were suffering from over-refinement, surfeit and moral corruption. Because the Germans had retained their original Teutonic dullness, the clergy could not altogether succeed in infecting them with the

GERMAN RELIGIOUSNESS AND MORALITY.

poison of their vicious teaching. Their lower clergy, compared with that of other European countries, was more chaste and modest. The innate love of family life and genial association, which the Germans have in common with Jews, preserved them from that moral depravity to which the Romance nations had already succumbed. In the educated circles of Italy, especially at the papal court, Christianity and its doctrines were sneered at; the political power they conferred alone being valued. But in Germany, where there was little laughter, except in taverns, Christianity was treated as a more serious matter; it was looked upon as an ideal, which had once been alive, and would live again.

But these moral germs in the German race were so deeply buried that it needed favorable circumstances to bring them to light, and cause them to stand forth as historical potencies. However much the Germans themselves may ignore it, the Talmud had a great share in the awakening of these slumbering forces. We can boldly assert that the war for and against the Talmud aroused German consciousness, and created a public opinion, without which the Reformation, like many other efforts, would have died in the hour of birth, or, perhaps, would never have been born at all. A paltry grain of sand caused the fall of an avalanche, which shook the earth around. The instrument of this mighty change was an ignorant, thoroughly vile creature, the scum of the Jewish people, who does not deserve to be mentioned in history or literature, but whom Providence seems to have appointed like some noisome insect involuntarily to accomplish a useful work.

Joseph Pfefferkorn, a native of Moravia, was by trade a butcher, and, as may easily be surmised, illiterate. His moral turpitude was even greater than his ignorance. He committed a burglary, was caught, condemned to imprisonment by Count de Guttenstein, and released only at the urgent prayers of his relatives, and on payment of a fine. It appears that he hoped to wash away this disgrace with baptismal water; the church was not scrupulous, and received even this despicable wretch, when at the age of thirty-six he presented himself, with wife and children, to be received into Christianity (about I505?)· He seems to have been baptized at Cologne ; at any rate, he was kept and made much of by the ignorant, proud and fanatical Dominicans of that city. Cologne was an owls' nest of light-shunning swaggerers, who endeavored to obscure the dawn of a bright day with the dark clouds of superstition, hostile to knowledge. At their head was Hochstraten (Hoogstraten), an inquisitor or heretic-hunter, a violent, reckless man, who literally longed for the smell of burning heretics, and in Spain would have been a useful Torquemada. His counterpart was Amold of Tongern (Tungern), a Dominican professor of theology. The third in the coalition was Ortuin de Graes, of Deventer (who Latinized his name to Ortuinus Gratius), the son of a clergyman. Ortuin de Graes entertained so violent a hatred against Jews that it could not have been due solely to religious zeal. He made it his special business to stir up the wrath of the Christians by anti-Jewish writings. But as he was too ignorant to concoct a book or even a pamphlet, he surrounded himself with baptized Jews, who had to supply him with materials. A Jew, who, during a persecution or for some reason, had become a convert to Christianity in his fiftieth year, and assumed the name of Victor von Karben, though he had but little Hebrew and rabbinical learning, was dubbed rabbi, in order to give more weight to his attacks on Judaism and to his confession of Christianity. It is not precisely known whether Victor von Karben, who sorrowfully stated that on his conversion he left his wife, three children, brothers and dear friends, voluntarily

PFEFFERKORN'S FIRST PAMPHLET.

or by compulsion reproached the Jews with hating Christians and reviling Christianity. He supplied Ortuinus Gratius with materials for accusations against them, their Talmud, their errors and abominations, which Ortuinus worked up into a book. But Victor von Karben appears, after all, not to have been of much service, or he was too old (born 1442, died 1515) to assist in the execution of a deep scheme, destined to bring profitable business to the Dominicans, the heresy-judges of men and writings. But they needed a Jew for this purpose; their own order had not long before got into rather bad odor. Pfefferkorn was the very man for them. He lent his name to a new anti-Jewish publication, written in Latin by Ortuinus Gratius. It was entitled "A Mirror for Admonition," inviting the Jews to be converted to Christianity. This first anti-Jewish book with Pfefferkorn's name dealt gently with the Jews, even sought to show the groundlessness of the frequent accusations with regard to stealing and murdering Christian children. It entreats Christians not to banish the Jews, nor to oppress them too heavily, since to a certain extent they are human beings. But this friendliness was only a mask, a feeler put forth to gain firm ground. For the Cologne Dominicans aimed at the confiscation of the Talmudic writings, as in the days of Saint Louis of France. This was distantly pointed to in Pfefferkorn's first pamphlet, which endeavored to throw suspicion on the Talmud, and adduced three reasons to explain the stiff-necked unbelief of Jews: their practice of usury, the fact that they were not compelled to go to church, and their attachment to the Talmud. These obstacles once removed, Jews would throng to church in crowds. The pamphlet, therefore, admonished princes and people to check the usury of the Jews, to compel them to attend church and listen to sermons, and to burn the Talmud. It admitted that it is not just to infringe upon the Jews' claim to their writings, but Christians did not hesitate, in certain cases, to do violence to Jews, and compared with that the confiscation of the Talmudic books was a venial offense. This was the sole object of the pamphlet under Pfefferkorn's name. It was generally believed in Germany that the Cologne owls expected to do a good stroke of business ; if they could induce the ruling powers to sequestrate all copies of the Talmud, Dominicans, as inquisitors, would have the disposal of them, and the Jews, who could not do without the Talmud, would pour their wealth into Dominican coffers to have the confiscation annulled. Hence, in the succeeding two years, still putting Pfefferkorn forward as the author, they published several pamphlets, wherein it was asserted to be a Christian duty to expel all Jews, like so many mangy dogs. If the princes would not do so, the people were to take the matter into their own hands, solicit their rulers to deprive the Jews of all their books except the Bible, forcibly take from them all pledges, above all, see that their children be brought up as Christians, and expel the adults as incorrigible rogues. It was no sin to do the worst to Jews, as they were not freemen, but body and soul the property of the princes. If they refused to listen to the prayer of their subjects, the people were to assemble in masses, even create a riot, and impetuously demand the fulfillment of the Christian duty of degrading the Jews. The masses were to declare themselves champions of Christ, and carry out his will. Whoso did an injury to Jews was a follower of Christ; whoso favored them was worse than they, and would hereafter be punished with eternal suffering and hell fire.

But Pfefferkorn, Ortuinus Gratius and the Cologne Dominicans had come too late in the day. Riots for the killing of Jews, though they were no less hated and despised than in the times of the crusades and of the Black Death, were no longer the

fashion. Princes were little disposed to expel the Jews, since with them a regular revenue would disappear. Zeal for the conversion of Jews had considerably cooled down; in fact, many Christians pointed scornfully at baptized Jews, saying that they resembled clean linen: as long as it is fresh the eye delights in it, after a few days' wear it is cast aside as soiled. Thus a converted Jew, immediately after his baptism, is cherished by the Christians; when some days have passed he is neglected, avoided, and finally made sport of.

The German Jews, dreading new dangers from Pfefferkorn's zeal, endeavored to thwart him. Jewish physicians, usually held in high favor at the courts of princes, appear to have exerted their influence with their patrons to show the falsity of Pfefferkorn's accusations, and to render them ineffectual. Even Christians manifested their dissatisfaction with the machinations of the baptized Jew, and loudly proclaimed Pfefferkorn to be a worthless fellow and a hypocrite, who was not to be believed, his object being simply to delude the foolish, and fill his own purse. He, therefore, published a new pamphlet (March, 1509), which he impudently entitled "he Enemy of the Jews." This venomous libel reiterated all his former accusations, and showed how the Jews, by charging interest on interest, impoverished the Christians. He blackened the character of Jewish physicians, saying that they were quacks, who endangered the lives of their Christian patients. It was, therefore, necessary to expel the Jews from Germany, as Emperor Maximilian had driven them from Austria, Styria and Carinthia; or if allowed to remain, they were to be employed in cleansing the streets, sweeping chimneys, removing filth and carrion, and in similar occupations. But, above all, every copy of the Talmud, and all books relating to their religion, the Bible excepted, were to be taken from them. In order effectually to carry out this step, house to house visitation was to be made, and the Jews were to be compelled, if necessary by torture, to surrender their books. Ortuinus Gratius had a hand in the drawing up of this pamphlet, too.

These venomous writings in German and Latin were but means and preliminaries to a plan which was to realize the hopes of the Dominicans of Cologne, the public burning of the theological books of the Jews, or their conversion into a source of profit. They urged Emperor Maximilian, who did not easily lend himself to the commission of a deed of violence, to deliver the Jews, together with their books and purses, to their tender mercies. For this purpose they called in the aid of the bigotry of an unfortunate princess.

Kunigunde, the beautiful sister of Maximilian and favorite daughter of Emperor Frederick, in her youth had been the cause of much affliction to her aged sire. Without her father's knowledge she had married his declared enemy, the Bavarian duke, Albert of Munich. For a long time her deeply offended father would not allow her name to be mentioned. When her husband died in the prime of manhood (1508), his widow, perhaps repenting her youthful error, entered a Franciscan convent at Munich. She became abbess of the nuns of Sancta Clara, and castigated her body. The Dominicans hoped to turn to good purpose the gloomy character of this princess. They furnished Pfefferkorn with letters of introduction to her. With poisoned words he was to detail to her the shameful doings of the Jews, their blasphemies against Jesus, Mary, the apostles and the church in general, and to demonstrate to her that the Jewish books which contained all these abominations deserved to be destroyed. A woman, moreover a superstitious one, whose mind has been dulled in convent walls, is easily persuaded. Kunigunde readily believed the calumnies against

EMPEROR MAXIMILIAN'S MANDATE.

the Jews and their religious literature, especially as they were uttered by a former Jew, who could not but be acquainted with their habits and wickedness, and who assured her that after the destruction of the Jewish books all Hebrews would gradually be converted to Christianity. Pfefferkorn easily obtained from the bigoted nun what he wanted. She gave him a pressing letter to her imperial brother, conjuring him to put a stop to Jewish blasphemies against Christianity, and to issue a decree that all their writings, except the Bible, be taken from the Jews and burnt, lest the sins of blasphemy daily committed by them fall on his crowned head. Furnished with this missive, Pfefferkorn straightway went to Italy, to the camp of the emperor.

The fanatical letter of Kunigunde and the calumnies of Pfefferkorn succeeded in extorting from Maximilian a mandate, dated August 19th, 1509, giving the baptized miscreant full power over Jews. He was authorized to examine Hebrew writings anywhere in the German empire, and to destroy all whose contents were hostile to the Bible and the Christian faith. The Jews were enjoined, under heavy penalties to person and property, to offer no resistance, but to submit their books to Pfefferkorn's examination. Pfefferkorn, with the emperor's authority, returned triumphantly to Germany, to open his campaign against Jewish books or Jewish purses. He began his business, which promised profit, with the community at Frankfort, then the most important of Germany, where many Talmud scholars, consequently many copies of that work, besides many rich Jews, were to be found. On Pfefferkorn's demand, the senate assembled all the Jews in the synagogue, and communicated to them the emperor's order to surrender their books.

In the presence of clergymen and members of the senate, all prayer-books found in the synagogue were confiscated. It happened to be the eve of the Feast of Tabernacles (Friday, September 28th). By his own authority, or pretending to hold it from the emperor, Pfefferkorn forbade the Jews to attend the synagogue on the day of the feast; he intended to hold a house to house visitation on that day, for he was very anxious to get hold of copies of the Talmud. The clergymen present, however, were not so inconsiderate as to turn the feast of the Jews into mourning, but deferred the search for books till the following Monday. How did the Jews act? That they dared protest against this arbitrary proceeding proves that a new order of things had arisen. No longer as formerly in Germany did they submit, with the dumb submission of lambs, to spoliation and death. They appealed to the charters of various popes and emperors, granting them religious liberty, which included possession of their prayer-books and text-books. They demanded a delay of the confiscation in order to appeal to the emperor and the supreme court of judicature. The directors of the community of Frankfort immediately sent a deputy to the elector and archbishop of Mayence, Uriel von Gemmingen, in whose diocese Frankfort was situated, to induce him to forbid the clergy to co-operate in this injustice. When Pfefferkorn began his house to house visitation, the Jews protested so energetically that it had to be deferred until the senate decided whether or not their objection was to be allowed. The decision of the sapient senate was unfavorable; but when the confiscation was about to be commenced, a letter from the archbishop arrived, prohibiting the clergy from lending Pfefferkorn any assistance. This frustrated the scheme; for the senators also withdrew from the transaction as soon as they knew that the highest ecclesiastical dignitary in Germany sided with the Jews. The latter were not idle. For, though they did not know that the powerful Dominicans stood behind Pfefferkorn, they suspected

BISHOP URIEL VON GEMMINGEN.

that persons, hostile to the Jews, used this spiteful wretch to stir up persecution against them. They at once dispatched a defender of their cause to the emperor, and another to the German communities, far and near, to appoint a general synod, to be summoned for the succeeding month, to consider what steps should be taken, and to raise funds.

Temporarily this unpleasant business seemed to take a turn favorable to the Jews. The senate of Frankfort remained passive, except in laying an embargo on the packets of books belonging to Jewish booksellers, and forbidding their sale. The conduct of the archbishop was what benefited them most. Either from a sense of justice--he was generally fair in his dealings--from a kindly feeling for the Jews, from a dislike of Dominican heretic-hunting, or, finally, from jealousy of the emperor's interference with his functions, in giving so miserable a wretch as Pfefferkorn spiritual jurisdiction in his diocese, Uriel von Gemmingen took the part of the Jews. He addressed a letter to the emperor (October 5th), wherein he gently insinuated that he was to blame for having given full powers to so ignorant a man as Pfefferkorn, and asserted that to his knowledge no blasphemous or anti-Christian writings were in the possession of the Jews of his diocese, and hinted that if the emperor absolutely insisted on the examination and confiscation of Hebrew literature, he must employ an expert. He was so zealous on behalf of the Jews as to write to Von Hutten, his agent at the imperial court, to assist the Jews in laying their case before the emperor. In the meantime, not to betray his partisanship, he invited Pfefferkorn to Aschaffenburg, and informed him that his mandate from the emperor was faulty in form, whereby it became ineffectual, for the Jews would dispute its validity.

At this interview the name of Reuchlin was mentioned for the first time, whether by the archbishop or by Pfefferkorn is uncertain. It was suggested to request the emperor to appoint Reuchlin and Victor von Karben Pfefferkorn's coadjutors in the examination of Jewish books. Pfefferkorn, or the Dominican friars themselves, thought it necessary to secure the co-operation of a man whose learning, character and high position would render their proceedings more effective. Reuchlin, the pride of Germany, was to be made their associate, so as to disarm possible opponents. It was part of their scheme, too, to throw discredit, in one way or another, on the man whom obscurantists looked upon with disfavor, and who, to their vexation, first stimulated German and then European Christians in general to study the Hebrew language. But by these very artifices Pfefferkorn and his patrons not only spoilt their game, but raised a storm, which in less than a decade shook the whole edifice of the Catholic Church. It was justly said afterwards that the semi-Jewish Christian had done more injury to Christianity than all the blasphemous writings of the Jews could have done. John Reuchlin assisted in making the transition from the Middle Ages to modern times, and, therefore, his name is famous in the annals of the sixteenth century; but in Jewish history also he deserves honorable mention.

John Reuchlin, of Pforzheim (born 1455, died 1522), or Capnion, as his admirers, the students of the *humaniora,* called him, with his younger contemporary, Erasmus of Rotterdam, delivered Germany from the reproach of barbarism. By their example and incitement they proved that, with regard to knowledge of ancient Greek and Latin, a pure style and humanistic culture in general, Germans could not only rival, but surpass Italians. Besides his astonishing learning in classical literature and his elegant diction, Reuchlin had a pure, upright character, nobility of mind, integrity which was proof against temptation,

JOHN REUCHLIN.

admirable love of truth, and a soft heart. More versatile than Erasmus, his younger colleague, in preparing for and spreading humanistic and esthetic culture in Germany, Reuchlin also devoted himself to the study of Hebrew to acquire mastery of the language blessed by God, and thus emulate his pattern, the Church Father Jerome. His love for Hebrew grew into enthusiasm, when on his second journey to Rome he became acquainted at Florence with the learned youth, Pico di Mirandola, Italy's prodigy, and learned from him what deep, marvelous secrets lay hidden in the Hebrew sources of the Kabbala. After that Reuchlin thirsted for Hebrew literature, but could not quench his thirst. He could not even obtain a printed copy of the Hebrew Bible. Only in his mature age he found opportunities of acquiring a more profound knowledge of Hebrew. During his stay at Linz, at the court of the aged emperor, Frederick III, he made the acquaintance of the imperial physician and Jewish knight, Jacob Loans, and this Jewish scholar became his teacher of Hebrew language and literature.

Reuchlin devoted every hour that he could snatch from his avocations at court to this study, and mastered it so thoroughly that he was soon able to do without a teacher. His genius for languages stood him in good stead, and enabled him to overcome difficulties. He endeavored to turn to speedy account the Hebrew learning acquired with such zeal. He wrote a small work, "The Wonderful Word," a spirited panegyric of the Hebrew language, its simplicity, depth and divine character. "The language of the Hebrews is simple, uncorrupted, holy, terse and vigorous; God confers in it direct with men, and men with angels, without interpreters, face to face, ... as one friend converses with another." A Jew devoted to the antiquities of his race could not have spoken more enthusiastically. The work consists of a series of discussions between an Epicurean philosopher, a Jewish sage (Baruchias), and a Christian (Capnion), and its object is to prove that the wisdom of all nations, the symbols of pagan religions and the forms of their worship are but misconceptions and travesties of Hebrew truth, mysteriously concealed in the words, in the very shapes of the letters of the Hebrew tongue.

Reuchlin may have felt that his knowledge of Hebrew still left much to be desired; he, therefore, as ambassador of the elector palatine, whom he represented at the court of Pope Alexander VI (1498-1500) continued his study of Hebrew literature. Obadiah Sforno, of Cesena, then residing at Rome, became Reuchlin's second teacher of Hebrew. Thus the German humanist, already a famous man, whose Latin discourses were the admiration of Italians, sat at the feet of a Jew to perfect himself in Hebrew, nor did he disdain to accept instruction from a Jew whenever the opportunity offered, so highly did he esteem the Hebrew language.

Being the only Christian in Germany, or we may say in all Europe, sufficiently familiar with the sacred language, Reuchlin's numerous friends urged him to compile a Hebrew grammar, to enable the studiously inclined to instruct themselves. The first Hebrew grammar by a Christian, which Reuchlin designated as "a memorial more lasting than brass" (finished in March, 1506), was a somewhat poor affair. it gave only the essentials of pronunciation and etymology, together with a vocabulary, the imperfections of which need not surprise us, as it is the work of a beginner. But the grammar produced important results: it aroused a taste for Hebrew studies in a large circle of scholars, who thenceforth zealously devoted themselves to it; and these studies supplied a new factor towards the Lutheran Reformation. A number of disciples of Reuchlin, such as Sebastian Munster and Widmannstadt, followed in his footsteps, and raised the Hebrew language to the level of Greek.

REUCHLIN'S PREJUDICE.

But though Reuchlin went down into the Jews' lane to carry off a hidden treasure, he was at first no less intensely prejudiced against the Jewish race than his contemporaries. Forgetful of its former glory, and blind to the solid kernel, because enveloped in a repulsive shell, Reuchlin looked on the Jewish people as utterly barbarous, devoid of all artistic taste, superstitious, mean and depraved. He solemnly declared that he was far from favoring the Jews. At the same time as his Hebrew grammar he wrote an epistle, in which he traced all the misery of the Jews to their blind unbelief, instead of looking for its source in Christians' want of charity towards them. Reuchlin, no less than Pfefferkorn, charged the Jews with blasphemy against Jesus, Mary, the apostles and Christians in general; but a time came when he regretted this indiscreet lucubration of his youth. For his heart did not share the prejudices of his head. Whenever he met individual Jews, he gave them his affection, or at least his esteem; he probably found that they were better than Christians represented them to be. His sense of justice did not allow him to let wrong be done to them, much less to help in doing it.

When Pfefferkorn and the Cologne Dominicans approached Reuchlin, he was at the zenith of his life and fame. High and low honored him for his rectitude; Emperor Frederick had ennobled him; Emperor Maximilian appointed him counselor and judge of the Swabian League; the circle of humanists, the order of free spirits within and without Germany, loved, worshipped, almost deified him. Though hitherto no shadow of heresy had fallen on Reuchlin, who was on the best of terms with the Dominicans, yet the friends of darkness instinctively saw in him their secret enemy. His cultivation of science and classical literature, his anxiety for an elegant Latin style, his enthusiasm for Greek, by which all Germany had been infected, and worse than all, his introduction of Hebrew, his preference for " Hebrew truth," for the Hebrew text over the corrupt Latin Vulgate, which the church held as canonical and unassailable, were considered by the obscurantists as crimes, for which the Inquisition could not, indeed, directly prosecute him, but which secured him a place in their black book.

The order given to Pfefferkorn, the secret agent of the Dominicans of Cologne, to implicate Reuchlin in the examination of blasphemous Jewish writings, as said above, was a cunningly devised trap. On his second journey to the imperial camp, Pfefferkorn waited on Reuchlin at his own house, endeavored to make him a confederate in his venomous schemes against the Jews, and showed him the imperial mandate. Reuchlin declined the proposal somewhat hesitatingly, though he approved of destroying Jewish libels on Christianity ; but he pointed out that the emperor's mandate was faulty in form, and that, therefore, the authorities would not willingly enforce it. Reuchlin is said to have hinted that, if invited to do so, he would interest himself in the matter. Pfefferkorn, in consequence, applied to the emperor for a second mandate, correct in form and unassailable. But the Jews had not been idle in endeavors to induce the emperor to revoke the mandate and restore their books.

The community of Frankfort had appointed Jonathan Levi Zion, a zealous member, to advocate their case with the emperor. The community of Ratisbon also had sent an agent to the imperial court. Isaac Triest, a man greatly beloved by the persons surrounding the emperor, took great pains to frustrate Pfefferkorn's plans. The Jewish advocates were supported by influential Christians, including the representative of the archbishop and the Margrave of Baden. They first adduced the charters

guaranteeing religious liberty, granted to the Jews by emperors and popes, in accordance with which even the emperor had no right to interfere with the management of their private affairs, or to attack their property in the shape of religious books. They did not fail to inform the emperor that their accuser was a worthless person, a thief and burglar. The Jewish advocates thought that they had attained their end. The emperor had listened to their petition in an audience, and promised them a speedy reply. Their friendly reception led them to look for an immediate settlement of this painful affair; moreover, it was a good omen that Uriel von Gemmingen, their protector, was appointed commissary.

But they did not understand Maximilian's vacillating character. As soon as Pfefferkorn appeared before him, armed with another autograph letter from his sister, wherein the ultra-pious nun conjured him not to injure Christianity by the revocation of his mandate, the scales were turned against the Jews. The emperor was in reality secretly piqued that the despised Jews of Frankfort, in contempt of his mandate, had refused to give up the books found in their houses.

He thereupon issued a second mandate (November 10th, 1509), wherein he reproached the Jews with having offered resistance, and ordered the confiscation to be continued. But he appointed Archbishop Uriel as commissioner, and advised him to obtain counsel from the universities of Cologne, Mayence, Erfurt and Heidelberg, and to associate with himself learned men, such as Reuchlin, Victor von Karben, and the inquisitor, Hoogstraten, who was wholly ignorant of Hebrew. With this mandate in his pocket, Pfefferkorn hastened back to the scene of his activity, the Rhenish provinces. Archbishop Uriel appointed Hermann Hess, chancellor of the University of Mayence, his delegate, to direct the confiscation of Jewish books. Accompanied by him, Pfefferkorn again repaired to Frankfort, and the book-hunt began afresh. Fifteen hundred manuscripts, including those already seized, were taken from the Frankfort Jews, and deposited in the town hall.

Worse than the emperor's vacillating conduct was the apathy shown by the large communities of Germany in the appointment of delegates to a conference to discuss and frustrate the malicious plans of Pfefferkorn, or rather, of the Dominicans. Smaller communities had contributed their share towards the expenses occasioned by this serious matter, but the larger and richer communities of Rothenburg on the Tauber, Weissenburg and Furth, on which the Jews of Frankfort had counted most, displayed deplorable indifference. But when, in consequence of the second mandate, Jewish books were confiscated not only at Frankfort but also in other communities, more active interest was manifested. First the Frankfort senate was influenced in their favor. The Jewish booksellers were accustomed to bring their bales of books for sale to the spring Fair at Frankfort. Pfefferkorn threatened to confiscate these also, but the senate of Frankfort refused to assist in the measure, being unwilling to break the laws regulating the Fair. The Jewish booksellers, moreover, had safe-conducts each from the prince of his own country, protecting not only their persons, but also their property. The archbishop maintained sullen silence, but was inclined to favor the Jews. He did not call together the learned men whom the emperor had mentioned to examine the Jewish books, and did no more than he could help. Many princes, also, whose eyes had been opened to the ultimate results of this strange confiscation, seem to have made representations to the emperor. Public opinion was particularly severe on Pfefferkorn. But he and the Dominicans were not idle; they endeavored to win over the emperor and public opinion, and it is

MAXIMILIAN'S THIRD MANDATE.

remarkable that the enemies of publicity should have opened the mouth of that hitherto silent arbitress, and rendered her powerful.

For this purpose there appeared another anti-Jewish pamphlet, with Pfefferkorn's name on the title-page, entitled, "In Praise and Honor of Emperor Maximilian." It blew clouds of incense into the emperor's face, and regretted that the charges against the Jews, from indifference and ignorance, were so little noticed in Christian circles. It reasserted that the Talmud, the usury of the Jews, and their facilities for making money, were the causes of their obstinately refusing to become Christians. Thus the Cologne Dominicans--always standing behind Pfefferkorn--by means of public opinion again attempted to put moral pressure on Maximilian.

But this public opinion must have spoken so strongly in favor of the Jews, that Maximilian was induced to take a step unusual for an emperor, namely, in a measure revoke his former commands, by directing the senate of Frankfort to restore to the Jews their books (May 23d, 1510), "till the completion of our purpose and the inspection of the books." Great was the joy of the Jews. They had escaped a great danger: not their religious books only, so dear to their hearts, but their position in the Holy Roman Empire had been at stake, since the Dominicans, in case of success, would not have stopped at tile confiscation of books, but would have indicted new humiliations and persecutions.

But the Jews triumphed too soon; the Dominicans and their confederate and tool, Pfefferkorn, would not so readily surrender the advantages already secured. A regrettable occurrence in the Mark of Brandenburg supplied fresh energy to their machinations, and a pretext for formulating an accusation. A thief had stolen some sacred emblems from a church, and when questioned as to the holy wafer, he confessed having sold it to Jews in the Brandenburg district. Of course, the thief was believed, and the bishop of Brandenburg entered on the persecution of the Jews with fiery fanaticism. The elector of Brandenburg, Joachim I, an ardent heretic-hunter, had the accused brought to Berlin. The accusation of reviling the host was soon supplemented by the charge of infanticide. Joachim had the Jews tortured, and then ordered thirty to be burnt. With firmness, songs of praise on their lips, these martyrs of Brandenburg met their fiery deaths (July 10th, 1510), except two, who, with the fear of the stake upon them, submitted to baptism, and suffered the seemingly more honorable fate of being beheaded. This is the first mention of Jews in Berlin and Brandenburg. The occurrence made a great stir in Germany, and the Cologne Dominicans employed it to induce the emperor to issue a new mandate for the confiscation of Jewish books, seeing that to the Talmud alone could be attributed the alleged hostility of the Jews to Christianity. They sheltered themselves behind the same go-between; the bigoted nun, the ducal abbess Kunigunde, to whom the diabolical wickedness of the Jews, as revealed by the above occurrence, was presented in the most glaring colors. The Dominicans suggested to her how detrimental to Christianity must be the fact that the host-reviling and child-murdering Jews could boast of having had their books restored to them by order of the emperor, who thus, to a certain extent, approved of the abuse of Christianity which they contained. The abbess thereupon fairly assailed her brother, and at their interview at Munich besought him on her knees to reconsider the matter of the Jewish books. Maximilian was perplexed. He was loath to refuse his dearly beloved sister what she had so much at heart; on the other hand, he was not highly edified by Pfefferkorn's tissue of lies about the Jews. He found an expedient to appear just to both parties.

REUCHLIN'S OPINION.

He issued a new mandate, the fourth in this affair (July 6th, 1510), addressed to Archbishop Uriel, directing him to resume the inquiry, but in another form. The indictment was not to be considered as proved, but was to be thoroughly investigated. The archbishop of Mayence was to take the opinions of the German universities named, and also of Reuchlin, Victor von Karben and Hoogstraten, to whom the emperor sent a special summons in official form. The final decision as to the character of the Jewish writings was to be communicated to him by Pfefferkorn, the originator of the inquiry. The Jews had reason to look forward with anxiety to the issue; their weal and woe depended on it.

It was fortunate for the Jews that the honest, truthful Reuchlin, so enthusiastically prepossessed for Hebrew and Kabbalistic literature, was asked to give his opinion of Jewish literature. The Cologne Dominicans, who had proposed him, thereby frustrated their own design, and as a further effect made him the enemy of their hostile endeavors. As soon as Reuchlin received the emperor's command, he set to work to answer the question, "Whether it was godly, laudable, and advantageous to Christianity to burn the Jewish writings," whereby the Talmud especially was meant. His judgment was extremely favorable to the writings in question, nor did he miss the chance of bestowing sundry side blows on the vile instigator Pfefferkorn. Jewish literature, the mistress of his heart, was to be charged as a culprit, and should he fail to defend her with all the powers of his mind ? Reuchlin's opinion is conceived in the pedantic, heavy, juridical style then prevailing, but does not lack ability. He started from the correct point of view, that, in answering the question, the Jewish writings were not to be treated in the aggregate as a homogeneous literature, but that, excluding the Bible, they were to be divided into six classes. The class of exegetic works, such as those by R. Solomon (Rashi), Ibn-Ezra, the Kimchis, Moses Gerundensis and Levi ben Gershon, far from being detrimental to Christianity, he declared to be indispensable to Christian theology, the most learned Christian commentators of the Old Testament having taken the best of their work from the Jews, as from fountains whence flow the real truth and understanding of the Holy Scriptures. If from the voluminous writings of Nicholas de Lyra, the best Christian exegetist, all borrowed from Rashi were to be excised, the part left, which he himself had composed, might be comprised in a few pages. He, indeed, considered it a disgrace that many doctors of divinity, from ignorance of Hebrew and Greek, interpreted the Scriptures wrongly. The class of Hebrew writings on philosophy, natural sciences and the liberal arts were in no way distinguished from what might be found in Greek, Latin, or German works. With regard to the Talmud, against which the chief accusation was laid, Reuchlin confessed his inability to understand it; but other learned Christians understood no more of it than they might learn from its accusers, including Pfefferkorn. He was acquainted with many who condemned the Talmud without understanding it. But could one write against mathematics without having knowledge thereof? He was, therefore, of opinion that the Talmud was not to be burnt, even if it were true that it contained libels on the founders of Christianity. "If the Talmud were deserving of such condemnation, our ancestors of many hundred years ago, whose zeal for Christianity was much greater than ours, would have burnt it. The baptized Jews, Peter Schwarz and Pfefferkorn, the only persons who insist on its being burnt, probably wish it for private reasons."

To defend Kabbalistic writings, and save them from being burnt, was easy enough. Reuchlin had but to point to occurrences at the papal court,

scarcely two decades ago. The learned and eccentric Count Pico di Mirandola had aroused enthusiastic admiration for the Kabbala, maintaining that it contained the most solid foundation of the chief doctrines of Christianity. Sixtus IV had caused some of the Kabbalistic writings to be translated into Latin. Reuchlin concluded his opinion by advising that their books should not be taken from the Jews, nor burnt, but that at every German university two professors of Hebrew be appointed for ten years, who might also be asked to teach modern, or rabbinical Hebrew; and thus the Jews might be led by gentle means and by conviction to embrace Christianity.

Unquestionably, since Jews had been ill-used and persecuted by Christians, they had not found so friendly an advocate as Reuchlin, who declared himself in their favor in an official document, intended for the chancellor of the empire, and the emperor himself. Two points on which Reuchlin laid stress were especially important to Jews. The first was, that the Jews were citizens of the Holy Roman Empire, and were entitled to its full privileges and protection. This was the first stammering utterance of that liberating word of perfect equality, which required more than three centuries for its perfect enunciation and acknowledgment. The medieval delusion, that the Jews, by Vespasian and Titus' conquest of Jerusalem, had become the bondmen of their successors, the Roman and German emperors, was hereby partly dispelled. The recognition that Jews also had rights, which the emperor and the state, the clergy and the laity must respect, was the first faint, trembling ray of light after a long, dark night. The second point, which Reuchlin emphasized more positively, was of equal importance: that the Jews must not be considered or treated as heretics. Since they stood without the church, and were not bound to hold the Christian faith, the ideas of heresy and unbelief--those terrifying and lethal anathemas of the Middle Ages--did not apply to them.

Of what use this judgment of Reuchlin was to the Jews, we discover by the decision of the faculties consulted--faculties to whom the Talmud, of course, was a book with seven seals. The Cologne Dominicans in a body, the theological faculty, the inquisitor Hoogstraten, and the gray-haired convert Victor von Karben, all mouthpieces of one mind, did not trouble themselves to prove that the Talmud was hostile to Christianity; they assumed it, and, therefore, quickly arrived at their decision, that the Talmudic writings, and all others, probably of the same stamp, were to be seized and burnt. But they went further; Hoogstraten, in particular, had the assurance to say that the Jews should be indicted. Experts were to extract and arrange heretical passages from the Talmud and other Jewish books; then the Jews were to be questioned whether or not they admitted the perniciousness of books containing such doctrines. If they admitted it, they could raise no objection to have them committed to the flames. If they obstinately persevered in treating such passages as portions of their creed, the emperor was to surrender them as convicted heretics for punishment to the Inquisition.

The faculty of the university of Mayence delivered a similar sentence, but went much further. They pronounced not only all Talmudic and rabbinical writings to be full of errors and heresy, but that even the Scriptures must have been contaminated and corrupted by them, especially in articles of faith; wherefore these were to be taken from the Jews, examined, and if their expectation was realized, the Jewish Bibles were to be thrown into the flames.

THE HEBREW BIBLE THREATENED.

It was a clever trick on the part of the Dominicans to get rid of the inconvenient Hebrew text, the "Hebrew truth". Had the theologians of Mayence and Cologne succeeded in enforcing their views, the Book received on Sinai, the words of the

Prophets, the Psalms, monuments of a time of grace, would have been cast upon a blazing pyre, and a bastard, the corrupt Latin Vulgate, substituted for it. The Dominicans appear to have suspected that the plain sense of the words of the Bible would bring ruin upon them. Fortunately, the Cologne Dominicans themselves defeated their cunningly laid plan by an act of villainy.

Reuchlin had sent his opinion on Jewish literature in a sealed packet, and by a sworn messenger, to Archbishop Uriel, assuming that, being an official secret, it would be opened and read only by the archbishop and the emperor. But Pfefferkorn, who believed himself to be on the eve of avenging himself on the Jews, had it open in his hand even before the emperor had read it. How this occurred has never been cleared up. Reuchlin in plain words denounced the Cologne priests as unscrupulous seal-breakers. We ought almost to be grateful to them for having dragged an affair, originally enveloped in official secrecy, into publicity, thereby calling in another tribunal, and turning the peril of the Jews into a peril to the church. They had grown desperate over Reuchlin's opinion, because his voice had great weight with the emperor and his advisers. Therefore, the Dominicans, armed at all points, set to work to publish a refutation of Reuchlin's defense of the Jews and their books. It was written in German to render the cause popular, and incense the multitude so as to render it impossible for the emperor to listen to Reuchlin.

This libel, entitled "Handspiegel," spread abroad in thousands of copies, on a man so highly placed and honored, a judge of the Swabian League, a scholar of eminence, naturally caused a great sensation. Since the invention of printing it was the first furious attack on a dignitary, and being written in German, everyone could understand it. The Cologne Dominicans had permitted themselves to be guided by their envenomed hatred rather than by prudence. Reuchlin was compelled to take steps against such attacks, by which his honor was too deeply wounded for silence. He hastened to the emperor, and complained of Pfefferkorn, the rancorous calumniator, the ostensible author of the "Handspiegel". The emperor, by words and gestures, betrayed his indignation, and quieted the excited Reuchlin by the promise that the matter should be inquired into by the bishop of Augsburg. But amidst the press of business, in the confusion of Italian quarrels, the emperor forgot Reuchlin, the mortification he had suffered, and the redress promised him. The Frankfort autumn Fair was approaching, at which Pfefferkorn intended to offer for sale the remainder of the copies, and nothing had been done for or by Reuchlin.

Thus Reuchlin was compelled to make the Talmud a personal question, to appeal to public opinion, and thereby render the matter one of almost universal interest. He prepared a defensive and offensive reply to the " Handspiegel" for the Frankfort Fair. At the end of August, or beginning of September, 1511, his controversial pamphlet, entitled "Augenspiegel" (or Spectacles, a pair of spectacles being represented on the title page), which has acquired historical celebrity, made its appearance. He designed to reveal to the German public the villainy of Pfefferkorn and his coadjutors. It was a pamphlet which, we may say without exaggeration, was equivalent to a great action. It was directed against Pfefferkorn, and by implication against the Cologne Dominicans, the patrons and instigators of his calumnies. It relates in plain, honest language the progress of the whole affair: how the baptized "Jew " had made every effort to prove the Talmud dangerous, desiring to have it burnt, and had meant to turn Reuchlin to account in the matter. He publishes the missives of the emperor and of the archbishop addressed to him, and also his "Opinion." He reports how Pfefferkorn by dishonest means obtained possession of the "Opinion," and misused it to concoct a libel, containing no less than thirty-four untruths about him (Reuchlin). The tone of the "Augenspiegel" expresses the just indignation of a man of honor against a villain who has set a trap for him.

What roused the indignation of Reuchlin most was the charge that he had been bribed to write his defense of the Talmud. With honest anger he protested that at no time during his whole existence had he received from Jews, or on their behalf, a single penny, or any other reward. No less hurt was Reuchlin at the contempt expressed for his Hebrew scholarship, especially at the accusation that he had not himself composed his Hebrew grammar. His defense of the Jews is dignified. The scoundrel Pfefferkorn had reproached him with having learnt Hebrew from Jews, with whom, then, he must have had intercourse in defiance of the canon law. Thereupon Reuchlin says: "[He] writes that Divine law forbids our holding communion with Jews; this is not true. Every Christian may go to law with them, buy of or make presents to them. Cases may occur where Christians inherit legacies together with Jews. It is allowed to converse with and learn from them, as Saint Jerome and Nicholas de Lyra did. And lastly, a Christian should love a Jew as his neighbor; all this is founded on the law."

It may be imagined what excitement was created by Reuchlin's "Augenspiegel", written in German, when it appeared at the Frankfort Fair, the meeting-place of hundreds of thousands, at a time when there was no public press, and everyone readily lent his ear to a scandalous tale. To find that so distinguished a man as Reuchlin would set an accuser of the Jews in the pillory as a calumniator and liar, was something so new and surprising as to make readers rub their eyes, and ask themselves whether they had not hitherto been dozing. The Jews greedily bought a book in which for the first time a man of honor entered the lists on their behalf, and with powerful voice stigmatized the charges against them as calumnies. They rejoiced at having found a champion, and thanked God that He had not forsaken them in their tribulation. Who would find fault with them for laboring in the promulgation of Reuchlin's pamphlet? But by preaching against it in their pulpits, and by prohibiting its sale as far as they could, bigoted priests of the stamp of the Cologne Dominicans did most to disseminate it. From all directions, in learned and unlearned circles, congratulations were sent to Reuchlin,with expressions of satisfaction that he had so boldly and firmly settled the impudent Pfefferkorn and his abettors.

With the publication and circulation of Reuchlin's treatise, and his defense of the Talmud, commenced a struggle which every day became more serious, and at last assumed far greater proportions than the subject justified. For the bigots, still in the full power of their terrorizing might, did not hesitate to

PFEFFERKORN PREACHES.

take up the challenge. Pfefferkorn's cause was also theirs. Yet a man had dared step forward boldly, not only to disapprove of the condemnation of the Talmud, but also to declare that the persecution of the Jews was unchristianlike; and that they ought, on the contrary, to be treated with sympathy and love. What audacity! It aroused in them such virtuous indignation that they shot beyond the mark, and committed such blunders that they damaged their cause irreparably.

Pastor Peter Meyer, of Frankfort-on-the-Main, who had not been able to obtain the prohibition of the sale of the "Augenspiegel," made the second mistake. He announced from the pulpit during service that Pfefferkorn would preach on the eve of the next "Feast of our Lady" against Reuchlin's Jewish writings, and he exhorted the faithful to attend in great numbers. Nothing could be more fatal than this error. Pfefferkorn with his disagreeable, repulsive face, distinctly Jewish features and coarse, vulgar look, preach before a Christian congregation in his Jewish-German jargon ! Each word and each movement would provoke his hearers to laughter, and drive away even sincere devotion. Moreover, was it in accordance with Catholic law that a layman, above all a married layman, should officiate in the church? Not long before this a simple shepherd had been sentenced to be burned on account of unsanctioned preaching. To keep the letter of the law Pfefferkorn preached on the appointed day (September 7th,1511), not in the church, but before the entrance, to a great crowd of people. It must have been very droll to see how this ill-favored Jew made the sign of the cross over believers, and spoke of the Christian faith in the Jewish jargon. Pfefferkorn's chief desire was to make the Jews and their well-wishers detestable, and to excite the hatred of his hearers against them.

Until now thd chief mover of the whole scandal, the venomous and malicious master heretic-hunter, Jacob Hoogstraten, had kept behind the scenes, but had sent his followers to the front one by one: first Pfefferkorn, then Ortuinus Gratius and Amold von Tongern. Henceforth he stood in the foreground himself, his insolent demeanor seeming to assume that priests and laymen must all bow aefore him, and sink under his frown in the dust, and that he had the right to tread statutes and customs under his feet. To save, by violent measures, the weakened authority of the order, all Dominicans had to make common cause, and apply their energy to carry through the condemnation of Reuchlin and the Talmud. The conflict spread over a wider area, and became an affair of the whole order.

Authorized by the provincial of his order, Hoogstraten, in his capacity as inquisitor, suddenly issued (September l5th, l513) a Summons to Reuchlin to appear at Mayence within six days, at eight o'clock in the morning, to be examined on the charge of heresy and of favoring the Jews. On the appointed day Hoogstraten, with a host of Dominicans, appeared in Mayence; they were confederates, chosen to sit as judges in the commission. Hoogstraten opened the session, acting at once as judge and accuser. He had prepared an unassailable bill of indictment against Reuchlin and the Talmud, and taken the precaution to seek allies, so that he might not stand alone in this weighty contest. Shortly before, he had addressed letters to four universities, begging them to express their opinion on Reuchlin's book, "Augenspiegel," in accordance with his own views, and all had fulfilled his expectations.

The accusation which he brought forward was, of course, that which Pfefferkorn and Amold von Tonern had already made. It had for its basis: Reuchlin favors the Jews too much, treats "the insolent people" almost as members of: the church, and as

men on an equality with others, while his writings savor too much of heresy. Hoogstraten, therefore, instructed the court to pronounce sentence upon Reuchlin's "Augenspiegel": that it was full of heresy and error, too favorable to the unbelieving Jews, and insulting to the church, and therefore ought to be condemned, suppressed, and destroyed by fire. One must not overlook the great difference between a German and a Spanish inquisition court. Torquemada or Ximenes would have made short work of it, and condemned the book together with the author to the stake. Hoogstraten was not too kindhearted for such a sentence; but he dared not venture so far, because he would have had all Germany, the ecclesiastical as well as the temporal rulers against him.

General indignation was aroused at the injustice of a trial carried on in violation of all rules. The students of the Mayence University, not yet tainted by the corruption of theology, their judgment not warped by casuistry, and not influenced by foreign considerations, loudly proclaimed their displeasure at this shameless proceeding of the Inquisition. They carried the doctors of jurisprudence with them, and this induced other earnest men to interfere.

To the surprise of the Dominicans, the aged, venerable Reuchlin appeared in Mayence, accompanied by two respected counselors of the Duke of Wurtemberg. The chapter now took great trouble to effect a reconciliation. But Hoogstraten, who wished to see smoke rise from the fagots, would agree to nothing, and delayed the negotiations till the 12th of October, the time when the final sentence would be pronounced. The inquisitor commanded all the ecclesiastics in Mayence to announce from the pulpit that everyone, Christian or Jew, if he would escape punishment, must give up all copies of the "Augenspiegel" to the flames. The people were promised thirty days' indulgence, if they assembled on the appointed day at the church square to celebrate the auto-da-fe and increase its splendor. On the 12th Of October the place before the church in Mayence was thronged with spectators--the curious, the sympathetic, and the seekers after indulgence! Decked out like peacocks, the

Fathers and Brothers of the Dominican order, and the theologians of the universities of Cologne, Louvain, and Erfurt, strutted along to the tribunal erected for them, and "the earth trembled under their feet." Hoogstraten, till now the accuser, again took his place among the judges. They were about to pronounce the formula of the curse, and have the fire kindled, when a messenger hastily arrived, bringing a letter from Archbishop Uriel, which turned them speechless.

Uriel von Gemmingen, like most bishops of his time, was more worldly-minded than spiritual, and had no canonical fanaticism against Jews. The presumptuousness of the Dominicans of Cologne and their unjust proceedings against Reuchlin angered him, too. Therefore, he issued a proclamation to the commissioners selected from his chapter, ordering that judgment be delayed for one month until a new agreement might be arrived at. If they did not consent, this letter deprived them of their privileges as judges of the inquisitorial court, and every thing hitherto decreed was null and void. Utterly dumbfounded, the Dominicans listened to the notary's reading of the document, which entirely frustrated their schemes and machinations. Hoogstraten alone boldly dared express his anger at the denial of their rights. The other confederates slunk away ashamed, followed by the jeers of the street boys, and the cry of the men, "O that these Brothers, who wished to outrage a just man, might be burnt at the stake."

Reuchlin was by no means so situated as to be able to triumph over his enemies and those of the Jews. Though subdued for the moment, they were certainly not vanquished. He knew their cunning and malignity too well to give himself up to inactive enjoyment of his victory. He knew that their persecutions would only be redoubled in the future. Therefore, he hastened to announce his appeal to the pope, so that silence might be imposed from that quarter on his embittered enemies. But Reuchlin justly feared that with the vacillation and venality of the Vatican his cause would go badly, if the investigation were conducted beyond the jurisdiction of the pope by the Dominicans of Cologne. Therefore, he sent a Hebrew letter to Benet de Lates, the Jewish physician of Pope Leo X, begging him to plead for the pope's favor in his cause.

Leo, of the celebrated family of the Medici, about whom his father had said that he was the wisest of his sons, had succeeded to the papal chair only a few months before. He was an aristocrat, more interested in politics than in religion, a Roman pagan rather than a Catholic priest, looking down with contempt from his Olympian heights on theological controversy as child's play. He only considered how best to steer between the two warring states or houses of Hapsburg and Valois, without endangering the temporal interest of the Roman Catholic hierarchy. With candor that would surprise us today, the pope ventured to say, "It is well known how useful this fable of Christ has been to us and ours ! " With him now rested the decision, whether Reuchlin's "Augenspiegel" savored of heresy, and whether he duly or unduly favored the Jews. Leo, whose pontificate fell in a time when theological questions threatened to embroil all Europe, perhaps knew less of them than his cook. Much, therefore, depended on the light in which the conflict between Reuchlin and the Dominicans was placed before him. For this reason Reuchlin begged the physician Benet de Lates, who had access to the pope and care of "the person of his Holiness," to win over Leo X, so that the trial might not take place in Cologne or its vicinity, where his cause would be lost. Reuchlin laid all the circumstances before him: how Pfefferkorn and the Cologne Dominicans had conspired against the Jews and the Talmud, and how only his extraordinary efforts had saved the Talmud from destruction. Had the Dominicans been able to get hold of and read this letter, they could have brought forward incontestable proof of Reuchlin's friendliness towards the Jews, for in it he wrote much that he had publicly denied.

It is natural that Benet de Lates brought all his influence to bear in favor of Reuchlin. And it was probably owing to his zeal that Leo so soon (November 21st, 1513) issued instructions to the bishops of Speyer and Worms on the controversy between Reuchlin and Hoogstraten. Leo ordered that they be examined separately or together, by the bishops or by judges appointed by them, who, without the intervention of any other tribunal, were to pronounce judgment, to be accepted without appeal. The bishop of Worms, a Dalburg, with whom Reuchlin was on friendly terms, did not care to accept the commission. So the young bishop of Speyer, George, elector palatine and duke of Bavaria, appointed two judges, who summoned both parties to appear within a month before the tribunal in Speyer. Reuchlin came punctually, accompanied by a procurator and friends. Hoogstraten, on the other hand, trusting to the power of the Dominicans, did not present himself, nor send a competent representative. The judges commenced the suit, not with becoming energy, but with a certain half-

heartedness, perhaps from fear of the revenge of the Dominicans. The trial was spun out over three months (January to April, 1514).

Only after Reuchlin had written two German papers on the matter in dispute and the progress of the proceedings, did the bishop deign to notice the evidence and pass judgment, which was wholly in favor of Reuchlin. He stated that the "Augenspiegel" contained not an iota of heresy or error, that it did not unduly favor the Jews, that, therefore, Hoogstraten had slandered the author, and silence should be imposed on him in this matter; that the writings might be read and printed by everyone, and that Hoogstraten be charged with the costs (111 Rhenish gold florins).

The Dominicans of Cologne gnashed their teeth, stormed and raged at the issue of the suit, and used every effort to overthrow the judgment of the apostolic court. At that time, on account of the disunion in Germany, it was very difficult to put into execution a judicial decree, and the Dominicans were not inclined to lessen the difficulty when the sentence was given against themselves. They laughed at the bishop of Speyer, calling him a stupid fellow. The notice of the verdict was torn down by the bold Pfefferkorn. Hoostraten had unofficially--that is to say, without giving notice to the bishop of Speyer, then acting as apostolic judge--appealed to the pope, although he had scouted the idea of such an appeal before. His hope of winning the suit against Reuchlin and securing the condemnation of the "Augenspiegel" was founded on the venality of the Vatican. "Rome will do anything for money," he frankly said; "Reuchlin is poor, and the Dominicans are rich; justice can be suppressed by money." Hoogstraten could also count on the good will of the cardinals, who inveighed against free inquiry. At all events, they could be depended upon to drag out the suit so long that Reuchlin's means would not suffice to meet the costs. Besides this, the Dominicans relied on obtaining from the universities, in particular the leading one of Paris, the condemnation of the "Augenspiegel," and using it to exert pressure upon the pope. All Dominicans, Thomists and obscurantists, both in and outside Germany, made common cause to work the downfall of Reuchlin.

This union of the Dominican party had the effect of binding together the friends of learning, the enemies of scholasticism, bigotry and church doctrine--in one word, the Humanists--and inducing them to take concerted action. Virtually a society of Humanists, a Reuchlinist party, was formed in western Europe, the members of which silently worked for one another and for Reuchlin: "One supported the other, and said to his comrade, Be brave." "All we who belong to the ranks of learning are devoted to Reuchlin no less than soldiers to the emperor." It was a formal alliance, which the supporters of Reuchlin loyally adhered to. So, in consequence of Pfefferkorn's bitter hostility to the Jews and the Talmud, two parties were formed in Christendom, the Reuchlinists and the Arnoldists, who waged fierce conflict with each other. It was a struggle of the dark Middle Ages with the dawn of a better time.

Young Germany was working with all its might on behalf of Reuchlin and against the bigots: besides Hermannvon Busche, and Crotus Rublanus (Johann Jager), there was the fiery Ulrich von Hutten, the most energetic and virile character of the time. In fact, Hutten's energy first found a worthy aim in the passionate feud between Reuchlin and the Dominicans. Formerly his fencing had consisted of passes in the empty air; his knightly courage and fiery genius had met only phantom adversaries. Now, for the first time, the knightly phantom youth of

ULRICH VON HUTTEN.

six-and-twenty had a clear perception of the relation of things ; he saw a real enemy, to meet whom with his knight's sword and the sharper weapon of his intellect, in a life and death struggle, would be a praiseworthy, glorious undertaking. To destroy the Dominicans, priests and bigots, and establish the kingdom of intellect and free thought, to deliver Germany from the nightmare of ecclesiastical superstition and barbarism, raise it from its abjectness, and make it the arbiter of Europe, seemed to him the aim to toil for. As soon as Hutten was clearly conscious of this, he worked ceaselessly for his object, the first step towards its realization being to help Reuchlin, the leader in the struggle for humanism, to gain the victory over his mortal foes. A cardinal, Egidio de Viterbo, who delighted in the Hebrew language and in the Kabbala, openly sided with Reuchlin. He wrote to him, "The Law (Torah) revealed to man in fire was first saved from fire when Abraham escaped the burning furnace, and now a second time, when Reuchlin saved, from the fire, the writings from which the Law received light, for had they been destroyed eternal darkness would again have set in. So, exerting ourselves for your cause, we are not defending you, but the Law, not the Talmud, but the church." It is remarkable that the whole Franciscan order, from hatred of the Dominicans, took up Reuchlin's cause.

In almost every town there were Reuchlinists and anti-Reuchlinists, whose mutual hatred brought them at times to blows. The motto of one was, "Rescue of the 'Augenspiegel' and preservation of the Talmud", and of the other, "Damnation and destruction to both." Involuntarily the Reuchlinists became friends of the Jews, and sought grounds on which to defend them. The adherents of the Dominicans became fiercer enemies to the Jews, and sought out obscure books to prove their wickedness.

The report of this contest spread through Europe. At first limited to Germany, the controversy soon reached both Rome and Paris. Hoogstraten and the Dominicans worked with energy to have the judgment of Speyer overthrown, in the latter place by the greatest university, in the former by the papal see, and to have Reuchlin's writings sentenced to the flames. In both places they had powerful and influential allies, who devotedly and zealously worked for their party.

Reuchlin, although his suit had been lawfully won in the apostolic court in Speyer, was forced to take steps to counteract the appeal instituted by the intrigues of his enemies. And his friends succeeded in influencing the pope. Leo X appointed the cardinal and patriarch Dominico Grimani as judge of the inquiry. It was well known that this ecclesiastical prince cultivated rabbinical literature, and, as patron of the Franciscan order, hated the Dominicans, and took Reuchlin's side. Without doubt prominent Jews were working in Rome for Reuchlin, but, like the German Jews, they had the good sense to keep in the background, so as not to imperil the cause by stamping it as Jewish. Cardinal Grimani issued (June, 1514) a summons to both parties, but in consideration of Reuchlin's advanced years permitted him to send a representative, while Hoogstraten had to appear in person. Furnished with recommendations and a well-filled purse, the inquisitor appeared in Rome with undiminished confidence of obtaining a victory. What could not be obtained in Rome for money?

Reuchlin had nothing of the kind to offer; he was poor. He had not the magic wand which commands the gold of bigoted women, nor the conjurer's formula over father-confessors, who are apt treasure-diggers. But there was no lack of recommendations from his friends and well-wishers. Emperor Maximilian, who, much to his own regret, had originated

all this disturbance, by lending ear to Pfefferkorn's stupidities and his sister's hysterical piety, often interceded with the pope for Reuchlin. The emperor wrote that he believed that the Cologne people wished to prolong the controversy illegally and through intrigue, in order to crush the excellent, inoffensive, learned and orthodox Reuchlin; that what he had written (in favor of the Hebrew

Scriptures) had been written at the emperor's command, with a good object, and for the benefit of Christendom.

But the Dominicans defied public opinion, the commission appointed by the pope, and the pope. They spoke of the pope as of a schoolboy under their authority. If he did not give a decision in their favor, they threatened to withdraw their allegiance, and desert him, even risking a rupture with the church. They went so far as to threaten that in case Reuchlin proved victorious, they would ally themselves with the Hussites in Bohemia against the pope. So blinded was this faction by revengeful feelings, that from sheer obstinacy they would undermine Catholicism. Nor did they spare the majesty of the emperor; when they learned that Maximilian had interceded for Reuchlin with the pope, they heaped abuse on him.

The Dominicans built their hopes on the verdict of Paris, the head of all European universities. If this important school of divinity condemned Reuchlin's writings and the Talmud, then even the pope would have to submit. Every influence was, therefore, brought to bear to obtain a favorable opinion from Paris. In particular, the king of France, Louis XII, was worked on by his confessor, Guiliaume Haquinet Petit, to influence the school of divinity in favor of the Dominicans. The political events which had set the German emperor and the French king at variance were also brought into play. Because the emperor of Germany was for Reuchlin, the king of France decided for the Dominicans and against the Talmud. But this decision was not easily obtained, for Reuchlin numbered many warm friends in Paris. The consultation was prolonged from May to the beginning of August, 1514.

Many of the voters spoke in favor of Reuchlin, and at the same time expressed their indignation at the unlawful proceedings ; but they were cried down by the fanatics. Many French divines were guided by the example of Saint Louis, who, at the instigation of the baptized Jew, Nicholas Donin, and by command of Pope Gregory IX, had ordered the Talmud to be burnt three centuries before. The Parisian doctors, therefore, gave sentence that Reuchlin's "Augenspiegel," containing heresy, and defending with great zeal the Talmudic writings, deserved to be condemned to the flames, and the author to be forced to recant.

Great was the joy of the Dominicans, particularly those of Cologne, over this judgment. They believed their game to be won, and that the pope himself would be forced to submit. They did not delay in making known to the public this concession, so hardly won, by means of another libelous pamphlet.

The lawsuit, allowed to lag in Rome, was willfully delayed still more by the Dominicans. The commission appointed had a close translation of the "Augenspiegel" prepared by a German in Rome, Martin von Gronigen; but the opposition found fault with it. Numerous hindrances blocked the progress of the suit, and at this stage cost Reuchlin 400 gold florins. The Dominicans had hoped so to impoverish their adversary, the friend of the Jews, that he would be incapacitated from obtaining justice. The prospect of seeing Reuchlin's cause triumphant at Rome diminished. Reuchlin's friends were, therefore, anxious to create another tribunal, and appeal from the badly advised or intimidated pope to public opinion.

"EPISTOLE OBSCURORUM VIRORUM."

During this tension of minds in small and great circles, whilst high and low ecclesiastics, princes and citizens, anxiously awaited news as to how the Reuchlin lawsuit had ended, or would end in Rome, a young Humanist (most likely Crotus Rubianus, in Leipsic), wrote a series of letters, which, for wit, humor and biting satire, had not been equaled in all literature. The "Letters of Obscurantists" (*Epistole Obscurorum Virorum*), published in 1515, in a great measure directed against the rascally Ortuinus Gratius, laid bare, in the language of the unpolished monks, their own baseness and insolence, their astonishing ignorance, their lust, their animosity and vileness, their despicable Latin, and still more contemptible morality, the absurdity of their 1ogic, their foolish chatter--in short, all their intolerable vices were made so evident, and described so clearly, that even the half-educated could comprehend. All Reuchlin's enemies. Hoogstraten, Amold von Tongern, Ortuinus Gratius, Pfefferkorn, their accomplices, and the Paris University, were lashed with whips and scorpions, so that no spot on them remained sound. This clever satire, containing more than Aristophanian scorn, made the stronger an impression as the Dominicans, the Thomists, the Doctors of Divinity, revealed themselves in their own persons, in their miserable meanness, placing themselves, metaphorically speaking, in the pillory. But it was inevitable that, in deriding the bigots and the papacy, the whole tyranny of the hierarchy and the church should be laid bare. For, were not the Dominicans, with their insolent ignorance and shameless vices, the product and natural effect of the Catholic order and institution? So the satire worked like a corroding acid, entirely destroying the already rotting body of the Catholic Church.

The Jews and the Talmud were the first cause of the Reuchlinist quarrel; naturally, they could not be left out of account in the letters of the Obscurantists. So it happened that the much despised Jews became one of the topics of the day.

A roar of laughter resounded through western Europe at the reading of these satirical letters. Everyone in Germany, Italy, France and England who understood Latin, was struck with the form and tenor of these confessions of Dominicans and scholastics. Their awkward vulgarity, dense stupidity, egregious folly, impurity of word and deed, stood so glaringly in contrast with their presumed learning and propriety, that the most serious men were moved to mirth. It is related that Erasmus, who, at the time of reading the letters, suffered from an abscess in the throat, laughed so heartily that it broke, and he was cured. The merry Comedy of the Fools put Reuchlin entirely in the right, and the Dominicans were judged by public opinion, no matter how the pope might deal with them. All were curious to know who could be the author. Some thought it was Reuchlin himself, others Erasmus, Hutten, or one of the Humanist party. Hutten gave the right answer to the question as to the author: "God himself." It appeared more and more clearly that so slight a cause as the burning of the Talmud had taken a worldwide significance, the will of the individual serving only to further the interests of all. In Rome and Cologne, far-seeing Reuchlinists discerned in it the work of Providence.

Only the German Jews could not indulge in merriment. The Dominicans had meantime worked in another way to obtain their object, or at least to have revenge on the Jews. Of what avail was it to the Jews that some enlightened Christians, having had their attention drawn to Judaism, were seized with so great a predilection for it that they gave expression to their new convictions in writing? Christendom as a whole was irrevocably prejudiced against Jewish teachings and their adherents. Erasmus rightly said,

" If it is Christian to hate the Jews, then we are true Christians." Therefore, it was easy for their enemies to injure them. Pfefferkorn had often pointed out that there were in Germany only three great Jewish communities, at Ratisbon, Frankfort and Worms, and that with their extermination, Judaism in the German kingdom would come to an end.

To bring about the expulsion of the Jews from Frankfort and Worms, their enemies had discovered effective means. The young Margrave, Albert von Brandenburg, hitherto bishop of Magdeburg, who later attained melancholy renown in the history of the Reformation, had been elected to the archbishopric of Mayence. The enemies of the Jews, acting probably on a suggestion from Cologne, induced Archbishop Albert to issue an invitation to religious and secular authorities and to towns, principally Frankfort and Worms, to attend a diet in Frankfort, to discuss how the Jews might be banished and never be permitted to return. Obeying the invitation (January 7th, 1516), many deputies appeared. The program was to this purport: All the estates were to unite and take an oath to relinquish the privileges and advantages derived from the Jews, to banish all Jewish subjects and never, under any pretext, or for any term, permit them to return. This resolution was to be laid before the emperor for his confirmation.

The Jews of these places saw certain danger hanging over their heads. If at other times the German princes and rulers were disunited and indolent, in the persecution of Jews they were always united and energetic. Nothing remained for the Jews but to send a deputation to Emperor Maximilian, and implore him to grant them his favor and support them against so malevolent a measure. The emperor happily remembered that the Jews, even when ruled by various great or petty rulers, were in reality the servants of himself and the empire, and that their banishment would be an encroachment on his suzerainty. Maximilian hastened, therefore, to send a very forcible dispatch to Elector Albert and the chapter of Mayence, to the religious and secular authorities, and to the towns (January, 1516), expressing his displeasure at their conference, and forbidding them to meet again at the appointed time, So the Jews were for the moment saved. But the archbishop of Mayence, or in his absence the chapter, did not give up the pursuit of the desired object The enemies of the Jews, the friends of the Cologne

Dominicans, still hoped to turn the emperor against them. But the hope was vain; the Jews were not banished for the present.

Reuchlin's lawsuit, although delayed by the struggles of the two parties, whose time was taken up in plotting against each other's intrigues, made slow but perceptible progress. Hoogstraten, seeing that the commission would decide in favor of Reuchlin, vehemently demanded a decision by council, inasmuch as it was a question. not of law, but of faith. Pope Lee, who did not care to be on bad terms with either party, in opposition to his own repeated command had to yield to a certain extent, On the one side Emperor Maximilian and many German princes insisted upon having Reuchlin declared blameless and silencing the Dominicans; on the other side the king of France and young Charles (at that time duke of Buraundy), the future emperor of Germany, king of Spain and America, used threatening language towards the pope, demanding that the matter be taken up seriously, and that Reuchlin's book be condemned. Leo, therefore, considered it advisable to escape from this critical position. He submitted the matter for final decision to a court of inquiry, formed of members of the Lateran Council, then in session. Thus the dispute about the Talmud became the concern of a general council, and was raised to the dignity of a European question.

REUCHLIN'S SUIT IN ABEYANCE.

The council committee finally declared in favor of Reuchlin. Before Leo X could confirm or reject its decision, Hoogstraten and his friends influenced him to issue a mandate suspending the suit. This temporizing exactly suited Leo's character and his position between the excited rival parties. He hated excitement, which he would have brought on himself; if he had decided in favor of either party. He did not wish to offend the Humanists, nor yet the bigots, nor the German emperor, nor the king of France, nor the ruler of Spain. So the suit was suspended, and at any favorable opportunity could be taken up again by the Dominicans. Hoogstraten had to leave Rome in disgrace and dishonor, but he did not give up the hope of winning his cause in the end. He was a strong-willed man, who could not be discouraged by humiliations, and so unprincipled that falsehood and misrepresentations came easy to him.

If Pope Leo believed that at his dictation the conflict would cease, he overestimated the authority of the papacy and mistook the parties as well as the real issue involved. Feeling ran too high to be quieted by a word from those in power. Neither party wished for peace, but for war, war to the knife. When Hoogstraten returned from Rome, his life was in danger. Furious Reuchlinists often conspired against him, and sought by polemical leaflets to exasperate public opinion still more against the Dominicans. Hutten, since his mature judgment had taken in the situation at Rome, was most eager to bring about the downfall of ecclesiastical domination in Germany.

The secret could be no longer kept, it was given out from the house-tops that there was dissension in the church. Not their foes, but the provincial of the Dominican order, Eberhard von Cleve, and the whole chapter, represented in an official letter to the pope that the controversy had brought them, the Dominicans, into hatred and contempt; that they were held up to the mockery of all, and that they--so very undeservedly!--were decried, both in speech and writing, as the enemies of brotherly love, peace and harmony; that their preaching was despised, their confessional avoided, and that everything they undertook was derided, and declared to be only the result of pride and meanness.

Meanwhile the contention between Reuchlin and the Dominicans, especially Hoogstraten, developed in another direction, and affected Judaism at another point. The Kabbala formed the background of this movement. Out of love for this secret doctrine, supposed to offer the key to the deepest knowledge of philosophy and Christianity, Reuchlin had wished to spare the Talmud, because in his opinion it contained mystical elements. The youthful Kabbala became the patroness of the old Talmud. Reuchlin understood but little of Kabbalistic doctrines, but his eagerness for knowledge and his zeal spurred him on to study. Moreover, the attack by his adversaries upon his orthodoxy, honesty and erudition, had made it an affair of honor for him to prove convincingly that the Kabbala agreed with Christianity. But he was unfortunate in the choice of his Hebrew models. For a long time he sought a guide, until chance brought him to the most confused source of information: the foolish writings of the Kabbalist, Joseph Jikatilla, of Castile, which the convert Paul Riccio had lately translated into Latin. As soon as Reuchlin heard of this literary treasure of Joseph Jikatilla, he did not rest till he had obtained it, and again set about proving that the Kabbala was in agreement with Christianity.

Believing that the Kabbala reveals and confirms the highest truths, the mysteries of Christianity, Reuchlin composed a work on Kabbalist science, and dedicated it to Pope Leo X, giving new emphasis to

THE REFORMATION.

his contention that the Jewish writings, instead of being burnt, should be cherished.

Reuchlin must have counted on the approval of the pope, to whom he dedicated the work, for having found new support for the tottering faith. He hoped that Leo X would at length grant him peace and rest by pronouncing judgment in the suit between himself and the Dominicans, which, though suppressed, was persistently urged by the latter. The Christian-like Kabbala was to be his intercessor at the Vatican. He did not stand alone in his foolish fondness for the secret doctrine. Not only the cardinals but the pope himself expected to gain much for Christianity by proper research into the Kabbala.

As the interest in the Reuchlin controversy began to flag, another movement started in Germany, continuing, as the other had begun, to shake the firm pillars of the papacy and the Catholic Church, and prepare the regeneration of Europe. The discussion aroused by the Talmud created an intellectual medium favorable to the germination and growth of Luther's reform movement. Destined soon to become a force in the world's history, even the Reformation arose from small beginnings, and needed most powerful protection not to be nipped in the bud.

Martin Luther was a strong, straightforward, obstinate and passionately excitable character, holding with tenacity to his convictions and errors. By the opposition which he met, Luther finally came to the conclusion that each individual pope, consequently the papacy, was not infallible, and that the basis of faith was not the pope's will, but the Scriptural word.

The death of the old emperor, Maximilian, who had been unequal to the task of grappling with the theological perplexities called forth by himself, and the election of a new emperor, spun out for half a year, drew politics into the arena, and gave rise to a confusion in which the friends and foes of free religious thought and of gloomy orthodox faith were not distinguishable. Hutten and the Humanists favored Charles V, in whose own country, Spain, the Dominicans still had the upper hand, and where the flames from the stake were still unextinguished; but he was opposed by the pope. The Reuchlinist and the Lutheran cause, as it were, the Talmud and the Reformation, were merged into each other. So great a change had taken place that the electors assembled to elect an emperor declared against the obscurantists of Cologne and in favor of Reuchlin.

Instead of condemning the Talmud, Pope Leo X encouraged the printing of the work. Thus, through a movement incomprehensible to all its contemporaries, the unexpected took place: Reuchlin was justified, and the Talmud was justified, and in a measure favored by the pope. Indeed, Daniel Bomberg, a rich Christian publisher in Antwerp, in the same year brought out a complete edition of the Babylonian Talmud in twelve folio volumes, the model of all later editions.

A clever pantomime, which first appeared in Latin or French, and was soon translated into German, portrays Reuchlin as the originator of the great and growing movement. It represents a doctor, on whose back may be read the name of Capnion (Reuchlin), throwing a bundle of straight and crooked sticks on the stage, and then going away. Another figure (Erasmus), having in vain endeavored to put the bundle in order, shakes his head over the chaos, and disappears. Hutten also comes in. Luther appears in monk's dress, and with a firebrand kindles the crooked twigs. Another figure, in imperial robes, strikes with its sword the spreading fire, only giving it wider play. At length comes the pope, who, wishing to extinguish the fire, seizes a vessel, and pours the oil in it upon the flames, then clasps his hands

on his head, while the bright flames shoot up never again to be stifled. Pfefferkorn and the Talmud should not have been missing in this dumb show, for they were the fuse that started the conflagration.

The situation was such that the slightest breath made the flames leap up. Luther had gained firmness and courage at the imperial diet of Worms, and by his speech, revealing fearlessness, completed the rupture with the papacy. Although urged by his own bigotry, besieged by obscurantists and exhorted by princes, Emperor Charles was disposed to condemn the reformer to the stake as a heretic, yet partly from consideration for Frederick, elector of Saxony, partly from policy, hoping thereby to hold the pope in check, he only declared him an exile a month later. Meanwhile Luther was already on his Patmos, the Wartburg, hidden and protected. Whilst in solitude he worked at a German translation of the Bible, ultra-reformers overthrew church regulations, altered the church services, did away with masses and priestly decoration, abolished the vows of monks, and introduced the marriage of priests--that is to say, the priests publicly acknowledged their former secret mistresses as their wives. The time was ripe for the Reformation, and it took firm hold of North Germany, Denmark and Sweden, extending to Prussia, Poland, and, on the other hand, to France and even Spain, the country of darkest and most bigoted ecclesiasticism and the home of persecution. Zwingli, the reformer of Switzerland, after much wavering, declared himself against the papacy; so, in that country, too, where there was more freedom of action than in submissive Germany, the new church service was introduced, the marriage of priests permitted, pictures and crucifixes destroyed, and monasteries done away with. A new order of things had set in; all powerful Rome stood impotent before the new spirit. The enthusiasm of the Anabaptists began to arouse public feeling and transform all relations of life.

At first, Luther's Reformation affected the Jews but slightly. Catholics and innovators in every town, especially in Germany, were so occupied with fighting each other, that they had no leisure for the persecution of Jews; so there came a pause. Luther, whose voice even then was more powerful than that of the princes, at first defended them from numerous accusations. In his plain-spoken and fervent way, he said:

> *"This rage (against the Jews) is still defended by some silly theologians, and advocated by them; they declare insolently that the Jews are the servants of the Christians, and subject to the emperor. I beg you to tell me who will join our religion, be he the most amiable and patient of men, when he sees that they are treated so cruelly and inimically, and not only in an unchristian way, but even brutally. Most of the Passion preachers (in Holy Week) do nothing but make the sin committed by Jews against Christ heavier and greater, and embitter the hearts of believers against them."*

In one of his works, the title of which, calculated to startle their antagonists, ran, "Jesus was born a Jew," Luther expressed himself against the indelible hatred of the Jews still more sharply:

> *"Those fools, the papists,bishops, sophists and monks, have hitherto so dealt with Jews, that every good Christian would rather have been a Jew. And if I had been a Jew, and seen such stupidity and such blockheads reign in the Christian Church, I would rather have been a pig than a Christian. They have treated the Jews as if they were dogs, not men: they have done nothing but revile them. They are blood-relations of our Lord; therefore, if it were proper to*

boast of flesh and blood, the Jews belong to Christ more than we. I beg, therefore, my dear papists, if you become tired of abusing me as a heretic, that you begin to revile me as a Jew.

"Therefore, it is my advice," continued Luther, "that we treat them kindly. Now that we drive them by force, treating them deceitfully and ignominiously, saying that they must have Christian blood to wash away the Jewish stain, and I know not what more nonsense,--prohibiting them from working amongst us, from living and having social intercourse with us, forcing them to be usurers, how can we expect them to come to us? If we would help them, so must we exercise, not the law of the pope, but that of Christian love --show them a friendly spirit, permit them to live and to work, so that they may have cause and means to be with us and amongst us."

HEBREW STUDIED BY CHRISTIANS.

These were words which the Jews had not heard for a thousand years. They show unmistakable traces of Reuchlin's mild intercession in their favor. Many hot-headed Jews saw in Luther's opposition to the papacy the extinction of Christianity and the triumph of Judaism. Three learned Jews went to Luther, and tried to convert him. Enthusiastic feelings were aroused among the Jews at this unexpected revulsion, especially at the blow dealt the and the idolatrous worship of images and the boldest hopes were entertained of the speedy downfall of Rome, and the approaching redemption by the Messiah.

But the Jewish religion gained much more by the Reformation than the Jewish race. Despised before, it became fashionable, so to say, in the early days of the Reformation. Reuchlin had expressed the modest wish that at the few German universities a professor of the Hebrew language might be appointed. Through his zeal for Hebrew (he had published, shortly before his death, a work on Hebrew accents and prosody), and through the increasing conviction that without this knowledge the Bible must remain a sealed book, princes and universities sought teachers, and instituted Hebrew professorships not only in Germany and Italy, but also in France and Poland. The light, graceful, classic muse,which had withdrawn many hearts from the church, was more and more neglected, and the serious Hebrew mother was sought out instead. Young and old did not hesitate to seek Jews from whom to learn Hebrew. A friendly connection was formed between Jewish masters and Christian pupils, to the intense vexation of bigots on both sides ; and many prejudices died out by these means. The principal teacher of the Christians was a grammarian of German descent, Elias Levita (born 1468, died 1549). This poor man, who had to struggle for his daily bread, laid the foundation of the knowledge of the Hebrew language. The plundering of Padua-where, perhaps, he was born--brought him, by way of Venice, to Rome, where Cardinal Egidio de Viterbo, wishing to advance in his grammatical and Kabbalistic studies, took him into his house, supporting him and his family for more than ten years. Not only this church dignitary, but many other Christians of high position sat at Levita's feet. One was George de Selve, bishop of Lavour, the French ambassador, as learned as he was statesman-like. Against the reproach of some bigoted rabbis, Levita defended himself by the remark that his Christian pupils all were friends of the Jews, and tried to promote their welfare. On the inducement of his patron, Egidio, he worked at a Hebrew grammar in the Hebrew language, the greater part of which was translated into Latin by Reuchlin's pupil, Sebastian Munster. Elias Levita had not a mind of great depth, nor did he propound a new theory on the structure of the Hebrew language. He rigorously adhered to the grammatical system of the Kimchis, because he did not know their predecessors. His usefulness consisted in his command over the whole Scriptural vocabulary, his pedagogic skill, and his gift of vivid presentation. Beyond the elements he did not go, but they perfectly satisfied the wants of the time. Only one deviation did Levita make from the beaten track. Against the firm belief of the time that the accents and the vowel signs in the Hebrew Bible were of ancient origin, having been revealed on Mount Sinai, or at all events, introduced by Ezra, he maintained that they had not been known even at the time of the Talmud, because they had been superfluous when Hebrew was a living language. It can easily be imagined what a storm this opinion raised. It at once upset all preconceived notions. The bigots raised a cry against him as though he had by his assertion disowned Judaism. Elias Levita was, therefore, little liked by his brother

Jews, and associated more with learned Christians, which brought much blame from the over-pious, and produced evil consequences for his descendants.

He was not the only teacher of the Hebrew language and literature to Christians. As before him, Obadiah Sforno had given Reuchlin instruction in Hebrew, so at the same time as Levita, Jacob Mantino and Abraham de Baimes were engaged in instructing Christians.

Throughout Christendom there was a desire to know the Hebrew language. The printers reckoned on such good sales that in several places in Italy and Germany, even where there were no Jews, new and old Hebrew grammatical writings were published. Everyone wished to know Hebrew and to understand the Hebrew language and literature. Some years before the representatives of the church had considered the knowledge of Hebrew superfluous, or even a pernicious evil touching on heresy; but through the Reformation it became a necessary branch of divinity. Luther himself learnt Hebrew to be able to penetrate the meaning of the Bible.

The change of mind was most evident in France. The Paris university, the leader of thought, had by a majority condemned Reuchlin's "Augenspiegel" in favor of the Talmud and Hebrew studies ; scarcely six years later there was a professorship and a printing press for Hebrew, and the confessor of King Louis, William Haquinet Petit, though a Dominican, the one whose slander had brought about the condemnation of Reuchlin's work, appeared as a patron of Hebrew literature.

At his advice King Francis I invited the bishop of Corsica, Augustin Justiniani, a man well read in Hebrew literature, to come to France. This young king felt, or at least showed, interest in learning and also in the study of Hebrew. He invited Elias Levita to come to France, and fill the professorship of Hebrew there, probably at the instigation of his admirer, De Selve. One must take into consideration what this signified at that time. In France proper, for more than a century, no Jew had been permitted to dwell, nor even to make a passing stay, and now a Jew was invited, not merely to reside there, but to accept an honorable post and instruct Christians. What heresy! Elias Levita, however, declined this flattering proposal ; he would not have felt at ease there as the only Jew, and to urge the admission of Jews into France was not in conformity with his character. Justiniani undertook the task of introducing the study of Hebrew into France.

At the University of Rheims the French students made attempts to speak Hebrew. As there were not sufficient grammars, Justiniani had the wretched Hebrew grammar of Moses Kimchi printed. Yet more remarkable is it that in Paris, where three hundred years previously the Jewish orthodox party, with the help of the Dominicans, had burnt Maimuni's religious philosophical work, "Guide of the Perplexed," the Dominican Justiniani now caused a Latin translation of the same to be published (1520). Naturally, the Christian teachers of the Hebrew language remained dependent on their Jewish masters; they could not take a single step without them. Paulus Fagius, a reforming priest and disciple of Reuchlin, wishing to establish a Hebrew press in Isny, called upon Elias Levita to go there. This offer was accepted, for Levita was in difficulties, and could find no publisher for his Chaldean and Rabbinical dictionaries. Paulus Fagius was particularly pleased with these works, because they appeared to him to offer the key to the Kabbala, so much sought for by Christian scholars.

Through the agitation by Reuchlin and Luther the neglected science of the Bible was to a certain extent cultivated. Judaism and Christianity are both founded on the Sacred Writings, yet they were quite strange to the followers of both religions.

TRANSLATIONS OF THE BIBLE.

The glorious memorial of a much favored time was so shrouded and surrounded with a network of senseless explanations, so disfigured by these accessories, that its full value was completely unknown. Because everything was looked for in, and imported into, the Holy Scriptures, the true meaning was not discovered. To the Christian laity the Bible had been inaccessible for a long time, because the papacy, with instinctive fear, had forbidden its translation into the vernacular. So the faithful knew only fragments or isolated texts, and, owing to distorted interpretations, these not always correctly. It was, therefore, a work of great importance that occupied Luther in his solitude on the Wartburg--the translation of the Bible, the Old and New Testaments, into German. For this purpose Luther had to learn Hebrew, and seek information from Jews. To his contemporaries it seemed as if God's Word had for the first time been revealed; this clear voice they had never before heard. A breath of fresh air was wafted on men, when the ramparts were broken down that had so long held its spirit imprisoned. Classical antiquity had improved the taste of a small circle. Hebrew antiquity rejuvenated the whole generation, once more infusing love of simplicity and naturalness. The Bible was soon translated into all European languages; the Catholics themselves were obliged to disregard the papal command, and render it into intelligible language for the people's use. The Jews also felt the want of the Holy Scripture in the vernacular. A translation into Spanish was made in Ferrara, by a Marrano, Duarte de Pinel, who had escaped from Portugal, and called himself Abraham Usque as a Jew.

The demand for Hebrew Bibles was so great that Daniel Bomberg undertook the great work of publishing the Old Testament, with the commentaries of Rashi, Ibn-Ezra, Kimchi, Gersonides, and others. The sale of this rabbinical Bible was so rapid that new editions were continually appearing.

IV. CHAPTER XV

DAVID REUBENI.

The traveler David Ruebeni in Rome--Solomon Molcho--His Relations with David Reubeni--Clement VII--Molcho in Ancona and Rome--His favor with the Cardinals--Death of Molcho--The Enthusiastic Regard in which he was held

1524 C.E.

Coming from the far East, and emerging from obscurity, appeared a man of whom it is hard to say whether he was an impostor or a foolish fanatic, and whether he intended to play the role of a Messianic or of a political adventurer, but he caused a great stir among Jews, affecting the Marranos in the extreme West. David, an Oriental by descent, long resident in Arabia and Nubia, suddenly appeared in Europe in a peculiar character, and by means of both fiction and truth started the wildest hopes. He declared himself a descendant of the old Hebrew tribe of Reuben, which, he alleged, still flourished in Arabia in independence, and he claimed to be a prince, the brother of a reigning Jewish king. He, therefore, called himself David Reubeni.

Loving travel and adventure, he journeyed much in Arabia, Nubia and Egypt, and came finally to Italy. The report was that he had been sent by his brother, who commanded 300,000 chosen warriors, and by the seventy elders of the land of Chaibar, to the European princes, especially to the pope, to obtain firearms and cannon with which to fight the Mahometan people, who hindered the union of the Jewish race on both sides of the Red Sea, and to assist the brave Jewish army to drive the Turks out of the Holy Land.

David Reubeni's appearance and manner were such as to inspire confidence. In both, there was something strange, mysterious and eccentric. He was of dark complexion and dwarfish in stature, and so excessively thin that continuous fasts reduced him almost to a skeleton. Possessed of courage and intrepidity, he had at the same time a harsh manner that admitted of no familiarity. He only spoke Hebrew, and that in so corrupt a jargon that neither Asiatic Jews nor those of southern Europe understood him. He came to Rome (February, 1524), and accompanied by a servant and an interpreter, rode on a white horse to the Vatican, and requested an interview with Cardinal Giulio, in the presence of other cardinals. Pope Clement also gave him audience, and accepted his credentials.

Clement VII (1523-1534), one of the most excellent popes, an illegitimate scion of the Florentine Medicis, was sensible and kind, and earnestly desired to see Italy freed from the barbarians, that is, the Germans. But he reigned at a time when Europe had lost its balance. On the one side Luther and his Reformation, which gained ground daily, threatened to undermine the papacy; and on the other, Charles V's powerful realm, Spain and Germany with Burgundy and a part of America, almost crushed Italy into servile dependence. If Clement quarreled with the emperor, the latter favored the Reformation, and set about restraining the papal power. If the pope became reconciled to him, the liberty of Italy was menaced. Thus, notwithstanding his firm character, he was continually wavering, and like most of his contemporaries had recourse to astrology, in order to learn from the stars what was beyond the wisdom of men.

To Pope Clement VII, David Reubeni seems to have handed letters of introduction from Portuguese captains or business agents, whom he may have met in Arabia or Nubia. These credentials the pope sent to the Portuguese court, and when they were there declared trustworthy, David was treated with the greatest distinction, and received all the

honors due an ambassador. He rode through Rome on a mule, accompanied by ten Jews and more than two hundred Christians. The plan of a crusade against Turkey, by which the most dangerous enemy of Christianity would be driven out of the Holy Land by an Israelitish army, attracted the pope, because it promised to restore to him the control of military affairs, but its execution was thwarted by the complexities of his position. Even the most incredulous of the Jews could not conceal from themselves the astonishing fact that a Jew was treated with respect and politeness by the Vatican, and were convinced that there must be at least a grain of truth in David's report. Roman and foreign Jews pressed round him who seemed to open a hopeful future to them. Senora Benvenida Abrabanela, wife of the rich Samuel Abrabanel, sent him great sums of money from Naples, a costly silk banner embroidered with the Ten Commandments, and many rich garments. He, however, played his part in a masterly manner, keeping the Jews at a respectful distance.

At length a formal invitation came from the king of Portugal, summoning David Reubeni to his court. The latter left Rome, traveling by sea with a Jewish flag on his ship. In Almeirin, the residence of king Joao III near Santarem, where David arrived, like a wealthy prince, with a numerous retinue bearing beautifully embroidered banners, he was also treated with the greatest honor, and a scheme was discussed with him as to how the weapons and cannons could be transported from Portugal for the Israelite army in Arabia and Nubia. David's appearance in Portugal seems to have changed the feeling towards the Marranos, and Joao was persuaded to give up the intended persecution of them. For so great an undertaking Joao would need their support, their money and their advice. If he wished for an alliance with the Hebrew king and people, he must not persecute the half-Jews in his own country. So his zeal for the establishment of the Inquisition in Portugal suddenly cooled. One can imagine the astonishment and joy of the Marranos in Portugal, when they understood that not only might a Jew be admitted into Portugal, but that he was received at court, and treated with respect. Thus, then, had came the hour of deliverance of which they had so long dreamed. Unexpected help had come to them, freedom and deliverance from their anguish; they breathed again. Whether or not David Reubeni had declared himself the forerunner of the Messiah, did not matter to the Marranos; they believed it, and counted the days to the time when he would make them behold the new Jerusalem in all its splendor. They pressed round him, kissed his hands, and treated him as if he were their king. From Portugal the supposed message of salvation passed to Spain to the still more unfortunate Marranos there, who received it with ecstasies of joy. These poor people had fallen into a morbid, eccentric, irresponsible state of mind. Daily and hourly they suffered torments of soul, through having to join in religious customs which they abhorred with their whole heart. It was no wonder that many of them lost their mental balance, and became quite mad. In the vicinity of Herrara, a Marrano maiden proclaimed herself a prophetess; fell into trances and had visions; declared that she had seen Moses and the angels, and promised to lead her suffering companions into the Holy Land. She found many believers among the Marranos, and when this was discovered, she was burned together with thirty-eight adherents. Messianic expectation, that is, redemption through a miracle, made the atmosphere in which the Marranos breathed and lived. At the news of the arrival of an ambassador from a Jewish kingdom at the Portuguese court, a crowd of Spanish converts fled to Portugal to be near their supposed

redeemer. David, who enjoyed the privilege of traveling about in Portugal, appears to have behaved very circumspectly: he gave them no promises, and did not encourage them openly to acknowledge Judaism. He knew well that he was walking on the edge of a precipice, and that one expression, one act of his directed towards bringing back new-Christians to Judaism might cost him his life. Nevertheless, all eyes were fastened on him; all were aroused and excited by the wonderful events which would certainly come to pass.

David Reubeni's appearance and the hopes it awakened took strongest hold upon one noble, talented, handsome youth ; indeed, the whole course of his existence was changed. Diogo Fires (born about 1501, died a martyr, 1532) whose glowing, poetic imagination under more favorable circumstances might have accomplished much in the domain of the beautiful, became a tool in the hands of the self-proclaimed envoy from Chaibar. Fires, who was born a new-Christian, had acquired a good education; he understood and could speak Latin, the universal language of the time. He had risen to be royal secretary at a high court of justice, and was a great favorite at court. With Hebrew and rabbinic literature he must have been familiar from his earliest youth, and he had been initiated into the Kabbala, probably by one of the Marrano teachers. At the time when David and his chimerical plans made so much stir in Portugal, Diogo Fires was completely possessed by wild dreams and visions, all of which had a Messianic background. He hastened, therefore, to David, to ascertain whether his mission was in accordance with these visionary revelations. David Reubeni appears to have treated him with coldness, and to have told him plainly that his military embassy had nothing to do with Messianic mysticism. But Diogo Fires fancied the coldness of the alleged envoy to be owing to the circumstance that he had not accepted the sign of the covenant, and he forthwith proceeded to undergo the dangerous operation of circumcision. The consequent loss of blood laid him on a sick bed. David was highly incensed when Fires told him of this, as both of them would be in danger, if it came to the king's ears that a Marrano had so emphatically and openly declared himself a Jew; for it would be asserted that David had persuaded him to take this course.

After circumcision Fires (who took the name of Solomon Molcho) had yet more terrible visions, owing presumably to his bodily weakness. Their import always had reference to the Marranos and their redemption by the Messiah. According to his own account a strange being (Maggid), who communed with him from Heaven in a dream, charged him to leave Portugal and set out for Turkey. David Reubeni also had advised that he should leave Portugal with all speed, as the act of circumcision might involve also David in danger, and frustrate his schemes. Leaving Portugal cannot, then, have been difficult for Marranos. Diogo Fires (or Solomon Molcho) reached Turkey, and hoped for a Messianic mission and a martyr's death.

A great sensation was made there by this enthusiastic, handsome young Kabbalist, the new Jewish recruit. At first he gave himself out as a delegate from David Reubeni, of whose good reception at the papal and Portuguese courts rumors were current even in the East, and had not failed to inflame people's imagination. In Salonica, Joseph Taytasak's Kabbalistic circle took possession of him, and greedily listened to his dreams and visions. At Adrianople Molcho converted to the Kabbala the sober-minded Joseph Karo, who had left Spain when a boy, and had hitherto busied himself entirely with Talmudic learning.

Enthusiasm is infectious. Karo fell into the same Kabbalistic enthusiasm as Molcho.

SOLOMON MOLCHO.

He also had his dream-prompter (Maggid), who taught him inelegant, mystical interpretations of Scriptural passages, and revealed the future. He was so faithful an imitator that, like Molcho, he lived in the most certain expectation of being burnt at the stake as a "burnt-sacrifice of a sweet savor unto the Lord." Molcho inoculated his followers with a longing for martyrdom. His captivating person, pure enthusiasm, romantic disposition, past career, astonishing knowledge of the Kabbala (though born a Christian), everything connected with him, raised up a host of adherents, who greedily listened to his mystic utterances, and believingly accepted them. He often preached, and words flowed like a torrent from his lips. Gray-headed men went with questions to the youth, seeking explanations of obscure verses of Scripture, or revelations of the future. At the urgent request of his friends in Salonica he published a brief abstract of his Kabbalistic sermons, the substance of which was: The advent of the Messiah is at hand; his reign will begin at the end of the year 5300 dating from the creation (1540)· The sack and havoc of Rome (May 5th, 1527), confirmed the Messianic hopes of Kabbalistic zealots. Rome, the iniquitous Catholic Babylon, filled with the spoils of the whole earth, was taken by storm by German soldiers, mostly Lutherans, and was treated almost as a hostile city by order of the Catholic emperor, Charles V. The fall of Rome, according to Messianic and apocalyptic principles, had been predicted as a sign of the Messiah's advent. Now Rome had fallen. In Asia, Turkey, Hungary, Poland, and Germany, hopes of the coming of the Messiah were stirring in Jewish hearts, and were associated with the name of Solomon Molcho, who was to bring about their realization.

In Spain and Portugal the Marranos held yet more firmly to their visions of Messianic redemption, and to David Reubeni, whom, with or without his consent, they took for a forerunner of the Messiah. Their illusion was so complete that they boldly inaugurated enterprises which could only end in death for themselves. Several Spanish Marranos, condemned to the stake, had curiously enough found a place of refuge in Portugal (in Campo-Mayor), where they were suffered to remain unmolested. A company of young people from among them ventured to attack Badajoz, whence they had fled, for the purpose of rescuing some Marrano women languishing in the Inquisition dungeons. Their eruption greatly alarmed the inhabitants, but they succeeded in rescuing the unfortunate victims. The incident made a great stir in both countries, and led to most prejudicial results for the pseudo-Christians. This occurrence, as well as the denunciation of several Marranos for disrespect to an image of the Virgin Mary, again induced the king to consider the scheme of establishing a court of Inquisition. David Reubeni's favor with the king of Portugal was of brief duration. He was at first received by Joao III with extraordinary friendliness, and often admitted to audience (when conversation was carried on by means of an Arab and Portuguese interpreter), and received the distinct promise that eight ships and 4,000 firearms should be placed at his disposal to enable his brother, the alleged king of Chaibar, to make war upon the Turks and Arabs, but the king gradually cooled down. Miguel de Silva, Portuguese ambassador at the papal court while David was at Rome, had held the alleged Jewish prince of Chaibar to be an adventurer. He was recalled to Portugal, and opposing the other councilors, who were deluded by David's daring character, made strenuous efforts to deprive him of the king's favor. Moreover, the homage so remarkable and openly offered to him by the Marranos had roused suspicion concerning him. Miguel de Silva, entrusted with the commission to establish the In-

DAVID REUBENI LEAVES PORTUGAL.

quisition in Portugal, pointed out that the king himself, by favoring the alleged Jewish prince, plainly fortified the Marranos in their unbelief, or adherence to the Jewish cause. Then came the circumcision and flight of the royal secretary, Diogo Fires (Solomon Molcho). This occurrence gave great offense at the Portuguese court, and it was insinuated to the king that David had been his abettor.

Thus it came to pass that David Reubeni suddenly received orders to quit Portugal after he had tarried there and been treated with distinction for nearly a twelve-month. Only two months' grace before embarkation was granted him. The ship that carried him and his retinue was cast away on the Spanish coast, and David was taken prisoner in Spain, where he was forced to appear before the Inquisition. However, before that could take place, Emperor Charles set him free, and David Reubeni betook himself to Avignon, under papal jurisdiction. As soon as King Joao broke with David Reubeni, every reason for sparing the Marranos vanished. The vacillating king was hard-pressed by the queen, the Dominicans, and some of the nobles, to decide on introducing the Inquisition. The bishop of Ceuta, Henrique, formerly a Franciscan monk and a fanatical priest, brought about the decision. In his diocese of Olivenca five new-Christians were suspected of Jewish practices. He made short work of them. Without greatly troubling as to whether the tribunal of the Inquisition was or was not sanctioned by the pope, and legally established by the king, he prepared stakes and fagots, and burnt the victims to death, having condemned them without regular trial (about 1530)· The people jubilantly applauded him, and celebrated the murder of these Jewish-Christians with bull-fights. Far from wishing to hide his deed, Henrique boasted of it, and pressed the king to commence in earnest the chastisement of the heretical and sinful new-Christians. Joao decided to address himself to Pope Clement respecting the organization of commissions of inquiry in Portugal.

But there were still some priests left from the previous reign who loudly raised their voices against this violent treatment of the Marranos. Two especially deserve to have their names made known to posterity--Ferdinand Coutinho, bishop of Algarve, and Diogo Pinheiro, bishop of Funchal. They had been witnesses of the inhuman cruelties with which, under Manoel, the Jews were driven to baptism, and in no way could recognize them as Christians, neither when there was question of punishing them for relapsing into heresy, nor of entrusting them with judicial power or spiritual benefice. Coutinho, untiring in ridicule of the mistaken zeal of the younger priests, reminded the king that Pope Clement VII himself had not long before allowed several Marranos to acknowledge Judaism openly in the very city of Rome. This pope, convinced of the injustice shown to new-Christians, with the consent of the college of cardinals had given them an asylum at Ancona, permitting them freely to confess themselves Jews. In Florence and Venice also they could live without molestation. Nay, the papal consistory itself had given out that the Portuguese Marranos were to be regarded as Jews. He considered, so Coutinho expressed himself in his friendly consideration of the question, that instead of the new-Christians, accused of outraging what Christians hold sacred, the witnesses ought to be punished for bearing false testimony. The new-Christians should be won to the true faith only by gentle means. At length the king decided to submit the question to the pope, who, should he sanction the establishment of the Inquisition, would at the same time absolve him from the promises made to the Marranos. The Portuguese ambassador at Rome, Bras Neto, received orders to obtain a bull

to that effect from the pope. But what so easily, by a stroke of the pen, had been conceded to Spain, cost the king of Portugal many efforts and a struggle, and he was never able full to enjoy his Inquisition.

Now the weak hand the amiable Kabbalist Solomon Molcho seized the spokes of this revolving wheel. From the East he had gone to Italy to fulfill the Messianic mission with which he was inspired, or with which he was credited. He wished to speak fearlessly before princes, in the capital of Christendom, of the approaching redemption. At Ancona, where he arrived with followers towards the end of 1529, certain malevolent persons, according to his own story, persecuted him. They were in fact prudent men, who were informed of his life in the East, and feared that, as a result of his impetuous striving for martyrdom, evil consequences would ensue for Jews all over the world, or at least for the Marranos in Italy, Portugal and Spain. Molcho, when cited, is understood to have confessed fearlessly that he preferred Judaism because it taught the truth. Bishop of Ancona discharged him as one of the Portuguese Marranos to whom freedom of religious confession had been allowed by the pope and the cardinals, but forbade him to preach against Christianity. Molcho remained some time at Ancona, where his preaching became very popular, even priests and Christians of the higher classes coming to the synagogue. However, he seems to have compromised himself, and in consequence repaired to Pesaro with the duke of Urbino, Francesco Maria della Revere I, who thought a settlement of Marranos in his little state would be advantageous. But there was no rest for Molcho ; he burnt with impatience to be at Rome to prepare the way for the coming of the Messiah, though without any clear conception of what to do. He waited for some prompting from on high, which, he believed, could not fail him. In obedience to a vision he abandoned his retinue at Pesaro, and set out alone on horseback for Rome. At the first sight of the Eternal City his feelings overcame him, for Molcho, like Luther, held Rome to be the seat of anti-Christ; he sank into fervent prayer, imploring redemption and forgiveness of sin for Israel. A voice broke in upon his prayer, predicting in verses of the Bible, "Edom (Rome) shall be the heritage of Israel, his foot shall be unsteady, but Israel will gain the victory." In this mood he entered Rome, and took up his abode at an inn kept by Christians. He put on a tattered suit, blackened his face, wrapped dirty rags around his feet, and leaving his horse and clothes at the inn, he took his stand among the tribe of beggars on the bridge over the Tiber, opposite the pope's palace. This equipment was in accordance with Messianic tradition, which had it that the Messiah would tarry amongst the lepers and ragged beggars of Rome, to be summoned thence to triumph. For thirty consecutive days the Portuguese enthusiast led this miserable existence, neither eating: meat nor drinking wine, but contenting himself with the scantiest and poorest fare, and waiting for the prophetic ecstasy.

In this condition of bodily tension and mental exaltation, Molcho fell into a deep sleep, and had a confused dream, noteworthy because part of it was afterwards fulfilled to the very letter. It was predicted in this vision that a devastating flood would break over Rome and a northern country, and his native land be panic-stricken by an earthquake, that when he himself reached his thirtieth year he would be raised to a higher degree, and clad in Byssus. because of his own free w he had devoted himself to death. He would return to Rome, but leave It again before the flood took place. Then the Holy Spirit, the spirit of wisdom and understanding, would rest on the Messianic king, the dead would rise from the dust, and God give His people glory.

MOLCHO AT ROME.

Next morning, enfeebled by his long mortification and his troubled sleep, Molcho dragged himself back to his inn, and rested. He laid aside his disguise, and went out to hold converse with Jews (February, 1530)· Being still a complete stranger in Rome, and in order to avoid the denunciation of his opponents, he gave himself out as a messenger from Solomon Molcho. In spite of this he was recognized, and denounced to the Inquisition as a seditious Marrano. He had some time previously entered into intercourse with the pope and some of the cardinals, to whom he predicted the flood. Clement VII, who for several years had been drinking of the cup of sorrow, and experiencing humiliations such as had fallen to the lot of few popes before him, who had been forced to crown at Bologna his deadly enemy, Charles V, as king of Italy and emperor of Rome (February 22d-24th, 1530), was but too readily inclined to listen to dreams and visions. Other unknown relations may have existed between the pope and Molcho, in consequence of which the latter was regarded with surprising favor by the pope. Molcho had friends also among the cardinals. Lorenzo Pucci, for example, grand penitentiary of the papal see, who had taken Reuchlin's part against the Dominicans, was attached to him. Hence, while the papal police were lying in wait for Molcho, at the gates of Rome, he escaped over the walls, and hastened to the pope, from whom he obtained a pontifical passport that guaranteed him against harm.

Furnished with this, Molcho came back secretly to Rome, and one Saturday suddenly appeared in the chief synagogue, where, to the astonishment of all present, he preached on a text taken from the prophetical portion. His adherents in Rome increased so largely that he preached in the synagogue every Sabbath until autumn, without meeting with opposition. He inspired his hearers, yet seemed powerless to disarm his opponents. Molcho was the Jewish Savonarola. He spoke with unshakable certainty of his visions, and even announced to the king of Portugal (through the ambassador, Bras Neto) the earthquake which threatened Lisbon, so that precautionary measures might be taken. Molcho was himself so firmly convinced that the flood would come to pass that, when the predicted time approached, he went to Venice, Molcho and David Reubeni, who meanwhile had returned from Avignon to Italy, again met face to face. They looked at each other coldly and with amazement; each expected miracles from the other. Each desired the other to acknowledge his sublime mission. They were both embarrassed. Molcho's eyes were opened on this occasion to the true character of his once-admired master. He no longer believed in Reubeni's ignorance, but felt convinced that, Talmudic and Kabbalistic learning not being in keeping with his character as an Arabian prince, it was assumed by him in order to deceive people. Molcho even recanted his declaration that he was David's emissary. " Before the God of heaven and earth I proclaim the truth, that my circumcision and the abandonment of my country were not counseled by flesh and blood (David), but took place at the express command of God." Molcho was a deluded enthusiast, whereas David was an adventurer intentionally deceiving others. After his unsuccessful attempt to win over the king of Portugal and Charles V to his schemes, David went to Venice with the purpose of influencing the president of that republic, which had close relations with the East. Remarkably enough he found sympathy there; the Venetian senate sent a man well acquainted with the country to question him respecting his plan and means of conquest in the East (1530)·

Both Molcho and David were harassed by the more temperate Jews, who apprehended danger for

themselves and their religion. While at Venice Molcho was poisoned by Jewish hands, and fell into a dangerous illness.

Meanwhile the inundation of Rome predicted really took place, transforming the city into a stormy lake, and causing great havoc (October 8th, 1530)· At the same time a brilliant comet appeared, shooting out rays of light till the heavens seemed about to open. In Portugal the earth shook thrice, and the earthquake destroyed a number of houses in Lisbon, many persons being buried beneath the ruins (January 26th, 1531)·

After the inundation of Rome, Molcho again appeared in that city, where he was honored as a prophet. The pope, to whom he had predicted the calamity, seems to have lavished his affections upon him, and he bestowed public marks of honor upon him. The Portuguese ambassador, Bras Neto, told him that if the king of Portugal had known how favored a man in God's sight was Molcho, and how well able to read the future, he would have permitted him to dwell in his dominions. And this was the moment when the ambassador received the mandate from his sovereign to work secretly for a bull from the papal see introducing the Inquisition against the Marranos! A more unfavorable time could not have been chosen. The affair was laid for decision before the grand penitentiary, Cardinal Lorenzo Pucci. But the latter, as well as Pope Clement, influenced by Solomon Molcho, strongly opposed the proposal from the beginning. Pucci straightforwardly said to the Portuguese ambassador, "The king of Portugal, like the king of Spain, is more attracted by the Marranos' wealth than concerned about the orthodoxy of their creed; let him rather leave them free to live according to their own law, and punish only those who, after voluntarily embracing Catholicism, relapse to the Jewish faith." For the moment Bras Neto was powerless. He even feared Molcho's influence with the pope, and kept his doings secret, lest anything come to the ears of the Marranos in Portugal, and they supply Molcho with money wherewith to bribe the pope's retainers to work against the establishment of the Inquisition.

All this time Molcho was untiringly persecuted by his fellow-believers, more especially by his enemy, Jacob Mantin, the learned but unscrupulous physician and philologist. This revengeful man came from Venice to Rome for no other purpose than to cause the ruin of him whom he gratuitously hated. He took the Portuguese ambassador fairly to task for allowing a former Portuguese Christian, who preached against Christianity, to remain at liberty in Rome. As the ambassador would not listen to him, Mantin carried his complaint to the inquisition. He procured witnesses from Portugal who testified that Solomon Molcho had lived as a Christian in Portugal, and managed to have him cited before the congregation. Hereupon Molcho exhibited his passport from the pope, trusting with such support to remain unmolested; but the Inquisitors tore it from his hands, and betook themselves to the pope, to whom they represented how indecent it was that he should protect a scoffer at Christianity. Clement replied that he needed Molcho for a secret purpose, and requested that he be left undisturbed. When the Inquisition showed itself inclined to disregard his denunciation, Mantin raised new points against Molcho He contrived to set possession of the letter which some years before Molcho had written from Monastir to Joseph Taytasak, respecting his past life and his return to Judaism, translated it into Latin, and laid it before the tribunal. As the letter undoubtedly contained abuse against Edom, i.e., against Rome and Christianity, the Inquisition was forced to take notice of it; and Clement also no longer dared set his face

against Mantin's denunciation. The congregation now proceeded with the case, and sentenced Molcho to be burnt to death. A funeral pile was built up, and the fagots kindled. People came in crowds to the place to witness the attractive sight. A wretched victim brought thither in penitential shroud was thrown without ceremony into the fire. One of the judges informed the pope that the act of faith had been completed by the offender's death. The judge and the witnesses of the execution are said to have felt no small astonishment when Solomon Molcho alive was encountered in the pope's apartments.

It seems that Clement, to save his favorite's life, foisted in some one else, who ascended the scaffold, whilst Solomon Molcho was kept hidden in the pope's chambers.

The pope himself communicated this fact to the perplexed judge, enjoining silence in order that Jews and Christians might not have fresh fuel to feed their excitement. Solomon Molcho was saved, but he dared no longer remain in Rome; that was plain even to him, and he begged the pope to let him go. Escorted by a few faithful servants of the pope, Solomon Molcho rode out of Rome at night (February or March, 1531)·

After Molcho's departure from Rome, especially after the death of Cardinal Lorenzo Pucci (August, 1531), a different feeling towards the Marranos sprang up. A Portuguese agent obtained from the pope, who was urged thereto by Emperor Charles and the grand penitentiary, Antonio Pucci, the successor to his uncle, the bull establishing the Inquisition, so long prayed for (December 17th, 1531), although Cardinals Egidio de Viterbo, Elias Levita's disciple, and Geronimo de Ghinucci,had declared against it. As though this mild-tempered pope were ashamed of allowing his former proteges to be persecuted, he bracketed the Lutherans with them. He was careful, too, not to permit the fanatical Dominicans to acquire power over the Marranos. The king's confessor, a Franciscan, the gentle-minded Diogo de Silva, was appointed inquisitor general of Portugal. Three tribunals were established, at Lisbon, Evora, and Coimbra, with the "Constitutions " of the Spanish courts introduced by Torquemada, and improved, that is, made severer, by his successors. After the king and the grandees had withdrawn their protection, the Portuguese Marranos were in a far worse plight than their Spanish brethren. The populace had long so hated them that even otherwise upright Christians turned informers, whereas in Spain spies had to be specially hired for the purpose.

When the Inquisition began its execrable work many of the Marranos naturally contemplated leaving the country. But flight was not easy ; it was with them as with their forefathers when they came out of Egypt--the foe behind, the sea, with all its dangers and terrors, in front. A law was made (June 14th, 1532), strictly forbidding emigration to Africa, not even excepting the Portuguese colonies. Captains were warned, under penalty of death, not to carry Marranos, and all Christians were prohibited from buying real estate of new-Christians; these were not permitted to send their goods away to foreign countries, nor effect exchanges at home. Nevertheless, many of them prepared for emigration, in order "to flee from the land touched by the poisonous serpent" (the Inquisition); but before they could even set foot on board ship, they and their wives and children were seized, and hurried away to gloomy dungeons, whence they were dragged to the stake. Others perished of the sea before they could reach the was to bring them to a place of safety. Many were drawn forth from the most hidden retreats, and burnt to death. Those who escaped from the claws of this bloodthirsty monster found no relief in

strange lands--they were imprisoned in Flanders, arrested in France, unkindly received in England. In addition to such torments many lost their fortunes, and, in consequence, their lives. Those who reached Germany succumbed in extreme misery on the Alps, leaving wives about to become mothers, who, on cold and deserted roads, brought forth children, and endured a new form of misfortune. Nevertheless, the Marranos did not intermit their attempts to escape, but prosecuted them with increased caution. No other way out of their troubles was left. Appeals to justice and humanity, and the urging of their chartered rights and privileges, found none but deaf ears in the cabinet.

Marranos who escaped to Rome made bitter complaints to Pope Clement of the inhumanity with which the Inquisition persecuted them and their brethren, and urged that the king had obtained the bull by fraud, inasmuch as the facts of the case had not been set before the papal consistory in a proper light. They especially complained that emigration was prohibited, in direct opposition to the legal equality which had been granted. Clement VII, who regretted that he had issued the bull, to which he had been forced, sympathized with their grievances. He may have felt, too, that the fires of the Inquisition, employed against those who were neither Catholics nor willing converts, branded the Catholic Church, and gave the Lutherans more material to continue their hostile assaults, to depict it as bloodthirsty and a just object of hatred. Moreover, he was well aware that the Inquisition had been introduced into Portugal only because Spain and his arch-foe, Emperor Charles, desired it, with the object of placing Portugal in an unequivocally dependent condition. Hence Clement revolved a plan to revoke the bull. At this time Solomon Molcho and David Reubeni resumed their mystical activity, and conceived the daring scheme of going to the emperor at Ratisbon, where the Reichstag was then assembled. With a floating banner, embroidered with the letters "Machbi " (initials of the Hebrew words of the verse, " Who is like unto thee among the gods, O Lord"), they traveled from Bologna, by way of Ferrara and Mantua, to Ratisbon. Emperor Charles gave them audience, and they probably pleaded the cause of the Jews earnestly. An unwarranted and improbable report affirms that they attempted to convert the emperor to the Jewish faith. But they were not so heedless as to make this attempt. They simply petitioned the emperor to permit the Marranos to arm themselves, and, joining the Jewish tribes, attack the Turks. Joslin of Rosheim, who was also in Ratisbon, vainly warned them not to make this request. The end was that Charles put them both in chains (June-September, 1532), and carried them fettered to Mantua. The banner was left at Ratisbon. An inquisition, at the emperor's wish, was set on foot at Mantua, and Molcho was condemned to be burnt to death for relapse and heresy. While the emperor was diverting himself by triumphal processions, festivals, hunting, plays, and all imaginable merry-makings, the funeral pile of the Lisbon Marrano was built up, and set on fire. They led him to the place of execution with a gag in his mouth, for his eloquence was so powerful and persuasive that emperor and tribunal feared its effect on the crowd. He was, therefore, forced to keep silence. But when the executioners were ready to throw him into the blazing fire, a courier from the emperor arrived, removed the gag, and asked him in the emperor's name, whether he repented of his transgressions and was willing to return to the bosom of the church; if so, he should be pardoned. As might have been expected, Molcho replied that he had longed to die a martyr, "a burnt-sacrifice, of a sweet savor unto the lord," that he repented him of only one thing

MOLCHO'S DEATH.

--that he had been a Christian in his youth. Come life; come death, he commended his soul unto God. Then he was thrown into the midst of the flames, and died with unshaken constancy.

Molcho was the victim of a phantasma,aoria, a delusion, into which, at feud with reality, he allowed himself to fall. The rich gifts bestowed on him by nature--a handsome person, glowing imagination, quick perception, ready enthusiasm--which would have been steps on the ladder of fortune for any character less fantastical, only served to ruin him, because, swept into the vortex of the Kabbala, he fondly hoped to accomplish the work of redemption. David Reubeni had not even the martyr's crown. Charles carried him to Spain, and cast him into a dungeon of the Inquisition, in which he was still living three years afterwards. It appears that he was at length put to death by poison. As a Jew, the Inquisition had no power over him. But many of the Spanish Marranos who had had intercourse with him, and whose names he probably betrayed on the rack, were burnt to death.

Enthusiasm for Molcho was so great that a mistaken faith was pinned to him, and various fictions respecting him were invented. In Italy and Turkey numbers believed that he had on this occasion, as once before, escaped death. Some said that they had seen him a week after his auto-da-fe; others gave out that he had visited his bride at Safet. Joseph Karo, whose name was soon to be widely known, longed for martyrdom like Molcho's. Even the circumspect Joseph Cohen of Genoa, a careful historian, averse to belief in miracles, was dazed, and knew not what to think of the affair. An Italian Kabbalist, Joseph of Arli, would not abandon the hope that the time of the Messiah, as announced and prepared by Molcho, would soon dawn on the Jewish world. Molcho's death, according to him, would soon find avengers. By a childish transposing of the letters of two verses in Isaiah (Notaricon), he predicted the downfall of the religion of Jesus from various causes: Luther's agitation, the many new sects springing up among Christians, the recent sack of Rome, and the mutually inimical attitude of the pope and the emperor.

IV. CHAPTER XVI.

STRIVINGS OF EASTERN JEWS FOR UNITY. SUFFERING IN THE WEST.

Efforts towards Unity--Jacob Berab proposes the Re-introduction of Rabbinical Ordination into Palestine--Successful Opposition of Levi ben Chabib--Joseph Karo--His Connection with Solomon Molcho and his Messianic Visions--Karo's Religious Code-Converts to Judaism at the Era of the Reformation-Expulsion of the Jews from Naples and Prague--Their Return to the latter Town--Dr. Eck--Martin Luther and the Jews

1538--1566 C.E.

EVERY fresh column of smoke rising from the fires of the Inquisition in Spain and Portugal drove Marranos, singly or in groups, far away to the East, to Turkey. They no longer felt safe even in Italy, since the popes, against their own higher convictions, allowed themselves to be overborne concerning the Inquisition. In Turkey a little Jewish world was thus by degrees formed, on which even the sultan's despotic rule did not encroach, however much individuals might be exposed to arbitrary treatment. Here, as in Palestine, where numbers and prosperity had raised them in their own estimation, they could indulge in dreams of obtaining some degree of independence, might strive for national and religious unity, and hope to realize their wild Messianic fancies. The career of the Mantuan martyr, Solomon Molcho, did not fail to leave an impression; his words echoed in the ears of his brethren. At Safet, the largest congregation in Palestine, where he had made a long stay, forming intimate relations and awakening hopes, the fulfillment of his Messianic predictions was looked for even after his death. The completion of the round number 5300 from the creation of the world (1540) seemed to be a suitable year for the coming of the Messiah. But the Messianic period, according to then prevailing ideas, would not come suddenly; the Israelites had to do their part in preparing the way. Maimuni, the highest authority, had taught that the Messianic time would or must be preceded by the establishment of a universally recognized Jewish court of justice, or Synhedrion. Hence the necessity was felt of having authorized and duly appointed judges, such as existed at the time of the Temple and the Talmud in Palestine, of re-introducing, in fact, the long-disused ordination (Semichah). There was no hindrance to be feared from the Turkish state. As it was, the rabbis had their own civil and even criminal jurisdiction ; but these rabbis (who were also judges), being appointed by the community, had not the warrant of authority required by Talmudic rules. Obedience was given them, but they also met with opposition. Authority was conventional, not built on the foundation of Talmudic Judaism. No unity of legislation and exposition of the Law was possible while every rabbi was absolute in his own congregation, not subject to some higher authority. It was, therefore, a need of the times to create a sort of religious supreme court, and where should that be done but in Palestine? The sacred memories connected with that country could alone lend the dignity of a Synhedrion to a college of rabbis. Teaching that was to meet with universal acceptance could proceed from Zion alone, and the word of God only from Jerusalem.

How excellent and necessary it was to re-introduce the ordination of rabbis by a higher authority bad been discussed by many, but only one, the acute-

ORDINATION RE-ESTABLISHED.

minded but obstinate and daring Jacob Berab, had the energy to set about doing the thing. After much journeying from Egypt to Jerusalem, and thence to Damascus, Berab, in his old age, settled at Safet. He was in good circumstances, and, owing to his wealth and intellect, enjoyed marked respect and consideration. He determined to give a definite direction to the aimless ideas floating in men's minds with regard to the coming of the Messiah. This was certainly a praiseworthy aim, but some little ambition was undoubtedly mixed up in his plan : to be himself the highest authority, perhaps the chief of the Synhedrion in Palestine, and consequently revered throughout the East, and even by the whole Jewish race. The first step was difficult. Ordination could be lawfully given only by those who themselves had been ordained, and there had been no such for a very long time. An utterance of Maimuni happily offered ground for a new departure, viz., when wise men gathered together in Palestine shall agree to ordain one of their number, they have the right to do so, and the ordained rabbi can also ordain others. At that time no community in Palestine, in point of numbers, could compare with Safet, which had grown through frequent immigrations till it contained more than 1,000 Jewish families. Safet, or rather the Talmudists of that city, therefore, had it in their own hands, if they could only agree, to re-establish the dignity of the Synhedrion, even in the face of opposition from other congregations, because the Safet party was in the majority. The officiating and non-officiating rabbis of Safet, men without name or fame had far too high a respect for Berab's intellectual power, Talmudic 1earning, and wealth, to gainsay his proposition, or put any obstacle in his path. A hint from him sufficed to bring together five and twenty men ready to confer on him the dignity of an ordained judge and rabbi. Thus ordination was reestablished (1538), and the focus for a new Synhedrion determined. It rested with Jacob Berab to ordain as many colleagues as he pleased. From principles laid down in the Talmud he demonstrated in a lecture the legality of the step, and confuted every possible objection. One after another, Talmudists in other congregations in Palestine announced their assent to this innovation. By this step Berab and his followers thought that they had reached the first stage of preparation for the Messianic age. In fact, this renewal of ordination, if not able to bring about the Messianic times, might very well have been the nucleus of Jewish unity. A re-established Synhedrion in the Holy Land would have had a grand sound in Europe, might have exercised special attraction, and brought still more immigrants to Palestine. Persecutions of Jews in Italy and Germany, the war of extermination against Marranos in Spain and Portugal, a thirst for what was eccentric and out of the common in an age distinguished by strongly excited longing for the Messiah, all this would have been sufficient inducement to allure rich, educated Jews from western lands to the East. With the help of their capital, and founded on the authority of a Synhedrion, a Jewish community having the character of a state might have been organized, and Berab was the right person to carry out so great a scheme with perseverance --not to say stubbornness.

But difficulties immediately arose. It was to be expected that if the congregation at Jerusalem and its representatives were not consulted with regard to an act so pregnant with consequences, there would be danger that the whole arrangement would be declared null and void, for the Holy City should have the first vote in a matter of such weight for the Holy Land. Jacob Berab saw this perfectly well, and proposed, as the first exercise of his newly-acquired dignity, to ordain the head of the Jerusalem college of rabbis. Levi ben Jacob Chabib, who

LEVI BEN CHABIB.

held that position, was born in Zamora, and was of about the same age as Berab. As a youth, in the times of forced baptism, under King Manoel, he had become a pseudo-Christian, received a baptismal name, made the sign of the cross, and performed other ceremonies of the Catholic Church with a heart full of despair. At the first favorable opportunity he fled from Portugal, cast off his assumed garb of Christianity, sought safety in Turkey, and finally betook himself to Jerusalem. There, by virtue of the wide range of his Talmudic learning, more extensive than profound, he became as rabbi the first person in the community. He deserved its gratitude by caring for the physical and spiritual welfare of his congregation, especially for piloting it through the disturbed state into which it was in danger of falling afresh through the new arrivals from various countries, who were disinclined to submit to law and order. Levi ben Chabib had also some knowledge of mathematics, astronomy, and the calculation of the calendar. Between himself and Jacob Berab, with whom he had lived for some time in Jerusalem, there was no friendly relationship. On several occasions they had come into collision, though Levi ben Chabib had always behaved in a friendly, unassuming manner, and avoided whatever might wound his opponent. Their relations of late years had been more intimate, but Levi ben Chabib could not forget how slightingly Jacob Berab had treated him.

And now, as chief rabbi of Jerusalem, he was invited to recognize the election of Jacob Berab as the first lawfully ordained rabbi-judge, member of the Synhedrion, and by his consent to approve of the same. Jerusalem was thereby subordinated to Safet and he himself to Jacob Berab. This was a real offense, for Berab had not thought it worth while to ask the consent of the Jerusalem college beforehand, but had haughtily made his innovation known through a decree, in which, by virtue of the dignity conferred upon him, he designated Levi ben Chabib an ordained judge. At the same time he had made it evident that disapproval from Jerusalem would disturb him but little, since it could only be regarded as the opposition of a minority to the majority at Safet. The moment for taking an important step towards Jewish unity had come, and it found Levi ben Chabib, whose vote at all events was of importance, wanting in magnanimity. Resentment gained the upper hand; he forgot that in earlier days it had been also his desire to re-establish the ordination of rabbis. As soon as a notification of the act at Safet reached him, he immediately and emphatically declared himself against the election. His antagonism seems, however, to have found no response in Jerusalem, for only one of his rabbinical colleagues, Moses de Castro, adopted his view, the remainder acquiesced in Berab's action. In Talmudical and rabbinical law arguments could not fail to be discoverable against the revival of ordination and the Synhedrion. Such a confused host of opinions exists therein, that arguments may be found for or against almost anything. Berab and the electors obedient to his nod themselves furnished their opponents with an objection. The Jews of Safet dared not give utterance to their underlying hope that through ordination the Messianic time would be brought nearer. Though the rabbis might be filled with Messianic hopes, such a motive for the re-introduction of ordination would have sounded too fantastic and ridiculous in their own ears. Other plausible grounds were not just then to be found. The calendar of festivals, which had formerly been prepared by ordained members of the college, had been fixed for a thousand years, and could not now be meddled with. Other cases where the Talmud required an ordained judge were

of too rare occurrence to permit that the necessity of ordination be proved on that head. The people of Safet, therefore, made the most of a reason meant to appear practical and suited to the times, which was nevertheless very far-fetched. Many Marranos were to be found in Palestine who had been forced during their outward assumption of Christianity to commit what according to the Talmud were deadly sins. With contrite hearts they repented of their transgressions, and longed for forgiveness and atonement--they had not given up the Catholic doctrine of outward penance when they cast off the mask of Christianity. Such forgiveness of sins, however (Berab made it appear), could be theirs only when the scourging prescribed by the Law (39 stripes) was inflicted; again, this punishment could be decreed only by a lawfully ordained college. Therein lay the necessity for ordination.

If Levi ben Chabib was disposed to extend his antipathy from the originator to the execution of his work, there would be no difficulty in proving this reason for the scheme invalid. Not content with this, he brought forward a host of sophistries. Jacob Berab had not expected such antagonism at Jerusalem from Levi ben Chabib and his colleague, Moses de Castro, because he credited them either with less courage or more self-denial, and it embittered him extremely. It was all the more painful to him since their opposition was calculated to wreck his whole undertaking. How could he hope to prove it acceptable to Asiatic, European, and African Jews, when Jerusalem, the Holy City, would have none of it? And without such acceptance, how could he make it the central point of a re-organization ? Besides, his life was in danger at Safet, probably through denunciation to the Turkish authorities, who were willing to grasp at any opportunity to get hold of his property. Berab had to leave Palestine for a time. He consecrated four Talmudists, as Judah ben Baba had done in Hadrian's time, so that the practice of ordination might not immediately fall to the ground. These four were chosen not from the elder, but from the younger rabbis, among them Joseph Karo, the enthusiastic adherent of Solomon Molcho and his Kabbalistic Messiahship, who entered heart and soul into the ordination scheme. Such preference, shown to younger and more pliable, if more gifted men, stirred up still more ill-will in Jerusalem. The two rabbis of Palestine in the epistles exchanged on the subject (written with a view to publication) grew more and more bitter against each other, so offensive indeed that the most passionate excitement cannot excuse their language. In reply to Levi ben Chabib's censorious remark, "One who is consecrated and ordained should have not only learning, but holiness also," Jacob Berab made a spiteful reference to Levi's compulsory adoption of Christianity: "I have never changed my name; in the midst of distress and despair I kept always in the way of the Lord." He upbraided Levi ben Chabib with still having somewhat of Christian dogma sticking to him. This thrust reached his opponent's heart. The latter confessed that in the day of forced baptisms in Portugal his name had been changed, that he had been made a Christian, and that he had not been able to die for the religion of his fathers. But he brought forward his youth as an excuse; he had not been twenty years old, had remained a pseudo-Christian scarcely a year, and he hoped that the flood of tears which he had shed since then, and which he still shed, would wipe out his sin before God. After this humiliation Levi ben Chabib's violence against Berab knew no bounds. He flung the grossest insults at him, and declared that he hoped never more to meet him face to face. Through this intemperate violence of the chief rabbi of Jerusalem and Berab's death, which followed immediately after (January, 1541), the system of ordination fell to the ground.

JOSEPH KARO.

Joseph Karo alone, one of the ordained, refused to give in. This remarkable man, who later on had so deep an influence on Jewish history (born 1488, died 1575) when a child, was driven from Spain with his parents. He early learned the bitter lessons of suffering, and after long traveling about, came to Nicopolis in European Turkey. He studied the text of the Mishnah so assiduously that he knew it by heart. Later on Karo left Nicopolis to settle at Adrianople, where, on account of his extraordinary Talmudical learning, he was looked up to with respect, and found disciples. In his thirtieth year he undertook the gigantic work of furnishing Jacob Asheri's Code with a commentary, authorities, and corrections, to which he devoted twenty years of his life (1522--1542). Twelve years more were spent in a further revision (1542--1554). His imagination, kept in entire inactivity by such a dry task, was fired by the appearance of Solomon Molcho. That young enthusiast from Portugal made so overpowering an impression upon him, that Karo allowed himself to be initiated into the tortuous mazes of the Kabbala and to share Molcho's Messianic dreams. After this time his mind was divided between dry rabbinical scholarship and the fantastic ideas of the Kabbala. He kept up a correspondence with Molcho during the latter's stay in Palestine, and formed plans for going thither himself. Like Molcho, he prepared for a martyr's death, "as a burnt-sacrifice, an offering made by fire, of a sweet savor unto the Lord," and like Molcho, he had strange visions, which, according to his belief, were inspired by some superior being. This superior being (Maggid) was not an angel, or an imaginary voice, but--oddly enough--the Mishnah personified, who descended to him, and generally at night whispered revelations, because he had devoted himself to its service. Joseph Karo had these visions (which he for the most part committed to paper), not for a short period of time, but at intervals, to the end of his life, for nearly forty years. Part of them were afterwards published, and it is melancholy to see what havoc the Kabbala played with the intellect of that day. The superior being (or the Mishnah) laid the heaviest penances on Karo, forbade him to indulge in meat and wine, and went to the extent of prohibiting much drinking of water. If he was guilty of any fault, sleeping too long, being late at prayers, or slightly neglecting his study of the Mishnah, the mother Mishnah appeared, and made the most tender remonstrances. She certainly made astonishing revelations to him. These predictions were far from being mere deceptions, but were the promptings of a tumultuous epoch, or an excited imagination, such as is found in the warm, luxurious East oftener than in the cold, sober North.

Joseph Karo was so full of the thought that he was called to play a part in Palestine, and die as a martyr, during the time of preparation for the Messiah as begun by Solomon Molcho, that he left Adrianople. He stayed for some time at Salonica, a place swarming with Kabbalists. At length, he arrived in Safet, that nest of Kabbalists, with a companion of like mind, Solomon Alkabez, a dull, spiritless writer, whose song of welcome for the Sabbath bride (Lecha Dodi) has become more famous than its author. At Safet, Joseph Karo experienced the joy of seeing part of his fantastic dreams fulfilled; he was ordained by Berab as a member of the Synhedrion. After Berab's death Karo dreamed of nothing but his future greatness; he was to bring about ordination, and to be recognized by the sages of Palestine and foreign countries as a patriarch and leader of the Jews in Palestine. He would educate the best Talmudists, so that disciples of his school only would be accepted. Everyone would do him reverence as the holy likeness (Diokna Kadisha), and he would work miracles. Like Molcho, he was to die a martyr's death, that the name of

JOSEPH KARO'S CODE.

God might be hallowed; but his resurrection would soon afterwards follow, and he would enter into the Messianic kingdom.

All these advantages and prerogatives were to be won by a single achievement, which of itself would make the Jews into one great people, and gain him universal admiration. When his thorough commentary on Jacob Asheri's Code was completed, printed, published, and in circulation, when he had elaborated a comprehensive code of religious law grounded on that work, he would surely be acknowledged as patriarch and lawgiver in all Israel. His guardian angel had whispered to him that he would be made worthy to train many disciples and to see his writings printed and circulated throughout Israel. Even the supernatural worlds would ask, "Who is the man with whom the King of kings is well pleased, the patriarch of Palestine, the great writer of the Holy Land?" He would be enabled to publish his commentary, elucidations, and decisions without fault or error.

Devoted piety, fantastical imagination, and some degree of ambition inspired the author, who elaborated, for the whole Jewish race, the final code of religious law, destined to end all wavering, uncertainty, and antagonism of opinion. Kabbalistic enthusiasm combined with the Messianic hopes excited by Solomon Molcho, and the ceremony of ordination administered by Berab, gave Karo no rest, until by means of a comprehensive written work he had accomplished these hopes, at least so far as religious unity was concerned. Yet several decades were to elapse before the Jewish world received this Sift, a colossal work which required years for its completion. Joseph Karo's astounding, incessant industry had to eke out lack of genius. Such a work could be accomplished only by religious devotion and inspiration united with a fantastic imagination. Of all his lofty dreams one only was actually realized, that he would be chief rabbi of Safet after Jacob Berab's death, and would be acknowledged as a rabbinical authority, the latter coming about only gradually. But his authority was not absolute; he had a rival in Berab's best disciple, Moses de Trani.

THE MARRANOS AT NAPLES.

In Naples, where the Spaniards ruled, the ultra-Catholic party had long tried to introduce the Inquisition against the Marranos who resided there. When Charles V returned from his victorious expedition in Africa, this party tried to induce him to banish the Jews from Naples, because the Marranos were but strengthened in their unbelief by intercourse with them. But Donna Benvenida, the noble wife of Samuel Abrabanel, who was held in high respect by the Spaniards, so ardently entreated the emperor to revoke the decree of banishment, and her young friend, the daughter of the viceroy, so warmly supported her request, that he could not refuse them. It is also possible that Abrabanel's money may have had something to do with it. But a few years afterwards, Charles ordered the Neapolitan Jews to wear the badge of shame on their dress, and in case of transgression to suffer punishment in their person and property, or leave the country. They chose the latter alternative, probably by the advice of Samuel Abrabanel. They probably realized that persecution would not end there, but that it would form the prelude to harsher treatment. But this voluntary exile was turned into banishment, and every Jew who should venture to show himself again in Naples, was threatened with severe punishment (1540--1541). Many turned their steps towards Turkey, a few went to Ancona, under papal protection, or to Ferrara, under the rule of Duke Hercules II, who passed for a friend of the Jews. Those who emigrated by sea suffered much hardship, and many of them were taken by pirates, and carried to Marseilles. The Marranos who were living there did much for them, and King Henry II also treated them humanely. As he could not keep them in his country, he sent them in his ships to Turkey. Samuel Abrabanel also left Naples, although he was offered the exceptional license to remain there; but he refused to separate himself from the lot of his unhappy co-religionists. He settled in Ferrara, and lived there for about ten years. His noble wife, highly respected by Leonora, the daughter of the viceroy of Naples, now the Duchess of Tuscany, survived him.

A year later, the Jews of Bohemia experienced a milder, so to speak, more decent form of hatred. There had been many fires in the towns, especially in Prague. The Jews and shepherds were accused of having hired incendiaries. The Jews were also charged with having betrayed to the sultan the secret preparations for war against the Turks. The Bohemian diet therefore resolved to banish all Jews from Bohemia, and King Ferdinand, brother of Charles V, gave his assent. They were compelled to start on their exile with all their belongings (Adar, 1541) for of the numerous Jews of Prague only ten persons or families received permission to remain there. Many of them found their way into Poland and Turkey, then the two most tolerant countries. The innocence of those who had suffered death and

THE BLOOD ACCUSATION.

of the banished Jews, was established in the course of the same year. A few of the notables interceded for their recall, for they were more indispensable than trade jealousy, fanaticism, and the hatred of race would confess. Thus those who had settled near the Bohemian frontier were able to return to their home. But for this favor they were obliged to pay a tax of 300 schock groschen, and were ordered to wear a badge of yellow cloth as a mark by which they might be distinguished.

At the same time two persons of exalted rank and great influence, the one on the Catholic, the other on the Protestant side, attacked the Jews so mercilessly, that it is a marvel that they were not exterminated to a man. The cause of provocation in one instance was as follows: About Easter, a peasant boy, four years old, from the duchy of Neuburg in Bavaria, was missed, and suspicions arose that he was with the Jews. After Easter the boy was discovered by means of a dog, and enemies of the Jews pretended to see signs of Jewish torture on his body. Upon this the bishop of Eichstadt caused certain Jews to be seized and dragged to his residence that they might be tried, and sent a request to the neighboring princes to seize the Jews in their domains. But the inquiry did not prove the guilt of the Jews. On this occasion Duke Otto Henry of Neuburg warmly espoused the cause of the Jews, and exerted his influence to oppose the bishop of Eichstadt. The latter moved heaven and earth to have them banished at least. A courageous writer, probably at the suggestion of the duke, boldly defended the Jews against the prejudice of Christians in a pamphlet. This publication, " Little Book about the Jews," the author of which was a Lutheran pastor (perhaps Hosiander), for the first time placed the whole falsehood and malice of the accusation of the murder of Christian children in a clear light. The author, who professed to have had much intercourse with Jews, and to have become thoroughly acquainted with their language, laws, and customs, declared emphatically that a shameful injustice was done to Jews by these perpetual accusations of child-murder. The wealth and the pure faith of the Jews were the reasons. On the one hand, avaricious and cruel princes, or impoverished nobles or citizens, who owed money to Jews, invented such tales in order to be able to use violence against them; and on the other, such fables were invented by monks and the secular clergy in order to make new saints and fresh shrines for the encouragement of pilgrimages. In the long period since the dispersion of the Jews among Christians, no one had asserted, till within the last 300 years, that they had murdered Christian children. These idle tales had become current only since monks and priests practiced so much deception with pilgrimages and miraculous healings. Therefore, it was fair to assume that priests had invented the story of the murder of the child in the province of Neuburg. The author further points out that till the third century the Christians were accounted child-murderers and shedders of blood in the heathen world. The confessions of Jews themselves, which were quoted in confirmation of the accusations, had been made under torture, and could not be received as evidence.

Fanatical Catholic priests, especially the bishop of Eichstadt, saw with indignation that Jews, instead of being abhorred and persecuted, were glorified in this book, and hastened to efface the impression. Dr. John Eck, so notorious in the history of the Reformation, a favorite of the bishop of Eichstadt,

DR. ECK'S LIBEL.

was commissioned to write an answer, to prove the crime of bloodguiltiness, and to defame the Jews. This lawyer-theologian, with the broad shoulders of a butcher, the voice of a seditionist, and the disputativeness of a sophist, who had brought the Catholic Church, which he intended to defend against the Lutherans, into discredit by his vanity and his intemperate habits, this unprincipled disputant gladly undertook to belabor the Jews. In 1541 he wrote a hostile reply to the above-intentioned pamphlet, in which he set himself to prove "the evil and wickedness brought about by Jews in all the German territories and other kingdoms." He revived the old accusations against baptized Jews, patched together old wives' tales about the cruel nature of the Jews, raked up the false stories about Trent and Ratisbon uttered by Jews when undergoing torture, and added his own experiences to them. Eck was so shameless as to bring proofs of the cruelty of the Jewish character from the Old Testament. To cast infamy upon them he even slandered the Old Testament heroes held sacred by the church. In verbose language and with a false show of learning he maintained that Jews mutilated the children of Christians, and used their blood in the consecration of their priests, to assist their wives in child-birth, and to heal sickness; and that they desecrated the host. He exclaimed indignantly: "It is a great mistake that we Christians leave the Jews so much freedom, and grant them protection and security." Probably on the petition of Jews against these accusations, the emperor, Charles V, renewed their privileges, and declared them innocent of shedding the blood of Christians.

It is not edifying to find that Luther, the champion against obsolete prejudices, the founder of a new faith, agreed on the subject of Jews with his mortal enemy, Dr. Eck, who, with the same effrontery, had employed similar falsehood against himself. Luther had become greatly embittered with advancing age. He had lost much among his own followers by his obstinacy and persistent caviling, had disturbed the unanimity of those of the same way of thinking, and in his own camp created a breach which caused infinite harm to the Reformation for several centuries. He became enraged when his colleagues, Karlstadt, Munzer, etc., referred to the year of Jubilee, and the enfranchisement of the slaves and serfs. A pamphlet, in the form of a dialogue, in which Judaism was involved in a contest with Christianity, probably written by a Christian, was now sent to him; this was too much for him. Could Judaism be so bold as to think of measuring itself against Christianity? Luther at once set about writing a passionate, stinging pamphlet, "Concerning the Jews and their Lies" (1541), which, in spitefulness, exceeded the writings of Pfefferkorn and Eck.

Luther began by saying that he had made up his mind not to write anything further about Jews, nor against them, but because he had learnt that "this miserable, wicked people" dared entice Christians to join them, he wished to warn weak-minded men not to allow themselves to be fooled. Luther's principal argument, in proof of the truth of Christianity against the denial of Jesus by the Jews, is written in very monkish style. Because the Christians, for more than a thousand years, had robbed them of all the rights of man, had treated them as evil beasts, had trodden them under foot, lacerated, and slain them: in a, word, because they had fallen into distress

through the harshness of Christians, therefore, they must be rejected, and the Savior of the world must have appeared!

This is medieval logic. But it exceeds the limits of indulgence towards the peculiarities of a strong character, when Luther, in his uncharitableness towards Jews, employs language such as was usual with those who burnt Jews at the stake. What is to be done with this wicked, accursed race, which can no longer be tolerated? asked Luther, and he gave an answer to the question which shows equal want of charity and wisdom. First of all the reformer of Wittenberg recommended that the synagogues be reduced to ashes, "to the honor of God and of Christianity." Next, Christians were to destroy the houses of the Jews, and drive them all under one roof, or into a stable like gypsies. All prayer-books and copies of the Talmud and the old Testament were to be taken from them by force (as Luther's opponents, the Dominicans, had advised), and even praying and the use of God's name were to be forbidden under penalty of death. Their rabbis were to be forbidden to teach. The authorities were to prohibit the Jews from traveling, and to bar the roads against them, so that they must stay at home. Luther advised that their money be taken from them, and that this confiscated wealth be employed to establish a fund to maintain those Jews who should embrace Christianity. The authorities were to compel able-bodied Jews and Jewesses to forced labor, and to keep them strictly employed with the flail, the axe, the spade, the distaff and spindle, so that they might earn their bread in the sweat of their brow, and not live in idleness, feasting, and splendor. Christians were not to show any tender mercy to Jews. Luther urged the emperor

LUTHER ADVISES VIOLENT MEASURES.

and the princes to expel them from the country without delay, and drive them back into their own land. Luther even stirred up the robber-nobles against them. He had heard that a rich Jew was traveling through Germany with twelve horses. This Jew was known as the wealthy Michael, of Frankfort, the protege of the Margrave of Brandenburg; if the princes did not close the road against him and his fellow-believers, Luther urged the robber-knights to do so, for Christians might learn from his pamphlet how depraved was the Jewish nation. These absurd charges Luther ascribed to a worthless convert, Anton Margaritha, the son of a rabbi of Ratisbon. He had become a Catholic, and being punished on account of calumnies, had turned Lutheran, and written a foolish book against the Jews, and from this book Luther had taken his unjust attacks upon them.

Shortly before his death he exhorted his hearers in a sermon to drive out the Jews:

> *" Besides all this you still have the Jews. who do great evil in the land. If they could kill us all, they would gladly do so, aye, and often do it, especially those who profess to be physicians--they know all that is known about medicine in Germany; they can give poison to a man of which he will die in an hour, or in ten or twenty years; they thoroughly understand this art. I say to you lastly, as a countryman, if the Jews refuse to be converted, we ought not to suffer them, or bear with them any longer."*

In the reformer and regenerator of Germany, then, the Jews had almost worse enemy than in the Pfefferkorns, Hoogstratens, and Ecks, certainly worse than in the popes till the middle of the century.

IV. CHAPTER XVII

A JEWISH STATE PROJECTED

The Jews in Turkey--Joseph Karo compiles the Shulhan Aruch--Isaac Lurya--the Jewish Dark Age--Spread of the Kabbala--Chayim Vital Calabrese

1566-1600 C.E.

JOSEPH of Naxos long cherished the thought of founding a Jewish state. The Jew and the statesman in him yearned for this, and the enormous wealth of his mother-in-law, over which he had control, was to serve him as the means for its execution. Even when a fugitive Marrano he had seriously put before the Republic of Venice the request that it give him one of its numerous islands, so that he might people it with Jewish inhabitants. When later on Joseph stood high in favor with Prince Selim, and also with Sultan Solyman, he obtained from them, besides seven villages, the ruins of the city of Tiberias, for a small Jewish state to be peopled only with Jews. He sent one of his agents to supervise the rebuilding of Tiberias. The Turkish prince gave the pasha of Egypt strict orders to assist the building in every way. The Arab occupants of the neighboring villages were compelled to render forced labor, and the new and beautiful houses and streets of the city of Tiberias were completed in a year. Joseph of Naxos wished to make it a manufacturing town to compete with Venice. He planted mulberry-trees for the cultivation of silk-worms, and introduced looms for the manufacture of silks ; he also imported wool from Spain for the making of fine cloth.

Joseph does not seem to have directed his full energy to the little Jewish state; his plans were far more extensive, and thus New Tiberias never became an important place. He next endeavored to obtain the island of Naxos as a dukedom, together with the adjacent islands of the Aegean Sea, and when he was fortunate enough to be appointed duke by Sultan Selim, he thought no more about peopling his little island state with Jews ; perhaps it was not practicable. His mind was next set on becoming king of Cyprus. It is possible that he might have transformed this island of the goddess of beauty into a Jewish state had he obtained possession of it, but his enemy, the grand vizir, Mahomet Sokolli, prevented this. Thus his dreams of founding an independent Jewish state were dispelled. In reality, Joseph of Naxos did nothing of lasting importance for Judaism. He made various attempts, and then relaxed in his endeavors, or misspent his means.

The fact that Jews occupied an exceedingly favored position in Turkey for so long a period did not result in correspondingly enduring progress. They did not produce a single great genius who originated ideas to stimulate future ages, nor mark out a new line of thought for men of average intelligence. Not one of the leaders of the different congregations was above the level of mediocrity.

The rabbis and preachers were deeply learned in their particular subjects, but kept to the beaten track, without making a new discovery or bequeathing an original contribution, even in their own department. Only one rabbi left to posterity an epoch-making work, which even yet possesses significance, disputed though it be; but even this work contained nothing new or original. Joseph Karo, chief rabbi of the city of Safet, in Palestine, completed, after many years of toil, a new book of religious ordinances, the "Shulchan Aruch." Religious impulses, mystical fanaticism, and ambition, had equal shares in the making of this book. For Joseph Karo was still subject to strange visions; he still believed that he would be recognized everywhere as the highest authority by the compilation of his religious code, a norm for Jewish religious life; and that, by this means, he would accomplish the revival of rabbinical ordination, in which Jacob Berab had failed; restore, in fact, the unity of Judaism, and thereby hasten the coming of the Messiah. He spent the whole of his life in collecting the vast material, in weighing the pros and cons of arguments, drawing conclusions and arranging them in their proper places. By doing this he supplied a serious want. There was no manual that embraced the whole field of religious observance. As the Talmud and the later religious codes to an even greater extent favored differences of opinion upon nearly every single point in matters of religion, ritual, law and the marriage state, disputes constantly occurred which led to altercation and divisions in the communities, for it rarely happened that two rabbis agreed upon any question that came up for discussion. Each was able to adduce reasons for or against any argument from the vast mass of rabbinical literature.

It was this confusion and divergence of opinion that Joseph Karo wished to check by means of his

"THE SHULCHAN ARUCH."

new religious Code. He embraced the whole of the vast field of Talmudic and rabbinical literature, although his intellect could not master it. By birth a Spaniard, he involuntarily preferred the views of Spanish authorities to those of French and German writers. Hence he allowed partiality to creep into his compilation. As a matter of course, too, Karo admitted various elements of mysticism, though only sparingly, as if unwilling to place the Zohar upon a level with the Talmud in matters of practical religious observance. He has embodied in his Code excellent precepts in regard to sanctity, chastity, brotherly love, morality, and honesty in business, drawn from the Talmud and the rabbinical writings; but they disappear in a sea of casuistical details and mere externals, in a patchwork of divisions and subdivisions, of "ifs" and "buts." In this work there appears an altogether different kind of Judaism from that revealed on Sinai, announced by the prophets, or even taught by Maimuni. But this Judaism thoroughly suited the ideas of the Jews of that period, and therefore Karo's Code was immediately hailed with delight, disseminated, and received as the infallible standard authority in Turkey, throughout the East, in Italy, and even in Poland.

Thus religious life received a certain finality and unity, but at the expense of spirituality and freedom of thought. From Karo Judaism received the form maintained up to the present time. His dream was partially fulfilled. His rabbinical writings became the common property of Judaism, and gave it religious unity. But he himself did not become the leader and head, as the "Spirit of the Mishnah" had repeatedly promised him: he was only honored as one authority among many others. Still less did he restore the ordination of rabbi-judges as members of a Synhedrion, or hasten in any way the coming of the Messiah.

At that time there was a man in Italy, who not only surpassed all his Jewish contemporaries in his spirit of inquiry and desire for truth, but who would have been able to purify Judaism from the dress of centuries of hardship, if the tendency of the age had not run counter to this endeavor, or if he had had greater courage in opposing it. Azarya ben Moses dei Rossi (born at Mantua about 1514, died in 1578), descended from an old Italian family, had buried himself so deeply in books, that his body bore traces of severe suffering from over-study. Feeble, yellow, withered, and afflicted with fever, he crept about like a dying man. Yet in this living corpse a powerful and healthy mind worked with great activity. He had thoroughly mastered the whole of Jewish literature, besides being well read in Latin historical works, and he had also practiced medicine. At the same time he led a wandering life. He dwelt for some rime at Ferrara, then in Bologna, had to leave that city in consequence of the persecution and expulsion of the Jews under Pius V, and finally settled again permanently in Ferrara. He held intercourse with the greatest Jews, Christians, and Marranos of his age, and was regarded by all with astonishment as a marvel of learning. He did not allow the treasures of his knowledge to lie dead within him, but let them grow and spread luxuriantly. Ancient history possessed special attraction for him. But even more admirable than his vast reading was the use he made of it. He was the first to bring into contact and connection with one another two provinces of literature which were far apart--the Talmud and its offshoots, with Philo, Josephus, and the works of the Church Fathers, proving the truth of historical narratives from the mouths of many witnesses. Dei' Rossi, too, was the only one not satisfied with the data of tradition; he accepted nothing as truth till he had subjected it to a searching examination.

But how could a sober, critical method of inquiry have found favor in an age when the mystic, dazing Kabbala was the first authority, bidding men esteem blind credulity as the highest virtue, and exciting visionary enthusiasm to the highest pitch of fanatical intoxication? The visions of Solomon Molcho and Joseph Karo and their fond enthusiasm about the Messiah were sober compared with the excitement which reigned after their death, and celebrated a veritable witches' Sabbath. During the last three decades of the sixteenth century the Kabbala gained sole mastery in Palestine, conjured up apparitions, and encouraged orgies of mysticism. It spread thence over the whole of Turkey, Poland, Germany, and Italy, darkening and confusing men's minds, having an evil influence even upon their hearts, allowing no healthy thought to appear, or branding such thought as heretical and sinful. It was a period of Kabbalistic mania, coincident with profligacy and moral degradation, and its victims despised not only the sciences, but even the Talmud with its exhortations to sobriety. Then for the first time the Jewish world entered on a "dark age" of its own, with all the appropriate credulity, while only the last traces of such darkness were visible in Europe generally. This tendency was exaggerated by two men, who by their fanaticism and visionary extravagance infected a continually widening circle. These were Isaac Lurya and his disciple Chayim Vital Calabrese.

Isaac Lurya Levi (born in Jerusalem in 1534, and died 1572) was descended from a German family. Left an orphan at an early age by the death of his father, young Isaac came to Egypt, to the house of a rich uncle, Mardochai Francis, a tax-farmer, and began to study the Talmud. The dry study of the Talmud, which filled the mind with voluminous learning, unfruitful hair-splitting, and mere formulas, yet failed to satisfy the wants of the heart, seems to have become repugnant to Lurya, and to have driven him to fantastic mysticism. He preferred the awful loneliness of the Nile country to the noise of the school; abstraction in worlds of mysticism and devout praying to working out intellectual problems. He was greatly attracted by the Zohar, which had then been printed for the first time, and, widely spread abroad, had become accessible to everybody. The more familiar he became with the Kabbala through his absorption in the sounding emptiness of the Zohar, the more did he seek solitude, and the less intercourse had he with men. He even neglected his young wife, only visited his house from Sabbath to Sabbath, and spoke little, that little being only in Hebrew. Lurya is said to have spent several years in solitude in this manner, and the result was that like all whose reason is weaker than their imagination, he became a confirmed visionary. The mystic book, the Zohar, his constant companion in this seclusion, aided in exciting his imagination. Firmly convinced of its authenticity as the work of Simon bar Yochai, and also of the divine character of all the fantasies and follies therein revealed, Lurya persisted in seeing in it high allusions and profound wisdom. In his heated imagination he

ISAAC LURYA.

even saw Elijah, the teacher of mysteries, face to face.

But what did the prophet Elijah, or the Zohar, or rather his own heated imagination, reveal to him? First he took the trouble to put system, unity, and logical order into the confusion and intricacies of the Zohar, as if connected thought could be expected in the idle chatter of a half imbecile. The hermit of Cairo sought to deduce from it how God had created and ordered the world by means of the mystic numbers (Sefiroth), or how the Godhead revealed itself in the forms of substances, or how it concentrated itself within itself in order to project the finite nature of created things from its own infinitude. Thus he evolved an extraordinarily complicated system of powers and opposing powers, forces and counterforces, forms and degrees (Parsophin), in the four spheres of Separation, Creation, Formation, and Transformation; and he clothed these empty abstractions with such wondrous names, that he afterwards complained, with reason, that no one could understand his mystic system. Yet Lurya looked upon this intricate and complex theory of the creation as only a kind of introduction to what seemed to him a much more important and practical part of the Kabbala, whereby the divine order of the world (Olam ha-Tikkun) could be brought about. This practical Kabbala of Lurya rests upon a not less marvelous doctrine of souls, also based upon the visions of the Zohar.

Our souls, he says, reflect the close connection between the finite and the infinite, and, therefore, have a manifold character. The whole of the soul material to appear in temporal life was created with Adam, but each soul, according to its higher or lower degree, was fashioned in, from, or with the first man, out of high or low organs and forms. Accordingly, there are souls of the brain, the eyes, the hands, and the feet. Each of these must be regarded as an effluence, or spark (Nizuz), from Adam. By the first sin of the first man--for the Kabbala finds original sin necessary for its fanciful creations--the higher and the lower, the superior and the inferior souls, good and evil, became confused and mingled together. Even the purest beings thereby received an admixture of evil and the devilish element of the "husk" (Kelifa). But the moral order of the world, or the purification of the first man, cannot be brought about till the consequences of original sin, the confusion of good and evil, are obliterated and removed. From the most evil part of the soul material emanates the heathen world ; the people of Israel, on the other hand, come from the good part. But the former are not quite without an admixture of the original good, while the latter are not free from an admixture of the corrupt and demoniac. This imperfection gives the continual impulse towards sin, and hinders the chosen fragment of the human race from following the law of God, the Torah. The Messianic period will put an end to the disturbance of divine order arising from the first sin, or abolish the disorder which has since crept in, and will introduce, or see introduced, the divinity of the world. Therefore, a complete separation of good from evil must take place, and this can only happen through Israel, if it or each of its members will lose or cast away the admixture of evil. For this purpose, men's souls (especially those of the Israelites) have to wander through the bodies of men and animals, even through rivers, wood, and stones. The doctrine of the transmigration of souls forms the center and basis of Lurya's Kabbala, but he has a peculiar development of the idea. According to this theory even the souls of the pious must suffer transmigration, since not even they are free from the taint of evil; there is none righteous upon earth, who does only good, and sins not. In this way, Lurya solved the difficulty, which former Kabbalist writers could not overcome.

TRANSMIGRATION OF SOULS.

But this separation of the good and evil elements in the world's soul material, the expiation and obliteration of original sin, or the restoration of the divine order in Adam, would require a long series of ages, owing to the impulse towards sin continually present. There are, however, means of hastening this process, and this was the really original doctrine that Lurya enunciated. Besides the transmigration of our souls, sinful and subject to demoniac forces as they are, there is another mode of expiation, the elevation or impregnation of the soul (Ibbur, super-foetatio). If a purified soul has neglected various religious duties here on earth, or has had no opportunity of fulfilling them, it must return to the earthly life, attach itself to the soul of a living human being, and unite and coalesce with it in order to retrieve this neglect. Or again, the departed spirits of men freed from sin appear again on earth to support the weak and waver in souls which cannot attain to good by thoir own efforts, strengthen them and lead them to the final goal. These pure spirits combine with weaker souls still struggling, and form a union with them, provided that they have some affinity with one another, i. e., if they originate from the same spark or organ of Adam, since as a rule only similar (homogeneous) souls attract each other, while on the other hand dissimilar (heterogeneous) souls repel each other. According to this theory the banishment and dispersion of Israel have for their purpose the salvation of the world or of men's souls. The purified spirits of pious Israelites unite with the souls of men of other nationalities in order to free them from the demoniacal impurities that possess them.

Isaac Lurya imagined a complete system of the transmigration and combination of souls. It also seemed to him important to know the sex of a soul, for feminine souls are found in masculine bodies, and vice versa, according to the transmigration and attraction in each case. It is especially important in contracting a marriage to know whether the souls of man and wife harmonize with each other in respect of origin and degree. By means of this secret the visionary of Cairo expected to solve the other mystery, namely, how good spirits may be conjured down from heaven, and in a measure compelled to enter the bodies of living men, and thus made to divulge revelations of the world beyond, Hereby he believed that he held the key to the kingdom of the Messiah and the regeneration of the world. Lurya also believed that he possessed the soul of the Messiah of the branch of Joseph, and that he had a Messianic mission. He saw spirits everywhere, and heard their whispers in the rushing of the waters, the movements of the trees and grass, in the song or twittering of birds, even in the flickering of flames. He saw how at death the souls were set free from the body, how they hovered in the air, or rose out of their graves. He held intimate intercourse with the saints of the Bible, the Talmud, and with the rabbis, in particular with Simon bar Yochai. In short, Lurya was a ghost-seer and raiser of the dead, a second Abraham Abulafia, or Solomon Molcho, arousing hopes of the coming of the Messiah by Kabbalistic jugglery, but with all this fanaticism he was sober and sophistical. He introduced the casuistry of the Talmud into the Kabbala.

In Egypt, Isaac Lurya found little or no favor with his labyrinth of higher worlds and his theories of creation and redemption. To realize his scheme of redemption he migrated with his wife and child to Safet, the Jerusalem of mysticism, where the mystic doctrine flourished, and the Zohar, the spurious work of Moses de Leon, was exalted to the same level as the Law of Moses ben Amram. Almost the whole college of rabbis and the chief leaders of Safet were

Kabbalists. This place was at the time a flourishing city inhabited only by Jews. The members

of the community knew little of oppression or the cares of life, and so the Kabbalists could spin mystical theories to their hearts' content. They felt as safe under the favor that the Jewish Duke of Naxos found with the sultan, as if in a state of their own, politically independent. The Kabbalists had gone so far in their imitation of Catholicism that they had adopted auricular confession and the adoration of martyrs. And this was the stage on which Lurya, the creator of the new Kabbala, was to originate new aberrations.

At first (about 1569), he appears to have received little attention in the city of Kabbalists. Only through his acquaintance and connection with a still greater visionary, perhaps not quite so honest as himself, did he become a person of consequence, and infect everyone with his waking dreams. This man was the Italian Chayim Vital Calabrese (born 1543, died 1620), whose father, a copyist of the scrolls of the Law, had traveled to Palestine from Italy. Vital had learned nothing thoroughly in his younger days; he had only gained a smattering of the Talmud and mystic lore. He possessed a wild, extravagant imagination, and a decided inclination for adventure and sensation. For two years and a half Vital had occupied his time with alchemy and the art of making gold. From this mystic art he turned to Lurya's Kabbala. It is not known which of these two men first sought the other, but it is certain that each, without wishing it, deceived the other. Together they visited desolate places and graves, particularly the grave of Simon bar Yochai, the feigned author of the Zohar, in Meiron. This was Lurya's favorite spot, because there he fancied he could draw down upon himself the spirit of this supposed chief of the mystics. Now and again Lurya sent forth his disciple to conjure up spirits, and for this purpose delivered to him certain formulas made up of the transposed letters of the name of the Deity. Of course, evil spirits fled before Vital's gaze, whilst good spirits attached themselves to him, and communicated their secrets.

It was Vital who spread sensational reports concerning the extraordinary, almost divine gifts of his master, and of his power over departed and living souls; doing so, it appears, with an artful calculation of effect and publicity. Lurya, once so isolated, now found himself surrounded by crowds of visitors; Kabbalists, young and old, came to listen to the new revelation. Several disciples attached themselves to him, and he communicated to them his confused thoughts, assigned to each the original Adamite soul that dwelt in him, the transmigrations which it had undergone before its present corporeal existence, and its functions on earth. It never occurred to these people, already enmeshed in the Kabbalistic net, to doubt the truth of these communications. The disciples that gathered round him Lurya formed into two classes: the " initiated " and the "Novices."

Mystical conversations and notes, the interviewing and summoning of spirits, formed the occupation of Lurya and his followers. In short, Lurya was on the eve of founding a new Jewish sect. On the Sabbath he dressed in white, and wore a fourfold garment to symbolize the four letters of the name of God. The underlying fact of all his revelations and exertions was that he was the Messiah of the race of Joseph, the forerunner of the Messiah of David's line. This, however, he only furtively hinted to his disciples. His delusion was that the Messianic period would commence at the beginning of the second half of the second period of a thousand years since the destruction of the Temple, i. e., in 1568.

The sudden death of the mystic, at the age of thirty-eight, conduced still more to his glorification. Death is wont to transfigure natures like his, and

veneration for them increases as years roll on. With Eastern exaggeration, his disciples regarded him as even more than a worker of wonders; they called him the "Holy and Divine," and sought, for their own glory, to win adherents for him and his visionary extravagances. They declared that, if Lurya could only have lived five years longer, he would have improved the world so effectually, that the Messianic period would certainly have begun. Abraham Abulafia, who had evolved a Kabbalistic medley from his own consciousness, was declared a heretic, and persecuted. Isaac Lurya, who had done the same thing with the Zohar as a foundation, was almost deified.

After Lurya's death, Vital Calabrese came to the fore. He immediately usurped a kind of authority over his fellow-disciples, pretended that Lurya on his deathbed had appointed him his successor, and, in feigned obedience to a dying request of his master, took away from them the written notes given them by Lurya. Vital let it be understood that he was the Messiah of the race of Joseph. However, some disciples did not pay any attention to this, and forthwith taught in various countries what they had received from Lurya himself. This was especially done by Israel Saruk in Italy, whither he had traveled.

The harm that the Kabbalistic doctrines of Lurya caused in Jewish circles is inexpressible. Judaism became surrounded with so thick a husk of mysticism, that it has not even yet succeeded in entirely freeing itself, and showing its true kernel. Through Lurya influence there was formed, side by side with the Judaism of the Talmud and the rabbis, a Judaism of the Zohar and the Kabbala. For it was due to him that the spurious Zohar was placed upon a level with, indeed higher than, the Holy Scriptures and the Talmud.

The mysticism of Lurya laid stress upon an idea which has been strangely neglected in Jewish circles, viz., devotion in prayer, but even this devotion degenerated into Kabbalistic trifling. Every word and every syllable of the ordained prayers was to be meditated on devoutly, so that one might reflect upon the worlds of the Sefiroth, the number of the names of God hidden therein, and many other things. Lurya's Kabbala certainly inculcated the preservation of an unruffled disposition, and interdicted dejection, or outbreaks of anger and ill-humor. But this serenity, from its mystical setting, received a touch of constraint and unpleasantness, like the laughter of a madman. The Sabbath, with its prayers and meals, forms the central point of Lurya's mystic teaching. He looked upon it as the visible representation of the world of the Sefiroth, as the embodiment of the Divinity (Shechinah) in temporal life, and all actions done or left undone on that day had an influence upon the higher world. Lurya's followers welcomed the Sabbath, " the mystic bride," with chanting, and for this purpose Lurya composed Chaldaic songs full of obscure and meaningless formulas. His Kabbala also introduced a second Day of Atonement, The "Day of Hosannas," the seventh day of the Feast of Tabernacles, was formerly observed as a day of festivity. Even Joseph Karo did not venture in his code to attribute a higher, mystical, religious function to this day. Lurya's school first raised it, on the authority of the Zohar, to the rank of a minor day of expiation, introduced the practice of holding a mystic vigil the previous night, and perceived in every leaf of the willow branches, and in the seven-fold processions round the scrolls of the Law, a higher, mystical meaning. In relation to morality, too, the mysticism of Lurya had a corrupting influence. It demanded a "harmony of souls" as a condition of marriage, and, therefore, whenever disagreement showed itself in married life, it was said that the marriage was not a union foreordained by the harmony of the Sefiroth.

DEATH OF JOSEPH NASSI.

Kabbalists, therefore, separated from their wives in consequence of the smallest dissension in married life, to seek out the harmonious soul predestined for them. Thus divorce became frequent in Kabbalistic circles. Kabbalists often left their wives and children in the West, and, migrating to the East, contracted a new marriage, or several new marriages, and the children of the different marriages knew nothing of one another.

These corrupting mystic doctrines did not remain a dead letter, but were forthwith put into practice by their adherents. Thus, the brilliance shed by the Jewish Duke of Naxos and other influential Jews at the Turkish court over their fellow-believers in the East, came to resemble the light of the will-o the-wisps that make the waters of a stagnant marsh gleam with a flickering light. The religious stagnation at the time was glaring indeed; there was a complete relapse into heathenism; and what was worse, there sounded no warning voice which recognized the mischief, or stigmatized, though ever so feebly, the corruption as it really was. Perhaps the feeling of complete security in which the Jews in Turkey reposed under mighty protectors of their own race had encouraged this religious disorder. In any case, it did not decrease as this protection gradually disappeared, when the influence of Joseph of Naxos ceased on the death of Sultan Selim in 1574· His successor, Sultan Murad III (I574--1595), left the Jewish duke in possession of his rank and offices according to his father's dying request. But he no longer had direct influence over the divan ; he was supplanted by his adversary, the grand vizir, Mahomet Sokolli, and his rival, Solomon Ashkenazi, and could accomplish nothing without intrigues through the agency of the harem. Joseph Nassi did not long survive his partial disgrace; he died of calculus, on August 2d, 1579, sincerely lamented by the Jews.

V. CHAPTER 1

CHMIELNICKI AND THE PERSECUTION OF THE JEWS OF POLAND BY THE COSSACKS

The Study of the Talmud in Poland--Jews and Cossacks--Chmielnicki--Sufferings of the Jews in consequence of his Successes--the Tartar Haidamaks--Fearful Massacres in Nemirov, Tulczyn, and Homel--Prince Vishniovieki--Massacres at Polonnoie, Lemberg, Narol, and in other Towns--John Casimir--Lipmann Heller and Sabbatai Cohen--Renewal of the War between Cossacks and Poles--The Polish (Jewish) Fugitives

1648-1656 C.E.

By reason of their great number, their importance, and their compact union, the Jews in Poland formed a state within a state; The general synod, which assembled twice a year at Lublin and Jaroslaw, formed a legislative and judicial parliament from which there was no appeal. At first called the Synod of the Three Countries, it became in the first quarter of the seventeenth century the Synod of the Four Countries (Vaad Arba Arazoth). An elective president (Parnes di Arba Arazoth) was at the head, and conducted public affairs. The communities and rabbis had civil, and, to a certain extent, criminal, jurisdiction, at least against informers and traitors, Hence no Jew ventured to bring an accusation against one of his race before the authorities of the country, fearing to expose himself to disgrace and contempt from public opinion, which would have embittered his life, or even entailed death. Almost every community had its college of judges, a rabbi with two assessors, before whom every complaint was brought, but the final decision rested with the synod. The synod also concerned itself about honesty in dealing and conduct, and in weight and measure, wherever Jews were affected.

The study of the Talmud in Poland, established by Shachna, Solomon Lurya, and Moses Isserles, reached a pitch attained at no previous time, nor in any other country. The demand for copies of the Talmud was so great that in less than twenty years three editions had to be printed, no doubt in thousands of copies. The study of the Talmud was a greater necessity in Poland than in the rest of Europe. The rabbis, as has been already said, had jurisdiction of their own, and decided according to Talmudical and Rabbinical laws. The great number of Jews in Poland, and their fondness for litigation, gave occasion to intricate law cases. The rabbi-judges were obliged to go back to the source of law, the Talmud, to seek points of support for such cases. The contending parties being themselves well informed and acute, the reasoning of the rabbis had to be flawless to escape criticism. Hence Rabbinical civil law in Poland met with extraordinary cultivation and extension, to adapt it to all cases and make it available for the learned litigants. Thus the ever-growing subtlety of the method of Talmud study depended on current conditions and wants, and on the circumstance that each Talmudist wished to surpass all others in ingenuity.

It would be tedious to enumerate the Rabbinical authors of Poland in the first half of the seventeenth century. The cultivation of a single faculty, that of

hair-splitting judgment, at the cost of the rest, narrowed the imagination, hence not a single literary product appeared in Poland deserving the name of poetry. All the productions of the Polish school bore the Talmudical stamp, as the school regarded everything from the Talmudical point of view. The disciples of this school looked down almost with contempt on Scripture and its simple grandeur, or rather it did not exist for them. How, indeed, could they have found time to occupy themselves with it? And what could they do with these children's stories, which did not admit the application of intellectual subtlety? They knew something of the Bible from the extracts read in the synagogues, and those occasionally quoted in the Talmud. The faculty for appreciating the sublimity of biblical doctrines and characters, as well as simplicity and elevation in general, was denied them. A love of twisting, distorting, ingenious quibbling, and a foregone antipathy to what did not lie within their field of vision, constituted the character of the Polish Jews. Pride in their knowledge of the Talmud and a spirit of dogmatism attached even to the best rabbis, and undermined their moral sense. The Polish Jews of course were extraordinarily pious, but even their piety rested on sophistry and boastfulness. Each wished to surpass the other in knowledge of what the Code prescribed for one case or another. Thus religion sank, not merely, as among Jews of other countries, to a mechanical, unintelligent ceremonial, but to a subtle art of interpretation. To know better was everything to them ; but to act according to acknowledged principles of religious purity, and exemplify them in a moral life, occurred to but few. Integrity and right-mindedness they had lost as completely as simplicity and the sense of truth.

The corruption of the Polish Jews was avenged upon them in a terrible way, and the result was, that the rest of the Jews in Europe were for a time infected with it. With fatal blindness Polish Jews offered the nobility and the Jesuits a helping hand in oppressing the Zaporogian Cossacks in the Ukraine and Little Russia. The magnates wished to make profitable serfs of the Cossacks, the Jesuits hoped to convert the Greek heretics into Roman Catholics, the Jews settled in the district expected to enrich themselves and play the lord over these pariahs. They advised the possessors of the Cossack colonies how most completely to humiliate, oppress, torment, and ill-use them; they usurped the office of judges over them, and vexed them in their ecclesiastical affairs. No wonder that the enslaved Cossacks hated the Jews, with whom their relations were closest, almost more than their noble and clerical foes. The Jews were not without warning what would be their lot, if these embittered enemies once got the upper hand. In an insurrection of the Zaporogians under their Hetman in about 1638, despite its brief duration, they slew 200 Jews, and destroyed several synagogues. Nevertheless, Jews lent a hand, when in consequence of the insurrection the further enslavement of the sufferers was determined upon. In the year 1648, fixed by that lying book, the Zohar, they expected the coming of

BOGDAN CHMIELNICKI.

the Messiah and the time of redemption, when they would be in power, and, therefore, they were more reckless and careless than was their custom at other times. Bloody retribution was not long delayed, and struck the innocent with the guilty, perhaps the former more severely than the latter.

It proceeded from a man who understood how to make use of the increasing hatred of the Cossacks for his purposes, and who was regarded by his countrymen as their ideal. Bogdan Chmielnicki (Russian Chmel),born about 1595,died 1657,before whom all Poland trembled for several years, gave Russia the first opportunity of interfering in the Polish republic, and was a frightful scourge for the Jews. Chmielnicki, brave in war and artful in the execution of his plans, impenetrable in his schemes, at once cruel and hypocritical, had been vexed by Jews, when he held the subordinate position of camp secretary (Pisar) of the Cossacks subject to the house of Koniecpolski. A Jew, Zachariah Sabilenki, had played him a trick, by which he was robbed of his wife and property. Another had betrayed him when he had come to an understanding with the Tartars. Besides injuries which his race had sustained from Jewish tax farmers in the Ukraine, he, therefore, had personal wrongs to avenge. His remark to the Cossacks, "The Poles have delivered us as slaves to the cursed breed of Jews," was enough to excite them. Vengeance-breathing Zaporogians and booty-loving Tartars in a short time put the Polish troops to flight by successful maneuvers (May 18, 1648). Potocki, the lieutenant-general, and 8,000 Poles, according to agreement, were delivered to the Tartars. After the victory the wild troops went eastward from the Dnieper, between Kiev and Pultava, plundering and murdering, especially the Jews who had not taken flight; the number of the murdered reached several thousand. Hundreds underwent baptism in the Greek Church, and pretended to be Christians, in order to save themselves. Fortunate were those who fell into captivity with the Tartars; they were transported to the Crimea, and ransomed by Turkish Jews. Four Jewish communities (Porobischa and others) of about 3,000 souls resolved to escape massacre by surrendering to the Tartars with all their property. They were well treated, and sold into Turkey, where they were ransomed in a brotherly manner by those of their own race. The Constantinople community sent a deputy to Holland to collect money from the rich communities for the ransom of captives.

Unfortunately for the Poles and Jews, King Vladislav, for whom Chmielnicki had shown some respect, was removed by death. During the interregnum of several months, from May to October, 1648, the usual Polish dissension occurred, which crippled every attempt at resistance. At first Chmielnicki drew back, apparently inclined to negotiate with the crown, but he gave his creatures full power to ravage the Polish provinces. Regular troops of murderers, called Haidamaks (the Tartar word for partisans), were formed under brutal leaders who cared not a straw for human life, and who reveled in the death-struggles of their Polish and Jewish foes. In the name of religion they were urged by the Greek popes to murder Catholics and Jews. The commander of each troop had his own method of exercising cruelty. One had thongs slung round the necks of Catholic and Jewish women, by which they were dragged along; this he called "presenting them with a red ribbon." A few weeks after the first victory of the Cossacks, a troop under another of these chiefs advanced against the stronghold of Nemirov, where 6,000 Jews, inhabitants and fugitives from the neighborhood, had assembled; they were in possession of the fortress, and closed the gates. But the Cos-

sacks had an understanding with the Greek Christians in the town, and put on Polish uniforms in order to be taken for Poles. The Christian inhabitants urged the Jews to open the gates for their friends. They did so, and were suddenly attacked by the Cossacks and the inhabitants of the town, and almost entirely cut down amid frightful tortures (Siwan 20-June 10, 1648).

Another Haidamak troop under Kryvonoss attacked the town of Tulczyn, where about 600 Christians and 2,000 Jews had taken refuge in the fortress. There were brave Jews among them, or necessity had made them brave, and they would not die without resistance. Nobles and Jews swore to defend the town and fortress to the last man. As the Cossack peasants understood nothing of the art of siege, and had repeatedly suffered severely from the sorties of Jews and Poles, they resorted to a trick. They assured the nobles that their rage was directed only against the Jews, their deadly foes ; if these were delivered up, they would withdraw. The infatuated nobles, forgetful of their oath, proposed that the Jews should deliver up their arms to them. The Jews at first thought of turning on the Poles for their treachery, as they exceeded them in numbers. But the rabbi of Tulczyn warned them against attacking the Poles, who would inflict bloody vengeance, and all Poland would be excited against the Jews, who would be exterminated. He implored them to sacrifice themselves for their brethren in the whole country; perhaps the Cossacks would accept their property as ransom. The Jews consented, and delivered up their arms, the Poles thereupon admitting the troops into the town. After the latter had taken everything from the Jews, they set before them the choice of death or baptism. Not one of them would purchase life at that price ; about 1,500 were tortured and executed before the eyes of the Polish nobles (Tamuz 4--June 24)· The Cossacks left ten rabbis alive, in order to extort large sums from the communities. The Poles were immediately punished for their treachery. Deprived of the assistance of the Jews, they were attacked by the Cossacks and slain, proving that violators of their word cannot reckon on fidelity towards themselves. This sad event had the good effect that the Poles always sided with the Jews, and were not opposed to them in the course of the long war.

At the same time another Haidamak troop, under a leader named Hodki, had penetrated into Little Russia, and caused dreadful slaughter in the communities of Homel, Starodub, Czernigov, and other places east and north of Kiev. The Jews of Homel are said to have suffered martyrdom most firmly, on the same day on which the Tulczyn community was annihilated. The leader of the troop had all the Jews of Homel, inhabitants as well as fugitives, stripped outside the town, and surrounded by Cossacks, and called upon them to be baptized or to expect a most frightful death. They all, men, women, and children, to the number of about 1,500, preferred death.

Prince Vishnioviecki, the only heroic figure amongst the Poles at that time, a man of penetration, intrepid courage, and strategic ability, defended the cause of the persecuted Jews with devoted zeal. He took the fugitives under the protecting wings of his small, but brave force, with which he everywhere pursued the Cossack bands to destruction. But, because of his limited power, he could accomplish nothing of lasting import. Through petty jealousy, he was passed over at the election of the commander-in-chief against the Cossack insurrection, and instead of him three were chosen, of a character calculated to help on Chmielnicki to further victories.

Annoyed at the pitiful policy of the regent, the primate of Gnesen, Vishniovecki followed his own course, but was compelled to retreat before the

PRINCE VISHNIOVIECKI.

overpowering number of the roving troops and the Greek Catholic population in sympathy with them, and so destruction was brought on the Jews, who had reckoned on his heroic courage. In the fortress of Polonnoie, between Zaslav and Zytomir, 10,000 Jews, partly inhabitants, partly fugitives from the neighborhood, are said to have perished at the hand of the besieging Haidamaks and the traitorous inhabitants (Ab 13--July 22).

The unfortunate issue of the second war between Poles and Cossacks (September, 1648), when the Polish army, more through dread of the Tartars under Tugai Bey and the incapacity of its generals, than through Chmielnicki's bravery, was scattered in wild flight, and collected only behind the walls of Lemberg, prepared a bloody fate even for Jews who thought themselves safe at a distance from the field of battle. There was no escape from the wild assaults of the Zaporogians, unless they could reach the Wallachian borders. The blood of slaughtered and maltreated Jews marked the vast tract from the southern part of the Ukraine to Lemberg by way of Dubno and Brody; in the town of Bar alone from two to three thousand perished. It scarcely need be said that the brutal cruelty of the regular Cossacks, as well as of the wild Haidamaks, made no distinction between Rabbanites and Karaites. The important community of

Lemberg lost many of its members through hunger and pestilence, and its property besides, which it had to pay to the Cossacks as ransom.

In the town of Narol the Zaporogians caused a revolting butchery. It is said that in the beginning of November 45,000 persons, among them 12,000 Jews, were slain there with the cruelest tortures. Among the corpses remained living women and children, who for several days had to feed on human flesh. Meanwhile the Haidamaks roamed about in Volhynia, Podolia, and West Russia, and slaked their revenge in the blood of nobles, Catholics, clergy, and Jews, to thousands and tens of thousands. In Crzemieniec an inhuman monster slew hundreds of Jewish children, scornfully examined the corpses as Jews do with cattle, and threw them to the dogs. In many towns Jews, as well as Catholics, armed themselves, and drove the bloodthirsty Cossacks away.

The election of a king, which finally was effected--and, though the Polish state was on the brink of an abyss, it took place amidst fights and commotions--put an end to bloodshed for the moment. Although for the most part in a drunken condition, Chmielnicki retained sobriety enough to dictate, among his conditions of peace, that no Catholic church should be tolerated, nor any Jew live, in the Cossack provinces. The commission, unable to accept the conditions, departed without settling the business (February 16, 1649). The Jews, who had reckoned upon a settlement, and returned to their homes, paid for their confidence with death, for the Cossacks surrounded the towns with death-cries. Thus, a second time, many Jews and nobles perished at Ostrog (March 4, 1649)·

The breaking off of the negotiation with Chmielnicki led to a third encounter. Although the Polish army this time appeared better armed on the field of battle, it had as little success as before. In the battle at Sbaraz it would have been completely destroyed by the Zaporogians and Tartars, if the king had not wisely come to an understanding with the Tartar chief. Thereupon followed the peace (August, 1649), which confirmed Chmielnicki's program, among other points that concerning the Jews. In the chief seats of the Cossacks (i. e., in the Ukraine, West Russia, in the district of Kiev, and a part of Podolia) they could neither own or rent landed estates, nor live there.

In consequence of this convention, the Poles and

CONVERTS RETURN TO JUDAISM.

Jews were unmolested for about a year and a half, although on both sides schemes were harbored to break the agreement at the first opportunity. As far as residence was allowed them, the fugitive Jews returned to their homes. King John Casimir allowed the Jews baptized according to the Greek confession openly to profess Judaism. In consequence, the baptized Jews fled from the Catholic districts to Poland to be free from compulsory Christianity. This permission was especially used by Jewish women whom the rude Zaporogians had married. The Jews brought back into Judaism many hundreds of children, who had lost their parents and relatives, and had been brought up in Christianity, investigated their descent, and hung the indication of it in a small roll round their necks, that they might not marry blood relations of forbidden degrees. The general synod of rabbis and leaders which assembled at Lublin in 1650 occupied itself entirely with the attempt to heal, at least partially, the wounds of Judaism. Many hundreds, even thousands, of Jewish women did not know whether their husbands lay in the grave, or were begging in the East or West, in Turkey or Germany, whether they were widows or wives, or they found themselves in other perplexities created by the Rabbinical law. The synod of Lublin is said to have hit upon excellent arrangements. Most probably the lenient Lipmann Heller, then rabbi of Cracow, strove to effect a mild interpretation of the law relating to supposed death. At the instigation of the young, genial rabbi Sabbatai Cohen (Shach), the day of the first massacre at Nemirov (Siwan 20) was appointed as a general fast day for the remnant of the Polish community. The hoary Lipmann Heller, at Cracow, Sabbatai Hurvitz, at Posen, and the young Sabbatai Cohen drew up penitential prayers (Selichoth), mostly selected from older pieces, for this sad memorial day.

After a pause of a year and a half, the war between Cossacks and Poles broke out in the early part of the year 1651, the first victims again being Jews, as Chmielnicki and the wild Zaporogians now fell upon the Polish territory where Jewish communities had again settled. The massacre, however, could not be so extensive as before; there no longer were thousands of Jews to slaughter. Moreover the evil days had inspired the Jews with courage; they armed a troop of Jewish soldiers, and enlisted them in the king's service. The fortune of war turned against the Cossacks, and they were obliged to accept the peace dictated by the king (November 11, 1651). John Casimir and his ministers did not forget to guard the rights of the Jews in the treaty. They were to be permitted to settle anywhere in the Ukraine, and to hold property on lease.

This treaty also was concluded and ratified only to be broken. Chmielnicki had accepted it to strengthen himself and restore his reputation with the Cossacks. As soon as he had gained his first object, he began hostilities against the Poles, from which Jews always suffered most severely. In two years after the first insurrection of the Zaporogians, more than 300 communities were completely destroyed by death or flight, and the end of their suffering had not yet arrived. The Polish troops could not withstand the violent attacks or skillful policy of Chmielnicki. When he could no longer hope for help from the Tartars, he combined with the Russians, and incited them to a war against unhappy Poland, divided against itself. In consequence of the Russian war in the early part of 1654 and 1655, those communities suffered which had been spared by the Cossack swarms, i. e., the western districts and Lithuania. The community of Wilna, one of the largest, was completely depopulated (July, 1655) by slaughter on the part of the Russians and

by migration. As if fate were then determining upon the partition of Poland, a new enemy was added to the Cossacks and Russians in Charles X of Sweden, who used Poland as the first available pretext to slake his thirst for war. Through the

Swedish war, the communities of Great and Little Poland, from Posen to Cracow, were reduced to want and despair. The Jews of Poland had to drink the cup of poison to the dregs. The Polish general, Czarnicki, who hated the Jews, ill-used those spared by Cossacks, Russians, and the wild Swedes of the Thirty Years' War, under the pretense that they had a traitorous understanding with the Swedes. The Poles also behaved barbarously to the Jews, destroyed the synagogues, and tore up the holy scriptures. All Poland was like a bloody field of battle, on which Cossacks, Russians, Prussians, Swedes, and the troops of Prince Ragoczi of Transylvania wrestled; the Jews were ill-used or slain by all. Only the Great Elector of Brandenburg behaved leniently towards them. The number of Jewish families said to have perished in ten years of this war (600,000) is certainly exaggerated, but the slaughtered Jews of Poland may well be rated at a quarter of a million. With the decline of Poland as a power of the first rank, the importance of Polish Judaism diminished. The remnant were impoverished, depressed, and could not recover their former position. Their need was so great, that those who drifted to the neighborhood of Prussia hired themselves to Christians as day laborers for field work.

As at the time of the expulsion of the Jews from Spain and Portugal every place was filled with fugitive Sephardic Jews, so during the Cossack-Polish war fugitive Polish Jews, wretched in appearance, with hollow eyes, who had escaped the sword, the flames, hunger, and pestilence; or who, dragged by the Tartars into captivity, had been ransomed by their brethren, were seeking shelter everywhere. Westwards, by way of Danzig and through the Vistula district, Jewish-Polish fugitives wandered to Amsterdam, and were forwarded thence to Frankfort-on-the-Main and other Rhenish cities. Three thousand Lithuanian Jews came to Texel in the Netherlands, and were hospitably received. Southwards many fled to Moravia, Bohemia, Austria, and Hungary, and wandered from those places to Italy. The prisoners in the armies of the Tartars came to the Turkish provinces, and some of them drifted to Barbary. Everywhere they were received by their brethren with great cordiality and love, cared for, clothed, and supported. The Italian Jews ransomed and supported them at great sacrifice. Thus, the community of Leghorn at this time formed a resolution to collect and spend a quarter of their income for the liberation and maintenance of the unfortunate Polish Jews. The German and Austrian communities, also, although they had suffered under the calamities of the Thirty Years' War, exercised that brotherly feeling which they rarely professed with their lips, but cherished the more deeply in their hearts.

The number and misery of those escaped from Poland were so great, that the German communities and probably others were obliged to devote the money intended for Jerusalem to the maintenance of Polish Jews. The Jews of Jerusalem dependent on alms, who were drained by the pasha and his subordinates, felt the want of their regular support from Europe. They soon fell into such distress, that of the 700 widows and a smaller number of men living there nearly 400 are said to have died of hunger.

The Cossack persecution of the Jews, in a sense, remodeled Judaism. It became Polonized, so to speak. The Polish-Rabbinical method of study had long dominated the Talmudical schools of Germany. Now, through the fugitives, most of whom were Talmudical scholars, it became authoritative. Whoever wished to acquire thorough Talmudic and Rabbinical knowledge was obliged to sit at the feet of Polish rabbis. Through their influence, scientific knowledge and the study of the Bible declined still more than previously. In the century of Descartes and Spinoza, when the three Christian nations, the French, the English, and the Dutch, gave the death-blow to the Middle Ages, the Jewish-Polich immigrants brought a new middle age over European Judaism, which maintained itself in full vigor for more than a century, to some extent lasting to our own time.

V. CHAPTER II.

SETTLEMENT OF THE JEWS IN ENGLAND AND MANASSEH BEN ISRAEL.

Obstacles to the Resettlement of Jews in England--Manasseh ben Israel--His Character and Attainments-Christian Students of Jewish Literature--Enthusiastic Friends of the Jews-The Puritans--Cromwell and Holmes--Nicholas' Protection of the Jews-"The Hope of Israel"--Fresh Victims of the Inquisition-Manasseh ben Israel's Negotiations with the English Parliament--He journeys to London, and is graciously received by Cromwell--A Council sits at Whitehall to decide the Question of the Readmission of the Jews--Prynne's anti-Jewish work--Controversial Pamphlets--Manasseh's Vindication--The Re-admission of the Jews connived at.

1655-1657 C.E.

At the very time when the Jews of Poland were trodden down, slaughtered, or driven through Europe like terrified wild beasts, a land of freedom was opened, from which the Jews had been banished for more than three centuries and a half. England, which the wise queen Elizabeth and the brave Cromwell had raised to be the first power in Europe, a position very different from that of crumbling Poland, again admitted Jews, not indeed through the great portal, yet through the back door. But this admission was so bruited abroad, that it was like a triumph for Judaism. The Jews of Amsterdam and Hamburg looked with longing to this island, to which they were so near, with whose merchants, shipowners, and scholars they were in connection, and which promised wide scope for the exercise of their varied abilities. But settlement there seemed beset with insuperable obstacles. The English Episcopal church, which exercised sway over

the English conscience, was even more intolerant than the popery which it persecuted, Not granting freedom to Catholics and Dissenters, would it tolerate the descendants of those aspersed in the New Testament? The English people, who for centuries had seen no Jew, shared to the full the antipathy of the clergy. To them every Jew was a Shylock, who, with hearty goodwill, would cut a Christian to pieces--a monster in human form, bearing the mark of Cain. Who would undertake to banish this strong prejudice in order to render people and rulers favorable to the descendants of Israel? The man who undertook and executed this difficult task did not belong to the first rank of intellectual men, but possessed the right measure of insight and narrowness, strength of will and flexibility, knowledge and imagination, self-denial and vanity, required for so arduous an undertaking. Manasseh ben Israel, second or third rabbi at Amsterdam, who at home played only a subordinate part, the poor preacher who, to support his family, was obliged to resort to printing, but obtained so little profit from it, that he wished to exchange pulpit oratory for mercantile speculation, and was near settling in Brazil; he it was who won England for Judaism, and, if he did not banish, diminished the prejudice against his race. To him belongs the credit for a service not to be lightly estimated, for there were but few to help him. The release of the Jews from their thousand years' contempt and depreciation in European society, or rather the struggle for civil equality, begins with Manasseh ben Israel. He was the Riesser of the seventeenth century. As has been stated, he was not in the true sense great, and can only be reckoned a man of mediocrity. He belonged to the happily constituted class of persons, who do not perceive the harsh contrasts and shrill discords in the world around, hence are confiding and enterprising. His heart was deeper than his mind. His power rested in his easy eloquence, his facility in explaining and working out ideas which lay within his narrow field of vision, and which he had acquired rather than produced. Manasseh ben Israel had complete grasp of Jewish literature., and knew the Christian theology of his time, and what was to be said on each point, i. e., what had been said by his predecessors. On the other hand, he had only a superficial knowledge of those branches of learning which require keenness of intellect, such as philosophy and the Talmud. His strength was in one respect his weakness, His facility in speaking and writing encouraged a verbose style and excessive productiveness. He left more than 400 sermons in Portuguese, and a mass of writings that fill a catalogue, but discuss their subjects only superficially. Manasseh's contemporaries looked upon his writings with different eyes. The learning amassed therein from all literatures and languages, and the smoothness of form riveted their attention, and excited their admiration. Among Jews he was extraordinarily celebrated; whoever could produce Latin, Portuguese, or Spanish verse, made known his praise. But even Christian scholars of his time over-estimated him.

In Holland, which, by the concurrence of many circumstances, and especially through the powerful impulse of Joseph Scaliger, the prince of philologists, had become in a sense the school of Europe, the foundation was laid in the seventeenth century for the wonderful learning contained in voluminous folios. At no time had there been so many philologists with early-matured learning, iron memory, and wonderful devotion to the science of language, as in the first half of the seventeenth century, which seems to have been specially appointed to revive what had so long been neglected.

THE PURITANS.

The greatest number of ardent admirers of "God's people" were to be found in England, precisely among those who now had powerful influence in the army council and the camp. At the time when the Germans were fighting each other on account of difference of creed, invoking the interference of foreigners, and impairing their own freedom and power, England was gaining what could never be taken away, religious and, at the same time, political freedom, and this made it a most powerful and prosperous country. In Germany the religious parties, Catholics, Lutherans, and Calvinists, in selfish blindness demanded religious freedom each for itself alone, reserving oppression and persecution for the others,. These internecine quarrels of the Germans were utilized by the princes to confirm their own despotic power. In England, the same selfishness prevailed among the Episcopalians, Presbyterians, and Catholics, but a fourth party arose whose motto was religious freedom for all. The senseless despotism of Charles I and the narrow-mindedness of the Long Parliament had played into the hands of this intelligent and powerful party. England, like Germany, resembled a great blood-stained battle-field, but it had produced men who knew what they, wanted, who staked their lives for it, and effected the rejuvenescence of the nation. Oliver Cromwell was at once the head which devised, and the arm which executed sound ideas. By the sword he and his army obtained religious freedom, not only for themselves, but also for others. He and his officers were not revengeful freebooters or blood-thirsty soldiers, but high-minded, inspired warriors of God, who waged war against wickedness and falseness, and hoped for, and undertook to establish a moral system of government, the kingdom of God. Like the Maccabees of old, the Puritan warriors fought " sword in hand, and praise of God in their mouth." Cromwell and his soldiers read the Bible as often as they fought. The great heroes of the Old Testament, with fear of God in their hearts and the sword in their hands, at once religious and national champions, served as models for the Puritans: the Judges, freeing the oppressed people from the yoke of foreign domination ; Saul, David, and Joab, routing the foes of their country; and Jehu, making an end of an idolatrous and blasphemous royal house-these were favorite characters with Puritan warriors. In every verse of the books of Joshua, Judges, Samuel, and Kings, they saw their own condition reflected; every psalm seemed composed for them, to teach them that, though surrounded on every side by ungodly foes, they need not fear while they trusted in God. Oliver Cromwell compared himself to the judge Gideon, who first obeyed the voice of God hesitatingly, but afterwards courageously scattered the attacking heathens; or to Judas Maccabeus, who out of a handful of martyrs formed a host of victorious warriors.

To bury oneself in the history, prophecy, and poetry of the Old Testament, to revere them as divine inspiration, to live in them with every emotion,

yet not to consider the people who had originated all this glory and greatness as preferred and chosen, was impossible. Among the Puritans, therefore, were many earnest admirers of "God's people," and Cromwell was one of them. It seemed a marvel that the people, or a remnant of the people, whom God had distinguished by great favor and stern discipline, should still exist. A desire was excited in the hearts of the Puritans to see this living wonder, the Jewish people, with their own eyes, to bring Jews to England, and, by making them part of the theocratic community about to be established, stamp it with the seal of completion. The sentiments of the Puritans towards the Jews were expressed in Oliver Cromwell's observation, " Great is my sympathy with this poor people, whom God chose, and to whom He gave His law; it rejects Jesus, because it does not recognize him as the Messiah." Cromwell dreamt of a reconciliation of the Old and the New Testament, of an intimate connection between the Jewish people of God and the English Puritan theocracy. A Puritan preacher, Nathaniel Holmes (Holmesius), wished, according to the letter of many prophetic verses, to become the servant of Israel, and serve him on bended knees. The more the tension in England increased through the imprisonment of the king, the dissensions between the Presbyterian Long Parliament and the Puritan army, the civil war, the execution of King Charles, and the establishment of a republic in England, the more public life and religious thought assumed Jewish coloring. The only thing wanting to make one think himself in Judea was for the orators in Parliament to speak Hebrew. One author proposed the seventh day as the day of rest, and in a work showed the holiness of this day, and the duty of the English people to honor it. This was in the beginning of 1649. Parliament, it is true; condemned this work to be burnt as heretical, scandalous, and profane, and sentenced the printer and author to punishment. But the Israelite spirit among the Puritans, especially among the Levelers, or ultra-republicans, was not suppressed by these means. Many wished the government to declare the Torah to be the code for England.

These proceedings in the British islands, which promised the exaltation of Israel at no distant period, were followed by Manasseh with beating heart. Did these voices not announce the coming of the Messianic kingdom? He hoped so, and put forth feverish activity to help to bring about the desired time. He entertained a visionary train of thought. The Messiah could not appear till the punishment of Israel, to be scattered from one end of the earth to the other, had been fulfilled. There were no Jews then living in England. Exertions must be made to obtain permission for Jews to dwell in England, that this hindrance to the advent of the Messiah might be removed. Manasseh therefore put himself into communication with some important persons, who assured him that "the minds of men were favorable: to the Jews, and that they would be acceptable and welcome to Englishmen." What especially justified his hopes was the "Apology" by Edward Nicholas, former secretary to Parliament, "for the honorable nation of the Jews." In this work, which the author dedicated to the Long Parliament, the Jews were treated, as the chosen people of God, with a tenderness to which they were not accustomed. Hence the author felt it necessary to affirm at the end, that he wrote it, not at the

instigation of Jews, but out of love to God and his country. The opinion of the apologist was, that the great sufferings brought upon England by the religious and civil war were a just punishment for English persecution of the saints and favorites of God, i. e., the Jews, and an urgent admonition to atone for this great sin by admitting them and showing them brotherly treatment. The author proved the preference and selection of Israel by many biblical quotations. He referred to a preacher who had said in Parliament in connection with the verse: "Touch not mine anointed, and do my prophets no harm," that the weal or woe of the world depended upon the good or bad treatment of God's people. God in His secret counsel had sustained this people to the present day, and a glorious future was reserved for them. Hence it was the duty of Englishmen to endeavor to comfort them, if possible give them satisfaction for their innocent blood shed in this kingdom, and enter into friendly intercourse with them. This work also defends the Jews against the accusation of having crucified Jesus. The death of Jesus took place at the instigation of the Synhedrion, not of the people. In most impressive terms it urges the English to comfort the afflicted and unhappy Jews. The pope and his adherents, he said, would be enraged at the kind treatment of the Jews, for they still inflicted cruelty and humiliation upon the people of God, the popes compelling the Jews to wear opprobrious badges, and Catholics avoiding all contact with them, because they abhorred idols and heathen worship.

This work, which, more than friendly, absolutely glorified the Jews, excited the greatest attention in England and Holland. Manasseh hen Israel was delighted with it, thinking that he was near his object, especially as his friend Holmes at once communicated with him on the subject, saying that he himself was about to prepare a work on the millennium, in which he would emphasize the importance of the Jews in the molding of the future. Manasseh ben Israel immediately set to work to do his share towards the realization of his object. He, however, as well as the Christian mystics in England, had one anxiety; what had become of the lost Ten Tribes banished by the Assyrian king Shalmanassar? A restoration of the Jewish kingdom without these Ten Tribes seemed impossible, nay, their discovery was the guarantee of the truth of the prophetic promises. The union of Judah and Israel which some of the prophets had impressively announced would remain unfulfilled if the Ten Tribes had ceased to exist. Manasseh, therefore, laid great stress upon being able to prove their existence somewhere. Fortunately he was in a position to specify the situation of the Ten Tribes. Some years before, a Jewish traveler, named Montezinos, had affirmed on oath that he had seen native Jews of the tribe of Reuben, in South America, and had held communication with them. The circumstantiality of his tale excited curiosity, and inclined his contemporaries to belief. Antonio de Montezinos was a Marrano, whom business or love of travel had led to America. There he had stumbled upon a Mestizo (Indian), who had excited in him a suspicion that members of his race were living in America, persecuted and oppressed by the Indians, as the Indians had been by the Spaniards, and later experiences confirmed the suspicion.

Antonio de Montezinos, or Aaron Levi, had brought the surprising news to Amsterdam, and had related it under oath to a number of persons, among them Manasseh ben Israel (about 1644· Afterwards he went to Brazil, and there died. On his deathbed he repeatedly asserted the truth of the existence of some Israelite tribes in America. Manasseh ben Israel was firmly convinced by the statement of this man, and made it the foundation of a work, entitled "Israel's Hope", composed to pave the way for the Messianic time.

"ISRAEL'S HOPE."

He sent this Latin treatise on the existence of the Ten Tribes and their hopes to a prominent and learned personage in England, to be read before Parliament, which was under Cromwell's influence, and before the Council of State. In an accompanying letter Manasseh explained to Parliament his favorite idea, that the return of the Jews to their native land--the time for which was so near--must be preceded by their complete dispersion. The dispersion, according to the words of Scripture, was to be from one end of the earth to the other, naturally including the island of England, in the extreme north of the inhabited world. But for more than 300 years no Jews had lived in England; therefore, he added the request that the Council and Parliament grant Jews permission to settle in England, to have the free exercise of their religion, and to build synagogues there (1650). Manasseh made no secret of his Messianic hopes, because he could and did reckon on the fact that the saints or Puritans themselves wished for the "assembling of God's people" in their ancestral home, and were inclined to help and promote it. He also intimated in his letter, that he was resolved to go to England, to arrange for the settlement of the Jews.

Manasseh ben Israel had not reckoned amiss. His request and dedication were favorably received by Parliament. Lord Middlesex, probably the mediator, sent him a letter of thanks with the superscription, "To my dear brother, the Hebrew philosopher, Manasseh ben Israel." A passport to England, was also sent to him. The English ambassador in Holland, Lord Oliver St. John, a relative of Cromwell, told him that he wished to go to the Amsterdam synagogue, and gave him to understand, probably according to Cromwell's instructions, that England was inclined to gratify the long-cherished wish of the Jews. Manasseh took care that he be received in the house of prayer with music and hymns (about August, 1651). However, the goal to which he seemed so near was removed by political complications. England and Holland entered into a fierce war, which broke off the connection between Amsterdam and London. Manasseh's relations to his elder colleague, Saul Morteira (1652), and the president, Joseph da Costa--it is not known on what account--became strained, and in an angry mood he formed the resolution to leave Amsterdam. The directors of the community succeeded in establishing a tolerable understanding between the two chachams, but Manasseh had neither the cheerfulness required nor a favorable opportunity to resume his adventurous scheme.

But when Oliver Cromwell, by the illegal but necessary dissolution of the Long Parliament, assumed the chief power in April, 1653, and showed an inclination to conclude peace with the States General, Manasseh again took up his project. Cromwell had called together a new parliament, the so-called Short, or Barebones, Parliament, which was composed wholly of saints, i. e., Puritan preachers, officers with a biblical bias, and millennium visionaries. The partiality of Cromwell's officers for the old Jewish system is shown by the serious proposition that the Council of State should consist of seventy members, after the number of the Jewish Synhedrion. In Parliament sat General Harrison, a Baptist, who, with his party, wished to see the Mosaic law introduced into England. When Parliament met (July 5, 1653), Manasseh hastened to repeat his request, that Jews be granted permission to reside in England. The question of the Jews was immediately put on the program of business. Parliament sent Manasseh a safe conduct to London,

that he might conduct the business in person. As the war between England and Holland still continued, his relatives and friends urged him not to expose himself to the danger of a daily change of affairs, and he again put off his voyage to a more favorable time. The Short Parliament was soon dissolved (December 12, 1653), and Cromwell obtained kingly power under the title of Protector of the Realm. When he concluded peace with Holland (April, 1654), Manasseh thought the time well suited for effecting his wishes for the redemption of Israel. He was encouraged by the fact that three admirals of the English fleet had drawn up a petition in October, 1654, to admit Jews into England. Manasseh presented his petition for their admission to Cromwell's second, still shorter Parliament, and, probably at his instigation, David Abrabanel Dormido, one of the leading men at Amsterdam, at the same time presented one to the same effect, which Cromwell urgently recommended to the Council for speedy decision (November 3, 1654)· Manasseh reveled in intoxicating dreams of the approaching glorious time for Israel. He regarded himself as the instrument of Providence to bring about its fulfillment. In these dreams he was upheld and confirmed by Christian mystics, who were eagerly awaiting the millennium. The Dutchman, Henry Jesse, had shortly before published a work, "On the Speedy Glory of Judah and Israel," in the Dutch language. The Bohemian physician, mystic, and alchemist, Paul Felgenhauer, went beyond the bounds of reason. Disgusted with the formal creed of the Evangelical Church, and the idolatrous tendency of Catholicism, he wrote during the Thirty Years' War against the corruption of the Church and the Protestant clergy, and wished for a spiritual, mystical religion. By a peculiar calculation, Felgenhauer was led to believe that the year six thousand and the advent of the Messiah connected with it were not far off. Persecuted in Germany by Catholics and Protestants, he sought an asylum in Amsterdam, and there formed the acquaintance of Manasseh ben Israel. Between these men and a third visionary, Peter Serrarius, the speedy coming of the Messianic time was often the subject of conversation. Felgenhauer then composed an original work (December, 1654) entitled "Good News of the Messiah for Israel! The redemption of Israel from all his sufferings, his deliverance from captivity, and the glorious advent of the Messiah are nigh for the comfort of Israel. Taken from the Holy Scriptures of the Old and New Testament, by a Christian who is expecting him with the Jews." Felgenhauer places the Jewish people very high, as the seed of Abraham, and considers true believers of all nations the spiritual seed of Abraham. Hence Jews and Christians should love, not despise, one another. They should unite in God. This union is near at hand. The bloody wars of nation against nation by sea and land in the whole world, which had not happened before to anything like the same extent, are signs thereof. As further signs he accounted the comets which appeared in 1618, 1648, and 1652. Verses from the Bible, especially from Daniel and the Apocalypse, with daring interpretations, served him as proofs. Felgenhauer denied an earthly Messiah, nor did he allow the claim of Jesus to the title.

As this half-insane work was dedicated to Manasseh, he was obliged to answer it, which he did with great prudence (February 1, 1655), gladly welcoming the pages favorable to Jews, and passing over the rest in silence. The good news concerning the near future was the more welcome to his heart, he said, as he himself, in spite of the afflictions of many centuries, did not cease ardently to hope for better times.

THE FIFTH MONARCHY.

Manasseh ben Israel had the courage to express without ambiguity Jewish expectations in opposition to the opinions held by Christian enthusiasts. They, for the most part, imagined the fifth monarchy, which they alleged was about to commence, as the millennium, when Jesus would again appear and hand over the sovereign power to the saints. The Jews would have a share in it; they would assemble from the ends of the earth, return to their ancestral home, and again build Jerusalem and the Temple. But this would be only an intermediate state, the means to enable the whole Twelve Tribes to acknowledge Jesus as Messiah, so that there be but one flock under one shepherd. Against this Manasseh ben Israel composed a treatise, ended April 25, 1655, on the fifth kingdom of the prophecy of Daniel, interpreting it to mean the independence of Israel. In this work, called "The Glorious Stone, or the Image of Nebuchadnezzar," and dedicated to Isaac Vossius, then in the service of the queen of Sweden, he put forth all his learning to show that the visions of the "four beasts," or great kingdoms, had been verified in the successive sway of the. Babylonians,

Persians, Greeks, and Romans, and therefore the coming of the fifth kingdom also was certain. This was shown in Daniel plainly enough to be the kingdom of Israel, the people of God. In this Messianic kingdom all nations of the earth will have part, and they will be treated with kindness, but the authority will ever rest with Israel. Manasseh disfigured this simple thought by Kabbalistic triviality and sophistry. It is singular that not only did a learned Christian accept the dedication of this essentially Jewish work, but the celebrated painter Rembrandt supplied four artistic engravings representing Nebuchadnezzar's, or Manasseh's, vision.

Manasseh had received a friendly invitation from the second Parliament assembled by Cromwell; but as it had meanwhile been dissolved, he could not begin his journey until invited by the Protector himself. He seems to have sent on in advance his son, Samuel ben Israel, who was presented by the University of Oxford, in consideration of his knowledge and natural gifts, with the degree of doctor of philosophy and medicine, and according to custom, received the gold ring, the biretta, and the kiss of peace. It was no insignificant circumstance that this honor should be conferred upon a Jew by a university strictly Christian in its conduct. Cromwell's will appears to have been decisive in the matter. He sent an invitation to Manasseh, but the journey was delayed till autumn. Not till the end of the Tishri festivals (October 25-31, 1655) did Manasseh undertake the important voyage to London, in his view, of the utmost consequence to the world. He was received in a friendly manner by Cromwell, and had a residence granted him. Among his companions was Jacob Sasportas, a learned man, accustomed to intercourse with persons of high rank, who had been rabbi in African cities. Other Jews accompanied him in the hope that the admission of Jews would meet with no difficulty. Some secret Jews from Spain and Portugal were already domiciled in London, among them being the rich and respected Fernandez Carvajal. But the matter did not admit of such speedy settlement. At an audience, Manasseh delivered to the Protector a carefully composed petition, or address. He had obtained the authorization of the Jews of

MANASSEH BEN ISRAEL IN LONDON.

the different countries of Europe to act as their representative, so that the admission of Jews into England might be urged not in his own name alone, but in that of the whole Jewish nation. In his petition he skillfully developed the argument, by means of passages from the Bible and the Talmud, that power and authority are conferred by God according to his will; that God rewards and punishes even the rulers of the earth, and that this had been verified in Jewish history; that great monarchs who had troubled Israel had met with an unhappy end,as Pharaoh, Nebuchadnezzar, Antiochus Epiphanes, Pompey, and others. On the other hand, benefactors of the Jewish nation had enjoyed happiness even here below, so that the word of God to Abraham had been literally fulfilled:–"I will bless them that bless thee, and curse them that curse thee." "Pagans have of old .... granted free liberty even to apostate Jews: .... how much more then may we . . . hope it from your Highness and your Christian Council, since you have so great knowledge of, and adore the same one only God of Israel, together with us."

At the same time Manasseh ben Israel circulated through the press a " Declaration " which served to explain the reasons for admitting Jews, and to meet objections and allay prejudices against their admission. All his reasons can be reduced to two--one mystical and one of trade policy. The mystical reason has been repeatedly explained. His opinion coincided with that of many Christians, that the return of the Israelites to their home was near at hand. The other reason was put in this form: that through the Jews the trade of England would greatly increase in exports and imports from all parts of the world. He developed this point of the advantage which the Jews might bestow at great length, showing that on account of their fidelity and attachment to the countries hospitable and friendly to them they deserved to be treated with consideration. Besides, they ought to be esteemed, on account of their ancient nobility and purity of blood, among a people which attached importance to such distinctions.

Manasseh ben Israel considered the commerce to which Jews were for the most part devoted from a higher point of view. He had in mind the wholesale trade of the Portuguese Jews of Holland in the coin of various nations (exchange business), in diamonds, cochineal, indigo, wine, and oil. Their money transactions were not based on usury, on which the Jews of Germany and Poland relied. The Amsterdam Jews deposited their capital in banks, and satisfied themselves with five per cent interest. The capital of the Portuguese Jews in Holland and Italy was very considerable, because Marranos in Spain and Portugal invested their money with them, to evade the avarice of the Inquisition. Hence Manasseh laid great weight on the advantages which England might expect from his enterprising countrymen. He thought that trading,

the chief occupation, and, to a certain extent, the natural inclination, of the Jews of all countries since their dispersion, was the work of Providence, a mark of divine favor towards them, that by accumulated treasures they might find grace in the eyes of rulers and nations. They were forced to occupy themselves with commerce, because, owing to the insecurity of their existence, they could not possess landed estates. Accordingly, they were obliged to pursue trade till their return to their land, for then "there shall be no more any trader in the house of the Lord," as a prophet declares.

Manasseh ben Israel then took a survey over all the countries where Jews, in his time, or shortly before, by means of trade, had attained to importance, and enumerated the persons who had risen to high positions by their services to states or rulers. However, much that he adduced, when closely considered, is not very brilliant, with the exception of the esteemed and secure position which the Jews occupied in Holland. Then he quoted examples of the fidelity and devotedness of Jews in ancient and modern times towards their protectors. We forcibly refuted the calumny that the Jews had been banished from Spain and Portugal for treachery and faithlessness. It was easy for him to show from

Christian authors that the expulsion of the Jews, and their cruel treatment by Portugal, were at once criminal and foolish, and most emphatically condemned by wise rulers. He took occasion to defend his brethren against three other charges: usury, child murder, and proselytism. To wipe off the stain of usury, he made use of the justification employed by Simone Luzzatto, a contemporary Jewish Italian author, that usury was objectionable not in itself, but in its excess. Of great weight was the fact which he adduced, that the Portuguese Jews, for whom he was pleading, abhorred usury as much as many Christians, and that their large capital had not been obtained from it. Manasseh could repudiate with more vehemence the charge of murdering Christian children.

Manasseh reminded the Christians that there had been a time when they, too, had been charged by heathens with being murderers of children; sorcerers, and conjurers, and had been punished by heathen emperors and officials. He was able to refer to a case of his own time, that of Isaac Jeshurun, of Ragusa, a Jew repeatedly tortured for child murder, whose innocence had come to light, and filled the judges with remorse. Manasseh denied the accusation of the conversion of Christians to Judaism, and referred to the injunction of the Jewish law to dissuade rather than attract proselytes.

> *"Now, because I believe, that with a good conscience I have discharged our nation of the Jews of those three slanders. ... I may from these two qualities, of Profitableness and Fidelity, conclude, that such a nation ought to be well entertained, and also beloved and protected generally of all. The more, considering they are called in the Sacred Scriptures the sons of God. . . I could add a third (point), viz., of the Nobility of the Jews, but because that point is enough known amongst all Christians, as lately it has been shown by that worthy Christian minister, Mr. Henry Jessey. . . and by Mr. Edw. Nichloas, Gentleman. Therefore I will here forbear and rest on the saying of Solomon .... 'Let another man's mouth praise thee, and not thine own.' "*

Cromwell was decidedly inclined to the admission of the Jews. He may have had in view the probability that the extensive trade and capital of the Spanish and Portuguese Jews, those professing

Judaism openly as well as secretly, might be brought to England, which at that time could not yet compete with Holland. He was also animated by the great idea of the unconditional toleration of all religions, and even thought of granting religious freedom to the intensely hated, feared, hence persecuted Catholics. Therefore, he acceded to the wish of the Jews to open an asylum to them in England. But he was most influenced by the religious desire to win over the Jews to Christianity by friendly treatment. He thought that Christianity as preached in England by the Independents, without idolatry and superstition, would captivate the Jews, hitherto deterred from Christianity.

Cromwell and Manasseh ben Israel agreed in an unexpressed, visionary, Messianic reason for the admission of Jews into England. The Kabbalistic rabbi thought that in consequence of the settlement of Jews in the British island, the Messianic redemption would commence, and the Puritan Protector believed that Jews in great numbers would accept Christianity, and then would come the time of one shepherd and one flock. To dispose the people favorably towards the Jews, Cromwell employed two most zealous Independents, his secretary, the clergyman Hugh Peters, and Harry Marten, the fiery member of the Council, to labor at the task.

At last the time came to consider the question of the admission of Jews seriously. They had been banished in the year l290 in pursuance of a decree enacting that they should never return, and it was questionable whether the decree was not still in force. Therefore, Cromwell assembled a commission at Whitehall (December 4, 1655), to discuss every aspect of the matter. The commission was composed of Lord Chief Justice Glynn, Lord Chief Baron Steel, and seven citizens, including the Lord Mayor, the two sheriffs of London, an alderman, and the recorder of the city, and fourteen eminent clergymen of different towns. Cromwell mentioned two subjects for discussion: whether it was lawful to admit Jews into England, and, in case it was not opposed to the law, under what conditions the admission should take place. Manasseh had formulated his proposal under seven heads: that they should be admitted and protected against violence; that they should be granted synagogues, the free exercise of religion, and places of burial; that they should enjoy freedom of trade ; and that their disputes should be settled by their own rabbis and directors; and that all former laws hostile to Jews should be repealed for their greater security. On admission, every Jew should take the loath of fidelity to the realm.

There was great excitement in London during the discussion on the admission of the Jews, and popular feeling was much divided. Blind hatred against the crucifiers of the Son of God, and blind love for the people of God; fear of the competition of Jews in trade, and hope of gaining the precedence from the Dutch and Spaniards by their means, prejudiced ideas that they crucified Christian children, clipped coin,or wished to make all the English people Jews--these conflicting feelings disturbed the judgment for and against them. Cromwell's followers, and the Republicans in general, were for their admission; Royalists and Papists, secretly or openly his enemies, were opposed to the proposal. The people crowded to the hall where the Jewish question was publicly discussed. At the very beginning the legal representatives declared that no ancient law excluded the Jews from England, for their banishment had been enacted by the king, without the consent of Parliament. The city representatives remained silent; the most violent were the clergy, who could not rid themselves of their hatred against Jews. Cromwell, who most earnestly wished to see them admitted, therefore added three clergymen, among them Hugh Peters, from whom he expected a vote favorable to the Jews. The question was not brought to a decision in three sittings. Cromwell therefore ordered a final discussion (December 18; 1655), at which he presided. The majority of the clergy on this day, too, were against the admission of Jews, even the minority favoring it only with due precautions. Cromwell, dissatisfied with the course of the discussion, first had the theological objections refuted by Manasseh ben Israel, then expressed himself with much warmth, and reprimanded the clergy. He said that he had hoped to receive enlightenment for his conscience; instead, they had made the question more obscure. The main strength of his arguments was : The pure (Puritan) gospel must be preached to the Jews, to win them to the church. " But can we preach to them, if we will not tolerate them among us?" Cromwell thereupon closed the discussion, and resolved to decide the matter according to his own judgment.

He had not only the opposition of the fanatical clergy to contend against, but also that of the multitude, who shared their prejudiced feeling. The enemies of the Jews made every effort to win over the people against their admission. They spread the report that the Jews intended to buy the library of the University of Oxford, and, if possible, turn St. Paul's into a synagogue. They sought to bring Cromwell's friendship for the Jews under suspicion, and circulated the report that an embassy had come to England from Asia and Prague to find out whether Cromwell was not the expected Messiah of the Jews. A clerical pamphleteer, named William Prynne, stirred up a most fanatical excitement against the Jews. He composed a venomous work, " A Short Demurrer," in which he raked up all false accusations against them of counterfeit coining, and the crucifixion of Christian children, and briefly summarized the anti-Jewish decrees of the thirteenth century, so as to make the name of Jew hated. From other quarters, also, various publications appeared against them. John Hoornbeek, a Dutchman, composed a book on the conversion of the Jews, in which he pretended to be their friend, but actually sought to asperse them. John Dury, an Englishman residing at the time at Cassel, was also resolved to make his voice heard about the Jews; he weighed arguments for and against their admission, and at last inclined to the view that it was a serious matter to permit Jews to enter England. His work was printed and distributed. Probably at Cromwell's suggestion, Thomas Collier wrote a refutation of Prynne's charges, dedicating it to the Protector. He concluded his work with a passage in the taste of that time :

> *" Oh, let us respect them; let us wait for that glorious day which will make them the head of the nations. Oh, the time is at hand when every one shall think himself happy that can but lay hold on the skirt of a Jew. Our salvation came from them! Our Jesus was of them! We are gotten into their promises and privileges! The natural branches were cut off, that we might be grafted on! Oh, let us not be high-minded, hut fear. Let us not, for God's sake, be*

unmerciful to them! No! let it be enough if we have all their [spiritual] riches."

While the admission of Jews met with so many difficulties in England, the Dutch Government was by no means pleased with Manasseh ben Israel's efforts to bring it to pass, fearing, doubtless, that the Amsterdam Jews would remove to England, with all their capital. Manasseh was obliged to pacify the Dutch ambassador in an interview, and to assure him that his exertions concerned not Dutch Jews, but the Marranos, watched with Argus eyes in Spain and Portugal, for whom he wished to provide an asylum. Manasseh waited six months in London to obtain from Cromwell a favorable decision, but without success. The Protector found no

leisure to attend to the Jewish question, his energies were devoted to obtaining the funds necessary for the government and foreign wars, refused by one Parliament after another, and to frustrating the royalist conspiracy against his life. Manasseh's companions, who had given up all hopes of success, left London; others who, having fled from the Pyrenean peninsula, were on their way thither, turned back, and settled in Italy or Geneva.

But the friends of the Jews were unwearied, and hoped to produce a change of mind in the people. One of "the saints " published a small work (April, 1656), in which he briefly summarized the proceedings at the discussion on the admission of Jews, and then added: " What shall be the issue of this, the most high God knoweth; Rabbi Manasseh ben Israel still remains in London, desiring a favorable answer to his proposals; and not receiving it he hath desired, that if they may not be granted, he may have a favorable dismission, and return home. But other great affairs being now in hand, and this being business of very great concernment, no absolute answer is yet returned to him."

To elicit a thorough refutation of all the charges advanced by the enemies of the Jews and the opponents of toleration, a person of high rank, in close relation with the government, induced Manasseh ben Israel to publish a brief but comprehensive work, in defense of the Jews. In the form of a letter he stated all the grounds of accusation. These included the current slanders: the use of the blood of Christians at the Passover, curses upon Christians and blasphemy against the God of the Christians in Jewish prayers, and the idolatrous reverence alleged to be shown the Torah scrolls. The defense of the Jews, which Manasseh ben Israel composed in reply (April 10), and which was soon afterwards circulated through the press, is perhaps the best work from his pen. It is written with deep feeling, and is, therefore, convincing; learned matter is not wanting, but the learning is subordinate to the main object. In the composition of this defense Manasseh must have had peculiar feelings. He had come to England the interpreter or representative of the people of God, expecting speedily to conquer the sympathy of Christians, and pave the way for the lordship of Israel over the world, and now his people was placed at the bar, and he had to defend it. Hence the tone of this work is not aggressive and triumphant, but plaintive. He affirmed that nothing had ever produced a deeper impression on his mind than the letter addressed to him with the list of anti-Jewish charges.

> *" It reflects upon the credit of a nation, which amongst so many calumnies, so manifest (and therefore shameful), I dare to pronounce innocent And in the first place, I cannot but weep bitterly, and with much anguish of soul lament, that strange and horrid accusation of some Christians against the dispersed and afflicted Jews that dwell among them, when they say (what I tremble to write) that the Jews are wont to celebrate the Feast of Unleavened Bread, fermenting it with the blood of some Christians whom they have for that purpose killed."*

To this false charge so often made, among others by Prynne, the greatest part of his defense is devoted, and it is indeed striking. He traced the accusation to false witnesses or the confession of accused persons under torture. The innocence of the accused was often brought to light, but too late, when they had been executed. Manasseh confirmed this by an entertaining story. The physician of a Portuguese count had been charged by the Inquisition as a Judaizing Christian. In vain the count pledged himself for his orthodoxy, he was nevertheless tortured, and himself confessed that he was a Judaizing sinner. Subsequently the count, pretending serious illness, sent for the inquisitor, and in his house, with doors closed, he commanded him in a threatening tone to confess in writing that he was a Jew. The inquisitor refused ; then a servant brought in a red-hot helmet to put upon his head. Thereupon the inquisitor confessed everything demanded by the

count, who took this opportunity to reproach him with his cruelty and inhumanity.

This last work of Manasseh ben Israel produced in England the favorable effect desired. Though Cromwell, amidst the increasing difficulties of his government, could not fully carry out the admission of the Jews, he made a beginning towards it. He dismissed Manasseh with honorable distinctions, and granted him a yearly allowance of one hundred pounds (February 20, 1657) out of the public treasury. The Jews were not admitted in triumph through the great portal, but they were let in by Cromwell through a back door, yet they established themselves firmly. This was in consequence of an indictment brought against an immigrant Marrano merchant, Antonio Robles, that he, a Portuguese Papist, had illegally engaged in business pursuits in England, but he was acquitted by the Protector on the ground that he was not a Catholic, but a Jew. Thus the residence of such Jews was suffered ; they could therefore drop the mask of Catholicism. Two respected Marranos, Simon de Caceres and Fernandez (Isaac) Carvajal, in fact received Cromwell's permission to open a special burial-ground for the Sephardic Jews settled in London (1657)· In consequence of this permission it was no longer necessary to make a show of attending church or of having their newly-born children baptized. But they occupied an anomalous position. Being strangers, and on account of their insignificant numbers, they lived not exactly on sufferance, but were ignored. Thus Manasseh ben Israel's endeavors were not entirely in vain. He did not draw the pension awarded him, nor did he live to witness the coming up of the seed scattered by him, for on the way home he died, at Middelburg, probably broken down by his exertions and the disappointment of his hopes, even before he reached his family (November, 1657)· His body was afterwards brought to Amsterdam, and an honorable epitaph was put over his grave. But his zealous activity, outcome though it was of Messianic delusions, bore fruit, because it was sincere. Before he had been dead ten years, Jews were gradually admitted into England by the monarchy which succeeded the republic. A community was assembled which soon became organized, a room was fitted up in King street as a synagogue, and Jacob Sasportas, the wanderer from Africa, Manasseh hen Israel's companion, was chosen rabbi. The branch community of London took as its model that of Amsterdam. From this second stronghold, occupied by Portuguese Jews, afterwards proceeded the agitation for popular freedom and the liberation of the Jews.

V. CHAPTER IV.

SPINOZA AND SABBATAI ZEVI

Spinoza's Youth and Education--His Intellectual Breach with Judaism--The Rabbis and Spinoza--Excommunication--Spinoza's "Tractate" and "Ethics"--Spinoza's Writings Concerning Judaism--Spinoza's Contemporaries in Amsterdam--The Mystical Character of the Years 1648 and 1866--Sabbatai Zevi's early Career--The Jerusalem Community--Sabbatai's Travels--Nathan Ghazati--Sabbatai announced in Smyrna as the Messiah--Spread of Enthusiastic Belief in the pseudo-Messiah--Manoel Texeira--Ritual Changes introduced by the Sabbatians--Sabbatai proceeds to Constantinople-Nehemiah Cohen--Shabbatai Zevi's Apostasy to Islam and its Consequences--Cotinuation of the Sabbatian Movement--Death of Sabbatai and Spinoza--Results of the Sabbatian Imposture.

1656-1677 C.E.

WHILST Manasseh ben Israel was zealously laboring to complete the fabric of Judaism by hastening on the Messianic era, one of his disciples was applying an intellectual lever to destroy this edifice to its foundation and convert it into a shapeless dust heap. He was earnest about what was only amusement for Leo Modena. The Jewish race once more brought a deep thinker into the world, one who was radically to heal the human mind of its rooted perversities and errors, and to prescribe a new direction for it, that it might better comprehend the connection between heaven and earth, between mind and matter. Like his ancestor Abraham, this Jewish thinker desired to break to pieces all idols and vain images, before which men had hitherto bowed down through fear, custom, and indolence, and to reveal to them a new God, not enthroned in heaven's height beyond their reach, but living and moving within them, whose temple they themselves should be. His influence was like that of the storm,

BARUCH SPINOZA

deafening and crushing down, but also purifying and refreshing.

The lightning flashes of this great philosophical genius did greatest injury to Judaism which was nearest to him. In the degradation of the religion of his day and its professors, even his searching gaze could not recognize the fair form concealed beneath a loathsome exterior.

This great thinker, the most famous philosopher of his time, who brought about a new redemption, was Baruch Spinoza (really Espinosa, born in Spain 1632, died 1677)· He belonged to a family eminent for neither intellect nor wealth. No sign at his birth portended that he would reign for more than two centuries a king in the realm of thought. With many other boys, he attended the Jewish school, consisting of seven classes, recently established in Amsterdam, whither his parents had migrated. With his extraordinary talents he surely kept pace with the requirements of the school, if he did not exceed them. In his thirteenth or fourteenth year he was probably introduced by Manasseh ben Israel to the study of the Talmud, and initiated into Hebrew grammar, rhetoric, and poetry. He received final instruction in Rabbinical lore from Saul Morteira, the greatest Talmudist of his time in Amsterdam. Together with Spinoza Morteira taught others who later had more or less influence on Jewish history, but were of quite another stamp.

Thirst for knowledge stimulated Spinoza to venture beyond the limited circle of studies pursued in Morteira's lecture-room. He plunged into the writings of older Jewish thinkers, three of whom alike attracted and repelled him: Ibn-Ezra with his free-thinking and his reticence, Moses Maimuni with his artificial system, aiming at the reconciliation of faith and science, of Judaism and philosophy, and Chasdai Crescas with his hostility to traditional philosophy. Spinoza was also at home in the Kabbala, the main doctrines of which had been rendered accessible through Abraham de Herrera and Isaac Aboab. These various elements heaved and fermented in his mind, which strove for insight, and excited in his breast tormenting doubts, to which Ibn-Ezra's covert unbelief mainly contributed. A youth of fifteen, Spinoza is said to have expressed his doubts in the form of questions to his master Morteira, which may have not a little perplexed a rabbi accustomed to beaten tracks. To these elements of skepticism, conveyed to him from Jewish literature, others were added from without. Spinoza learned Latin, in itself nothing remarkable, since, as has been remarked, nearly all the Jewish youths of Amsterdam, as well as Christians of the educated classes of Holland, regarded that language as a means of culture. But he was not contented with superficial knowledge; he desired to drink deep of classical literature. He sought the instruction of an eminent philologist of his time, Dr. Franz van den Enden,

SPINOZA'S STUDIES.

who lectured in Amsterdam to noble youths, native and foreign. Here he learned, in contact with educated Christian youths, to adopt a different point of view from that which obtained in Morteira's lecture-room and in Jewish circles. Van den Enden also strongly influenced his mind. Though not an atheist, he was a man of skeptical and satirical vein, who turned religious customs and prejudices to ridicule, and exposed their weaknesses. But what with him was the object of humor and wit, excited Spinoza's susceptible and analytical mind to deep reflection and meditation. The natural sciences, mathematics, and physics, which he pursued with devotion, and the new-born, imposing philosophy of Descartes (Cartesius), for which his mind had special affinity, extended his circle of vision and enlightened his judgment. The more he imbibed ideas from various sources, assimilating them with those innate in him, and the more his logical understanding developed, the more did he become alienated from Judaism, in its Rabbinical and Kabbalistic trappings, and love of Van den Enden's learned daughter was not needed to make him a pervert from Jewish belief.

Independent, judicial reason, which disregards what is traditional or hallowed by time, and follows its own laws, was his mistress. To her he dedicated pure, undivided worship, and she led him to break with inherited views. All that cannot be justified before the inexorable tribunal of clear human vision, passed with him for superstition and clouded thought, if not actual frenzy. His ardent desire for truth, pure truth and certainty, led him to a complete breach with the religion endeared to him from childhood ; he not only rejected Talmudical Judaism, but also regarded the Bible as the work of man. The apparent contradictions in the books of Holy Scripture appear to have first raised his doubts as to their inspiration. It must have cost him a hard struggle to give up the customs and opinions endeared to him through manifold ties, and to become, to a certain extent, a new man. For Spinoza was quite as much a moral character as a deep thinker. To hold anything as false in theory, and yet from fear, custom, or advantage to adopt it in practice was impossible for him. He was differently constituted to his revered master Descartes, who kept away from the church the torch of truth which he had kindled, made a gap between theory and practice to avoid offending that church, and, for example, vowed a pilgrimage to our Lady of

Loretto for the success of his system and its destructive tendency. According to Spinoza's idea every action ought to be a true reflection of reason. When he could no longer find truth in Judaism, he could not bring himself to follow its ritual precepts. He ceased to attend the synagogue, cared no longer for the Sabbath and the festivals, and broke the laws concerning diet. He did not confine himself to the renunciation of Judaism, but imparted his convictions to young men who sought his instruction.

The representatives of the community of Amsterdam were the more concerned at the daily increasing report of Spinoza's estrangement from, and hostility to Judaism, as they had in a measure looked upon the gifted youth as their exponent, and as a firm support to the jeopardized religion of their fathers. Now it was to be feared that he would abandon it, go over to Christianity, and devote his intellectual gifts to doing battle against his mother faith. Could the representatives of that faith, the college of rabbis and the secular heads of the community, behold with indifference this systematic neglect of Judaism in their midst?

The college of rabbis, in which sat the two chief Chachams, Saul Morteira and Isaac Aboab--Manasseh ben Israel was then living in London--had ascertained the fact of Spinoza's change of opinion, and had collected evidence. It was not easy to accuse him of apostasy, as he did not proclaim his thoughts aloud in the market-place, as Uriel da Costa had announced his breach with Judaism. Besides, he led a quiet, self-contained life, and associated little with men. His avoidance of the synagogue, the first thing probably to attract notice, could not form the subject of a Rabbinical accusation. It is possible that, as is related, two of his fellow-students (one, perhaps, the sly Isaac Naar) thrust themselves upon him, drew him out, and accused him of unbelief, and contempt for Judaism. Spinoza was summoned, tried, and admonished to return to his former course of life. The court of rabbis did not at first proceed. with severity against him, for he was a favorite of his teacher, and beloved in the community on account of his modest bearing and moral behavior. By virtue of the firmness of his character Spinoza probably made no sort of concession,

SPINOZA AND THE RABBIS.

but insisted upon freedom of thought and conduct. Without doubt he was, in consequence, laid under the lesser excommunication, that is, close intercourse with him was forbidden for thirty days. This probably caused less pain to Spinoza, who, self-centered, found sufficient resource in his rich world of thought, than to the superficial Da Costa. Also, he was not without Christian friends, and he, therefore, made no alteration in his manner of life. This firmness was naturally construed as obstinacy and defiance. But the rabbinate, as well as the secular authorities of the community did not wish to exert the rigor of the Rabbinical law against him, in order not to drive him to an extreme measure, i. e., into the arms of the Church. What harm might not the conversion to Christianity of so remarkable a youth entail in a newly-founded community, consisting of Jews with Christian reminiscences ! What impression would it make on the Marranos in Spain and Portugal? Perhaps the scandal caused by Da Costa's excommunication, still fresh in men's memories, may have rendered a repetition impracticable. The rabbis, therefore, privately offered Spinoza, through his friends, a yearly pension of a thousand gulden on condition that he take no hostile step against Judaism, and show himself from time to time in the synagogue. But Spinoza, though young, was of so determined a character, that money could not entice him to abandon his convictions or to act the hypocrite. He insisted that he would not give up freedom of inquiry and thought. He continued to impart to Jewish youths doctrines undermining Judaism. So the tension between him and the representatives of Judaism became daily greater; both sides were right, or imagined they were. A fanatic in Amsterdam thought that he could put an end to this breach by a dagger-stroke aimed at the dangerous apostate. He waylaid Spinoza at the exit the theater, and struck at the philosopher with his murderous weapon. But the latter observed the hostile movement in time, and avoided the blow, so that only his coat was damaged. Spinoza left Amsterdam to avoid the danger of assassination, and betook himself to the house of a friend, likewise persecuted by the dominant Calvinistic Church, an adherent of the sect of the Rhynsburgians, or Collectants, who dwelt in a village between Amsterdam and Ouderkerk. Reconciliation between Spinoza and the synagogue was no longer to be thought of. The rabbis and the secular authorities of the community pronounced the greater excommunication upon him, proclaiming it in the Portuguese language on a Thursday, Ab 6th (July 24th), 1656,shortly before the fast in memory of the destruction of Jerusalem. The sentence was pronounced solemnly in the synagogue from the pulpit before the open Ark. The sentence was as follows: "The council has long had notice of the evil opinions and actions of Baruch d'Espinosa, and these are daily increasing in spite of efforts to reclaim him. In particular, he teaches and proclaims dreadful heresy, of which credible witnesses are present, who have made their depositions in presence of the accused."

All this, they continued, had been proved in the presence of the elders, and the council had resolved to place him under the ban, and excommunicate him.

The usual curses were pronounced upon him in presence of scrolls of the Law, and finally the council forbade anyone to have intercourse with him, verbally or by writing, to do him any service, to abide under the same roof with him, or to come within the space of four cubits' distance from him, or to read his writings. Contrary to wont, the ban against Spinoza was stringently enforced, to keep young people from his heresies.

Spinoza was away from Amsterdam, when the ban was hurled against him. He is said to have received the news with indifference, and to have remarked that he was now compelled to do what he

THE THEOLOGICO-POLITICAL TREATISE.

would otherwise have done without compulsion. His philosophic nature, which loved solitude, could easily dispense with intercourse with relatives and former friends. Yet the matter did not end for him there. The representative body of the Portuguese community appealed to the municipal authorities to effect his perpetual banishment from Amsterdam. The magistrates referred the question, really a theological one, to the clergy, and the latter are said to have proposed his withdrawal from Amsterdam for some months. Most probably this procedure prompted him to elaborate a justificatory pamphlet to show the civil authorities that he was no violator or transgressor of the laws of the state, but that he had exercised his just rights, when he reflected on the religion of his forefathers and religion generally, and thought out new views. The chain of reasoning suggested to Spinoza in the preparation of his defense caused him doubtless to give wider extension and bearing to this question. It gave him the opportunity to treat of freedom of thought and inquiry generally, and so to lay the foundation of the first of his suggestive writings, which have conferred upon him literary immortality. In the village to which he had withdrawn, 1656-60, and later in Rhynsburg, where he also spent several years, 1660-64, Spinoza occupied himself (while polishing lenses, which handicraft he had learned to secure his moderate subsistence) with the Cartesian philosophy and the elaboration of the work entitled "The Theologico-Political Treatise." His prime object was to spread the conviction that freedom of thought can be permitted without prejudice to religion and the peace of the state ; furthermore, that it must be permitted, for if it were forbidden, religion and peace could not exist in the state.

The apology for freedom of thought had been rendered harder rather than easier for Spinoza, by the subsidiary ideas with which he crossed the main lines of his system. He could not philosophically find the source of law, and transferred its origin to might. Neither God, nor man's conscience, according to Spinoza, is the fountain of the eternal law which rules and civilizes mankind; it springs from the whole lower natural world. He made men to a certain extent "like the fishes of the sea, like creeping things, which have no master." Large fish have the right, not only to drink water, but also to devour smaller fish, because they have the power to do so; the sphere of right of the individual man extends as far as his sphere of might. This natural right does not recognize the difference between good and evil, virtue and vice, submission and force. But because such unlimited assertion on the part of each must lead to a perpetual state of war of all against all, men have tacitly, from fear, or hope, or reason, given up their unlimited privileges to a collective body, the state. Out of two evils--on the one hand, the full possession of their sphere of right and might, tending to mutual destruction, and its alienation, on the other--men have chosen the latter as the lesser evil. The state, whether represented by a supreme authority elected for the purpose, such as the Dutch States General, or by a despot, is the full possessor of the rights of all, because of the power of all. Every one is bound by his own interest to unconditional obedience, even if he should be commanded to deprive others of life ; resistance is not only punishable, but contrary to reason. This supreme power is not controlled by any law. Whether exercised by an individual, as in a monarchy, or by several, as in a republic, it is justified in doing everything, and can do no wrong. But the state has supreme right not merely over actions of a civil nature, but also over spiritual and religious views ; it could not exist, if everyone were at liberty to attack it under the pretext of religion. The government alone has the right to control religious affairs, and

SPINOZA'S THEORY OF THE STATE.

to define belief, unbelief, orthodoxy, and heresy. What a tyrannical conclusion! As this theory of Spinoza fails to recognize moral law, so it ignores steadfast fidelity. As soon as the government grows weak, it no longer has claim to obedience; everyone may renounce and resist it, to submit himself to the incoming power. According to this theory of civil and religious despotism, no one may have an opinion about the laws of the state, otherwise he is a rebel. Spinoza's theory almost does away with freedom, even of thought and opinion. Whoever speaks against a state ordinance in a fault-finding spirit, or to throw odium upon the government, or seeks to repeal a law against its express wish, should be regarded as a disturber of the public peace. Only through a sophistical quibble was Spinoza able to save freedom of thought and free expression of opinion. Every man has this right by nature, the only one which he has not transferred to the state, because it is essentially inalienable. It must be conceded to everyone to think and judge in opposition to the opinion of the government, even to speak and teach, provided this be done with reason and reflection, without fraud, anger, or malice, and without the intention of causing a revolution.

On this weak basis, supported by a few other secondary considerations, Spinoza justified his conflict with Judaism and his philosophical attacks upon the sacred writings recognized by the Dutch States. He thought that he had succeeded in justifying himself before the magistrates sufficiently by his defense of freedom of thought. In the formulation of this apology it was apparent that he was not indifferent to the treatment which he had experienced from the college of rabbis. Spinoza was so filled with displeasure, if not with hatred, of Jews and Judaism, that his otherwise clear judgment was biased. He, like Da Costa, called the rabbis nothing but Pharisees, and imputed to them ambitious and degraded motives, while they wished only to secure their treasured beliefs against attacks. Prouder even than his contemporaries, the French and English philosophers, of freedom of thought, for centuries repressed by the church, and now soaring aloft the more powerfully, Spinoza summoned theology,in particular, ancient Judaism before the throne of reason, examined its dogmas and archives, and pronounced sentence of condemnation upon his mother-faith. He had erected a tower of thought in his brain from which, as it were, he wished to storm heaven. Spinoza's philosophy is like a fine net, laid before our eyes, mesh by mesh, by which the human understanding is unexpectedly ensnared, so that half voluntarily, half compulsorily, it surrenders. Spinoza recognized, as no thinker before, those universal laws, immutable as iron, which are apparent in the development of the most insignificant grain of seed no less than in the revolution of the heavenly bodies, in the precision of mathematical thought as in the apparent irregularity of human passions. Whilst these laws work with constant uniformity, and produce the same causes and the same phenomena in endless succession, the instruments of law are perishable things, creatures of a day, which rise, and vanish to give place to others: here eternity, there temporality; on the one side necessity, on the other chance; here reality, there delusive appearances. These and other enigmas Spinoza sought to solve with the penetration that betrays the son of the Talmud, and with logical consecutiveness and masterly arrangement, for which Aristotle might have envied him.

The whole universe, all individual things, and their active powers are, according to Spinoza, not merely from God, but of God; they constitute the infinite succession of forms in which God reveals Himself, through which He eternally works according

to His eternal nature--the soul, as it were, of thinking bodies, the body of the soul extended in space. God is the indwelling, not the external efficient cause of all things; all is in God and moves in God. God as creator and generator of all things is generative or self-producing nature. The whole of nature is animate, and ideas, as bodies, move in eternity on lines running parallel to or intersecting one another. Though the fullness of things which have proceeded from God and which exist in Him are not of an eternal, but of a perishable nature, yet they are not limited or defined by chance, but by the necessity of the divine nature, each in its own way existing or acting within its smaller or larger sphere. The eternal and constant nature of God works in them through the eternal laws communicated to them. Things could, therefore, not be constituted otherwise than they are; for they are the manifestations, entering into existence in an eternal stream, of God in the intimate connection of thought and extension.

What is man's place in this logical system ? How is he to act and work? Even he, with all his greatness and littleness, his strength and weakness, his heaven-aspiring mind, and his body subject to the need of sustenance, is nothing more than a form of existence (Modus) of God. Man after man, generation after generation, springs up and perishes, flows away like a drop in a perpetual stream, but his nature, the laws by which he moves bodily and mentally in the peculiar connection of mind and matter, reflect the Divine Being. Especially the human mind, or rather the various modes of thought, the feelings and conceptions of all men, form the eternal reason of God. But man is as little free as things, as the stone which rolls down from the mountain: he has to obey the causes which influence him from within and without. Each of his actions is the product of an infinite series of causes and effects, which he can scarcely discern, much less control and alter at will. The good man and the bad, the martyr who sacrifices himself for a noble object, as well as the execrable villain and the murderer, are all like clay in the hands of God ; they act, the one well, the other ill, compelled by their inner nature. They all act from rigid necessity. No man can reproach God for having given him a weak nature or clouded intellect, as it would be irrational if a circle should complain that God has not given it the nature and properties of the sphere. It is not the lot of every man to be strong-minded, and it lies as little in his power to have a sound mind as a sound body.

On one side man is, to a certain extent, free, or rather some men of special mental endowments can free themselves a little from the pressure exercised upon them. Man is a slave chiefly through his passions. Love, hate, anger, thirst for glory, avarice, make him the slave of the external world. These passions spring from the perplexity of the soul, which thinks it can control things, but wears itself out, so to speak, against their obstinate resistance, and suffers pain thereby. The better the soul succeeds in comprehending the succession of causes and effects and the necessity of phenomena in the plan of the universe, the better able is it to change pain into a sense of comfort. Through higher insight, man, if he allows himself to be led by reason, can acquire strength of soul, and feel increased love to God, that is, to the eternal whole. On the one hand, this secures nobility of mind to aid men and to win them by mildness and benevolence; and creates, on the other, satisfaction, joy, and happiness. He who is gifted with highest knowledge lives in God, and God in him. Knowledge is virtue, as ignorance is, to a certain extent, vice. Whilst the wise man, or strictly speaking, the philosopher, thanks to his higher insight and his love of God, enjoys tranquillity of soul, the man of clouded intel-

lect, who abandons himself to the madness of his passions, must dispense with this joyousness, and often perishes in consequence. The highest virtue, according to Spinoza's system, is self-renunciation through knowledge, keeping in a state of passiveness, coming as little as possible in contact with the crushing machinery of forces--avoiding them if they come near, or submitting to them if their wild career overthrows the individual. But as he who is beset by desires deserves no blame, so no praise is due the wise man who practices self-renunciation; both follow the law of their nature. Higher knowledge and wisdom cannot be attained if the conditions are wanting, namely, a mind susceptible of knowledge and truth, which one can neither give himself, nor throw off. Man has thus no final aim, any more than the eternal substance.

Spinoza's moral doctrines--ethics in the narrower sense--are just as unfruitful as his political theories. In either case, he recognizes submission as the only rational course.

With this conception of God and moral action, it cannot surprise us that Judaism found no favor in Spinoza's eyes. Judaism lays down directly opposite principles--beckons man to a high, self-reliant task, and proclaims aloud the progress of mankind in simple service of God, holiness, and victory over violence, the sword, and degrading war. This progress has been furthered in many ways by Judaism in the course of ages. Wanting, as Spinoza was, in apprehension of historical events, more wonderful than the phenomena of nature, and unable as he therefore was to accord to Judaism special importance, he misconceived it still further through his bitterness against the Amsterdam college of rabbis, who pardonably enough, had excommunicated him. Spinoza transferred his bitterness against the community to the whole Jewish race and to Judaism. As has been already said, he called the rabbis Pharisees in his "Theologico-Political Treatise" and in letters to his friends, and gave the most invidious meaning to this word. To Christianity, on the contrary, Spinoza conceded great excellencies; he regarded Judaism with displeasure, therefore, detected deficiencies and absurdities everywhere, while he cast a benevolent eye upon Christianity. Spinoza, therefore, with all the instinct for truth which characterized him, formed a conception of Judaism which, in some degree just, was, in many points, perverse and defective. Clear as his mind was in metaphysical inquiries, it was dark and confused on historical ground. To depreciate Judaism, Spinoza declared that the books of Holy Scripture contain scribes' errors, interpolations, and disfigurements, and are not, as a rule, the work of the authors to whom they are ascribed--not even the Pentateuch, the original source of Judaism. Ezra, perhaps, first collected and arranged it after the Babylonian exile. The genuine writings of Moses are no longer extant, not even the Ten Commandments being in their original form. Nevertheless, Spinoza accepted every word in the Bible as a kind of revelation, and designated all persons who figure in it as prophets. He conceded, on the ground of Scripture, that the revelation of the prophets was authenticated by visible signs. Nevertheless, he very much underrated this revelation. Moses, the prophets, and all the higher personages of the Bible had only a confused notion of God, nature, and living beings; they were not philosophers, they did not avail themselves of the natural light of reason. Jesus stood higher; he taught not only a nation, but the whole of mankind on rational grounds. The Apostles, too, were to be set higher than the prophets, since they introduced a natural method of instruction, and worked not merely through signs, but also through rational conviction.

THE JEWISH THEOCRACY.

It was only Spinoza's bitterness against Jews which caused him to depreciate their spiritual property and overrate Christianity. His sober intellect, penetrating to the eternal connection of things and events, could not accept miracles, but those of the New Testament he judged mildly.

In spite of his condemnatory verdict on Judaism, he was struck by two phenomena, which he did not fully understand, and which, therefore, he judged only superficially according to his system. These were the moral greatness of the prophets, and the superiority of the Israelite state, which in a measure depend on each other. Without understanding the political organization, in which natural and moral laws, necessity and freedom work together, Spinoza explains the origin of the Jewish state, that is, of Judaism, in the following manner: When the Israelites, after deliverance from slavery in Egypt, were free from all political bondage, and restored to their natural rights, they willingly chose God as their Lord, and transferred their rights to Him alone by formal contract and alliance. That there be no appearance of fraud on the divine side, God permitted them to recognize His marvelous power, by virtue of which He had hitherto preserved, and promised in future to preserve them, that is, He revealed Himself to them in His glory on Sinai; thus God became the King of Israel and the state a theocracy. Religious opinions and truths, therefore, had a legal character in this state, religion and civic right coincided. Whoever revolted from religion forfeited his rights as a citizen, and whoever died for religion was a patriot. Pure democratic equality, the right of all to entreat God and interpret the laws, prevailed among the Israelites. But when, in the overpowering bewilderment of the revelation from Sinai they voluntarily asked Moses to receive the laws from God and to interpret them, they renounced their equality, and transferred their rights to Moses. Moses from that time became God's representative. Hence, he promulgated laws suited to the condition of the people at that time, and introduced ceremonies to remind them always of the Law and keep them from willfulness, so that in accordance with a definite precept they should plough, sow, eat, clothe themselves, in a word, do everything according to the precepts of the Law. Above all, he provided that they might not act from childish or slavish fear, but from reverence for God. He bound them by benefits, and promised them earthly prosperity--all through the power and by the command of God. Moses was vested with spiritual and civil power, and authorized to transmit both. After the death of Moses the Jewish state was neither a monarchy, nor an aristocracy, nor a democracy; it remained a theocracy. The family of the high-priest was God's interpreter, and the civil power, after Joshua's death, fell to single tribes or their chiefs.

This constitution offered many advantages. The civil rulers could not turn the law to their own advantage, nor oppress the people, for the Law was the province of the sacerdotal order--the sons of Aaron and the Levites. Besides, the people were made acquainted with the Law through the prescribed reading at the close of the Sabbatical year, and would not have passed over with indifference any willful transgression of the law of the state. The army was composed of native militia, while foreigners, that is, mercenaries, were excluded. Thus the rulers were prevented from oppressing

the people or waging war arbitrarily. The tribes were united by religion, and the oppression of one tribe by its ruler would have been punished by the rest. The princes were not placed at the head through rank or privilege of blood, but through capacity and merit. Finally, the institution of prophets proved very wholesome. Since the constitution was theocratical, every one of blameless life was able through certain signs to represent himself as a prophet like Moses, draw the oppressed people to him in the name of God, and oppose the tyranny of the rulers. This constitution offered a further advantage, because the land was equally divided, and no one could be permanently deprived of his portion through poverty, as restitution had to be made in the year of jubilee.

Hence, there was little poverty, or such only as was endurable, for the love of one's neighbor had to be exercised with the greatest conscientiousness to keep the favor of God, the King. Finally, a large space was accorded to gladness. Thrice a year and on other occasions the people were to assemble at festivals, not to revel in sensual enjoyments, but to accustom themselves to follow God gladly; for there is no more effectual means of guiding the hearts of men than the joy which arises from love and admiration.

After Spinoza had depicted Israel's theocracy quite as a pattern for all states, he was apparently startled at having imparted so much light to the picture, and he looked around for shade. Instead of answering in a purely historical manner the questions, whence it came that the Hebrews were so often subdued, and why their state was entirely destroyed; instead of indicating that these wholesome laws remained a never realized ideal, Spinoza suggests a sophistic solution. Because God did not wish to make Israel's dominion lasting, he gave bad laws and statutes. Spinoza supports this view by a verse which he misunderstood. These bad laws, rebellion against the sacerdotal state, coupled with bad morals, produced discontent, revolt, and insurrection. At last matters went so far, that instead of the Divine King, the Israelites chose a human one, and instead of the temple, a court. Monarchy, however, only increased the disorder; it could not endure the state within the state, the high-priesthood, and lowered the dignity of the tatter by the introduction of strange worship. The prophets could avail nothing, because they only declaimed against the tyrants, but could not remove the cause of the evils. All things combined brought on the destruction of the divine state. With its destruction by the Babylonian king, the natural rights of the Israelites were transferred to the conqueror, and they were bound to obey him and his successors, as they had obeyed God. All the laws of Judaism, nay, the whole of Judaism, was thereby abolished, and no longer had any significance. This was the result of Spinoza's inquiry in his "Theologico-Political Treatise." Judaism had a brilliant past, God concluded an alliance with the people, showed to them His exalted power, and gave them excellent laws; but He did not intend Israel's pre-eminence to be permanent, therefore He also gave bad laws. Consequently, Judaism reached its end more than two thousand years ago, and yet it continued its existence! Wonderful! Spinoza found the history of Israel and the constitution of the state

excellent during the barbarism of the period of the Judges, while the brilliant epochs of David and Solomon and of King Uzziah remained inexplicable to him. And, above all, the era of the second Temple, the Maccabean epoch, when the Jewish nation rose from shameful degradation to a brilliant height, and brought the heathen world itself to worship the one God and adopt a moral life, remained to Spinoza an insoluble riddle. This shows that his whole demonstration and his analysis (schematism) cannot stand the test of criticism, but rests on false assumptions.

Spinoza might have brought Judaism into extreme peril; for he not only furnished its opponents with the weapons of reason to combat Judaism more effectually, but also conceded to every state and magistrate the right to suppress it and use force against its followers, to which they ought meekly to submit. The funeral piles of the Inquisition for Marranos were, according to Spinoza's system, doubly justified; citizens have no right on rational grounds to resist the recognized religion of the state, and it is folly to profess Judaism and to sacrifice oneself for it. But a peculiar trait of Spinoza's character stood Judaism in good stead. He loved peace and quiet too well to become a propagandist for his critical principles. "To be peaceable and peaceful" was his ideal; avoidance of conflict and opposition was at once his strength and his weakness. To his life's end he led an ideally-philosophica1 life; for food, clothing, and shelter, he needed only so much as he could earn with his handicraft of polishing lenses, which his friends disposed of. He struggled against accepting a pension, customarily bestowed on learned men at that time, even from his sincere and rich admirers, Simon de Vries and the grand pensionary De Witt, that he might not fall into dependence, constraint, and disquiet. By reason of this invincible desire for philosophic calm and freedom from care, he would not decide in favor of either of the political parties, then setting the States General in feverish agitation. Not even the exciting murder of his friend John de Witt was able to hurry him into partisanship. Spinoza bewailed his high and noble friend, but did not defend his honor, to clear it of suspicion. When the most highly cultivated German prince of his time, Count-Palatine Karl Ludwig, who cherished a certain affection for Jews, offered him, " the Protestant Jew," as he was still called, the chair of philosophy in the University of Heidelberg under very favorable conditions, Spinoza declined the offer. He did not conceal his reason: he would not surrender his quietude. From this predominant tendency, or, rather, from fear of disturbance and inconveniences and from apprehension of calling enemies down upon him, or of coming into collision with the state, he refused to publish his speculations for a long time. When at last he resolved, on the pressure of friends, to send "The Theologico-Political Treatise" to press, he did not put his name to the work, which made an epoch in literature, and even caused a false place of publication, viz., Hamburg, to be printed on the title-page, in order to obliterate every trace of its real authorship. He almost denied his offspring, to avoid being disturbed.

As might have been foreseen, the appearance of "The Theologico-Political Treatise" (1670), made an extraordinary stir. No one had written so distinctly and incisively concerning the relation of religion to philosophy and the power of the state, and, above all, had so sharply condemned the clergy. The ministers of all denominations were extraordinarily excited against this "godless" book, as it was called, which disparaged revealed religion. Spinoza's influential friends were not able to protect it; it was condemned by a decree of the States General, and forbidden to be sold--which only caused it to be read more eagerly. But Spinoza was the more reluctant to publish his other writings, especially his philosophical system. With all his strength of character, he did not belong to those bold spirits, who undertake to be the pioneers of truth, who usher it into the world with loud voice, and win it adherents, unconcerned as to whether they may have to endure bloody or bloodless martyrdom. In the unselfishness of Spinoza's character and system there lurked an element of selfishness, namely, the desire to be disturbed as little as possible in the attainment of knowledge, in the happiness of contemplation, and in reflection upon the universe and the chain of causes and effects which prevail in it. A challenge to action, effort, and resistance to opposition lay neither in Spinoza's temper, nor in his philosophy.

Without suspecting it, Spinoza possessed In the East an ally, diametrically his opposite, who labored to disintegrate Judaism, and succeeded in throwing the whole Jewish race into a turmoil, which long interfered with its progress. Sabbatai Zevi was at once Spinoza's opposite and his ally. He possessed many more admirers than the philosopher of Amsterdam, became for a space the idol of the Jewish race, and has secret adherents even to the present time. Sabbatai Zevi (born Ab 9, 1626, died 1676), of Smyrna, in Asia Minor, was of Spanish descent, and became the originator of a new Messianic frenzy, the founder of a new sect. He owed the attachment which he inspired even as a youth, not to his qualities of mind, but to his external appearance and attractive manner. He was tall, well formed, had fine dark hair, a fine beard, and a pleasant voice, which won hearts by speech and still more by song. But his mind was befogged by reason of the predominance of fancy; he had an enthusiastic temperament and an inclination to what was strange, especially to solitude. In boyhood Sabbatai Zevi avoided the company and games of playmates, sought solitary places, and what usually has charms for the young did not attract him. He was educated by the current method. In early youth he studied the Talmud in the school of the veteran Joseph Eskapha, a staunch Talmudist of Smyrna, but did not attain to great proficiency. The more was he attracted by the confused jumble of the Kabbala. Once introduced into the labyrinth of the Zohar, he felt himself at home therein, guided by Lurya's interpretation. Sabbatai Zevi shared the

SABBATAI ZEVI.

prevailing opinion that the Kabbala can be acquired only by means of asceticism. He mortified his body, and bathed very frequently in the sea, day and night, winter and summer. Perhaps it was from sea-bathing that his body derived the peculiar fragrance which his worshipers strongly maintained that it possessed. In early manhood he presented a contrast to his companions because he felt no attraction to the female sex. According to custom Sabbatai Zevi married early, but avoided his young, good-looking wife so consistently, that she applied for divorce, which he willingly granted her. The same thing happened with a second wife.

This aversion to marriage, rare in the warm climate of the East, his assiduous study of the Kabbala, and his ascetic life, attracted attention. Disciples sought him, and were introduced by him to the Kabbala. Twenty years old he was the master of a small circle. He attached disciples to himself partly by his earnest and retiring manner, which precluded familiarity, partly by his musical voice, with which he sang in Spanish the Kabbalistic verses composed by Lurya or himself. Another circumstance must be added. When Sultan Ibrahim ascended the throne, a violent war broke out between Turkey and Venice, which made the trade of the Levant unsafe in the capital. Several European, that is, Dutch and English, mercantile houses in consequence transferred their offices to Smyrna. This hitherto insignificant city thereby acquired importance as a mart. The Jews of Smyrna, who had been poor, profited by this commercial development, and amassed great riches, first as agents of large houses, afterwards as independent firms. Mordecai Zevi, Sabbatai's father, from the Morea, originally poor, became the Smyrna agent of an English house, executed its commissions with strict honesty, enjoyed the confidence of the principals, and became a wealthy man. His increasing prosperity was attributed by the blind father to the merit of his Kabbala-loving son, to whom he paid such great reverence, that it was communicated to strangers. Sabbatai was regarded as a young saint. The more discreet, on account of his folly, declared him to be mad. In the house of his English principal, Mordecai Zevi often heard the approach of the millennium discussed, either he himself or some of his people being enthusiastic believers in the apocalypse of the Fifth Monarchy. The year 1666 was designated by these enthusiasts as the Messianic year, which was to bring renewed splendor to the Jews and see their return to Jerusalem. The expectations heard in the English counting house were communicated by Mordecai Zevi to the members of his family, none of whom listened more attentively than Sabbatai, already entangled in the maze of the Luryan Kabbala, and inclined to mistake enthusiastic hopes for prosaic fact. What if he himself were called upon to usher in this time of redemption? Had he not, at an earlier age than any one before, penetrated to the, heart of the Kabbala? And who could be more worthy of this call than one deeply immersed in its mysteries?

The central point of the later Kabbala was most intense expectation of the Messiah; Lurya, Vital, and their disciples and followers proclaimed anew, "The kingdom of heaven is at hand." A peculiar redemption was to precede and accompany it--the redemption of the scattered elements of the original soul (Nizuzoth) from the fetters of original evil, the demon nature (Kelifoth), which, taking a hold on men through the fall of the angels or divine elements, held them in captivity, impeded their upward flight, and necessitated the perpetual transmigration of souls from body to body. As soon as the evil spirit was either consumed, annihilated, rendered powerless, or at least existed by itself without admixture of the divine, then the Kabbalistic

order (Olam ha-Tikkun) would prevail, streams of mercy would pour forth without let or hindrance upon the lower world through the channels of the Sefiroth, and fructify and miraculously quicken it. This work of redemption can be accomplished by every truly pious man (Zaddik), who having an enlightened soul, and being initiated into the Kabbala, stands in close union with the world of spirits, comprehends the connection between the upper and lower world, and fulfills all religious exercises (Kewanoth) with concentrated devotion and with due regard to their influence upon the higher powers. Still more effectually the Messiah, the son of David, will accomplish the annihilation of demoniacal powers and the restoration of lost souls, or rather the collection of the scattered elements of the universal soul of Adam. For to the Messiah, in whom dwells a pure, immaculate soul, are unfolded the mysterious depths of the higher worlds, essences, and divine creation, even the Divine Being Himself. The Messiah of the seed of David would, to a certain extent, be the original man (Adam Kadmon) incarnate, part of the Godhead.

This Luryan mysticism dazzled the bewildered brain of the Smyrna youth, and produced such confusion and giddiness, that he thought he could easily usher in this spiritual redemption, which would be immediately followed by that of the body. In what manner this haughty wish to play the part of a Messiah germinates and breaks forth in enthusiastic minds, is an impenetrable riddle. Sabbatai Zevi was not the first to believe himself able to reverse the whole order of the world, by mystical hocus-pocus, and partly to succeed in the endeavor. Certain it is that the extravagant notions entertained by Jews and Christians with regard to the near approach of the time of grace worked upon Sabbatai's weak brain. That book of falsehoods, the Zohar, declared that in the year of the world 5408 (1648) the era of redemption would dawn, and precisely in that year Sabbatai revealed himself to his train of youthful companions as the Messianic redeemer. It happened in an apparently insignificant manner, but the mode of revelation was of great import to the initiated. Sabbatai Zevi uttered the full four-lettered name of God in Hebrew (YHWH, the Tetragrammaton) without hesitation, although this was strictly prohibited in the Talmud and by the usage of ages. The Kabbalists attached all sorts of mystical importance to this prohibition. During the dispersion of Israel, the perfection of God Himself was to a certain extent destroyed, on account of the sinfulness of men and the degradation of the Jewish people, since the Deity could not carry out His moral plan. The higher and lower worlds were divided from each other by a deep gulf; the four letters of God's name were parted asunder. With the Messianic period of redemption the moral order of the world, as God had laid it down in the plan of the universe, and the perfection and unity of God would be restored. When Sabbatai Zevi permitted himself to pronounce the name of God in full, he thereby proclaimed that the time of grace had begun with him.

However, despite his pious, mystical life, he had too little authority at the age of two and twenty for the rabbis to allow an infraction of the existing order of things, which might lead to further inroads. When Zevi's pretensions became known some years later, the college of rabbis, at their head his teacher Joseph Eskapha, laid him and his followers under a ban. Many bickerings ensued in the community, the particulars of which are not known. Finally he and his disciples were banished from Smyrna (about 1651). The Messianic delusion appeared to have been extinguished, but it smoldered on, and broke out again, about fifteen years later, in a bright, consuming flame. This persecution, far from terrifying

ABRAHAM YACHINI.

Sabbatai Zevi, gave him a sense of his dignity. The idea of a suffering Messiah had been transplanted from Christianity to Judaism; [or vice-versa--ed.] it was the accepted view that humiliation was the precursor of the Messiah's exaltation and glorification. Sabbatai believed in himself, and his disciples, amongst them Moses Pinheiro, a man of mature age, highly esteemed for scientific acquirements, shared the belief with tenacity. If the Messiah had been obliged to beg his way through the world, his illusion would not have long held its ground. But Sabbatai was richly provided with means, he could maintain his independence and his presumed dignity, and win adherents to his cause. At first, however, he kept himself in concealment, did not say much about his Messiahship, and thereby escaped ridicule. Whither he betook himself after his banishment from his native city is not quite certain; probably to the Turkish capital, where dwelt the largest Jewish community, in which were so many clean and unclean elements, that everyone could find companions for plans and adventures. Here he made the acquaintance of a preacher, Abraham Yachini, who confirmed him in his delusion. Yachini stood in high repute on account of his talent as a preacher. He was a needy and artful fellow, and made neat transcriptions for a Dutch Christian, who dabbled in Oriental literature. From selfish motives or delight in mystification, and to confirm Sabbatai Zevi in his delusion,Yachini palmed off upon him an apocryphal manuscript in archaic characters, which he alleged bore ancient testimony to Sabbatai's Messiahship.

This document, which the young fanatic himself appears to have taken for a genuine revelation, became later on the source of many mystifications and impostures. However, it appeared inadvisable to the dupe and the deceiver that he should appear in Constantinople. Salonica, which had always paid homage to mysticism, seemed a more suitable field for Kabbalistic extravagances. Here, therefore, Sabbatai resided for some time, gained adherents, and came forward with greater boldness. Here he enacted one of his favorite scenes, by which he afterwards worked upon the imagination of the Kabbalists. He prepared a solemn festival, invited his friends, sent for the sacred book (Torah), and intimated to those present, that he was about to celebrate his mystical marriage with it. In the language of the Kabbala this meant that the Torah, the daughter of heaven, was to be united indissolubly with the Messiah, the son of heaven, or En-Sof. This scene displeased the discreet rabbis of Salonica, and they decreed his banishment. Thence he betook himself to the Morea, probably to relatives and friends of his father, and resided for some time at Athens, where at that time there was a Jewish community. When the Jews of this region heard of the sentence pronounced upon him, they gave him no encouragement. This opposition, far from discouraging him, only served to make him bolder; he probably regarded his sufferings as necessary for the glorification of the Messiah.

At last, after long wandering, a prospect of realizing his dream presented itself at Cairo. In the Egyptian capital there was a Jewish mint-master and tax-farmer, with the title of Saraph-Bashi, similar to the Alabarchs at Alexandria in earlier ages. At that time (after 1656) the office was held by Raphael Joseph Chelebi, of Aleppo, a man of great wealth and open-handed benevolence, but of unspeakable credulity, and ineradicable propensity to mysticism and asceticism. Fifty learned Talmudists and Kabbalists were supported by him, and dined at his table. Everyone who sought his compassion found help and relief in his need. While riding in the royal chariot, and appearing in splendid robes, he wore sackcloth underneath, fasted and bathed much, and frequently at night scourged himself. Samuel Vital, a son of Chayim Calabrese, superintended his constant penances according to the Kabbalistic precepts of Lurya (Tikkun Lurya). These were intended, as has been stated, to hasten the coming of the Messiah. To be in Cairo and not to make Raphael Joseph's acquaintance was an inconceivable course for a Kabbalist. Sabbatai Zevi thus came into his circle, and won his confidence the sooner, as, owing to his independent position, he did not desire anything of him. He appears to have partially revealed his Messianic plans to Raphael. He had grown older, more mature, and wiser, and knew how to make men amenable to his wishes. The Apocalyptic year, 1666, was drawing near, and it was important to use the auspicious moment.

He betook himself to Jerusalem, perhaps under the delusion that in the Holy Land a miracle would take place to confirm his greatness. The community at Jerusalem was at that time in every way poor and wretched. Besides being ground down by the oppressions and extortions of Turkish officials, it suffered because the supplies from Europe were exhausted on account of the constant massacres of the Jews in Poland. The consequence was that the best men emigrated, leaving the government of the community to thorough-going Kabbalists, devoted adherents of Lurya and Vital, or to a licentious set, who followed the impulses of bare-faced selfishness. There were at that time very few men of repute and authority in Jerusalem. A Marrano physician named Jacob Zemach appears to have stood at their head. He had leapt, so to speak, in one bound from a Portuguese church into the nest of Kabbalists at Safet, and there, as later at Jerusalem, had become an unconscious tool for the mystifications practiced by Vital. Abraham Amigo, a Talmudist of the second or third rank, had similar aims. A man of some importance, to be sure, was Jacob Chages (1620-1674), who had migrated from Italy to Jerusalem, and who wrote Spanish well. Chages, however, had no official position, but lived the life of a recluse in an academy, which two brothers named Vega, of Leghorn, had founded for him. The thoughtless credulity of the people of Jerusalem of that time is instanced by the gross deception practiced upon them by Baruch Gad, one of their alms-collecting emissaries, which they, the learned and the unlearned, not only credited, but swore to as true. Baruch Gad had gone on a begging Journey to Persia, where he pretended that he had experienced many adventures, and had been saved by a Jew of the tribe of Naphtali, who had given him a Kabbalistic letter from one of the "Sons of Moses" at the miraculous river Sabbation. It contained much about the riches, splendor, and daily miracles of the Sons of Moses, and said that they were momentarily awaiting the commencement of the Messianic epoch as a signal for coming forth. This story, certified by a circular, was brought by Baruch Gad to Jerusalem, where it found unquestioning credence. When the community of Jerusalem had fallen into great want in consequence of the Cossack massacre, ten so-called rabbis, Jacob Zemach at their head, sent to Reggio to their envoy Nathan Spira, of Jerusalem, a copy of this document from the Sons of Moses, which was kept in careful custody. It was to serve as a bait to draw more abundant alms.

The miracle which Sabbatai Zevi was expecting for himself in the Holy City was present in the credulity and mania for miracles on the part of the people of Jerusalem, who were inclined, like the lowest savages, to accept any absurd message as a

SABBATAI'S HABITS.

divine revelation, if only it was brought before them in the right manner. At first the Smyrna enthusiast kept himself quiet, and gave no offense. He lived according to the precepts of the Kabbala, imposed the severest mortifications on himself, and often stayed by the graves of pious men in order to draw down their spirits. Thereby, aided by his pleasing, attractive, and reverential behavior and taciturn manner, he gradually gathered round him a circle of adherents who had blind faith in him. One of his devoted followers related with credulous simplicity, that Sabbatai Zevi shed floods of tears in prayer. He sang Psalms the whole night with his melodious voice, while pacing the room now with short, now with long strides. His whole conduct was out of the ordinary groove. He was also wont to sing coarse love songs in Spanish, with a mystical meaning, about the emperor's fair daughter Melisselda, with her coral lips and milk-white skin, as she rose out of the bath. Sabbatai used another means to win hearts. When he showed himself in the streets he distributed sweet-meats of all sorts to the children, who in consequence ran after him, and he thus gained the favor of their mothers.

An incident brought his eccentric ideas nearer their realization. The community at Jerusalem was sentenced by one of the pashas or some minor official to one of those oppressive exactions which frequently carried torture or death in their train. The impoverished members rested their hopes solely on Raphael Joseph Chelebi at Cairo, known to have the means and inclination to succor his afflicted brethren, especially the saints of Jerusalem. A messenger was to be sent to him, and Sabbatai Zevi was universally regarded as the most fitting, particularly as he was a favorite with the Saraph-Bashi. He undertook this task willingly, because he hoped to get the opportunity to play the part of savior of the Holy City. His worshipers date from this journey to Egypt the beginning of his miraculous power, and assert that he accomplished many miracles at sea. Sabbatai however traveled not by water, hut by land, by way of Hebron and Gaza, probably joining a caravan through tile desert. He excited so much attention that all the Jews of Hebron, in order to observe him, refrained from sleep during the night of his stay. Arrived at Cairo, he immediately received from Chelebi the sum required for the ransom of the community at Jerusalem, and, besides, an extraordinarily favorable opportunity presented itself to confirm his Messianic dreams.

During the massacre of the Jews in Poland by Chmielnicki, a Jewish orphan girl of about six was found by Christians, and put into a nunnery. Her parents were dead, a brother had been driven to Amsterdam, the whole community broken up and put to flight, and no one troubled himself about the forsaken child, so that the nuns of the convent regarded the foundling as a soul brought to them and gave her a Christian convent education. The impressions received in the house of her parents were so lively, that Christianity found no entrance into her heart; she remained faithful to Judaism. Nevertheless, her soul was nourished by fantastic dreams induced by her surroundings, and her thoughts took an eccentric direction. She developed into a lovely girl, and longed to escape from the cloister. One day she was found by Jews, who had again settled in the place, in the Jewish cemetery. Astonished at finding a beautiful girl of sixteen lightly clad in such a position, they questioned her, and received answer that she was of Jewish extraction, and had been brought up in a convent. The night before, she said, she had been bodily seized by her father's ghost, and carried out of bed to the cemetery. In support of her statement, she showed the women nail-marks on her body, which were said to come from her father's hands.

SABBATAI'S WIFE.

The Jews thought it dangerous to keep a fugitive from the convent in their midst, and sent her to Amsterdam. There she found her brother. Eccentric by nature and excited by the change in her fortunes, she continually repeated the words, that she was destined to be the wife of the Messiah, who was soon to appear. After she had lived some years in Amsterdam under the name of Sarah, she came--it is not known for what purpose--by way of Frankfort-on-the-Main to Leghorn. There, as credible witnesses aver, she put her charms to immoral use, yet continued to maintain that she was dedicated to the Messiah, and could contract no other marriage. The strange history of this Polish girl circulated amongst the Jews,and penetrated even to Cairo. Sabbatai Zevi, who heard of it, gave out that a Polish-Jewish maiden had been promised to him in a dream as his spiritual wife. He sent a messenger to Leghorn, and had Sarah brought to Cairo.

By her fantastical, free, self-confident behavior and by her beauty, Sarah made a peculiar impression upon Sabbatai and his companions. He himself was firmly convinced of his Messiahship. To Sabbatai and his friends the immoral life of this Polish adventuress was not unknown. This also was said to be a Messianic dispensation; he had been directed, like the prophet Hosea, to marry an unchaste wife. No one was so happy as Raphael Joseph Chelebi, because at his house the Messiah met his bride, and was married. He placed his wealth at the disposal of Sabbatai Zevi, and became his most influential follower. The warm adhesion of so dignified, respected, and powerful a man brought many believers to Sabbatai. It was rightly said, that he had come to Egypt as a messenger, and returned as the Messiah. For, from this second residence at Cairo dates his public career. Sarah, also, the Messiah's fair bride, brought him many disciples. Through her a romantic, licentious element entered into the fantastic career of the Smyrna Messiah. Her beauty and free manner of life attracted youths and men who had no sympathy with the mystical movement. With a larger following than when he started, Sabbatai returned to Palestine, bringing two talismans of more effective power than Kabbalistic means--Sarah's influence and Chelebi's money. At Gaza he found a third confederate, who helped to smooth his path.

At Jerusalem there lived a man named Elisha Levi, who had migrated thither from Germany. The Jews of the Holy City dispatched him to all parts of the world with begging letters. Whilst he was roaming through northern Africa, Amsterdam, Hamburg, and Poland, his son Nathan Benjamin Levi (1644--1680) was left to himself, or the perverse education of that time. He developed, in the school of Jacob Chages, into a youth with superficial knowledge of the Talmud, acquired Kabbalistic scraps, and obtained facility in the high-sounding, but hollow, nonsensical Rabbinical style of the period, which concealed poverty of thought beneath verbiage. The pen was his faithful instrument, and replaced the gift of speech, in which he had little facility. This youth was suddenly raised from pressing poverty to opulence. A rich Portuguese, Samuel Lisbona, who had moved from Damascus to Gaza, asked Jacob Chages to recommend a husband for his beautiful, but one-eyed daughter, and he suggested his disciple Nathan Benjamin. Thus he became connected with a rich house, and in consequence of his change of fortune, lost all stability, if he had had any. When Sabbatai Zevi,with a large train of followers, came to Gaza on his way back from Cairo, posing as the Messiah, and accepted as such by the crowds gathering about him, Nathan Ghazati (i.e, of Gaza) entered into close relationship

NATHAN GHAZATI.

with him. In what way their mutual acquaintance and attachment arose is not explained. Sabbatai's disciples declared that Nathan had dug up a part of the ancient writing, wherein Zevi's Messiahship was testified. It is probably nearer the truth, that Sabbatai, to convince Ghazati of his mission, palmed off on him the spurious document received from Abraham Yachini. At any rate Nathan became his most zealous adherent, whether from conviction or from a desire to play a prominent part, can no longer be discerned in this story, in which simple faith, self-deception, and willful imposture, border so close on one another.

After Nathan Ghazati and Sabbatai had become acquainted, the former a youth of twenty, the latter a man of forty, prophetic revelations followed close upon one another. Ghazati professed to be the risen Elijah, who was to pave the way for the Messiah. He gave out that he had received a call on a certain day (probably the eve of the Pentecost, 1665), that in a year and a few months the Messiah would show himself in his glory, would take the sultan captive without arms, only with music, and establish the dominion of Israel over all the nations of the earth. The Messianic age was to begin in the year 1666. This revelation was proclaimed everywhere in writing by the pretended prophet of Gaza, with the addition of wild fantasies and suggestive details. He wrote to Raphael Joseph acknowledging the receipt of the moneys sent by him, and begging him not to lose faith in Sabbatai; the latter would certainly in a year and some months make the sultan his subject and lead him about as a captive. The dominion would be entrusted to Nathan, until he should conquer the other nations without bloodshed, warring only against Germany, the enemy of the Jews. Then the Messiah would betake himself to the banks of the river Sabbation, and there espouse the daughter of the great prophet, Moses, who at the age of thirteen would be exalted as queen, with Sarah as her slave. Finally, he would lead back the ten tribes to the Holy Land, riding upon a lion with a seven-headed dragon in its jaws. The more exaggerated and absurd Nathan's prophetic vaporings were, the more credence did they find. A veritable fit of intoxication took possession of nearly all the Jews of Jerusalem and the neighboring communities. With a prophet, formerly a shy youth, proclaiming so great a message, and a Messiah, more profoundly versed in the Kabbala than Chayim Vital, who could venture to doubt the approach of the time of grace ? Those who shook their heads at this rising imposture were laughed to scorn by the Sabbatians.

The rabbinical leaders of the Jerusalem community were unfavorably struck by this Messianic movement, and sought to stifle it at its birth. It was sufficient to prejudice them against Sabbatai that he stood in the foreground, and put them in the shade. He is said to have distributed the money from Egypt according to his own discretion, and in the division to have unduly favored his own followers. Jacob Chages and his college threatened him with the heaviest excommunication if he should persist in his course. Sabbatai Zevi appears to have cared little for this, especially as a ban could have no effect if the community was on his side. Even Moses Galante, the son-in-law of Jacob Chages, esteemed as an authority in the Holy Land, regarded him with respect, although, as he afterwards declared, he did not believe in him unconditionally. Sabbatai Zevi saw clearly that Jerusalem was not the right place for his plans, as the rabbis would place obstacles in his way. Nathan Ghazati thereupon proclaimed in an ecstasy that Jerusalem had lost its importance as the sacred city, and that Gaza had taken its place. At Smyrna, his native city--an important gathering-place for Europeans and

SAMUEL PRIMO.

Asiatics--Sabbatai thought he could obtain greater success. His rich brothers prepared a good reception for him by the distribution of money amongst the poor and needy, and Nathan's extravagant prophetic letters had kindled the imagination of the people. But before he left Jerusalem, Sabbatai took care to dispatch active missionaries of a fanatical and fraudulent character, to predict his Messianic appearance, excite men's minds, and fill them with his name. Sabbatai Raphael, a beggar and impostor from the Morea, enlarged in mountebank fashion on the Messiah's greatness; and a German Kabbalist, Matathias Bloch, did the same in blind simplicity.

Thus it came to pass that when Sabbatai Zevi left Jerusalem--of his own accord, as he pretended, banished, as others said--he was at once received in triumph in the large Asiatic community of Aleppo. Still greater was the homage paid him in his native city (autumn 1665). The ban pronounced against him was not remembered. He was accompanied by a man of Jerusalem, Samuel Primo, who became his private secretary, and one of his most zealous recruiting agents. Samuel Primo understood the art of investing trifles with an air of official seriousness and by a flowery style to give world-wide importance to the Messianic imposture. He alone remained sober in the midst of the ever-increasing fanaticism, and gave aim and direction to the enthusiasts. Primo appears to have heralded Sabbatai's fame from conviction; he had a secret plan to be accomplished through the Messiah. He appears to have made use of Sabbatai more than to have been employed by him. Sabbatai had tact enough not to announce himself at once at Smyrna as the Messiah; he commanded the believing multitude not to speak of it until the proper time. But this reserve, combined with other circumstances-the ranting letters of Nathan, the arrival of some men of Jerusalem who brought him the homage of the Holy City (though without being commissioned to do so), the severe mortifications which the people inflicted on themselves, to atone for their sins and become worthy of the coming of the Messiah--all this worked upon the minds of the multitude, and they could scarcely wait for the day of his revelation. He had the Kabbalists on his side through his mystical utterances. At length Sabbatai Zevi declared himself publicly in the synagogue, with blowing of horns, as the expected Messiah (New Year, September, or October, 1665), and the multitude shouted to him, " Long live our King, our Messiah !" The proverb that a prophet is least honored in his own country was for once belied. The madness of the Jews of Smyrna knew no bounds. Every sign of honor and enthusiastic love was shown him. It was not joy, but delirium to feel that the long-expected Messiah had at last appeared, and in their own community. The delirium seized great and small. Women, girls, and children fell into raptures, and proclaimed Sabbatai Zevi as the true redeemer. The word of the prophet, that God at the end of the world will pour forth his spirit upon the young, appeared fulfilled. All prepared for a speedy exodus, the return to the Holy Land. Workmen neglected their business, and thought only of the approaching kingdom of the Messiah. The confusion in men's brains showed itself in the way in which the Sabbatians of Smyrna strove to merit a share in the time of grace. On the one hand, they subjected themselves to incredible penances--fasted several days in succession, refrained from sleep for nights, in order that, by Kabbalistic prayers (Tikkunim) at midnight, they might wipe away their sins, and bathed in extremely cold weather, even with snow on the ground. Some buried themselves up to the neck in the soil, and remained in their damp graves until their limbs were

stiff with cold. On the other hand, they abandoned themselves to the most extravagant delight, and celebrated festival after festival in honor of the Messiah, whenever Sabbatai Zevi showed himself--always with a large train of followers--or walked through the streets singing Psalms, " The right hand of the Lord is exalted, the right hand of the Lord bringeth victory," or preached in a synagogue, and proved his Messiahship by Kabbalistic interpretations of Scripture. He showed himself only in procession in public, waved a fan to cool himself, and whoever was touched with it was sure of the kingdom of heaven. The delirious joy of his followers knew no bounds. Every word of his was repeated a thousand times as the word of God, expounded, exaggerated, and intensified. All that he did was held as miraculous, published, and believed. The madness went so far that his adherents in Smyrna and elsewhere, as at Salonica, that Kabbalist hotbed of old, married their children of twelve, ten, and even younger, to one another--seven hundred couples in all--that, according to Kabbalistic ideas, they might cause the souls not yet born to enter into life, and thereby remove the last obstacle to the commencement of the time of grace.

The activity of Sabbatai Zevi in electrifying the minds of simple believers, now by public pomp and pageantry, now by silent retirement, was supplemented by Sarah, his wife, who by her loose conduct worked on the passions of the male population. The bonds of chastity, drawn much tighter among Eastern Jews than in Europe, were broken. The assembling of persons of both sexes in great multitudes, hitherto unheard of, was a slight innovation. In Messianic transports of delight men and women danced with one another as if mad, and in mystical fervor many excesses are said to have been committed. The voice of censure and caution was gradually silenced; all were drawn into the vortex, and the unbelievers were rendered harmless. The rabbi Aaron de la Papa (died 1674), an aged and respectable man, who at first spoke against this Messianic madness, and pronounced the ban against its originator, together with other rabbis, was publicly reviled in a sermon by Sabbatai, removed from office, and obliged to leave Smyrna.

Most unworthy was the behavior of the rabbi Chayim Benvenisti (1603-1673), a very considerable authority on the Talmud, and of astonishing learning, who, because he was a literary opponent of De la Papa, not only suffered the latter's removal from office, but allowed himself to be appointed in his place by Sabbatai. Though at first harshly disposed towards the new Messiah, he became a believer, and led the multitude by his authority. The latter were instigated by Sabbatai to bloodthirsty fanaticism. Because a noble, rich, and respected man in Smyrna, Chayim Penya, who had liberally supported Chayim Benvenisti, opposed the widespread delusion with obstinate incredulity, he was suddenly attacked in the synagogue, persecuted, and nearly torn to pieces by the raging multitude. Sabbatai Zevi, the pretended incarnation of piety, commanded the synagogue to be broken open and the vile heretic to be seized. But when Penya's daughters, likewise attacked by the madness, fell into raptures, and prophesied, the father had no choice but to put a good face upon the wretched business. He also assumed the air of a zealous adherent. After Penya's subjugation Sabbatai Zevi became sole ruler in the community, and could lead the Jewish population at will for good or for evil. In this humor which lasted for some months, the Jews of Smyrna feared their tyrants, the Turkish cadis, very little; if they offered to check the prevailing tendency, they were induced by rich presents to remain inactive.

These events in the Jews' quarter at Smyrna

SABBATAI'S ADHERENTS.

made a great sensation in ever-widening circles. The neighboring communities of Asia Minor, many members of which had betaken themselves to Smyrna, and witnessing the scenes enacted in that town, brought home exaggerated accounts of the Messiah's power of attraction and of working miracles, were swept into the same vortex. Sabbatai's private secretary, Samuel Primo, took care that reports of the fame and doings of the Messiah should reach Jews abroad. Nathan Ghazati sent circulars from Palestine, while the itinerant prophets, Sabbatai Raphael and Matathias Bloch, filled the ears of their auditors with the most marvelous accounts of the new redeemer. Christians also helped to spread the story. The residents, the clerks of English and Dutch mercantile houses, and the evangelical ministers, reported the extraordinary occurrences in Smyrna, and though they scoffed at the folly of the Jews, could not withhold half-credulous sympathy. Did they not see with their own eyes the ecstasies, and hear with their own ears the predictions, of the prophets and prophetesses of Sabbatai Zevi, the true redeemer? On the exchanges in Europe men spoke of him as a remarkable personage, and eagerly awaited news from Smyrna or Constantinople. At first the Jews were dazed by the reports that suddenly burst upon them. Was the long cherished hope, that one day the oppression and shame of Israel would be removed, and that he would return in glory to his home, at length to be realized? No wonder that nearly everywhere scenes similar to those in Smyrna were repeating themselves, that men's minds were filled with credulity, accepting mere rumors as accredited facts, or that wild excitement, ascetic living, and almsgiving to the needy, by way of preparation for the time of the Messiah, were followed here and there by prophetic ecstasies. Not only the senseless multitude, but nearly all the rabbis, and even men of culture and philosophical judgment, fell a prey to this credulity.

At that time not a single man of weight and importance recognized that the primary source of all these phenomena lay in the Kabbala and the Zohar. Jacob Sasportas, originally from Africa, had lived in Amsterdam and London and, at this time, was in Hamburg. He was born about 1620, and died 1698. A man of courage and keen penetration, whose word had weight through his Talmudical learning, Sasportas from the first combated this Messianic rage with passionate warmth. He was unwearied in sending letter after letter to the various communities and their guides in Europe, Asia, and Africa, to unmask the gross deceptions practiced, and to warn against the sad consequences. But even he was entangled in the snares of the Kabbala, and adopted its principles. On the ground of this spurious philosophy, thoroughgoing enthusiasts were more in the right than half-hearted adherents. Spinoza, who might have scattered this thick mist with his luminous ideas, was not only estranged from Judaism and his race, but even hostile to them, and regarded the prevailing perplexities with indifference or malice.

The accounts of Sabbatai Zevi and the Messianic excitement either came direct, or in a roundabout way by Alexandria, to Venice, Leghorn, and other Italian cities.

Venice was led by the bigoted Kabbalist Moses Zacut, Spinoza's very uncongenial fellow-student, who had formed the design of migrating from Amsterdam through Poland to Palestine, but stopped short in Venice. Far from opposing the delusion of the multitude, he encouraged it, as did the rabbinate of Venice. The news from Smyrna had most striking effect upon the great and the lesser Jerusalem of the North. The prophet of Gaza, who was not devoid of sober calculation, had directed his

THE AMSTERDAM SABBATIANS.

propagandist circulars to the most considerable and the richest communities--Amsterdam and Hamburg. These entered into close relationship with the new Messianic movement. The Jews of Amsterdam and Hamburg received confirmation of the extraordinary events at Smyrna from trustworthy Christians, many of whom were sincerely rejoiced thereat. Even Heinrich Oldenburg, a distinguished German savant in London, wrote to his friend Spinoza (December, 1665):--"All the world here is talking of a rumor at the return at the Israelites, dispersed for more than two thousand years, to their own country. Few believe it but many wish it. . .Should the news be confirmed, it may bring about a revolution in all things."

The number of believers in Amsterdam increased daily among the Portuguese no less than among the Germans, and numbers of educated people set the example; the rabbis Isaac Aboab and Raphael Moses D'Aguilar, Spinoza's fellow-student Isaac Naar, and Abraham Pereira, one of the capitalists of Amsterdam and a writer on morals in Spanish, all became believers. Even the semi-Spinozist Dionysius Musaphia became a zealous adherent of the new Messiah. In Amsterdam devotion to the new faith expressed itself in contradictory ways--by noisy music and dancing in the houses of prayer, and by gloomy, monkish self-mortification. The printing presses could not supply enough copies of special prayer-books in Hebrew, Portuguese and Spanish, for the multitude of believers. In these books penances and formulas were given by which men hoped to become partakers in the kingdom of the Messiah. Many Sabbatian prayer-books (Tikkunim) printed Sabbatai's likeness together with that of King David, also the emblems of his dominion, and select sentences from the Bible. In confident expectation of speedy return to the Holy Land, the elders of one synagogue introduced the custom of pronouncing the priestly blessing every Sabbath.

At Hamburg, the Jews went to still greater lengths of folly, because they wished to make a demonstration against the bigoted Christians, who in many ways tormented them with vexatious restrictions, and when possible compelled them to listen to Christian sermons. Whoever entered the synagogue, and saw the Jewish worshipers hop, jump, and dance about with the roll of the Law in their arms, serious, respectable men withal, of Spanish stateliness, had to take them for madmen. In fact, a mental disease prevailed, which made men childish; even the most distinguished in the community succumbed to it.

Manoel Texeira, also called Isaac Senor Texeira, was born about 1630, and died about 1695. Some months before the death of his father, Diego Texeira, a Marrano nobleman who had emigrated from Portugal and settled at Hamburg, Manoel became resident minister, banker, and confidant of Christina, former queen of Sweden. She valued him on account of his honesty, his noble bearing, and his shrewdness. She exchanged letters with him on important affairs, conferred with him on the political interests of Europe, and credited him with deep, statesman-like views. During her residence at Hamburg she took up her abode in Manoel Texeira's house, to the vexation of the local ecclesiastical authorities--who were hostile to the Jews--and remained quite unconcerned, although the Protestant preachers censured her severely from the pulpits. Men of the highest rank resorted to Texeira's house, and played with him for high stakes. This Jewish cavalier also belonged to Sabbatai's adherents, and joined in the absurd dances; as also the skillful and famous physician Bendito de Castro (Baruch Nehemiah), now advanced in years, for a time the physician of the queen during her residence in Hamburg. De Castro was at that time director of the Hamburg community, and by his order the

SABBATIANS IN ENGLAND.

Messianic follies were practiced in the synagogue. Jacob Sasportas, who because of the outbreak of the plague in London at that time resided in Hamburg, used serious arguments and satire against this Messianic delusion; but he could not make his voice heard, and only just escaped rough handling by the Sabbatians. The community recently established in London in the reign of Charles II, which had elected Jacob Sasportas as chief rabbi, was no less possessed with this craze. It derived additional encouragement from contact with Christian enthusiasts who hoped to bring about the millennium. Curious reports flew from mouth to mouth. It was said, that in the north of Scotland a ship had appeared, with silken sails and ropes, manned by sailors who spoke Hebrew. The flag bore the inscription,"The Twelve Tribes or Families of Israel." Believers living in London in English fashion offered wagers at the odds of ten to one that Sabbatai would be anointed king at Jerusalem within two years, and drew formal bills of exchange upon the issue. Wherever Jews dwelt, news of the Kabbalistic Messiah of Smyrna penetrated, and everywhere produced wild excitement. The little community of Avignon, which was not treated in the mildest manner by the papal officers, prepared to emigrate to the kingdom of Judah in the spring of the year 1666.

If Sabbatai Zevi had not hitherto firmly believed in himself and his dignity, this homage from nearly the whole Jewish race must have awakened conviction. Every day advices, messengers, and deputations came pouring in, greeting him in most flattering terms as king of the Jews, placing life and property at his disposal, and overwhelming him with gifts. Had he been a man of resolute determination and strength of will, he might have obtained results of importance with this genuine enthusiasm and willing devotion of his believers. Even Spinoza entertained the possibility, with this favor able opportunity and the mutability of human things, that the Jews might re-establish their kingdom, and again be the chosen of God. But Sabbatai Zevi was satisfied with the savor of incense. He cherished no great design, or rather, he lived in the delusion that men's expectations would fulfill themselves of their own accord by a miracle. Samuel Primo and some of his confidants appear, however, to have followed a fixed plan, namely, to modify the Rabbinical system, or even to abolish it. That was in reality implied in the reign of the Messiah. The fundamental conception of the Zohar, the Bible of the Kabbalists, is that in the time of grace, in the world of order (Olam ha-Tikkun), the laws of Judaism, the regulations concerning lawful and forbidden things, would completely lose their significance. Now this time, the Sabbatians thought, had already begun; consequently, the minute ritualistic code of the Shulchan Aruch ought no longer to be held binding. Whether Sabbatai himself drew this conclusion, is doubtful. But some of his trusted adherents gave this theory prominence. A certain bitterness towards the Talmud and the Talmudic method of teaching prevailed in this circle. The Sabbatian mystics felt themselves confined by the close meshes of the Rabbinical network, and sought to disentangle it loop by loop. In their wanton extravagance the Kabbalists had so entirely changed the conception of the deity, that it had dwindled away into nothing. On the other hand, they had so exalted and magnified the Messiah, that he was close to God. The Sabbatians, or one of them (Samuel Primo?), built on this foundation. From the Divine bosom (the Ancient of Days), they said, a new divine personage had sprung, capable of restoring the order in the world intended in the original plan of Divine Perfection. This new

person was the Holy King (Malka Kadisha), the Messiah, the Primal Man (Adam Kadmon), who would destroy evil, sin, and` corruption, and cause the dried-up streams of grace to flow again. He, the holy king, the Messiah, is the true God, the redeemer and savior of the world, the God of Israel; to him alone should prayers be addressed. The Holy King, or Messiah, combines two natures--one male, the other female; he can do more on account of his higher wisdom than the Creator of the world. Samuel Primo, who dispatched circulars and ordinances in the name of the Messianic king, often used the signature, "I, the Lord, your God, Sabbatai Zevi." Whether the Smyrna fanatic authorized such blasphemous presumptuousness cannot be decided, any more than whether in his heart he considered the Jewish law null and void. For, although some Sabbatians, who uttered these absurdities, pretended to have heard them from his own lips, other disciples asserted that he was an adherent of traditional Judaism.

The truth probably is that Sabbatai Zevi, absorbed in idle ruminating, accepted everything which the more energetic among his followers taught or suggested. They began the dissolution of Judaism by the transformation of the fast of the tenth of Tebeth (Asara be-Tebeth) into a day of rejoicing. Samuel Primo, in the name of his divinity, directed a circular to the whole of Israel in semi-official form:

"The first-begotten Son of God, Sabbatai Zevi, Messiah and Redeemer of the people of Israel, to all the sons of Israel, Peace ! Since ye have been deemed worthy to behold the great day and the fulfillment of God's word by the prophets, your lament and sorrow must be changed into joy, and your fasting into merriment, for ye shall weep no more. rejoice with song and melody, and change the day formerly spent in sadness and sorrow, into a day of jubilee, because I have appeared."

So firmly rooted in men's minds was faith in Sabbatai Zevi, that the communities which the letter reached in time discontinued this fast, although they believed that they could enter into the kingdom of the Messiah only by strict abstinence. The staunch orthodox party, however, was shocked at this innovation. They could not conceive the Messiah as other than a pious rabbi, who, if possible, would invent fresh burdens. A thousand times had they read in the Zohar, and repeated to one another, that in the time of the Messiah the days of mourning would be changed into days of feasting, and the Law in general would be no longer binding; but when words were changed into deeds, horror seized them. Those rabbis who before had regarded the movement half incredulously, or had not interfered with the penances and deeds of active benevolence to which many of the Sabbatians had felt prompted, thereby giving silent assent, now raised their voice against the law-destroying Messiahship. There began to be formed in every large community a small party of unbelievers (Kofrim), chiefly men learned in the Talmud, who desired to guard the established religion against attacks and disruption.

Rabbinical Judaism and the Kabbala, hitherto in close confederation, began to be at variance with each other; this doubtful ally showing herself at last in her true form as the enemy of Rabbinism. But this sobering discovery, that the Kabbala was a serpent nursed into life by the rabbis themselves, was recognized only by a few. They still remained true to her, imputing the growing hostility to the Shulchan Aruch to Sabbatai and his aiders and abettors. It was too late, their voices were drowned in shouts of joy. Solomon Algazi, and some members of the Smyrna rabbinate who shared his opinions, tried to oppose the abolition of the fast, but were nearly stoned to death by the multitude of believers, and were obliged, like Aaron de la Papa, to leave the city in haste.

But the Messiah was at last forced to tear himself out of his fool's paradise and the atmosphere

SABBATAI SUMMONED TO CONSTANTINOPLE.

of incense in Smyrna, in order to accomplish his work in the Turkish capital--either because his followers compelled him to put his light, not under a bushel, but upon it, that the world at large might see it, or because the cadi could no longer endure the mad behavior of the Jews, and did not wish to bear the sole responsibility. It is said that the cadi gave Sabbatai Zevi three days to go to Constantinople and appear before the highest Turkish authorities. In his delusion, Zevi perhaps believed that a miracle would fulfill the prophecies of Nathan Ghazati and other prophets, that he would easily be able to take the crown from the sultan. He prepared for his journey. Before he left Smyrna, he divided the world among his six-and-twenty faithful ones, and called them kings and princes. His brothers, Elijah and Joseph Zevi, received the lion's share, the former was named king of kings, the latter king of the kings of Judah. To his other faithful followers he disclosed, in Kabbalistic language, which soul of the former kings of Judah or Israel dwelt in each of their bodies, that is, had passed into them by transmigration. Among the better known names were those of the companion of his youth, Isaac Silveira, and Abraham Yachini at Constantinople, who had imparted to him the art of mysticism. Raphael Joseph Chelebi could least of all be passed over; he had been the first firm supporter of the Messiah, and was called King Joash. A Marrano physician, who had escaped from Portugal, and was his devoted adherent, received the crown of Portugal. Even his former opponent Chayim Penya received a kingdom of his own. A beggar, Abraham Rubio of Smyrna, was likewise raised to a throne, under the name of Josiah, and was so firmly convinced of his approaching sovereignty that he refused large sums for his imaginary kingdom Sabbatai Zevi appears purposely to have started on his Messianic journey to Constantinople exactly at the beginning of the mystic year 1666. He was accompanied by some of his followers, his secretary Samuel Primo being in his train. He had announced the day of his arrival at Constantinople, but circumstances proved false to him. The ship in which he sailed had to contend with bad weather, and the voyage was prolonged by weeks. At some place on the coast of the Dardanelles the passengers of the weather-beaten vessel were obliged to land, and there Sabbatai was arrested by Turkish officers, sent to take him prisoner. The grand vizir, Ahmed Coprili, had heard of the excitement of the Jews in Smyrna, and desired to suppress it. The officers had strict orders to bring the pretended redeemer in fetters to the capital, and therefore hastened to meet the ship by which he came. According to orders, they put him in fetters, and brought him to a small town in the neighborhood of Constantinople, because the eve of the Sabbath was near. Informed by a messenger of his arrival at Cheknese Kutschuk, his followers hastened from the capital to see him, but found him in a pitiable plight and in chains. The money which they brought with them procured him some alleviation, and on the following Sunday (February, 1666), he was brought by sea to Constantinople--but in how different a manner to what he and his believers had anticipated ! However, his coming caused excitement. At the landing-place there was such a crowd of Jews and Turks who desired to see the Messiah, that the police were obliged to superintend the disembarkation. An under-pasha commissioned to receive him welcomed him with a vigorous box on the ear. Sabbatai Zevi is said, however, to have wisely turned the other cheek to the blow. Since he could not play the part of the triumphant, he at least wished to play that of the suffering Messiah with good grace. When brought before the deputy-vizir (Kaimakam), Mustapha Pasha, he did not stand the first test brilliantly. Asked what his intentions were, and why he had roused the Jews to such a pitch of excitement, Sabbatai is said to have answered that he was nothing more than a Jewish Chacham, come from]Jerusalem to the capital to collect alms; he could not help it if the Jews testified so much devotion to him. Mustapha thereupon sent him to a prison in which insolvent Jewish debtors were confined.

Far from being disappointed at this treatment, his followers in Constantinople persisted in their delusion. For some days they kept quietly at home, because the street boys mocked them by shouting, "Is he coming ? is he coming? " (Gheldi mi, Gheldi mi.) But they soon began again to assert that he was the true Messiah, and that the sufferings which he had encountered were necessary, a condition to his glorification. The prophets continued to proclaim the speedy redemption of Sabbatai and of all Israel. A Turkish dervish filled the streets of Constantinople with prophecies of the Messiah, whose enemies said that Sabbatai's followers had bribed him. Thousands crowded daily to Sabbatai's place of confinement merely to catch a glimpse of him. English merchants whose claims were not satisfied by their Jewish debtors applied to the Messiah. An order in his handwriting, admonishing defaulters to do justice to their creditors, as otherwise they would have no share in his joy and glory, had the best effect. Samuel Primo took care that most fabulous accounts should reach the Jews of Smyrna and those at a distance, of the reverence paid the Messiah by the Turkish authorities. At heart, he wrote, they were all convinced of his dignity. The expectations of the Jews were raised to a still higher pitch, and the most exaggerated hopes fostered to a greater degree. It was looked upon as a palpable miracle that summary Turkish justice allowed him, the rebellious Jew, to live. Did not this act of mercy prove that he was feared? The Turkish government in fact seems to have stood in awe of the Jewish Messiah. The Cretan war was impending, which demanded all the energy of the half-exhausted Turkish empire. The prudent grand vizir, Ahmed Coprili, did not like to sentence him to death, thus making a fresh martyr, and causing a desperate riot among the Jews. Even the Turks, charmed by Sabbatai's manner, and deceived by extraordinary miraculous manifestations, especially by the prophecies of women and children, joined the ranks of his worshipers. It seemed to Coprili equally dangerous to leave Sabbatai, during his absence at the war, in Constantinople, where he might easily add fuel to the ever-increasing excitement in the capital. He therefore commanded, after Sabbatai had been imprisoned in Constantinople for two months--from the beginning of February to April 17--that he be taken to the castle of the Dardanelles at Abydos, where state-prisoners were wont to be kept in custody. It was a mild confinement; some of his friends, among them Samuel Primo, were allowed to accompany him thither. The Sabbatians called this fortress by a mystical name, the Tower of Strength (Migdal Oz).

If Sabbatai Zevi had doubted himself for a moment, his courage rose through his change of abode, the respectful clemency shown him by the divan, and the steady and increasing devotion of the Jews. He felt himself the Messiah again. On his arrival at the castle of the Dardanelles on April 19, the day of preparation for the Passover, he slew a Paschal lamb for himself and his followers, and ate it with the fat, which is forbidden by the laws of the Talmud. He is said, while doing so, to have used a blessing which implied that the Mosaic, Talmudic, and

Rabbinical law was abrogated--"Blessed be God, who hath restored again that which was forbidden". At Abydos he held regular court with the large sums of money which his brothers and his rich adherents sent him with lavish hand. His wife Sarah, who was allowed to remain with him, demeaned herself as the Messianic queen, and bewitched the multitude by her charms. From the Turkish capital a number of ships conveyed his followers to the castle of the Dardanelles. The fare on vessels rose in consequence daily. From other countries and continents, too, crowds of Jews streamed to the place of his captivity, in the hope to be deemed worthy of beholding him. The governor of the castle reaped advantage thereby, for he charged the visitors entrance money, and raised it to fifteen or thirty marks a head. Even the inhabitants of the place profited, because they could earn high prices for board and lodging. A veritable shower of gold poured into Abydos. The impression which these facts, industriously circulated and exaggerated, made on the Jews in Europe, Asia, and Africa, and the effect which they produced, are indescribable. With few exceptions all were convinced of Sabbatai's Messiahship, and of a speedy redemption, in two years at the latest. They argued that he had had the courage to go to the Turkish capital, although he had openly proclaimed the dethronement of the sultan, yet had not forfeited his life, but had been left in a sort of mock imprisonment. What more was needed to confirm the predictions of prophets of ancient and modern times? The Jews accordingly prepared seriously to return to their original home. In Hungary they began to unroof their houses. In large commercial cities, where Jews took the lead in wholesale business, such as Amsterdam, Leghorn, and Hamburg, stagnation of trade ensued. In almost all synagogues his initials, S and Z, were posted up with more or less adornment. Almost everywhere a prayer for him was inserted in the following form: "Bless our Lord and King, the holy and righteous Sabbatai Zevi, the Messiah of the God of Jacob." In Europe the eyes of all communities were directed to Amsterdam, the representatives of which adhered to the movement most enthusiastically. Every post-day which brought fresh letters was a holiday for them. The Amsterdam Jews showed their joy openly, and were afraid neither of the Christian population nor of the magistrates. Isaac Naar, of Amsterdam, and the rich Abraham Pereira, prepared themselves for a journey to the Messiah, and the former ironically announced it to the unbelieving Jacob Sasportas. The Hamburg community always imitated that of Amsterdam, or went beyond it. The council introduced the custom of praying for Sabbatai Zevi, not only on Saturday, but also on Monday and

Thursday. The unbelievers were compelled to remain in the synagogue and join in the prayer with a loud Amen. And all this was done at the suggestion of the educated physician Bendito de Castro. The believers went so far as to threaten their opponents if they ventured to utter a word of censure against Sabbatai. At Venice, on the Sabbath, a quarrel broke out between the Sabbatians and their opponents, and one of the latter nearly lost his life. When Sabbatai was asked how the Kofrim (unbelievers) should be dealt with, he, or Samuel Primo, answered that they might be put to death without ado, even on the Sabbath; the executors of such punishment were sure to enjoy eternal bliss. A learned Talmudist at Buda, Jacob Ashkenazi of Wilna, whose son and grandson became zealous persecutors of the Sabbatians, was guided by the decision, and declared a member of the community worthy of death, because he would not say the blessing for Sabbatai Zevi. In Moravia (at Nikolsburg) there were such violent dissensions and tumults in consequence of

the craze about the Messiah, that the governor of the province was obliged to post up notices to calm men's minds. At Salee, in the north-western part of Africa, the ruling Emir Gailan (Gailand) ordered a persecution of the Jews, because they too openly displayed the hope of their coming redemption.

The attention bestowed by educated classes of Christians upon the extraordinary events, which were published as news of the day, in turn enhanced the credulity of the Jews. In short, every circumstance tended to increase the deception. Only Jacob Sasportas raised his warning voice against the imposture. He sent letters in all directions, here to point out the absurdity of current rumors, there to collect exact information. He failed to obtain striking evidence of Sabbatai's, or Nathan's, roguery. Forged letters and documents were the order of the day ; conscientiousness and uprightness had utterly disappeared. Thus the mist of false belief grew thicker and thicker, and one was no longer able to get at the truth.

For three months, from April to July, Sabbatai had been leading the life of a prince in the castle of the Dardanelles, intent only upon his own apotheosis. Either from caprice or at Samuel Primo's suggestion, he declared the fast of the 17th Tammuz to be abolished, because on this day he had realized his Messianic character. Was this a mere freak, or was it done with the intention of accustoming his adherents to the abolition of Rabbinical Judaism ? At all events, he appointed the 23d of Tammuz (July 25th), a Monday, to be kept as a strict Sabbath. More than four thousand Jews, men and women, who happened to be at Abydos, celebrated this new Sabbath with great scrupulousness. Sabbatai, or his secretary, sent circulars to the communities directing them to celebrate the next fast, the ninth of Ab, his birthday, as a festival by a special service, with Psalms specially chosen, with eating of choice meats, and the sound of the harp and singing. He is said to have contemplated the annulling of all the Jewish festivals, even the Day of Atonement, and the introduction of others in their stead. But before this could be done, he was guilty in his pride of an act of folly which caused the whole fabric to collapse.

Among the many thousand visitors from far and near, two Poles from Lemberg made a pilgrimage to him, to confirm their faith and feast on his countenance. One was Isaiah, son of a highly-esteemed Rabbinical authority, the aged David Levi (Ture Zahab), and grandson of the no less celebrated Joel Serkes; the other, his half-brother, Leb Herz. From these two Poles Sabbatai heard that in the distant land from which they came, another prophet, Nehemiah Cohen, was announcing the approach of the Messiah's kingdom, but not through Sabbatai. He gave Isaiah Levi a laconic letter to take to his father, in which he promised the Jews of Poland revenge for the massacre by the Cossacks, and peremptorily ordered Nehemiah to come to him with all speed. He laid so much stress on Nehemiah's coming, that he made his followers eager for his arrival. The two Poles traveled back delighted to Lemberg, and everywhere told of the splendor amid which they had seen the Messiah. Nehemiah was ordered to hasten to Sabbatai, and he was not

NEHEMIAH COHEN.

deterred by the length of the journey. When he arrived at Abydos at the beginning of September, he was immediately admitted to an audience which lasted several days. The Polish prophet and the Smyrna Messiah did not laugh in one another's faces, like two augurs, but carried on a grave discussion. The subject of their mystical conversation remained unknown, as may be imagined. It was said to concern the forerunner of the Messiah--the Messiah of Ephraim--whether or not he had appeared and perished, as had been predicted. Nehemiah was not convinced by the long argument, and did not conceal the fact. On this account, the fanatical Sabbatians are said to have secretly made signs to one another to do away with this dangerous Pole. He fortunately escaped from the castle, betook himself forthwith to Adrianople, to the Kaimakam Mustapha, became a Mahometan, and betrayed the fantastic and treasonable designs which Sabbatai Zevi cherished, and which, he said, had remained unknown to the government, only because the overseer of the castle of Dardanelles had an interest in the concourse of Jews.

The Kaimakam conveyed the intelligence to the sultan, Mahomet IV, and the course to he pursued with regard to Sabbatai was maturely considered, the mufti Vanni being also admitted to aid the deliberations. To make short work with the rebellious schemer appeared impracticable to the council, particularly as Mahometans also followed him. If he should fall as a martyr, a new sect might arise, which would kindle fresh disturbances. Vanni, a proselytizing priest, proposed that an attempt be made to bring Sabbatai over to Islam. This advice was followed, and the sultan's physician (Hakim Bashi), a Jewish renegade, by name Guidon, was employed as the medium. A messenger suddenly appeared at Abydos, drove away the Jews, who were besieging the Messiah with homage, conveyed him to Adrianople, and brought him first to the Hakim Bashi, who, as a former co-religionist, would be able to convert him the more easily. The physician represented to him the dreadful punishment that would inevitably befall him if he did not appease the wrath of the sultan by adopting Islam. It is not known whether this call to apostatize from Judaism cost the conceited Messiah great mental conflict. He had not much manly courage, and Judaism, in its existing form, was perhaps dead for him. So he adopted Guidon's advice. The following day (Elul 13, September I4, 1666) he was brought before the sultan. He immediately cast off his Jewish head-dress, in sign of contempt; a page offered him a white Turkish turban and a green instead of the black mantle which he wore, and so his conversion to the Mahometan religion was accomplished. When his dress was changed, it is said that several pounds of biscuit were found in his loose trousers. The sultan was highly pleased at this termination of the movement, gave him the name of Mehmed Effendi, and appointed him his door-keeper--Capigi Bashi Otorak--with a considerable monthly salary; he was to remain near the sultan. The Messiah's wife, Sarah, the Polish rabbi's fair daughter of loose behavior, likewise became a Mahometan, under the name of Fauma Kadin, and received rich presents from the sultana. Some of Sabbatai's followers also went over to Islam. The mufti Vanni instructed them in the Mahometan religion. Sabbatai is said to have married a Mahometan slave, in addition to his wife Sarah, at the command of the mufti. Nehemiah Cohen, who had brought about this sudden change, did not remain in Turkey, but returned to Poland, took off the turban, and lived quietly without breathing a word of what had happened. He disappeared as suddenly as he had come forward. The ex-Messiah

impudently wrote, some days after his conversion, to his brothers at Smyrna: "God has made me an Ishmaelite ; He commanded, and it was done. The ninth day of my regeneration." Nearly at the same time the rabbis and presidents of schools at Amsterdam assembled, and sent a letter of homage to Sabbatai Zevi, to testify their belief in and submission to him. The semi-Spinozist Dionysius (Benjamin) Musaphia, vexed at not being invited, wrote a separate letter to Sabbatai Zevi, signed by himself and two members of the school (Elul 24th). A week later, twenty-four distinguished men of Amsterdam sent another letter of homage to the apostate Messiah. At their head was Abraham Gideon Abudiente. Did these letters reach the Mahometan Mehmed Effendi! At Hamburg, where likewise his conversion was not suspected, the blessing was five times pronounced over the renegade Sabbatai, on the Day of Atonement (October 9, 1666).

But when the rumor of his apostasy went the rounds of the communities, and could no longer be denied, confidence was succeeded by a bewildering sense of disenchantment and shame. The highest representative of Judaism had abandoned and betrayed it! Chayim Benvenisti, the rabbi of Smyrna, who had invested the false Messiah with authority from motives far from honorable, almost died of shame. Mahometans and Christians pointed with scorn at the blind, credulous Jews. The street boys in Turkey openly jeered at Jewish passers-by. But this ridicule was not all. So widespread a commotion could not die out and leave no trace. The sultan thought of destroying all the Jews in his empire, because they had formed rebellious plans, and of ordering all children under seven to be brought up in Islam. The newly converted Mahometan, Mehmed Effendi, in order to revenge himself, is said to have betrayed his own plans, and the consent of the Jews thereto. Two councilors and the sultana-mother are reported to have dissuaded the sultan from his design by the observation that the Jews ought to be regarded as having been misled. Fifty chief rabbis, however, because they had neglected their duty in teaching the people, were to be executed--twelve from Constantinople, twelve from Smyrna, and the remaining twenty-six from the other communities in Turkey. It was regarded as a special miracle that this resolution remained a dead letter, and that the Jews did not even have to pay a fine. The division in the communities might have had even worse consequences, if the unbelievers had heaped scorn and mockery upon the late devotees. But the colleges of rabbis in the East interposed, and sought to appease and reconcile, and threatened to excommunicate any one who, by word or deed, offended a former Sabbatian.

Although men's minds were calmed for the moment, it was long before peace was restored. After the first surprise at Sabbatai's conversion was over, his zealous followers, especially at Smyrna, began to recover. They could not persuade themselves that they had really been running after a shadow. There must be, or have been, some truth in Sabbatai's Messianic claims, since all signs so entirely agreed. The Kabbalists easily got over objections. Sabbatai had not turned Mahometan; a phantom had played that part, while he himself had retired to heaven or to the Ten Tribes, and would soon appear again to accomplish the work of redemption. Others, such as Samuel Primo, Jacob Faliachi, Jacob Israel Duchan, who had designed, through him, to bring about the fall of Rabbinical Judaism, and would not abandon their plan lightly, still

clung to him. The prophets, who had been manifestly proved false through his conversion, were most interested in remaining true to him. They did not care quietly to renounce their functions and withdraw into obscurity, or be laughed at. The prophets residing at Smyrna, Constantinople, Rhodes, and Chios were silenced; but the itinerant prophets, Nathan Ghazati and Sabbatai Raphael, did not choose to abdicate. The former had remained in Palestine during Sabbatai's triumph in order to be paid homage on his own account. After the deception was unmasked he regarded himself as no longer safe ; he made preparations to go to Smyrna, and continued to send out his mystical, bombastic letters. From Damascus he warned the Jews of Aleppo by letter not to allow themselves to be discouraged by strange circumstances in their belief in the Messiah; there was a deep mystery shortly to be revealed; but wherein the mystery consisted could not yet be disclosed. By these circulars the credulous were confirmed afresh in their delusion. In Smyrna many synagogues continued to insert the blessing for Sabbatai in their prayers. Hence the rabbis were obliged to interfere vigorously, especially the rabbinate of the Turkish capital. They laid under a ban all who should even pronounce the name of Sabbatai', or converse with his followers, and threatened to hand them over to the secular arm. Nathan Ghazati, in particular, was excommunicated, and everyone warned against harboring him or approaching him (Kislev 12, December 9, 1666). These sentences of excommunication were so far effectual that Nathan could not stay anywhere for any length of time, and even in Smyrna he could remain only a short time in secret at the house of a believer. But the rabbis were not able entirely to exorcise the imposture. One of the most zealous Sabbatians, probably Samuel Primo, who was ready in invention, threw out a more effective suggestion than that of mock conversion. All had been ordained as it had come to pass. Precisely by his going over to Islam had Sabbatai proved himself the Messiah. It was a Kabbalistic mystery which some writings had announced beforehand. As the first redeemer Moses was obliged to reside for some time at Pharaoh's court, not as an Israelite, but to all appearance an Egyptian, even so must the last redeemer live some time at a heathen court, apparently a heathen, "outwardly sinful, but inwardly pure." It was Sabbatai's task to free the lost emanations of the soul, which pervade even Mahometans, and by identifying them with himself, as it were, bring them back to the fountain-head. By redeeming souls in all circles, he was most effectually furthering the kingdom of the Messiah. This suggestion was a lucky hit; it kindled anew the flame of the imposture. It became a watchword for all Sabbatians enabling them, with decency and a show of reason, to profess themselves believers, and hold together.

Nathan Ghazati also caught up this idea, and was encouraged to resume his part as prophet. He had fared badly so far; he had been obliged secretly to leave Smyrna, where he had been in hiding several months (end of April, 1667). His followers, consisting of more than thirty men, were dispersed. But by this new imposture he recovered courage, and approached Adrianople, where Mehmed Effendi presided, attended by several of his adherents, who as pretended Mahometans lived and made fantastic plans with him. The representatives of the Jewish community at Constantinople and Adrianople rightly feared fresh disturbances from the presence of the false prophet, and desired to get rid of him. Nathan Ghazati, however, relied on his prophecy, which might possibly, he said, be fulfilled at the end of the year. He expected the Holy Spirit to descend upon the renegade Mehmed on the Feast of

Weeks (Pentecost), and then he also would be able to show signs and wonders. Until then, he defiantly replied to the deputies, he could entertain no propositions. When the Feast of Weeks was over, the people of Adrianople again urged him to cease from his juggleries. After much labor they obtained only a written promise to keep at a distance of twelve days' journey from the city, not to correspond with Sabbatai, not to assemble people round him, and if by the end of the year the Redeemer did not appear, to consider his prophecies false. In spite of his written promise, this lying prophet continued his agitation, and admonished the Sabbatians in Adrianople to make known their continued adhesion by the suspension of the fast on the 17th of Tammuz. In this city there was a Sabbatian conventicle under the leadership of a former disciple, who stood in close connection with Mehmed Effendi. The rabbinate of Adrianople did not know how to check the mischievous course of this daring sect, and were obliged to have recourse to falsehood. They announced that the renegade had suddenly appeared before the Jewish communal council, had repented of his imposture, and laid the blame on Nathan and Abraham Vachini, who had made him their dupe. In this way the rabbinate succeeded in deceiving the Sabbatians. The effect did not last long. Nathan on the one hand, and Mehmed Effendi's circle on the other, awakened new hope, the number of believers again increased, and they made a special point of not fasting on the 9th of Ab, the birthday of their Messiah. The rabbinates of Constantinople and Smyrna sought to repress this imposture by the old means--excommunication and threats of punishment (end of July)--but with little success. The Sabbatians had a sort of hankering after martyrdom in order to seal their faith. The false prophet renewed his propagandism. He still had some followers, including two Mahometans. At Salonica, the home of a swarm of Kabbalists, he fared badly. The more easily did he find a hearing in the communities of the islands of Chios and Corfu. His hopes were however directed principally to Italy.

Here also confusion continued to reign. The first news of Sabbatai's defection had not been confirmed, as in consequence of the war in Crete the ships of the Christians had been captured by the Turks. Thus the Sabbatians were left free to maintain their faith and denounce the report as false, especially as encouraging letters arrived from Raphael Joseph Chelebi of Cairo and others. The most absurd stories of Sabbatai's power and dignity at the Porte were published in Italy, and found credence. Moses Pinheiro, Sabbatai's old companion, Raphael Sofino at Leghorn, and the Amsterdam fanatics, Isaac Naar and Abraham Pereira, who had gone to Italy to search for the Messiah, had a special interest in clinging to straws; they feared ridicule as dupes. The ignorant mountebank and strolling prophet, Sabbatai Raphael, from the Morea, then residing in Italy, was bent upon deception and fraud, and appears to have reaped a good harvest there. When at last there could be no doubt of Sabbatai's change of religion, Raphael turned his steps to Germany, where, on account of defective postal arrangements and the slight intercourse of Jews with the outer world, they had only a vague idea of the course of events, and took the most foolish stories for truth. Sabbatai Raphael was there regarded as a prophet; but, as he expected greater gain from the rich Amsterdam community, he betook himself thither (September, 1667). Here also the imposture continued. Ashamed that they, the shrewd and educated Portuguese, should have been so signally deceived, they at first placed no faith in the news of Sabbatai's treachery. Even the rabbis Isaac Aboab, Raphael Moses d'Aguilar, and the

NATHAN GHAZATI IN ITALY.

philosophical skeptic Musaphia, remained staunch. Justly Jacob Sasportas laughed them to scorn, especially Musaphia, on account of his present unshaken faith as contrasted with his former incredulity.

Meanwhile Nathan Ghazati, the prophet of Gaza was pursuing his mischievous course in Italy. Coming from Greece, he landed at Venice (end of March, 1668), but the rabbinate and the council, who had had warning of him, would not allow him to enter the Ghetto. A Sabbatian interceded for him with some Christians of rank, and under such protection he could not be expelled. To cure those who had shared in the delusion, the rabbinate wrung from him a written confession, that his prophecies of Sabbatai Zevi's Messiahship rested on a freak of his imagination, that he recognized them as such, and held them to be idle. This confession was printed with an introduction by the rabbinate of Venice, in order at last to open the eyes of the Sabbatians in Italy. But it was not of much avail. The delusion, resting as it did on the Kabbala, was too deeply rooted. From Venice Ghazati was sent to Leghorn, with the suggestion to render him innocuous there, where Jews enjoyed more freedom; but Nathan Ghazati secretly escaped to Rome, cut off his beard, disguised himself, and is said to have thrown notes written in Chaldee into the Tiber, to bring about the destruction of Rome. The Jews recognized him, and, since they feared danger for themselves on papal soil from his fraudulent absurdities, they procured his banishment. Then he went to Leghorn, and found followers there also. Promising himself more honor and profit in Turkey, or more opportunity to satisfy his restless mind, Nathan returned to Adrianople. He did not pay great regard to word and oath. Nathan Ghazati compiled much Kabbalistic nonsense, but acquired no fame. He is said to have died at Sophia, and to have been laid in a vault dug by himself (1680). Other men appeared at the head of the Sabbatians who far surpassed him, and pursued a definite end.

Sabbatai, or Mehmed Effendi, at this time began his revolutionary chimeras afresh. Immediately after his apostasy he was obliged, under the direction of the mufti Vanni, to acquire Mahometan ways, and guard carefully against any appearance of inclination to Judaism and the Jews. He therefore figured as a pious Mahometan. Gradually he was permitted greater freedom, and to give utterance to his Kabbalistic views about God and the universe. Vanni, to whom much was new, heard his expositions with curiosity, and the sultan also is said to have listened to his words attentively. Probably Sabbatai won over some Mahometans to his Kabbalistic dreams. Weary of quiet, and anxious to play an active part again, he once more entered into close relations with Jews, and gave out that he had been filled anew with the Holy Spirit at Passover (end of March, 1668), and had received revelations. Sabbatai, or one of his aiders and abettors, published a mystical work (" Five Evidences of the Faith," Sahaduta di Mehemnuta) addressed to the Jews and couched in extravagant language, in which the following fantastic views were set forth: Sabbatai had been and remained the true Redeemer; it would be easy to prove himself such, if he had not compassion on Israel, who would have to experience the same dreadful sufferings as the Messiah; and he only persisted in Islam in order to bring thousands and tens of thousands of non-Jews over to Israel. To the sultan and the mufti, on the other hand, he said that his approximation to the Jews was intended to bring them over to Islam. He received permission to associate with Jews, and to preach before them at Adrianople, even in synagogues. Thus he played the part of Jew at one time, of Muslim at another. If Turkish spies

ABRAHAM MICHAEL CARDOSO.

were present, his Jewish hearers knew how to deceive them. They threw away their Jewish headdress, and put on the turban. It is probable that many Jews were seriously converted to Islam, and a Jewish-Turkish sect thus began to form round Sabbatai Zevi. The Jews who had hitherto felt such horror of apostatizing, that only the outcasts amongst them went over to Christianity or Islam, became less severe. They said without indignation that so and so had adopted the turban. Through such jugglery Sabbatians at Adrianople, Smyrna, Salonica, and other cities, even in Palestine, allowed themselves to be confirmed in their obstinate faith in the Messiah. Even pious men, learned in the Talmud, continued to adhere to him.

As though this complication were to become more involved, and the Kabbalistic-Messianic disorder were to be pursued to its utmost limits, a Sabbatian champion unexpectedly appeared in a man of European culture, not wanting in gifts, Abraham Michael Cardoso. He was an original character, a living personification of the transformation of the Portuguese Jews after their expulsion. Born of Marrano parents in a small town of Portugal, Celarico, in the province of Beira, Mislel Cardoso, like his elder brother Fernando, studied medicine. While the latter devoted himself earnestly to science, Miguel dawdled away his days amidst the luxury of Madrid, sang love-songs with the guitar under the balconies of fair ladies, and paid very little heed to Kabbala or Judaism. What influenced him to leave Spain is not known. Perhaps his more serious and thoughtful brother, who, after making a name in Spain as a medical and scientific author, out of love to Judaism migrated to Venice, where he plunged deeply into Jewish literature, infected him with enthusiasm. Both brothers assumed Jewish names after their return to the religion of their forefathers. The elder, Isaac Cardoso, gave up his name Fernando; the younger took the name of Abraharn in addition to that of Miguel (Michael). Both composed verses in Spanish. While the elder brother led a regular life, guided by moral principles and a rational faith, the younger fell under the sway of extravagant fancy and an eccentric manner of living. Isaac Cardoso (born 1615, died after 1680) conferred renown on Judaism, while Abraham Michael Cardoso (born about 1630, died 1706) was a disgrace to it.

The latter lived as a physician at Leghorn, but not flourishing he accepted the position of physician in ordinary to the Bey of Tripoli. His warm-blooded, dissolute nature was a hindrance to his advancement. Contrary to the custom of African Jews, he married two wives, and instead of employing himself with his difficult science, he revolved fantastical schemes. Cardoso appears to have been initiated into the Kabbala and the Sabbatian delusion by Moses Pinheiro, who was living at Leghorn.

He continually had dreams and visions, which increased in frequency after the public appearance of Sabbatai at Smyrna and Constantinople. He communicated his delusion to his wives and domestics, who likewise pretended to have seen all sorts of apparitions. The apostasy of the false Messiah from Judaism did not cure Cardoso of his delusion; he remained a zealous partisan, and even justified the treachery of the Messiah by saying that it was necessary for him to be counted among sinners, in order that he might atone for Israel's sin of idolatry, and blot it out. He sent circulars in all directions, in order to support the Messianic claim of Sabbatai, and figure as a prophet. In vain his more sober brother, Isaac Cardoso, warned and ridiculed him, asking him ironically, whether he had received the gift of prophecy from his former gallantries and from playing the guitar for the fair maidens of Madrid. Abraham Cardoso's frivolity was in no way

lessened, he even assumed a didactic tone towards his grave elder brother, who despised the Kabbala as he did alchemy and astrology, and sent him numberless proofs, from the Zohar and other Kabbalistic writings, that Sabbatai was the true Messiah, and that he must necessarily be estranged from Judaism. By his zeal he gained many adherents for the Sabbatian delusion in Africa; but he also made enemies, and incurred dangers. He continued to prophesy the speedy commencement of the Messiah's reign, although often proved false by reality. He put off the event from year to year, performed Kabbalistic tricks, set up a new God for Israel, and at last declared himself the Messiah of the house of Ephraim, until he was rigorously prosecuted by an opponent of these vagaries. Cardoso was driven back to his former uncomfortable position, forced to lead an adventurer's life, and win bread for himself and his family, so to speak, by his delusions, going through all sorts of jugglery, at Smyrna, at Constantinople, in the Greek islands, and at Cairo, and promoting the Sabbatian delusions with his abundant knowledge, eloquent tongue, and ready pen. Thanks to his education in Christian schools, he was far superior to other Sabbatian apostles, and knew how to give an air of rationality and wisdom to nonsense, thus completely blinding the biased, and stultifying even those averse to the Sabbatian movement.

Encouraged by the support of the Jews, continued in spite of his change of religion, Sabbatai persisted in keeping up his character as Messiah, and associated more and more with Jews. His weak brain had been turned by the overwhelming rush of events, and he completely lost balance. At one time he reviled Judaism and the God of Israel with foul words of abuse, and is said even to have informed against Jews as blasphemers of Islam before Turkish magistrates. At other times he held divine service according to the Jewish ritual with his Jewish followers, sang psalms, expounded the Zohar, ordered selections from the Torah to be read on the Sabbath, and frequently chose seven virgins for that purpose. On account of his constant intercourse with Jews, whom he was not able to bring over wholesale to Mahometanism, as he may have boastfully asserted, Mehmed Effendi is said to have fallen into disfavor, forfeited his allowance and been banished from Adrianople to Constantinople. He finally married another wife, the daughter of a man learned in the Talmud, Joseph Philosoph of Salonica. The Turkish patrol having surprised him in a village (Kuru Cisme) near Constantinople, while singing psalms in a tent with some Jews, and the Bostanji Bashi (officer) having reported it, the grand vizir commanded the Kaimakam to banish him to Dulcigno, a small town in Albania, where no Jews dwelt. There he died, abandoned and forsaken, it was afterwards said, on the Day of Atonement, 1676.

Spinoza, who had likewise broken away from Judaism, may well have looked with great contempt on this Messianic craze of his contemporaries. If he had cared to dig the grave of Judaism and bury it, he would have been obliged to recognize Sabbatai Zevi, his private secretary, Samuel Primo, and his prophets, as allies and abettors. The irrationality of the Kabbala brought Judaism much more effectually into discredit than reason and philosophy. At this time, when two forces of Jewish origin were antagonizing Judaism in the East and the West, the Portuguese community, increased to the number of four thousand families, undertook (1671) the building of a synagogue, and after some years finished work, which had been interrupted by war The dedication of the synagogue (Ab 10, August 2, 1675),

was celebrated with great solemnity and pomp. Neither the first Temple of Solomon, nor the second of Zerubbabel, nor the third of Herod, was so much lauded with song and eloquent speech as the new one at Amsterdam, called Talmud Torah. Copper-plate engravings, furnished with inscriptions in verse, were published. Christians likewise took part in the dedication. They advanced money to the Jews in the times of need, and a poet, Romein de Hooghe, composed verses in honor of the synagogue and the Jewish people in Latin, Dutch, and French.

Spinoza lived to see this rejoicing of the community from which he had become a pervert. He happened to be at Amsterdam just at the time. He was engaged in seeing through the press a treatise (Ethics) which reversed the views hitherto prevailing, and the second, enlarged edition of his other work, chiefly directed against Judaism. He may have laughed at the joy of the Amsterdam Jews, as idle; but the building of this synagogue in a city which a hundred years before had tolerated no Jews and had supported a Spanish Inquisition, was loud testimony of the times, and contradicted many of his assertions. He died not long afterwards, or rather, passed gently away as with a divine kiss (February 21, 1677), about five months after Sabbatai Zevi. Against his will he has contributed to the glory of the race which he so unjustly reviled. His powerful intellect, logical acumen, and strength of character are more and more recognized as properties which he owed to the race from which he was descended. Among educated Jews, Isaac Orobio de Castro alone attempted a serious refutation of Spinoza's philosophical views. Though his intention was good, he was too weak to break through the close meshes of Spinoza's system. It was left to history to refute it with facts.

V. CHAPTER VII:

THE AGE OF LUZZATTO AND FRANK

Poetical Works of Moses Chayim Luzzatto--Luzzatto ensnared in the Kabbala--His Contest with Rabbinical Authorities--Luzzatto's last Drama--Jacob Frank Lejbowicz and the Frankists--Excesses of the Frankists.

1727-1760 C.E.

Moses Chayim Luzzatto (born 1707, died 1747) was the son of very wealthy parents, natives of Padua. His father, who carried on an extensive silk business, spared no expense in educating him. The two ancient languages, Hebrew and Latin, which in Italy were in a measure a literary necessity, the one among Jews, the other among Christians, Luzzatto acquired in early youth; but they had an influence on his mind altogether different from that which they obtained over his contemporaries. Both enriched his genius, and promoted its higher development. Latin opened for him the realm of the beautiful, Hebrew the gates of the sublime. Luzzatto had a poet's delicately-strung soul, an Aeolian harp, which responded to every breath with harmonious, tuneful vibrations. His poetic gift displayed at once power and sweetness, wealth of fancy and richness of imagery, combined with due sense of proportion. A believer in the transmigration of souls might have said that the soul of the Hebrew-Castilian singer, Yehuda Halevi, had been born again in Luzzatto, but had become more perfect, more matured, more tender, and endowed with a more delicate sense of harmony, encompassed as he was by the musical atmosphere of his Italian fatherland. Even in early boyhood every event, joyful or sad, was to him a complete picture, a little work of art, wherein color and euphony were revealed together. A youth of seventeen, he discerned with such remarkable clearness the hidden charm of language, the laws of harmony, deducible from the higher forms of eloquence as from poetry, and the grace of rhythm and cadence, that he composed a work on the subject, and illustrated it by beautiful examples from sacred poetry. He contemplated introducing a new meter into modern Hebrew poetry, in order to obtain greater variety in the succession of long and short syllables, and thus produce a musical cadence. The Hebrew language is usually classified among the dead tongues. [This was written in the mid-19th century--ed]. To Luzzatto, however, it was full of life, vigor, youth, clearness, and euphony. He used Hebrew as a. pliant instrument, and drew from it sweet notes and caressing melodies; he renewed its youth, invested it with a peculiar charm, in short, lived in it as though his ear had absorbed the rich tones of Isaiah's eloquence. Incomparably more gifted than Joseph Penso de la Vega, Luzzatto, likewise in his seventeenth year, composed a drama on the biblical theme of Samson and the Philistines. This early work gives promise of the future master. The versification is faultless, the thoughts original, and the language free from bombast and redundancy. His Hebrew prose, too, is an agreeable contrast to the insipid, ornate, and laboriously witty style of his Jewish contemporaries; it has much of the simplicity, polish, and vivacity of the biblical narrative. Before his twentieth year Luzzatto had composed one hundred and fifty-hymns, which are only an imitation of the old psalter, but the language of which is marked by fervor and purity. It was

ENSNARED BY THE KABBALA.

perhaps during the same period that he composed his second Hebrew drama, in four acts--"The High Tower, or The Innocence of the Virtuous"--beautiful in versification, melodious in language, but poor in thought. The young poet had not yet seen life in its fullness, nor keenly studied its contrasts and struggles. He was acquainted only with idyllic family life and academic peace. Even virtue and vice, love and selfishness, which he desired to represent in his drama, were known to him but by hearsay. His muse becomes eloquent only when she sings of God's sublimity. Isolated verses are faultless, but the work as a whole is that of a schoolboy. He was too dependent on Italian models--still walked on stilts.

This facility and versatility in clothing both platitudes and original thoughts in new as well as borrowed forms, and the over-abundance of half-matured ideas, which, if he could have perfected them, might have proved a blessing to Judaism and to himself, were transformed into a curse. One day (Sivan, 1727) he was seized with the desire to imitate the mystic language of the Zohar, and he succeeded as well as in the case of the psalms. His sentences and expressions were deceptively similar to those of his model, just as high-sounding, apparently full of meaning, in reality meaningless. This success turned his head, and led him astray. Instead of perceiving that if the Kabbalistic style of the Zohar is capable of imitation, that book must be the work of a clever human author, Luzzatto inferred that his own creative faculty did not proceed from natural endowments, but, as in the case of the Zohar, was the product of a higher inspiration. In other words, he shared the mistaken view of his age with respect to the origin and value of the Kabbala. Isaiah Bassan, of Padua--who instructed Luzzatto in his early years--had infused mystical poison into his healthy blood. However, any other teacher would also have led him into the errors of the Kabbala, from which there was no escape. The air of the Ghettos was impregnated with Kabbala. From his youth upwards Luzzatto heard daily that great adepts in mysticism possessed special tutelar spirits (Maggid), who every day gave them manifestations from above. Why should not he, too, be vouchsafed this divine gift of grace? Some of the mystical writings of Lurya, at that time still a rarity, fell into his hands. He learnt them by heart, became entirely absorbed in them, and thus completed his derangement. Luzzatto was possessed by a peculiar delusion. His naturally clear and methodical intellect, his fine sense of the simplicity and beauty of the poetry of the Bible, and his aesthetic conceptions with regard to Italian and Latin literature urged him to seek clearness and common sense even in the chaos of the Kabbala, the divine origin of which was accepted by him as a fact. He in no way resembled the wild visionaries Moses Zacut and Mordecai of Eisenstadt ; he did not content himself with empty formulas and flourishes, but sought for sound sense. This he found rather in his own mind than in the Zohar or in the writings of Lurya. Nevertheless, he lived under the delusion that a divine spirit had vouchsafed him deep insight into the Kabbala, solved its riddles, and disentangled its meshes. Self-deception was the cause of his errors, and religious fervor, instead of protecting, only plunged him in more deeply. His errors were fostered by the conviction that existing Judaism with its excrescences would be unintelligible without the Kabbala, the theories of which could alone explain the phenomena, the strife, and the contradictions in the world, and the tragical history of the Jewish people. Israel--God's people--the noblest portion of creation, stands enfeebled and abased on the lowest rung of the ladder of nations; its religion misjudged, its struggles fruitless. To account for this

THE NEW ZOHAR.

bewildering fact, Luzzatto constructed a system of cobwebs.

It flattered the vanity of this young man of twenty to gain this insight into the relations of the upper and the lower worlds, to explain them in the mystical language of the Zohar, and thus become an important member in the series of created beings. Having firmly convinced himself of the truth of the fundamental idea of the Kabbala, he accepted all its excrescences--transmigration of souls, anagrams, and necromancy. He wrote reams of Kabbalistic chimeras, and composed a second Zohar (Zohar Tinyana) with appropriate introductions (Tikkunim) and appendices. The more facility he acquired, the. stronger became his delusion that he, too, was inspired by a great spirit, and was a second, perhaps more perfect Simon bar Yochai. Little by little there crept over him in his solitude the fantastic conviction that he was the pre-ordained Messiah, called to redeem, by means of the second Zohar, the souls of Israel and the whole world.

Luzzatto could not long bear to hide his light under a bushel. He began operations by disclosing to Israel Marini and Israel Treves, two young men of the same way of thinking as himself that his guardian spirit had bidden him grant them knowledge of his new Zohar. His disciples in the Kabbala were dazzled and delighted, and could not keep the secret. The result was that Venetian Kabbalists sought out the young and wealthy prodigy at his home in Padua, and thus confirmed him in his fanaticism. A vivacious, energetic, impetuous Pole, Yekutiel (Kussiel) of Wilna, who had come to Padua to study medicine, joined Luzzatto's circle. To hear of the latter,join him, abandon his former studies, and devote himself to mysticism was for the Pole a rapid, easy resolution. It was far harder for him to keep the secret. No sooner had he been initiated by Luzzatto than he blazoned forth this new miracle to the world. Kussiel circulated extravagant letters on the subject, which came into the hands of Moses Chages in Altona. The latter, who had stoutly opposed and effectually silenced Chayon and the other Sabbatian visionaries, was, so to speak, the recognized official zealot, whose utterances were decisive on matters of faith; and the rabbi of the so-called "three communities" of Altona, Hamburg, and Wandsbeck, Ezekiel Katzenellenbogen, who had excommunicated Moses Meir Kamenker and his confederates, was subservient to him. Chages therefore requested the Venetian community to suppress the newly-born brood of heretics before the poison of their doctrine could spread further.

The Venetian community, however, was not disposed to denounce Luzzatto as a heretic, but treated him with great forbearance, probably out of consideration for his youth, talents, and the wealth of his family, and merely ordered him to justify himself. The enthusiastic youth rebelled against this demand, proudly gave Chages to understand that he did not recognize his authority, repudiated the suspicion of Sabbatian heresy, and insisted that he had been vouchsafed revelations from Heaven. He referred him to his instructor Bassan, who would never refuse to testify that his orthodoxy was above suspicion. In this Luzzatto was perfectly right. Bassan was so infatuated with his pupil that he would have palliated his most scandalous faults, and encouraged rather than checked his extravagances. In vain Chages and Katzenellenbogen threatened him and the Paduan community with the severest form of excommunication, if he did not abandon his pretensions to second sight and mystical powers. Luzzatto remained unmoved: God had chosen him, like many before, to reveal to him His mysteries. The other Italian rabbis showed themselves as lukewarm in the matter as those of Padua and Venice. Moses Chages called on three rabbis to form a tribunal,

LUZZATTO UNDER SURVEILLANCE.

but all three declined to interfere. He exerted himself so zealously, however, that he persuaded several German rabbis (June, I730) to excommunicate all who should compose works in the language of the Zohar in the name of angels or saints. This threat proved effectual. Isaiah Bassan was obliged to repair to Padua and obtain a promise from his favorite disciple to discontinue his mystical writings and his instruction of young Kabbalists, or emigrate to the Holy Land. At last the Venetian rabbinate was stirred up to intervene, and sent three representatives to Padua--Jacob Belillos, Moses Menachem Merari, and Nehemiah Vital Cohen--in whose presence Luzzatto was obliged to repeat his promise under oath. He was compelled to deliver his Kabbalistic writings to his teacher Bassan, and they were placed under seal. Thus the storm which had threatened him was averted.

Luzzatto appears to have been sobered by these events. He occupied himself with his business, wrote more poetry, and resolved to marry. He was a happy father, lived in concord with his parents and brothers and sisters, and was highly respected. The evil spirit, however, to whom he had sold himself would not release him, and led him back to his youthful follies. A quarrel in the family and business misfortunes in connection with his father's house, in which he was a partner, appear to have been the cause of this renewal of his former studies. Disquieted and troubled in the present he sought to learn the future by means of Kabbalistic arts. He began once more to write down his mystical fancies, and ventured to show them to Bassan, from whom he obtained permission to publish them. It was whispered that Luzzatto performed incantations by means of magic, and that his teacher had handed him for publication some of the sealed writings in his custody. The Venetian council of rabbis, owing to certain reports, was especially excited and prejudiced against him. Luzzatto had written a sharp reply to Leon Modena's forcible work against the Kabbala; and as the latter was a Venetian rabbi, though of doubtful sincerity, the members of the Venetian council, Samuel Aboab and his five colleagues, considered any attack upon him an insult to their own honor. Their esprit de corps roused them to greater activity than had zeal for their faith, when seemingly in peril. True Venetians, they had in their service a spy, Salman of Lemberg, who watched and reported Luzzatto's movements to them. As long as he was prosperous and surrounded by friends the Venetian rabbis had treated him with remarkable indulgence,and bestowed on him a title of honor; but after his family fell into misfortune, when he was on the verge of ruin, and deserted by his friends and flatterers, their regard for him ceased, and they could not find enough stones to throw at him. They believed one of their number who asserted that he had found implements of magic in Luzzatto's house. Absurdly enough, too, they reproached Luzzatto with having learnt Latin; to a man who had studied this language of Satan no angel, they said, could appear ! The members of the Venetian council of rabbis believed, or pretended to believe that Luzzatto had boasted that in the Messianic age his psalms would take the place of David's psalter. They now showed themselves as active as they had previously been negligent in the persecution of the unfortunate author. They sent three inquisitors to Padua to examine him, search his house for writings, and make him declare on oath that he would publish nothing without first submitting it to the censorship of the Venetian council of rabbis. The poet, deeply mortified, haughtily answered that this council had no authority whatever over him, a member of the community of Padua. The Venetian rabbis then excommunicated him, and condemned his writings to the flames

LUZZATTO EXCOMMUNICATED.

(December, 1734), taking care to give notice of their proceedings to all the communities in Germany, particularly to the "big drum," Chages. The Paduan community also abandoned the unfortunate Luzzatto. To the honor of his teacher Isaiah Bassan be it said, that he adhered to him as staunchly in misfortune as in prosperity. The rabbi Katzenellenbogen, or rather his crier Chages, on this occasion made the sensible suggestion that the study of the Kabbala be altogether forbidden to young men, to prevent their falling into deplorable errors, as had hitherto been the case ; but the proposition failed to meet with the approbation of other rabbis. Twenty years later the evils produced by the Kabbala became so patent, that the synod of Polish Jews enacted a decree to the above effect without encountering opposition.

The unfortunate, excommunicated dreamer was obliged to leave his parents, his wife and child, and go forth a wanderer; but what grieved him even more was separation from his fellow Kabbalists and his mystic conventicle. He cherished the hope of being able to print his Kabbalistic writings in Amsterdam. Alas for his want of experience! Who would help him after fortune had turned her back ! At Frankfort-on-the-Main he was rudely awakened from his pleasant dream. As soon as the rabbi, Jacob Kahana, heard of his arrival, he insisted that he should promise on oath to abandon his Kabbalistic illusions, and to refrain from writing on or instructing any one in the doctrines of the Zohar (January 12, 1735)· One liberty, however, Luzzatto reserved for himself: to pursue his favorite studies at the age of forty in the Holy Land. Many rabbis of Germany, Poland, Holland, and Denmark, who were informed of Luzzatto's concessions, agreed in advance to his excommunication in case he should break his word. The name of Chages was of course upon the list.

Deeply humiliated and disappointed, Luzzatto repaired to Amsterdam. Here a gleam of sunlight smiled on him again. The Portuguese community received him kindly, as though desirous of atoning for the injustice he had experienced at the hands of the Germans and Poles. They granted him a pension; and he found a hospitable home in the house of Moses de Chaves, a wealthy Portuguese, and became instructor to his son. To be independent, he applied himself, like Spinoza, to the polishing of lenses, and this led him to study physics and mathematics. He found himself so comfortably settled that he induced not only his wife, but also his parents to come to Amsterdam, and they were well received by the Portuguese community. This favorable turn in his fortunes encouraged him to resume his chimerical theories. He repeatedly exhorted his disciples in Padua to remain true to their Kabbalistic studies; whereupon the council of rabbis at Venice, which had received intelligence of his proceedings, pronounced sentence of excommunication in the synagogues and in the Ghetto against all who possessed Kabbalistic writings or psalms of Luzzatto, and failed to deliver them to the council.

In addition to his various occupations, with the Kabbala for his spiritual wants and the polishing of lenses for his temporal needs, Luzzatto published a masterpiece second to none in Hebrew poetry; a drama, perfect in form, language, and thought ; a memorial of his gifts calculated to immortalize him and the language in which it is composed. Under the unpretentious form of an occasional poem in honor of the wedding of his disciple, Jacob de Chaves, with the high-born maiden Rachel de Vega Enriques, he published his drama, "Glory to the Virtuous" (La-Yesharim Tehilia). It differs materially from his earlier works. The poet had in the interval enjoyed various opportunities of gaining

LA-YESHARIM TEHILLA.

pleasant and painful experiences, and of enriching his mental powers. His muse, grown more mature, had become acquainted with the intricacies of life. Luzzatto had learnt to know the vulgar herd well enough to see that it resembles a reed swaying to and fro in the water, and is kept by the fetters of Deceit in a state of ignorance and infirmity against which Wisdom herself is powerless. He had been taught by experience how Folly yoked with Ignorance makes merry over those born of the Spirit, and mocks at their labors, when they measure the paths of the stars, observe the life of the vegetable world, behold God's works, and account them of more value than Mammon. Superficiality sees in all the events of life and of nature, however powerfully they may appeal to the heart, only the sport of Chance or the inflexible laws of heartless Necessity. Luzzatto had proved in his own case that Craft and Pride closely united can deprive Merit of its crown, and place it on their own heads. None the less he cherished the conviction that Merit, though misjudged and calumniated, at last wins the day, and that its acknowledgment (Fame) will fall to its share like a bride, if only it allows itself to be led by Reason and her handmaid Patience, averting its gaze from ignoble strife, and becoming absorbed in the wonders of Creation. "Could we, with undimmed eyes, for a moment see the world as it is, divested of pretense, we should see Pride and Folly, which speak so scornfully of Virtue and Knowledge, deeply humbled." Through an extraordinary occurrence, a. kind or miracle, Truth is revealed, Deceit unmasked, Pride becomes a laughing-stock, and the fickle mob is led to recognize true Merit.

Luzzatto in his dramatic parable clothes and vivifies this train of ideas, and enunciates them in monologues and dialogues through the mouth of acting, or, more correctly, speaking characters. Luzzatto's masterpiece is indeed not a drama in the strict sense of the word. The characters represented are not of flesh and blood, but mere abstractions: Reason and Folly, Merit and Deceit, are placed on the stage. The dramatic action is slight. It is in truth a beautiful wreath of fragrant flowers of poesy, a series of delightful monologues and dialogues. In it Luzzatto embodies deep thoughts, difficult to quicken into life or to paint in poetical colors ; but he succeeded. The wonderful evolution of the vegetable world, the extraordinary phenomena of light, are treated in dramatic verse by Luzzatto with the same facility as the appropriate subjects for poetry, and this too in the Hebrew language, not readily lending itself to new forms of thought, and with the self-imposed fetters of a meter never sinned against. His style is dignified, and he employed a diction quite his own, replete with youthful charms, beauty, and harmony. Thereby he supplied a new impulse for the coming age. When the mists of error passed away, the general chaos of thought was reduced to some sort of order, and a happier period opened, young poets derived inspiration from the soft warm rays diffused by the genius of Luzzatto. A modern

Hebrew poet who helped to accomplish the transition from the old to the new period, David France Mendes, owes his inspiration to Luzzatto.

What might not Luzzatto have accomplished if he could have liberated his mind from the extravagant follies of the Kabbala ! But it held him captive, and drew him not long after the completion of his drama (about 1744) to Palestine. Here he hoped to be able to follow unmolested the inspirations of his excited fancy, or play the ro1e of a Messiah. From Safet, too, he continued his communications with his band of disciples ; but before he could commence operations he fell a victim to the plague, in the fortieth year of his age. His body was buried in Tiberias. The two greatest modern Hebrew poets,

LUZZATTO'S FOLLOWERS.

Luzzatto and Yehuda Halevi, were to rest in Hebrew soil. Even the tongues of the slanderous Jews of Palestine, to whom Luzzatto, with his peculiarities, must have seemed an enigma, could only speak well of him after his death. Nevertheless he sowed bad seed. His Italian followers reintroduced the Kabbala into Italy. His Polish disciple, Yekutiel of Wilna, whose buffooneries had first got him into trouble, is said to have led an adventurer's life in Poland and Holland, playing scandalous tricks under the mask of mysticism. Another Pole, Elijah Olianow, who belonged to Luzzatto's following, and proclaimed him as Messiah and himself as his Elijah, did not enjoy the best of reputations. This man took part in the disgraceful disorders which broke out in Altona after Luzzatto's death, and which, again stirring up the Sabbatian mire, divided the Jews of Europe Into two hostile camps.

Jankiev Lejbovicz (that is, Jacob son of Leb) of Galicia, was one of the worst, most subtle, and most deceitful rascals of the eighteenth century. He could cheat the most sagacious, and veil his frauds so cleverly that after his death many still believed him an admirable man, who bore through life, and carried to the grave, most weighty secrets. He understood the art of deception even in his youth, and boasted how he had duped his own father. As a young man he traveled in Turkey in the service of a Jewish gentleman, and in Salonica entered into relations with the Sabbatians or Jewish Moslems there. If he did not learn from them how to work deceptive and mystifying miracles, he at all events learnt indifference towards all forms of religion. He became a Mahometan, as afterwards a Catholic,

JACOB FRANK.

for so long as it served his purpose, and changed his religion as one changes one's clothes. From his long sojourn in Turkey he acquired the name of Frank, or Frank. Ignorant of Talmudical literature, as he himself confessed, he was acquainted with the Zoharist Kabbala, explained it to suit his purpose, and took peculiar pleasure in the doctrine of metempsychosis, by virtue of which the successive Messiahs were not visionaries or impostors, but the embodiment of one and the same Messianic soul. King David, Elijah, Jesus, Mahomet, Sabbatai

Zevi, and his imitators, down to Berachya, were one and the same personality, which had assumed different bodily forms. Why should not he himself be another incarnation of the Messiah ? Although Jacob Frank, or Lejbovicz, loved money dearly, he accounted it only a lever by which to raise himself; he wished to play a brilliant part and surround himself with a mysterious halo. Circumstances were exceptionally favorable to him. He married in Nicopolis (Turkey) a very beautiful wife, through whom he attracted followers. He collected by degrees a small number of Turkish and Wallachian Jews, who shared his loose principles, and held him to be a superior being--the latest embodiment of the Messiah. He could not, however, carry on his mischievous schemes in Turkey, where he was persecuted.

Frank appears to have obtained intelligence of the schism in Poland caused by the Eibeschiitz controversy, and thought that he might utilize the propitious moment to gather round him the Sabbatians of Podolia, and play a part among them, and by means of them. He came suddenly amongst them, visiting many towns of Podolia and the Lemberg district, where secret Sabbatians resided, with whom he may have been in communication previously. They fell, so to speak, into his arms. Frank needed followers, and they were seeking a leader. Now they found one who had come to them with a full purse, of the contents of which he was not sparing. In a trice he won the Sabbatians of Podolia. Frank disclosed himself to them as the successor of Sabbatai, or, what was the same thing, as the new-born soul of the Sabbatian chief Berachya. What this manifestation signified was known to the initiated. They understood by it the blasphemous and at the same time absurd theory of a kind of "Trinity", consisting of the Holy and Most Ancient One, a Holy King, and a female person in the Godhead. Frank, like his predecessors, attributed the chief importance to the Holy King, at once the Messiah and God incarnate, and possessed of all power. Frank ordered his followers to address him as the Holy Lord. In virtue of his participation in the Godhead, the Messiah was able to do all things, even miracles, and Frank did perform miracles, as his followers maintained. The adherents whom he brought in his train, and whom he gathered round him in Poland, believed so strongly in his divine nature that they addressed to him mystic prayers in the language of the Zohar, with the same formulas that the Donmith of Salonica were wont to address to Jacob Querido and Berachya. In short, Frank formed a sect from the Sabbatians of Podolia, called by his name, "Frankists." Their founder taught his disciples to acquire riches for themselves, even by fraudulent and dishonest means. Deceit was nothing more than skillful artifice. Their chief task was to undermine rabbinical Judaism, and to oppose and annihilate the Talmud. This task they undertook with a passion which perhaps owed its origin to the constraints imposed upon them through fear of persecution. The Frankists opposed the Zohar to the Talmud, and Simon bar Yochai, its alleged author, to the other authorities of the Talmud, as though in earlier times the former had combated the latter and accused them of being the falsifiers of Judaism. The true teaching of Moses was said to be contained only in the Zohar, which had declared the whole of rabbinical Judaism to be on a lower level--a fact which blundering Kabbalists had so long overlooked. The Frankists, more clear-sighted, had discovered the half-concealed secret of the Zohar. They rightly called themselves anti-Talmudists as well as Zoharites. With a certain childish forwardness they did exactly those things which rabbinical Judaism strongly prohibited, and neglected those which the latter prescribed, not only in points of ritual, but also with regard to marriage and the laws of chastity. Among these anti-Talmudic Frankists were found rabbis and so-called preachers (Darshanim, Maggidim), Jehuda Leb Krysa, rabbi of Nadvorna, and Rabbi Nachman ben Samuel Levi of Busk. Of especial reputation among Polish Sabbatians was Elisha Schor of Rohatyn, an aged man, descended from distinguished Polish rabbis. He, his sons, his daughter Chaya (who knew the Zohar by heart, and was considered a prophetess), his grandson, and sons-in-law were from an early period thoroughgoing Sabbatians, to whom it was a positive pleasure to deride rabbinical precepts.

During the first months after his return to Poland, Frank held secret conferences with the anti-Talmudists of Podolia, as a public demonstration was attended with danger. One day, he with about twenty of his followers was surprised in Laskorun in a conventicle. The Frankists declared that they had been singing psalms in the Zohar language, while their adversaries asserted that they had been performing an indecent dance around a half-naked woman, and kissing her. Many gathered about the inn to force their way in; others ran to the police to give information that a Turk had stolen into Podolia to pervert the Jews to the Mahometan religion and make them emigrate to Turkey, and that those who had joined him were leading an Adamite, that is to say dissolute, life. The police immediately interposed, broke open the barricaded doors, and expelled the Frankists. Frank was dismissed next day as a foreigner, and repaired to the neighboring Turkish territory; and the Podolian Frankists were kept in custody. The incident made a sensation, and was perhaps intentionally exaggerated. Like wildfire the news concerning the Sabbatians spread. It can be imagined what this defiance of Rabbinical Judaism meant in those days, especially in Poland, where the most insignificant religious rites were sedulously observed. It was now discovered that, in the midst of the excessive piety which characterized the Poles, a number of persons, brought up in the knowledge of the Talmud, scoffed at the whole system of Rabbinical Judaism. The rabbis and elders forthwith began to employ the usual weapons of excommunication and persecution against the offenders, and the secret heretics were hunted out. Won over by large sums, the Polish authorities energetically supported the persecutors. Those in distress showed signs of repentance, and made public confession of their misdeeds, which, be they accurate or exaggerated, present a sad picture of the deterioration of the Polish Jews. Before the council of rabbis in Satanov, in open court, several men and women stated that they and their friends had not only treated the rites of Judaism with contempt, but had abandoned themselves to fornication, adultery, incest, and other iniquities, and had done so in accordance with Kabbalistic-mystic teachings. The penitents declared that Frank had taught his followers to scoff at chastity.

In consequence of this evidence a solemn sentence of excommunication was pronounced in Brody against the Frankists: no one might intermarry with them, their sons and daughters were to be

treated as bastards, and none who were even suspected could be admitted to the post of rabbi, to any religious office, or to the profession of teacher. Everyone was in duty bound to denounce and unmask the secret Sabbatians. This excommunication was repeated in several communities, and finally ratified by a great synod in Konstantinov on the Jewish New Year (September, 1756). The document was printed, distributed, and ordered to be read aloud every month in the synagogues for observance. This sentence of excommunication contained one point of great importance. No one under thirty years of age was to be permitted to study the Kabbala. Necessity at length opened the eyes of the rabbis to the recognition of the impure spring, which since the time of Lurya had poisoned the sap of the tree of Judaism. More than four centuries had passed since philosophical inquiry had been forbidden, and the young Kabbala encouraged. In their blindness, the rabbis had imagined that they were strengthening Judaism in placing folly oil the throne of wisdom. This course produced that book of lies, the Zohar, which impudently set itself above the Holy Writings and the Talmud. Finally, the delusions of the Kabbala declared a life and death war against rabbinical Judaism. Such were the fruits of blindness. The members of the synod of Konstantinov turned in their perplexity to Jacob Emden, who, since his controversy with Eibeschiitz, was accounted the representative of sound orthodoxy. He, too, enjoyed a triumph, though of an altogether different from the one his antagonist was at the same time celebrating in the midst of his noisy admirers. The Polish Jews at last began to be aware that secular knowledge and cultivated eloquence are after all not altogether objectionable, since they can render assistance to Judaism. They were desirous that a cultured Portuguese should come to Poland, endowed with knowledge and readiness of speech, who would represent them before the Polish magistracy and clergy, in order to suppress the dangerous Frankist sect.

Jacob Emden, deeply affected by the despairing appeal of his Polish brethren, came to a conclusion great importance for succeeding ages. Sabbatians of all shades appealed to the Zohar as a sacred authority, as the Bible of a new revelation, excusing all their blasphemies and indecencies by quotations from it. What if the Zohar should prove not to be genuine, but only a supposititious work? And this was the conclusion to which Emden came. The repulsive incidents in Poland first suggested the inquiry to him, and it became clear to him that at least a portion of the Zohar was the production of an impostor.

To the question whether it would be lawful to persecute the Frankists, Jacob Emden answered emphatically in the affirmative. He held them, according to the accounts received from Poland, to be shameless transgressors of the most sacred laws of decency and chastity, turning vice into virtue by means of mystical jugglery. No persuasion, however, was required from him; when persecution became necessary in Poland the will to indict it was never wanting. The Frankists were denounced to the magistracy and clergy as a new sect, and handed over to the Catholic Inquisition, and the bishop of Kamieniec, Nicolas Dembowski, in whose diocese they were apprehended, had no objection to erect a stake. Frank was cunning enough to avert from his followers the blow aimed at them and to direct it against their enemies. From Chocim, where after a brief imprisonment he had settled in safety, he counseled them to emphasize two points in their defense: that they believed in a "Trinity", and that they rejected the Talmud as a compilation full of error and blasphemy. His counsel

meeting with opposition, he secretly assembled some of his followers in a small town in Poland, and reiterated his advice, with the addition that twenty or thirty of them must quickly be baptized to give more emphasis to their assertions that they acknowledged the Trinity and rejected the Talmud. To Frank change of religion was a small matter. The Talmud Jews of the district heard of Frank's secret conference with his confederates, collected a band, attacked them, and after using them roughly placed them in confinement. This proceeding provoked the anti-Talmudists to revenge. They would not, indeed, be baptized, but they declared before the tribunal of Bishop Dembowski that they were almost Christians, that they believed in a "Divine Trinity", that the rest of the Jews, who repudiated this doctrine, did not hold the true faith, and persecuted them on account of their superiority. To make their breach with Judaism unmistakable, or to revenge themselves in a very sanguinary way, they made false accusations, namely, that believers in the Talmud make use of the blood of Christians, and that the Talmud inculcates the murder of Christians as a sacred duty. There was no difficulty in trumping up evidence in favor of the accusation. It was only necessary that some Christian child should be missing. Something of the kind must have occurred in Jampol in Podolia (April, 1756), and immediately the most respected Jews of the town were placed in chains, and the other communities menaced. Bishop Dembowski and his chapter, rejoiced at their good luck, favored the Frankists in every way in return for their false evidence, freed them from prison, protected them from persecution, allowed them to settle in the diocese of Kamieniec, permitted them to live as they pleased, and were delighted to foster their hatred of the Talmud Jews. The bishop flattered himself that, through the Frankists, among whom were several rabbis, he would be able to convert many Polish Jews to Catholicism. The new sect passed into the state in which the persecuted becomes the persecutor.

In order to drive their adversaries to desperation, the Frankists (1757) petitioned Bishop Dembowski to arrange a disputation between themselves and the Talmudists, and bound themselves to prove both the doctrine of the Trinity and the harmful nature of the Talmud, from the Scriptures and the Zohar. To this the bishop willingly consented. One of the Frankist rabbis--perhaps old Elisha Schor, of Rohatyn--composed a confession of faith, which, almost unequaled for audacity and untruthfulness, is so artful in its explanation of Sabbatian-Kabbalistic doctrines as to have led the bishop to suppose that they were in consonance with the Catholic faith, and to drive their adversaries into a corner. The Frankist confession of faith contains nine articles. The religion revealed by God to man contains so many deep mysteries, that it must be thoroughly searched out and examined ; without higher inspiration, however, it cannot be understood. One of these mysteries is that the Godhead consists of three Persons, equal to one another, at once a Trinity and a Unity. Another mystery is that the Godhead assumes human form to manifest itself visibly to all men. Through the mediation of these deities incarnate, mankind is redeemed and saved--not through the Messiah expected to assemble the Jews and lead them back to Jerusalem. The latter is a false belief: Jerusalem and the Temple will never be rebuilt. The Talmud, indeed, interprets revealed faith otherwise; but its interpretation is baneful, and has led its adherents into error and unbelief. The Talmud contains most revolting statements ; such as that Jews are permitted, indeed, obliged, to deceive and slay Christians. The Zohar, which is diametrically opposed to the Talmud, offers the only true and correct interpretation of the Holy

Writings. All these absurd statements, the Frankist confession of faith supported by passages from the Bible and the Zohar; and to vilify the Talmud, passages in it were intentionally misrepresented. The creed was printed and published in the Hebrew and the Polish language. The representatives of the Polish community--the Synod of the Four Countries--were painfully sensible, in their desperate situation, of the want of education prevalent among them. They could not produce a single man who could expose the imposture of the Frankists and the hollowness of their creed in well-turned or even tolerable language. The proud leaders of the Synod behaved like children in their anxiety. They helplessly devised extravagant schemes, wished to appeal to the pope, and to incite the Portuguese in Amsterdam and Rome to protect them from the machinations of their vindictive enemies.

Bishop Dembowski consented to the proposition of the Frankists, and issued a command that the Talmudists send deputies to a disputation at Kamieniec, failing which he would punish them and burn the Talmud as a book hostile to Christianity. In vain the Polish Jews referred to their ancient privileges, screened themselves behind great nobles, and spent large sums of money. They were obliged to prepare for the disputation and render account to the enemies they had so greatly despised. Only a few rabbis appeared. What could the representatives of the Talmud, with their profound ignorance and halting speech, effect against the audacious denunciations of the Frankists, particularly as they also acknowledged the Zohar as a sacred book, and this, as a matter of fact, formulates the doctrine of a kind of Trinity ! What happened at the disputation of Kamieniec has never transpired. The Talmudists were accounted as vanquished and refuted. Bishop Dembowski publicly declared (October 14, 1757), that, as the anti-Talmudists had set down in writing and proved the chief points of their confession of faith, they were permitted everywhere to hold disputations with the Talmudists. Copies of the Talmud were ordered to be confiscated, brought to Kamieniec, and there publicly burned by the hangman. Dembowski was permitted arbitrarily to favor the one party and condemn the other. The king of Poland and his minister, Count Bruhl, troubled themselves but little about internal affairs, still less about the Jews. Hence Dembowski, who at about that time was made archbishop of Lemberg, was allowed with the aid of the clergy, the police, and the Frankists, to search for copies of the Talmud and other rabbinical writings in the towns of his bishopric, collect them at Kamieniec, and drag them through the streets in mockery. Only the Bible and the Zohar were to be spared, as in the time of the Talmud persecution under Popes Julius IV and Pius V. Nearly a thousand copies of the Talmud were thrown into a great pit at Kamieniec and burnt by the hangman. The Talmudists could do nothing, but groan, weep, and proclaim a rigorous fast-day on account of "the burning of the Torah." It was the Kabbala that had kindled the torches for the funeral pile of the Talmud. The clergy, in conjunction with the anti-Talmudists, daily made domiciliary visits into Jewish houses to confiscate copies of the Talmud.

To free themselves and all other Jews from the oft repeated, and as often refuted, accusation of child-murder, which the abject Frankists had confirmed, the Jewish Talmudists sent Eliakim Selig (Selek) to Benedictus XIV, to procure an official exposure of the falsehood of the charge brought against Jews. Eliakim's determination and persistence succeeded in obtaining this authoritative acquittal in Rome at the end of 1757.

Suddenly Bishop Dembowski died (November 17, 1757) a violent death, and this led to a new developoment

FRANKIST PERSECUTIONS.

in the controversy. Persecution of the Talmudists immediately ceased, and from that time the Frankists were persecuted, imprisoned, and declared outlaws. Their beards were shaved off as a mark of disgrace and to make them easily recognizable. The majority, no longer able to maintain themselves in Kamieniec, fled to the neighboring province of Bessarabia. But they were even more disturbed under Turkish jurisdiction. Their persecutors informed the Jewish community of the arrival of the anti-Talmudists in their district and of their injuriousness to Judaism, and the former had only to notify the Pasha and the Cadi that these supposed Polish Jews were not under the protection of the Chacham Bashi (chief rabbi) of Constantinople in order to invite the Turks to fall upon the newcomers and mercilessly rob and ill-treat them. In despair the Frankists wandered restlessly about the borderlands of Podolia and Bessarabia. At length they addressed the king of Poland, and implored him to confirm the privilege tolerating their worship granted them by Bishop Dembowski. Augustus III, the weakling and martyr of the seven years' war, thereupon issued a decree (June 11, 1758) permitting the Frankists to return unmolested to their homes, and reside in Poland wherever they pleased. The decree was not enforced with sufficient energy, and the Frankists continued to be persecuted by their opponents aided by the nobles. In their trouble some of their body were sent to beg Frank, who had so long forsaken them, to assist them with his advice. While affecting to demur, he willingly obeyed their call and repaired again to Podolia (January, 1759)·

With his appearance the old game of intrigue began once more. Frank was from that time the life and soul of his followers, and without his commands they undertook nothing. He saw clearly that the hypocrisy of simply declaring that the anti-Talmudists believed in the Trinity must not be repeated, but that they must make more of a concession to Christianity. By his advice six Frankists, the majority foreigners, repaired to Wratislav Lubienski, Archbishop of Lemberg, with the declaration (February 20, 1759), "in the name of their whole body," that they were all willing, under certain conditions, to be baptized. In their petition they used phrases savoring of Catholicism, and breathed vengeance against their former co-religionists. Lubienski had this petition of the Zoharites printed, in order, on the one hand, to proclaim the victory of the Church, on the other, to keep the members of this sect to their word; but he did nothing for them. Although in their Catholic and Kabbalistic language they declared that they were languishing for baptism "like the hart for the water-brooks," they did not in the least contemplate an immediate formal secession to Christianity. Frank, their leader, whom they blindly followed, did not consider the time ripe for this extreme measure. He reserved it to extort favorable terms, which were embodied in an address presented to the king and Archbishop Lubienski (May 16, 1759) by two deputies. They insisted especially on a disputation with their opponents, adducing as a reason, that they wished to show the world that they were led to embrace Christianity, not from necessity and poverty, but through conviction. They wished, moreover, to give an opportunity to their secret confederates to publicly avow themselves believers in Christianity, which they would infallibly do if their righteous cause should triumph in public argument. Finally they hoped in this way to open the blinded eyes of their antagonists. To this cunningly devised petition breathing malice against their enemies, the king made no reply, while Lubienski answered evasively that he could only promise, them eternal salvation if they allowed themselves to be baptized;

the rest would follow as a matter of course. He displayed no zeal whatever for the conversion of these ragged fellows whom he believed to be dissemblers. The papal nuncio in Warsaw, Nicholas Serra, did not regard with favor the idea of the conversion of the anti-Talmudists.

The position of affairs changed; however, when Lubienski withdrew to Gnesen, his arch-episcopal seat, and the administrator of the archbishopric of

Lemberg, the canon De Mikulski, showed more zeal for conversion. He immediately promised the Frankists to arrange a religious conference between them and the Talmudists, if they would exhibit a sincere desire for baptism. On this the deputies, Leb Krysa and Solomon of Rohatyn, in the name of the whole body, made a Catholic confession of faith (May 25). It closed with these words: "The Talmud teaches the use of the blood of Christians, and whosoever believes in it is bound to use this blood." Thereupon Mikulski, without consulting the papal nuncio Serra, made arrangements for a second disputation In Lemberg (June, 1759)· The rabbis of this diocese were summoned to appear, under pain of a heavy fine, and the nobility and clergy were requested in case of necessity to compel them. The nuncio Serra, to whom the Talmudists complained, was in the highest degree dissatisfied with the idea of the disputation, but did not care to prevent it because he wished to learn with certainty whether the Jews used the blood of Christians. This appeared to him the most important point of all. Just at this time Pope Clement XIII had given a favorable answer on this question to the Jewish deputy Selek. Clement XIII proclaimed that the Holy See had examined the grounds on which rested the belief in the use of human blood for the feast of the Passover and the murder of Christians by Jews, and that the Jews must not be condemned as criminals in respect of this charge, but that in the case of such occurrences legal forms of proof must be used. Notwithstanding this, the papal envoy at this very time, deceived by the meanness of the Frankists, partially credited the false accusation, and notified the Curia of it.

The religious conference which was to lead to the conversion of so many Jews, at first regarded with indifference, began to awaken interest. The Polish nobility of both sexes purchased admission cards at a high price, the proceeds to go to the poor people who were to be baptized. On the appointed day the Talmudists and Zoharites were brought into the cathedral of Lemberg; all the clergy, nobility, and burghers crowded thither to witness the spectacle of Jews apparently belonging to the same religion, hurling at each other accusations of the most abominable crimes. In reality it was the Talmud and the Kabbala, formerly a closely united pair of sisters, who had fallen out with each other. The disputation failed miserably. Of the Frankists, who had boastfully given out that several hundreds of their party would attend, only about ten appeared, the rest being too poor to undertake the long journey and attire themselves decently. Of the Talmudists forty were present owing to their dread of the threatened fine. How Judaism had retrograded in the century of "enlightenment" when compared with the thirteenth century! At that time, on a similar occasion, the spokesman of the Jews, Moses Nachmani, proudly confronted his opponents at the court of Barcelona. In Lemberg the representatives of Talmudic Judaism stood awkward and disconcerted, unable to utter a word. They did not even understand the language of the country --their opponents, to be sure, were in like case--and interpreters had to be employed. But the

ZOHARITES BAPTIZED.

Catholic clergy in Poland and the learned classes also betrayed their astounding ignorance. Not a single Pole understood Hebrew or the language of the rabbis sufficiently to be an impartial witness of the dispute, whilst in Germany and Holland Christians acquainted with Hebrew could be counted by hundreds. The Talmudists had a difficult part to play in this religious conference. The chief thesis of the Frankists was that the Zohar teaches the doctrine of the Trinity. Could they dare to deny this dogma absolutely without wounding the feelings of the Christians, their masters? And that leanings toward this doctrine were to be found in the Zohar they could not deny. Of course, they might have refuted completely the false charge of using the blood of Christian children and of the bloodthirsty nature of the Talmud, or might have cited the testimony of Christians and even the decisions of popes. They were, however, ignorant of the history of their own suffering, and their ignorance avenged itself on them. It is easy to believe that the Talmudic spokesmen, after the three days' conference, returned home ashamed and confused. Even the imputation of shedding Christian blood continued to cling to their religion.

The Zoharites who had obtained their desire were now strongly urged by the clergy to perform their promise, and allow themselves to be baptized. But they continued to resist as if it cost them a great struggle, and only yielded at the express command of their chief, Frank, and in his presence. The latter appeared with great pomp, in magnificent Turkish robes, with a team of six horses, and surrounded by guards in Turkish dress. He wished to impress the Poles. His was the strong will which led the Frankists, and which they implicitly obeyed. Some thousand Zoharites were baptized on this occasion. Frank would not be baptized in Lemberg, but appeared suddenly, with dazzling magnificence, in Warsaw (October, 1759), aroused the curiosity of the Polish capital, and requested the favor that the king would stand godfather to him. The newspapers of the Polish capital were full of accounts of the daily baptisms of so many Jews, and of the names of the great nobles and ladies who were their godparents. But the Church could not rejoice in her victory. Frank was watched with suspicion by the clergy. They did not trust him, and suspected him to be a swindler who, under the mask of Christianity, as formerly under that of Islam, desired to play a part as the leader of a sect. The more Frank reiterated the demand that a special tract of country be assigned to him, the more he aroused the suspicion that he was pursuing selfish aims and that baptism had been but a means to an end. The Talmud Jews neglected nothing to furnish proofs of his impostures. At length he was unmasked and betrayed by some of his Polish followers, who were incensed at being neglected for the foreign Frankists, and showed that with him belief in Christianity was but a farce, and that he had commanded his followers to address him as Messiah and Holy Lord. He was arrested and examined by the president of the Polish Inquisition as an impostor and a blasphemer. The depositions of the witnesses clearly revealed his frauds, and he was conveyed to the fortress of Czenstochow and confined ill a convent (March,

1760)· Only the fact that the king was his godfather saved Frank from being burnt at the stake as a heretic and apostate. His chief followers were likewise arrested and thrown into prison. The rank and file were in part condemned to work on the fortifications of Czenstochow, and partly outlawed. Many Frankists were obliged to beg for alms at the church doors, and were treated with contempt by the Polish population. They continued true, however, to their Messiah or Holy Lord. All adverse events they accounted for in the Kabbalistic manner: they had boon divinely predestined. The cloister of Czenstochow they named mystically,"The gate of Rome." Outwardly they adhered to the Catholic religion, and joined in all the sacraments, but they associated only with each other, and like their Turkish comrades, the Donmah, intermarried only with each other. The families descended from them in Poland, Wolowski, Dembowski, Dzalski, are still at the present day known as Frenks or Shlibs. Frank was set at liberty by the Russians, after thirteen years' imprisonment in the fortress, played the part of impostor for over twenty years elsewhere, in Vienna, Brun, and at last in Offenbach; set up his beautiful daughter Eva as the incarnate Godhead, and deceived the world until the end of his life, and even after his death; but with this part of his career Jewish history has nothing to do.

V. CHAPTER IX.

THE NEW CHASSIDISM

The Alliance of Reason with Mysticism--Israel Baalshem, his Career and Reputation--Movement against Rabbinism--The "Zaddik"--Beer Mizricz, his Arrogance and Deceptions--The Devotional Methods of the Chassidim--Their Liturgy-Cossack Massacres in Poland--Elijah Wilna, his Character and Method of Research--Circumstances Prove Favorable to the Spread of the New Sect--Vigorous Proceedings against them in Wilna--Death of Beer Mizricz--Progress of Chassidism despite the Persecution of its Opponents

1750-1786 C.E.

The founders of the new Chassidism were Israel of Meidziboz (born about 1698; died 1759) and Beer of Mizricz (born about 1700; died 1772). The former received, alike form his admirers and his antagonists, the surname of "The Wonder-worker by means of Invocations in the Name of God", Baal-Shem, or Baal-Shemtov, in the customary abbreviated form, Besht. As ugly as the name, Besht, was the form of the founder and the order that he called into existence.

The Graces did not sit by his cradle, but the spirit of belief in wonder-working, and his brain was so filled with fantastic images that he could not distinguish them form real, tangible beings. The experiences of Israel's youth are unknown. So much, however, is certain: he was left an orphan, poor and neglected, early in life, and passed a great portion of his youth in the forests and caves of the Carpathian mountains. The spurs of the Carpathian hills were his teachers. Here he learnt what he would not have acquired in the dark, narrow, dirty hovels called schools in Poland--namely, to understand the tongue which nature speaks. The spirits of the mountains and the fountains whispered secrets to him. Here he also learned, probably from the peasant women who gathered herbs on the mountain-tops and on the edges of rivers, the use of plants as remedies. As they did not trust to the healing power of nature, but added conjurations and invocations to good and evil spirits, Israel also accustomed himself to this method of cure. He became a miracle-doctor. Necessity, too, was his teacher; it taught him to pray. How often, in his forsaken and orphaned condition, may he have suffered from want even of dry bread, how often may he have been surrounded by real or imaginary dangers! In his distress he prayed in the usual forms of the synagogue ; but he spoke his words with fervor and intense devotion, or cried them aloud in the solitude of the mountains. His audible prayer awakened the echoes of the mountains, which appeared as an answer to his supplications. He seems to have been often in a state of rapture, and to have induced this condition by frantic movements of the whole body while praying. This agitation drove the blood to his head, made his eyes glitter, and wrought both body and soul into such a condition of over-excitement that he felt

a deadly weakness come over him. Was this magnetic tension of the soul caused by the motions and the shouting, singing, and praying?

Israel Baalshem asserted that, in consequence of these bodily agitations and this intense devotion, he often caught a glimpse of infinity. His soul soared upward to the world of light, heard and saw Divine secrets and revelations, entered into conversation with sublime spirits, and by their intervention could secure the grace of God and prosperity, and especially avert impending calamities. Israel Miedziboz also boasted that he could see into the future, as secrets were unveiled to him. Was this a deliberate boast, self-deception, or merely an over-estimation of morbid feelings? There are persons, times, and places, in which the line of demarcation between trickery and self-delusion cannot be distinguished. In Poland, in Baalshem's time, with the terrible mental strain created by the Kabbala in connection with the Sabbatian fraud, the feverish expectation of imminent Messianic redemption, everything was possible and everything credible. In that land the fancy of both Jews and Christians moved among extraordinary and supernatural phenomena as in its natural element. Israel steadfastly and firmly believed in the visions seen when he was under mental and physical excitement; he believed in the power of his prayers. In his delusion he blasphemously declared that prayer is a kind of marriage union (Zivug) of man with the Godhead (Shechina), upon which he must enter whilst in a state of excitement. Equipped with alleged higher knowledge of secret remedies and the spirit world, to which he thought he had attained through Divine grace, Israel entered the society of men to prove his higher gifts. It must be acknowledged to his credit that he never misused these talents. He did not make a trade of them, nor seek to earn his livelihood with them. At first he followed the humble occupation of a wagoner, afterwards he dealt in horses, and when his means permitted it he kept a tavern.

Occasionally, when specially requested, he employed his miraculous remedies, and thereby gained so great a reputation that he was consulted even by Polish nobles. He became conspicuous by his noisy, delirious praying, which must have so transfigured him that men did not recognize the wagoner or horse-dealer whom they knew. He was admired for his revelation of secrets. In Poland not only the unlearned and the Jews considered such gifts and miracles possible; the Jesuits and the Kabbalists had stultified the Christians and the Jews of their country, and plunged them into a state of primitive barbarism.

It would have been a remarkable thing if such a wonder-doctor, who appeared to have intercourse with the spirit world, had not found adherents, but he can hardly have designed the formation of a new sect. He was joined by persons of a similar disposition to his own, who felt a religious impulse, which could not be satisfied, they thought, by a rigorous, penitential life, or by mechanical repetition of prescribed prayers. They joined Israel, in Miedziboz, to pray with devotion, i. e., in a sing-song tune, clapping their hands, bowing, jumping, gesticulating, and uttering cries. Israel need not have been a trickster to obtain followers. Mysticism and madness are contagious. He particularly attracted men who desired to lead a free and merry life, at the same time hoping to reach a lofty aim,

DOB BEER.

and to live assured of the nearness of God in serenity and calmness, and to advance the Messianic future. They did not need to pore over Talmudical folios in order to attain to higher piety.

It became the fashion in neo-Chassidean circles to scoff at the Talmudists. Because the latter mocked at the unlearned chief of the new order, who had a following without belonging of the guild of Talmudists, without having been initiated into the Talmud and its appendages, the Chassidim depreciated the study of the Talmud, avowing that it was not able to promote a truly godly life. Covert war existed between the neo-Chassidim and the Rabbanites; the latter could not, however, harm their opponents so long as Israel's adherents did not depart from existing Judaism. After the death of the founder, when barbarism and degeneracy increased, the feud grew into a complete rupture under Beer of Mizricz.

Dob Beer (or Berish) was no visionary like Israel, but possessed the faculty of clear insight into the condition of men's minds. He was thus able to render the mind and will of others subservient to him. Although he joined the new movement only a short time before Israel's death, yet, whether at his suggestion or not, Israel's son and sons-in-law were passed over, and Beer was made Israel's successor in the leadership of the neo-Chassidean community. Beer, who transferred the center to Mizricz--a village in Volhynia--was superior to his master in many points. He was well read in Talmudical and Kabbalistic writings, was a fluent preacher (Maggid), who, to further his purpose, could make the most far-fetched biblical verses, as also Agadic and Zoharic expressions, harmonize, and thus surprise his audience. He removed from the Chassidim the stigma of ignorance, especially disgraceful in Poland, and secured an accession of supporters . He had a commanding appearance, did not mingle with the people, but lived the whole week secluded in a small room--only accessible to his confidants--and thus acquired the renown of mysterious intercourse with the heavenly world. Only on the Sabbath did he show himself to all who longed to be favored with his sight. On this day he appeared splendidly attired in satin, his outer garment, his shoes, and even his snuff-box being white, the color signifying grace in the Kabbalistic language. On this day, in accordance with the custom introduced by Israel Besht, he offered up prayers together with his friends, with the strangers who had made a pilgrimage to him, with the new members, and those curious to see the Kabbalistic saint and wonder-worker. To produce the joyous state of mind necessary to devout prayer, Beer indulged in vulgar jokes, whereby the merriment of the bystanders was aroused; for instance, he would joke with one of the circle, and throw him down. In the midst of this child's play he would suddenly cry out, " Now serve the Lord with gladness." Under Beer's guidance, the constitution of Chassidism remained apparently in the same form as under his predecessor: fervent, convulsive praying, inspiration (Hithlahabuth), miraculous cures, and revelations of the future. But as these actions did not, as with Israel, flow from a peculiar or abnormal state of mind, they could only be imitated-artifice or illusion had to supply what nature withheld. It was an accepted fact that the Chassidean leader, or Zaddik, the perfectly pious man, had to be enthusiastic in prayer, had to have ecstatic dreams and visions. How can a clever plotter appear inspired? Alcohol, so much liked in Poland, now had to take the place of the inspiring demon. Beer had not the knowledge of remedial herbs, which his teacher had obtained in the Carpathian mountains. He, therefore, devoted himself to medicine, and if his remedies did not avail, then the sick person died of his sinfulness. To predict the future was a more

THE "ZADDIK."

difficult task, yet it had to be accomplished; his reputation as a thaumaturgist depended upon it. Beer was equal to the emergency. Among his intimates were expert spies, worthy of serving in the secret police. They discovered many secrets, and told them to their leader; thus he was enabled to assume an appearance of omniscience. Or his emissaries committed robberies; if the victims came to the "Saint" in his hermitage to find them out, he was able to indicate the exact spot where the missing articles were lying. If strangers, attracted by his fame, came to see him, they were not admitted, as mentioned, until the following Saturday, to take part in the Chassidean witches' Sabbath. Meantime his spies, by artful questions and other means, gleaned a knowledge of the affairs and secret desires of these strangers, and communicated them to the Zaddik. In the first interview Beer, in a seemingly casual manner, was able, in a skillfully arranged discourse, to bring in allusions to these strangers, whereby they would be convinced that he had looked into their hearts, and knew their past. By these and similar contrivances, he succeeded in asserting himself as omniscient, and increasing the number of his followers. Every new convert testified to his Divine inspiration, and induced others to join.

In order to strengthen respect for him, Beer propounded a theory, which in its logical application is calculated to promote most harmful consequences. Supported by the Kabbalistic formula, that "the righteous or the pious man is the foundation of the world," he magnified the importance of the Zaddik, or the Chassidean chief, to such an extent that it became blasphemy. "A Zaddik is not alone the most perfect and sinless human being, he is not alone Moses, but the representative of God and His image." All and everything that the Zaddik All and everything that the Zaddik does and thinks has a decided influence upon the upper and lower worlds. The Deity reveals Himself especially in the acts of the Zaddik; even his most trifling deeds are to be considered important. The way he wears his clothes, ties his shoes, smokes his pipe, whether he delivers profound addresses, or indulges in silly jokes--everything bears a close relation to the Deity, and is of as much moment as the fulfillment of a religious duty. Even when drawing inspiration from the bottle, he is swaying the upper and nether worlds. All these absurd fancies owed their origin to the superstitious doctrines of the Kabbala, which, in spite of the unspeakable confusion they had wrought through Sabbatai Zevi and Frank, in spite of the opposition which their chief exponent, the Zohar, had encountered at about this time at the hands of Jacob Emden, still clouded the brains of the Polish Jews. According to this theory, the Zaddik, i. e., Berish Mizricz, was the embodiment of power and splendor upon earth. In his "Stubel," or" Hermitage," i. e., in his dirty little retired chamber, he considered himself as great as the papal vicar of God upon earth in his magnificent palace. The Zaddik was also to bear himself proudly towards men; all this was "for the glory of God." It was a sort of Catholicism within Judaism.

Beer's idea, however, was not meant to remain idle and unfruitful, but to bring him honor and revenue. While the Zaddik cared for the conduct of the world, for the obtaining of heavenly grace, and especially for Israel's preservation and glorification, his adherents had to cultivate three kinds of virtues. It was their duty to draw nigh to him, to enjoy the sight of him, and from time to time to make pilgrimages to him. Further, they were to confess their sins to him. By these means alone could they hope for pardon of their iniquities. Finally, they had to bring him presents, rich gifts, which he knew how to employ to the best advantage.

SPREAD OF THE NEW CHASSIDISM.

It was also incumbent upon them to attend to his personal wants. It seems like a return to the days of the priests of Baal, so vulgar and disgusting do these perversities appear. The saddest part of all is that this teaching, worthy of a fetish worshipping people, met with approbation in Poland, the country distinguished by cumbersome knowledge of Jewish literature. It was just this excess, this over-activity of the spiritual digestive apparatus, that produced such lamentable phenomena. The intellect of the Polish Jews had been so over-excited, that the coarsest things were more pleasing to them than what was refined.

Beer dispatched abroad as his apostles bombastic preachers who seasoned his injurious teachings with distorted citations from the Scriptures. Simple-minded men, rogues and idlers, of whom there were so many in Poland,attached themselves to the new Chassidim; the first from inclination to enthusiasm and belief in miracles ; the cunning, in order to procure money in an easy way, and lead a pleasant existence; and the idlers, because in the court of the Zaddik they found occupation, and gratified Their curiosity. If such idlers were asked what they were thinking of, as they strolled about pipe in mouth, they would reply with seriousness, "We are meditating upon God." The simple people, however, who hoped to win bliss through the Chassidean discipline, engaged continually in prayer, until through exhaustion they dropped unconscious.

Neo-Chassidism was favored by two circumstances, the fraternization of the members and the dryness and fossilized character of Talmudic study as carried on in Poland for more than a century. At the outset the Chassidim formed a kind of brotherhood, not indeed with a common purse, as among their prototypes, the Essenes and the Judaeo-Christians, but having regard to the wants of needy members. Owing to the closeness of their union, their spying system, and their energy, it was easy for them to provide for those who lacked employment or food. On New Year and the Day of Atonement people, even those who dwelt at long distances, undertook pilgrimages to the Zaddik, as formerly to the Temple, and left their wives and children to pass the so-called holy days in the company of their chief, to be edified by his presence and actions. Here the Chassidean disciples learned to know one another, discussed local affairs, and rendered mutual help. Well-to-do merchants found opportunity at these assemblies, in conversation with fellow-believers, upon whose fidelity and brotherly attachment they could rely, to discover fresh sources of income. Fathers of marriageable daughters sought and easily found husbands for them, which at that time in Poland was considered a highly important matter. The common meals on the afternoons of Saturdays and the holidays strengthened the bonds of loyalty and affection among them. How could meals for so many guests be provided? The wealthy Chassidim regarded it as a duty to support the Zaddik liberally. A special source of income was the superstitious belief prevalent among the Chassidim that the Zaddik for certain sums (Pidion, Redemption) could ward off threatening perils and cure deadly diseases. Pressure was brought to bear upon wealthy but weak-minded persons, and they were terrified into believing that they could escape impending calamities only by rich gifts. Whoever desired to enter upon a hazardous transaction consulted the Zaddik as an oracle, and had to pay for his counsel. The cunning Chassidim knew everything, were ready with counsel in any emergency, and by their craftiness were able to afford real assistance. The Zaddik, however miserly he might be, had to assist the poor and distressed with his revenues. Thus every member received help here. Full of enthusiasm

they returned home from their journey; the feeling that they belonged to a brotherhood elevated them, and they ardently looked forward to the return of the holy time. The poor and forsaken, the fanatical and the unprincipled, could not do better than join this union, this easy-going yet religious order.

Earnest men, also, desirous of satisfying their spiritual wants, felt themselves attracted to the Chassidim. Rabbinical Judaism, as known in Poland, offered no sort of religious comfort. Its representatives placed the highest value upon the dialectic, exposition of the Talmud and its commentaries Actual necessity had besides caused that portion of the Talmud which treated of civil law to be closely studied, as the rabbis exercised civil jurisdiction over their flocks. Fine-spun decisions of new, complicated legal points occupied the doctors of the Talmud day and night. Moreover, this hair-splitting was considered sublimest piety, and superseded everything else. If any one solved an intricate Talmudic question, or discovered something new, called Torah, he felt self-satisfied, and assured of his felicity hereafter. All other objects, the impulse to devotion, prayer, and emotion, or interest in the moral condition of the community, were secondary matters, to which scarcely any attention was paid The mental exercise of making logical deductions from the Talmud, or more correctly from the laws of Mine and Thine, choked all other intellectual pursuits in Poland. Religious ceremonies had degenerated, both amongst Talmudists and the unlearned, into meaningless usages, and prayer into mere lip-service. To men of feeling this aridity of Talmudic study, together with the love of debate, and the dogmatism and pride of the rabbis arising from it, were repellent, and they flung themselves into the arms of the new order, which allowed so much play for the fancy and the emotions. Especially preachers, semi-Talmudists who were looked upon and treated by erudite rabbi-Talmudists as inferior and contemptible, who eked out a wretched living, or almost starved, leagued themselves with the neo-Chassidim, because among them their talents of preaching were appreciated, and they could obtain an honorable position, and be secured against need. By the accession of such elements the circle of neo-Chassidim became daily augmented. Almost in every town lived followers of the new school, who occasionally had intercourse with their brother members and their chief.

With advancing strength the antipathy of the neo-Chassidim to the rabbis and Talmudists increased. Without being aware of it they formed a new sect, which scorned intercourse with the Talmud Jews. With Beer at their head, they felt themselves strong enough to introduce an innovation, which would naturally bring down the anger of the rabbis upon them. Since prayer and the rites of Divine service were the chief consideration for them, they did not trouble themselves about the prescriptions of the ritual law as to how many prayers should be said, nor at what time the different services should commence and terminate, but were entirely guided by the feeling of the moment. Through their daily ablutions, baths, and other preparations for public worship they were seldom ready for prayer at the prescribed time, but began later, prolonged it by the movements of their bodies and their intoning, and suddenly came to an end after omitting several portions. They were especially averse to the harsh interpolations in the Sabbath and festival prayers (the Piyutim). These insertions interrupt the most important and suggestive portions of the service. To abolish these at a blow, Beer Mizricz introduced the prayer-book of the arch-Kabbalist, Isaac Lurya, which for the

STATE OF POLAND.

greater part conforms to the Portuguese ritual, and does not contain poetical (poetanic) additions. In the eyes of the ultra-orthodox this innovation was an enormous, or rather a double crime, permitting, as it did, the omission of interpolations hallowed by custom, and the exchange of the German ritual for the Sephardic.

This innovation would probably have been severely visited upon the neo-Chassidim, but that at this time, when the political power of Poland lay crushed, the firm political connection of the Polish Jews had also been dissolved. Poland was distracted by civil war. "In this country," as the Primate of Gnesen complained at the opening of the Reichstag, March, 1764, "freedom is oppressed, the laws are not obeyed, justice cannot be obtained, trade is utterly ruined, districts and villages are devastated, the treasury is empty, and the coin of the realm has no value." It had been enfeebled by the Jesuits, and was already regarded by Russia as a sure prey. Its king--Stanislaus Augustus Poniatowski--was a weakling, the plaything of internal factions and external foes (September, 1764)· In the first year of his reign, Poniatowski among other laws issued a regulation which destroyed the communal union of the Polish Jews. The synod of the Four Countries, composed of delegates, rabbis and laymen (Parnassim), with authority to pronounce interdicts and levy fines, was not permitted to assemble, pass resolutions, or execute them.

The dissolution of the synod was very fortunate for the neo-Chassidim. They could not be excommunicated by the representatives of the Polish Jewish world, but each individual congregation had to proceed against them and forbid their meetings. Even this step was not taken at once, as the terrible death-struggle in which Poland engaged before its first partition was severely felt by the wealthy Jews, who trembled for their lives. The Confederation War broke out, which made many districts a desert; Poland was punished by eternal Justice in the same way as it had sinned. In the name of the pope and the Jesuits it had always persecuted dissenters, and excluded them from public offices, and, in the name of the dissenters, Catherine plunged the land into fratricidal war. The Russians, for the second time, let loose against Poland the Zaporogian Cossacks--the savage Haidamaks--who inflicted death, by every known method, upon the Polish nobles, the clergy, and the Jews. The Haidamaks hung up together a nobleman, a Jew, a monk, and a dog, with the mocking inscription, "All are equal." Most inhuman cruelties were inflicted upon captives and the defenseless. In addition came the Turks, who, in the guise of saviors of Poland, murdered and plundered on every side. The Ukraine, Podolia, in general the southern provinces of Poland, were turned into deserts.

These misfortunes were more advantageous than injurious to the neo-Chassidim. They spread in the north, and whilst hitherto they had been able to carry on their cult only in small, comparatively young communities, from this time they gained ground in the large and old congregations. Their numbers had already grown to such an extent that they formed two branches--the Mizriczians and the Karlinians The former called after their original home, the latter after the village of Karlin, near Pinsk. The Karlinians spread as far as Wilna and Brody. At first they proceeded cautiously. As soon as at least ten persons had assembled, they looked for a room (Stubel) in which to conduct their services; there they practiced the rites of their creed, and sought to gain new adherents; but all this was skillfully done, so that nothing came to light before they had secured a firm foothold. In Lithuania their system was not yet known, and thus at first they aroused no suspicion.

ELIJAH WILNA.

The first violent attack upon them was made by a man whose influence was blessed during his lifetime, and even after death, and who, in a more favorable environment, might, like Mendelssohn, have effected much for the moral advancement of his co-religionists. Elijah Wilna (born 1720; died 1797), whose name, with the title of "Gaon," is still mentioned by the Lithuanian Jews with reverence and love, was a rare exception among the mass of the Polish Jews. He was of the purest character, and possessed high talents, which he did not put to perverted uses. It suffices to say of his character that in spite of his comprehensive and profound Talmudical erudition, he refused a post as rabbi, in contrast to most scholars in Poland, who were office-seekers, and obtained rabbinates by artifice. In spite of the marvelous fertility of his pen in many domains of Jewish literature, he allowed nothing to be published during his lifetime, again in contradistinction to contemporary students, who, in order to make a name and to see their ideas in print, scarcely waited till the ink of their compositions was dry. In his disinterestedness, Elijah Wilna realized the ideal of the Talmud, that a teacher of Judaism "should use the Law neither as a crown to adorn himself therewith, nor as a spade to dig therewith." In spite of the superiority of his knowledge and the full and general recognition accorded him, he modestly and conscientiously avoided asserting himself. The gratification that results from research, from the seeking of knowledge, completely satisfied him. His intellectual method corresponded in its unaffected simplicity with his character and life. As a matter of course, the Talmud and all the branches connected with or dependent on it filled his mind. But he disliked the corrupt method of his countrymen, who indulged in hairsplitting, casuistry, and subtleties. His sole aim was to penetrate to the simple sense of the text; he even made an attempt at the critical examination and emendation of texts, and by his undistorted explanations he blew down the houses of cards which the subtle Talmudists had erected upon quicksand.

It required extraordinary mental force to swim against the high tide of custom and rise above the aberrations into which all the sons of the Talmud in Poland had fallen. In point of fact Elijah Wilna stood isolated in his time. It seemed as though from his youth he had been afraid of following the errors of his compatriots, for he attached himself to no special school, but, strange to say, was his own teacher in the Talmud. Talmudical studies did not exclusively occupy his mind. Elijah Wilna devoted great attention to the Bible--a rarity in his circle--and, what was still more unusual, he acquainted himself with the grammar of the Hebrew language. Unlike his compatriots, he by no means despised a knowledge of extra-Talmudic subjects, but studied mathematics, and wrote a book upon geometry, algebra, and mathematical astronomy. He exhorted his disciples and friends to interest themselves in profane sciences, and openly expressed his conviction that Judaism would be the gainer from such studies, only his scrupulous piety, his immaculate conduct, his unselfishness, and his renunciation of every office and position of honor, saved him from the charge of heresy on account of his pursuing extra-Talmudical branches of knowledge.

Elijah Wilna, above all, implanted a good spirit in the Lithuanian Jews. He taught his sons and disciples to seek simplicity and avoid the casuistry of the Polish method. In Elijah Wilna the beautiful Talmudical saying was exemplified, " He who flees from honors is sought out by them." At an early age he was recognized, even outside of Poland, as an authority and a man of truth. Yet even Elijah was subject to the delusion that the hateful

THE CHASSIDIM ATTACKED.

Kabbala was a true daughter of Judaism, and contained true elements. He deeply lamented the moral ruin wrought by the Kabbala among Podolian and Galician Jews, through the rascally Frank, who had driven them into the arms of the Church, and made them enemies to the Synagogue; yet he could not free himself from it. Even when the danger of these false doctrines was brought home to him by the rise of the Chassidim, and he was compelled openly to oppose them, he could not relinquish his blind fondness for the Kabbala.

The neo-Chassidim, or Karlinians, had crept into Wilna, and had established a secret "Stubel" for their noisy conventicles. A trusty friend of their leader, and an emissary sent by him, had stealthily introduced their cult into the town, and won over several members of the Wilna community. Their meetings, their proceedings, and their derision of the Talmudists, were betrayed. The whole congregation were greatly excited at this. They were indignant that the Karlinians impudently asserted of the respected Elijah Wilna, that, like his occupation and his belief, his life was a lie. The elders and rabbis forthwith took counsel. The Chassidic conventicles were straightway attacked, investigations set on foot, and trials instituted. Writings were found among the Chassidim, which contained the principle that all sadness was to be avoided, even in the repentance for sins. But greatest uneasiness was aroused by the alterations in the liturgy and the disrespectful utterances against the rabbis. Elijah Wilna, who, although he filled no official position, was always invited to the council meetings, and had an important voice in its decisions, took a very serious view of the matter. He beheld in the Chassidic aberration a continuation of Frank's excesses and corrupting influence. The otherwise gentle and meek man became a veritable fanatic. The rabbis and the chiefs of the community, together with Elijah Wilna, addressed a letter to all the large communities, directing them to keep a sharp eye upon the Chassidim, and to excommunicate them until they abandoned their erroneous views. Several congregations immediately obeyed this injunction. In Brody, during the fair, in the presence of many strangers, the ban was published against all those who prayed noisily, deviated from the German synagogue ritual, wore white robes on Sabbath and the festivals, and were guilty of other strange customs and innovations. Elijah Wilna's circle launched a vigorous denunciatory pamphlet against the offenders. This was the first blow that the Chassidim experienced. In addition, their leader, Beer Mizricz, died in the same year (1772)--the rabbis imagined in consequence of the excommunication and thus they felt themselves utterly deserted. Owing to the weakness of the king, and the greed of the neighboring nations, the kingdom of Poland was dismembered. Through this disorganization the union of the Chassidim was broken, and the separated members became dependent upon the legislature, or the arbitrary treatment, of various governments.

However, this storm did not crush them; they remained firm, and did not display the slightest sign of submitting to their opponents (Mithnagdim). On the contrary, the struggle made them more active and energetic. They were not deeply moved by the ban under which they had been placed; this weapon, blunted since the contest for and against Jonathan Eibeschutz, could no longer inflict wounds. The Chassidim, grown to the number of fifty or sixty thousand, formed themselves into small groups, each with a leader, called Rebbe. Their itinerant preachers encouraged the individual communities to persevere in their tenets, and to accept persecution as a salutary trial. The connection of the groups with one another was maintained

in this way; a chief from the family of Beer Mizricz was placed at the head as the supreme Zaddik, to whom the various Rebbe were subordinate, and for whose use they were to set aside a portion of their income. The possible apostasy of members through the onslaughts from Wilna was met by the order that the Chassidim might read no work that had not received the approval of the Chassidic authorities. Obedience towards their leaders had taken so deep a root in the minds of the Chassidim that they never transgressed this prohibition. Their chiefs distributed among them the sermons or collections of sayings supposed to have been written by Israel Baalshem, or Beer Mizricz, which emphasized the high importance of the Zaddik, of the Chassidic life, and of scorn for the Talmudists--vile writings, which were nevertheless read with admiration by the members, who were kept in a constant state of intoxication. What had hitherto been optional and individual was raised by these writings to the rank of statutes and stringent laws.

After Beer's death, two men chiefly contributed to the exaltation of Chassidism, one through his unbounded enthusiasm, the other by his scholarship. These men, neither of whom is open to suspicion, were Israel of Kozieniza (north of Radom) and Salman of Liadi, both Beer's disciples.

So strong did the Chassidim again become, that a second interdict had to be fulminated against them. This time also the persecution originated in Wilna, and was instigated by Elijah Wilna. The Chassidim were declared to be heretics, with whom no pious Jew might intermarry (summer of 1781)· Two messengers were sent from Wilna to the Lithuanian congregations to induce them to support the ban. In consequence of this, the collections of Chassidic sermons and other writings, although they contained sentences from Holy Writ, were publicly burnt in Brody and Cracow. In Selvia, near Slonim, during the fair, in the presence of large numbers of Jews, the ban was publicly promulgated against the Chassidim and their writings (August 21, 1781); but these obsolete methods were of little use. In the Austrian Polish provinces (Galicia) other means were employed by the disciples of the Mendelssohn school against the stultifying system of the Chassidim. The decree of Joseph II, that schools for instruction in German and elementary subjects be established in all Jewish communities, encountered vigorous resistance from all Jews, but especially from Chassidim. In the belief that culture would improve the demoralized and barbarous state of the people, a small body of men, Mendelssohn's admirers, strove zealously to oppose them. Among the most ardent workers for the enlightenment of the Galician Jews was Alexander Kaller and his associates probably obtained a decree from the court at Vienna, commanding that no Chassidic or Kabbalistic writings be admitted into Galicia (1785)· After the second partition of Poland, denunciations were also leveled against the Chassidim in Russian Poland as dangerous to the state. Salman of Liadi was dragged in chains to St. Petersburg. Elijah Wilna is said to have been the instigator of this charge, too; indeed, he persecuted the sect as long as he lived. After his death the Chassidim took vengeance upon him by dancing upon his grave, and celebrating the day of his decease as a holiday, with shouting and drunkenness. All efforts made to suppress the Chassidim were in vain, because in a measure they represented a just principle, that of opposing the excesses of Talmudism. Before the end of the eighteenth century they had increased to 100,000 souls. At the present day they rule in congregations where they were formerly persecuted, and they are spreading on all sides.

V. CHAPTER XI:

THE FRENCH REVOLUTION AND THE EMANCIPATION OF THE JEWS

The Jewish Question and the National Assembly--Efforts to equalize Paris Jews--Jewish Question deferred--Equalization of French Jews--Bonaparte in Palestine

1791-1805 C. E.

At the outbreak of the Revolution, there lived in France scarcely 50,000 Jews--almost half of whom (20,000) dwelt in Alsace--under the most oppressive yoke. In Metz, the largest, "the pattern community," only 420 Jewish families were tolerated, and in the whole of Lorraine only 180, and these were not allowed to increase. In Paris, in spite of stringent prohibitions, a congregation of about 500 persons had gathered (since 1740); about as many lived in Bordeaux, the majority of them of new-Christian or Portuguese descent. There were also some communities in the papal districts of Avignon and Carpentras. In Carpentras there dwelt about 700 families (over 2,000 souls) with their own rabbinate. Those in the best condition were the Jews of Bordeaux and the daughter community of Bayonne. Among the Jews of the various provinces there was as little connection as among those in other European countries. Misfortune had separated them. Thus it happened that no concerted action was taken to obtain naturalization from the National Assembly at once, although Gregoire, the Catholic priest, true love for mankind in his heart, exhorted them to seize this favorable opportunity. They indeed boasted men of energy, filled with love for their race, and ready for self-sacrifice, men of tact, such as Cerf Berr, Furtado, Isaac Berr, and David Gradis, but at first no measures were taken. An appeal for united action may possibly have been made, but the pride of the Portuguese probably made it ineffectual. Therefore, in the first stormy months of the Revolution, nothing was undertaken for the emancipation of the Jews. The deputies in the States General or the National Assembly were sufficiently occupied without thinking of the Jews. Besides, they adhered rather closely to the program enumerating the wishes of their electors, on which the emancipation of the Jews was not mentioned. The deputies of Alsace and Lorraine, in fact, had received instructions to attack the Jews. The assaults made upon the Jews in the German provinces, as a result of the disorders of the Revolution, first moved the victims to bring their complaints before the National Assembly. It was, perhaps, an advantage that the ripe fruit of liberty did not fall into their laps, but that they had to exert themselves energetically to obtain it; for thus liberty became the more precious to them.

The storming of the Bastille had finally torn the scepter from the deluded king, and handed it over

to the people. The Revolution had tasted blood, and began to inflict punishment upon the tyrants. In many parts of the land, as if by agreement, castles were burnt down, monasteries destroyed, and the nobility maltreated or slain. The people, brought up in ignorance by the Church, and now released from the chains of slavery, knew not how to distinguish friend from foe, and rushed recklessly upon what lay nearest their stupid gaze. In Alsace the lower classes of the people at the same time made a fierce attack upon the Jews (beginning of August, 1789)--perhaps incited by secret Jew-haters--destroying their houses, plundering their property, and forcing them to flee half-naked. They, who hitherto had been humiliated and enslaved by the nobles and the clergy, were now fellow-sufferers with their tyrants. The Alsatian Jews mostly escaped to Basle, and although no Jew was allowed to live there, the fugitives were sheltered and sympathetically treated. Complaints were made to the National Assembly of the excesses after the first draught of liberty; from that Assembly all expected help, no longer from the monarchy, which had already become a mere shadow. Every deputy received detailed reports of disquieting, sometimes sanguinary, events. The ill-treated Jews of Alsace had turned to Gregoire, and he sketched (August 3) a gloomy picture of the outrages upon the Jews, and added that he, a servant of a religion which regards all men as brothers, requested the interference of the powerful arm of the Assembly on behalf of this despised and unhappy people. He also published a pamphlet, called "Proposals in Favor of the Jews," to influence public opinion. Then followed the memorable night of the Fourth of August, which covered the French nation with eternal fame, when the nobles sacrificed their privileges on the altar of freedom, and acknowledged the equality of all citizens--the birth-hour of a new order of things. In consequence of this agitation, and dreading that they might fall victims to anarchy, the Jews of the various provinces resolved to present petitions for admission into the fraternity of the French people; but again they acted singly, and to some extent preferred contradictory requests. The Jews of Bordeaux had already joined the National Guard, and one was even appointed captain. They had only one desire, that their equalization be sealed by law, and this wish their four deputies, David Gradis, Furtado, Lopes-Dubec, and Rodrigues, publicly expressed. About a hundred Parisian Jews were also enrolled in the National Guard, and rivaled the other citizens in patriotism and revolutionary spirit. They sent eleven deputies to the National Assembly, who prayed for the removal of the ignominy which covered them as Jews, and for equalization by law, saying that the example of the French people would induce all the nations of the earth to acknowledge the Jews as brothers. The community of Metz desired besides that their oppressive taxes be removed, and the debts which they had contracted in consequence of the taxes be made void. The communities of Lorraine sent a delegate to the National Assembly, Berr Isaac Berr (born 1744; died 1828), who, a man of many virtues and merits, and an admirer of Mendelssohn and Wessely, had great influence. He drew up a petition containing the special request that the authority and autonomy of the rabbis in internal affairs be established and recognized by law. The deputies for Luneville and an adjacent community protested against this. It was a long time, however, before the Jewish question became the distinct order of the day. The National Assembly seemed to shrink from discussing the point, for fear of stirring up public opinion still more passionately in the German provinces with their obstinate prejudices and hatred of Jews.

Religious intolerance manifested itself even in

FREEDOM OF WORSHIP.

the Assembly. On the 23d of August an exciting sitting was held. The subject of debate was whether the inviolable rights of man, to be placed at the head of the constitution, were to include religious freedom of conscience and freedom of worship. A deputy, De Castellane, had formulated this point plainly: " No man shall be molested on account of his religious opinions, nor disturbed in the practice of his belief." Against this motion a storm arose on the part of the Catholic Clergy and other representatives of Catholicism. They continually spoke of a dominant religion or confession, which, as hitherto, should be supported by the State, whilst other creeds might be tolerated. In vain Mirabeau raised a bold protest against such presumptuousness. "The unrestricted freedom of belief is so sacred in my eyes, that even the word tolerance sounds despotic to me, because the very existence of an authority empowered to tolerate, insults freedom, in that it tolerates, because it might do the reverse"

But his powerful voice was drowned by the opposing clamor. The clever speech of another deputy, Rabaud Saint Etienne, however, gained the victory for freedom of conscience. He spoke also on behalf of the Jews. "I demand liberty for the nation of the Jews, always condemned, homeless, wandering over the face of the whole globe, and doomed to humiliation. Banish forever the aristocracy of thought, the feudal system of opinion, which desires to rule others and impose compulsion upon them."

Amidst strong opposition the law was passed, which has since become the basis of the European constitution :

" No one shall be molested on account of his religious opinions, in so far as their outward expression does not disturb public order as established by law."

Therewith one point in the petition of the French Jews was disposed of. But when the Jewish question afterwards came on for treatment (September 3), it was postponed, and handed over to a committee. Three weeks later the Assembly was again obliged to deal with the Jewish question. Persecutions which the Jews underwent in certain places forced it upon them. Those in

Nancy were threatened with pillage, because they were reproached with having bought up provisions and raised the prices. The Jewish question became so pressing, that the order of the day (on September 28) was interrupted by it. It was again Gregoire who defended the persecuted. He was supported by Count Clermont-Tonnerre, a sincere friend of liberty. With glowing eloquence he pointed out that Christian society was guilty of the degradation of the Jews, and that it must offer them some atonement. The Assembly thereupon resolved that the president address a circular letter to the various towns, stating that the declaration of the rights of man, which the Assembly had accepted, comprehended all men upon earth, therefore also the Jews, who were no longer to be harassed. The king, with his enfeebled authority, was asked to protect the Jews from further persecutions. This action, however, produced no results for the sufferers. The Jews of Alsace remained exposed to attack, as before. The Jewish representatives of the three bishoprics of Alsace and Lorraine lost patience, seeing that their equalization was being constantly deferred. They therefore strove to obtain a hearing for themselves. Introduced by the deputies of Lorraine to the National Assembly (October 14), Berr, the indefatigable advocate of his co-religionists, delivered a speech, in which he portrayed the sufferings of a thousand years, and implored humane treatment for them. He worthily fulfilled his task. He was obliged to be brief; the Assembly, which had to establish a new edifice upon the ruins of the old kingdom, could not spare time for long speeches. President Preteau replied that the Assembly would

feel itself happy to be able to afford rest and happiness to the Jews of France. The meeting applauded his words, permitted the Jewish deputies to be present as guests at the proceedings, and promised to take the equalization of the Jews into consideration at the next sitting. From this time the French Jews confidently hoped that their emancipation would be realized.

Meanwhile, the Revolution had again made a gigantic stride forward: the people had brought the proud French sovereign like a prisoner from Versailles to Paris. The deputies also moved to Paris, and the capital became more and more infected with revolutionary fever. The youthful Parisian Jews, as well as the immigrants, took great interest in all occurrences. Even the middle classes aided the cause of the fatherland by supplying funds. At length the Jewish question was to be settled. A deputy was appointed to report upon it, and a special sitting called. But it was brought into connection with another question, namely, the franchise of executioners, actors, and Protestants, to whom the Catholic population in some towns did not wish to grant permission to vote.

The report was sent in by Clermont-Tonnerre, and spoke most logically in favor of all four classes. All sincere friends of liberty, Robespierre, Duport, Barnave, and, of course, Mirabeau, expressed themselves in favor of the Jews and their fellow-sufferers. The followers of the old school opposed them with determination, chief among them Abbe Maury, Bishop LaFare of Nancy, and the bishop of Clermont. Only one ultra-revolutionist, Reubell, from Alsace, spoke against the Jews, maintaining that it was dangerous forthwith to grant complete rights of citizenship to those resident in Alsace, against whom there was deeply-rooted hatred. Abbe Maury produced utterly false, or partially true statements, as arguments for unfriendly behavior towards the Jews. He even quoted Voltaire's anti-Jewish writings in order to prejudice the Assembly. The Assembly hesitated; it feared to attack the gross prejudice entertained by the populace of the eastern provinces against the Jews. At the representation of one of the deputies, the equalization of the Jews was separated from that of the Protestants, and the resolution ran in this equivocal manner: that the Assembly reserved to itself the right of deciding about the Jews, without determining upon anything new concerning them. This reservation was repeated at the discussion of the laws for the election of municipal officers (January 8, 1790), from which Jews were excluded.

This evasive decision grossly offended the Portuguese Jews of Bordeaux. Hitherto they had tacitly enjoyed all the rights of citizens, and in their turn fulfilled all their duties with self-sacrificing readiness. Now they were to be kept in uncertainty about their civil status, in company with the German Jews, against whom they bore an antipathy not less than that of hostile Christians. They therefore hastily dispatched a deputation to Paris to cause this injurious resolution to be rescinded. As the population were on better terms with the Portuguese, their request was easily obtained. The deputy for Bordeaux, De Seze, spoke warmly on their behalf. Talleyrand, then bishop of Autun, was appointed to report upon the matter, and concisely suggested (February 28), that those Jews who had hitherto enjoyed civil rights as naturalized Frenchmen should continue to enjoy that privilege. The enemies of the Jews, of course, opposed this motion, fearing that it would apply also to German Jews.

Nevertheless, the majority decided that those Jews in France who were called Portuguese, Spaniards, or Avignonese (of Bordeaux and Bayonne) should enjoy full privileges as active citizens, and the king at once approved of this law. It was

GODARD.

the first legal recognition of the Jews as citizens, and, though only a partial recognition, it at least would serve as a precedent.

The deputies of the Jews from German districts did not so easily attain success ; they had to struggle hard for equality. At the same time they lighted upon a means whereby to bring pressure to bear upon the National Assembly, and induce them to concede them full citizenship. There were five men who worked most perseveringly to remove all obstacles. They won over to their side the fiery, eloquent advocate Godard, to plead their cause with pen and tongue. They knew that power was no longer in the hands of the National Assembly, but had been seized by the parties of the capital, who, with their revolutionary ardor, held complete sway over Paris, the deliberating Assembly, the king, almost the whole country. The Jewish representatives from Paris, Alsace, and Lorraine therefore turned to them for help. They had Godard draw up a petition to the National Assembly, stating that the emancipation of the Jews was not only demanded by the principles of the Constituent Assembly and by justice, but that it was cruelty to withhold it. For, so long as their equality was not legally established, the people would believe that they were indeed the outcasts their enemies had described them to be. But even more efficacious than this petition was a scene which the Parisian Jews arranged with their advocate, before the General Assembly of the Paris Commune; it decided the question. Fifty Jewish members of the National Guards, adorned with cockades, among them Salkind Hurwitz, the Pole, appeared as deputies before the Assembly of the Commune, and petitioned that the city of Paris itself should energetically set about obtaining equality for the Jews. Godard delivered a fiery speech in their support. The president of the General Assembly, Abbe Mulot, replied to this vigorous address with the fervid eloquence peculiar to the orators of the Revolution : "The chasm between their religious conceptions and the truth which we as Christians profess, cannot hinder us as men from approaching each other, and even if we reproach each other with our errors and complain of each other, at least we can love each other." In the name of the meeting he promised to support the petition of the Paris Jews for equalization. Next day (January 29,1790), the Jews of Paris obtained a certificate, couched in most flattering terms, and testifying to their excellent reputation, from the inhabitants of the district of the Carmelites, where most Jews dwelt at this time.

The six deputies appointed for the district of the Carmelites then went to the City Hall, to support the resolution in favor of the Jews. One of them, Cahier de Gerville, afterwards a minister, delivered an impressive address. "Do not be surprised," said he, " that this district hastens to be the first to make public recognition of the patriotism, the courage, and the nobility of the Jews who dwell in it. No citizen has proved himself more zealous for the gaining of liberty than the Jew. . . none has displayed more sense of order and justice, none shown more benevolence towards the poor, and readiness in voluntarily contributing towards the expenses of the district. Let us attack all prejudices, and attack them with determination. Let not one of the monstrosities of despotism and ignorance survive the new birth of liberty and the consecration of the rights of man . . . Take into consideration the just and pressing demands in favor of our new brethren, and join your wishes to their petition, so that thus united they may come before the National Assembly. Do not doubt but that you will obtain, without trouble, for the Jews of Paris that which was not denied the Jews of Portugal, Spain, and Avignon. What reason is there for

showing a preference for this class? Do not all Jews hold the same doctrines? Are not our political conditions alike for the one as for the other? If the ancestors of those Jews on whose behalf we plead experienced more bitter suffering and persecution than the Portuguese Jews, then this long, cruel oppression which they have sustained should give them a new claim to national justice. For the rest, look to the origin of these strange and unjust distinctions, and see whether any one today dares set up a distinction of rights between two classes of the same people, two branches of the same stem, basing his action upon apocryphal tradition, or rather upon chimeras and fables."

To this speech the President Abbe Mulot replied, bringing into prominence the fact that the report from the district of the Carmelites was to be considered of great weight in favor of the Jews.

The next speech, that of Abbe Bertolio, at length induced the meeting to add its favorable testimony to the Jews of Paris, and to express the wish to the National Assembly that these Jews, most of them of German birth, be put on an equal footing with the Portuguese. Mayor Bailly and his committee on the same day passed the resolution, that as soon as the other districts announced their approval, the whole weight of the influence of the municipality of Paris be exerted on behalf of the equalization of the Jews. In the course of the following month all the city districts, with the exception of that of the Halles, sent in their approval of the decision of the Carmelite district. Accordingly, a deputation of the Commune, together with its president, Abbe Mulot, officially commissioned by the capital (February 25), presented itself at the meeting of the National Assembly, to request, or rather by moral suasion to compel, that body to extend to Jews resident in Paris the decree declaring the Portuguese Jews full citizens.

After some delay, certain deputies demanded (April 15) that the Jewish question be placed on the order of the day. Abbe Maury again opposed the motion, and promised to present a memorial which the Jews should be called upon to answer. In order, however, to protect the Jews of Alsace from the attacks of mobs, the Assembly again decreed that they were under protection of the laws, and that the magistrates and the National Guard were to take precautions for their security. In this way they appeased their consciences. The king forthwith sanctioned (April 18) the law of protection for the Alsatian Jews, after which the question was not broached for three months.

Fortunately the Jewish question did not stand isolated, but was connected with other questions. The Jews of Alsace, especially those of Metz, had to pay high protection-taxes. When the subject of finances came on for discussion, the Assembly had to determine whether this tax should continue or cease. They came to a liberal decision, although the deputies were sorely troubled about the deficit thus created. The secretary of the committee of the crown land, Vismes, first showed how unjust it was that the community of Metz, which Louis XIV, once when in good humor, had given to the Duke of Brancas and the Countess De Fontaine, should pay annually to the house of Brancas 20,000 francs. He therefore proposed that the Jew taxes should be remitted without any indemnification, and that every tribute, under whatever name--protection money, residence-tax, or tolerance-money--should cease. This proposal was passed into law (July 20) almost without opposition. Louis XVI, who by this act saw another remnant of the Middle Ages vanish, at first showed himself tardy in confirming the law (August 7). Ten years previously the Jews of Alsace had in vain presented a memorial to the state council detailing the misery of their condition;

it received no notice. Owing to the sudden revolution of affairs, they now achieved in less than an hour more than they had ever dared hope for.

But the National Assembly would not proceed to deal with the chief demand of the Jews of the Lower Rhine--as these districts were then called--to grant them civil rights. Several had expressed themselves favorably, when the Duc de Broglie intervened with a violent speech. He asserted that the proposed resolution would engender new causes of excitement in Lorraine and Alsace, already in a state of ferment owing to the action of the clergy who refused to take the oath. Strasburg was likewise greatly excited on account of the Jews, who desired to settle there, where hitherto no Jew had been permitted. De Broglie further remarked that the general body of Jews in Alsace was utterly indifferent to citizenship ; that the petition presented in their name was an intrigue carried on by four or five Jews; especially one, who had amassed a great fortune at the expense of the state (Cerf Berr), was scattering large sums of money most liberally in Paris, to gain adherents for the scheme of equalization. His motion to adjourn this question till the Constitution was finished was carried.

But the Constitution was definitely fixed and ratified by the king (September, 1791), and the German-speaking Jews of France did not obtain the equality so often promised. Only the paragraph in the "Rights of Man," which said that no one might be molested on account of his religious opinions, benefited them. At last, a few days before the dissolution of the National Assembly, the Jews were remembered by one of the friends of liberty, Duport, a member of the Jacobin Club, formerly a parliamentary councilor. In a speech of a few words he procured the equality they so much desired. He drew the natural conclusion from the above-quoted rights of religious freedom, and said, " I believe that freedom of thought does not permit any distinction in political rights on account of a man's creed. The recognition of this equality is always being postponed. Meanwhile the Turks, Moslems, and men of all sects, are permitted to enjoy political rights in France. I demand that the motion for adjournment be withdrawn, and a decree passed that the Jews in France enjoy the privileges of citizenship (citoyens actifs)." This proposition was accepted amid loud applause. In vain did Reubell strive to oppose the motion, he was interrupted. Another member suggested that every one who spoke against this motion be called to order, because he would be opposing the Constitution itself. Thus the National Assembly adopted (September 27, 1791) Duport's proposal, and next day formulated the law that all exceptional regulations against Jews be abrogated, and that the German Jews be admitted to the oath of citizenship. Two days later the National Assembly was dissolved, to make way for a still more violent revolutionary assembly. A few days later Louis XVI confirmed this full equalization of the French Jews (November 13, l791)· They were not required to swerve one iota from their religion as the price of emancipation; all demanded of them being that they forego certain ancient privileges.

Berr Isaac Berr was justified in rejoicing at this success, in which he had had a large share. He at once dispatched a letter of congratulation to his co-religionists, to rouse enthusiasm for their newly attained freedom, and at the same time incline them to appropriate improvements:

BERR ISAAC BERR

"This nation asks no thanks, except that we show ourselves worthy citizens."

Berr added certain important, timely remarks, in which he gently pointed out to his French co-religionists faults growing out of their former wretched plight, and admonished them to remove these faults.

He also supplied the French Jews with means to enable them to become thorough Frenchmen and at the same time remain members of the House of Jacob. The Bible was to be rendered into French on the basis of Mendelssohn's German translation, and put into the hands of the young, so that the corrupt German language which they used might be completely banished from their midst. Berrthus attacked a foolish prejudice which regarded the German or Jewish-German dialect as akin in sanctity to the Hebrew, therefore a more worthy organ for Divine Service than the language of Voltaire.

With great assiduity and self-sacrifice, most of the French Jews interested themselves in the welfare of the state which had given them a fatherland, liberty, and equality. They destroyed at one blow all the calumniations of their opponents, who had asserted that as Jews they would not be able to fulfill the duties of citizens. They came to the front whenever the state stood in need of help.

Together with the victorious French troops of the Republic, the deliverance of the Jews, the most oppressed race of the ancient world, advanced from one place to another. It took firm root in Holland, which had been changed into a Batavian Republic (beginning of 1795). Here several energetic Jews, among them Asser (Moses and Carolus), De Lemon, and Bromet, had joined a club, called Felix Libertate, which had taken the motto of the French Republic--Liberty, Equality, Fraternity.

NAPOLEON IN PALESTINE.

The name of the invincible French, who had achieved wonderful victories in Italy, quickly spread abroad, even beyond Europe, and aroused terror and surprise in the most remote countries. A new Alexander, the Corsican Bonaparte, a god of war when scarcely thirty years old, set out with a comparatively small army to subdue Egypt, and hoped to penetrate to India. In less than six months (July--November, 1798) Egypt lay crushed at his feet. But a Turkish army was on its way to meet him, against which Bonaparte advanced into Palestine. Thus, through a marvelous series of historical events, the Holy Land became the scene of a bloody war between the representatives of the old and the new spirit in Europe.

El Arish and Gaza in the southwest of Palestine fell into the hands of the French army, which scarcely numbered l2,000 men (17th and 25th February, 1799). The Jewish community of Gaza had fled. In Jerusalem the news of French victories and cruelty created a panic. It was rumored that Napoleon was about to enter the Holy City. At the command of the sub-pasha, or Motusallim, the inhabitants began to throw up ramparts, the Jews taking part in the work. One of their rabbis, Mordecai Joseph Meyuchas, encouraged and even assisted them in their operations. The Turks had circulated the report that the French treated Jews particularly in a cruel manner. Bonaparte had issued a summons to the Asiatic and African Jews to march under his banners, promising to give them the Holy Land, and restore ancient Jerusalem to its pristine splendor. But the Jews in Jerusalem appear either not to have trusted in these flattering words, or to have been utterly ignorant of the proclamation. Probably it was only a trick on the part of Bonaparte, intended to win over to his side the Jewish minister of the pasha of Acco, Chayim Maalem Farchi (assassinated in 1820), the soul of the defense of the important sea-fortress of Acco. Had Bonaparte succeeded in conquering Syria and carrying the war into the heart of Turkey, he would perhaps have assigned a share in his government to members of the Jewish nation upon whom the French could rely. But the appearance of Bonaparte in Palestine was like that of a terrible meteor, which disappears after causing much devastation. His dream to become Emperor of the East, and restore Jerusalem to the Jews, quickly faded away.

V. CHAPTER XII.

THE JEWISH-FRENCH SYNHEDRION AND THE JEWISH CONSISTORIES.

Assembly of Notables-Italian Deputies--The Twelve Questions--Debate on Mixed Marriages--The Paris Synhedrion--Its Constitution-Napoleon and his enactments--Emancipation in Germany

1806-1813 C.E.

Jewish affairs now assumed a serious complexion. Napoleon laid the Jewish question for discussion before his council, which entrusted it to a young member, a Count Mole, known in later French history as the prototype of ambiguity. To the surprise of all the elder and more influential members of the council, Mole, whose great-grandmother was a Jewess, presented a report decidedly hostile to the Jews, suggesting that all French Jews be placed under exceptional laws, which meant that their legally acknowledged and practically realized equality was to be taken from them. His report was received with deserved derision by the oldest members of the council, who were so imbued with the principle of absolute equality sanctified by the Revolution, that they could not conceive that a creditor suing for payment from his debtor could have a right to inquire into his religious belief. They suspected that Mole was in league with the reactionary politicians Fontanes and Bonald, who was anxious to offer up the Jews as the first sacrifice to their retrograde policy. Mole, however, appears to have sought to curry favor with the emperor, who, as he knew, was not kindly disposed towards the Jews, Although all the councilors were in favor of their unabridged civil rights, the Jewish question was to be brought up at the regular session of the state council under the presidency of Napoleon (April 30, 1806), who attached great importance to the matter.

It was a fateful moment when these questions, settled long ago, came up for discussion. The weal and woe not alone of the French and Italian Jews, but of those in all Europe, depended upon the issue of this consultation. For if the equalization of the Jews of the former countries was in any way threatened, those of other countries would be doomed to remain in a state of degradation and oppression for a long time to come.

NAPOLEON ORDERS A JEWISH ASSEMBLY.

At a second sitting of the state council (May 7, 1806) Napoleon spoke in a milder tone of the Jews. He rejected the proposal made to him to expel Jewish peddlers, and endow the tribunals of justice with unlimited authority over usurers. He desired to do nothing that might be disapproved by posterity, or darken his fame. Nevertheless, he could not free himself from the prejudice that the Jewish people, from the most ancient times, even from the days of Moses, had been usurers and extortioners. He was, however, determined not to permit any persecution or neglect of the Jews. He then conceived the happy thought--or it may have been suggested to him--to bring together a number of Jews from various provinces, who were to tell him whether Judaism demanded of its adherents hatred and oppression of Christians. The Jews themselves, through the medium of their representatives, were to decide their fate.

OPENING OF THE JEWISH PARLIAMENT.

Thus the first Jewish Parliament in Paris assembled on a Sabbath, in a room of the Hotel de Ville, decorated with appropriate emblems. The deputies attended in full force, none were absent ; some of them intentionally came in carriages. Some of the stricter members again tried to have the first meeting postponed, but in vain. The dread of Napoleon's authority terrified those who as a rule paid scrupulous regard to religious ordinances. Under the chairmanship of

Rabbi Solomon Lipmann, the oldest member, the election now proceeded. The orthodox had provided themselves with ballot tickets, but most of the others wrote them out unabashed before the very eyes of the rabbis [thus violating the Sabbath--ed.], whilst a few had theirs written for them. Only two men were qualified for the presidency, Berr Isaac Berr and Furtado. The former was supported by the orthodox party, the latter by the politicians. Furtado obtained the majority of votes. With parliamentary tact he presided over the meeting. The deputies became fully conscious of the grave responsibility resting upon them, and proved themselves equal to their task. All were animated by a strong desire for unanimity.

Even the German rabbis, who hitherto had been buried in the seclusion of the academies amidst the Talmud volumes, quickly adapted themselves to the new circumstances and to parliamentary forms. Certain deputies contributed to impress all present with a feeling of concord. The speech of the deputy Lipmann Cerf Berr had a remarkable effect, especially the following words:--"Let us forget our origin! Let us no longer speak of Jews of Alsace, of Portugal, or of Germany. Though scattered over the face of the globe, we are still one people worshipping the same God, and as our law commands us, we are to obey the laws of the country where we live."

When the officer of the guard of honor furnished for the meeting approached the newly-elected president to receive his orders, and when at the departure of the deputies, the guard greeted them with military honors and beat of drums, they felt themselves exalted, and their fear was turned to hope.

This joyful expectation revived their courage, and enabled them to oppose the attacks of Jew-hating writers. Meantime the whole body of deputies from the kingdom of Italy arrived, and created a favorable impression by their bearing. Amongst them the spirit of the age manifested itself in difference of religious views and opinions, although not so sharply marked as among the French and German Jews.

The most distinguished among the Jewish-Italian deputies was Abraham Vita di Cologna (born 1755, died in Trieste, 1832). He was well versed both in Rabbinical and scientific learning, of prepossessing appearance, and an elegant speaker. While rabbi of Mantua, he was elected a member of the Parliament of the Italian kingdom. His Talmudical and secular knowledge, however, was neither comprehensive nor deep. Cologna was in favor of the new tendency, which removed Judaism from its isolated position to imbue it with European ideas; but both the means and end were not clearly defined in his mind, and he took no steps to carry out his wishes. An elder member of the Italian notables, Joshua Benzion Segre (born about 1724 died 1809), at once owner of an estate, rabbi, and municipal councilor of Vercelli, was also in favor of scientific studies, and belonged to the advanced party, The follies of the Kabbala still found many supporters among educated Italian Jews, although its first opponents had come from Italy. Benzion Segre was averse to the study, while the Italian deputy Graziadio (Chanannel) Nepi, rabbi and physician in Cinto (born 1760, died 1836), was a firm believer in it. He was exceedingly well read in Jewish literature, and compiled an alphabetical register of the names of Jewish authors of ancient and modern times.

TWELVE QUESTIONS.

At the second sitting (July 29), the three imperial commissioners solemnly propounded twelve questions, which the Assembly were to answer conscientiously. The chief points were, whether the French Jews regarded France as their country, and Frenchmen as then brothers; whether they considered the laws of the state as binding upon them, and, by way of deduction from these two points, the incisive third question, "Can Jews legally intermarry with Christians," and, lastly, whether usury in the case of non-Jews is permitted or forbidden. The remaining points referred to polygamy, divorce, and the authority of the rabbis, and were of a subordinate nature. Most of the members could not listen to these queries without feeling pain that their love of country and their attachment to France should be called into question, notwithstanding that Jews had attested their patriotism by shedding their blood upon battlefields. From many sides rose a cry at these questions, "Aye, unto death." The address delivered by Mole on submitting these twelve questions was cold and to some extent offensive. Its contents were nearly as follows:--The charges against various Jews had been proved. The emperor was, however, not satisfied to check the evil himself, but desired the assistance of the deputies. They were to state the whole truth in replying to the questions laid before them. The emperor permitted full liberty of discussion, but wished them to bear in mind that they were Frenchmen, and would be relinquishing that honor unless they showed themselves worthy of it. The assembly now knew what was expected. They were brought face to face with the alternative of renouncing their equality or damaging Judaism.

Furtado, in his reply to the speech of the commissioner, very cleverly turned the mistrust of the emperor into a semblance of trust. He said that the Jews welcomed the opportunity of answering these questions, to lay bare all errors and put an end to the prejudices entertained against them. The speech which Berr Isaac Berr delivered at this meeting was more sincere, more manly, and altogether more fervent. Furtado represented the Jews, but not Judaism; he caused it to be understood that the Assembly should consider it a duty and an honor to obey every hint of the emperor. Berr gave dignified expression to the claims of Judaism. The duty of replying to the questions was assigned to a commission, which included, besides the president, the secretary, and the auditors, the four most eminent rabbis, Sinzheim, Andrade, De Cologna, and Segre, and two learned laymen.

This commission handed over the chief part of their work to Rabbi David Sinzheim, the most scholarly and esteemed member of the assembly, who in a very short time completed his task to the satisfaction of his colleagues, of the imperial commissioners, and eventually of the emperor (July 30 till August 3). His report was submitted to the commissioners, who reported it to the emperor before it was brought up for public discussion. Napoleon was so pleased with the behavior of the Assembly that he announced his intention to grant an audience to all the members. In fact, their parliamentary tact, as displayed in the proceedings, filled him with such high regard towards them that he partially overcame his prejudices against the Jews. He had always pictured them as ragmen and usurers, with cringing, bent forms, or as sly, cunning flatterers lying in ambush for their prey ; and to his astonishment he beheld among the members men of fine character, intelligence, and imposing appearance. He thus acquired a better opinion of the Jews. It must be admitted that the incense offered him by the Assembly, as to a deity, did not leave him unmoved. On the other hand, the serious task placed before the Jewish deputies made them greater, exalted them above the common level, idealized

them. Their harmonious work aroused their enthusiasm, the orations intoxicated them, and even the sober German members became infected.

At the third sitting (August 4), at the debate upon the replies to the various questions, the deputies were filled with self-confidence and the certainty of victory. No difficulty was offered by the first two questions--whether polygamy was allowed among Jews, and whether the validity of a divorce granted by the French law was acknowledged by their religious and moral code. These were decided according to the desire of the emperor without any injury to Judaism. But the third question aroused painful excitement, and revealed the opposition which had divided the Jews since the time of Mendelssohn--"May a Jewess marry a Christian, or a Christian woman a Jew?" This question had given rise to heated debates in the commission, how much more in public assembly. Even the orthodox party felt that to reply unconditionally in the negative would be extremely perilous. The commission, however, had already supplied a clever answer, and if it is owing to Sinzheim's efforts, it redounds to his intellect and tact. At the outset it was skillfully explained that, according to the Bible, only marriages with Canaanite nations were forbidden. Even by the Talmud intermarriages were allowed, because the nations of Europe were not considered idolaters. The rabbis, to be sure, were opposed to such unions, seeing that the usual ceremonies could not be performed. They would refuse to bless such an union, as the Catholic priests refused their assistance on such occasions. This refusal, however, was of little consequence, as civil marriages were recognized by: the state. At all events, the rabbis considered a Jew or Jewess who had contracted a union of this kind as a full co-religionist.

The remaining questions were settled without any excitement in two sittings (August 7th and 12th). The questions whether the Jews regarded Frenchmen as their brothers, and France as their country, were answered by the Assembly with a loud, enthusiastic affirmative. They were able to refer to the doctrines of Judaism, which in its three phases--Biblical, Talmudical, and Rabbinical--had always emphasized humanity and the brotherhood of man. Only one point in the report of the commission gave rise to a certain amount of friction, viz., that which seemed to ascribe a kind of superiority to the Portuguese Jews, as if through their conduct they were held in higher esteem by Christians than the German Jews. This clause was therefore struck out.

In answering the two questions relative to usury, the Assembly was able to demolish a deeply-rooted prejudice and place Judaism in a favorable light.

The commissioner Mole, the first to yield to Jew-hatred and propose to exclude Jews from state offices, had now to declare publicly (September 18) that the emperor was satisfied with the intentions and zeal of the assembly. His speech on this occasion struck quite a different note to former ones. "Who, indeed," he exclaimed, "would not be astonished at the sight of this assembly of enlightened men, selected from among the descendants of the most ancient of nations? If an individual of past centuries could come to life, and if this scene met his gaze, would he not think himself transplanted within the walls of the Holy City ? or might he not imagine that a thorough revolution in the affairs of man had taken place?" " His Majesty," continued Mole, "guarantees to you the free practice of your religion and the full enjoyment of your political rights; but in exchange for these valuable privileges, he demands a religious surety that you will completely realize the principles expressed in your answers."

What could the surety be? Napoleon then

THE SYNHEDRION.

announced a surprising message, which filled the assembly with joyful astonishment and electrified them. "The emperor proposes to call together the great Synhedrion !" This part of their national government, which had perished together with the Temple, and which alone had been endowed with authority in Israel, was now to be revived for the purpose of transforming the answers of the Assembly into decisions, which should command the highest respect, equally with those of the Talmud, with Jews of all countries and throughout all centuries. Further, the Assembly was to make known the meeting of the great Sanhedrion to all the synagogues in Europe, so that they send to Paris deputies capable of advising the government with intelligence, and worthy of belonging to this assembly. That the revived Synhedrion might possess the honorable and imposing character of its model, it was to be constituted on the pattern of the former one; it was to consist of seventy-one members, and have a president (Nasi), a vice-president (Ab-Beth-Din), and a second vice-president (Chacham). This announcement made the deputies feel as if the ancient glory of Israel had suddenly risen from the tomb and once more assumed a solid shape. Three months previously they had been summoned to rescue their civil rights which were endangered, and now a new vista opened before them; they seemed to behold their glorious past revived in the present, and assisted in the accomplishment of the dream; and they were filled with amazement.

Naturally, on receipt of this announcement, the Assembly passed enthusiastic motions and votes of thanks. They expressed their approval of everything which the commissioners had proposed or intimated. The Synhedrion was to be composed of two-thirds rabbis and one-third laymen, and was to include all the rabbis in the Assembly of Notables, together with others to be afterwards elected. The true importance of the Assembly now came to an end; its duties now were merely perfunctory. The proclamation issued to the whole Jewish world (Tishri 24-October 6) was its only momentous action thereafter. It aimed at rousing the Jews to take an interest in the Synhedrion and to send deputies. This proclamation was written in four languages, Hebrew, French, German, and Italian, and expressed the feelings which animated members of the Assembly, and the hopes entertained for the great Synhedrion.

The Jewish Parliament, and the re-establishment of a Synhedrion created much interest in Europe. The world was accustomed to Napoleon's feats of war and brilliant victories; the power of his arms had ceased to astonish men. But that this admired and terrible hero should descend to the most ancient people, to raise and restore them to some of their lost splendor, caused, perhaps, more general surprise among Christians than among Jews. It was looked upon as a miraculous event, as marking a new era in the history of the world, in which a different state of things would prevail. Some Christian writers in Bamberg, at their head a. Catholic priest (Gley), expected such abundant and important results from the Jewish assembly in Paris that they established a special newspaper, a kind of journal for the Jews. Only the liberal Berlin intelligensia--David Friedlander's circle--experienced an uncomfortable sensation at the news, because they feared

that, through the Synhedrion in France, ancient Judaism might be revived in a new garb. They therefore declared the Synhedrion a juggler's performance, provided by Napoleon for his Parisians. Patriotism was also involved in this sense of uneasiness, for the Prussian Jews participated in the deep grief into which the people of Prussia and the royal family had been plunged by the defeats at Jena and Auerstadt (October 14, 1806)

Four days after the dissolution of the Assembly of Notables (Adar 9--February 9, 1807) the Great Synhedrion, very different in character, assembled. It consisted, as mentioned above, for the greater part of rabbis, most of whom had been members of the Assembly of Notables. Twenty-five from the same Assembly were added, ratification of the answers to the twelve questions according to the wishes of Napoleon was secured. To all appearances the great Synhedrion was to assemble and transact business according to its own pleasure. The commissioners were not to have any communications with it. The minister of the interior had chosen only the first three officials: Sinzheim as President (Nasi), the gray-headed Segre as first Vice-President (Ab-Beth-Din), and Abraham di Cologna as second Vice-President (Chacham).

After attending the synagogue, the Assembly made its way to the Hotel de Ville, and there the seventy members, in a hall specially decorated for them, took their seats according to seniority, by ancient custom in a semi-circle around the president. The sittings were public, and many spectators were present at them. The members of the Synhedrion were suitably attired in black garments, with silk capes and three-cornered hats. The meeting was opened by a prayer specially composed by Sinzheim. The speeches of Sinzheim and Furtado, with which the first meeting commenced, were entirely appropriate to the situation.

The second sitting (February 12) was occupied with the reading of the motions which the Synhedrion was to sanction, together with the presentation of addresses from different congregations in France, Italy, and the Rhineland, and especially in Dresden and Neuwied, expressing their agreement with the assembly, and the reception of messengers to the Synhedrion from Amsterdam.

The Synhedrion felt itself at a loss for subjects to discuss. The new matters which they had proposed to settle were left untouched. The Franco-Prussian war had caused the emperor to be forgetful of the Synhedrion and the Jews in general. There only remained for the members of the Synhedrion to convert the replies of the previous assembly into definite, inviolable laws. The question as to the power of the new Synhedrion to impose binding laws, or whether it could be placed on the same basis as the ancient one, was not debated. The rabbis overcame this scruple by arguing that each generation was permitted by the Talmud to institute suitable ordinances and make new decisions, and therefore, without further discussion, they declared themselves as constituted. Without demur, the Synhedrion adopted Furtado's disintegrating view, that]udaism consisted of two wholly distinct elements--the purely religious and the political-legislative laws. The first mentioned are unalterable; the latter, on the other hand, which have lost their significance since the downfall of the Jewish state, can be set aside. The inferences from this difference, however, could not be drawn by any individual, but only by an authorized assembly, a great Synhedrion, which owing to unfavorable circumstances had never been able to assemble. The Synhedrion was, therefore, no innovation. The following highly important paragraph with reference to marriage was also passed without opposition: That not only must the civil marriage precede the religious ceremony, but that intermarriages between

DECISIONS OF THE SYNHEDRION.

Jews and Christians were to be considered binding, and although they were not attended by any religious forms, yet no religious interdict could be passed upon them. In this evasive manner the Synhedrion satisfied its own conscience and the suspicions of the imperial officers.

As the Synhedrion had no actual business to transact, the time of the sittings was filled up with speeches delivered by Furtado, Hildesheimer, the deputy from Frankfort, Asser, the deputy from Amsterdam, and finally by Sinzheim, who made the closing speech. The new decisions of the Synhedrion, drawn up in French and Hebrew, enacted the following: That it is prohibited for any Jew to marry more than one wife;that divorce by the Jewish law was effective only when preceded by that of the civil authorities ; and that a marriage likewise must be considered a civil contract first; that every Israelite was religiously bound to consider his non-Jewish neighbors, who also recognize and worship God as the Creator, as brothers; that he should love his country, defend it, and undertake military service, if called upon to do so ;that Judaism did not forbid any kind of handicraft and occupation, and that, therefore, it was commendable for Israelites to engage in agriculture, handicrafts, and the arts, and to forsake trading; and finally, that it was forbidden to Israelites to exact usury either from Jew or Christian.

These new laws of the Synhedrion were of very limited scope. The Synhedrion had in view only the present, and did not look into the distant future. The Jews in general were not satisfied with its action and results. An English Jew, in a letter addressed to the members, boldly reproached them for having disowned, not alone Judaism, but all revealed religion. " Has any one of our brethren in Constantinople, Aleppo, Baghdad, Corfu, or one of our (English) communities been sent as a deputy to you, or have they recorded their approval of your decisions ?"

The French Government, however, had obtained the surety stipulated before the rights of citizenship would be legally recognized anew. At the proposition of the commissioners the Synhedrion and their resolutions were submitted to Napoleon, whose attention had been fixed on the Prusso-Russian war, until owing to the decisive battle of Prussian Friedland the delusive peace of Tilsit was concluded. During Napoleon's absence, plans were secretly laid with the purpose of restricting the rights of the French Jews. The Jewish deputies, however, discovered this, and the indefatigable Furtado, together with Maurice Levy of Nancy, hastened from the Seine to the Niemen to acquaint the emperor with the agitation against the Jews ; and he remained prepossessed in favor of Judaism.

After the dissolution of the Synhedrion the Assembly of Notables again convened to present their formal report to the authorities (March 25-April 6, 1807).

After the interval of a year, Napoleon announced to the Jews his intentions with reference to legislation on their behalf. He expressed (March 17, 1808) his approval of the wretched consistorial organization which degraded the officials of the synagogue to the level of policemen, and regulated the civil position of the Jews, or rather made encroachments on their hitherto favorable condition, although he repeatedly assured them that their equalization would suffer no restrictions. He had deceived all the world, and everywhere trodden freedom under foot; how could he be expected to keep his word with the Jews and to leave their freedom unmolested ? The law suggests that the Jew-hating Mole framed it. It contained no word about the equalization of the Jews. No French Jew henceforth was to engage in any species of trade without having obtained the permission of the prefect, and his consent was to be granted only on the testimony of the

civil magistrates and the consistory as to the good character of the applicant. Contracts of Jews who could not show a patent were null and void. The taking of pledges as security for a loan was also surrounded by limitations which savored of the Middle Ages. Further, no foreign Jew was to settle in German departments,nor any from those departments in another district. Finally, the Jewish people were not allowed to procure substitutes for military service ; each Jew who was chosen as a soldier had to enter the ranks. These restrictive laws were to remain in force for ten years, " in the hope that by the end of that period, and by the enforcement of various regulations, no difference whatever would exist between the Jews and the other citizens."

Thus the Jews of France, the anchor of hope of their brethren in other countries, were once again humiliated and placed under exceptional legislation. The law enacted, indeed, that the Jews of Bordeaux and certain other departments who had given no cause for complaint should not be included under these new restrictions. Shortly afterwards, owing to their loud complaints, exceptions were made in favor of the Jews of Paris, Livorno, the department of the Lower Pyrenees, and of fifteen other districts in France and Italy, so that only the scapegoats, the German-speaking Jews in France, were deprived of their civil rights. But the odious stain which had been again fastened to the Jews adhered to the emancipated as well. Their opponents, who zealously strove to check the elevation of the Jews, could now point to France, and urge that the race was indeed incapable of amendment, seeing that even where its members had been emancipated long since, they had to be deprived of their rights of equality.

But Napoleon's arm, powerful though it was, could not stem the flood once set in motion, by the liberation of oppressed nationalities and classes.

The first German prince who voluntarily conceded to the Jews at least a restricted amount of freedom was Duke Charles of Raden, one of the dependents of the family of Napoleon. Baden being on the borders of France became accustomed to the recognition of the Jews of the latter country as citizens ; and public opinion was more favorable to them there than in other parts of Germany. To be sure, the German Prince of Raden was not so free from

THE FRANKFORT JEWS.

prejudice as the member of the Napoleon family who occupied a German throne. He declared the Jews citizens of the state, but did not give them the freedom of the cities, so that they could not dwell in such towns as had hitherto been closed to Jews; and even where they had always been tolerated, they were only to be regarded as "protected citizens." The duke, however, reserved the right to confer the freedom of the cities upon those who should give up petty trading. Their religious peculiarities were to be respected, "only in so far as they agreed with the Mosaic Law, but not with the Talmudical interpretations of the same."

Even the city of Frankfort for a moment succumbed to the equality intoxication, although petty, pedantic hatred of Jews was incorporated in every patrician. This hatred had greatly increased in intensity since the spread of revolutionary principles. The subjection of the Jews was to compensate for loss of independence. Not a single badge or ceremony which perpetuated Jewish degradation was removed from the Jews, who numbered about five hundred families. The laws of "Stattigkeit," defining their dependent status, which had existed for two hundred years, were still annually read in the synagogue. Every newly admitted Jew was compelled to take the oath of allegiance to the Senate. Restrictions continued to be imposed on Jewish marriages. Jew-taxes had to be paid, as if the Holy Roman Empire still held sway, instead of the all-powerful will of the Corsican, crushing emperors and kings. The Jews were obliged to dwell in the narrow, dirty, unhealthy Jewish quarter,and every Christian, however degraded, had the right of crying to the most refined Jew, " Mach Mores, Jud! " ; of treating him as a despicable object, and even banishing him from the better parts of the city and from the parks.

The French general Jourdan had indeed freed the Frankfort Jews from the Ghetto for a few years, when he bombarded the city and destroyed that portion of it. Under the eyes of the French victors, the patricians, sorely against their will, permitted Jews to rent houses in other districts ; under no condition could they purchase or erect houses. When the Holy Roman Empire melted away like a snowflake before the breath of Napoleon, when Frankfort fell under the sovereignty of the Arch-Chancellor or Prince Primate of the Rhenish Confederation, and the powerful aldermen themselves became subject, the serfdom of the Jews came to an end, though the change was not expressed in legal enactments. Karl von Dalberg, a liberal-minded man, and most favorably disposed towards the Jews, would gladly have removed their yoke, indeed he wrote to Gregoire, the advocate of emancipation, upon this subject. However, he was too well aware of the stubborn hatred of the Frankfort patricians towards the Jews, to venture upon their complete emancipation. He had only promised in a general way at the so-called coronation that the members of the Jewish nation should be protected against injury and insulting treatment. The urgent necessity of regulating the status of the Jews by law, was apparent to this Prince Primate, who discharged his duty only by half measures, such as were characteristic of the Germans. By the publication of a new order for the government and protection of the Jews, he conceded, in the spirit of the new era, that "previous laws, being opposed to the modern constitution of the Jewish nation," should be abrogated. At the same time he figured as the adherent of the anti-Jewish party by stating " that complete equality could not be granted so long as the Jews did not show themselves worthy of it, by forsaking their peculiarities and adopting the customs of the country." By these new ordinances they were treated as strangers on sufferance, who might enjoy the benefits of the law of

nations and of humanity, but not the rights of citizens. The only relief measure was that the various protection-taxes were consolidated into an annual impost of 22,000 florins. Even the Ghetto was again held out to them as their residence; they were cautioned not to renew their leases in town with Christian landlords, because the day would soon dawn when they would have to return to their prison. Naturally, the Jews of Frankfort used their utmost endeavors to have these exceptional laws annulled, the more as their co-religionists in the neighboring kingdom of Westphalia were enjoying equality. When the Rhenish

Confederation was dissolved and the Duchy of Frankfort created with a constitution of its own, recognizing the equality of all inhabitants, of whatever belief, Amschel, Gumprecht, and Rothschild (the first court-agent who made princes subject to himself), as representatives of the Jews, did not rest until they had induced the Archduke Dalberg and his council to establish their equalization by a special law in spite of all opposition. The new archduke being in want of funds, besides desiring the freedom and equality of the Jews, consented to grant these privileges for the sum of 440,000 florins (being twenty times the amount of the annual tax of 22,000 florins), 150,000 to be paid at once, then 50,000, and the remainder in annual payments of 10,000 florins. The law (published December 28, 1811) decreed, "that all Jews living in Frankfort under protection, together with their children and descendants, should enjoy civil rights and privileges equally with other citizens." The Jews took the oath of citizenship, entered upon their privileges and duties, and Louis Baruch (Borne), a Jew, was employed in the ducal police. The Jew-street, or what remained of it, lost its mournful privileges, and was swept out of existence or joined to adjacent quarters. The proud patricians gnashed their teeth at such unheard-of innovations. They had suffered a double loss by the abolition of serfdom and of the old laws regarding the Jewish inhabitants ; but for the time they had to acquiesce.

The northern Hanse Towns, where German guild-narrowness joined to ossified Lutheranism scarcely allowed the Jews to breathe, were compelled by order of the French garrison to grant them equality. Hamburg agreed to place all its inhabitants, including Jews, upon an equal level (1811), and also admitted them to seats in the civic council.

The small town of Lubeck showed more opposition to the settlement and emancipation of a few Jews under French protection. Hitherto only about ten families were tolerated in the town as "protection Jews," who were forbidden to engage in trade, join the guilds, or obtain possession of houses. These privileges were regarded as exclusively Christian; no Jews dared claim them. Only three Jews were allowed to come daily into Lubeck from the neighboring town of Moisling (under the dominion of Denmark or Holstein), and these were compelled to pay a sort of poll-tax at the gate. Any deputy of the merchants' guild could lay hands upon them, and take them before the police, if they sold goods, and everything found in the possession of such suspects was confiscated. With the advent of the French (1811-1814), about forty-two Jews from Moisling and fourteen foreigners with their families moved to Lubeck, thus bringing the number of families in Lubeck up to sixty-six. These sixty-six Jews aroused the fierce rage of the Lubeck patricians even more than Napoleon's sovereignty. The embargo laid by Napoleon upon the Continent to

annoy England had attracted several Jewish families to North Germany, hitherto unfriendly to Jews.

In the Hanse Town of Bremen, which until then had known only traveling Jews, who paid toll on entering the town, Jews took up residence under French protection, not indeed in great numbers, but too many for the bigotry of the patricians. Here, too, they were allowed equal rights with other citizens. Even the Duke of Mecklenburg, Frederick Franz, granted the equalization of the Jews (February 22, 1812), and allowed marriages between Jews and Christians, a greater concession than those made by any other code. Prussia also could no longer resist the tide in favor of the Jews. In Prussia they had displayed much greater love for their native land, and brought more sacrifices during the times of trouble than many of the corrupt nobility, who had ingratiated themselves with their victorious enemies. But a long time elapsed before King Frederick William III could overcome his aristocratic and religious repugnance to them. He only abolished the insulting cognomen of "protection Jews," declaring them not only admissible to the citizenship of towns, but under compulsion to perform its duties. They were forced to take the oath as citizens of towns and to share in the burdens of the cities in which they lived. But they were not to be recognized as state citizens, their position being the reverse of that of the Jews in Baden. The prospect of equalization as state citizens was continually held out to them, but the promise remained unfulfilled for several years. When Hardenberg again assumed control of the disturbed affairs of the state, and insisted upon the repeal of decayed laws and the removal of rotten conditions, he favored the removal of the civil disabilities of the Jews, so that by their help new strength should be infused into the mutilated, bleeding, impoverished territory,--help which it could ill spare in its wretched state of deep depression. David Friedlander and his friends, Berlin capitalists, used their utmost efforts to bring about the state equalization so long promised. The king again and again delayed the ratification of the law submitted to him by the chancellor. At length--moved, it is said, by the interest taken by the Berlin Jews in commemorating the death of the much-suffering, lamented Queen Louise--Frederick William gave his assent (March 11, 1812) to the equalization of all Jews at that time settled in Prussia. They were to be admitted to posts in schools and colleges; but the king withheld the privilege of admission to state offices. With the privileges, they were to assume the duties, especially as soldiers. Their religious affairs were to be regulated afterwards: " When the plan for their religious organization is drawn up, such Jews as enjoy public confidence both on account of their knowledge and probity will be consulted."

Three German princes alone withstood the spirit of the age: those of Bavaria, Austria, and Saxony. The first, Maximilian Joseph, appointed king of Bavaria by Napoleon, promulgated an edict (June 10, 1813), which appeared to concede equality to Jews, at least to those who possessed the right. of settlement. But it was equality with many limitations. In cities to which no Jew bad hitherto been admitted, their settlement was to depend upon the royal pleasure, and even in those places where they had dwelt for a long time their numbers were not to be increased, but rather diminished. In Austria, Leopold II and Francis I, the successors of Emperor Joseph, who had somewhat loosened the chains of the Jews, left the favorable intentions of their predecessor unexecuted, and imposed new humiliations. In addition to the unendurable burden of taxes in Bohemia, Moravia, Silesia, and Galicia,--taxes upon candles, upon wine, and meat--a collection-tax was imposed in Vienna, which was a toll upon every Jew who entered the capital. Spies closely watched

the Jew who stayed in Vienna for a short time unprovided with a passport, and treated him like a criminal. Marriages among Jews were still restricted, and could be contracted only by the eldest son of the family, or by one able to pay heavy bribes. Although Austria was so often overrun by the soldiers of liberty, yet, impenetrable as the wall of China, it resisted every innovation.

In the newly created kingdom of Saxony all the restrictions imposed in the time of the Electoral princes and the Lutheran Church were maintained in their fullest rigor. Saxony was rightly called the Protestant Spain of the Jews. Indeed they were not suffered to dwell in the country at all; only a few privileged Jews were admitted to the two towns of Dresden and Leipsic, but under the express condition that they could be expelled at any time. They were not allowed to have a synagogue, but only to meet for prayer in small rooms, on condition that they made no noise. In Leipsic and Dresden every privileged Jew was compelled to pay annually seventy thalers for himself, besides other sums for his wife, children, and servants. The Jews were rigidly constrained in their choice of trades and occupations, and were placed under strict supervision while traveling. When all other German districts had abolished the poll-tax, Saxony still retained it. The example of the two neighboring countries--Westphalia and Prussia--had no influence upon this district, which at that time was rendered doubly selfish by trade jealousy and religious prejudice. The reactionary movement found plenty of fuel in Germany.

V. CHAPTER XV.

REFORM AND YOUNG ISRAEL

Israel Jacobson--His Reforms--The Hamburg Reform Temple Union --Eleazar Libermann--Aaron Chorin--Lazarus Riesser--Party Strife--Isaac Bernays--His Writings--Bernays in Hamburg

1818-1830 C.E.

The changes in Judaism, like those in the Jews, began in Germany. The first to undertake some sort of reform was Israel Jacobson. He was especially fitted for the leadership of a new party by his attachment to his faith, his admiration for beauty and external qualities, his activity, wealth, and high position. Immediately after the Westphalian Consistory had been appointed, and he had been placed at its head, he came forward with innovations of a two-fold nature. From the public service in the synagogue connected with the newly-erected school in Cassel, he removed all objectionable and noisy features, especially the sing-song reading so in use. He naturally insisted upon the delivery of sermons in German. He also introduced new forms and methods borrowed from the Church, such as German as well as Hebrew prayers, insipid German songs by the side of the psalms pregnant with thought, and the ceremony of confessing the faith (Confirmation) for half-grown boys and girls--an idea without meaning in Judaism.

Jacobson exercised such power over his associates in the Westphalian Consistory, that they unresistingly accepted these innovations. He then proceeded to introduce his reforms into all the communities of Westphlia, with the threat that he would have such synagogues as refused to adopt his regulations closed. This compulsion, however, aroused the feelings of the orthodox party; the introduction of the German language into divine service being particularly objectionable to the majority A rabbi of mild temperament Samuel Eger of Brunswick (died 1842), had the courage to protest against the arbitrary conduct of the president of the consistory. He prophetically expressed the conviction, that by employing German prayers and hymns the Hebrew language would fall into disuse, and finally die out, and the bond uniting the Jews dispersed throughout the world would thereby be relaxed. Jacobson appears to have paid no heed to these warnings and signs of opposition. The dissatisfied Jews must have lodged complaints about him and his new schemes with King Jerome, for the king reprimanded him for his autocratic interference in matters of conscience and his ardor for reform.

Jacobson's glory ended with the speedy downfall of the Westphalian kingdom. Having moved to Berlin, he furnished a room in his house as a synagogue (1815), although he had formerly been

opposed to private synagogues, and introduced his reformed service with German prayers, songs, and a choir. At first there was no room for an organ. Afterwards Jacob Beer, the banker, the father of Meyer Beer, provided a large chamber (1817), where an organ could be put up. After the victory of the Germans over Napoleon, it became the fashion to be religious, and it infected Jews who had previously not experienced the slightest necessity for devotional exercises, and had been quite indifferent to religious ceremonial. Such sentimentalists, who had no regard for Judaism, attended the services of

Jacobson, in order to "edify themselves," and "be devout," as the new phrases ran. The "Society of Friends" furnished members. This was the origin of a Reform party, a tiny community within the community, which however, as could be easily foreseen, had a future, owing to the energy displayed at the commencement and the repulsive form of the ordinary divine service. The great attraction in the new form of service was the German sermon, which Jacobson usually delivered. His addresses exercised great power, because the so-called "homiletic discourses" of the rabbis and the Polish or Moravian itinerant preachers, werc dull and unattractive.

But the private synagogue in Berlin, owing to complaints made by some of the orthodox party, was closed by the Prussian government. The king of Prussia, Frederick William III, was averse to all innovations, even in Jewish circles, and hated them as being revolutionary plots. A young preacher from the school of Jacobson thereupon betook himself to Hamburg, having been invited to conduct a free school established by certain rich Jews. Here he set on foot the plan of erecting a reform temple on the model of Jacobson's.

This young minister, Kley, had brought from Jacobson's synagogue a complete scheme, which included German hymns and prayers, sermons, and the organ. He composed a so-called "religious song-book," in imitation of the Protestant liturgy, an empty and feeble work, suited only to a race of children, ignorant of the psalms, the pattern sources of religious devotion. But there were men in Hamburg who, although they approved of modern ideas, were yet unwilling to break entirely with Judaism and its past, and who decidedly objected to the omission of Hebrew in their prayers. The chiefs of this movement were M. J. Bresselau, himself a good Hebrew stylist, and Saeckel Frankel (died in Hamburg, 1833), likewise a Hebrew scholar, who had re-translated several of the Apocryphal books into the sacred language. These two men compiled a selection from the Hebrew prayers in use, in order to amalgamate them with the newly-adopted German songs and prayers, a discordant medley in contents and form, which somewhat called to mind a friendly compromise among contending parties. About fifty families joined, and thus arose the Reform Temple Union in Hamburg. This mongrel birth was ushered into the world without love and enthusiasm. Its promoters were so prosaic that the anniversary of the battle of Leipsic was chosen for the day of the consecration of the Temple (October 18, 1818). The preacher Kley, in order to have ample material for a discourse, had to use as a starting point the German wars of freedom, which had caused the Jews in Germany to retrograde rather than to advance. Young maidens sang hymns with the young men, in order to create the sensation which the cause itself could not awaken, and this gave great offense. Kley could not have kept the Temple community together for long, had not the Templars, as they were called, found an efficient preacher in Gotthold Salomon, of Dessau (died 1862), who was well acquainted with biblical and Jewish literature, and knew how to conceal the bareness of the new movement. On the one hand, he invested the Temple with Protestant attributes, and on the other, by reason of his conceit and ostentation, he gave it an aggressive character. With Salomon the influence of the preacher among the German Jews commenced; the pulpit took the place of the school, and from it there often resounded the hollow phrases which conceal thought, or the lack of thought. The Temple Union had officially given up the belief in the Messiah, without exactly defining what position Judaism was to assume with reference to Christianity. Some of the zealous reformers meditated a complete rupture, and the refusal to contribute to the communal funds.

The originators and leaders were filled with the delusive idea, which at first appeared justifiable, that the Temple, through its modern and attractive form of service, would bring back to the fold those alienated from Judaism. They hoped that the less stringent religious forms would overcome the dislike felt by worldly men against everything Jewish. In a few instances those who had fallen away from Judaism were restrained from overstepping the threshold into the Church, but it was not a remedy with permanent effect. Nevertheless, the achievements of the Hamburg Temple, commonplace though its origin was, are not to be underrated. At one stroke, without much hesitation, it banished the rubbish of centuries from the synagogue, swept away with youthful impetuosity the holy cobwebs which no one had ventured to touch, and awakened a taste for a well-regulated service, for decorous behavior at divine worship, and for order and simplicity. The injury inflicted on Judaism by the aping of foreign customs, and the dilution of its own strength, cannot be altogether attributed to it.

Naturally the establishment of the Hamburg Temple produced a split in the Jewish world. Hitherto there had existed only the "old-fashioned" and the "new-fashioned " people, as they termed each other, but no distinct sects possessing a banner, a password, and a confession of faith. Not even the old-fashioned orthodox section constituted a definite party. For, although the adherents of the past, who would not swerve a hair's breadth from former practices, were so numerous, that even in Hamburg they might have suppressed the innovators if they had chosen, they did not act as a body. Only the faint remonstrance of single individuals was heard lamenting the ruin of Judaism through its betrayers, and these oft-repeated wailings were pitiful. The old party had no chiefs, no leaders; respect for the rabbis had vanished in a single generation. The wretched dispute for and against Jonathan Eibeschutz, and the satires of Hebrew writers of the period of the Measfim, had completely undermined their authority. In the larger German congregations the empty rabbinical chairs were permitted to remain untenanted. They no longer wished to have rabbis from Poland, because these could not speak the language of the land, and in Germany there were no great rabbis of recognized authority. Berlin set the example, which was followed by the community of Prague, after the death of the wise Ezekiel Landau, by Hamburg after the retirement of the zealot Raphael Cohen, and by Frankfort-on-the-Main after the death of the ultra-orthodox (Chassidic) Pinchas Hurwitz. The assistants (Dayanim) of the rabbis administered the rabbinical office-hybrid creatures, too dependent to have an opinion of their own, and too weak to oppose the demands of reckless leaders of communities.

As a result of the disregard in which the rabbis were held, the Talmudical schools fell into decay. Gifted Jewish youths, whose education formerly had begun with the Talmud, preferred to attend the gymnasiums and universities, and learned to despise the Talmud and Judaism. The most famous Talmudical

THE ORTHODOX LEADERS.

academies in Prague, Frankfort, Altona and Hamburg, Furth, Metz, and Halberstadt, which had boasted at least several hundred pupils (Bachurim), were gradually closed. This desolation spread to Poland, as the Talmud students no longer had hope of finding employment in Germany and France. They made their way to Germany, but with the intention of studying science (Chochmoth), or if they remained at home, they devoted themselves to the ensnaring mysticism of Neo-Chassidism. There were but four rabbis of the younger generation who, on account of their profound knowledge of the Talmud and their pure, patriarchal character, enjoyed widespread authority: Mordecai Benet, in Nikolsburg, Jacob Lissa, Akiba Eger, and his son-in-law, Moses Sofer, of Frankfort-on-the-Main . These four rabbis, by their ingenious methods, kept alive the zeal for Talmudical study. Akiba Eger, owing to his astoundingly ingenious mind and high virtues --among which modesty was preeminent--enjoyed almost divine reverence from the thousands of disciples who came from his academies in Friedland and Posen. He was a quiet man, who never took the initiative, and was averse to aggressive opposition. Moses Sofer, on the other hand, was a fanatical zealot and an active heretic-hunter. He possessed courage and determination which disregarded consequences. He might have been a useful leader, but, like his companions, he was at too great a distance from the scene of action, to take part in the contest, or even to set up a standard. These rabbis had not the slightest conception of the new tendency which the times and the Jews had developed, and were therefore ignorant of the importance of the cause which they represented. They did not know the enemy whom they attacked, or despised him too much to be dangerous opponents. When a serious question or a critical situation arose, they were at a loss what to do, brought out their old rusty weapons, and damaged their cause by revealing its weakness. This awkwardness created an impression of feebleness and decrepitude. Thus the old orthodox party (as their opponents, borrowing the name from phraseology, termed them), or conservatives, were without a head, without a banner or a plan, utterly without unanimity or discipline, without consciousness of their own strength. They especially lacked eloquence, the indispensable means by which public opinion is influenced and ruled, and its follies and hollow emptiness are made apparent. Their utter want of education avenged itself bitterly upon the rigidly pious party.

On the other hand, the opposing section, the ardent innovators, the party of Jacobson, possessed what was wanting in the others: a daring leader, unity, and especially a wealth of passwords and phrases, such as, "spirit of the times, enlightenment," by which the thoughtless are captivated. Their victory and ultimate success could be foreseen. The confidence and the courage of youth, were bold, and not over-particular as to the means employed. Jacobson, their chief, knew how to pursue and achieve an end, and how to utilize the means at his disposal. He saw that the Hamburg Temple would encounter difficulties, and would be condemned as heretical by the old rabbis. Jacobson was in correspondence with the founders, and knew that the Senate, instigated by the orthodox party, would, like the king of Prussia, forbid innovations. He also saw that many of the Hamburg Templars were too lukewarm to struggle against great difficulties. For this reason he strove to obtain in advance the ratification of the Temple ritual. Among the rabbis of Germany he could find no voice of approval for the new order of service. He, therefore, connected himself --a fact which throws no favorable light upon the cause--with a base adventurer, who, it appears, was bribed to help him. Eleazar Libermann from

AARON CHORIN.

Austria, a gambler, became his apostle of reform. To characterize the man, it suffices to note that he afterwards was baptized. At the bidding of the reformers, Libermann traveled in Austria. From him they learned that in Hungary and Italy there were rabbis or would-be rabbis, willing to pronounce a favorable opinion upon the new ritual. Jacobson addressed his inquiries to them, and his wishes were fulfilled. The first who allowed himself to be used by Libermann was Aaron Chorin (from Chorin), rabbi in Arad, Hungary, a tedious talker of superficial culture and mediocre Talmudical scholarship, who was capable of repeating absurdities in three languages--in Hebrew, German, and the Jewish-German jargon. He was devoted to the new movement without clearly understanding its bearings. Two Italian rabbis of low attainments also spoke in favor of the innovations. The opinions of all these men--not one of whom was of wholly sound mind--showed that the introduction of the organ was not against Rabbinical law. Chorin alone produced authorities in favor of the other reforms, and for German prayers. Libermann collated these opinions, strengthened them by his own pretended learning, adding the falsehood that not only all the rabbis of Leghorn, but even those of Jerusalem, had declared it permissible to use the organ in Jewish divine service. These opinions, which were printed and scattered broadcast, were intended to exonerate the Hamburg Reform Temple from blame at its very birth, and to remove the blot of illegitimacy which, as might have been foreseen, the rabbis of the old school would affix to it.

Whilst the reformers energetically tried to forestall every obstacle, the conservatives remained idle, and allowed the dangers which threatened their convictions to gather unnoticed. As already observed, Hamburg had at this time no rabbi at its head, but a college of three assistants (Dayanim) of little repute. Although these official representatives of Judaism had almost the entire Hamburg community to support them, they opposed the innovations with little vigor. Shortly after the opening of the Temple, the college ordered a feebly-written proclamation to be put up in the synagogues (October 26, 1818), that the new prayer-book should not be used by Israelites of pious sentiments, because contrary to usage essential passages had been omitted or altered. But this declaration lost its effect, when the lay heads of the community--whose assistance the Dayanim had not been able to win took it down, and rebuked the authors, because "they had been guilty of intolerable presumption." The lay heads, at the recommendation of the college, afterwards invited the leaders of the Temple (November 8th) to a meeting, and requested them to discontinue the use of the prayer-book, as it did not agree with the ritual accepted by all Jewish communities. The Templars, however, laughed this demand to scorn.

The Temple Union unexpectedly received moral support from a person having great influence in Hamburg. Lazarus Riesser, the father of the indefatigable champion for the emancipation of the Jews in Germany, had always been reckoned one of the old orthodox party. As the son-in-law of Rabbi Raphael Cohen and his right hand, he was absorbed in the Talmud. He had published a Hebrew life of Raphael Cohen, in which he eulogized not only the author, but also his rabbinical views, and declared himself his faithful follower. How astonished, therefore, were the Hamburg Jews of both parties when a letter from Riesser suddenly appeared, entitled "To my co-religionists in Hamburg" (the beginning of 1819), applauding the Temple innovations, and sharply rebuking the rabbinical college which had opposed them ! He frankly called the opponents "sanctimonious hypocrites" who "nourish

contentions in Israel, and bar the way of the sons desirous of returning to the favor of their father." It appears that he wished to wreak a petty revenge upon the members of the rabbinical college of Hamburg, by whom he perhaps thought himself kept in the background.

The orthodox party in Hamburg who imagined that no rabbi in the whole of Europe would approve of the reforms, were bitterly disappointed; owing to the activity of Jacobson and Libermann, the Jewish public discovered that several rabbis in various districts upheld them. The old rabbis were so listless and indolent in the matter, that they had to be addressed twice, before they pronounced judgment against the Temple. In the first excitement the Hamburg rabbis had unwisely condemned the innocent and commendable customs which were introduced into the Temple, such as the Portuguese pronunciation of Hebrew, the omission of intoning in reading from the Bible. To rectify these mistakes, they afterwards limited their complaints to three points--the abridgment of the prayers, especially with reference to the omission of Messianic passages, prayers in German, and the use of the organ. To this program the agreement of numerous distinguished rabbis and rabbinates was at length secured ; four in Germany (Furth, Mayence, Breslau, and Hanau), five in Italy (Trieste, Modena, Padua, Mantua, and Leghorn), three in Prussian Poland (Posen, Lissa, and Rawitz), and two in Moravia (Nikolsburg and Trietsch). Moses Sofer in Presburg, the German rabbi in Amsterdam, and the French chief rabbis of the consistory of

Wintzenheim, also signed the document. They all declared the reforms in the Temple to be distinctly heterodox. Libermann's falsehoods now became apparent, as the Leghorn rabbinate had not given its assent to the use of the organ. Samun, a would-be rabbi of Leghorn, and Chorin of Arad, probably under moral compulsion, revoked their former testimonials. The most zealous in their denunciations of the Temple were Sofer of Presburg and Benet of Nikolsburg, who declared the slightest deviation from ancient usages as heresy. But the impression which the authors of this document had hoped for did not follow. It had been delayed too long, more than seven months having elapsed before sentence of heresy was promulgated; and meantime the Temple Union established itself. Eighteen antagonistic rabbinates (in all forty rabbis) did not seem many; and the most eminent of all, the Central Consistory of France, had remained silent. The signers of the protest asserted that more opinions had been received; but this belated statement was of no avail. The arguments adduced by the rabbis against the Temple service were for the most part void, some were thoroughly childish. The letter of the law spoke against them. The diversity of opinions among rabbinical authorities of various ages and countries, always made it possible to find reasons for and against any question.

This weakness was mercilessly exposed by M. J. Bresselau, one of the originators of the Hamburg reform. In a Hebrew letter (1819) written in beautiful Hebrew style and with such skillful manipulation of biblical verses, that it seemed as though the prophets and psalmists themselves were scourging the delusions of the obtuse rabbis, Bresselau treated them now as ignorant boys, now as false prophets, and especially as disturbers of the peace. Every sentence in this seemingly earnest but bitingly satirical epistle was a dagger-thrust against the old perversions and their defenders. The reformers also obtained reinforcement from Poland. The old-fashioned party, on the other hand, were unable to present a single Hebrew writer to defend their cause. Even the Hebrew style used in the document of the opposing rabbis was rugged and

coarse. The Dayanim of Hamburg, indeed, caused the testimonial to be in part translated into German--a concession that betrayed the weakness of their cause--but the German version was not calculated to create a good impression. For this they had to employ Shalom Cohen, a turn-coat, who had formerly belonged to the ranks of the reformers. In short, the conservatives were unfortunate, because they were unskillful and imprudent.

It also happened that the Temple quarrel took place in the year when the " Hep, hep !" cry was being raised, and Hamburg also participated in it. The wealthy and worldly Jews were thereby restricted to the society of their own people, and actively supported the banner that had been unfurled. The Jewish merchants of Hamburg, members of the Temple Union, who were accustomed to attend the fair at Leipsic during the chief festivals in the spring and autumn,joined some Berlin merchants of similar opinions, and established a branch synagogue (September 20, 1820). Meyerbeer composed the songs for the opening ceremony. They appointed a so-called fair-preacher (Messprediger), Jacob Auerbach, and from this gathering-place of Jews from various countries, the innovations spread to a wider circle. The Hamburg reforms thus were adopted in some parts; and in other communities, such as those of Carlsruhe, Konigsberg, and Breslau, where the entire program was not carried out, at least the rite of confirmation, imitated from the Church, was introduced.

The first attempt to set up an opposing party, so as to dam the overflowing stream of reform, and make it subside into a quiet bed, commenced on account of the Temple innovations. This opposing party was established by a man who had himself partially forsaken rabbinical Judaism, but who strove to strengthen and vindicate it, under the correct impression that development must take place upon its own soil, with due regard to historical conditions, and along its peculiar lines, and especially without aping foreign Church forms. Isaac Bernays (born at Mayence, 1792; died at Hamburg, 1849) was the man who intelligently opposed the prevailing flaccidity of semi-enlightened reform and thought.

Germany, in contradistinction to North Germany with its love for formal statements of doctrines, which never rose beyond the commonplaces of rationalism, a mystic philosophical school had been established, which promoted visionary notions. In all things, the smallest and the greatest, in nature and history, in the grouping of things, in numbers, colors, and names, this philosophy beheld a system, germs of ideas, the shattered ruins of a gigantic mirror reflecting fundamental thoughts in huge size. Isaac Bernays belonged to this school. To his vision Judaism in its literature and historical progress revealed itself half unveiled. Bernays' mind, with its overflowing wealth of ideas, found in all phenomena the harmonious systemization and development of a fundamental thought, which to manifest all its latent possibilities permeated passing events and historical achievements, and which had developed from the beginning of creation to the most recent fact. Bernays, much profounder than Mendelssohn, was the first to recognize the important role of Judaism in the history of the world, and at a glance to measure the range of its literature. His fault was, perhaps, that he was too rich in ideas, that therefore he sought out and discovered too much, and was not equal to the task of clothing his ideas in fitting form and language. From his superior altitude he looked with contemptuous pity upon the poverty of thought of Jewish reformers, who desired to contract and confine the giant spirit of Judaism (of which they had no conception) within the narrow bounds of a catechism for big and little children. In his eyes the followers of Friedlander

were the embodiment of insipidity and narrowness. They impressed Bernays with the idea of a rabble who dwell in a Pyramid. and fit it up for petty household purposes.

The train of thought by which Bernays reconstructed Judaism in his mind from its original sources and history, is little known to us. He preferred oral to written instruction, and was averse to put his thoughts on paper. The " Biblical Orient," which is ascribed to him, is, so to speak, only the foundation of the vestibule of a reverence-inspiring temple. This work, odd as it was in form, is distinguished for its depth and originality; it starts with the idea, that to Judaism is allotted the task of bringing back to God men created in his image, and that the Jewish people was to serve as a type to mankind, showing how the lost likeness to God may be regained. The "Biblical Orient" endeavored to establish a more thorough comprehension of the Bible than had been effected by the Mendelssohnian school. They had regarded it merely from its poetical side, and had failed to see that it portrays the collision between two views of life. Bernays believed that his criticism dethroned the Mendelssohn school, together with its founder; for Mendelssohn himself, by his superficial treatment of Hebrew literature, had been the first to contribute to the enervation of Judaism.

According to the opinion of Bernays, the Hebrew cult differed from that of the heathen, and was intended to be a contrast. Idolatry expressed itself in plastic, Judaism in ritual, symbolism. Therefore the very aspect of Judaism which the reformers desired to abolish as unfitting and unworthy, should be preserved. Everything which in the course of Jewish history had been assimilated and developed, according to Bernays, ought to have a place assigned to it, being a necessary part of the whole, even Talmudism and the Kabbala.

This book contains many immature and unpolished ideas, much that borders on the ridiculous. But if the author only succeeded in awakening the idea that Judaism has an historical mission as an apostle to the nations, it should suffice to procure for him a place of honor in the records of Jewish history. Not that he could claim this as a new discovery, for the text-book of Judaism plainly points to it. It is the essence of the messages proclaimed by the prophets. It has been verified by history that European and Asiatic nations have been delivered from their darkness by the light that came from Judaism. But the accumulated sufferings of the Jews, and the servile form assumed by Judaism, had caused this fact to be so entirely forgotten, that its own sons had no idea thereof. The merit of the man who again called it to mind is therefore of no mean degree.

The extraordinary talents and original ideas of Bernays directed the attention of Jewish society to him. Afterwards, it is true, he denied the authorship of the "Biblical Orient"; but if he did not actually compose it, he might have done so, for it is flesh of his flesh, or spirit of his spirit.

The Hamburg community, which sorely needed a power to withstand the Temple Union, in consequence of his renown chose Bernays for their spiritual guide. It was a good move on their part, and bore important results. The rabbis of the old school were ill prepared for the contest between two justifiable principles, the preservation of Judaism in its peculiar manifestations, and the assimilation of European culture by the Jews. Their weapons had grown rusty, and injured the owners more than their opponents. Fresh forces were

BERNAYS' SERMONS.

therefore required in their cause--men cognizant of the wants of the age, who could utilize them for the honor and purification of Judaism. The appointment of

Bernays to the Hamburg rabbinate (November, 1821) created a stir: he was the first rabbi with a well-ordered secular education. It was a sign of the times that he dispensed with the title of rabbi and preferred to be called Chacham, as was customary among the Portuguese Jews : he did not wish the despised title of rabbi to be a hindrance to his activity. True to his aversion for slavish imitation, he eschewed all clerical mummery in costume and gestures, to which the reform preachers attached great importance in the pulpit. Bernays did not claim to be the guardian of souls, only the teacher of his congregation. He also delivered sermons, but the contents, form, and other details differed entirely from those introduced by the Jacobson school. Owing to his peculiar mode of thought, his addresses were not understood by the multitude; but thoughtful hearers at least conceded to him the merit of originality, which contrasted favorably with the insipidity of the Temple preachers. When Heine, who at this time was still interested practically in Judaism, was staying in Hamburg, he was induced to hear Bernays' sermons, and to compare them with those of other preachers. Heine understood the method and form of his thoughts, and the opinion of the lyrical satirist ran as follows: " I have heard Bernays preach ..., none of the Jews understand him, he desires nothing for himself, and will never play any other part; but he is a man of mind, and has more life in him than Kley, Salomon, and Auerbach."

By unobtrusive work, Bernays succeeded in gaining the respect, not only of the community, but also of the rigidly pious party elsewhere. Their suspicious natures found nothing to blame in the religious conduct of the Chacham. The changes that he introduced, in reality reforms, met with approval and imitation in orthodox congregations. By his penetration and his great erudition he exercised deep influence over the rising generation, to whom he opened up the rich treasures of Jewish literature, then but little known. He thereby imbued his disciples with joyous attachment to Judaism. As already stated, he did not care for writing. If his courage had kept pace with his knowledge and wealth of ideas, his activity would have had greater influence on modern Jewish history.

But his election as head of the Hamburg community, and Mannheimer's activity in establishing the order of service in the Vienna synagogue, gradually aroused the emulation of other German communities. Educated rabbis were preferred, and they restored dignity to the synagogue. And so these new German Jewish innovations gradually spread, and made their influence felt in France and Italy, sparking similar reforms there.

V. CHAPTER XVII.

THE YEAR 1844 AND THE BLOOD ACCUSATION AT DAMASCUS

Mehmet Ali--Ratti Menton--Damascus- Father Tomaso--His Disappearance--Blood Accusation against the Jews of Damascus--Imprisonment of Accused--Their Tortures and Martyrdom--Blood Accusation in Rhodes--In Prussia--Adolf Cremieux-Meeting of English Jews--Moses Montefiore--Nathaniel de Rothschild--Merlato, the Austrian Consul--Plots--Thiers-Steps taken by the Jews in Paris and London--Bernard van Oven--Mansion House Meeting--Montefiore, Cremieux, and others sent to Egypt--Solomon Munk.

1840 C.E.

An unforeseen event, insignificant at the beginning, but of vast importance in its results, gave the lie to the false prophets and quacks, and showed how wondrous the force which holds the members of the Jewish race in an indissoluble union; how strong the invisible bond which without their knowledge embraces them; and how a serious menace Judaism arouses the patriotism of the reformer

MEHMET ALI.

and the orthodox, of the politician who appears to have forsaken his faith and the recluse engrossed only in the Kabbala or the Talmud, of the Jew in frivolous France and of him in serious Asia. Strangely enough, the despised " Jewish Question" became interwoven in the complicated threads of European and Asiatic politics, and the Russian despot Nicholas as also the American Republic had to take up the cause of the Jews in Damascus. He who remembers this time, and can appreciate the marvels of history, cannot misunderstand the wonderful intermingling of events. Ratti Menton, an Italian naturalized in France, a reckless, unconscientious fortune-hunter; Hanna Bachari Bey, a renegade, who had passed from Christianity to Islam, a thorough knave and bitter Jew-hater; Mohammed El-Telli, a man of like caliber, who threatened a rich Jew in Damascus with a blood accusation unless he advanced money to relieve him of his difficulties; and finally a Christian Arab, Shibli Ajub, a worthless wretch panting for revenge, because he had been imprisoned on the charge of embezzlement preferred by a Jew; this is the list of fiends who originated a bloody drama, in which the part of martyrs was once more played by the Jews. But their sufferings induced courage, exaltation, and proud self-reliance.

Political events, as intimated, served as the background for this drama. The cunning Mehmet All, Pasha of Egypt, by splendid victories had wrested all Syria and Palestine from the Turkish sultan, his feudal lord. He oppressed the inhabitants of these countries more severely even than those of his own pashalic, in order to fill his coffers. The so-called Citizen King, Louis Philippe, equally cunning, in order to disarm the resentment of the legitimate princes of Europe, supported Mehmet All's plans of conquest, and French agents aided the Egyptian robbery system. These intrigues increased when the strong-minded but unfortunate Sultan Mohammed was dead, and hic weak, pampered son, Abdul Meg'id, only seventeen years old, ascended the throne (July, 1839). Then the Eastern Question commenced to wax warm. Russia supported feeble Turkey that it might not fall into the arms of Mehmet Ali. France, on the other hand, supported the Egyptian robber, in order to checkmate Russia. Austria and England were unsettled in their policy, and Prussia was the fifth wheel on the van of the European Pentarchy. Owing to the close union between Louis Philippe and Mehmet Ali, the Christians in Palestine and Syria, hitherto oppressed, could now raise their heads; for France delighted to pose as the protector of Christianity in the East in order to gain title and power, as she coquetted with the clerical party at home in order to suppress the friends of liberty. The clergy and monks of many orders in the East, especially the Catholics or Latins, until lately the oppressed, now, relying upon French protection, became the oppressors.

In Damascus, which at that time contained five thousand Jewish families, or about twenty thousand souls, the guardian of a Capuchin cloister, Father Tomaso (Thomas), of Sardinia, together with his servant, disappeared one day (February 5, 1840). He was no saint in the Catholic sense of the word, but a man of the world, more ready to take than to give money. He pottered in medicine, especially occupying himself with inoculation for small-pox, and as often visited in Jewish and Mahometan as in Christian quarters. What had become of the Father so well known to the whole population of Damascus? No one knew exactly. There was a rumor that Tomaso had some days before quarreled with a Turkish mule-driver, who was said to have sworn, "This Christian dog shall die by no other hand than mine." It was said that insults and violence

FATHER TOMASO'S DISAPPEARANCE.

followed. As soon as it was known that the Father had disappeared, and had probably met with a violent death, the monks besieged the unscrupulous Ratti Menton, the French consul in Damascus, with entreaties to search for the murderer. Attention was immediately directed to the Jews, some of them having innocently testified that they had seen Tomaso and his servant in the Jewish quarter, on the evening before they disappeared. The monks, chief among them a fanatical Jew-hater, Father Tusti, quickly caught up the suspicion against the Jews, hoping thereby to gain several ends. They could satiate their hatred against the Jews, suppress the inquiry as to whether Father Tomaso had indeed quarreled with Mussulmans and reviled them, and finally a new martyr, slain by the Jews, would be added to their list of saints, which was always a source of profit. Ratti Menton, in turn, from interested motives, quickly endorsed the suspicion against the Jews, and relinquished every other theory, although a clue had been given by the fact that the Turkish merchant, who had been present at the quarrel with the Father, had hanged himself. Sherif Pasha, the governor of Damascus, was readily induced to permit or carry on the persecution of the Jews from a desire to be on friendly terms with the French consul, and hoping to obtain profit for himself from a blood accusation against the Jews. To save appearances, the accusers quoted the evidence of a pious fraud, who assured them that Tomaso and his servant had been murdered in the Jewish quarter in such and such a house. This trick was probably perpetrated by Bachari Bey. The Turkish rascal, Mohammed El-Telli, offered his services as a spy to Ratti Menton, if he would free him from prison and debt. He willingly consented; the two scoundrels were worthy of each other.

Proofs soon accumulated. Christians testified that they had heard Jews say, "Let us shut the gates, and not go out, because danger is imminent," or that they had seen the monk in the house of a Jew shortly before his disappearance. The bill of accusation was quickly prepared: "The Jews have murdered Tomaso and his servant to use the blood for their Passover Festival,"–as though they would be so ridiculous as to keep it for six weeks ! Efforts were made to arouse the Christians and the Turkish populace. Several Jews were arrested, brought before Ratti Menton, and examined. A poor Jewish barber from inborn fear showed great confusion during the examination in the presence of the spies. But he firmly denied participation in, or knowledge of, the murder of the missing monk. Nevertheless the French consul handed him over for trial to Sherif Pasha, as a man under strong suspicion. The latter ordered him to receive the bastinado, five hundred blows with a stick upon the-soles of his feet. This torture, however, appeared too mild to Ratti Menton. The poor barber was subjected to the cruelest tortures, but he remained steadfast. He was then visited by Mohammed El-Telli, who was in prison for debt. Induced by deceitful speeches, the barber, afraid of fresh torture, agreed to name the guilty persons. He named, upon suggestion, seven distinguished and wealthy Jews, David Arari (Harari), with his son and brothers, then Moses Abulafia, Moses Saloniki, and Joseph Laniado, an old man of eighty years. When arrested and examined they denied their guilt. The bastinado was resorted to, but the executioners, fearing that the old men would sink under the blows, and that their confessions would be of no use, employed another method of torture. The accused, guarded by soldiers, were compelled to stand erect for thirty-six hours, without food or drink, and without being allowed to go to sleep. As this torture bore no result, the bloodthirsty villains

proceeded at Ratti Menton's orders to inflict a violent beating with switches; at the twentieth blow the unhappy victims fell to the ground unconscious. The French consul nevertheless ordered the scourging to be continued when they revived.

All this, however, did not extort a confession. Sherif Pasha invented a new species of torment, or employed one suggested to him. More than sixty children between the ages of three and ten were torn from their parents, shut up in a room, and deprived of food, so that the mothers, agonized by the piteous cries of the children, might be driven to make confessions, even though untrue ones. This means also failed. In spite of compassion for their children, the Jewish mothers in no way confirmed the horrible accusation. Only one woman and her daughter were driven by grief and love of their children into the arms of Islam. Sherif Pasha became enraged, and threatened that if the Father were not found, many Jewish heads should fall. With a band of soldiers (February 18) he marched into the Jewish quarter, and commanded the magnificent house of David Arari to be destroyed, in order to find the corpse of the monk or suspicious traces. The houses of the other accused were also ruined. Distressed by so much cruelty, a Jewish youth ventured to go to the Pasha and give evidence that he had seen Father Tomaso enter the shop of a Turk shortly before his disappearance. Instead of following this clue, Ratti Menton and his private secretary Baudin, tried to hush up the evidence. The youth was unmercifully flogged, and in the same night died, the first martyr in this tragedy.

Ratti Menton was inexhaustible in devices for extorting a confession from the Jews. He ordered an experiment to be tried upon David Arari's Turkish servant, Murad el Fallat. He had nothing to confess, and permitted himself to be scourged till his body was almost lacerated. Mohammed El-Telli then interviewed him, and by mingling friendly overtures and threats obtained some information from him. The servant accused himself of having murdered Tomaso at the command of David Arari in the presence of the other prisoners ; and the Jewish barber was persuaded to confirm this statement. Ratti Menton then caused the two mutilated men to be led to a place where the bones and skulls were supposed to have been thrown into a canal. He found a piece of bone and a fragment of cloth; Christian doctors declared that this bone belonged to a human body, and the patch was judged to be part of the monk's cowl. Positive proof of the murder having been thus found in the Jewish quarter, the seven accused were again examined, and subjected to cruel tortures. They were ordered to produce the flask of blood taken from the murdered men for the Passover Festival. The tortures killed the old man Joseph Laniado. Moses Abulafia, to escape further torture, assumed the turban. The others, worn out by suffering, said all that was demanded of them; they had become dull, and only desired a speedy death. Their confession, however, did not help them. The French consul wanted tangible evidence, such as the flask of blood and other proofs. But the poor prisoners, however willing, were unable to produce them.

New tortures were applied, the only result being that the wretched victims retracted their former confessions. As Ratti Menton needed new victims, Arari's servant was required to assist in supplying them early in March. Suspicion fell upon other distinguished Jewish families: upon the wealthy family of Farchi (Parchi), upon a young man named Isaac Levi Picciotto (Peixotto), and upon Aaron Stambuli. Three rabbis of Damascus, Jacob Anteri, Solomon and Azaria

Halfen, had been arrested earlier, and tortured, but the desired evidence was not obtained. Of the distinguished

THE AUSTRIAN CONSUL.

Jews said to be implicated in the charge of murder, only two could be found: Raphael Murad Farchi who, owing to his high position as consul, thought himself safe, and Picciotto, the nephew of the consul-general of Aleppo, who had been knighted for his services by the Austrian emperor. Picciotto alone remained steadfast, and boldly upbraided Ratti Menton and the Pasha with the inhumanity of their conduct. He was protected by the Austrian consul, an Italian named Merlato, who despite all threats and arguments refused to allow an Austrian subject to be tortured without substantial proofs of his guilt. This new complication produced a change in the horrifying drama. Merlato had long looked on calmly at the inhuman acts, like the other European consuls, especially the English consul named Werry, who was Ratti Menton's accomplice. But at length Merlato's patience was exhausted; he openly attacked the barbarous, horrible proceedings. Consequently he had to endure a good deal of abuse. The Christian populace heaped curses upon him, because he defended the Jews, and would not surrender his protege Picciotto into the hands of the cannibals. His house was surrounded by spies, and the Mahometan mob was also inflamed against the Jews by foul means.

Ratti Menton was indefatigable in inventing new charges and sham proofs. He ordered a contemptible book against the Jews, by Lucio Ferrajo, which had been shown him by the monks, to be translated into Arabic. This book proved from the Talmud that the Jews used blood, that they slew Christian children, and outraged the Host, which afterwards worked miracles. The Arabic translation was given by Ratti Menton to Sherif Pasha, and he circulated it among the Mahometan populace. To set on foot a thorough-going persecution, Franciscus of Sardinia, a venomous Capuchin monk, was brought from Beyrout, being well known for his ability to give an appearance of truth to perversions and falsehoods. The Pasha then commanded that the three imprisoned rabbis be separated, and directed to translate into Arabic certain suspicious passages in the Talmud, with the threat of death if they were caught in a deception. Thoughtful Turks shook their heads at this systematic persecution of the Jews; but they held their peace. Ratti Menton closed the proceedings, and pronounced judgment, as if it had been incontrovertibly proved, that the arrested and tortured Jews were the murderers of Father Tomaso. Those still alive were sentenced to be beheaded. Sherif Pasha obtained the assent of his lord, Mehmet Ali, to this deed.

As if to give verisimilitude to the blood-accusation against the Jews, and justify their destruction as bloodthirsty cannibals, a. similar incident occurred at about the same time on the island of Rhodes, which belonged to Turkey. A boy of ten years of age, the son of a Greek peasant, had hanged himself, and the Christians hastened to charge the Jews with his murder. The European consuls took the matter in hand, and demanded of the governor, Yussuf Pasha, a strict investigation against the Jews. Upon the evidence of two Greek women that the boy had followed a Jew of Rhodes, the man was arrested, tried, imprisoned, and, because of his denial, inhumanly tortured. His nostrils were pierced by an iron wire, red-hot coals placed upon his head, and a heavy stone upon his breast. This was done or approved by Europeans and Christians, consuls of the European powers, of England, France, and Sweden. Here, too, the Austrian consul took no part in the barbarous persecution. The torture was applied to the accused Jew by his officers without tho knowledge of the Pasha. The confession which they desired to obtain was that he had killed the Greek boy to send his blood to the chief rabbi at Constantinople. It was a sort of conspiracy

of the Christians in Turkey against the Jews, to bring them to the edge of the precipice, perhaps due to envy, because the young Sultan, Abdul Meg'id, on ascending the throne, in his congratulatory address (Hatti-Sherif of Gulhane) had conceded equal privileges to ail subjects of his kingdom, Jews included. The Greeks and Latins in Turkey thought but little of their freedom, because they had to share it with the hated Jews.

Induced by the cruel torture, the half lifeless Jew in Rhodes made a confession. He incriminated several Jews in the murder of the boy, hoping that they had already fled from fear of persecution. But some of them were still in Rhodes. As in Damascus, they were incarcerated, tortured, and brought near to death's door. Nevertheless they remained firm. The consuls then ordered the Ghetto to be closed, so that no one might pass in and out, and the Jews might be unable to lay their complaints before the Pasha, or even before the Sultan. For three days the Jews received no food from outside. Greeks were constantly prowling around the Ghetto to throw in bones, to be able to say afterwards that they were the bones of a murdered Christian. The Austrian consul, who at first had taken the part of the, Jews, was ultimately induced to join their enemies.

In consequence of this double accusation, a perfect storm arose against the Jews in Syria and Turkey. In Djabar, near Damascus, the mob broke into the synagogue, pillaged and destroyed it, and tore the scrolls of the Law to shreds. In Beyrout the Jews were protected from ill-treatment by the interposition of Laurilla, the Dutch consul, and Sason, the Prussian consul. The spirit of enmity spread as far as Smyrna, and was attended by many attacks upon the Jews.

Was it a mere accident that at the same time (beginning of March, 1840) a blood accusation was raised against a Jew in Rhenish Prussia, in Julich? A Christian girl, nine years of age, asserted that a Jew had stabbed her. Her little brother, six years old, confirmed her statement. A Jew and his wife, who happened to be journeying through Julich, were identified by the children as the criminals, and the girl added that the Jew at the same time had killed an old Christian with a knife. If truth speaks from the mouth of children, this Jew would have had to be sentenced as a murderer of Christians, a vampire. If the torture had been applied, an avowal of the crime would probably have been extorted from the Jew and his wife. But a strict judicial inquiry elicited that the statements of the children were idle falsehoods and deception. The Christian supposed to have been murdered was alive. The pretended wound on the girl's body was only a smudge of blood. The accused Jew was acquitted, and a rumor, referred to by the state attorney himself, charged two Christians from Dusseldorf with having drummed these horrible accusations into the children's heads.

In Rhenish Prussia the truth and the innocence of the Jews were brought to light quickly. In Damascus and Rhodes, on the other hand, the struggle was prolonged, because fiendish European Christians had intentionally woven such a network of lies, that even guileless persons were deceived. In vain the ill-treated Jews wrung their hands, and entreated their European brethren to aid them by means of their more favorable circumstances. They found it exceedingly difficult to bring the truth to light and to unmask villainy. Religious fanaticism, Judaeo-phobia, and political party passions, all combined to assist the triumph of falsehood. The underhand plotters employed the art of Guttenberg--whose four hundredth jubilee was then being celebrated--to circulate accusations throughout the world that Jews were eager drinkers of Christian blood.

THE PRESS AND THE BLOOD ACCUSATION.

Ratti Menton arranged that a report from Damascus presenting the events from his point of view be inserted in the French journals to inform the European world that the Jews had murdered a priest and his servant, and had collected the blood for their unleavened bread for the Passover. One corpse had been thrown into the canal in their Quarter, and the other into a Jew's cellar. They had confessed, acknowledging that they had committed the crime in order to celebrate the mysteries of their religion. Without Ratti Menton's zeal the culprits would not have been discovered, and without his interposition the Jewish quarter and all its inhabitants would have been destroyed. Not only the newspapers controlled by the Catholic clergy zealously spread this charge against the Jews, but also the liberal journals, in order to glorify the power of France in the East, published as facts all the distorted statements from Damascus. The eyes of Europe being at this time directed towards the entanglements in Turkey, the false reports rapidly spread through the veins of European journalism. The hatred of the Middle Ages against the Jews might have been easily re-awakened, and might have caused scenes of blood to be re-enacted. The Jews of Europe were filled with horror that in the broad daylight of the nineteenth century they had still to contend against the dark specter of the blood accusation, that it might not drag them down into the grave.

The press, which had been used by their adversaries, was now employed to greater advantage in the cause of the Jews. Calumnies and lying accusations against them could no longer be concealed under the veil of secrecy. There were courageous Jews who tore off the mask of virtue from falsehood and hypocrisy. Such a man was Adolf Cremieux (born 1796, died 1880), who shortly before this time had celebrated triumphs of eloquence. This extraordinary man was destined, as will be shown, to become the bold and powerful advocate of the Jews in their tribulation. The false charges brought against them in Damascus made him their advocate, and induced him to take an active part in the history of his co-religionists. Cremieux, who, among the many talented orators of France, was considered an exceptionally fine speaker, employed his great gifts in the defense of innocent prisoners, without distinction of creed, position, or party. Although Cremieux was at this time a member of the Franco-Jewish consistory, he had not hitherto troubled himself much about Jewish affairs ; his soul was filled with patriotism for France. The blood accusation at Damascus, which had been spread far and wide by the opponents of the Jews, first reminded him of his Jewish origin, and inspired him with courage and zeal to take up the cause of his brethren in religion and race, and developed in him a glowing patriotism for Judaism. At the first news of the dark proceedings in Damascus, thoroughly convinced that the Eastern like the European Jews were innocent of blood, Cremieux hastened to the French minister to ask him whether the government had more precise information on the matter. The minister replied that he had not received the slightest information on the subject from the consul or any other source. Thus it was made evident how this game was played. With all the glowing fire of his eloquence and the courage instilled by a righteous cause, Cremieux opposed the wide-spread slanders which echoed through France (April 7), and became the center of a patriotic movement of the French communities. Cremieux was then vice-president of the central consistory, and the Jews of France looked to him, their appointed representative, to rend asunder the network of lies which extended from Damascus to France.

Like the French Jews, those of England also

MEETING IN LONDON.

aroused themselves suddenly. By their wealth and honorable conduct they stood very high in public opinion. Some had been elected to fill the honorable post of sheriff; and it was to be expected that they would soon be admitted into Parliament. The most distinguished Jews of England, among them Baron Nathaniel Rothschild, Sir Moses Montefiore (who from a pious sentiment had undertaken a pilgrimage to the Holy Land), Salomons, and the highly-esteemed brothers Goldsmid, held a meeting (April 21), and resolved to appeal to the governments of England, France, and Austria, to use their influence to put a stop to the inhuman proceedings in Damascus. Cremieux came to London, and was present at the meeting, in order to consider a common course of action. The unanimity was noteworthy with which prominent Jews took up the cause of their persecuted brethren, and defended the purity of Judaism, of its Law, and the Talmud. On the same day (May 1), Cremieux presented himself before Louis Philippe, king of France, and a Jewish deputation waited on the English minister, Lord Palmerston, in order to obtain the protection of these two countries for the victims in Damascus. Louis Philippe replied with much feeling: " I do not know anything about the occurrence; but if anywhere there are unfortunate Jews who appeal to the protection of my government, and if anything can be effected by its means, I will conform with your wishes."

Whether the asseveration was seriously meant by this diplomatic monarch cannot be known. A vice-consul was, however, appointed to visit Damascus, investigate the matter, and draw up a report. But he was only a subordinate, whom, as might have been imagined, Ratti Menton could easily deceive, or venture to oppose. The answer of Lord Palmerston was more straightforward. He promised the Jewish deputation, who laid before him full proofs of the innocence of the accused at Damascus and Rhodes, that he would empower the English ambassador at Constantinople, as also the consul at Alexandria, to use every effort to check the continuance of such cruelties. In another quarter, less public, but more effective, steps were taken to obtain the support of Vienna and the Austrian cabinet. The Austrian consul in Damascus, Merlato, was the only one who had seen through the wickedness of Ratti Menton, his assistants, and the monks, and with true soldierly courage had offered firm resistance. In return, he was abused by his opponents both in the East and the West; they decried him as a Jew, to throw suspicion upon his defense of the Jews, and thus destroy its effects. But Merlato felt himself morally pledged to plead the innocence of the Jews as a personal matter. He issued a faithful and comprehensive report of the groundless attacks of the mob upon the victims at Damascus. This narrative, a defense of his conduct in protecting Picciotto, he dispatched to his superior, the consul-general of Egypt, and it was sent by the latter as a correct account to Metternich, the Austrian minister. Although adverse to publicity, Metternich had allowed all writings favorable to the Jews to be circulated in the newspapers. In this report Ratti Menton, whom the clerical intriguers had glorified as an angel of light, was shown to be an evil demon. A revolution ensued in public opinion which filled the Jews with courage, and foreshadowed the triumph of justice. It is difficult to say whether Metternich's intervention in this matter arose from his own impulse, from displeasure at the cruelty practiced, or from political hostility to France and a desire to break her power in the East, or, perhaps, from complaisance to the house of Rothschild, whose members were extraordinarily zealous on behalf of their co-religionists in this affair. At any rate, Metternich encouraged the Austrian agents in Egypt and Syria to stand up boldly in defense of the Jews.

REVISION OF THE RHODES TRIAL.

In Constantinople, at the divan of the Sultan, the representatives of European governments friendly to the Jews, obtained a revision of the trial for blood accusation in the island of Rhodes. Jewish deputies from Rhodes had at length succeeded in reaching Constantinople. Nathaniel de Rothschild also betook himself thither, and as a result Abdul Meg'id issued a Firman (July 27) that the Greek population should send to the capital three primates as accusers, and the Jews as many elders as defendants. A tribunal, under the presidency of Risaat Bey, was appointed to inquire into the matter, the result being that Yussuf Pasha was dismissed from his post of governor of Rhodes, and the Jews charged with child-murder were acquitted. Further, they were instructed to demand compensation for the losses sustained from those who had unjustly accused them, viz., some of the European consuls. In three months--from the beginning of May till towards the end of July--the affair was settled.

With Mehmet Ali there were greater difficulties to be encountered. He had, indeed, as early as the beginning of April, promised the Austrian consul general Laurin to put an end to the atrocities; but this was prevented by the French consul-general, Cochelet, and, foolishly trusting in France, he could not quarrel with the agents of the French government. But Laurin, acting on the instructions of Metternich, was untiring in his efforts to withdraw the Pasha of Egypt from the net of the French intriguers. At his instigation the Jews of Alexandria presented an eloquent and spirited address to Mehmet Ali. It was remarkable that the Egyptian Jews did not receive the bastinado for speaking the truth; Mehmet Ali well knew who supported them. A letter of Metternich to the Pasha produced a wonderfully favorable effect. In the settlement of the Eastern Question, the latter could not afford to break with Austria, from which country the Sultan could obtain reinforcements more quickly than from France.

Mehmet Ali therefore resolved to form a court of justice, consisting of the consuls of Austria, England, Russia, and Prussia, to carry on the trial according to European usages. The tribunal was empowered to dispatch a commission to Damascus, and institute an impartial examination of witnesses on the spot. An order was sent to Damascus to Sherif Pasha, commanding him to discontinue the torture of the prisoners, and in general to stop the persecution of the Jews. To suppress any riotous outbreak of the Christians, whose courage had increased, eight hundred soldiers were sent thither. The matter began to look as if the truth would be vindicated. The four consuls nominated as chief judges, diffident of their ability to conduct so complicated a trial, turned for aid to Vienna, and asked that four German judges, well versed in criminal law, investigate the matter, but a political interlude interrupted the proceedings.

A secret war was waged between the overwise king, Louis Philippe, and the cunning statesman Thiers, who was trifling with the minister's portfolio, and whose little person and big phrases so thwarted the king that he kept him as much as possible at arm's length. Just at this time (in May) Thiers played a trick on the king, and forced him to make him president of the cabinet. The little "fly," as he was called, began to hum and buzz, behaving as if he could acquire the Rhine as French property, and settle the Eastern Question according to the views of France. To secure a majority in the Chamber, Thiers was forced to gain the good graces of the clerical party, which was especially strong in the Chamber of Peers. Thus it happened that no strict investigation into the Damascus affair could be permitted, in order that the brutal behavior of Ratti Menton and the monks might not be

brought to light. At any rate, it had been a slight upon France that its consul had been excluded from the new court of justice. Besides this, Thiers was not on friendly terms with the financial world, that is, with the Rothschilds, and he desired to strike a blow to make them yield. The French consul general

Cochelet, in Alexandria, received instructions from Thiers to stay the hand of Mehmet Ali, and prevent the misdeeds in Damascus from being brought to light. The Egyptian Pasha, misled by Thiers' plotting, obeyed his orders, and withdrew the promise made to the four consuls. Thus the drama which had seemed to be approaching a conclusion was again prolonged, but its end was not favorable to Thiers and his protege.

Jews of every shade of opinion had become possessed of sufficient independence to defy the prevarications of a minister or of a consul. Achille Fould, who was bound to Judaism by only a slender tie, as well as the strictly orthodox Hirsch Lehren in Amsterdam, both regarded it as their duty to take a bold part in the defense of their persecuted co-religionists in Syria. In the French Chamber of Deputies (July 2) Fould questioned Thiers so sharply that the latter was forced to make excuses. "The French consul had ordered the torture, and after the French nation had set the example of obedience to the rule of 'equality before the law' as well as in religious matters, a Frenchman countenanced this exception to the rule, employed torture, and thus supported the executioners of the Pasha. This behavior was so deeply resented by the other European agents that the French ambassador was excluded from the council which had been established, because he was the accuser, whilst the others were the defending advocates."

To this statement Thiers was compelled to reply, but each word he uttered sounded like a falsehood. Two Christian deputies took the part of the Jews in this discussion. Count Delaborde, who had traveled in the East, highly praised the Jews of Turkey, and stated that well-deserved respect was accorded to them, and that, like Lamartine, he had received the most hearty and generous hospitality from their wealthy members. Thiers positive assertion that he was in possession of papers which proved the innocence of Ratti Menton, was met by another deputy, Isambert; he produced a report drawn up by the apostolical missionary, the successor of Father Tomaso, which stated "that the exertions and zeal of the French consul in torturing the Jews of Damascus surpassed all comprehension." The Chamber of Deputies, however, did not pass a vote of censure upon the minister, who so belied the courteous character of the French nation, but the looks of the deputies condemned him. Thiers felt such discomfort that he made a petty attack upon the Jews, "who had stirred up a storm throughout Europe, asking the assistance of the ministers of every state, and had thus shown that they possessed more influence than was asserted." The Jews, to be sure, had to unite and develop especial activity, seeing that the Catholic party in France, Italy, and Belgium had formally conspired, or received a hint from headquarters to enshroud in darkness the events in Damascus, and to represent the Jews in the East and in Europe as murderers and cannibals. Throughout Italy the documents in favor of the Damascus victims or against Ratti Menton were not allowed to be printed: the censorship, which was under the care of the clergy, forbade it. A French journal had called on baptized Jews to state upon oath and to the best of their knowledge, whether they had ever found among their former co-religionists or in Jewish writings, the slightest trace or precept concerning the abominable crime imputed to the unhappy people in

Damascus. Several Jews who had been converted to Protestantism, and even held ecclesiastical positions, asserted the innocence of the Jews of this crime-amongst them, Augustus Neander, known as Church historian and a man of tender conscience.

APPEALS FROM THE EAST.

The clerical enemies of the Jews now published a fresh accusation, that the Talmud which the European Jews knew and studied might indeed be free from passages hostile to Christians and advising the shedding of blood, which may have been expunged from the copies out of fear, but the Jews of the Orient, under Turkish rule, still possessed the Talmud in its original form, which was full of hatred against all men, especially against Christians.

Thus the Jews were forced to establish a bond of truth against the untrue, to make public the innocence of the martyrs in Damascus, and at the same time attest the purity of their own doctrines; in short, they had to help themselves. The French central consistory, which had received solemn promises from Louis Philippe, saw itself deceived in its hopes. Cremieux was compelled to make the painful statement to his brethren, "France is against us." The urgent cries of the Jews from Damascus, Beyrout, Alexandria, and Constantinople, in letters to the Rothschilds, to Moses Montefiore, Cremieux, and to Hirsch Lehren in Amsterdam, made it apparent that it was necessary for prominent European Jews to repair to the scene of action, in order to obtain more effective results. The central consistory therefore determined to send an emissary, with an escort, to Alexandria, whose burning eloquence might gain the favor of Mehmet Ali. Entrusted with this dangerous and honorable mission, Cremieux entered Into communication with the heads of the Jewish community in London.

Here a committee of the noblest and most distinguished Jews, including Montefiore and Rothschild, had been formed, who, in a meeting held in the vestibule of a synagogue (June 15), passed the following important resolution, that Montefiore, accompanied by a friend chosen by himself, should undertake the journey to Egypt together with Cremieux, " to represent the Jews of England at the court of the Pasha, and to defend their persecuted brethren in the East by means of his weighty influence and his zeal." It was also determined at this meeting to collect large sums of money, because it was seen that they would be wanted, not indeed as bribes in the pending trial at Damascus, but that large rewards might be offered to discover the murderer of Father Tomaso. A thousand pounds sterling were offered as a reward for the discovery of the criminal. The readiness of the Jews to contribute was on this occasion again manifested in a most conspicuous manner. Poor men as well as millionaires contributed to the just cause. The committee also caused unfalsified public opinion, as it exists in England, to make itself heard in Parliament on behalf of the Jews, and Sir Robert Peel, who exercised great influence, undertook this task.

The session of the House of Commons (June 22) affords an interesting contrast to the sitting of the French Chamber of Deputies at the same time and upon the same subject. Peel rightly introduced the questions to the ministers with the words, "that it was merely necessary to mention the matter in the Lower House, to reach the great ends of justice and humanity." Lord Palmerston answered in a totally different manner to Thiers: "I have already directed the English consul-general Hedges to represent to Mehmet Ali what effect the news of such atrocities must produce in Europe, and that it was in his own interest to inquire into the matter, and hand over to punishment the guilty parties, if they were discovered, whilst the innocent victims should be indemnified, if this were still possible. I have also sent instructions to Her Majesty's consul in Damascus to make a thorough investigation into all that has taken place, and to send home an exact report as to the part which the European consuls had taken in the matter."

The air of England rendered susceptible to feelings of liberty even those who were accustomed to

MEETING IN LONDON.

elevate the enslavement of bodies and minds to the rank of a dogma. O'Connell, the fiery Irish agitator for the emancipation of the Catholics in England, advocated in Parliament that a similar privilege be granted to the Jews. "Observations upon this subject would have been stronger, if a member of this House belonging to the creed of the accused had been able to make them. The Government ought to introduce a bill for the complete emancipation of the Jews."

Thus spake England by the mouths of its worthiest representatives.

Next day (June 23) a numerous assembly of the most distinguished Jews in London was held in the Great Synagogue to make final arrangements for sending Montefiore to Egypt. It was proved on this occasion what a noble circle of Jews England harbored, and that their minds were filled by lofty sentiments of attachment to Judaism and its adherents. Hitherto the English Jews had taken but little part in Jewish history, they had remained passive owing to their insignificant numbers. But when for the first time they asserted themselves, they displayed their independence, and gave a brilliant example to others. Montefiore, De Castro, Rothschild, Van Oven, Salomons, and many others, spoke and acted like Jews conscious of their dignity, who were ready to make the greatest sacrifices, in order to secure the triumph of their impugned belief. Cremieux had come over from Paris to be present. The meeting first acknowledged its gratitude to those men, Christians as well as Jews, who had zealously defended the unhappy people of Damascus, viz., James de Rothschild, who had largely contributed towards the support of the impoverished Jews in Damascus, Metternich and his agents, Laurin and Merlato, and also Hedges, the English consul. Bernard van Oven delivered a glowing speech, which, however, was to the point, and was received with much applause.

Many words were not required at this meeting. All were firmly resolved to make every effort and every sacrifice to obtain satisfaction for those falsely accused of shedding blood. This high-minded Jewish assembly in London was somewhat similar to that held in Alexandria exactly eighteen centuries before, when Judaism, in the time of the Emperor Caligula, was branded with disgrace by shameless, diabolical enemies. At that time, also, the most prominent Jews, famed for their culture, nobility of mind, and wealth, gathered together. But the Alexandrine assembly, surrounded by foes, had met with terror and fear, whilst the one in London was encouraged and supported by the good wishes and sympathy of the citizens of the capital. In the second Jewish congregation, that of Manchester, a similar meeting was held.

Assured of success by these signs, Montefiore set out on his important journey, provided with letters of recommendation from prominent men in the state, and accompanied by the good wishes of millions of persons, foremost among them Queen Victoria. On his departure she gave him audience, and placed at his disposal her vessel in which to cross the Channel--certainly an extraordinary mark of favor and sympathy for the misfortunes of the Jews, but at the time the feeling in their favor was so strong, that it did not create great surprise. Montefiore was accompanied by a gentleman of the legal profession and by his wife Judith, who insisted upon sharing her husband's hardships on this expedition in the cause of her nation. She was the ideal of a Jewish woman, cultured, noble-minded, proud of her confession and devotedly attached to her race, a brilliant contrast to the women of Berlin, who had brought disgrace upon Judaism. Before Montefiore and his escort left England, the two chief rabbis of the German and Portuguese communities, Solomon Herschel (died 1842), and David

Meldola, deemed it necessary to repeat the solemn oath which Manasseh ben Israel and Moses Mendelssohn had taken: that the blood accusation against the Jews had not a shadow of support in Talmudical writings, or in fact. in view of the baseness of the clerical French party and the venality of German newspapers, this oath was by no means superfluous. Catholic agitators in France and Belgium reviled the Jews, for a contemptible, yet comprehensible reason, and with a definite plan of entrapping the conscience of the free in their nets. But the German writers acted in this way from low motives, in order to utilize the misfortunes of others as a source of wealth. A certain Dr. Philibert had sent a letter to the house of Rothschild in Paris, stating that for a large sum of money he would undertake the defense of the Damascus Jews in every European journal, adding the threat that if this blood-money were refused he would influence public opinion in the opposite direction. Such miserable creatures were repulsed by the Jews with scorn. They felt that they could rely upon their own strength and the power of truth. Foiled in their expectations, the contemptible scribblers attacked the Jews, and increased the number of lies and slanders which had accumulated around the Damascus murder. The chief rabbis had therefore to swallow their pride, and to take an oath on a matter as clear as daylight.

However, if the Jews were attacked in the French and German newspapers, England afforded them sufficient cause to forget all the sufferings of the Jews throughout fifteen centuries. Distinguished merchants, proprietors of large banking-houses, and members of parliament, about two hundred and ten in all, preferred a request to the Lord Mayor of London, Marshall, to call a public meeting and enable them to express their feelings and their sincere sympathy with the persecuted Jews in Damascus, The Lord Mayor, being of their opinion in the matter, cordially assented, and a brilliant meeting was held in London (in the Mansion House, July 3) which was in itself a victory. Many ladies of rank were among the audience.

THE MANSION HOUSE MEETING.

Towards the end of the meeting O'Connell entered. He thought that his presence would be required to arouse enthusiasm. But when he saw that the zeal on behalf of the Jews had been raised to a high pitch, he merely added:

> *" After the testimony given to demonstrate the moral worth of the Jews, could any man be so insane as to believe that they use blood for their rites? Is not a Jew an example in every relation of life? Is he not a good father, a good son? Are they not true friends? Are they not honest, industrious? .... I appeal to all Englishmen to raise their voices in defense of the victims of that shameful oppression.. May the appeal go from one end of the British Isles to the other, and if the concurrence of an Irishman be wanting, here am I to testify to it."*

This three hours' meeting in the Mansion House forms a noteworthy episode in Jewish history. In the name of the meeting, the Lord Mayor communicated the resolutions which were passed, not only to the English government, but also to the ambassadors of all European powers, requesting them at the same time to obtain expressions of sympathy with the Jews from their respective nations and rulers. So effective was the result of unbiased public opinion, that the emperor of Russia, Nicholas, as well as the American Republic, felt themselves morally compelled to express their abhorrence at tortures indicted on Jews.

A few weeks later a similar meeting was held in Manchester, and, although most of the speakers were clergymen, the same sentiments with regard to the Jews were pronounced. Why had not such views predominated in the fourth and fifth centuries, when Christianity first became paramount? What tears and bloodshed would have been avoided! But the Jewish race was to be tested and strengthened by martyrdom.

Montefiore was enabled to begin his journey filled with courage. He was not only supported by the government, but was accompanied by the sympathies of the best men in England, and therefore he felt hope. For Cremieux the matter was not so easy. In fact, he was hampered by the French ministry. Thiers wished to show himself firm. Perhaps he was not so much to blame as was generally supposed; it is possible that Louis Philippe, who was very cunning, hindered him from yielding. He was reminded also in the Chamber of Peers (July

10) by honorable men, that by his defense of Ratti Menton, he was compromising the honor of France, but he continued in his ambiguous attitude. Events brought the cunning of Thiers and the king to naught. Whilst they thought that by petty intrigues, childish obstinacy, and by deceiving Mehmet Ali they were strengthening the position of France, the four remaining European powers--England, Russia, Austria, and Prussia--formed the Quadruple Alliance (July 15) against France, which agreed that Syria should be restored to the Sultan. The downfall of Thiers was imminent, while he was boasting of his successes.

A day before the conclusion of the alliance, Montefiore and Cremieux, with their respective escorts, set out for Egypt. In Cremieux's company was Solomon Munk, who worthily represented Jewish learning. Thus the Jewish embassy was not lacking in what is requisite for the success of a great enterprise--devotion, pure trust in God, eloquence, and deep scholarship. In their journey through France these noble-minded, gallant representatives of Judaism were received with enthusiasm in the Jewish communities, in Avignon, Nismes, Carpentras, and Marseilles, and were followed by good wishes. In Leghorn, where the royal ship anchored, the Portuguese community solemnly celebrated the day of their landing. Every distinction among the Jews disappeared in the unanimous admiration for men who had undertaken so difficult a task, and in the hope that they would succeed. All Israel was once more of one heart and soul. Orthodox rabbis

allowed prayers for Montefiore and Cremieux to be interpolated in the Divine service. Every Jew, even the most humble, was ready to bring some sacrifice in order to lighten the task.

On arriving at Cairo (August 4), they hastened on their mission, without taking any rest. Montefiore, strongly supported by the English consul-general Hodges, who had received instructions from Palmerston to that effect, at once solicited an interview with Mehmet Ali (August 6), by whom he was received, and to whom he handed a petition in the name of the Jewish community requesting permission to go to Damascus and there conduct an inquiry into the circumstances of the case. For this purpose a safe-conduct was required for himself and his friends, and also the privilege of speaking to the prisoners as often as was necessary, and of hearing evidence. Mehmet Ali was sorely perplexed. He would willingly have acceded to this request, because he earnestly wished to pose as a just prince before the eyes of Europe. But the French consul-general Cochelet--instructed by Thiers--checked this inclination, and made every effort to prevent the veil from being lifted. Cochelet, contrary to custom, would not even introduce Cremieux to the Pasha. Cremieux was therefore obliged to seek an audience for himself; but, like Montefiore, he received only evasive answers. The Eastern Question had at that time become extremely perplexing. Every moment Mehmet Ali was expecting the final decision of the European powers, that he should submit to the Sultan, surrender his independence, and give up Syria. He did not wish to break with those powers which took up the cause of the Jews, more especially with England and Austria, nor with Thiers, nor Louis Philippe, who would not forsake Ratti Menton and the monks. Owing to Mehmet All's indecision, matters dragged on for three weeks. The Jewish envoys received no definite reply. They were not discouraged, but sought to devise new means by which to attain their aim. Cremieux hit upon the best plan. All the European consuls, or as many as were willing to sign a petition, were to demand the liberation of the prisoners in Damascus. Nine consuls agreed to this, in fact all except the French consul. Mehmet Ali, however, obtained information of the proposed petition, and in order that it might not appear that he had yielded to the pressure of foreign powers, through their representatives, he determined to dispatch an order to Damascus (August 28) that the prisoners should forthwith be set at liberty.

The two envoys and their escort were filled with heartfelt joy. The three synagogues in Alexandria resounded with prayers of thanksgiving and blessings for Mehmet Ali, Metternich, and the Austrian consuls Laurin and Merlato, and all who had taken part in the deliverance and who were delighted at the result of their efforts.

Great was the astonishment, however, of the two Jewish representatives, when a Turkish copy of Mehmet Ali's order reached them, and Munk, who was a skilled linguist, read out the words, "Mr. Moses Montefiore and M. Cremieux have besought me to bestow mercy upon the Jews in Damascus and to grant them liberty," which implied that the accused Damascus Jews, though guilty, had been treated by the Pasha with mercy, instead of justice. The hand of Cochelet was visible in this attempt to shield Ratti Menton and the monkish executioners. Cremieux straightway hastened to the Pasha, explained to him how the expression "mercy" cast a slur upon the accused, and with them upon all Jews, because they were thus declared to be guilty. He asked that the words "liberty and peace" be substituted. Mehmet Ali ordered this alteration to be made in the Firman, and thus the last intrigues of Cochelet were destroyed.

THE DAMASCUS PRISONERS RELEASED.

As soon as the order arrived at Damascus, Sherif Pasha, who knew Mehmet Ali's severity, was obliged to liberate the nine Jewish prisoners who were still detained in jail (September 6) without consulting Ratti Menton. Seven of the men had been mutilated by the tortures, only two having escaped injury who had suffered persecution, while four victims had died. No sooner did the joyful news of their liberation get abroad in Damascus, than all the Jews and many Turks assembled before the prison, and accompanied the sufferers to the synagogue, to offer up thanks to God for their regained freedom, and to pray for Mehmet Ali and their Jewish protectors.

The joy of the Jews in all parts of the world, on hearing of the triumph of their just cause, may be imagined; it was a national rejoicing in which the best men, both in Europe and Asia, participated. All that remained to be effected was to obtain from Mehmet Ali the official statement that the blood accusation was a calumny, and of this there were ample proofs when everyone in Damascus could speak freely about the sad occurrence. The Jewish envoys also made it their duty to induce the Pasha to abolish torture altogether. But political complications prevented the accomplishment of this humane proposal. Mehmet Ali was obliged to surrender Syria as well as Crete to Turkey. Thus punishment overtook him for having complacently witnessed for nearly three months the scenes of blood in Damascus out of deference to France. Sherif Pasha, even before Damascus was captured by the Turks, was dragged in chains to Cairo, and there executed, it is said for treason. Francois Salins, one of the malicious French persecutors of the Jews in Damascus, was torn to pieces by the mob. The fanatical Catholics of this city, who under Mehmet Ali had been permitted to practice so much cruelty, were humiliated, or felt humiliated, when Raphael Farchi, the distinguished Jew, was again installed in his position as member of the city council. No longer able to torture the Jews, they cooled their hatred by inciting to a crusade against them. The representative of the Greek Patriarch, the Armenian bishop Vantabiet, the vicar of the Holy Land, the Syrian priest Jacob, and the representative of the Catholic Patriarch, the priest Maruni--in short, the representatives of three sects who bore deadly hatred against each other united in fastening a new calumny on the Jews, who were hated equally by all three. " The Jews of Damascus allowed themselves grossly to insult the Christians, to abuse them and subject them to all sorts of indignities. Several persons made complaints of the disgraceful behavior of the Jews, abominable behavior, which humiliates all Christians."

The majority of European Christendom were, however, sufficiently well acquainted with the veracity of the clergy of Damascus to pay no attention to this hypocritical lament, and the heads of Catholicism felt ashamed of having exposed themselves in the Damascus affair.

The Jewish envoys did not think their task completed, unless they sought to prevent, as far as lay in their power, the repetition of events which branded all Judaism with dishonor. Foreseeing that Syria, together with Damascus, would be restored to Turkey, Montefiore made his way to Constantinople, entered into communications with the Porte, to which he had influential letters of recommendation, and together with some distinguished Jews of the Turkish capital obtained an audience of the Sultan, when he asked for a Firman (November 6), which should in future secure the Turkish Jews from blood accusations.

Cremieux chose another field for his activity. The martyrdom of the Damascus Jews had the unexpected effect of strengthening the connection between the Jews in Europe and those in the East. The latter saw with astonishment how much their European brethren could accomplish by means of

SCHOOLS IN THE EAST.

culture, influence, and courage, and that they were treated with distinction by princes and the great, whilst they themselves bent their backs, unresistingly, to every blow. This reverent admiration of the Asiatic Jews for those of Europe,

Cremieux utilized in the attempt to emancipate the Egyptian Jews (or at least those in the two capitals of Alexandria and Cairo) from their state of ignorance, and render them susceptible to civilization. Their ignorance of even Jewish writings, a consequence of the immeasurable oppression under which they had labored, as well as of their indescribable poverty, was the cause of the intense contempt in which they were held by Mahometans and Christians. From this ignominy Cremieux hoped to free them, and he was powerfully supported by Solomon Munk, who appears to have been destined to be the intermediary between the European and the Egyptian Jews--between the past and the present. Munk addressed an eloquent Hebrew and Arabic circular letter (Elul 23) to the Jews of Egypt, in which he contrasted the former splendor of the Jews of that country in the time of the Second Temple, in the time of Philo and Maimuni, when they stood at the head of Jewish spiritual activity, with the darkness of their present misery, the consequence of their intellectual decay. He exhorted them to wake from their deathlike torpor and establish schools, where their children might obtain a knowledge of Judaism and of Jewish literature, and at the same time a secular and practical education. Munk effected for the Egyptian Jews what Wessely had done for those of Europe. But, unlike his predecessor, he was not denounced as a heretic for his efforts. On the contrary, the rabbi of Alexandria was the first to offer assistance in the work. A distinguished Jew, named Valensino, placed himself at the head of a society for establishing schools and supervising public education. Then Cremieux, together with Munk, repaired to Cairo, where there dwelt a large congregation of about 300 families, only about twelve of whom were very wealthy, while about 200 lived on charity. Here also the rabbi, Moses Joseph Algazi, an aged man of seventy-six, and a prominent man named Adda, readily assisted in founding schools. Owing to their exertions and those of other persons, two schools for boys were opened in Cairo (October 4), and one for girls; these were called the Cremieux schools. Here Munk succeeded in bringing about an important reconciliation. In spite of the fanaticism of the rigidly orthodox, he succeeded in having the children of Karaites admitted to the schools, there being only about a hundred persons of this sect left in Cairo. The rabbi Algazi also supported the innovation, which seemed to be a step tending to restore brotherhood between Rabbanites and Karaites. Stirred by these movements, the grand rabbi of Constantinople (Chacham Bashi),Moses Fresco, issued a circular letter (October 28) to the Turkish congregations, urging that it was the duty of the Jews to learn the language of the country (Turkish), in order to meet the Sultan's wishes, who, by his Firman Hatti-Sherif, had raised them from their abject state. The mixed language in which this circular letter of the Chacham Bashi was written (Old Spanish with Hebrew and Turkish words), proved sufficiently the necessity of a pure language for the Jews.

However, these beginnings were merely seeds scattered in the desert sand, and it was doubtful whether they would take root and grow. The efforts were resumed on a larger scale twenty years later, under the name of "The Universal Alliance of Israelites" (Alliance Israelite Universelle) The mission to Egypt produced practical and' lasting fruit for Jewish science, chiefly through Solomon

Munk (born at Glogau, 1802; died at Paris, 1867). It is doubtful whether the spotless character of this

SOLOMON MUNK.

man, or his devoted attachment to science, is to be more admired. He added to the number of great men produced among the Jews during the first half of the nineteenth century. His modesty was a marked feature, which grew in proportion to the increase of his scientific importance. For his patience in misfortune, and cheerfulness in the sufferings which he had incurred in the service of science, he was greatly admired in his native country, Germany, and in France, his adopted country, and he was loved as much as he was revered. Munk possessed all the virtues of the Jews without their faults. In the comprehensive range of Arabic literature he was one of the first masters of the day, and the most profound scholars in the same study recognized his equality, or awarded him the palm. As interpreter to the escort of Cremieux, he spoke and wrote Arabic like one born in an Arab tent. He divined the words and sense of any manuscript passage by a kind of instinct, which only increased in keenness when he lost his sight from pouring over manuscripts. His intellectual sight compensated for the loss of his physical power. The darkness which enshrouded him for nearly twenty years before his death did not prevent his vision from being clear and distinct.

The glory of Jewish history during the Middle Ages developed during the rule of the Arabs in the East and West; its dawn began with Saadiah, and it reached its zenith with Maimuni. Munk banished the obscurity in which this epoch had been enwrapped, and illumined it with the full light of his profound studies. The innermost thoughts of Maimuni, the awakener of intellects, to whom the Jewish race is chiefly indebted for its renaissance in modern days, were completely revealed only through the researches of Munk. He renewed in its original form what had been spoilt by continual emendations. The proud boast of Christendom, that even in the obscurity of the Middle Ages it had disseminated the bright germs of thought, Munk controverted by incontestable proofs that without Arabic and Jewish philosophy, the darkness of the Middle Ages would have been impenetrable. Another historical fact, the origin and development of the Karaite sect, which, notwithstanding the powerful influence it exercised upon thought in the Jewish Middle Ages, was known only in rough outlines, was brought to light by Munk; in a word, Jewish science is deeply indebted to him. He not only greatly added to it by his profound knowledge, but he also showed how to pursue a sound course of investigation. Munk discovered new Arabic sources, rendering them comprehensible and accessible, and thereby greatly adding to the knowledge of Judaism, which he loved with all his heart. Munk's sojourn in Alexandria and Cairo was of extraordinary value in his literary and historical researches. From that soil, which had lain unproductive as to intellectual results for many a day he excavated rich treasures for Jewish science. Munk fully recognized that the self-respect of the Jews would be confirmed only by self-knowledge, reached along the paths of science.

AFTERWORD BY THE EDITOR

It was Graetz's misfortune to have written only seconds before the hour struck for Israel--a few short years before the most significant events in Jewish history were to unfold, concluding with the reversal of the Diaspora and the re-establishment of the state of Israel. Such events would have seemed only idle dreams in Graetz's day; there was not even a breath of Zionism in the air. Hebrew, it was feared, would soon fall into disuse, once it disappeared from the synagogue services. Had someone prophesied that in a hundred years, no one would be alive who would know how to speak or read Hebrew, he might have been credited.

Neither did Graetz have very much to say about the American Jewish community. At the time when Graetz wrote, the great Russian pogroms which began after the assassination of Alexander II in 1881 were yet future; the place of Jews in Eastern Europe, if always precarious, seemed nevertheless deeply-rooted. Instead, within a narrow window of time (some thirty-five years, roughly), one-third of the Jewish population of Eastern Europe was suddenly convulsed by a compulsion to emigrate to America. These formed the basis for the American Jewish community, which was to become the largest and most influential in the world.

A scant twenty-years after the close of the emigration to America (which was effectively ended by the start of the First World War), Adolf Hitler was in power in Berlin. But it was too late for Hitler to complete his plans to annihilate all the Jews of the world; those thirty-five years had defeated him; as though, as the saying is, "even before the wound occurs, the remedy has been prepared". Perhaps for Graetz' sake, it was best that he could not have lived into this century, to see what became of his beloved Germany, and the depths to which that nation, having renounced the gospel of its savior, plunged.

(Editor)